Value and Values

EDITED BY
Roger T. Ames & Peter D. Hershock

Value & Values

Economics & Justice in an Age of Global Interdependence

University of Hawai'i Press &
East–West Philosophers' Conference
HONOLULU

Printed in the United States of America

20 19 18 17 16 15 6 5 4 3 2 1

Library of Congress Cataloging-in-Publication Data

East-West Philosophers' Conference (10th : 2011 : Honolulu, Hawaii)
Value and values : economics and justice in an age of global interdependence / edited by Roger T. Ames and Peter D. Hershock.
pages cm
Papers from the 10th East-West Philosophers' Conference, held in Honolulu, May 16–24, 2011.
Includes index.
ISBN 978-0-8248-3967-3 (cloth : alk. paper)
1. Economics—Moral and ethical aspects—Congresses. I. Ames, Roger T., editor. II. Hershock, Peter D. III. Title.
HB72.E23 2011
174'.4—dc23 2014019850

University of Hawai‘i Press books are printed on acid-free paper and meet the guidelines for permanence and durability of the Council on Library Resources.

Designed by George Whipple

Printed by Sheridan Books, Inc.

Contents

Acknowledgments *ix*

Introduction *1*
Roger T. Ames and Peter D. Hershock

Part I Interdependence and Relationality

1 The Mosaic and the Jigsaw Puzzle: How It All Fits Together *27*
Thomas P. Kasulis

2 Value, Exchange, and Beyond: Betweenness as Starting Point *49*
Meera Sushila Viswanathan

3 Triple Negation: Watsuji Tetsurō on the Sustainability of Ecosystems, Economies, and International Peace *68*
James McRae

4 Fouling Our Nest: Is (Environmental) Ethics Impotent against (Bad) Economics? *82*
Heidi M. Hurd

5 The Visible and the Invisible: Rethinking Values and Justice from a Buddhist-Postmodern Perspective *109*
Jin Y. Park

6 "You Ought to Be Ashamed of Yourself!" *125*
James Peterman

7 Filial Piety and the Traditional Chinese Rural Community: An Alternative Ethical Paradigm for Modern Aging Societies *142*
Yang Liuxin, Baoyan Cheng, and Xu Di

8 Doing Justice to Justice: Seeking a More Capacious Conception of Justice from Confucian Role Ethics *157*
Roger T. Ames

Part II Dynamism and Contextuality

9 Moral Equivalents *185*
Kathleen M. Higgins

10 A Critique of Economic Reason: Between Tradition and Postcoloniality *198*
Purushottama Bilimoria

11 Economies of Scarcity and Acquisition, Economies of Gift and Thanksgiving: Lessons from Cultural Anthropology *214*
Kenneth W. Stikkers

12 John Dewey, Institutional Economics, and Confucian Democracies *229*
Larry A. Hickman

13 The Responsible Society as Social Harmony: Walter G. Muelder's Communitarian Social Ethics as a Bridge Tradition for Confucian Economics *241*
Robert Smid

14 *Swaraj* and *Swadeshi:* Gandhi and Tagore on Ethics, Development, and Freedom *259*
Nalini Bhushan and Jay L. Garfield

15 Economics and Religion or Economics versus Religion: The Concept of an Islamic Economics *272*
Oliver Leaman

16 Two Challenges to Market Daoism *283*
James Behuniak Jr.

17 Buddhist, Western, and Hybrid Perspectives on Liberty Rights and Economic Rights *296*
Gordon Davis

18 The Conversation of Justice: Rawls, Sandel, Cavell, and Education for Political Literacy *312*
Naoko Saito

19 Social Justice and the Occident *324*
Paul Standish

20 Three-Level Eco-Humanism in Japanese Confucianism: Combining Environmental with Humanist Social Ethics *337*
T. Yamauchi

21 Economic Growth, Human Well-Being, and the Environment *351*
Workineh Kelbessa

Part III Equity and Diversity

22 The Moral Necessity of Socialism *377*
Karsten J. Struhl

23 Invaluable Justice: Heidegger, Derrida, and Daoism Thinking on Values and Justice *400*
Steven Burik

24 What Is It Like to Be a Moral Being? *418*
Amita Chatterjee

25 What Is the Value of Poverty? A Comparative Analysis of Aristotle's *Politics* and Dōgen's *Shōbōgenzō Zuimonki* *429*
Steve Bein

26 Economic Goods, Common Goods, and the Good Life *441*
May Sim

27 On the Justice of Caring Labor: An Alternative Theory of Liberal Egalitarianism to Dworkin's Luck Egalitarianism *460*
Wu Shiu-Ching

28 Aging, Equality, and Confucian Selves *483*
Steven F. Geisz

29 Institutional Power Matters: The Role of Institutional Power in International Development *503*
Lori Keleher

30 The Value of Diversity: Buddhist Reflections on More Equitably Orienting Global Interdependence *519*
Peter D. Hershock

List of Contributors *539*
Index *551*

Acknowledgments

This book would not have been conceivable were it not for the East-West Philosophers' Conference Series and its dedication to galvanizing intercultural reflection. Based on the conviction that a plurality of perspectives from different traditions and cultures can be brought into a conversation out of which all parties can be enriched and new insights offered to the wider community and a global audience, the EWPC Series has throughout its many iterations since the 1930s brought together some of the best minds from the world's diverse cultures to explore various pressing issues and problems in philosophy and society. This aim reflects the multicultural self-understanding of the University of Hawai'i and its community and was a primary reason for the choice of the University of Hawai'i as the physical site for the East-West Center. Support from both these institutions was crucial to the success of the Tenth East-West Philosophers' Conference, from which the contributions in this volume were selected.

Hosted in May 2011, the Tenth East-West Philosophers' Conference brought together scholars from different cultures and with different perspectives to consider how best to realize a productive and sustainable reltionship between economics and ethics. What is the appropriate correlation between worth (value) and what is worthwhile (values), between seeking a shared human prosperity and our different visions of what constitutes a moral life? The theme of the conference was selected for its intellectual merits, but also to initiate conversations that anticipated Hawai'i's serving as host to the Asia-Pacific Economic Cooperation (APEC) Leaders Meeting that convened in November 2011, bringing together a high-level international gathering of more than ten thousand participants from the Asia-Pacific region, including leaders from twenty-one APEC economies, senior government officials, business leaders, international economists, Asia-Pacific experts, and worldwide media. Jointly sponsored by the Department of Philosophy under the auspices of the College of Arts and Humanities at the University of Hawai'i at Mānoa, and the East-West Center, the conference involved some 250 participants from countries across the globe for an intensive weeklong engagement.

The planning, organization, and execution of a conference of this size is a formidable undertaking. Fortunately we had the guidance of the International Advisory Committee, chaired by former conference director Marietta Stepaniants of the Russian Academy of Sciences. At home, the Philosophy Department of the University of Hawai'i lent its full measure of resources and support to the event, including a quite incredible team of graduate students. The long tradition of the East-West Philosophers' Conference Series has been maintained since its inception by the support given from the local community in general, and its business community in particular. In many ways, the topic of the conference this year—reembedding and integrating economics to promote a flourishing society—reflects the spirit of the enlightened Honolulu business community, which has continued to support this conference series as it has grown exponentially over the past generation.

This support has been rallied by the late business leader Dr. Hung Wo Ching. On the occasion of the Seventh East-West Philosophers' Conference in 1995, he embraced the cosmopolitan vision of the conference series and graciously agreed to be the honorary chairman. Dr. Ching worked for the success of the conference and was involved in all the details of the project. The Ching family has continued this tradition, and the Hung Wo and Elizabeth Lau Ching Foundation supported the Tenth East-West Philosophers' Conference with a generous grant.

Over the past decade the Uehiro Foundation on Ethics and Education headquartered in Tokyo has been a benefactor of the University of Hawai'i Philosophy Department in supporting the Uehiro Academy for Philosophy and Ethics in Education, the annual Uehiro Cross-Currents Graduate Student Conference, the University of Tokyo–University of Hawai'i Graduate Student Summer Institute, and many other student-driven initiatives. The Uehiro Foundation was also generous on this occasion in its support for the Tenth East-West Philosophers' Conference.

The conference has also received the magnanimous support of the following sponsors: the Diamond Head Memorial Fund, the K. J. Luke Foundation, Warren and Carolyn Luke, the Chan Foundation in Vancouver, Canada, Professor Barbara B. Smith, University of Hawai'i Press, Mr. and Mrs. Gulab Watumull, the James and Juanita Wo Foundation, Ms. Fumiye Miho, Robert C. Solomon, and Roger and Bonnie Ames.

The opening ceremony and reception were hosted at the Imin Center by University of Hawai'i president M. R. C. Greenwood and were attended by community dignitaries including Hawai'i governor Neil Abercrombie and many of our donors and community leaders. The East-West Center's partnership in sponsoring the conference series has enabled us to convene our meetings at a truly world-class facility, bringing both elegance and professionalism to our event.

As is the long-standing custom, the conference was open to the Honolulu public, and many community members attended the panels. Moderators for the panels were drawn from the ranks of the most distinguished University of Hawai'i faculty and East-West Center scholars, making the conference an event belonging to the entire campus. A great deal of international talent made its presence known, but it was balanced by the inclusion of many local world-class scholars.

A special achievement at this iteration of the conference with the sponsorship of the Uehiro Foundation on Ethics and Education (and the help of Masato Ishida) was the inclusion of many faculty from Japan's most prestigious institutions. A total of eighteen faculty and graduate students from Tokyo and Kyoto Universities were listed on the formal program, with several of them presenting plenary papers.

The University of Hawai'i Press and many other university and trade presses helped us construct a large book exhibition for the participants, and the famous photographer/philosopher Cheung Chan Fai from the Chinese University of Hong Kong contributed an exhibition of his photographs, *From 30,000 Feet in the Sky,* challenging us to find new perspectives on the relationship between economics and a flourishing world society.

The inspired work of two colleagues in particular must be noted. Cindy Scheopner distinguished herself as the program and fiscal officer for the entire conference and carried out her responsibilities with professionalism and good humor. The standing ovation she received at the closing banquet was fair evidence of the enormous respect and affection felt for her by the participants of the conference. We also had occasion to share the host culture of the islands with our foreign guests. Aaron Sala did a marvelous job in organizing different kinds of Hawaiian music and hula programs for the various events, and the conference had an opportunity to visit the Bishop Museum during a break on the weekend.

Introduction

Roger T. Ames and Peter D. Hershock

Economics and Social Justice

Economics and ethics have not always been considered separate domains of inquiry and action. From antiquity through at least the eighteenth century, the fields of economics and ethics were in many cultures understood to be coterminous and mutually entailing. Rather than being assumed to be naturally distinct, "value" and "values" were seen as intimately related.

There are assertions in early Buddhist texts, for example, that poverty alleviation is prerequisite for the successful cultivation of wisdom, attentive mastery, and moral clarity, and for the expression of such wisdom in compassionate, responsive virtuosity. In Islamic societies, it traditionally has been assumed (and still is in much of the Muslim world) that a single set of principles should govern all actions, from the marketplace to the mosque—an explicit denial of the all-too-common practice of separating and compartmentalizing the secular and the sacred. In Confucian societies, the right to rule as enshrined in the celestial mandate (*tianming*) that legitimized the authority of the state was understood as a "divine," or cosmic, response to the moral propriety of those in power (*de*), the most telling index of which was not the claimed motivations of the powerful, but rather the sustained presence of social prosperity and communal flourishing. And even in the modern West, prior to the beginning of the nineteenth century, economics and ethics were understood as closely allied projects oriented to understanding how best to organize society. Adam Smith, while now best remembered as the visionary architect of market economics, erected his arguments for the superiority of free and competitive markets on explicitly historical and moral grounds, and as a statement of his deep and abiding concern with issues of poverty alleviation and the advancement of society as a whole.

Contemporary global dynamics, especially in the aftermath of what is now being called the Great Recession of 2008–2009, can be seen as demonstrating the tragically devastating effects of what Karl Polanyi termed the "disembedding" of markets from broader social, cultural, and political systems. Among these continuing effects are the growing disparities of wealth, income, resource use, and opportunity that have characterized the last half century of accelerating globalization and industrial modernization.

Statistics tell the tale. Today, 40 percent of the world's assets are owned by just 1 percent of the world's households; the top 2 percent own just over half the world's assets, and the top 10 percent more than 86 percent. The bottom 50 percent of households, representing nearly 3.5 billion people, possess just 1 percent of global wealth.[1] In terms of income, the richest 5 percent of the world's people earn approximately 30 percent of total global income, while the poorest 40 percent of the world's working population took home just 5 percent.[2] And, in terms of consumption, the top 10 percent of the world's people consume more than the rest of the world combined.[3]

It has been argued, and quite vehemently by some, that statistics such as these tell only a partial story. Industrial modernization and the global dominance of free-market economies have brought absolute gains in incomes, health, and expanding life options for all. Inequality, it might be argued, is not a matter of ethical concern; it is a developmental necessity that demands, if anything, a technical response. Yet there is also considerable evidence that, since the self-conscious divorce of economics and ethics in the early nineteenth century, the absolute gains ostensibly enjoyed by all of the world's people have been brought about in ways that have afflicted the global majority with a *decreasing share* of the benefits of industrialization and free-market globalization. In 1820, the wealth and income gap between the richest 20 percent of countries in the world and the poorest 20 percent stood at a ratio of 3 to 1. By 1913, that ratio had increased to 11 to 1; in 1950 it was 35 to 1; in 1973, 44 to 1; in 1992, 72 to 1; and in 1998, 86 to 1.[4] And this ratio is exponentially greater today.

To the extent that a relatively shrinking share of wealth, income, resources, and opportunity brings with it increasing relational disadvantage, it is entirely understandable that the world's majority would question the continued segregation of considerations on how best to bring about economic growth from those regarding how best to understand and secure the conditions for leading truly worthwhile lives. And, in fact, this debate has become a critical rallying point for such disparate mass movements as those associated with the Arab Spring and Occupy Wall Street. Yet if the project is one of questioning and perhaps working to overturn the divorce of economics from ethics, it must also be one that recognizes the need to engage in a critical discourse aimed at reconciling the quantitative and the qualitative—the pressing need to bring value and values into productive conversation.

This book has grown out of an effort to open and sustain precisely this kind of conversation. One of its guiding assumptions is that the discussion we need is one that must be historically situated. We need a conversation acknowledging that contemporary global dynamics cannot be fully understood or aptly addressed through any critical approach that fails to take account not only of how things are now, but also of how they have come to be as they are. A second assumption, however, is that the discussion we need will not consist in reviving one or another premodern discourse. It is a conversation that, however much it draws upon the past, must be original; that is, it must be both creative and primordial, with *creativity* connoting significant innovation and *primordial* implying the initiation of new relations (from the Latin *primus* + *ordiri*, or "the first to begin a web").

The need to *originate* a conversation between economics and ethics is in part a function of the fact that the conceptual bifurcation of value and values is itself of relatively recent mintage. While it is now unremarkable to distinguish between "value" (as what something is worth) and "values" (as determinants of what is considered worthwhile), this distinction was explicitly formulated only in the early part of the twentieth century and seems to have come about as part of the larger modern separation of the work done by economics and ethics.[5]

Value and Values: Some Historical Context

The concept of value is, of course, at least as ancient as bartering practices. But it was only at the end of the eighteenth and the beginning of the nineteenth century that economists such as Adam Smith and David Ricardo began to articulate a broad and critically robust concept of value as a calculable function of resource supplies, patterns of use, exchange advantages, and labor efficiencies. Indeed, the articulation of this formal economic concept of value was a crucial driver in consolidating a transition from morally informed efforts to understand, explain, and improve on market operations—as, for example, in Smith's *Wealth of Nations*—to "scientific" and mathematically grounded economic theories. This transition occurred against the background of the interdependent processes of modernization, industrialization, marketization, and nation-state building. Together, these processes served as powerful imperatives for investigating the dynamics of social cohesion and identity formation, and for responding to questions about already evident and anticipated patterns of economic predation and social disintegration.

The economic concept of value was modified by Marx and Engels to mount a critical assessment of the exploitative dimensions of global capitalism. With far-reaching historical ramifications, Marx and Engels formulated a relationally robust notion of value as a complex function of material inputs, infrastructure costs related to producing and marketing commodities, the amount and quality of labor invested in the production of goods and services, and the institutional dynamics (especially those of a political and social complexion) that frame and sustain specific patterns of consumption and use. In this sense, value is generated as a complex function of the total field of relationships brought into focus by a specific commodity and its transport from producers to consumers.

Over the first half of the nineteenth century, then, as economic thinkers grappled with the new realities of the industrial era—realities that highlighted expanding opportunities both for wealth generation and for a troubling interplay among the economic, social, cultural, and political spheres—the concept of value itself underwent changes that involved both greater internal articulation and a significant (if for many, still tangential) linkage to issues of fairness and justice. Toward the end of the nineteenth century, presaging what we would now call a sociological perspective, the historian and philosopher Wilhelm Dilthey argued that human societies, their institutions, and their processes of change reflect acts of interpretation that establish hierarchies of concern and senses of what is good. Because of this, these societies cannot be understood in purely material or mathematical terms.

By the beginning of the twentieth century, material and epistemic conditions were conducive to further movement in the direction of articulating a full-fledged concept of values. Accepting Dilthey's thesis, Georg Simmel took the crucial step of seeking to link the concept of value as economic worth with clusters of personal and social dispositions, and with experiences of felt significance, cognitive coherences, and symbolic resonances that inform what is deemed worthwhile in any given society at any particular point in time. In his monumental *Philosophy of Money*, published in 1900, Simmel argued (re-inflecting Marx's and Engels' insights) that value is ultimately derived from social relations as a complex function of subjective and intersubjective desirability. While money serves as a generic medium of interaction that allows a full rationalization of exchange processes, it also symbolizes interests in ways that disengage them from their natural settings, greatly facilitating social differentiation. Simmel's conclusion, a prescient one, is that accelerating monetary exchanges would both result from and result in accelerating and expanding options for choice and voluntary association.

This usage of value as an index of personally and socially manifest dispositions and desires was fully mainstreamed by the 1930s. For example, anticipating by a half century the now increasingly well-recognized need to frame social realities in terms of a fundamentally relational ontology, the social psychologist George Herbert Mead (1934) explicitly located values in processes of interaction conjoining the subjective and the objective, the personal and the social, and the private and the public. Such a conception of values then became a key element in post–World War II political discourse, prompting Isaiah Berlin to argue in 1950 in a seminal *Foreign Affairs* article that the atrocities of the war could be traced to "crumbling values" and a collapse of civilizational standards.[6]

Although we now readily distinguish between value and values, it is useful to keep this historical sketch of the origins of the distinction in mind, especially because of the peculiar ontological status of values. Like emotions, values seem to be utterly commonplace and well-understood aspects of our daily experience until we are asked to define them precisely or to explain their formation and the power of their effects on how and why we live as we do. Like emotions, values are not easily or satisfactorily mapped onto the ontological and epistemological dichotomy of experiencing subjects and experienced objects. And just as there is to date no universally agreed upon "taxonomy" of emotions—and indeed considerable debate among psychologists, anthropologists, sociologists, and philosophers as to what counts (or does not count) as an emotion—there is as yet no widely accepted classification schema for values. The concept of values has not undergone anything like the kind of theoretical evolution that has taken place with the economic concept of value. To be critically useful, any origination of conversation between economics and ethics must take this into responsible account.

Narrative Complexity: Some Imperatives for Conceptual Diversity

One of the liabilities of the brief historical sketch just given of the conceptual bifurcation of value and values is that it unfortunately suggests a linear movement, a genealogy seemingly purified of complex influences. A related liability is that such a sketch is undertaken from what necessarily amounts to a single synoptic perspective, the apparent "objectivity" of which suggests that it is the product of a neutral (albeit editorial) "view from nowhere." Whatever our convictions about the possibility of neutral and objective inquiry and knowledge, given the global nature of the dynamics that compel a contemporary conversation between economics and ethics, the historical context needed to effectively originate and sustain this conversation cannot be singular.

If data is history stripped of narrative, the imperative to originate a global and historically contextualized conversation on value and values is also a mandate to grapple with the challenges of collaborative storytelling. To make use of Jean-Luc Nancy's pregnant distinction, our mandate is to resist the temptations of crafting a *common* history, an essential history, and instead to undertake improvisations of a truly *shared* history: that is, an irreducibly relational history in which multiple voices have important and distinctive contributory shares. In short, the attempt to conversationally reconcile value and values, critically balancing the claims and considerations of economics and ethics, must be both cognitively and culturally diverse.

One of the insights afforded by the study of ecosystems is that diversity is not a function of the mere presence of various species; in fact, diversity is a function of relationships among species and their environments that are conducive to self-sustained flourishing. And, with important implications for deepening efforts to conserve and enhance cognitive and cultural diversity, the greatest biodiversity is found not toward the geographical "center" of an ecosystem but rather in "peripheral" regions where different ecosystems intersect and overlap. Likewise, the most fertile sites of cognitive and cultural creativity and growth are those wherein different disciplines and cultures come into significant and sustained interaction.

Comparative philosophy is just such a site of cognitive and cultural interaction. Granted this, it is fitting that the occasion of the Tenth East-West Philosophers' Conference was used to question the estrangement of economics and ethics and to begin a shared discussion of prospects for their productive reconciliation. There are, of course, many different approaches to ethics that could be placed in conversation with economics. A typical list would include virtue, deontological, utilitarian, pragmatist, and care ethics, with each of these dispositions being subject to internal and increasingly refined further differentiation. But these very differentiations in approaches to discerning how best to structure thought and activity are themselves products of a historical process in which European and American perspectives have long been predominant. Many of the ethical systems that emerged in the context of non-Western cultures—such as those that might be broadly classified as Buddhist, Hindu, Islamic, Confucian, Daoist, and many more—cannot be readily fitted into the conceptual spaces mapped by Western categories.

Generally speaking, recognizing and taking critical account of such differences becomes particularly significant in addressing the kinds of predicaments—such as climate change and persistent global poverty and hunger—that require resolutely coordinated responses across cultural and national boundaries, responses that entail articulations among systems of values, not just within them. And in the case of bringing ethics and economics into conversation, inclusiveness is particularly crucial.

It is now a commonplace observation that justice is a key dimension in our ethical evaluation of different modes and consequences of economic activity. For a host of historical reasons, the globally dominant approach to assessing the presence of economic justice is tied to gauging the degree of equity present within and among societies, where equity is understood as equality of opportunity. Yet this is but one possible conception of equity, a conception that links equity and justice to the presence of freedoms of choice, the exercise of autonomy, and the primacy of the individual agent as the basic unit of analysis. In global historical terms, these now familiar linkages are relatively recent and are by no means either universal or common.

In an example from within the Western tradition, Aristotle characterized equity as a positive corrective to the effects of strictly applied laws and principles that fail to bring about justice precisely because of their universality. That is, for Aristotle, equity involves qualitative considerations of particularity and difference in the pursuit of justice. This approach—one that has strong resonances with Asian ethical traditions—suggests that engaging issues of economic justice can be effectively mounted and sustained only on the basis of a conception of justice that itself values diversity. Such considerations of particularity and difference certainly define the approach that has been taken in selecting the essays gathered here to foster the emergence of conditions conducive to an original conversation between economics and ethics in our age of increasingly complex global interdependence.

The Essays

The principle of inclusion for the essays selected for this volume has been their perceived contribution to the governing theme of the relationship between economics and justice in an age of global interdependence. One of the critical readers for this volume was Karyn Lai, whose own conscientiousness as a reviewer required her to reveal her identity to the editors, thereby facilitating the process of revision. Her detailed evaluation and substantial suggestions for the editors and individual authors have gone far to making this a better volume.

One recommendation Lai made that we pondered long and hard was that the essays be organized in a way that better serves the argument of the volume. Her critique was that our original organization into sections on interdependence, environment, economics, ethics, justice, and rights in fact ironically followed and reinforced the fragmented disciplinary structure in Western scholarship that we have railed against. Her suggested alternative arrangement was three sections on the themes of interdependence and relationality, dynamicism and contextuality, and equity and diversity, a structure that captures and reflects current thematics in cross-cultural philosophical dialogues. Further, these three themes appear over and over again in the essays en bloc as key approaches and insights into how best to address disjunctions among the domains of economics, ethics, and the environment.

The first set of essays, on interdependence and relationality, aims to bring into clearer focus what we mean by an "age of global interdependence" and to register the consequences of having failed to adequately acknowledge the critical merits of attuning our values, intentions, and cultural practices and ideals to the shared realities of interdependence and relationality. The chapters in this section pivot on a turn toward relational and interdependent conceptions of personhood as the basis of critical engagement with environmental issues, economics, ethics, politics, and institutional life. These insights are enriched by drawing from Japanese, Confucian, and Buddhist philosophies to anticipate new paradigms for understanding and responding to human, global, and environmental realities. These essays embed human life within dynamic environmental contexts, challenge liberalist economic models, and support meaningful reconceptualizations of globalization, economic vitality, welfare, justice, and other contemporary issues.

In his essay "The Mosaic and the Jigsaw Puzzle: How It All Fits Together," Thomas P. Kasulis addresses the fundamental epistemic question of how we know the world around us. Our Enlightenment legacy is a *Wissenschaft* paradigm of knowing in which we uncritically assume the individual integrity of independent things that interact with one another according to a pattern of external relations. Kasulis draws upon East Asian Buddhist sources to challenge the hegemony of this objective "scientific" model of knowledge with a holographic paradigm of knowing that emerges from a focus on internal, constitutive relations. Kasulis contrasts the particularized knowing of the engaged potter with the universalizing knowing of the detached geologist in how they relate to clay. He asks how we might reconsider the complex problems of our age if we were to address them through the "potter's" epistemic paradigm so that the ideals of engagement, internal relatedness, and holographic interpenetration are shared across social, economic, and political organizations while at the same time allowing each individual organization to maintain its distinctive local character.

Meera Sushila Viswanathan begins her essay "Value, Exchange, and Beyond: Betweenness as Starting Point" with a rigorous exploration of the linguistic and cultural etymology of the term "value." This exegesis uncovers the transformation of this term historically from referencing an absolute intrinsic quality ("a good") of something to referencing a functional quality that derives its meaning from its place among and its relationship with other things—the relative aspect of value as value in exchange or value in use. Viswanathan introduces the sociologist and philosopher Georg Simmel, who in his *Philosophy of Money* regards money as a "category of thinking" that produces the impersonal relations from which the modern concepts of the individual, independence, and freedom emerge. She then turns to Watsuji Tetsurō, who like Simmel is challenged to find values that transcend specific cultures but who offers a radically different understanding of relationality and its social consequences that ultimately derives from the logic and the corollaries of giving primacy to the betweenness of persons.

James McRae, in his "Triple Negation: Watsuji Tetsurō on the Sustainability of Ecosystems, Economies, and International Peace," also invokes Watsuji to speak from the relatively new branch of environmental studies that deals with the relationship between national security and ecosystem sustainability. The demands of consumerism can overstress the environment to the point of collapse, thus promoting economic and political instability. This being the case, environmental ethics, business ethics, and international relations can be seen as interdependent fields of inquiry. McRae deploys the philosophy of Watsuji Tetsurō to explain this interrelationship and articulate a normative framework that might be used to promote both environmental sustainability and international peace. Making use of the notion of *kyōsei,* which has been developed at length in business ethics, he expands Watsuji's concept of double negation to incorporate environmental concerns. Since environmental mismanagement leads to the collapse of socio-economic systems, Watsuji's ethics can form the groundwork for a normative system that promotes both strong economies and secure states.

Heidi M. Hurd's essay "Fouling Our Nest: Is (Environmental) Ethics Impotent against (Bad) Economics?" sets out to address perhaps the two most pressing questions of our time: How is it possible that we have so fouled our Earthly nest? And why are we seemingly unable to make changes that will reverse the devastating effects of our own actions on the ecological health of the planet? Her answers are at once straightforward and complex: fix our failed economics and cure the anthropocentrism of our impotent ethics to extend appropriate moral concern to natural entities. Hurd outlines a series of market failures—externalities or "transaction spillovers" such as air pollution; open-access resources such as fishing grounds; nonrival and nonexcludable public goods such as climate stability and air quality; and information asymmetries in which consumers are blind to hidden costs—that seem to be well beyond the resolution capacity of the market-fixing mechanisms to which our democratically elected officials most commonly appeal. But even if we were able to get the markets "right," the deeper problem with the utilitarian standard of value that we are wont to apply is that it makes *human* preferences the touchstone of all valuation. The challenge is to formulate a theory of welfare that uncouples welfare from subjective well-being and that is sufficiently capacious to include all natural entities. Finally, Hurd explores and yet remains unconvinced by the merits of an aretaic theory of environmental care in which virtuous persons' knowledge about their place in the world is sufficiently robust to dissolve pretensions that everything is "all about us"—even if it is all about our virtue.

Jin Y. Park, in "The Visible and the Invisible: Rethinking Values and Justice from a Buddhist-Postmodern Perspective," brings Buddhist values into the discourse on justice. In her reflection on the reality of poverty in the midst of the seeming abundance of economic growth, she references Amartya Sen (a name that surfaces in many essays throughout this volume), who begins his book *Development as Freedom* with the observation: "We live in a world of unprecedented opulence, of a kind that would have been hard even to imagine a century or two ago. . . . And yet we also live in a world with remarkable deprivation, destitution and oppression." Park argues that what distinguishes the modern from the premodern in human history is a shift in the justification of private actions and social changes from invocations of a theological ground to appeals to such secular ideals as equality, freedom, democracy, and progress. Since such concepts exist only through systems that represent and claim to exercise such ideals—whether governments, law codes, social and moral norms, or economic structures—the issue she seeks to address is the very nature of a system. Despite the fact that traditional Buddhist doctrine does not overtly offer a theory of justice in a manner similar to the Western philosophical tradition, the Huayan Buddhist understanding of the nondual nature of existence, even of particular entities, resonates with the Derridean notion of justice and its relation to an apparatus created to implement justice. Noting that visible reality cannot fully represent the reality of existence, Park then notes that, when one's vision is limited by the visible, epistemological error is the inevitable result. From a Buddhist perspective, this is the cause of suffering. In a capitalist society in which production systems are kept largely out of sight, the visible reality of human existence becomes comparatively inflated, while its invisible aspects, which in fact are part of the identity of the visible, are consistently suppressed. Hunger and poverty become invisible behind the glitzy appearance of big cities and shopping malls filled with commodities, luring consumers of all ages and backgrounds. Park appeals to the Huayan idea of "cessation and contemplations" as a basis for adapting traditional Buddhist practices in the context of the current world and its invisible systems. While cessation is liberation from the mode of thinking that anchors itself on the subject-object dualism, Huayan Buddhist contemplation means seeing things as interdependent and interpenetrating rather than as isolated existents, opening space for effectively reconceiving justice.

James Peterman's "You Ought to Be Ashamed of Yourself!" is the first of the next three essays that turn to justice and the Confucian tradition. Peterman explores the Confucian tradition as an opportunity to reflect on contemporary ethical discussions of restorative justice and the legitimacy of shaming practices, especially Martha Nussbaum's argument that shaming punishments by the courts compromise human dignity. Peterman argues that, in establishing a distinction between a primitive notion of shame that erodes personal dignity and a healthy conception of shame that is under one's own control, Nussbaum has provided those interested in restorative justice with at least a few legal cases in which an appeal to shame might in fact be legitimate. But Nussbaum goes on to claim that the proper response to a guilty act is appropriate punishment attached to the guilty act, not shame attached to the person. In doing so, Peterman suggests, Nussbaum renders the restorative justice position incoherent because she is confusing guilt and shame. Peterman deploys Bernard Williams and Ludwig Wittgenstein to challenge the narrowness of Nussbaum's conceptual argument and her assumption that hers is the only way of understanding the guilt-shame relationship. What Peterman is able to draw from the Confucianism of the *Analects* is a robust sense of intervention that would invite liberal-minded persons such as Nussbaum to become involved in restorative justice practices, both as observers and as participants. By becoming familiar with the healthy outcomes of restorative justice in inviting individuals to engage in public expressions of shame, liberal critics might be able to view such expressions of shame as a means of sustaining human dignity rather than as its enemy.

Yang Liuxin, Baoyan Cheng, and Xu Di, in "Filial Piety and the Traditional Chinese Rural Community: An Alternative Ethical Paradigm for Modern Aging Societies," analyze the pressing ethical implications of aging in a modern society. They examine traditional Confucian ethics as well as local community ethics, and through reconstructing the central concept of filial piety (*xiao*), based on a close reading of the *Analects of Confucius,* they explore ethical possibilities for contemporary extensions of this foundational value and the lifestyle that traditionally ensued from it. Filial piety is grounded in the natural and biological networks that connect intergenerational life experiences with genealogical continuities and ties of mutual affection. In a Confucian context, human beings are understood as participants in living families and communities, and the traditional rural community is seen as the local extension of the family unit. In looking to resolve the ethical problems of aging in a modern society, Yang, Cheng, and Xu argue that it is essential to transcend individualism and the value of financial exchange that are foundational in currently dominant economic and ethical paradigms. They insist that the traditional Chinese value of filial piety and its ideal exemplification in the lifestyle of the local community offer a unique point of departure for considering new ethical and practical responses to aging.

The essay by Roger T. Ames, "Doing Justice to Justice: Seeking a More Capacious Conception of Justice from Confucian Role Ethics," opens with a discussion of the concrete example of injustices perpetrated on the Hawaiian people to show how contemporary discourses on justice grounded in an abstracted individuality not only fail to deliver justice but in fact perpetuate grave historical injustices. The two related levels of this individuality are the autonomous individual and principled justice, both of which, Ames argues, are anemic abstractions insufficiently capacious to give expression to real social justice. Indeed, having become an ideology, abstract individuality not only fails to promote distributive justice; it has begun generating pernicious consequences. In his recent publications, Amartya Sen has recognized this problem. While Sen's capabilities approach goes some distance in acknowledging the need to treat people as the unique creatures they are, he remains committed to a foundational individualism and lacks sufficient appreciation of the irreducibly social nature of persons. Ames presents Confucian role ethics and its holistic vision of the moral life as an alternative, sui generis vocabulary for pursuing social justice. Confucian philosophy begins from a fundamentally relational and gerundive notion of unique persons that stands in stark contrast to a foundational individualism that persists in Sen, and it culminates in insisting that any theorizing of the human experience must find its ultimate warrant empirically in the ordinary affairs of the day. Ames argues, however, that Confucian ethics is not itself the final answer and, respecting its own premises, needs to be reformed and reauthorized for an increasingly complex world.

The essays in the second part, "Dynamism and Contextuality," emphasize the importance of understanding contexts within which human values are articulated and realized. Some of the chapters focus on the need for environment, economics, law, and other social institutions to be conceived of not as static systems, but as alive and dynamic and thus sensitive to local and contextual features. Other chapters provide empirical and historical evidence for this need for dynamism and contextuality through articulating examples of localized contexts, including contemporary India, China, and Korea, and in Islamic and North American indigenous societies as well.

In "Moral Equivalents," Kathleen M. Higgins begins from William James' suggestion that enlisting the youth in public service projects could serve as the moral equivalent of war in strengthening the character of young people and making them socially responsible. By calling for a reevaluation of our institutions in terms of costs and benefits, James is raising a market exchange question: How can we as a society make better deals for ourselves? Higgins uses this capitalist logic of "getting the best deal" to explore the possibility of marketing environmentalism rather than asceticism as the moral equivalent of sacrifice for the common good and of regarding environmentally sound displays of wealth and humanitarian largesse as moral equivalents of conspicuous consumption. This strategy echoes Nietzsche, who contends that we should reconsider values that we have taken for granted, and the institutions that are constructed on them, with the ultimate aim of reassessing our values to achieve better outcomes. Higgins urges that we reconsider not only moral values, but also the economic ones enshrined in capitalist practices as well. Indeed, if we follow James' logic of moral equivalents, we might want to look for a better deal than capitalism itself.

Purushottama Bilimoria, in "A Critique of Economic Reason: Between Tradition and Postcoloniality," explores the relationship between economics and ethics by using the occasion of India's recent reemergence as a major force in the global economy to take a second look at the narrative frequently rehearsed about India's long history of poverty and its inability to rise to the economic standards of the West. Bilimoria gives an account of this adverse imaginary, which has been grounded in the negative thesis that traditional Indian values and ideals are obstacles to economic development, leaving the subcontinent mired in abject poverty. At the same time, the positive cultural conditions for development have been wholly ignored. Bilimoria links the economic renaissance to an approach to human flourishing that has deep roots in the organic model of society that prevailed in traditional India, with its emphasis on trust, compassion, hospitality, sensitivity to the distress of others, and advocacy of a host of personal and social virtues. He ascribes this spiritual foundation not just to India's Hindu culture but more inclusively to what Jain, Buddhist, Parsi, Christian, Muslim, Sikh, Gandhian, and quasi-secularist forays have contributed to what might be called "the gross economic wisdom," or GEW, of the subcontinent. While classical economists continue to believe in the myth of economic growth, Bilimoria cites economists such as Amartya Sen who argue that GDP by itself should not be the sole measure of economic and social well-being. Indeed, actual welfare should be the gauge of development: that is, the quality of life that follows from respect for human dignity along with forms of advocacy, education, and social engagement that enable actual human capabilities.

Kenneth W. Stikkers, with his "Economies of Scarcity and Acquisition, Economies of Gift and Thanksgiving: Lessons from Cultural Anthropology," responds to the old and familiar debate between capitalism and socialism that followed from contradictory claims about human nature by noting how cultural anthropology has emerged to contest the problematic isolation of a simple and unitary human nature committed to personal gain as a defining source of our economic life. Yet in spite of being forwarded as products of an empirical and eminently scientific discipline, mainstream economic theories persist in making use of untenable assumptions about so-called human nature even after they have been flatly rejected by more than a century of empirical findings in other social sciences. Indeed, Stikkers is able to establish a clear contrast between familiar assertions of modern Western economics that appeal to the unbounded character of human desire to acquire and consume amid the scarce resources of nature, and less familiar economic perspectives grounded in assumptions about gift giving and thanksgiving. Stikkers argues that sound economic theory must rest on sound philosophical anthropology and that cultural anthropology is highly useful to economic theorizing because it opens up possibilities for retooling basic assumptions in economic thought and policy making. Gift economies invite us to consider other definitions of wealth and prosperity than those that have dominated Western thinking since the advent of modernity, challenging us to ask: What can we learn from such economies, and what theoretical possibilities are opened by studying archaic economies that orthodox economics tend to preclude a priori?

Larry A. Hickman returns to the Confucian tradition by placing it in conversation with American Pragmatism. In "John Dewey, Institutional Economics, and Confucian Democracies," Hickman deplores the recent rightward tilting of the political landscape in the United States, much of which has been fueled by an almost militant libertarianism that embraces many of the assumptions and values of the right wing of the neoclassical synthesis in economics.

Hickman chooses to examine a pragmatic alternative (or perhaps better said, a pragmatic supplement) advanced by John Dewey and others, including Thorstein Veblen. Although Dewey was one of the twentieth century's most influential philosophers, educators, and public intellectuals, the relevance of his ideas to contemporary economic theory has not so far been sufficiently appreciated, a fact that may be due, at least in part, to the very dominance of the neoclassical synthesis. Hickman explores how the critiques of key assumptions of neoclassical economics by Dewey, Veblen, and others open an avenue for better appreciating current discussions about democracy and economic development in Confucian societies. Dewey himself called for the birth of a new Confucianism that, rejecting a blind reliance on ossified custom and rigid hierarchies, would better express the profoundest values of the Chinese people as a culture of thought and intellectual influence. Such a transformation would become the institutional and cultural matrix from whence the local development of science and technology would emerge.

In his essay "The Responsible Society as Social Harmony: Walter G. Muelder's Communitarian Social Ethics as a Bridge Tradition for Confucian Economics," Robert Smid turns to the contemporary Chinese economy and seeks to put a historical Confucianism in conversation with the two dominant economic systems of the twentieth century: communism and capitalism. In this effort, Smid does not see Confucianism as providing an alternative economic system to either but rather as offering resources that might stand as constructive correctives to the systemic weaknesses that have been increasingly evident in these dominant economic forms. He begins with a thorough examination of the etymology and the textual history of the central Confucian notion of *he,* a distinctively Confucian conception of harmony amid difference that serves the culture as a grounding economic value for distributive justice as it is captured in the traditional image of the well-field system. Such a notion of harmony is manifest not in the reconciliation of conflicts as such but rather in the continuous adjusting and reconciling of such tensions as they emerge in ever novel circumstances. Smid then turns to the theologian Walter G. Muelder's communitarian social ethics and social responsibility as a bridge tradition that might facilitate the development of a constructive Confucian critique of contemporary economics. For Smid, the virtue of drawing on traditions like Muelder's communitarianism may be the difference between the Confucian tradition having something interesting yet wistfully idealistic to say in the economic sphere and the development of a practicable and thus more forceful discourse concerning the ideal organization of that sphere.

In their coauthored essay "*Swaraj* and *Swadeshi:* Gandhi and Tagore on Ethics, Development, and Freedom," Nalini Bhushan and Jay L. Garfield return us to India and begin from three observations: first, that Gandhi introduced *swaraj* and *swadeshi* into the colonial Indian discourse as terms encapsulating his ethical and political theory and his approach to a new economics of postcolonial life; second, that while these terms became an important framework for academics and activists in their discussion and analysis of the Indian struggle for independence, there was little agreement on what these terms actually mean; and, finally, that although Tagore and Gandhi explicitly debated the meanings of these terms, interpretations of this exchange have remained inconclusive. Bhushan and Garfield then use an epistemological predicament articulated by K. C. Bhattacharyya as a platform for revisiting the Gandhi-Tagore debate, a predicament that Bhattacharyya argues is grounded on the fact that the colonial Indian subject was shaped by an educational system that fostered "cultural subjection" and "a slavery of the spirit" to such an extent that Indians were wholly alienated from the norms, ways of seeing, and habits of mind needed to live authentic intellectual lives. By invoking this predicament, Bhushan and Garfield are able to determine more clearly the agreement and the disagreement that remain between Tagore and Gandhi and to show why Tagore regarded Gandhi's ideology as not only *shortsighted*, but in fact *incoherent*. Ultimately, Tagore and Gandhi offer two distinct conceptions of freedom. For Gandhi, freedom at its core is self-mastery and requires a renunciation of the material and political attractions of modernity and the adoption of the accoutrements of a simpler, more local agrarian life. For Tagore, freedom first is freedom *from* poverty and isolation but, after that, is freedom *to* engage creatively with others and other cultures. Whereas Gandhi sees modernity as *antithetical* to freedom, Tagore sees it as a *vehicle* to that goal.

Oliver Leaman, in "Economics and Religion or Economics versus Religion: The Concept of an Islamic Economics," challenges two stereotypes about Islamic economics, one that is positive: Islamic banking was immune to the recent economic collapse that affected the rest of the world so dramatically; and one that is negative: Islam is so restrictive on what can be done with capital, property, and inheritance that it has prevented the economies of the Islamic world from flourishing. Alluding to the historical fact that the Prophet Muhammad was himself a trader, Leaman sets out the main criteria of an Islamic economy by exploring its defining vocabulary. In spite of the uniqueness of the Islamic institutions, however, Islamic trade and banking necessarily take place in contexts that include many forms of banking and as a practical consequence must share significant common ground with non-Islamic institutions. Turning to studies of living examples of Islamic economies, Leaman shows that while important differences exist among them, there is a common axis on issues such as *shari'ah* law, interest, risk, and speculation. Although the Qur'an seems to contemplate firmly a free-market economy and clearly advocates a middle position between extremes, it also makes passionate demands for justice and charity in the conduct of trade, envisioning Muslim commerce as informed by appropriate measures to help less fortunate members of society.

James Behuniak Jr. turns from Islam to Daoism to address another stereotype, offering us "Two Challenges to Market Daoism." In the scholarly literature, a cadre of libertarians and advocates of free-market capitalism have co-opted the *Daodejing* and its putative policy of "nonintervention," which they extrapolate from the central Daoist notion of *wuwei*—literally, "doing nothing"—as a classical expression of laissez-faire economics, proffering a homegrown doctrine of "market Daoism" that can be used to anticipate recent economic developments in China. Behuniak musters two substantial challenges to this rather tenuous inference. A theory of market Daoism flies in the face of the fact that Daoist philosophy with respect to economics is not very different from other early schools and their persistent prejudice against the merchant classes. Indeed, given the socio-economic ideal provided in the *Daodejing* and other historical evidence, Behuniak argues that even a cursory reading of this classical text—a text that supports a policy of local rule over small communities—does not admit the claim that it would endorse market-friendly policies, let alone free-market capitalism. Indeed, Behuniak provides a compelling philosophical argument that the idea of market Daoism ignores Daoist philosophy's advocacy for reducing desires, its clear antagonism toward the accumulation of wealth, and its stance toward the negative effects that greed has on the human community.

Gordon Davis, in his essay "Buddhist, Western, and Hybrid Perspectives on Liberty Rights and Economic Rights," joins the lively debate among contemporary Buddhist philosophers and commentators on Buddhist ethics as to whether a robust conception of human rights can be derived from and justified within any major Buddhist tradition. Similar debates on whether there is justification for a regimen of human rights have continued in various non-Western traditions of moral philosophy for decades. Davis argues that justifications offered by Buddhist philosophers are based on the indirect and contingent benefits of institutionalized rights rather than on the direct or intrinsic moral value of rights. Further, he argues that this defense both practically and theoretically may offer the soundest moral reasoning when it comes to justifying the majority of putative human rights and to granting comparable support for both economic rights and liberty rights. Davis rebuts two major objections to the claim that economic rights are defensible and valuable: the objection that it is possible that there are intractable conflicts between economic rights and other, supposedly more important, rights; and the objection that economic rights will not foster the same degree of agreement among different cultures as liberty rights. For Davis, both objections are often overstated, and Buddhist ethics with its distinctively teleological emphasis can add much to modern Western reflections on personhood, law, morality, and the public sphere.

In her essay "The Conversation of Justice: Rawls, Sandel, Cavell, and Education for Political Literacy," Naoko Saito takes up the theme of the conversation between economics and values in the age of global interdependence. As an illustration of a kind of conversation about justice that calls for diversity, she reports on what she calls the "Sandel boom" in contemporary Japan. Harvard philosopher Michael Sandel, whose books and lectures are occasioning a public conversation on justice and democracy, has become a celebrity. Saito calls attention to Sandel's and Stanley Cavell's different modes of critique of Rawls' liberal concept of justice and of the idea of the human subject found therein. Although she is concerned with the substance of their arguments, her focus is rather on *how* they use the language of justice and *how* their respective critiques of Rawls reveal different convictions about the role of philosophy in awakening our common political consciousness. In analyzing the contrasting perspectives of these three American philosophers, Saito begins with Rawls' and Sandel's approaches to the conversation *about* justice, and then proceeds to a discussion of Cavell's approach to the conversation *of* justice—a conversation that exceeds the dichotomization of the liberal and the communitarian and that invokes an alternative horizon of economy—one that is inseparable from ways of living. While Rawls and Sandel want to engage us in rational discourse *about* justice, Cavell wants justice to speak to us—to you and me—and hence wants us to find our own voices in moral encounter, with the language of *polemos* a condition for authorship. For Saito, Cavell's Emersonian perspective and his ordinary-language philosophy elucidate an alternative dimension of our political life—a dimension missing from both Rawls' and Sandel's accounts that provides us with an alternative and a richer perspective on justice, incorporating a perfectionist vision of education for political literacy from within. Acknowledging dissonance and what is *not* held in common, this is a vision of education for *citizenship without inclusion,* carrying us beyond discourses of inclusion and diversity.

Paul Standish, in "Social Justice and the Occident," begins from the high visibility of the term "social justice" in contemporary political and academic discussion. Indeed, given the overcrowded and environmentally depleted world, how are we to live together in justice, in our own countries and continents and in the world as a whole? The centrality of social justice in the modern world requires that this term receive due critical attention. Standish begins by examining how social justice as an idea has become influential in educational research and related fields. He argues that this influence cannot be separated from the global dominance of English, which then gives rise to the related question of translation. Standish underscores the particular pertinence of this investigation in turning to a topic that lies at the heart of thinking in philosophy and social science: that is, the very nature of subjectivity as it is evidenced in translation. He then returns to consider aspects of social justice in an effort to unsettle some of the dominant patterns of influence and to open the way toward a different kind of thinking about social justice.

In his essay "Three-Level Eco-Humanism in Japanese Confucianism: Combining Environmental with Humanist Social Ethics," T. Yamauchi attributes the success of the Edo model of a green and sustainable environment to policies based on *an eco-holistic environmental ethic* that had Japanese Confucianism as its source. He seeks to compare Edo-era Japan with contemporary "modernized" societies by examining Platonic cosmology as a primary source of modern Western thought and then comparing it with Japanese Confucian cosmology. In a conflicted Platonic cosmology—one that includes "the artificial moment on the one hand and the organismic moment on the other"—Yamauchi finds a tension between the apparent absence of any concern for the environment in Plato's cosmology and the organismic, ecological tendencies that are evident in his social and political philosophy. The focus of Japanese Confucianism, by contrast, is a purely organismic view of nature in which the cosmos is regarded as a huge living being: the great father and mother that is the source of all things. Introducing a "three-level eco-humanism" that is adapted from the Japanese Confucian Ogyū Sorai, Yamauchi discerns common ground between advocates of environmental ethics and advocates of humanistic thinking and in the process searches for the wisdom needed to engender a sustainable society. He uses Edo-era Japan as a concrete example of a society that solved the moral conflict between human interest and the welfare of nature.

The title of Workineh Kelbessa's chapter, "Economic Growth, Human Well-Being, and the Environment," fairly maps the landscape of his concerns. He asks after the ethical implications that have been largely ignored in mainstream studies assessing the dominant modes of development advanced through the policies and practices of major international institutions, national governments, and independent NGOs. Although development ethicists have examined the moral consequences of development and have advocated for the flourishing life of the human being, appreciating the fact that economic growth can be a means of human enrichment, they have paid insufficient attention to the impact of development on the natural environment. More attention must be given to the interconnection if not interdependence of growth, human flourishing, and the sustainability of the natural environment.

The chapters in the third and final section of this volume, "Equity and Diversity," draw upon a range of philosophical traditions—Buddhist, Daoist, Hindu, and Confucian—to challenge the nonflexible notions of personhood and justice assumed by exponents of liberal economics. These essays provide a compelling case for the recognition of diversity as a way in which equity might be achieved. Issues discussed include the intertwined nature of economics, ethics, individual and institutional health, spirituality, poverty, egalitarianism, and attitudes toward the aging.

Karsten J. Struhl contributes to this final section with an essay, "The Moral Necessity of Socialism," that like Kasulis' essay is focused on different ways of conceiving of "interdependence," arguing that, while socialism might not be the historical necessity often claimed in classical Marxist theory, it is in fact a moral imperative that humanity must strive to realize if we are to survive and to live well. Struhl identifies two pressing problems in our historical moment that cannot be resolved within the context of a global capitalism and that make socialism a moral necessity. The first problem is that our global culture approximates what Norman Geras has referred to as "the contract of mutual indifference," a post-Holocaust malaise in which appropriate mutual moral concern has been replaced by a bystander mentality to the extent that such indifference has degraded the human experience and smothered our moral culture. The second problem is an ecological crisis that threatens the very survival of humanity, and much more. For Struhl, only socialism, understood as a fundamental moral project, can begin to address these problems.

In "Invaluable Justice: Heidegger, Derrida, and Daoism Thinking on Values and Justice," Steven Burik asks the question: What can comparative philosophy contribute to thinking about values, economics, and justice? Can we apply philosophy in general, and comparative philosophy in particular, to these problems directly? Martin Heidegger, one of the protagonists in Burik's essay, has on occasion made it clear that philosophy is "useless." Burik thus begins from a quote from Heidegger: "Philosophy . . . cannot be directly applied, or judged by its usefulness in the manner of economic or other professional knowledge. But what is useless can still be a force, perhaps the only real force." Thinking beyond values or use for Heidegger, Derrida, and Daoism can thus seem useless from the perspective of thought that maintains this dichotomy. Comparing Heidegger, Derrida, and Daoism, the main theme of this essay is to rethink the familiar process of valorization that is in fact inimical to justice. Traditionally, justice has been understood as somehow based on equality, or equity, and the idea of valuation means making artificial and hierarchical distinctions between opposing structures. Against this normal sense of value, Burik's protagonists argue for the value of inclusion, relationality, and interdependence. Do not interfere with the natural inclination of things. Let them run their course without artificially, and hierarchically, valuing them. Although these philosophers express this in different ways, there is an overall tendency toward a more inclusive way of thinking that translates into justice not based on equality or sameness or equity, but rather a notion of justice grounded in difference and otherness.

Amita Chatterjee, like Ames in his essay, offers a critical yet appreciative critique of Amartya Sen's recent book, *The Idea of Justice*. In "What Is It Like to Be a Moral Being?" Chatterjee engages the Sen title, in which Sen uses insights derived from both Western and Indian moral and economic theories to criticize the Rawlsian theory of justice. She begins by identifying the important differences that separate Sen and Rawls. In broad terms, rather than waiting upon the construction of a perfect theory of justice, Sen recommends that we begin at the other end. Since reducing the quantum of injustice in the world involves real people in real-life situations, justice has to be relative to a situation. In more technical terms, while Sen appropriates the *nīti* and *nyāya* from the *Arthaśāstra* as an important pillar of his idea of justice, Chatterjee makes the case that in a close reading of this canonical text, this distinction in fact lends theoretical support to Rawls' "theory" rather than to Sen's "idea." But important recent experiments in cognitive developmental psychology do lend empirical support to Sen's position. Chatterjee agrees with Sen that, in our world full of inequities and inequalities, Rawls' original position is a useless myth. Some of us are strong, some are weak, some are smart, some are dumb, some have access to more knowledge, and some have less. It is not possible to place everyone on a par. While Sen is certainly taking the discourse of justice in the right direction, we still have a distance to go in formulating a fully developed theory of justice as a moral value.

Steve Bein's essay "What Is the Value of Poverty? A Comparative Analysis of Aristotle's *Politics* and Dōgen's *Shōbōgenzō Zuimonki*" begins from the observation that Dōgen and Aristotle appear to stand in diametrical opposition to each other on the value of poverty. While Dōgen repeatedly admonishes monks and nuns to be poor and advises laypeople that even they would be better off if they gave up all their worldly possessions, Aristotle famously describes poverty as "the parent of revolution and crime." Bein summarizes this seeming contrast in four propositions: (1) Dōgen is often characterized as a radical in many respects; (2) Aristotle's observation of the relationship between poverty and social upheaval is anything but radical; (3) Dōgen's monastic, individualized conception of poverty is not identical to Aristotle's sociological, politicized conception of poverty; and (4) despite the foregoing three propositions, we may still find it surprising that Dōgen's view and Aristotle's view seem to be diametrically opposed to each other. After a close reading of the texts—Dōgen's *Shōbōgenzō Zuimonki* and Aristotle's *Politics*—Bein introduces an important distinction: Aristotle's poverty, involuntary poverty, is a "poverty of" (that is, a lack of something), while Dōgen's poverty, voluntary poverty, is a "poverty for" (that is, a surrendering of something in order to achieve something else). *If* Aristotle and Dōgen are both concerned with volition and consent in moral decision making, then the strong views Aristotle expresses on involuntary poverty might not extend to voluntary poverty. In other words, Aristotle's position on voluntary poverty might not be as far from Dōgen's as it appears.

In "Economic Goods, Common Goods, and the Good Life," May Sim, in continuing the dialogue with Aristotle, begins with two fundamental questions: What is the relationship of economic goods like food and shelter that are necessary for life to such common goods as the virtues of justice, moderation, courage, and wisdom? And how do these economic and common goods in turn contribute to the good life? Drawing on the wisdom of Aristotle and Confucius as representative of disparate philosophical traditions, Sim explores the lessons their reflections offer for contemporary assessments of these goods. For Aristotle, external goods such as property and wealth are required for human flourishing, but because they originate from and cater to our nonrational bodily needs, they are merely means to the end of the good life and are inferior to internal goods that arise from the well functioning of the rational soul. Aristotle relegates economics to the household or private realm, which must be satisfied before one can engage in the activities that constitute happiness itself, namely, the life of politics and philosophy. Whereas Aristotle holds that it is not a government's job to secure external goods for its people, Confucius believes that the ruler is responsible for securing the people's external goods, as the political realm is simply the family writ large. That is, external goods belong to the public realm of politics for Confucius and are a clear sign of the legitimacy of the government. Given the priority of virtue over wealth for Confucius, however, he would agree with Aristotle that external goods are not to be pursued as ends in themselves. Aristotelians and Confucians both acknowledge our reliance on external goods for living and point to their proper use in living well, but each of them also directs us to the natural limits of human consumption, which are clear if we understand human nature. Both philosophies would recommend that, instead of a quantitative GDP measure that focuses solely on goods and wealth, a new measure of economic well-being is needed that is informed by the quality of virtue in oneself and others, including the nonhuman realm.

In "On the Justice of Caring Labor: An Alternative Theory of Liberal Egalitarianism to Dworkin's Luck Egalitarianism," Wu Shiu-Ching engages Ronald Dworkin's theory of resource equality, which claims that those who devote their lives to caring for vulnerable family members are no different from those who lead luxury lifestyles rather than work. Both are free to choose what they want to do, and as a result, neither is justified in receiving social compensations and both should be held responsible for suffering social and economic disadvantages due to their choices. Leading feminist philosophers argue that Dworkin's analogy is clearly false because caretakers, whether by force or by choice, provide a labor of love for dependent others, and, in their efforts as caretakers, they promote the public interests of society as a whole. Therefore, unlike in the case of those who elect to live a life of luxury in pursuit of their own happiness, the concept of good behind love's labor is the pursuit of the welfare of those who are dependent on someone else's care. Wu first summarizes the substance of the feminist objections to Dworkin's egalitarian theory, including the critique of dependence, the unequal division of sexual labor, and the capability approach to the just redistribution of public resources. Allowing for the apparent differences among feminist philosophers, Wu is able to abstract a substantial alternative theory of liberal egalitarianism from their critiques. This alternative theory would replace envy-free equality with altruistic care and social cooperation as the foundations for the theory of justice. It would also reinterpret what Dworkin means by sovereign virtue, not in terms of how the government should avoid envy among social members, but in terms of how the government should provide basic care for the protection of human dignity. Finally, with respect to human dignity in general and the dignity of those who provide care in particular, Wu's theory holds that the capability approach is better than resource equality as a form of just distribution of social resources.

In his essay "Aging, Equality, and Confucian Selves," Steven F. Geisz recalls the essay by Yang Liuxin, Baoyan Cheng, and Xu Di earlier in the volume with the question of whether the traditional value of filial piety (*xiao*) might have contemporary relevance. Geisz adds to the growing conversation between Confucian philosophy and liberal democracy by thinking specifically about ways in which a Confucian valuation of and deference to the elderly might challenge and inform liberal democracy. Geisz begins from the observation that liberal democracy at least ideally aims to treat all adult citizens as politically equal. Once citizens are over the age of majority, they are deemed full-fledged members of the community and in theory have equal standing with all other adult citizens when it comes to making policy and participating in the political realm in general. Geisz constructs his Confucian intervention around three interlinked questions: Is there any plausible alternative to a standard "all adult citizens have equal political standing" model of democracy that could be drawn from a specifically Confucian valuing of elder members of the community? Insofar as there is a plausible alternative, what might it reveal about differences between how liberalism and Confucianism think of persons as located in time? And what sort of difference would it make if the Confucian valuing of age were implemented via informal social norms, on the one hand, or via explicit institutional mechanisms and procedures, on the other?

Lori Keleher, in her essay "Institutional Power Matters: The Role of Institutional Power in International Development," argues that, while academics and practitioners working in international economic development often cite the critical role of empowerment within development, insufficient attention is given to a consideration of institutional power and its implications. Institutionalized power plays an important role in generating, reinforcing, and reproducing the inequalities that either prevent or limit various groups of individuals—most notably women—from acting as agents, from engaging in empowerment processes, and from being empowered. After exploring the key terms of art and explaining the concept of institutionalized power, Keleher enumerates some of the aspects of institutionalized power that require attention within international development. For example, institutions conflate social kinds with natural kinds and thereby allow social differences to appear to be fixed, natural, and objective facts about the way things are. Also, institutions defend current social systems with all their oppression and inequalities as essential to a valuable and valued culture, thereby allowing social differences to appear to be hard-won cultural assets that reflect the way things ought to be.

In "The Value of Diversity: Buddhist Reflections on More Equitably Orienting Global Interdependence," Peter D. Hershock weaves many of the themes of the volume together rather explicitly. Like Kasulis at the beginning of the volume, Hershock appeals to the Buddhist tradition and the concepts of interdependence, karma, and nonduality as resources for critiquing liberal assumptions about autonomy and individuality. He begins by providing a synoptic overview of statistics charting how income, wealth, and resource use have come to be distributed globally and within the United States, and perhaps even more alarmingly, how the trajectory of such distribution is trending exponentially. Making use of the Buddhist doctrine of karma, he argues that this trajectory is neither a historical accident nor a developmental necessity and that it can be altered. The combination of economic growth with widening inequality constitutes a predicament—an index of conflicts among widely held values and interests that cannot be "solved" technically. Rather, they can be resolved ethically only through deliberatively articulated and globally shared changes in globally dominant complexions of values, intentions, and practices. For guidance in reconciling the politics of recognition with that of redistribution, and for reconciling growth with justice, Hershock draws on Buddhist nondualism to provide a more nuanced conception of diversity and the basis of a qualitatively robust ethics of interdependence that emerges from a proper respect for relational equity.

This volume of thirty essays is remarkably wide-ranging in its philosophical exploration of the relationship between value and values. Rather than presenting a singular vision of that relationship, it offers prismatic access to global reflection on the imperatives for and merits of placing economics and ethics once again in open and sustained conversation. Economic theory and practice have over the last several centuries focused on understanding and establishing the conditions for quantitatively construed growth, predominantly depicting economic relations as universal phenomena that are both essential and common to all societies. As different in approach as the essays in this volume are, they are united in calling attention to the liabilities of this predominantly quantitative bias and calling for a restoration in economic discourse of significant qualitative concerns. Taken together, they present a chorus of approaches aimed correctively at aligning the interplay of economics and ethics with interculturally shared commitments to human-with-planetary flourishing—a diversity-enriching and equity-seeking East-West response to what may well be the defining challenge of the twenty-first century.

NOTES

1. James B. Davies with Susanna Sandström, Anthony Sharrocks, and Edward N. Wolff, "World Distribution of Household Wealth" (United Nations Discussion Paper 2008/3).

2. Branko Milanovic, "Global Income Inequality: A Review," *World Economics* 7, no. 1 (January–March 2006), 142. Accessed April 5, 2011, http://www2.unine.ch/repository/default/content/sites/inequality08/files/shared/documents/Milanovic1.pdf; United Nations Development Program, *Human Development Report, 2007/2008* (New York: Palgrave Macmillan, 2007).

3. World Bank, *World Development Indicators, 2008* (Washington, DC: World Bank, 2008).

4. United Nations Development Program, *Human Development Report, 1999* (New York: Oxford University Press, 1999).

5. The first systematic exposition of values in the contemporary sense implying both social origins and psychological attitudes was in William I. Thomas and Florian Znaniecki, *The Polish Peasant in Europe and America* (Chicago: University of Chicago Press, 1918–1920).

6. Isaiah Berlin, "Political Ideas in the Twentieth Century," *Foreign Affairs* 28, no. 3 (1950), 351–385.

PART I

INTERDEPENDENCE AND RELATIONALITY

The Mosaic and the Jigsaw Puzzle 1

How It All Fits Together

Thomas P. Kasulis

To understand and suitably engage our world—both natural and human—we need an effective strategy for knowing. That may seem obvious, but to forget it is to risk epistemic disaster. A Chinese proverb says a journey of a thousand *li* begins with one step, but that assumes the step must be in the right direction. For example, the tools we use to analyze political justice, economic equity, or ecological stability are all the legacy of the Enlightenment, what I will call the *Wissenschaft* paradigm of problem solving. That paradigm relies on fundamental, no longer consciously examined assumptions about the nature of relatedness, whether the relations are person to person, person to community, nation to nation, or humanity to nature. In other words, the *Wissenschaft* paradigm derives from an assumption about how everything fits together, and it proceeds in three steps. First, we analyze phenomena into their smallest parts. We then develop a model or framework to describe what connects those parts. Finally, we rebuild the picture of the whole by applying the relational framework to the individual components. In short: the *Wissenschaft* paradigm assumes the whole consists of its parts and a superstructure of external relations joining those discrete components. Such external relations as contracts, rules of exchange, principles of responsibility, criteria of fairness, or physical laws are the links in the superstructure. In the *Wissenschaft* paradigm, knowing arises from the analysis of the atomistic parts as viewed through an appropriate model, often a mathematical model, describing what holds the parts together.

What if we were to change the paradigm for knowing how things fit together? Suppose reality consists of not discrete, but overlapping or interdependent entities. Then we would have to adjust our method of knowing accordingly. To discover how things are related, we would look not outside the things, but more closely into each thing to see how it interpenetrates adjoining things. This would be a form of knowledge based on internal rather than external relations. To choose between the external and internal paradigms of relation is to choose whether reality is put together more like a mosaic or more like a jigsaw puzzle. Let us explore that analogy further.

The Mosaic and the Jigsaw Puzzle

Imagine we are in a Byzantine cathedral after significant damage from an earthquake. The huge mosaic backdrop to the altar is now in tiny pieces on the floor. The tiles, nearly identical in shape and differing only in color, lie in a heap at our feet. Studying the tiles alone, can we determine what the original mosaic portrayed? No. From the same pile of tiles, we could assemble many mosaics. To reconstruct it correctly, we would need information not found in the pieces themselves: perhaps a photograph or drawing of the mosaic before it was destroyed or perhaps the blueprint from when the mosaic was created. Even if we could find a subtle imprint of the tiles still on the wall, we would get only a hint of the overall configuration of the picture. Without knowledge of the colors, we still could not be sure exactly how to restore the mosaic. We might surmise it portrayed, for example, four human figures in robes. But which robe was red, which blue, which green? We might begin by counting the number of blue, red, and green tiles on the floor. Then we could try to map them onto any visible indentations on the plaster, counting the number of tiles needed for each set of outlined human figures. Analyzing the problem with a sophisticated computer model, we might be fortunate enough to succeed. More likely, we would still err in places, not knowing with certainty, for instance, where in the mosaic, other than in the robe, we should place identically colored tiles. Remembering intact church mosaics we had seen, we could try various alternatives, but there would likely remain many unknowns.

Now imagine instead we enter a home that had undergone similar devastation, but rather than a mosaic, the idiosyncratic owners had put together a twenty-thousand-piece jigsaw puzzle and mounted it on the wall much like a mosaic. Suppose again we had only the heap of pieces on the floor. Because these are jigsaw pieces rather than mosaic tiles, however, the combination of colors and shapes in each puzzle piece is unique. The question again is whether, based on the collection of jigsaw pieces alone, we can determine what the original jigsaw puzzle portrayed. In this case, we can. We would not need a blueprint or photograph to tell us how to assemble the pieces, because each jigsaw piece contains the information for connecting with its adjoining pieces. Not resorting to higher mathematics or computer-assisted modeling, we need only pay scrupulous attention to the details in the pieces themselves. All that would be required is patience and time, admittedly a lot of patience and time. Yet the reconstruction is possible because the details in the puzzle pieces reveal the interconnections, and, given the uniqueness of each piece, only one whole can be made from those pieces. To put together the mosaic, by contrast, we had to look outside the tiles to refer to an abstracted superstructure of relations represented in a blueprint or model. In other words, for the jigsaw puzzle, we discover how everything fits together by scrutinizing the details of each unique part. For the mosaic, on the other hand, we discover how everything fits together by distancing ourselves from the detail of very similar individual pieces. Assembling the jigsaw puzzle involves *engaged* knowing; the mosaic, *detached* knowing.

External and Internal Relations

Diagrams can depict how the mosaic and jigsaw images of the whole are built out of external and internal relations, respectively. Figure 1.1 shows how the two kinds of relations contrast. In an external relation, the related entities are discrete: *a* is *a* and *b* is *b*, regardless of whether they are related. Their relation (*R*) is something more, something outside what *a* is in itself and what *b* is in itself. In an internal relation, however, part of *a* is *b* and vice versa. Neither could be fully what it is without the other.

Figure 1.2 shows a whole built of externally related atomistic parts. We have already noted that the *Wissenschaft* paradigm of detached knowing begins by

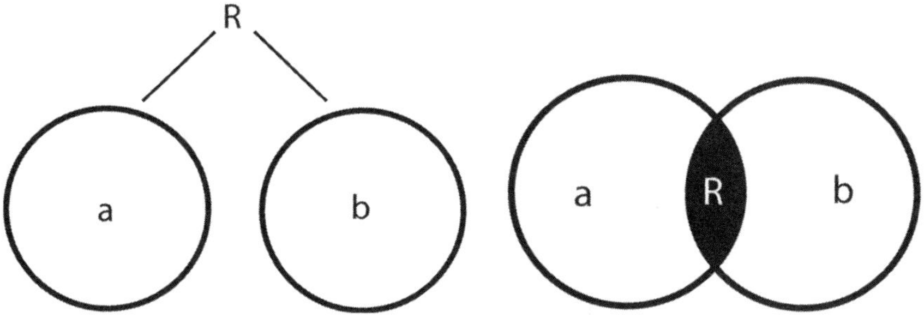

Figure 1.1. External Relation (left); Internal Relation (right)

breaking phenomena down to the smallest possible units, but the paradigm also presupposes that the further we reduce, the less variety we find among the parts. For example, suppose you were to look up from this book to survey the objects around you. You see many thousands of different things, but if you reduce that diversity to the level of elements, there can be no more than some 120 different atoms. Reducing further, those atomic elements can be analyzed on the quantum level to one or two dozen different subatomic particles. Each reduction yields less variety among its components, its goal being to reach the point when all constituents are essentially identical ("the basic building blocks of the universe"). Once reality is so atomistically analyzed, we can turn to the links among those basic building blocks, constructing a model that will describe the whole we started with, albeit in radically different terms. Viewed in this light, we see the beauty and efficacy of models built from mathematical functions: assuming the structure of the whole can be expressed as a function, an $f(x)$, the more our reductions have produced similar things, the more of reality fits into the range of the variable x. That is, the less the variety, the more the mathematical model can explain and the more adequately we can depict the full mosaic. As a result, the *Wissenschaft* paradigm has an aversion to variety and uniqueness.

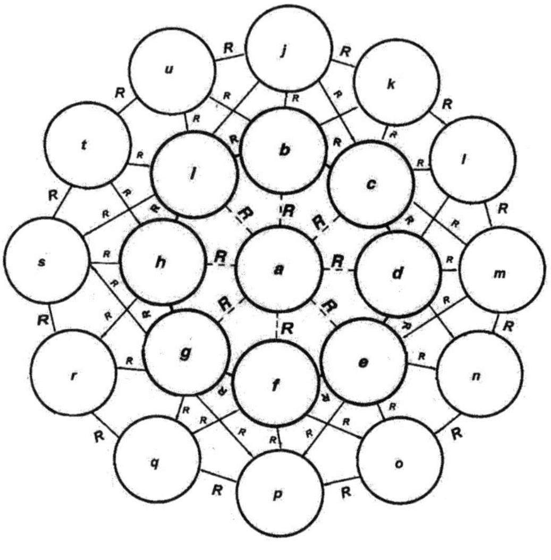

Figure 1.2. Externally Related Whole Consisting of Atomistic Parts

Figure 1.3, by contrast, shows a whole dependent on internal rather than external relations, more like the overlapping pieces in a jigsaw puzzle than the tiles in a mosaic. In such a view of how reality fits together, no single item exists discretely; to know a thing entails knowing something of its overlapping, interdependent adjacent entities. Knowledge of the whole arises, therefore, by analyzing the *uniqueness* of each entity in the whole, not by assuming the similarity of each entity. As Figure 1.3 shows, each part of the whole is unique because of its overlaps, that is, because of its interdependence, not its independence. For example, entity *b* differs from the other parts of the whole because only *b* overlaps with *a, i, j,* and *c*. Furthermore, because *b* cannot be *b* without *a, i, j,* and *c,* that specific interrelatedness yields its uniqueness. Figure 1.4 depicts the individual piece *e* of the mosaic paradigm: piece *e* is still piece *e* even if we strip it of its relations. In the jigsaw puzzle paradigm, by contrast, without its interrelations, *e* is not fully itself (Figure 1.5). To fill in what is missing (Figure 1.6), we must consider also *a, d, n, o,* and *f* (Figure 1.7), but if we want to fully consider those pieces, we have to include their adjacent pieces as well, and so on. In its uniqueness, the shape of *e* suggests its own interconnectedness. As the thirteenth-century Japanese Zen master Dōgen said,

> When we have not yet fully engaged phenomena with the body-mind, we think that is all there is to the phenomena. If we sufficiently engage them with the body-mind, however, we sense there is something more left out.[1]

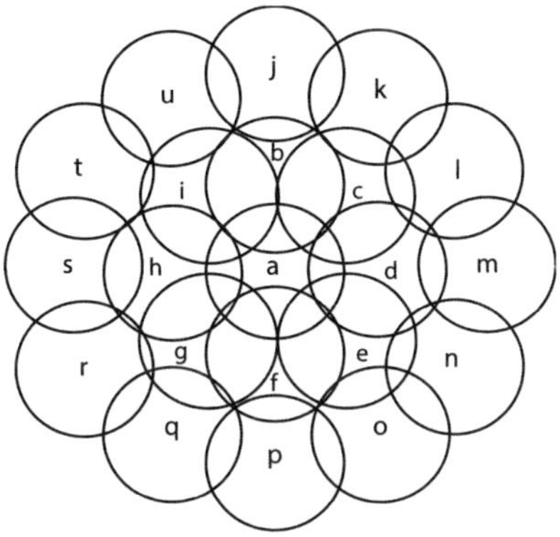

Figure 1.3. Internally Related Whole

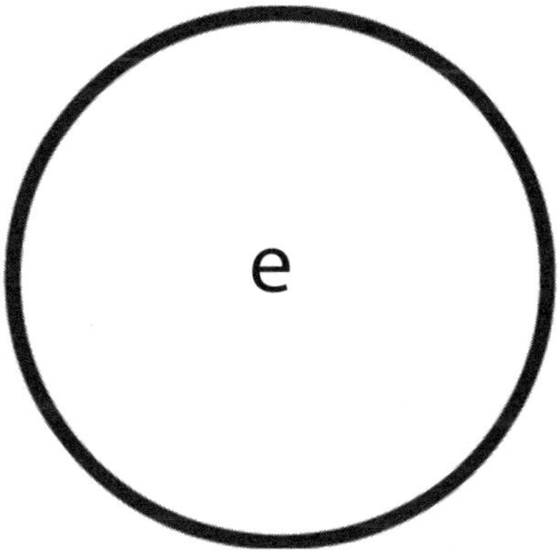

Figure 1.4. Piece *e* of the Mosaic without Its Relations

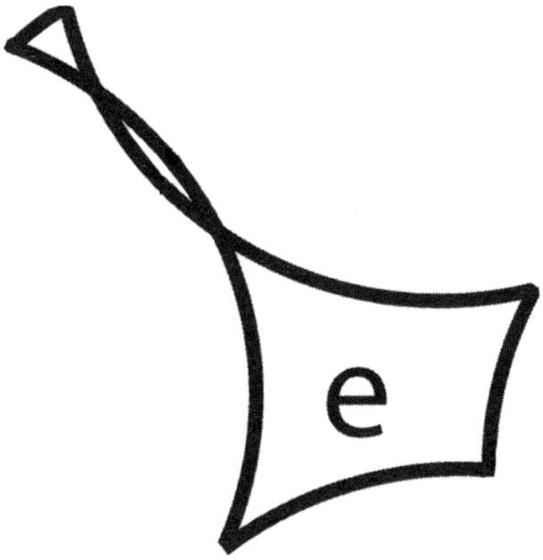

Figure 1.5. Piece *e* of the Jigsaw Puzzle without Its Relations

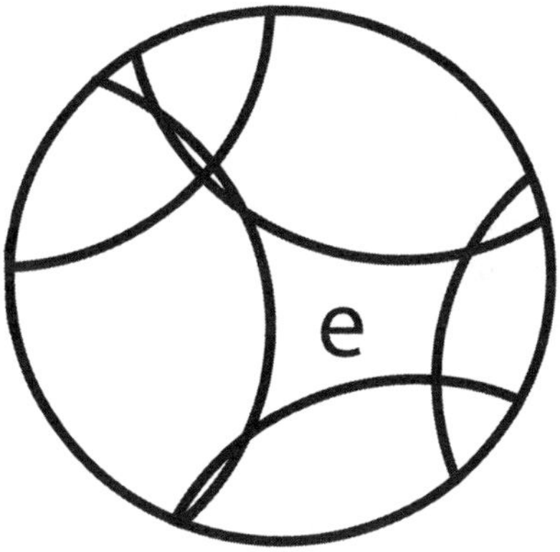

Figure 1.6. The Jigsaw Piece *e* in Its Fullness

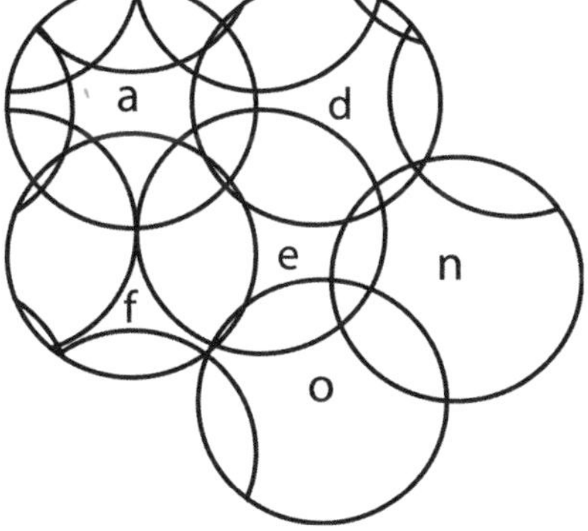

Figure 1.7. Jigsaw Piece *e* with Its Interrelations

Internally related wholes often have another special characteristic, a structure where not merely is the whole the sum of its parts, but its pattern is also in each of its parts. That is a "holographic" relation of whole and part.

The Holographic Whole

Figure 1.8 shows what happens when the pattern of Figure 1.3 is holographically inscribed in each of its parts. Given the recursive nature of the holographical, entity *k,* for example, contains the pattern of the whole—*a* through *u.* Taken together, Figures 1.3 and 1.8 reveal an intriguing characteristic of parts within a holographic whole: the combination of uniqueness and interchangeability. As already explained, each part is unique by virtue of its specific overlaps with its adjoining parts. Yet in its function of reflecting the pattern of the whole, each part is interchangeable with any other part: *every* individual part (*a, b, c, . . . u*) contains the pattern of *all* of the parts in the holographic whole (*a–u*). A concrete example will explain the paradox of each piece's being both unique and interchangeable.

Consider a sample of my blood compared with a sample of my saliva. Obviously, they are very different. In a test for cholesterol, for instance, a doctor would test a sample of my blood, not my saliva, because cholesterol internally relates to blood, but not saliva (as, in Figure 1.3, *c* has an internal relation with *b* but not

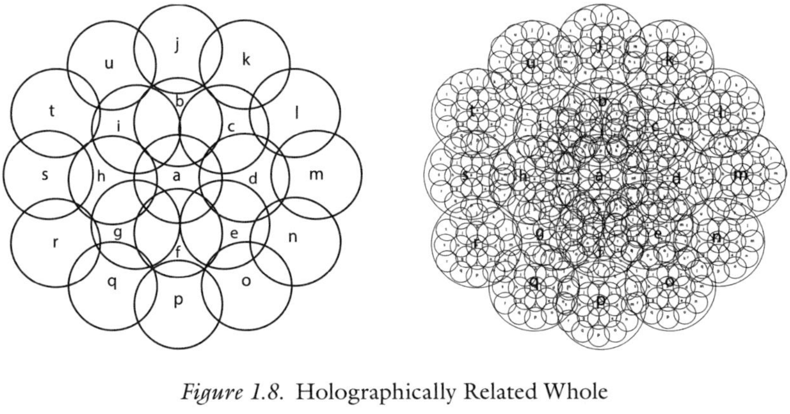

Figure 1.8. Holographically Related Whole

with *s*). Yet if we examine the blood and saliva more closely—*much* more closely—they are both holographically inscribed with identical DNA. For DNA samples, a drop of blood and a drop of saliva are interchangeable: either could yield key information for saving my life in a medical treatment or for landing me in jail after a forensic investigation. As parts internally related to other parts of my whole body, my saliva and blood cells relate to the rest of my body in radically different ways. Yet, as holographically inscribed parts of the same body, they match. This characteristic of uniqueness and interchangeability contrasts with mosaic constructions, in which the individual parts of the whole are ideally as alike as possible and difference lies in the superstructure of external relations. In organic chemistry, for example, every hydrogen atom or every carbon atom is identical in nature to all the other hydrogen atoms or carbon atoms; the rich variety of hydrocarbon compounds occurs because of the quantity of those atoms and how they are externally linked. In the holographic version of the jigsaw paradigm, to the contrary, uniqueness and variety lie in the individual parts, while sameness occurs in the whole as it is reflected by the parts. This contrast between the mosaic and holographic jigsaw paradigms leads to differences between detached and engaged knowing.

Detached and Engaged Knowing

Suppose we find ourselves in a forest or large grove where all we see around us is one individual tree after another. If we want to understand the grove's dispersion, we might begin by leaving it for higher ground, getting an aerial view for the sake of plotting its size and shape, relation to the surrounding terrain, and so forth. Then we can return to the grove to correlate its dispersion with light, water, ground cover, soil chemistry, and so forth. How did the seeds from the trees mature, disperse, and germinate so this species spread as it did in this place? We can try to model the prevailing wind patterns or animal behavior to see how they might have influenced this configuration. Such an approach seems both commonsensical and scientifically sound. If it were a stand of maple or oak, for example, those models of dispersion would yield excellent results. But what if it were instead a grove of aspens?

In that case, we would likely find that our previous models might not work so well, and we would have to tinker with them in hopes of making them more accurate, adding new parameters, or giving different weight to the factors we already have. It is no surprise that tinkering may be needed. The models we had developed for stands of maples, with their winged seeds, had to be adjusted when we worked with stands of oaks, with their acorns. The models of wind flow had been decisive in understanding the dispersal of the maple seeds, but for the acorns, displacement caused by foraging animals turned out to be more significant. For the aspens, however, our adjustments on the models would be less effective; we would not find any special external factors that, when added to the model, adequately explained the dispersion. The problem is that our mosaic paradigm had us looking for only *external* factors.

If we had begun not by distancing ourselves from the grove, but by focusing more intently on its internal details, we would have discovered that the individual aspens are not discrete entities but parts of a single organism. Like some fungi and mushrooms, these aspens are all outgrowths of a single root system. To understand one tree, we would need also to understand the trees next to it. The neighboring trees are not merely adjacent; they are part of one another. The aerial view we achieved by moving away from the grove could not show us this. No mathematical modeling based on seed dispersion, wind patterns, and animal behaviors could ever adequately explain how this grove of trees came to be the way it is. If we had never discovered the internal subterranean connections among the trees, we might have kept working on the mathematical models of external factors, making ever more complex formulas in hopes of getting closer to the truth. Yet the more we tweaked those models, the farther we got from the root of the answer.

Our tale of the aspen grove highlights the assumption made before we began to gather our empirical data, an assumption that skewed the results of our scientific modeling. We had assumed that the trees were like the individual, nearly identical tiles of a mosaic, linked by some external network of connections. We assumed that if we stepped back far enough and saw the patterns of all the external environmental factors, we could find those connections and map them through an adequate mathematical model. Then we would discover the blueprint that would tell us how the trees in the grove all fit together. If instead we had thought of the individual trees as more like jigsaw pieces than tiles in a mosaic, we would have assumed that in each tree we could find its connection to its neighboring trees. Then we would not have stood back and looked at the phenomena from a detached perspective, but instead engaged the trees by getting closer to them, digging into each one's individual character to discover the interlinkage among all the trees. Studying the individual would get us to the whole.

Let us review what our example has taught us about the two kinds of knowing. If we assume reality is atomistic, our study requires us to distance ourselves so we can assess the whole. The connections are not in the particulars, but in the external links that connect across the particulars. We have to detach ourselves from the variety of the phenomena so we can "see the forest for the trees." If we instead assume reality is a holographic jigsaw puzzle, however, our study begins with engaging the particular more closely so we can understand not only its inherent overlaps but also, by focusing in even more, the whole. In short, the mosaic paradigm encourages zooming out for the wide-angle view, whereas the holographic paradigm encourages zooming in to find the recursive microstructures revealing the structure of the whole.

The Holographic Paradigm in Asian Philosophy

The holographic relation of the whole in every one of its parts appears in many Asian philosophical traditions, most strikingly in the metaphor of Indra's net from the Indian Mahāyāna Buddhist *Flower Garland Sutra* (*Avataṃsaka Sūtra*). The imagery invites us to imagine each phenomenon (dharma) as a bejeweled node in a net. Each jewel has $n - 1$ facets, n being the totality of phenomena (the total number of jewels) in reality, and each facet reflects one other jewel. The result is that each jewel reflects all the other jewels and by examining every facet of any one thing, one can see in it the reflection of all things. Although Indian in origin, the holographic paradigm attained its fullest philosophical expression in East Asia with the Chinese Huayan (K. Hwaeom, J. Kegon) school of Buddhism and its theory of the four phenomenal worlds or worldviews (*dharmadhātu*).[2]

According to Dushun (CE 557–640), the founder of Huayan Buddhism, there are four levels to the phenomenal realm, each deeper in profundity than the one preceding it. On the surface there are just "things" or "events" (*shi*). These are like the individual phenomena labeled alphabetically in Figure 1.2, but without the links bridging them. This level resembles the first step of detached knowing: isolating the basic building blocks. On the second level, we have "patterns" (*li*) that form the connective tissue among things, in effect, the various *R*s in Figure 1.2. That connective tissue is what detached knowing portrays with its models: mathematical functions with variables, for instance. The third level is where the models and the individual phenomena mesh ("the interpenetration of *li* and *shi*"). The *Wissenschaft* paradigm, with its detached knowledge, aspires to this worldview: the fully expressed model of atomistic things connected by the external relations supplied by the superimposed template (Figure 1.2 as a whole). In the fourth and deepest phenomenal realm, however, the Huayan paradigm introduces internal relations. The interconnective web of external relations, the superstructure (*li*) connecting all phenomena, disappears, and we find instead the interpenetration of all phenomena without external connective links ("the interpenetration of thing and thing, of *shi* and *shi*"), an obvious reference to an internally related whole. Huayan Buddhism also assumes a holographic relation of whole and parts. As Dushun put it, "*Shi* [the thing] is completely identical, and not partially identical, with *li* [pattern]. Therefore, without causing the slightest damage to itself, an atom can embrace the whole universe."[3]

Huayan philosophy influenced East Asian aesthetics, especially Japan's emphasis on a simplicity taken even to the point of minimalism. In the evolution of the Japanese arts, we often find a transition from the complex to the simple, from the elaborate to the minimal. A case in point: Japanese forms of poetry historically began with long linked verse (*renga*) of unlimited lines that then were reduced to the *tanka* of eleven lines and then eventually down to the *haiku* form of just three lines. In Japanese painting as well, we find many examples of an ink-wash painting that is no more than a single withered branch with a few blossoms and a bird. And Zen paintings may be reduced to a simple circle. We miss the background assumptions if we see this artistic style as just a focus on the particular and the glorification of the simple. That would place such art on the most superficial of the four phenomenal realms, the domain of unconnected individual things. Instead, I would urge us to see this as the artistic representation of the fourth and deepest realm. Therefore, in a simple painting of a single branch, a blossom, and a bird, or in a *haiku* of just seventeen syllables, nothing is excluded because each individual is more than simply a discrete, isolated thing. If one fathoms the singular image, one fathoms the pattern of the whole. The perfect artistic expression, when properly appreciated, is a jewel in Indra's net that reflects all other things as well.

To sum up: the Huayan view recognizes something very close to the two paradigms of reality—the atomistic and holographic—that we have been developing, and it gives priority to the latter. Although perhaps no philosophical tradition in the West has given as sustained and focused an analysis of the two as has Huayan Buddhism, the distinction has not been completely ignored. Let us briefly examine one example.

Engaged Knowing in Western Philosophy

Consider how Henri Bergson emphasized a parallel distinction, his view being particularly relevant for introducing an affective and imaginative dimension to knowledge. In 1903 Bergson characterized the two kinds of knowing in this way: "Philosophers, in spite of their apparent divergencies, agree in distinguishing two profoundly different ways of knowing a thing. The first implies that we move round the object; the second that we enter into it."[4]

He exemplified the latter by applying it to knowing the motion of a moving object.

> I am attributing to the moving object an interior and, so to speak, states of mind; I also imply that I am in sympathy with those states, and that I insert myself in them by an effort of imagination. . . . And what I experience will depend neither on the point of view I may take up in regard to the object, since I am inside the object itself, nor on the symbols by which I may translate [it], since I have rejected all translations in order to possess the original. In short, I shall no longer grasp the movement [of the object] from without, remaining where I am, but from where it is, from within, as it is in itself.[5]

We might get to the core of Bergson's distinction by posing the question this way: Who better understands clay—a geologist or a potter? Geologists distance themselves from the object they try to understand, restricting their encounter with clay to looking at it with detachment, seeking the patterns or models that will help us discover how clay connects to other physical phenomena and is affected by external factors. The potter, by contrast, engages the clay with intellect, imagination, body, and feeling; knowing the clay is inseparable from working with the clay. The preposition is critical: a machine can perform the mechanical task of working *on* the clay, but a potter partners *with* the clay, seeking an expression that arises from their mutual engagement. As anyone who has tried to stubbornly impose his or her own will on an artistic medium can attest, the medium has a say in what it will become.

Both the potter and the geologist know clay, but they know it in different ways. We can even grant that each way has its advantages and limitations. Too often today, however, we philosophers slip into making a hierarchy that is, in the end, a thinly veiled criticism: we think of the potter's engaged knowing as, to use the argot, a "knowing-how" that is inferior to a "knowing-that." Engaged knowing, we imply, is no more than the lower kind of understanding the ancient Greeks called *tekhnē*, the applied knowledge and skill of an artisan. Yet, if we think of *tekhnē* as an engineering skill learned through technical training, then the modern *Wissenschaft* paradigm of knowing is also a candidate for being a *tekhnē*. After all, the forms of training in the *Wissenschaften* that typify most disciplines in the academy today are very much like learning a technical skill. To be trained as a chemist, a sociologist, or a philosopher generally involves a series of courses in methodology and mastery of the current models of the field. Throughout one's later career, one is expected to repeat and directly refer to that methodology and those models as the foundation for the validity for what one learns. Or at least, when conceiving a new model, to show how—according to the criteria of the *Wissenschaft*—the new model is superior to the former.[6] If we can grant, then, that there is no obvious reason to assess the detached form of knowing as *inherently* superior to the engaged form of knowing, why has the *Wissenschaft* paradigm achieved such scholarly dominance, including even in the study of philosophy?

Bergson not only contrasted the two kinds of knowing, but also observed that Western thinking was increasingly stressing the paradigm of moving around an object as the right way to know it. Indeed, we would have to say that this paradigm of detached knowing has become only more authoritative in the century since Bergson wrote those passages. How did this happen? In the last four centuries, and especially since the Enlightenment's stress on scientific empiricism, Western philosophy has progressively construed knowledge to be more an external than an internal relation. By rejecting medieval spirituality and institutions of authority, the modern West has stressed detached observation, public verifiability through replicable experiments, and an atomistic paradigm of both the natural and social worlds. We still recognize the importance of embodiment, affect, and intuition in daily life, but we usually believe knowledge is most dependable when it reflects a reality independent of the mind that knows it. Truth, then, lies in our ability to *refer to* what already is. The geologist, not the potter, really knows clay. Both the scientist and the clay preexist their relationship with each other, and knowledge becomes a link between them that leaves the integrity of both knower and known unchanged.

This shift in our dominant paradigm of knowledge has strikingly narrowed philosophy's scope. This narrowing is significant because most other disciplines in the academy originated within the *Wissenschaft* paradigm, but that is not so for philosophy. For the Greeks who named it, philosophy was the "love of wisdom," but it had to change its paradigm to gain credibility in the post-Enlightenment centers of learning. As a discipline in the modern university, philosophy has become a *Wissenschaft,* a "science" or "-ology" whose object is logic, language, empirical objects, and mental states. Ensconced as an academic department alongside the other *Wissenschaften* in the university, philosophy seems no longer to have a place for either love or wisdom. Instead it has become predominately the "study of knowledge," a literal translation of the word "epistemology." The Greek term *epistēmē,* of which epistemology is the science, apparently derives from *epi* (outside, beside, near) + *histanai* (to stand, to place). The etymology of the word suggests that epistemology studies the knowledge of bystanders or detached observers who place reality outside themselves. According to most academic philosophers today, reality preexists human engagement, and the best we can do is move about it, observing it with detachment in hopes of understanding it through our constructed models. That *Wissenschaft* paradigm of external relation maintains the integrity of the world and the integrity of the self. Let us now see how the pervasiveness of the mosaic paradigm contributes to today's global crises.

The Mosaic Paradigm's Role in Our Global Situation Today

Our world is rife with challenges to the ecology, to the economy, and to issues of equity and justice. We are scrambling to find innovative solutions and deeper understandings of our problems. We seek new and better models to make sense of the ever changing and, we fear, ever worsening circumstances in which we find ourselves. But in saying that, we may have already undermined our chances of success. Are we so committed to our *Wissenschaften* that we cannot even pause to consider whether they should be our primary, or even sole, approach to problems? If we find ourselves in ever-worsening circumstances, we already see ourselves as discrete entities being surrounded by external factors we need to control. After all, circumstances are what "stand around" (*circum* + *stances*) us, the word implying that the problems are separate from us and we need to take a stance vis-à-vis them; we need, in other words, to use a *Wissenschaft* as a *tekhnē* that applies models to the problems and cleverly manipulates them. Yet, are we like frustrated scientists analyzing the aspen grove by continuously tweaking our models without ever noticing the assumptions about whole and part that generated those models? Maybe our difficulties derive from how we go about trying to ameliorate crises, presuming that reality is like a mosaic. We might instead try to engage today's realities anew, to see them more as a jigsaw puzzle. What would that entail?

First of all, we would look for answers in the particular and the local, not the universal or transcultural. Whether we engage in macroeconomics or geopolitics, we too often blindly follow the *Wissenschaft* project of viewing phenomena as discrete pieces of a mosaic, nearly identical in nature and able to be understood and managed by imposing increasingly complex models that ignore local difference. Even our slogans portray our assumptions: "Think globally; act locally." That suggests we make a global model and then plug the mosaic tiles back up on the wall according to the template. It assumes there is nothing in the particularity that cannot be reduced to nearly identical atomistic units. I suggest we change our slogan to "Think locally; act globally." That is, taking the jigsaw approach or the vision of Huayan Buddhism's net of Indra as our starting point, why not focus ever more intently on the specifics of a problem in its own context: cultural, social, historical, human? The more profoundly we fathom the complexity and uniqueness of the particular, the more clearly we see how the particular overlaps with adjoining particulars and how they in turn fit into further pieces of the jigsaw puzzle that is the whole.

Consider taxation and the desire for economic equity. Why should we seek a *universal* model of the equitable distribution of wealth and taxation when local conditions vary so widely? What is effective in one culture might not be ideal in another, and given different local needs, the priorities of how wealth should be distributed and taxation designed might also vary. If we want to achieve better equity in practice, not merely theorize about its nature, we need to attend to the uniqueness of the local situation. In a society with a strong social system of extended families and care for the elderly by the family, for example, might not an investment in education or access to medical supplies be a more important priority than a government-run social security system for the aged? Why have the government administer elder care where the extended family always tries and wants to do that. Instead, in the local situation, let the government direct its resources to supporting and educating the younger generation who act as the caregivers. Conversely, in a society of nuclear families, the government might need to assume the role of directly supporting the elderly as a way to maintain their autonomy. Or, if we want to help people economically, why not start with addressing economic problems at the village level? In doing so, we will come to discover in the local details how that village depends on and interacts with neighboring villages, then how those issues interrelate with regional processes, then with national concerns, then international relations, and finally global issues. That would be "thinking locally; acting globally."

In understanding global issues, it is helpful to think not only about global changes, but also about what motivates them. What can we learn about those motives if we study them from the jigsaw-puzzle, rather than the mosaic, paradigm? For the sake of this discussion, let us consider three affective motivations: greed, fear, and love.

Greed. A theme in the recent occupy protest movement was the criticism of both financial and government institutions for their greed. The criticism was not just about avarice in individuals, but also about systemic avarice. From the detached standpoint of many current capitalist economic theories—the Chicago School of neoliberalism being the most stark example—greed is considered a positive force of growth; it drives competition and innovation in the marketplace. The result of applying that theory to models for global economic growth, however, is that its assumption that people are inherently greedy becomes in practice not a *descriptive* but a *prescriptive* claim. That is, if we think a vital world economy *requires* us to be greedy, the economic system will use marketing to feed individual covetousness and to stimulate the competitive desire to acquire more than others. That latter point is significant: Greed is not simply the desire to have more; more precisely, it is the desire to have *more than anyone else.* This distinguishes greed from other classic motivators like lust or gluttony, for example. An individual's lust does not envy, indeed it celebrates, other people's expressions of lust; the glutton desires merely more food, not necessarily more food than anyone else has. Lust or gluttony can be communal, in fact, as in an orgy or saturnalia. Therefore, although self-destructive, lust and gluttony are not intrinsically socially destructive. But greed is. It can thrive only by pitting one person against another, rending the fabric of an interwoven society.

Even when I have more than I can use, my greed is still unsatisfied if I know of people who have even more. If the *Forbes* listing of the world's wealthiest people indicates I am number fifty on the list, how much more money could I possibly need? Greed says "enough to make me number forty-nine next year."[7] Furthermore, an institutional system built on greed *requires* me to be greedy for my survival. For example, if the air quality were uniform around the globe (as presumably it might have been at one time in the long-ago past), I would not be greedy about air because it would be free and available equally to everyone. My one concern, then, would be that the overall quality of the air not deteriorate *for everyone* since my air is not separate from anyone else's air. In that way, my self-interest would accord with the common interest.

Now consider what happens when the air quality is not uniform; that is, some places have better, healthier air than others because of wind direction, altitude, topography, or distance from sources of pollution. Then those places become more desirable and consequently more expensive. For the sake of my health and that of my family, greed would drive me to accumulate enough wealth so we could afford to live in such a place. Moreover, once I financially invested in it, I would be motivated to keep the air there cleaner than elsewhere to preserve that investment, even if it meant the overall deterioration of air quality everywhere. That is, greed is driven not by the desire for cleaner air itself, but by the desire to have my air be cleaner than what others have. More pointedly, given a choice between everyone's having equal access to air of very good quality and my having access to air of merely good quality while others have poor air quality, greed would prefer the latter. If that seems irrational, that is because it is. What some have argued, and too many of us have been duped into believing, is not that greed itself is rational but that it is rational to think of greed as *good,* or at the least, absolutely necessary. Because of that argument, greed goes unbridled and we find people in finance acting in ways to maximize personal profit even if it might destroy the financial system itself. If the system crashes, that is okay because they will by then have accumulated enough wealth that they will still be better off than almost everyone else. Things might get so bad that their quality of life declines, but that, too, is acceptable if it declines less rapidly for them than for others. Greed does not concern itself with the overall amount of bread, but only with the desire to own the last piece. Greed (unlike gluttony or lust) is equally satisfied whether I get more or you get less. The Wall Street economic disaster derived from trying to satisfy greed in both directions, not merely making the rich richer but also making the poor poorer. Similarly, we find the directors of energy corporations working to maximize profits even if that means destroying everyone's environment, including their own. The environment will not decay evenly, however, and the wealthy will be able to afford what is necessary to survive longer, even if only a little longer. So greed's agenda, however irrational, can still be realized.

Some might rebut my analysis by saying although the word "greed" is sometimes used, that is not the best word for what such capitalist models are advocating. They really mean something more like "enlightened self-interest." That term needs to be unpacked, however. Does it describe a particular species of greed, one with a blend of reason and desire combined into a single function? I cannot see this as anything other than an oxymoron: greed and reason are so incompatible that they cannot be a single thing. Instead, I maintain, the idea of rational greed, or enlightened self-interest, is that the impulse of greed is *subjected to* or *controlled by* reflective rational analysis. That is, in enlightened self-interest, reason bridles greed, sometimes even denying greed's impulses entirely. This has been how almost all philosophical and spiritual traditions have understood greed throughout history and across the world: greed is bad, not good, and it must be controlled. Some traditions believe that we can reflect on the causes of greed and eradicate it completely. Buddhism treats "thirst" (*tṛṣṇā*) in that way, for example. Other thinkers, including such odd bedfellows as Hobbes, Kant, and Freud, believed greed could never be eradicated but could instead be restrained through rational structures. They respectively located those inhibitors in the state, in a sense of duty to universalizable moral principles, and in the civilizing function of the superego.

If the world's traditions of wisdom have so widely and persistently maintained the evils of greed and the need to squelch or at least control it, how did we arrive at the point where intelligent people would argue that greed is good? An important part of the answer to that question lies in what happened to the meaning of "self" in phrases like "enlightened self-interest." As we have discussed already, the *Wissenschaft* paradigm has achieved increasing dominance in academic thinking and scholarly research. A result is that the self is no longer merely the one who applies the *Wissenschaft* method but also an object of study for the method. Such a self is analyzed as an atomistic unit in various bridging relations with others: the self is a tile in a mosaic. In that root metaphor, my only connection with others is what the system of relational superstructures allows. Within myself, I have no inherent connection to others. Therefore, if the economic system advocates greed (in whatever form), my relation with others is understood to be connected by a system that requires greed for me to prosper. If I am not vigilant (as the advertising campaigns remind me incessantly), I will not have as much as others and both I and my family will suffer as a consequence. (I discuss the close relation between fear and greed later in the chapter.) Suppose on some introspective, personal level I may not want to be greedy and I consequently refuse to act according to greed's dictates. If my social system is based on a set of external rules built on the assumption that greed is necessary and good, however, my lack of greed endangers my very existence. Stuck in *Wissenschaft*'s atomistic paradigm of external relations, the rules for how to relate to others (other people, other nations, other segments of the global ecology) are imposed on me from outside. Those models, however much we refine them, always begin with the assumption that I am intrinsically a single tile in a mosaic, lacking connection with other tiles unless a master blueprint is imposed from without. The models also assume that my needs, motives, and aspirations are practically identical with those of every other tile in the social mosaic.

But what if reality fits together more like a jigsaw puzzle than a mosaic? What if we are more like a grove of aspen than a stand of oak? What if we break our robotic allegiance to the *Wissenschaft* paradigms and enter more intimately into the particularity of our internal connectedness? Then the major significance of my genes lies not in how they make me uniquely me, but instead in how they interlink me with my parents, my grandparents, my great-grandparents, and so on. If I trace those genetic links for just twenty generations (four hundred to five hundred years), I am internally linked with more than a million people. That number does not include siblings or cousins, only those whose DNA directly contributed to my *unique* DNA. (Remember that in holographic wholes, each entity is, on one hand, unique and, on the other, a reflection of the structure of the whole.) If I trace my genetic inheritance over thirty generations, my personal DNA chart includes more than a billion people. We can begin to see how the more particular our analysis, the more holographic the relation. I am not only part of humanity, but humanity as a whole is reflected in me. No external model, no contract, no world trade agreement, no economic system, no government, is needed to link me with others. Within myself, I am already interdependent and interrelated with humankind and, by a similar line of reasoning, with all of nature. If we start with that assumption about how it all fits together, even the idea of enlightened self-interest is transformed. The self now contains the interests of the whole because the self cannot be what it is without the whole.

Once we begin by thinking locally instead of globally, once we begin by analyzing particulars instead of by generalizing in universal models, once we begin with internal and holographic relations instead of external and atomistic relations, it is evident why so many religions and philosophers have deemed greed to be evil. When we zoom in on the individual jigsaw pieces, we find that greed breaks the intrinsic connectors within each piece that link it to the next. Greed cuts away what makes internal relations possible, robbing each piece of its interdependent uniqueness for the sake of making it into part of a set of nearly identical tiles that can fit the mosaic. Then my home is no longer a home, but merely real estate; real estate is merely a number in the ledger of some mortgage company; the numbers in the ledger, merely variables in some financial institution's subprime mortgage derivatives; and those derivatives, merely targets of opportunity for hedge funds. The mosaic model depersonalizes my home—the internal relations of family and shared biography—to make it fit a variable in some financial speculator's investment model. The speculator wagers either for or against foreclosure on my home without meeting me, without knowing my name, without even knowing the location of my home. It is impersonal; it is objective; it is just "the system"—greed without legal regulation, enacted without guilt or sense of personal responsibility.

Moreover, *Wissenschaft*'s paradigm of detached knowing subtly transforms self-interest into individual interest. Assuming each individual has the same needs and desires, detached knowing is inept at factoring in local differences, particularities, and intrinsic connections. It leaps to generality, obliterating the local expressions of ethnicity, race, culture, history, and religion that so strongly influence our particular needs, wishes, values, and motivations. The *Wissenschaft* paradigm cannot work otherwise: its mathematic models are built up from externally related atomistic parts, each discrete and functionally identical.

Fear. Let us consider now greed's consort: fear. For an example of how fear can shift a social context from internal to external relations, let us consider a situation from recent U.S. history. On September 10, 2001, New York City was its usual self of loosely related, inherently discrete activities and identities. Stockbrokers prowled Wall Street, artists hung out in Soho, designers and merchants kept the fashion district abuzz. The city had its Jewish jewelers and Irish cops, its Sikh cab drivers and Greek pizzeria owners. New York largely sustained its peaceful diversity by its people's benign disinterest in what others were doing. People lived and worked in their subgroups with intermittent transactions that put them in temporary external relations with others: performing a business exchange, rendering a service, taking money from a stranger and passing it down the row to the hotdog vendor in the aisle at the ballgame. The last example is particular revealing. Under what conditions would you hand over your money to a complete stranger, who would hand it to another, and then another, in hopes that the whole sequence would eventually be reversed so that you would get an item handed back to you in return? Probably only under the conditions of an ironclad contract. In this case, there exists such a contract, the unwritten social contract to which everyone in the ballpark silently assents. On September 10, New York was a society of individuals bound by such external relations.

Then came the attack on the World Trade Center. By September 12, everyone had suddenly become Americans and New Yorkers. People heroically helped their neighbors in a sobering display of grief and defiance. There was no such thing as "their pain" or "their survival" or "their defense," but rather, it was "our pain," "our survival," "our defense." The inhabitants of the city discovered the interdependence that had linked them all along: what I am is in part what you are. A similar feeling surged through the nation at large. Every American became a New Yorker in the spirit of John F. Kennedy's "*Ich bin ein Berliner.*" We were all in this together.

In the ensuing few months, the politicians and commentators orchestrated the politics of fear on a national scale, undermining the internal relations that had begun to dominate the society. They told us we were "at war with terror," a war that can have no clearly discernible enemy from a particular place in an identifiable uniform, a war that can have no conceivable end. The interdependent selves started to recede into their atomistic shells of individualistic self-preservation. The other was no longer part of me, but someone alien and unknowable, someone to be suspected, not trusted. Instead of being an engaged, interdependent community, New Yorkers—like everyone else in the nation—were told to be vigilant bystanders. The mentality of surveillance and suspicion replaced benevolence and trust. It reached a point where "they" wanted to build a mosque near "our" Ground Zero. Mistrust and outright hatred exploded with a destructive power beyond anything that happened on September 11.

Fear's emphasis on individual self-survival eroded the newly established community of interdependence. Political tacticians, with their personal or corporate agendas, fed fear to the electorate while the news media gorged itself on the political blood sport, giving every fringe group or crazed individual inordinate amounts of coverage. Every political gathering, every passing comment, every speech, was subject to the hermeneutics of fear: What was *really* going on? What is the secret agenda? How does this endanger *me*? Not only had the sense of internally related community disappeared, but there was no going back to the pre–September 11 contract society either. When hate and fear insinuate themselves into an integrity-based society, its fabric unravels. Integrity depends on external relations like contracts, but contracts require trust. When there is a flight to individualistic self-preservation, you can trust only those who think and feel *exactly* as you do. So small groups crop up, each with intense loyalty to a narrowly defined ideological creed. Broader connections, negotiations, and compromises with those who are different—the prerequisites for a successful society built on contract—dissolve, and atomistic, radical individualism prevails. If superstructure bonds atomistic units, then the disintegration of the superstructure turns self-interest into egocentric interest. What can counteract this societal disintegration? What might motivate a return to community, whether one built on intimate interdependence or one built on contractual agreement? Love perhaps?

Love. One consequence of an emphasis on engaged knowing over detached knowing is in how we care about others. To sharpen our understanding of the distinction, let us see how we may analyze the same statement in alternative ways, depending on whether we view care as an external or internal relation. Consider the instruction of Jesus of Nazareth to "love your neighbor as yourself." If we think of love as an external relation, we can say that Jesus was recommending that you analyze the self-love that connects you to yourself and then apply that love to connect yourself to others. In the terms of our Figure 1.1a, we can say that you examine the relationship of love (*R*) that connects you as subject (*a*) to yourself as object (*b*). Then you transfer that love to be the relation (*R*) between you (*a*) and your neighbor (the new *b*). In that interpretation, love is a thing; it is *what* links you first to yourself and then to others. You transpose that love from between you and yourself to between you and another.[8]

We sometimes understand charity along those lines. When we do, charity means seeing the other with the care or love one has when one looks at oneself. That kind of charity uses the imagination to "put yourself in the other's place" so you may understand the other's situation and treat that person as you would treat yourself. In this form of discourse, charity is love "extended" to others. As an external relation, such charity can be formalized into a principle, leading to a sense of *responsibility* or *duty* to "do unto others what you would have them do unto you."

Starting from the internal relations typical of the engaged knowing and the jigsaw-puzzle paradigm of reality, we can interpret Jesus' enjoinder differently. Specifically, to love your neighbor as yourself would imply discovering that your neighbor is part of yourself, as Figure 1.1b would suggest. The two relatents, you and your neighbor, are inseparable. To love yourself is, at least in part, to love your neighbor; to love your neighbor is, at least in part, to love yourself. Without that overlap, you cannot be fully yourself. Jesus' mandate, then, would be to dissolve the boundary of self or ego that keeps you from having a shared, interdependent existence with the other. In interpreting Jesus' command to love as arising from intimacy or internal relatedness, the mandate is not about *what* connects you to the other, but about *how* you and the other are so intertwined that loving one is loving the other. Love is not, as in an external relation, *extended* to another; it is discovered in the *already existing* ontology of what I really am, a being interlinked and inseparable (at least without loss) from everyone and everything else.

In the famous Buddhist text the *Vimalakīrti Sūtra,* we have the narrative of the profoundly wise and compassionate layperson, Vimalakīrti. The story is that Vimalakīrti is seriously ill, so much so that the bodhisattvas and deities in the heavens are worried. Yet, intimidated by his power to slice away all delusions and reveal any ignorance (even of gods and bodhisattvas), not one of them is anxious to visit Vimalakīrti and ask what is wrong. Finally, the deities consign the task to the bodhisattva Manjuśri, the incarnation of wisdom itself. Manjuśri goes down to see Vimalakīrti and asks, "Why are you sick?" Vimalakīrti's response echoes through the universe: "I am sick because beings are sick." Compassion is not *extending* one's love to suffering beings; compassion is the love that *feels* the suffering of others as one's own. Compassion is *how* one is, not *what* one does. Indeed, compassion is in my own self-interest insofar as it seeks to relieve the suffering I feel when in the presence of others' suffering. This again points to the importance of focusing on the particular and the local. On the level of an abstract, general model typical of the *Wissenschaft* mode of detached knowing, Vimalakīrti's compassionate engagement with the suffering of others as his own suffering would not be possible. Qualitatively speaking, a program of social services that applies a general model to every local situation is different in concept from a program arising from the specific local conditions themselves. The former arises out of charity, the latter out of love or compassion.

Conclusion: A Beginning without End

Assuming no large-scale change is on the immediate horizon, the rebuilding of social harmony must emerge gradually from a blossoming of small-scale community organizations. Compared to the new fear-based groups held together by ideological purity, intimacy-based groups with a sense of human interdependence are more likely to resuscitate social harmony and cohesion. Henri Bergson first articulated the connection between knowing and societal openness, his distinction between open and closed societies being the inspiration for Karl Popper's *The Open Society and Its Enemies.*[9] In our present conditions, when associations ground themselves in atomistic individualism and make ideological purity the basis of membership, they become dangerous fringe groups unwilling to trust, negotiate, or compromise. In the face of such chaos, the authoritarian closure of society seems the only route to stability and safety: freedom and rights are sacrificed to security. By contrast, a better prospect for long-range harmony lies in small-scale, intimacy-based social organizations built on internal relations. In them, personal thriving entails collective thriving. They grow by recognizing overlaps with adjoining groups, rather than by multiplying into ever more fanatic organizations. Furthermore, when engaged knowing serves as the cognitive side of internal relations, creativity and innovation can flourish more easily.

For such an engaged form of knowing to prosper, for the jigsaw puzzle to replace the mosaic, people from various sectors of society must be willing to take risks. Academics must be willing to risk their status in academia by challenging the hegemony of the *Wissenschaft* paradigm of knowing. Religious groups must be willing to take the risk of giving traditional teachings new interpretations, ones emphasizing engagement and compassion over detachment and charity. Philosophers, economists, and political thinkers must stress interconnectedness over autonomy. Ethicists must rethink their theories to stress responsiveness over responsibility. Political groups must discover the common ground they already share with their adversaries. Corporate organizations must cultivate policies and structures that see owners, managers, and workers as overlapping and interdependent identities in which the success of one sector is interdependent with all others. Social leaders must be willing to give up the ego-feeding idea that they "have the answers," that they have the universal model for what is best for everyone everywhere. True engagement involves listening and learning. It demands localized creativity and innovation, not the application of a preconceived master plan. Although the ideals of engagement, internal relatedness, and holographic interpenetration can be shared across social organizations, each individual organization must assume its distinctive local character. "Think locally; act globally." The whole can thrive only if that whole is not superimposed from outside, but is instead discovered in the details of local variation. Such organizations may share their experiences, but they cannot be expected to simply copy one another's solutions. Emphasis has to be on *how* to think about social organization, not on *what* structure has worked elsewhere. The engagement must be an end in itself, with the result always open. Obviously, this is an endless process.

There is the tale of a traveler who came upon a Zen monastery one winter morning and noticed the monks joyfully throwing shovelfuls of snow down a well. The man asked what they were doing. One monk responded with a big smile, "We're filling the well with snow." The man retorted, "That's impossible: the snow just melts and disappears into the water table. To fill a well with snow would be a never-ending task." The monks laughed heartily as they continued their shoveling, until one chimed out: "To do something, you don't need an ending—only a beginning."

NOTES

1. James W. Heisig, Thomas P. Kasulis, and John C. Maraldo, eds., *Japanese Philosophy: A Sourcebook* (Honolulu: University of Hawai'i Press, 2011), 146.

2. The Huayan philosophical system makes moot our Western philosophical distinction between "world" and "worldview." When we make that distinction, we think of

"world" as ontological and "worldview" as psychological, epistemological, or phenomenological. That is, we assume a difference between reality and our mental construction of reality. Based on this strong opposition, Western philosophers have conceived of different ways of construing the relation between the two. The most prominent theories are realism, which emphasizes "world" as the basis of knowledge, and idealism, which emphasizes "mental construction" as the basis of knowledge. The third theory is Kantian transcendentalism, which posits a reality—the noumenon—beyond what can ever appear phenomenally and therefore cannot be known; but even without direct access to the noumenal, there is objectivity and universality in human knowledge as filtered through the transcendental categories.

In Huayan philosophy (and many other Buddhist systems as well), the assumption is that reality shows itself as it is ("thusness," "as-ness"). To the extent it doesn't appear to us that way, it is because we have projected onto it our false delusions. That is, we delusionally experience what we seek and want to experience, regardless of what is actually presented to us by reality. From the standpoint of *buddhadharma,* that is, from the standpoint of what is actually presented and what would be directly perceived by a person without delusions (that is, by a buddha), reality shows itself and is known just as it is. Therefore, from that perspective, the "world" is identical to a "worldview without delusions projected into it."

3. From Dushun's *Concerning Meditation on the Phenomenal Realms,* trans. Garma C. C. Chang in *Buddhist Teaching of Totality: The Philosophy of Hwa Yen Buddhism* (University Park: Penn State University Press, 1971), 214. For an alternative translation, see Thomas Cleary, *Entry into the Inconceivable: An Introduction to Hua-yen Buddhism* (Honolulu: University of Hawai'i Press, 1983), 91.

4. Henri Bergson, *Introduction to Metaphysics,* trans. T. E. Hulme, Library of Liberal Arts 10 (Indianapolis: Bobbs-Merrill, 1955), 21.

5. Ibid., 21–22.

6. It is revealing that today philosophers often praise a new argument or theory as "clever" rather than "creative," or at least use the terms interchangeably. Since cleverness properly belongs to *tekhnē* it is a know-how trait.

7. This symptomology of greed is usually overlooked in arguments that heavily taxing the wealthy would lead to a decrease in entrepreneurial risk taking. That is, why would a wealthy person risk investing money to make more money if the resultant profit is then so heavily taxed that the rewards become increasingly small? That argument overlooks the nature of greed in the extremely rich: the only thing the very wealthy "need" is to become wealthier than people who currently have more wealth than they do. If taxation cut the assets of the superrich equally by 50 percent, that would not thwart number fifty on the *Forbes* list from desiring to become number forty-nine next year. For greed, assuming the basics for survival are adequate, the amount of wealth is less important than the level of *comparative* wealth.

8. Although the logic of this interpretation is clear and attractive to many people today, it is unlikely that Jesus of Nazareth could have understood his own statement in this way. Its assumptions about self-love and an individualistic self essentially independent of community, family, and friends would have no meaning in Jesus' time and place.

9. See Henri Bergson, *The Two Sources of Morality and Religion,* trans. R. Ashley Audra and Cloudesley Brereton, with the assistance of W. Horsfall Carter (New York: H. Holt and Company, 1935). Also see Karl R. Popper, *The Open Society and Its Enemies,* 2 vols. (London: Routledge and Kegan Paul, 1952).

Value, Exchange, and Beyond 2

Betweenness as Starting Point

Meera Sushila Viswanathan

Value and Exchange

"Is there a common value judgment for the cultures of different nations?"[1] So questioned the twentieth-century Japanese philosopher Nishida Kitarō. In the wake of global imperialism and expansionism in the latter half of the nineteenth century and the first half of the twentieth century, myriad nascent nation-states sought to create/integrate their indigenous traditions into the new world order, thereby necessarily shaping/reshaping it, as well as to situate themselves in the perceived existing hierarchy of nations. Accordingly, among Japanese intellectuals in the 1930s, such as Nishida Kitarō, Watsuji Tetsurō, Kuki Shūzō, Miki Kiyoshi, and Ienaga Saburō, the issues of value and national and individual identity become entwined. For each, the attempt to investigate and order "value" intellectually becomes both a moment of convergence and a moment of emergence, simultaneously individual and national. Value for each in different ways is absolute and at the same time contingent as a function of its context in human interaction and exchange.

Perhaps no term in the modern world, other than "human being," merits interest in as many academic fields as the notion of value in its linguistic, philosophical, scientific, mathematical, musical, aesthetic, and economic reverberations. From a sociolinguistic perspective, we may roughly trace the genealogy of its spectrum of meaning over time from simple "preference" (this versus that) to a "good" (conferring/embodying merit, whether social, religious/ethical, aesthetic, or material) to "utility" (a contextualized "good," i.e., good for something and someone somewhere at some time) to "worth" (a hierarchical notion in which relative values are organized according to their relationship with one another) to "price" (its translation into monetary currency and hence its fundamental translatability into a common register). We see the notion of value or the valuable, that which is desirable, pleasurable, laudable, optimal, or advantageous, evolve and alter, not only across disciplines or over time, but also across geo-cultural milieus.

Etymologically, we see a similar evolution with respect to the word "value" in English, deriving originally from the Latin verb *valere*, meaning "to be strong or well."[2] This state of being strong or well is not a comparative or relative measure but rather a quality in and of itself. But by the fourteenth century value appears in a variety of contexts, especially with regard to the notion of exchange, that is, "that amount of some commodity, medium of exchange, etc., which is considered to be an equivalent for something else; a fair or adequate equivalent or return."[3] Analogously, the German *Wert,* customarily used to translate the English "value," and cognate with the English "worth," has been thought to derive from the Proto-Germanic "*werthan-(pt. t. *warth, pp. *wurthanoz), to become, turn to; allied to L. vertere, to turn, uerti, to turn to."[4] In Old English, the earliest attested appearances of the equivalent *weorð* signify "equal in value to."[5] What these excursuses into linguistic origins suggest is the transformation of value historically from purely an absolute quality (a good) to one that may be juxtaposed among many others and deriving its significance from its relative place, just as *Wert,* or "worth," already etymologically beckons to a relational tie in the idea of turning toward. In other words, the elaboration of value seems necessarily to entail relation and relationship in various degrees of imbrication. One question to consider is whether therefore it is then possible to speak of absolute value at all, bringing us back to Nishida's query.

Sidestepping this conundrum, classical economists in Europe such as Adam Smith, while noting that value may be understood variously as value in use, value in exchange, and value as an independent or intrinsic entity, have privileged, with respect to the rational allocation of resources, exchange value, thereby underscoring the relative aspect of value.[6] In other words, intrinsic value has been elided and we understand value, not as an absolute, but instead only as turned or directed to some other end: either value in use, which is understood to be consonant with the notion of utility or instrumentality, or some generalized notion of good or, by contrast, value in exchange, in which value becomes equated with the quantity of labor it obtains in exchange.[7] Value in exchange does not just come to represent the analogical interchange of two abstract utilities between two individuals, but rather now is understood to abrogate the ratios by equating material commodities with labor, the effort expended by an individual or individuals, which is now in the service of the person in possession of such commodities.

Other classical economists such as David Ricardo[8] and, after him, Karl Marx, who understood labor to encompass all the costs of production, embrace the value-in-use/value-in-exchange dichotomy as well. For Marx, the focal point of the capitalist mode of production was the value of a commodity based on the cost of the aggregate amount of labor necessary to produce it and the ability to realize surplus value from it through exchange: ". . . it can equally well be said that all commodities, in exchange with living labour, buy more labour than they contain. This excess constitutes precisely surplus value."[9] For Hegel, it was the question of where history was progressing and where it was not, particularly in those critical moments of transition, which he saw as the product of what has been termed "irreconcilable value conflicts."[10] In more recent times, game theorists have sought to comprehend the idea of value as understood by two or more rational individuals in specific decision-making processes and the subsequent interaction of all the individual assessments of value in producing outcomes unforeseen by any of the individuals involved. What these have in common is their invocation of interstitial human interaction and exchange, not only in the determination of values and valuation, but also in the fundamental notion of value.

A discussion of how different theories of value have foregrounded the idea of human interaction and exchange in the course of Western intellectual history will then take us back to Nishida and to the question of how the issue was framed and developed by the Japanese thinker Watsuji Tetsurō and the novelist Natsume Sōseki in the first half of the twentieth century. We will come to understand, first, that the notion of value/worth has increasingly relied on the notion of exchange and relationship as it has developed historically; and second, that the classical economic understanding of the idea of value has underscored the notion of exchange value and hence the exchange of values, while obscuring the value of exchange itself (an inquiry undertaken by the newly burgeoning fields of sociology and anthropology in the latter part of the nineteenth and the early twentieth century), eventually in neoclassical economics, obviating the idea of relational exchange altogether. While economists and game theorists have tended to focus on negotiated exchanges (i.e., those that involve an explicit agreement that quantifies the values to be exchanged) and social scientists on reciprocal exchanges (i.e., exchanges in which, while there may or may not be expectation of some kind of future return, there is no evident quid pro quo), Watsuji's development of the idea of *aidagara,* or "betweenness," illuminates the underlying common premises of both kinds of exchange. And finally, as a coda we will explore briefly the novel *Kokoro* by Natsume Sōseki, Watsuji's friend and mentor, as an anticipatory rehearsal of Watsuji's later ideas about *aidagara* and, perhaps we may speculate, the genesis for some of his discussion of *rinrigaku,* or ethics.

The Exchange of Values

This idea of value as part of an evolving trajectory of the desirable has itself been subject to moral valuation. The historian Gertrude Himmelfarb argues in her philippic, *The De-moralization of Society: From Victorian Virtues to Modern Values,* that, at the beginning of the twentieth century, that same period in which modern Japanese philosophy begins to emerge, we begin to see a shift in moral understanding in which a substitution of values takes place for what she terms "virtues," whose consequence is the debasing of true morality in which relativist goods replace the absolute Good. She comments,

> "Values" brings with it the assumptions that all moral ideas are subjective and relative, that they are mere customs and conventions, that they have a purely instrumental, utilitarian purpose, and that they adhere to particular peoples—or, as we now say, they are race-, class-, and gender-specific. So long as morality was couched in the language of "virtue," it had a firm, resolute character . . . the word "virtue" carried with it a sense of gravity and authority, as "values" does not.[11]

Hence, the question raised by Nishida noted at the beginning of this essay from Himmelfarb's perspective is beside the point. Values may be culture based, but virtues are not. A universalist paradigm is conjured up in which historical/cultural/linguistic differences are elided in favor of an absolute and monolithic notion of morality, the question of a common value judgment addressed by Nishida is merely an empty and flabby gesturing at moral virtue that has already been eviscerated by reference to anything outside itself. It seems to be the relational quality of value, that "turning toward," that possibility of interchange and exchange, that precludes for Himmelfarb any authentic overarching moral weight or compass. For Himmelfarb, absolute value is an oxymoron whose ethical claims are meretricious.

This monetary model of value and exchange appears as well in the philosophy of Friedrich Nietzsche, whom Himmelfarb views as the primary culprit in the displacing of virtues in favor of values. In *The Genealogy of Morals* he suggests that the emergence of morals resulted from "a cultural regularization of exchange between individuals," arguing that "the feeling of guilt" originated "in the oldest and most primitive relationship among persons there is, in the relationship between buyer and seller, creditor and debtor."[12] Here the money economy not only offers a set of lenses from which one can reflect on everything in the world, but further it suggests that the very nature of human relations reflects a system of exchange and that the earliest form of tie resulted from an economic relation whose imbalances first give way to notions of personal culpability (*Schuld,* "to be guilty" from *Schulden,* "to be indebted"), from which the moral sense is born. Nietzsche argues, "For the first time, the individual stood and measured himself against individual."[13] Underlying the idea of exchange is his contention that "here we find the oldest variety of human acuteness, as well as the first indication of human pride, of superiority over other animals . . . man saw himself as the being that measures values, the 'assaying' animal."[14] In other words, he seems to be suggesting that we are in some sense human by virtue of our ability to evaluate, which in turn depends on our ability to effect reciprocal exchanges. To coin a phrase, in Nietzsche's understanding we are, by definition, *Homo pendens,* or "weighing man."

There is an echo in this idea of an economic exchange modeling the development of morality and ethics in Aristotle's description of reciprocality in conjunction with the issue of rectificatory justice in book 5 of the *Nicomachean Ethics* when he states:

> Now proportionate return is secured by cross-conjunction. . . . If, then, first there is proportionate equality of goods, and then reciprocal action takes place, the result we mention will be effected. If not, the bargain is not equal, and does not hold; for there is nothing to prevent the work of the one being better than that of the other; they must therefore be equated. . . . This is why all things that are exchanged must be somehow comparable.[15]

This idea of reciprocity, signified usually by the word *antipeponthos,* presupposes, as he notes, the possibility of comparability and equitability. Another usage of *antipeponthos,* as Nicholas Theocarakis points out, is as a mathematical term in geometry and physics designating relationships in the form of ratios, as in reciprocal angles of a polygon.[16] Hence, *antipeponthos* denotes a precise and explicit set of ratios underlying an exchange. A material exchange is instituted that restores the disequilibrium between persons on a contractual basis. What is needed is a mediating presence that allows for unlike things to be proportionately measured. Aristotle argues that the institution of money offers just such a means for rectifying an imbalance between individuals: "This is why all goods must have a price set on them; for then there will always be exchange, and if so, association of man with man."[17]

That ethical human relations can be modeled on the idea of negotiated financial exchange, as argued by Aristotle and Nietzsche, foreshadows and reflects, respectively, a series of shifts that takes place historically, according to Oswald Spengler in his work *Decline of the West.*[18] These shifts represent not simply a change within economics, but rather a developmental progression of modes of being in the world from the nomadic or seminomadic stage of development in which there is a sense of self-sufficiency to the move to settled life with the transmission of goods and then to the onset of urbanization and the appearance of commodities. He asserts, "With this goods become wares, exchange turnover, *and in place of thinking with goods we have thinking in money.*"[19]

The transformation to which Spengler alludes alters not only the relation of people to things but also the very fabric of human interaction, since "money aims at *mobilizing* all things."[20] We move from commodities to the commodification of virtually everything. But even as economists in the latter part of the eighteenth and the nineteenth century interrogated the notion of exchange value, philosophers during the same period grappled with the idea of value, in both relative terms as well as absolute. Two examples illustrate the spectrum:

one, Jeremy Bentham's utilitarian "felicific calculus,"[21] and the other, Immanuel Kant's formulation of the Categorical Imperative.[22] The former, which has been represented as a kind of responsive bookkeeping or accounting of human happiness, is put forward with various columns in which utilities or dis-utilities (pleasure- or pain-giving elements) are grouped, totaled, and then integrated in terms of various vectors (intensity, duration, etc.), reflecting the marketplace in which value now finds itself, an array whose possibilities are relative and instrumental. Jostling against this is the pursuit of absolute value as articulated by Kant in the form of what many understand as a deontological, nonconsequentialist imperative that is nonhypothetical, that is, that cannot be framed in terms of a conditional if-clause statement, and hence categorical, since it preempts notions of particular contexts and particular individuals at particular times and in particular places.

Ironically, with the advent of the latter part of the nineteenth century, as philosophy begins to privilege the notion of exchange in the understanding of value, neoclassical economics in the person of marginal utility theorists rejects the idea of value as being grounded in social relationships. Worth becomes determined by price defined as what a commodity will fetch in the marketplace rather than as labor or more generally exchange value, suggesting a new "objectivity" to the idea of value and worth. Exchange is no longer a social interaction between individuals or groups, but rather the exchange within the mind of the individual of relative utilities. Meanwhile, sociologists including Oswald Spengler and Georg Simmel and anthropologists such as Marcel Mauss[23] undertake an understanding of value and exchange that privileges the value of exchange rather than the exchange of value. For Spengler and Simmel, monetarization in its forming of new kinds of exchanges alters our very mode of being in the world, whereas for anthropologists such as Mauss it is the recognition that those "reciprocal," non-negotiated unequal exchanges, such as the potlatch, are central to the formation of society and have profound repercussions.[24]

The Value of Exchange

One way to comprehend the divide that emerged in the latter part of the nineteenth century is to consider further Spengler's observation:

> It is an error of all modern money-theories that they start from the value-token or even the material of the payment-medium instead of from the form of economic thought. In reality, money, like number and law, is a *category of thought*. . . . Only in the economy-picture of the townsman are there objective values and kinds of values which have an existence apart from his private needs, as thought-elements of a generalized validity.[25]

On the one hand, for Spengler the impact of urbanization with its accompanying monetarizing manifests itself not simply in the proliferation of coin but in the new perspective afforded individuals in which the totality of experience can be understood through the lens of a money economy and its translatability. On the other hand, the notion of absolute Good has now been transformed, not, as Himmelfarb might argue, into a welter of exchangeable values that can be equated through a kind of intangible bookkeeping, nor even into a dichotomy of relative and intrinsic values, but instead into what Spengler terms "objective values" and those values not of concern to the individual and his needs/desires/preferences but necessarily acknowledged to exist by the possibility of inclusion in the system of integrated understanding offered by the penumbra of money thinking.

The sociologist and philosopher Georg Simmel earlier took this idea of objectivity one step further by explicitly struggling to develop an explanatory model of value through exchange that resists simple relativism in his book *The Philosophy of Money:*

> The decisive fact in the objectivity of economic value, which makes economics a special area of investigation, is that its validity transcends the individual subject. . . . The equivalence of which we become aware, and in which we develop an interest through exchange, imparts to value its specific objectivity. . . . Exchange presupposes an objective measurement of subjective valuations, not in the sense of being chronologically prior, but in the sense that both phenomena arise from the same act.[26]

To wit, we overcome the problem of relativism by substituting the notion of the subjective versus the objective notion of value, from the assessments of the individual to the generalized assessments of the group.

But even individual assessment is a product of the moneyed economy and its values. Simmel suggests that, in an urbanized, moneyed economy, people lack self-sufficiency with respect to food, clothing, and shelter and are thus much more dependent than earlier individuals on others to accomplish the basic tasks of living. But at the same time, because the contributions of others are no longer part of an I-thou relation but instead reduced to an anonymous instrumental function (what Marx would have termed "alienation" associated with the production and consumption of commodities), there is the perception of self-containment and independence.

It is from this state of affairs that there emerges ironically a sense of freedom and from that a sense of individuality.

> If mere isolation does not produce a longing for others or satisfaction at being remote from others—in brief, a dependency of feeling—then man is placed completely beyond the question of dependency or freedom and actual freedom takes on no conscious value because it lacks its opposite—friction, temptation, proximity to

> differences. If freedom means the development of individuality, the conviction to unfold the core of our being with all its individual desires and feelings, then this category implies not a mere absence of relationships but rather a very specific relation to others. . . . Individual freedom is not a pure inner condition of an isolated subject, but rather a phenomenon of correlation which loses its meaning when its opposite is absent.[27]

Hence, he would concur with Spengler that it is through money as a "category of thinking" that the modern concept of the individual and his or her struggle with independence and freedom emerge: "Money is responsible for impersonal relations between people, and thus for individual freedom."[28] This, it should be clear, is not a Marxist indictment of the dehumanizing of society, but rather an etiological critique of the emergence of individual choice. For Simmel, money necessarily invokes the relationship between value and exchange, highlighting the relations between individuals. "The specific characteristic of the economy as a particular form of behavior and communication consists not only in exchanging *values* but in the value of *exchange*."[29]

The implications of exchange for Simmel are far-reaching, consisting of no mere swapping or matching of quid pro quo. Nor is exchange merely limited to the monetary sphere. Instead he asserts that exchange constitutes the basic form of human relations:

> It should be recognized that most relationships between people can be interpreted as forms of exchange. Exchange is the purest and most developed kind of interaction, which shapes human life when it seeks to acquire substance and content. . . . Every interaction has to be regarded as an exchange: every conversation, every affection (even if it is rejected), every game, every glance at another person. The difference that seems to exist, that in interaction a person offers what he does not possess whereas in exchange he offers only what he does possess, cannot be sustained. . . . It is the object of exchange to increase the sum of value: each party offers to the other more than he possessed before.[30]

Even more significant is his declaration that

> the philosophical significance of money is that it represents within the practical world the most certain image and the clearest embodiment of the formula of all being, according to which things receive their meaning through each other and have their being determined by their mutual relations.[31]

Whereas Himmelfarb saw value as relativizing and neutralizing significance, for Simmel it is through the exchange of values that we see the ultimate value of exchange: that meaning itself cannot exist in isolation or in any a priori fashion, that being is codetermined by the process of mutual relations made possible by monetary exchange.

In the view of Margaret Susman, it is in *Philosophie des Geldes* that "Simmel's relativism and thus, at the same time his relation to the absolute finds its most complete expression."[32] As he struggled to formulate his theory of value, Simmel wrote to his friend the neo-Kantian Heinrich Rickert,

> The concept of value seems to me to not only contain the same kind of *regressus in infinitum* as does that of causality but also contains a *circulus vitiosus* because, if one follows through the connections far enough one always finds the value of A is based on that of B or that of B is only based on that of A. . . . I see no end to the difficulties since, in any case, I am convinced of the fact that I can only maintain my relativism if it is capable, as it were, of solving all the problems which are presented by theories of absolutism.[33]

In other words, he noted, values derive from other values, and the pursuit of some originary value that stands by itself, some absolute value, entails a vicious circle that precludes anything but relativism. Ultimately he concludes, following Heraclitus' notion about the constancy of the river's change, that it is money itself, that embodiment of fluctuation and shifting values, whose value is only in its ability to effect value, that is the only constant.

> Money is the symbol in the empirical world of the inconceivable unity of being, out of which the world, in all its breath, diversity, energy and reality, flows. . . . [It is from this] that the what gains its "thatness." . . . Of all external practical things—for which any analogy to the absolute is only partially valid—money comes closest to this power of being.[34]

Beyond Values, Beyond Exchange: Nishida's Query and Watsuji's Response

Indirectly it was against the Western objectification of the idea of value that Nishida Kitarō asked his famous question, which we can now amplify:

> Is there a common value judgment for the cultures of different nations? . . . Tastes differ among different peoples. The taste that one nation espouses in its culture cannot be tasted by people from other nations. But if we allow this proposition to run its course to its logical conclusion, it will mean that we must deny the possibility of having a generally accepted value judgment and that no debate can be advanced on the issue of "taste." I do not accept this. . . . There must be a requirement for others that "everyone must feel in this manner." Only then can there be a value judgment. When we recognize an artistic value or a moral value in a certain thing, that in itself is an act to leave the self behind. One must be attracted to something that is infinitely greater than the self.[35]

In posing the question about values transcending cultures, Nishida posits the idea that particular cultural tastes (i.e., aesthetic goods) need not be relegated to the wasteland of cultural particularity, that in fact their value depends on their being recognized, felt, and understood by others. In other words, he gestures to the possibility of value as being both particular and relative, on the one hand, and transcendent and absolute, on the other. But he does not suggest that value entails exchange, rather that value is only a function of individual assessment and/or group concurrence.

The philosopher Watsuji Tetsurō responds to this challenge in his major opus *Ethics* (倫理学, *Rinrigaku*), putting forward his well-known formulation that "human being" (人間, *ningen*), written with the characters 人 (*nin*), "person," and 間 (*gen*, or *aida*), "space between," in Japanese, is what arises out of the spaces between persons, in other words, the betweenness, or 間柄 (*aidagara*). Though the word 存在 (*sonzai*) is often translated as "being," he resists the idea of conflating it with the concepts of *Sein* and *esse*. Rather,

> If it is tenable to hold that *son* is self-sustenance of the self and *zai* means to remain within human relations, then *son-zai* is precisely the self-sustenance of the self as betweenness. That is, it means that *ningen* possesses herself. We could also simply say that *sonzai* is "the interconnection of the acts of *ningen*."[36]

This radical interconnection or linking 連関 (*renkan*) does not follow from two individuals forming a relation, nor do social relations confer on them individual being. Human being consists of the simultaneous operation of individuals and societies working reciprocally through what he terms the principle of negation:

> What I have described as a human being's existence as betweenness is that which renders individuals and societies capable of occurring in their reciprocal negations. Therefore, for human beings, we cannot first presuppose individuals, and then explain the establishment of social relationships among them. Nor can we presuppose society and from there explain the occurrence of individuals. Neither the one nor the other has "precedence." . . . Insofar as individuals and society are already established, then society consists of the relations among the individuals constituting it, and individuals are individuals only within society.[37]

Watsuji argues that both individuals and society arise out of a double negation: first, the self's negation of its context results in the constitution of individuals and group or society, and then the negation of the negation in which the individual negates itself, heralding its reintegration with the whole. It is this ongoing, continuous dialectical formation of double negation that he avers to be the fundamental law of human being, which is always a becoming. This assertion would seem to parallel Simmel's emphasis on exchange and human relations and the idea of mutual reciprocity between individuals and society, that "things receive their meaning through each other and have their being determined by their mutual relations."[38]

But Watsuji critiques Simmel explicitly, rejecting his premise, and instead offers a radically different philosophical understanding of exchange and value in five areas with significant implications. First, as he notes,

> according to Simmel, "society consists of many individuals engaged in reciprocal activities." . . . It is evident in Simmel that individuals exist prior to reciprocal activities.[39]

Simmel, as remarked on earlier, sees the emergence of individuality, independence, and the notion of personal freedom as resulting from the impact of a modern moneyed economy in which our dependence on impersonal relations with others paradoxically births a sense of independence and freedom that constitute the individual. Watsuji, on the other hand, rejects this prefabrication of the individual:

> As a result, even though our betweenness-oriented being subsists between one individual and another, we cannot posit this individual as an individualistic being whose existence precedes the already existing betweenness.[40]

Second, they differ on the conceptions of freedom. For Simmel, freedom is simply the consequence of the perception of putative independence resulting from the alienation of modern individuals from one another by virtue of relating to others primarily through an instrumental approach. For Watsuji, there is as well a coercive aspect to society that compels the individual, offsetting its capacity "to unify, communalize and universalize,"[41] the former of which Simmel ignores in favor of idealizing the latter, what the sociologist Ralf Dahrendorf would call a utopian formulation in which social coherence emerges out of common shared values in contradistinction to the rationalist approach emphasizing dissension, conflict, power, and hegemony.[42] Like Dahrendorf, Watsuji finds both approaches inadequate to account for social construction and coherence. For Simmel, human beings remain the passive recipients of the communalizing process conferred by the *Gesellschaft* relationships of the modern era. Watsuji argues instead that individuals are able to reject such linkings. Hence, Watsuji defines freedom as movement toward negation first instituted by and simultaneously instituting the individual against the constraints of society. He notes, however, that this is only one kind of freedom:

> The various forms through which the concept of freedom is prescribed are roughly divided in two. One is the individual's emancipation from the whole, which may assume various forms, such as the state, a church, a family, and so forth. This sort of freedom is that with which moral philosophers in England have been mainly concerned. The economical and political position that has been promulgated as liberalism is also based on this concept of freedom. The other is freedom that has the capacity to self-initiate without a cause outside of itself. . . . This is the control of the self by the self, autonomy. . . . The first freedom is a negation that enables an individual to revolt against the whole. The second freedom is the negation which further negates the preceding negation. In either case, freedom is the movement of negation.[43]

While Simmel acknowledges this first kind of independence, it is only Watsuji who argues for the "freedom that has the capacity to self-initiate without a cause outside of itself."[44] This double negation, both relative and absolute, defines what he calls "betweenness."

Third, Watsuji notes that in Japanese a distinction is drawn clearly between instrumental good and absolute good rather than merely subjective and objective valuations.

> When the issue of goodness and badness is discussed in books concerned with ethics in contemporary Japan, time and again, writers define *goodness* as "something useful for achieving a specific purpose" or "something judged to be of value because it satisfies a desire." However, I do not think that the Japanese word *zen* ("goodness") is ordinarily used in this way. What those writers wish to advocate is a meaning for words such as *good, Gut, Agathon, Bonum,* which are almost equivalent to what the Japanese word *yoshi* (which means "to be good" and at the same time "approvable" in Japanese) signifies. . . .
>
> *Yoki* food, *yoki* clothing, a *yoki* house . . . , and so forth are regarded as *yoshi* on the ground that they are all of use for a specific purpose and satisfy a specific desire. However, we cannot correctly employ the word *zen* for either of these usages. . . . Hence when we take into account the concept of *zen,* it can be said that we have already forsaken the ethics of "*yoki* things," which is, the standpoint of *Guterethik*.[45]

In opposition to the idea of *yoshi* (善し), or goodness, understood in terms of instrumentality, we have the concept of absolute goodness in the concept of *zen* (譱). How are we to understand this notion of goodness implicit in *zen*? It is embodied in the idea of *makoto* (誠), or sincerity, in which the attitude of the self toward the world is understood as *shojiki* (誠), or radiating truthfulness or honesty.[46]

Fourth, according to Watsuji, in the West we see an antithesis between moral goodness and badness based on the idea of guilt. He echoes Nietzsche in seeing guilt (*Schulden*) as related to indebtedness and notes that the translation for guilt in Japanese is *zaiseki* (在籍), which carries no sense of debt or indebtedness. Watsuji argues that the notion of guilt that manifests itself in the West arises out of the abrogation of a biblical covenant with God and hence necessitates a kind of repayment for the act of disobedience against the divine. There is nothing, he stresses, of this kind of broken covenant in the Japanese understanding of badness. But at the same time he notes that there is a sense of badness associated with indebtedness in Japan as implied by the term *sumanai,* with which an individual usually excuses himself or herself for actions undertaken. In addition, he comments that *sumanai* is derived from the verb *sumasu* (済ます), related both to the idea of paying of a bill or the repayment of debt and to the idea of concluding or finishing something. *Sumanai* therefore embraces both indebtedness and incompleteness.[47]

This indebtedness, unlike the idea of *Schuld,* does not represent guilt over the breaking of the covenant with the divine but instead entails the notion of betrayal—betrayal of the trust implicit in the relationship between individual and individual and hence the individual and the group. It is both the mutual trust that constitutes the group and the group that provides the ground for mutual trust to emerge. The badness inheres not in the action of the breaking of rules but in the act of betrayal, understood as the imposition of pain on others through our actions, witting or unwitting. Hence, *zen* has at its core the notion of trust, *shinrai* (信頼), that which both constitutes and affirms the bond that gives rise to individuals and society and hence our humanity, even as the goodness of *zen* also encompasses the possibility of abrogation, badness or betrayal. "The negation of the whole is goodness when it is pierced through by the movement of coming back, but is badness in and by itself."[48]

The idea of trust in Watsuji's thinking differs from the kind of trust that prevails in the exchange of values remarked on by Aristotle, the classical economists, and thinkers such as Nietzsche. Trust may be understood as reposed faith or having trust in something or someone or, on the other hand, as trustworthiness. But as Virginia Held,[49] in discussing the problem of the prisoner's dilemma, suggests, there is a distinction to be made between accurate or reliable predictability and trust. Surely there is a self-consuming irony implicit in the idea of the "trustworthy" in contradistinction to the idea of trust. This former understanding would seem closer to the idea of the reliably predictable, in other words, based on prior behavior or history. But this realm of the trustworthy is precisely where trust is less called upon. If something has proven itself worthy of trust, surely trust is not required, or at least not to the same degree. It is when uncertainty and doubt prevail amid the possibility of betrayal that trust may emerge. We need only consider the paradox implied by "Trust but verify" to comprehend that in the exchange of values as discussed previously, we encounter a situation of enforced mutual trustworthiness rather than the unilateral and not necessarily mutual surrender, relinquishing, and self-abandonment entailed by actual trust.

Finally, for Watsuji, betrayal, implicit in the double negation of betweenness, calls forth the voice of conscience, not merely an accusing voice but literally in Greek and German "the knowing together." What is it we know through that togetherness, that mutuality? It is the knowledge of our guilt. Our badness, our betrayal, our "indebtedness" is not a function of things, but of ourselves: "that for which *I* is indebted to others, in the case of my subordination to others, is not things but *I* itself."[50] In the first negation, when we betray our relations to others, comes the loss of self that emerges from those very relations, and from the second betrayal, that negation of the earlier negation, comes the possibility of restoration of our authentic self in its relation to others through conscience. From betrayal comes guilt; from guilt comes the voice of conscience, which "forces us, too, to recognize the emptiness of our selves."[51] Watsuji notes also that "it is said that, in the voice of conscience, the authentic self is disclosed."[52] Emptiness is the ground of self not as an isolated being in the void but rather in its relational totality.

The most far-reaching observation within the work, I think, is Watsuji's comment that "if emptiness as the real feature of the self were truly realized, then self-abandonment and the practice of nonduality would immediately be there. That is to say, the practice of benevolence would arise, rather than the consciousness of guilt."[53] Here is where Watsuji is finally able to collapse the opposition between the relative and the absolute through an understanding of betweenness as a double negation in which the I neither/both possesses nor is possessed. The value of exchange or betweenness is in the possibility it offers through the disclosure of the fundamental emptiness of self and its implications for the emergence of authenticity in the notion of self-abandonment.

A literary presentiment of Watsuji's theory of ethics is given to us by the most acclaimed novelist of the modern period, Natsume Sōseki, who was a mentor and friend to Watsuji. As numerous scholars in Japan and elsewhere have pointed out, many of Watsuji's notions of ethics seem to be rehearsed in Sōseki's fiction. As he himself remarked in *Guzo Saiko* (*The Revival of Idols*),[54] in a section entitled "A Reminiscence on My Teacher Natsume" (Natsume sensei ni tsuioku), one of the most significant catalysts for his own philosophy is found in the 1912–1913 novel *Kōjin,* or *The Wayfarer.* In it, a young Japanese intellectual beset by existential angst quotes the German saying *Keine Brücke führt von Mensch zu Mensch,* "there is no bridge leading from man to man" (*hito to hito to no aida o tsunagu hashi wa nai*),[55] in the midst of his despair. This quotation and the implicit question it poses has struck a number of critics as one of the starting points for Watsuji's philosophy and can be understood as a rephrasing of Nishida's own query noted earlier. If we cannot bridge the divide between persons, how can we speak of aesthetics or ethics except as an amalgam of isolated individual value judgments? And if it is values and exchange that allow us to connect and transcend our discrete natures, must we assume necessarily a Rawlsian social contract that governs human relationships as Western liberalist theorists have done, one based on reciprocality and proportionality and the notion of exchange?

But Watsuji suggests a more fundamental dynamic of *aidagara,* or "betweenness," leading to an awareness of human being, *ningen,* as that dialectical double negation, which gives rise to both aesthetics and ethics as foreshadowed in Sōseki's 1914 novel *Kokoro.* It is not value and exchange that gives rise to human relationships, or even human relationships that give rise to value and exchange, but something more elemental, our very being in this world arising out of the concept of "betweenness." For Watsuji, value becomes understood in a new way that embraces both its relative and its absolute nature:

> The supreme value is absolute wholeness and an aspiration, or upward drive, or eagerness for it, is "goodness" . . . This can be illustrated through a simple expression, the Japanese term *nakayoshi,* which refers to the realization of socio-ethical unity.[56]

Initially we might imagine that this would seem to cede ground to a purely relative understanding of value that presumes a duality between "goodness," or that which promotes this "socio-ethical unity," and "badness," or that which threatens this unity. But Watsuji goes on to comment,

> The movement of absolute negativity, which is a return back to itself, is impossible apart from the moment of self-rebellion. Even though the union of love or self-sacrifice may be taken as goodness, it must be that what is requisite for the arising of this goodness is, above all, the independence of an individual, which is badness. If so, then badness turns out to be that which renders goodness possible, and hence, it ceases to be badness.[57]

Hence, Watsuji resolves the dualistic reasoning implicit in most considerations of value through the larger framework of absolute negativity and emptiness. We move from defining fundamental human being in what we earlier termed Nietzsche's *Homo pendens,* or "weighing man," to its implied equivalent in Watsuji's conception that we might term *Homo fidens,* or "trusting man."

In the novel *Kokoro,*[58] in which the central character, Sensei, struggles with issues of ethical goodness, trust, sincerity, and isolation emerge as dominant motifs. As the book progresses, we see a relationship develop between the narrator, "I," a hapless student, and his mentor and friend, Sensei, a relationship that many critics have viewed as based on that between Watsuji and Sōseki himself. Sōseki was a teacher at the prestigious First Higher School in Tokyo, which Watsuji attended, and Watsuji recollects standing outside the window of his classroom listening to his lectures when he had no other classes. But more than simply the identification of the characters with Watsuji and Sōseki, what is striking about the novel is how it functions virtually as a literary playing out of the scenarios that give rise to Watsuji's ethical theories. As Steve Odin astutely noted,[59] Sōseki himself moved from a position of modified Western "individualism" (個人主義, *kojinshugi*) and "egocentrism" (利己主義, *rikoshugi*) to later what he termed a "negation of self" (自己否定, *jiko hitei*), culminating in his final philosophical position, "follow heaven, depart from the self" (則天去私, *sokuten kyoshi*). For Watsuji, we might deduce, there is still a focus on the individual as individual here, even in the negation of and departure from self. Human being as such for Watsuji can be comprehended only as the continual double negation, first of others and then of self, allowing the dialectic of individual and group to be constituted as an ongoing "becoming."

The fictive treatment of the relationship between Watsuji and Sōseki as the putative "I" and Sensei is a perplexing one throughout the novel, in which I struggles to understand the agonizing lassitude experienced by his mentor and friend. There is little to connect them other than I's simpleminded and inexplicable devotion to Sensei, which Sensei regards with suspicion and doubt.

> "It is not you in particular that I distrust, but the whole of humanity." . . . "I don't even trust myself. And not trusting myself, I can hardly trust others." . . . "At any rate," he continued, "don't put too much trust in me. You will learn to regret it if you do. And if you ever allow yourself to feel betrayed, you will then find yourself being cruelly vindictive." . . . "You see, loneliness is the price we have to pay for being born in this modern age, so full of freedom, independence, and our own egotistical selves."[60]

Sensei is emotionally and spiritually paralyzed, I discovers eventually, first, as a result of Sensei's betrayal at the hands of his family, resulting in his rebellion against them, and then even more by Sensei's own subsequent betrayal of a friend and the attendant suicide of that friend. What seems to change Sensei is not a sharing or exchange with I, but instead the simple sincerity, *makoto,* of I's interest in him without reference to benefit or mutual return. Early on, I explains himself, saying,

> "No, sir, I am simply being sincere. And in all sincerity I wish to learn about life." . . . "I wonder if you are being really sincere," he said. "Because of what happened to me, I have come to doubt everybody. In truth, I doubt you too. But for some reason I do not want to doubt you. It may be because you seem so simple. Before I die, I should like to have one friend that I can trust. I wonder if you can be that friend. Are you really sincere?"[61]

Ironically, it is because Sensei trusts I that he reveals his cloaked past to him in a letter, a letter that is ultimately a suicide note. It is an act literally of self-negation, a departure from the self, though also figuratively a confession to self in that Sensei confides the truth to I. But sending the epistle is also an act of reposing trust, a unilateral crying out for help that serves no instrumental value. Sensei comments in a letter to his young friend about his struggles with guilt and his consequent awareness of the emptiness of self:

> Though I had resolved to live as though I were dead, my heart would at times respond to the activities of the outside world. . . . But as soon as I would try to break through the cloud that surrounded me, a frighteningly powerful voice would rush upon me from I know not where, and grip my heart tight until I could not move. . . . A voice would say to me: "You have no right to do anything. Stay where you are." . . . In fury and grief I would cry out: "Why do you stop me?" With a cruel laugh, the voice would answer, you know very well why. And I would bow in hopeless surrender.[62]

The novel ends with Sensei's presumptive suicide and I's reading of this final epistle on a train, stranded, going nowhere, speeding toward the now deceased Sensei. I remains suspended between his spiritual father, Sensei, who has abandoned him, betrayed him, through his suicide, and leaving behind, betraying, his own dying biological father. We end with a final recognition of the multiple instances of betweenness and the double negation underlying it, first of the self emancipating itself from the bonds of society and then of the awareness of the emptiness of self as a result of betraying the trust implicit in its relation to others. But how do we read Sensei's death, which has sometimes been interpreted as an instance of nihilism in the face of existential angst, in the light of Watsuji's ideas? As the ascendance of guilt culminating in its inevitable end? Or could we not read Sensei's suicide as well as a dissolution of self, the extinction of his "I" and narrative and its subsequent reformulation into the "I" and narrative of the young narrator within the text as an embodiment of the end of duality? Additionally, is not the narrative itself, which ends with Sensei's final epistle, whose painful honesty reflects the ideas of *makoto* and *shojiki,* the ultimate benediction for the young "I," even as the novel narrated retrospectively by the older "I," who has had to come to terms with his own emptiness, offers just such benediction, both aesthetic and ethical, to the reader?

NOTES

1. Nishida Kitarō, "Nihonteki no yukoto ni tsuite," reprinted in *Nishida Kitarō, Nihon no meicho,* ed. Kamiyama Shumpei (Tokyo: Chūō Kōron Sha, 1970), 47:443. Quoted in *Japan: A Documentary History: The Late Tokugawa Period to the Present* (Armonk, NY: M.E. Sharpe, 1997), 407.

2. *Oxford Dictionary of English Etymology* (Oxford: Oxford University Press, 1966), 321.

3. *Oxford English Dictionary,* 2nd ed. (Oxford: Oxford University Press, 1989), 19:415.

4. Walter W. Skeat, *An Etymological Dictionary of the English Language* (Oxford: Clarendon Press, 1901), 720.

5. *The Compact Edition of the Oxford English Dictionary* (Oxford: Oxford University Press, 1971), 2:3828.

6. Adam Smith, *The Wealth of Nations,* ed. Andrew Skinner (London: Penguin Books, 1970, reprinted 1999), book 1, chap. 4, 131–132; chap. 8, 169.

7. Ibid., chap. 4, 131; chap. 5, 133–134.

8. See David Ricardo, *Principles of Political Economy and Taxation, The Works and Correspondence of David Ricardo, ed. Piero Sraffa* (Indianapolis: Liberty Fund, 2005), 1:11.

9. See Karl Marx, *Theories of Surplus Value,* trans. and ed. G. A. Bonner and Emile Burns (London: Lawrence & Wishart, 1951), 4:128.

10. See Friedrich Hegel, *The Phenomenology of Mind,* trans. J. B. Baillie, "Independence and Dependence of Self-Consciousness: Lordship and Bondage" and "Objective Spirit: The Ethical Order" (London: Macmillan, 1931), 104–111, 254–266.

11. Gertrude Himmelfarb, prologue, "From Virtues to Values," in *The Demoralization of Society: From Victorian Virtues to Modern Values* (New York: Alfred A. Knopf, 1994), 11.

12. Friedrich Nietzsche, *On the Genealogy of Morals,* ed. Walter Kaufmann (New York: Random House, 1967), 8.

13. Ibid.

14. Ibid., 70.

15. Aristotle, *Nicomachean Ethics,* book 5.

16. Nicholas J. Theocarakis, "*Antipeponthos* and Reciprocity: The Concept of Equivalent Exchange from Aristotle to Turgot," *International Review of Economics* 55, no. 1 (2008), 29–44.

17. Aristotle, *Nicomachean Ethics,* book 5.

18. Oswald Spengler, *The Decline of the West,* vol. 2, *Perspectives of World History* (New York: Alfred A. Knopf, 1928).

19. Ibid., 481; emphasis mine.

20. Ibid., 485; emphasis mine.

21. See chapter 4 of Jeremy Bentham's *An Introduction to Principles of Morals and Legislation,* introd. by Lawrence J. Lafleur (New York: Hafner Publishing Co., 1948), 29–32.

22. See Immanuel Kant's *Groundwork for the Metaphysics of Morals,* ed. and trans. Allen W. Wood (New Haven, CT: Yale University Press, 2002), 33–37.

23. See Marcel Mauss' *The Gift: Forms and Functions of Exchange in Archaic Societies,* trans. Ian Gunnison (1923; repr., New York: W.W. Norton & Co., 1967), especially 10–12.

24. Ibid., chap. 4. See also Linda Molm's "Theoretical Comparisons of Forms of Exchange," *Sociological Theory* 21, no. 1 (March 2003), 1–17, for a discussion of the differences between negotiated exchanges and reciprocal exchanges across several disciplines.

25. Spengler, *Decline of the West,* 482; emphasis mine.

26. Georg Simmel, *The Philosophy of Money,* trans. Tom Bottomore and David Frisby (London: Routlege and Kegan Paul, 1978), 81.

27. Ibid., 298–299.

28. Ibid., 297.

29. Ibid., 80; emphasis mine.

30. Ibid., 82.

31. Ibid., 128–129.

32. Ibid., 25.

33. Ibid., 24.

34. Ibid., 497–498.

35. Nishida, "Nihonteki no yukoto ni tsuite."

36. Watsuji Tetsurō, *Watsuji Tetsurō's Rinrigaku: Ethics in Japan,* trans. Yamamoto Seisaku and Robert E. Carter (Albany: State University of New York Press, 1996), 21; Watsuji, *Rinrigaku* [Ethics], Jo and Ge (2 volumes), *Watsuji Tetsurō Zenshū* (*The Complete Works of Watsuji Tetsurō*) (Tokyo: Iwanami Shoten, 1962, vols. 10 and 11), 10:25.

37. Watsuji, *Ethics,* 102; *Rinrigaku,* 10:107.

38. Simmel, *Philosophy of Money,* 129.

39. Watsuji, *Ethics,* 105; *Rinrigaku,* 10:111.

40. Watsuji, *Ethics,* 83; *Rinrigaku,* 10:88.

41. Watsuji, *Ethics,* 108; *Rinrigaku,* 10:114.

42. Ralf Dahrendorf, "Out of Utopia: Towards a Re-Orientation of Sociological Analysis," *American Journal of Sociology* LXIV, no. 2 (September 1958), 115–127.

43. Watsuji, *Ethics,* 138; *Rinrigaku,* 10:145–146.

44. Watsuji, *Ethics,* 138; *Rinrigaku,* 10:146.

45. Watsuji, *Ethics,* 286; *Rinligaku,* 10:302–303.
46. Watsuji, *Ethics,* 272–282; *Rinligaku,* 10:286–298.
47. Watsuji, *Ethics,* 295–296; *Rinligaku,* 10:311–314.
48. Watsuji, *Ethics,* 284; *Rinligaku,* 10:300.
49. Virginia Held, "On the Meaning of Trust," *Ethics* 8, no. 2 (January 1968), 156.
50. Watsuji, *Ethics,* 302, 299; *Rinligaku,* 10:316.
51. Watsuji, *Ethics,* 299; *Rinligaku,* 10:316.
52. Watsuji, *Ethics,* 308; *Rinligaku,* 10:326.
53. Watsuji, *Ethics,* 300; *Rinligaku,* 10:317.
54. Tetsurō Watsuji, "Natsume sensei ni tsuioku," in *Guzo Saiko* (The revival of idols), *Watsuji Tetsurō Zenshū,* 17:85–99.
55. Natsume Sōseki, *The Wayfarer,* trans. Beongcheon Yu (Detroit: Wayne State University Press, 1967), 293. *Kōjin* can be found in vol. 7 of *Natsume Sōseki Zenshū* (Tokyo: Iwanami Shoten, 1985).
56. Watsuji, *Ethics,* 134; *Rinligaku,* 10:141–142.
57. Watsuji, *Ethics,* 134; *Rinligaku,* 10:142.
58. Natsume Sōseki, *Kokoro,* trans. Edwin McClellan (Washington, DC: Regnery, 1957). *Kokoro* can be found in vol. 9 of *Natsume Sōseki Zenshū* (Tokyo: Iwanami Shoten, 1985).
59. Steve Odin, *The Social Self in Zen and American Pragmatism,* SUNY Series in Constructive Postmodern Thought (Albany: State University of New York Press, 1996), 52.
60. Sōseki, *Kokoro,* 29–30.
61. Ibid., 68.
62. Ibid., 243.

Triple Negation 3

Watsuji Tetsurō on the Sustainability of Ecosystems, Economies, and International Peace

James McRae

Environmental security is a branch of environmental studies that explores how national security issues are affected by ecosystem sustainability and the demands placed on the natural world by human populations. The pursuit of consumer interests can often place stress on the environment, which can lead to a collapse of both ecosystems and economies, which in turn promotes political instability. For this reason, the fields of environmental ethics, business ethics, and international relations are ultimately intertwined. This essay draws from the philosophical anthropology of Watsuji Tetsurō's *Fūdo* to explain why human culture, economics, and the politics of warfare are so intimately tied to sustainability issues. The ethical principles of Watsuji's *Rinrigaku* are then used to articulate a normative framework that could be used to promote sustainability—and thereby maintain peace—on an international scale. By developing a relational understanding of environmental and business ethics that emphasizes roles and responsibilities over individual autonomy and rights, we can regulate business practices in a manner that is both environmentally and socially conscious. Because mismanagement of the environment leads to socio-economic problems that provoke global conflicts, the promotion of sustainability according to Watsuji's ethics can contribute to both a healthy economy and international security.

The Ethics of Watsuji Tetsurō

The Japanese word for ethics, *rinri* (倫理), consists of the characters for "fellows" and "principle," and thus ethics is the discipline that determines the principles for properly ordering human relationships.[1] Watsuji's philosophy of the person is deliberately opposed to Western ideas of ethical individualism and metaphysical dualism. He argues that the human mind and body are completely inseparable and that the "field of human relationships is superior to the individual."[2] This is clearly demonstrated in the terminology that he uses to discuss the idea of the person. In Japanese, there are two common terms used to designate the concept of "person": ***kojin*** and ***ningen:***

1. 個人 ***Kojin*** (individual): This word consists of the character ***hito*** (人)[3] preceded by the character 個, which is a counter used for enumerating random, inanimate objects. The word as a whole refers to an individual, a being set apart from the world "for the purposes of enumeration."[4] Watsuji thinks this has a decidedly lonely connotation: a person as ***kojin*** is fundamentally separated from other people and is, as a result, less than fully human. When used in this respect, the term "individual" has a cold and impersonal meaning. A focus on individual autonomy rather than social interrelation can easily degenerate to individualism, which leads to selfish, lonely despair. The only solution is through social interaction.[5]
2. 人間 ***Ningen*** (human being): ***Ningen*** is a combination of the words ***nin*** (人, also read ***hito***), or "person," and ***gen*** (間, also read ***aida/ma***), which means "the space in between things."[6] ***Ningen*** can be literally translated as "the space between persons" or "a person as in between." Thus, the "human being" as ***ningen*** is a person fundamentally defined by his relationship to a particular spatiotemporal context and the other beings within that context. ***Ningen*** thus refers to the interrelational nature of human beings.

Whereas ***kojin*** represents an individual self that is set apart from a particular context, ***ningen*** describes a person as a human being who is defined by his or her presence within space and who defines that space in return. Since we, as human beings, cannot avoid living in a certain portion of space-time, we must look to this spatiotemporal context as one of the essential defining factors of ourselves. As a result of this interpretation of the person, we must "abandon the modern European idea of seeing the world from the standpoint of self-consciousness. Instead, we must grasp the individual from the totality of human relationships."[7]

For Watsuji, in order to understand the human being, "we must first take note of the 'betweenness' (***aidagara***) in which people are located."[8] ***Aidagara*** (間柄) refers to the relationships that connect us to one another and allow us to interact with other persons in our contexts (our ***particular*** environments).[9] All beings exist within a ***basho*** (場所, life-field, place, or context) in space, such that "to exist ***within a body*** in a spatial ***basho*** is the most fundamental mode of human being."[10] A person's mind exists within his or her body (the first ground of context), and that body exists within the spatiotemporal world (the final ground of context). Other people naturally form an essential part of one's environment. Thus, one's relationship with one's ***basho*** (context) is characterized by the "betweenness" that one shares with one's natural environment and the other people that exist within that ***basho***.

Watsuji argues that climate (風土, *fūdo*) plays an essential role in the development of the person. He describes the person as defined by the two factors of climate and history:

> Here the space- and time-structure of human existence is revealed as climate and history: the inseparability of time and space is the basis of the inseparability of history and climate. . . . The human duality, of the finite and the infinite, is most plainly revealed as the historical and climatic structure.[11]

The history of an individual includes not only one's genealogy, but the history of the culture in which one lives. The climate in which one exists is the medium for self-discovery.[12] From the concept of *climate* springs Watsuji's theory of intersubjectivity: it is within the life-field (*basho*) that we find "the interconnected meanings of the life-world."[13] *Basho* is the ultimate ground of existence that fundamentally connects a human being to his or her environment through the vehicle of the body. It is this "betweenness" that unites human to human and allows one to be defined by the term "*ningen*" as a person within a context.[14] The only way for a person to truly exist as an individual in relation to the natural world is through this betweenness with one's environment as an extension of one's body. Any attempt to define oneself as an individual separate from this context results in *kojin,* a lonely being removed from the world and incapable of achieving authentic personhood. This is because *kojin* is a fictitious "self" that attempts to exist independent of the environment that defines all true selves. It is only by casting off the egoistic illusion of *kojin* and immersing oneself in one's *basho* that one can shape one's true identity as a person.[15]

It might be argued that Watsuji's definition of the person is overly anthropocentric and does not focus enough upon humankind's relationship to nature. This interpretation of Watsuji's philosophy of the person fails to take into account the emphasis that he places on the effects of nature on the person in his book *Fūdo.* One's natural surroundings play an essential role in the development of the person, to the extent that the different cultures of the world owe their distinct characters to the unique natural climates in which they make their homes. *Ningen* exists not only in the space between all persons, but also in the space between those persons and the natural world. In order to develop oneself, one must cultivate one's relationship with the totality of one's environment, not simply with selected parts of that environment.

Watsuji states that all human beings have a "double structure" of self in relation to their context: as *ningen* we are *individuals* completely defined by our *relationship* with our climate.[16] One is a fully developed human being only when one realizes this double structure and embraces one's context as an essential part of oneself. Yet in order to realize *ningen,* one must first make a movement from the individualism of *kojin* through a process of self-negation in which one denies the illusion of one's "individual" self:

> What is at stake here is the taking of a first step toward self-awareness. Apart from the self-awareness of an individual, there is no social ethics. The other moment is the individual's surrender to the totality. This is what has been called the *demand of the superindividual will,* or of total will. Without this surrender, there is also no social ethics.[17]
>
> An individual who does not imply the meaning of negation, that is, an essentially self-sufficient individual, is nothing but an imaginative construction.[18]

Many people, in an attempt to develop and define their selves, seek to do so by cutting that self off from its environment and constructing what they consider to be an autonomous self. However, because the individual is essentially defined by his or her environment, this fictitious, "individual" self is nothing more than an illusion, and the person becomes isolated from his or her environment. For Watsuji, the concept of the self as a lone individual that rises above or separates itself from its context is completely empty.

Here one might object: Does this view of anti-individualism mean that we do not exist apart from the larger "herd" of humanity? Not at all. Watsuji's betweenness implies that there is a space (*aida*) that exists between human beings, such that "we *can* come to meet in the between *and* that we are at a distance from one another."[19] We exist in this space and this space exists between us. Steve Odin states:

> According to Watsuji it is precisely this dialectical unity between the "self" (*ji*) and the "*other*" (*ta*) which constitutes the double character of *ningen* in its essential wholeness as an individual-society relationship.[20]

To exist in the world as *ningen* is to be completely defined by one's experiences in the world. Yet, because each person has a different web of interpersonal relations (betweenness) within a particular context, each individual has characteristically different experiences within his or her unique context that lead to a distinctively different person in each case. Each person is still a function of his or her betweenness with other people; it is simply that this betweenness is different for each person because of his or her different relations with different other persons as a function of the first ground of context, the body. Everyone is defined by context; what makes a person unique is the particular way in which he or she chooses to actively influence that context.

In his *Rinrigaku,* Watsuji defines ethics in terms of *ningen sonzai* (人間存在), "human beings existing":

> By the way, our question was "what is ethics?" and we found that this question asks about the fundamental structure of the *sonzai* of *ningen*.[21]
>
> [*Sonzai*] means "the maintenance or subsistence over against loss." . . . If it is tenable to hold that the *son* is the self-sustenance of the self and *zai* means to remain within human relations, then *son-zai* is precisely the self-sustenance of the

> self as betweenness. That is, it means that *ningen* possesses herself. We could also simply say that *sonzai* is "the interconnection of the acts of *ningen*."[22]

The ethical, for Watsuji, is the totality of actions within a particular context that allow the person as *ningen* to thrive and positively interrelate with his or her context. "Right" refers to those actions particular to an individual context that promote harmonious interrelation between *ningen* and the environment. "Wrong" refers to those relationships that hinder harmonious contextual interrelation. When Watsuji says that ethics is "the interconnection of the acts of *ningen*," he means it is the relationship of the good of all persons within a given context. Every act is "an interactivity between subjects."[23] No one can commit an action on a purely individual basis. Every action, via betweenness, affects other persons. Thus, the personal good immediately translates to the good of other persons and the environment.

Environmental Security

Environmental security studies the effects that environmental changes have on human conflict, which threatens the social, physical, and economic well-being of humans.[24] Figure 3.1 illustrates a hybrid theoretical model that explains the causal relationship between human activity, environmental impact, and violent conflict.[25] The black arrows show the causal relationship among human activity, environmental impact, negative social effects, and the promotion or avoidance of violent conflict. Since the 1970s, the environmental impact of human beings has been understood according to the simple equation of I = PAT: environmental impact is a function of population, affluence, and technology.[26] Current theoretical models in environmental security are substantially more complex, expanding upon the core idea of the I = PAT equation to explain how environmental degradation promotes violent conflict. Population growth leads to scarcity because it divides limited resources among more people. This is exacerbated by the fact that these resources are typically not equally distributed among the members of a society; the poor are impacted more quickly and significantly than are those with money and power.[27] Affluence amplifies the impact of population because consumer societies expect a higher standard of living, which places a greater strain on food, water, and energy sources. Technology refers to the processes used to obtain energy and resources from the natural environment. This can have either a negative effect (e.g., coal, oil, and nuclear power) or a positive effect (e.g., solar and wind energy). Taken together, population, affluence, and technology produce an environmental impact that can have negative results for human beings and other living things.

The term "environmental impact," or "environmental change" refers to a "human-induced decline in the quantity or quality of a renewable resource that

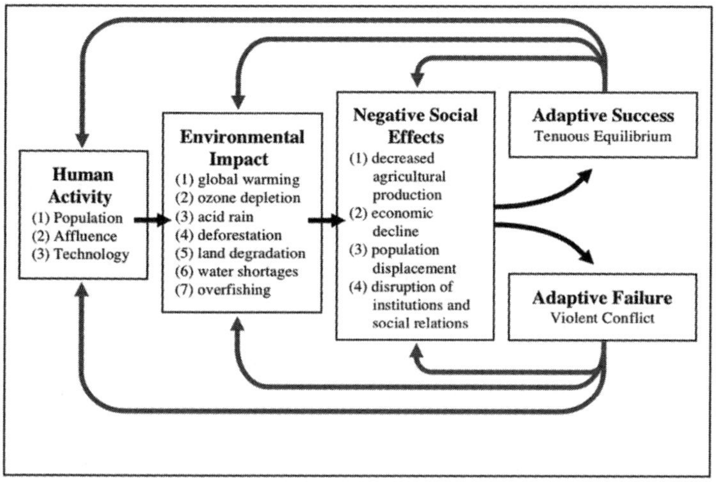

Figure 3.1. Environmental Impaction and Violent Conflict: A Hybrid Theoretical Model

occurs faster than it is renewed by natural processes."[28] Thomas F. Homer-Dixon argues that seven major environmental effects contribute to human conflict: global warming, ozone depletion, acid rain, deforestation, the degradation of arable land, water shortages, and overfishing.[29] These environmental pressures lead to conflict as a result of four interrelated social effects: decreased agricultural production, economic decline, population displacement, and the disruption of institutions and social relations. As natural resources and food become scarcer, the economy begins to decline. Environmental refugees are created as people move away from areas where there is no employment and there are few resources and extensive environmental degradation. Large population movements lead to group identity conflicts, which disrupt social relations. Unequal resource distribution intensifies the disparity between social classes, which promotes socio-political conflict. Poor countries are more vulnerable to environmental change and thus the developing world is more likely to suffer from conflicts due to environmental problems.[30] If left unchecked, these negative social effects ultimately promote violent conflict.

While Homer-Dixon suggests that the negative social effects of environmental change necessarily lead to violent conflict once they have reached a critical threshold, Richard A. Matthew, Ted Gaulin, and Bryan McDonald have suggested that there is a certain amount of adaptivity that can potentially mitigate the use of force. As the environment is progressively degraded by human activity, negative social effects begin to accumulate. If human beings are able to regulate their activity to minimize conflict and adapt to environmental change, they can achieve a tenuous equilibrium in which violence is averted. If they fail to adapt, violent conflict will be inevitable.[31] Homer-Dixon argues that environmental security is a feedback loop: population and activity per capita can stress vulnerable ecosystems, leading to negative environmental effects, which influence social effects, which can lead to conflict. The gray arrows in Figure 3.1 represent this feedback loop. Social effects and conflict affect human preferences, beliefs, social relations, and institutions, which in turn influence population and activity per capita.[32] Matthew, Gaulin, and McDonald echo this idea in their notion of adaptivity: successful adaptation has a positive effect on politics, the economy, and the environment, while unsuccessful adaptation leads to conflict, which has a deleterious effect on human beings, their institutions, and the natural world.

When interpreted from a Watsujian framework, the lessons of environmental security are not surprising: human beings affect and are profoundly affected by their environments. Because personhood and culture are a function of the natural and social environment in which one is radically contextualized, one should expect that harm inflicted on the environment will ultimately manifest itself socio-politically. While human beings have the ability to adapt to environmental pressures—a process that Watsuji explains at length in regard to the volatile climates of Japan and India—extreme, human-inflicted changes such as global warming or overfishing are likely to stress ecosystems beyond the critical threshold of adaptation. At this point, conflict becomes almost inevitable; even if we can temporarily avert disaster by reaching a tenuous adaptive equilibrium, the negative effects of human-induced environmental change produce a feedback loop that can disrupt this delicate balance.

Triple Negation: Watsuji, Environmental Ethics, and Security

Watsuji's understanding of ethics as the relationship between *ningen* (contextualized human beings) and *fūdo* (the natural and social environment) provides a normative framework that can help to promote both sustainability and peace. Watsuji's understanding of the person accurately reflects the biological reality of the human species. J. Baird Callicott, the leading interpreter of Aldo Leopold's Land Ethic, describes the ecological view of human beings:

> Ecology is the study of relationships of organisms to one another and to the elemental environment. . . . The ontological primacy of objects and the ontological subordination of relationships characteristic of classical western science is, in fact, reversed in ecology. Ecological relationships determine the nature of organisms rather than the other way around. A species is what it is because it has adapted to a niche in the ecosystem. The whole, the system itself, thus, literally and quite straightforwardly shapes and forms its component parts.[33]

Human beings, both as individuals and as a species, are defined by their relationships with one another and with the natural environment. Humans are a distinct species, but we are shaped by our environments in terms of morphology, diet, culture, and so forth. The anthropocentric worldview is characterized by a belief that human beings are separate from and superior to the rest of the planet, which makes the Earth little more than raw material to be exploited for human benefit. Watsuji's understanding of the person seems to anticipate Leopold's idea that human beings are merely plain citizens of the biotic community: instead of conquering the land as an "other" that can be used for our own benefit, we should strive to preserve the land as part of the interdependent process that is the ground for our very existence.[34]

Watsuji's understanding of *aidagara* (betweenness) is also reflected in the Land Ethic. The characters for *ningen* literally mean "person" (人) and "field" (間) in the sense of an electromagnetic field. Thus, one's notion of self is defined by concentric circles of interdependence that incorporate one's family, friends, community, and culture as well as one's local and global environment. This parallels Callicott's interpretation of Leopold's Land Ethic:

> Since individual organisms, from an ecological point of view, are less discrete objects than modes of a continuous, albeit differentiated, whole, the distinction between self and other is blurred. . . . As one moves, in imagination, outwardly from the core of one's organism, it is impossible to find a clear demarcation between oneself and one's environment. . . . The world is, indeed, one's extended body and one's body is the precipitation, the focus of the world in a particular space-time locale.[35]

Once human beings acknowledge their radical contextualization, they will be moved to revise their ethical systems to reflect the intrinsic value of the environment. Callicott argues that humans have evolved an "affective moral response to perceived bonds of kinship and community membership and identity."[36] If moral sympathy is, as Nitobe Inazō says, "sensitivity to the distress of others," humans can learn to be sensitive to the distress of the environment, even if it is not a person (since it has an objective well-being that ultimately affects our own).[37]

So how can human beings learn to live in harmony with the environment? One dominant paradigm that has been used extensively in business ethics is *kyōsei* (共生), or symbiosis. Surprisingly, this paradigm has received little attention in environmental ethics, even though it is grounded in the biological and ecological sciences. Japanese philosopher Hiroshi Abe has helped to pioneer the application of this concept to environmental ethics. Literally, symbiosis refers to different species "living together" for extended periods of time. While symbiotic relationships can be parasitic (in which one species benefits at the other's expense) or commensal (one species benefits while the other is neither harmed nor benefited), *kyōsei* refers to mutualism, in which both species benefit from their interaction. Drawing from Matsuda Hiroyuki, Abe defines mutualistic symbiosis as "interspecific interactions in which the benefits exceed the costs for both participants."[38] Abe stresses that *kyōsei* should be understood as mutualism in the broadest sense. It is not necessary for both species to gain an identical benefit from the relationship for it to be mutualistic, so long as the well-being of both species is enhanced. Even species that are not directly related to one another can interact in a mutually beneficial manner. Because matter is constantly circulated throughout an ecosystem, all living things are, to some extent, interdependent. While some species—like the classic example of the clownfish and sea anemone—form explicitly mutualistic symbiotic relationships, all species in an ecosystem affect one another to some extent.[39] Historically, human beings have acted in a manner that more closely resembles parasitism or commensalism, using the environment as raw material to satisfy strictly anthropocentric ends with little concern for the welfare of the other species affected. However, environmental security suggests that injury to the environment causally contributes to social destabilization and conflict, which means that even from an anthropocentric perspective, the good of human beings is closely tied to the good of the environment.

Kyōsei is not only a term that applies to cross-species interrelation; in business ethics, it has been used as a paradigm to promote harmonious relationships between human beings and nonliving entities such as corporations. It is the key paradigm in the Caux Roundtable Principles for Business, which have been voluntarily adopted by many of the world's largest corporations as a normative framework to guide international business. Within the context of the Caux Principles, *kyōsei* is broadly defined as " 'symbiosis,' which means 'different creatures living together' " or "living and working together for the common good."[40] The Caux Principles were first proposed by Ryuzaburo Kaku (chairman of Canon, Inc.), who argued that in business there must be a harmony between profit and ethical principles: "The common good is a necessary condition to make the world better, and kyosei is the sufficient condition."[41] These principles are grounded in stakeholder theory, a normative approach to business ethics that reconceptualizes the roles and relationships that define corporate obligations. Traditional shareholder theory argues that corporate executives have obligations only to those who have a financial share of the company and thus stand to profit from its success. Stakeholder theory expands upon this limited model to incorporate all those who have a stake in the outcome of the company's actions. While managers are responsible to stockholders, these are not the only people to whom they have moral obligations. The firm is at the hub of a wheel, the spokes of which are the stakeholders: financiers, suppliers, employees, communities, customers, and other groups that are affected by the actions of the business.[42] As Chester I. Barnard argues, the purpose of a corporation is to serve society, not vice versa.[43] All stakeholders must play a role in the solution of problems that affect the entire community: subsystem goals that actualize the good of a part of the community should be pursued only if they are consonant with overall system goals that promote the good of all stakeholders.[44]

Watsuji's ethics allows us to apply the notions of *kyōsei* and stakeholder theory to environmental ethics to create a set of normative principles like the Caux Roundtable Principles that can promote environmental sustainability and security. Watsuji recognizes human beings as radically contextualized. Ethics is designed to mitigate and minimize human conflict, so we need to recognize the connection between environmental change and scarcity if we wish to prevent warfare. Watsuji argues that ethics occurs in the tension between two poles, the "I" (or individual) and the "we" or social (see Figure 3.2). On one hand, we exist as individual human beings with goals that we wish to actualize and rights that we wish to protect. On the other hand, we are defined by our social, historical, and environmental context, in which individuality is subsumed. Ethics is created through a process of double negation, which involves two distinct movements: (1) the individual negates the community, which is necessary for normative concepts such as individual rights; then (2) the individual negates himself or herself to return to the community, which is essential for the creation of ethical notions such as the common good, generalizable goals, roles, and responsibilities.[45] Individuality is possible only by virtue of our relationships, which in turn can exist only because of individuality. This is what Watsuji means when he defines *ningen* as "persons in between." A guitar string functions only when it is placed under tension between the bridge and the nut; attaching the string at only one end makes it impossible to play. Similarly, human beings can function ethically only in the tension between the individual and the community; embracing then negating both egoistic individuality on one end and empty conformism on the other makes ethics impossible.

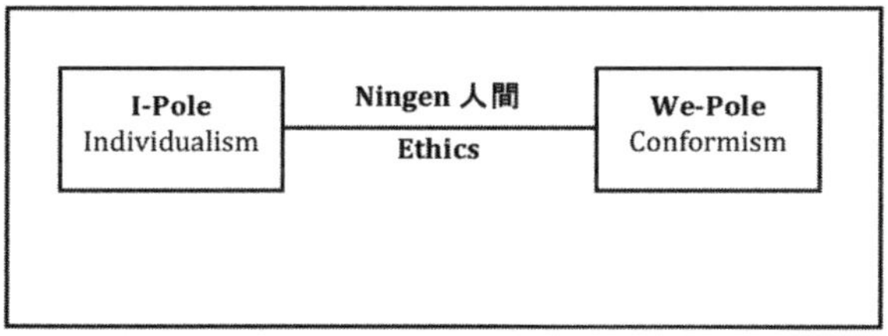

Figure 3.2. Watsuji's Double Negation

A similar process of negation needs to take place for environmental ethics to be possible. Watsuji argues that human beings are defined by their relationships not only with other people, but also with the natural environment in which their culture has developed. While the ethics of *ningen* is created by the double negation of the individual human and the collective, environmental ethics is created by a process of triple negation in which the individual and society both negate themselves in relation to the natural environment.[46] The good of the individual and the good of human society must be balanced with the good of the environment because these goods are all ultimately interdependent. The paradigm through which this balance can occur is *kyōsei:* the good of the individual is maximized when one strives to live in a mutually symbiotic relationship with other people and with the environment. Focusing only on the individual good leads to egoism, which is problematic because it prizes the good of one person (or a select few) over the good of others. Purely anthropocentric environmental ethics are problematic because they fail to take into account the full range of stakeholders who stand to either benefit from a healthy ecosystem or suffer from negative environmental changes. True symbiosis is attained only through an ecocentric ethic that values the environment itself and other living beings as stakeholders. While human beings should act from a fundamental respect for the intrinsic value of other humans and the natural environment, there is also a benefit to the self-interest of the agent in the sense that the maintenance of a healthy environment minimizes the negative social effects that lead to violent conflict.

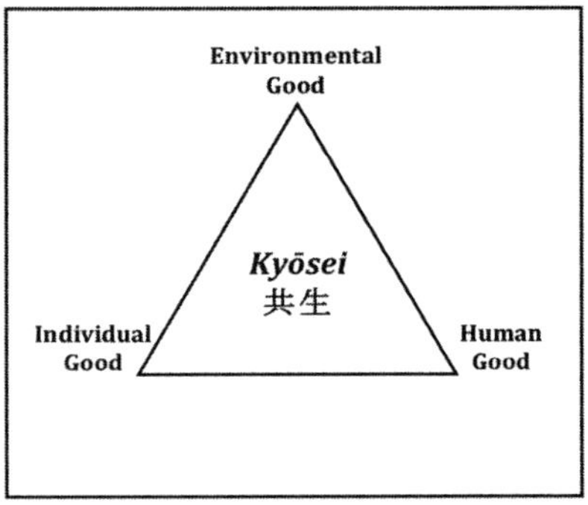

Figure 3.3. Triple Negation

Conclusions

Watsuji argues for a fundamental reevaluation of the philosophical anthropology that grounds our understanding of ethics. By reconceptualizing the notion of the autonomous, rational agent as *ningen,* a radically contextualized being, it is evident that one's natural environment plays a critical role in the promotion of one's well-being. Humans are ultimately defined through a process of triple negation between the individual, community, and natural environment: the good of all three entities is promoted only through the harmonious interrelation of *kyōsei* (see Figure 3.3). This means that we must view other human beings and the natural world as stakeholders in the common good rather than as raw material for the satisfaction of self-interest. The practical advantage of this view is that it promotes environmental security. By regulating human activity according to *kyōsei,* we can minimize our environmental impact and thereby reduce the negative socio-economic effects that promote violent conflict.

Ultimately, human beings need to adopt a set of moral principles that promote *kyōsei* on a local, national, and international scale. As indicated earlier, the Caux Roundtable Principles have been immensely successful at promoting stakeholder theory in international business ethics, and it might be possible to create a set of environmental ethical principles that could be voluntarily adopted by businesses and governments to promote sustainability and thereby minimize the negative social effects that generate conflict. It is beyond the scope of this essay to generate an exhaustive set of principles; ideally, these principles should be determined in an international dialogue like the one that generated the Caux Principles. However, there are several principles that would be essential to any environmental ethic that is designed to promote both sustainability and security. All human beings are stakeholders in the welfare of the environment, socio-economic stability, and international security. It is morally irresponsible to profit at the expense of other individuals or the environment upon which we all depend for natural resources. Poor countries are more likely to suffer from the negative environmental impact of unchecked population growth, consumerism, and unsustainable technologies. This means that poor countries are at a greater risk for the negative social effects that lead to violent conflict, which threatens the security and economic stability of other nations. It is thus in the interest of each nation to promote the economic and environmental sustainability of other countries. In the final analysis, it is only by protecting the environment that we can protect ourselves.

NOTES

1. Robert Carter, *Encounter with Enlightenment: A Study of Japanese Ethics* (Albany: State University of New York Press, 2001), 130.

2. Yasuo Yuasa, *The Body: Towards an Eastern Mind-Body Theory,* trans. Nagatomo Shigenori and T. P. Kasulis (Albany: State University of New York Press, 1987), 24.

3. This is simply the generic term for "human." It is the term that one would use when saying "Who is that *person* over there?" See T. P. Kasulis, *Zen Action, Zen Person* (Honolulu: University Press of Hawai'i, 1981), 5.

4. Ibid., 5–6.

5. Carter, *Encounter with Enlightenment,* 125.

6. Tetsurō Watsuji, *Watsuji Tetsurō's Rinrigaku: Ethics in Japan,* trans. Yamamoto Seisaku and Robert E. Carter (Albany: State University of New York Press, 1996), 18–19.

7. Yuasa, *The Body,* 23.

8. Ibid., 37.

9. Carter, *Encounter with Enlightenment,* 130.

10. Yuasa, *The Body,* 45.

11. Tetsurō Watsuji, *Climate and Culture: A Philosophical Study,* trans. Geoffrey Bownas (New York: Greenwood Press, 1988), 9–10.

12. Watsuji, *Climate and Culture,* 14.

13. Watsuji, *Rinrigaku,* 38.

14. Ibid., 37–38.

15. Watsuji, along with the rest of the Kyōto School, is sometimes interpreted as fascist because he ostensibly downplays the role of the individual and overemphasizes the importance of the collective. However, this is based on a misrepresentation of Watsuji's work, which emphasizes the simultaneous negation of *both* individualism *and* conformism (this concept of double negation is discussed at length later in this chapter). The Japanese government selectively appropriated Watsuji's work for political ends during the Second World War, but we can no more indict Watsuji for this than we can criticize Nietzsche for being misused by Hitler. As Robert Carter argues, "It must be kept in mind that [Watsuji's] intent was not to advocate tyranny or fascism, but to seek out an ethical and social theory whereby human beings as human beings could interact easily and fruitfully in the space between them, creating as a result a society, and a world-wide association of societies which selflessly recognized the value of the individual and the crucial importance of the well-being of the whole" ("Watsuji Tetsurō," in *The Stanford Encyclopedia of Philosophy* [Spring 2011 ed.], ed. Edward N. Zalta, http://plato.stanford.edu/archives/spr2011/entries/watsuji-tetsuro/. For a detailed discussion of Watsuji's philosophy in the context of *nihonjinron* studies and World War II politics, see Graham Parkes, "The Putative Fascism of the Kyoto School and the Political Correctness of the Modern Academy," *Philosophy East and West* 47, no. 3 (1997), 305–336.

16. Ibid., 22.

17. Ibid., 23.

18. Ibid., 22.

19. Robert Carter, "Interpretive Essay: Strands of Influence," in *Watsuji Tetsurō's Rinrigaku,* 338.

20. Steve Odin, *The Social Self in Zen and American Pragmatism* (Albany: State University of New York Press, 1996), 54–55.

21. Watsuji, *Rinrigaku,* 31.

22. Ibid., 20–21.

23. Ibid., 235.

24. Thomas F. Homer-Dixon, "On the Threshold: Environmental Changes as Causes of Acute Conflict," *International Security* 16, no. 2 (Fall 1991), 76–116, http://www.library.utoronto.ca/pcs/thresh/thresh1.htm.

25. Figure 3.1 represents a synthesis of the theoretical models of several leading theorists in environmental security. Homer-Dixon's analysis of the causal relationship between environmental stress, negative social effects, and violent conflict has been modified by Richard A. Matthew, Ted Gaulin, and Bryan McDonald's explanation of the role that adaptation plays in mitigating conflict. The details of these theories will be explained later in this section.

26. Paul R. Ehrlich and John P. Holdren pioneered this concept in their article "Impact of Population Growth," *Science* 171 (January 1971), 1212–1217.

27. Thomas F. Homer-Dixon, "Environmental Scarcities and Violent Conflict: Evidence from Cases," *International Security* 19, no. 1 (Summer 1994), 5–40, http://www.library.utoronto.ca/pcs/evidence/evid1.htm.

28. Ibid.

29. Homer-Dixon, "On the Threshold" and "Environmental Scarcities and Violent Conflict."

30. Homer-Dixon, "Environmental Scarcities and Violent Conflict."

31. Richard A. Matthew, Ted Gaulin, and Bryan McDonald, "The Elusive Quest: Linking Environmental Change and Conflict," *Canadian Journal of Political Science* 36, no. 4 (September 2003), 857–878.

32. Homer-Dixon, "On the Threshold."

33. J. Baird Callicott, *In Defense of the Land Ethic* (Albany: State University of New York Press, 1989), 87.

34. Aldo Leopold, *Sand County Almanac* (New York: Random House, 1990), 239–240.

35. Callicott, *In Defense of the Land Ethic,* 112–113.

36. Ibid., 83.

37. Nitobe Inazō, *Bushido: The Soul of Japan* (Rutland, VT: Tuttle, 1969), 47. Nitobe is specifically talking about the way that *bushidō,* the ethic of the Japanese samurai, interprets the Confucian virtue of *jin* (仁), which is often translated as "benevolence," "compassion," or "humaneness."

38. Hiroshi Abe, "From Symbiosis (Kyōsei) to the Ontology of 'Arising Both from Oneself and from Another,'" *Interdisziplinäre Phänomenologie* 4 (2007), 109–129.

39. Abe, "From Symbiosis," 119–120.

40. Henri-Claude de Bettignies, Kenneth E. Goodpaster, and Toshio Matsuoka, "The Caux Roundtable Principles for Business: Presentation and Discussion," in *International Business Ethics: Challenges and Approaches,* ed. Georges Enderle (Notre Dame, IN: University of Notre Dame Press, 1999), 133.

41. Kenneth E. Goodpaster, "Bridging East and West in Management Ethics: Kyosei and the Moral Point of View," in *International Business Ethics,* 150–151.

42. Thomas M. Jones, Andrew C. Wicks, and R. Edward Freeman, "Stakeholder Theory: The State of the Art," in *The Blackwell Guide to Business Ethics,* ed. Norman E. Bowie (Malden, MA: Blackwell, 2002), 19–20.

43. Ibid., 22.

44. Ibid., 23.

45. Watsuji, *Rinrigaku,* 114–115. Bernard Bernier addresses Watsuji's concept of double negation in his essay "Transcendence of the State in Watsuji's Ethics," in *Frontiers of Japanese Philosophy 2: Neglected Themes and Hidden Variations,* ed. Victor Sōgen Hori and Melissa Anne-Marie Curley (Nagoya, Japan: Nanzan University Press, 2008), 94–100.

46. Watsuji discusses only the double negation that occurs between the individual and the community. This concept of triple negation represents my own extension of his philosophy to environmental ethics.

Fouling Our Nest 4

Is (Environmental) Ethics Impotent against (Bad) Economics?

Heidi M. Hurd

I worry that our best ethics are not up to the task of protecting the global environment from our worst economics. This is not a practical claim; it is a philosophical one. My concern is that moral philosophy lacks the ability to explain or account for the moral significance of the planet upon which we live and the natural resources upon which we depend. It is hard to find a natural resource on the Earth that is not being exploited or that is not an object of commercial greed. Today, more than 60 percent of vital ecosystem goods and services are being used unsustainably; this means, by definition, that we are threatening today the ability of those tomorrow to meet basic needs and simple wants. We are depleting groundwater supplies, degrading agricultural soils, overfishing the oceans, cutting forests faster than they can regrow, leveling mountains for nonrenewable sources of energy, and filling in coastal and wetland areas in ways that exacerbate the devastating effects of floods and hurricanes. Our dependence on fossil fuels has motivated ecologically destructive drilling and mining methods, caused air and water pollution hazardous to the health of humans and that of other life forms, and blanketed the globe with greenhouse gases that are affecting global temperatures and threatening catastrophic changes in the Earth's climate patterns. Our conversion of forests, grasslands, and wetlands to agriculture and urban development has increased the species extinction rate by as much as one thousand times background rates, and we are currently threatening the precipitous extinction of one-third of the mammal, bird, amphibian, and wild plant populations on the globe. And as we ravenously consume the Earth's natural resources, we grow in number. The world's population has doubled in the past forty years to 7 billion and is presently growing by 80 million people a year, making the projected population in 2050 9.3 billion. Inasmuch as those who have less are understandably seeking to catch up to those who have more, one has to wonder how our increasingly stressed planet will be able to support an additional 2.3 billion people.

How is it possible that we have so fouled our Earthly nest? And why are we seemingly unable to make changes that will reverse the devastating effects of our own actions on the ecological health of the planet? In this essay, I want to outline two answers: (1) failed economics and (2) impotent ethics. Inasmuch as I am not an economist, my primary goal is to explore how our failure, as philosophers, to construct a robust account of environmental ethics is aiding, rather than arresting, the efforts of those who are inflicting long-term environmental damage in the name of short-term economic gains. I shall begin with a reminder of the lessons of Econ 101 in order to provide an appreciation of why our present environmental practices appear "uneconomical" by the measure of economics itself—why, that is, market mechanisms appear unable to ensure that our environmental practices in fact reflect our environmental preferences. As I shall outline, numerous present practices are not Pareto efficient because they are a product of market failures—externalities, open-access resources, nonrival and nonexcludable public goods, and information asymmetries (to name only a few). As such, we have cause to believe that economists themselves should be disappointed in the market's environmental performance, for its inefficiencies suggest that the market is failing to realize the utilitarian agenda to which economics is a handmaiden.

One answer is to fix our failed economics, to correct the market failures that presently make our environmental practices wasteful. This is, of course, the calling of environmental economists, who seek to eliminate "dirty subsidies" that encourage, rather than discourage, environmentally wasteful practices and who variously propose the use of command-and-control regulations, pollution quotas, taxes and tariffs, and better defined property rights as means of correcting market imperfections. One cannot help but wonder, however, whether there are not some environmental entities that ought not to be valued by the market at all. Perhaps some environmental entities ought not to be for sale; perhaps their moral worth ought not to be judged by their commercial value, however accurately that value can be assessed through pricing mechanisms. In the second part of this essay, I shall turn to the ways in which our environmentally destructive market practices may be a product of our philosophical failure to settle the ethical significance of natural entities. As I shall discuss, our leading forms of ethical reasoning and our leading schools of ethical thought are anthropocentric. As such, it takes a good deal of fancy philosophical footwork to avoid the conclusion that such theories, at least in principle, license the exploitation of natural entities so long as that exploitation does not violate the individual rights, majoritarian preferences, or personal interests by which leading utilitarian and rights theories specify the conditions of justice.

It is tempting to try to cure the anthropocentrism of the leading ethical theories by, for example, expanding their reach to environmental entities so as to argue that such entities command moral respect in their own right. If successful, we could then demand on behalf of Mother Nature the same concern that we demand for ourselves and that we accord to others. As I shall demonstrate, however, efforts to accord moral considerability to natural entities, conceived of either individually or collectively (as individual plants and animals, species, forests, mountains, coral reefs, wetlands, ecosystems, or biomes), invite credible philosophical complaints. However much one can stretch the domain of those who count, utilitarian theories are likely to fall short of ensuring the protection of all of the environmental entities that seemingly require protection. While some nonhuman entities may be thought to experience pain and pleasure and to have simple preferences (e.g., individual animals), many of these do not appear capable of experiencing the sort of happiness that utilitarians from Mill onward have demanded of those whose utility must be weighed equally in a utilitarian calculus. And many nonhuman entities (e.g., soils, mangroves, and rivers) do not have subjective experiences of any sort and so cannot be thought to possess welfare at all—at least so long as welfare is judged subjectively. One might stretch utilitarianism by suggesting that such entities have objective welfare interests, but one will run the risk of stretching it to the breaking point, for the notion that a fjord can have an interest at all surely strains the notion of welfare beyond practical recognition.

It is also hard to argue that such entities possess the essential capacities required of rights holders under the "will theory" of rights. And even under the more permissive "interest theory" of rights, many environmental entities will fall short of having interests that credibly support claims of right (notwithstanding Bolivia's enduring insistence that the United Nations accord Mother Earth the same rights as are accorded human beings). What's more, those who think that the recognition of environmental rights will prohibit environmental exploitation will surely find themselves surprised not just by the practical obstacles to rights enforcement, but also by the philosophical obstacles. For even deontologists recognize and themselves exploit multiple means of narrowing the scope of categorical duties so as to permit consequentially justified trade-offs.

As I canvass these traditional schools of thought, I will try to chart possible means of overcoming the obstacles to employing them in the name of environmental entities. But at the end of the day, while utilitarian and rights theories may require us to value and protect natural entities, there is little doubt that they do so most readily only by doing so instrumentally. They give us solid grounds to conserve environmental entities if (but only if) so doing is for the sake of persons; they do not readily give us grounds to value and protect individual nonhuman creatures, species, ecosystems, and biomes for their own sakes. And as such, they fail to arm us with means by which to dispute environmentally destructive practices that will be of net benefit to *persons* (as judged best, perhaps, by their market practices).

In employing a broad brush to paint the difficulties that must be overcome in order to apply traditional ethical concepts to environmental entities, my goal is to be neither a critic nor a naysayer. On the contrary, it is to examine why environmental ethics has lacked teeth when we have most needed its bite within corporate boardrooms, legislative chambers, and courtrooms. My hope is that this brush-clearing exercise will reveal the promise of alternative arguments (both new and old) that will give philosophical muscle to deeply held intuitions concerning the ethical impermissibility of allowing consumer preferences to be the sole measure of the Earth's value and the sole source of our Earthly obligations. This contribution will close with one such candidate—the possibility that on our best aretaic theory we ought to cultivate virtues of character that are inconsistent with actions that treat the environment as a means to our ends.

Bad Economics, Bad Environmental Practices

Consider our relationship to coal, from which half of America's electricity is generated. Coal is both less expensive per Btu and more abundant than natural gas or oil. Right now, we know about, we have mapped, and we can immediately access two hundred years' worth of reserves, and estimates suggest there may be 10 trillion metric tons of coal beneath the planet's surface. But to price coal by its ample supply and comparatively inexpensive Btus is to grossly misrepresent its true costs.

Coal fires in underground mines are expected to burn for centuries and currently contribute as much CO_2 to the atmosphere as do all American vehicles. Such climatic costs *are not included in the price of coal.* Fatalities are common, and black lung disease severely compromises the quality and duration of many miners' lives. The premature deaths of one thousand miners per year *are not included in the price of coal.*

While 30 percent of coal is still mined underground, companies can obtain two and a half times more coal per worker per hour through "mountaintop removal and valley fill." A mountain is first clear-cut, its lumber sold, and slash burned. The loss of its forest habitat and migratory resting places, the annihilation of its animal inhabitants, the ensuing landslides and floods, and the atmospheric emissions caused by the massive mining equipment *are not included in the price of coal.* To remove the layers of topsoil and shale that overburden the coal seams below, twenty-five hundred tons of explosives are detonated each day in the Appalachian region alone. The damage caused to local home foundations and wells and the increased local rates of lung cancer and chronic heart, lung, and kidney disease caused by the fog of silica dust in which local citizens are forced to live *are not included in the price of coal.*

To expose the veins of coal, 8-million-pound, twenty-story-high machines with gymnasium-sized bases unburden coal companies of the "overburden" by dumping it into adjacent valleys. To date, more than twelve hundred miles of Appalachian headwater streams have been buried in highly acidic mining waste. The costs of transforming incomparably beautiful, environmentally essential mountain ecosystems into biologically dead moonscapes *are not included in the price of coal.* Runoff pollutes downstream waters with silt high in iron and sulfur, the costs of which *are not included in the price of coal.* "Coal washing" produces thousands of gallons of sludge thick in carcinogenic chemicals and heavy metals, floods of which have killed or injured thousands and caused hundreds of millions of dollars of damage. Declared "acts of God," these costs *are not included in the price of coal.*

The two-lane roads required to support the enormous trucks that haul the coal from mining sites to "loadouts" and on to market destinations cost $500,000 per mile, as compared to four-lane highways, which cost $100,000 per mile. And the service life of coal-haul roads is between two and four years, rather than the standard twenty. These industry-specific infrastructure costs *are not included in the price of coal.* And when these ancient organic remains of the peat bogs of the Carboniferous Period reach the coal-fired power plants that convert 88 percent of the world's coal into electricity, they become the principal source of human-caused CO_2 emissions and thus the principal source of global warming. And the potentially catastrophic costs of global climate change *are not included in the price of coal.*

Were all the costs of coal reflected in its price—and in the price of electricity and other goods and services that depend upon it—we would clamor for clean energy, the price of which would seem a bargain by comparison. Classical economics promises us that well-functioning markets price things so as to allow us to make informed consumer choices, choices that cumulatively result in an allocation of resources that is Pareto efficient (such that no redistribution could make someone better off without making someone else worse off). Markets are supposed to reveal and satisfy our preferences by allowing us to vote with our dollars. We are supposed to be able to rely on their ability to put resources to their most valued uses so as to achieve the greatest good for the greatest number. But if coal (and the electricity that it produces) is not priced to include its true costs, consumers are not making fully informed choices when they turn on their lights. They are thus likely "voting" for more injuries to persons and property and more irreversible ecological destruction than they would if the true costs of coal were revealed in its price.

The question is: Why are these costs not included in the price of coal? And the short answer is: market failures. The real market underprices coal because it does not satisfy the conditions under which perfect markets would indeed match prices to preferences. Consider four such market failures, all of which suggest that if we are justifying our use of coal by pointing to its market price, we are guilty of bad economics.

Market Failures

Externalities. Most obviously the ecological and human costs I have described constitute negative externalities, or "transaction spillovers." Externalities are nonconsensual third-party effects of others' transactions. They can be positive, as when, for example, the values of homes in a neighborhood increase because a local school makes significant improvements in its educational resources. And they can be negative, as in the textbook example of air pollution, which is borne by many who do not reciprocally reap the benefits of the industries that cause it.

As a result of positive externalities, the market underproduces valuable goods, because producers and buyers do not take into account the full benefits associated with their transactions (e.g., the ways in which good schools increase the attractiveness of neighborhoods, elevating home prices and the profitability of local businesses). Negative externalities inversely result in the overproduction of harmful products, because producers do not have to pay for, or price their goods to include, injuries sustained by third parties. Thus, while the lease prices paid by coal companies to mountaintop landowners may compensate those landowners for the diminishment in aesthetic pleasure *the owners* take from their devastated lands, the increased risks to *their* health from the ensuing air and water pollution, the destruction of plant and animal species *they* may value, and the effects of climate change on *their* welfare, such lease prices do not include the value of these losses to those in the larger community to whom such costs spill over, or the value of these losses to nonhuman species whose moral concern may be the concern of no one. The result is cheap coal at others' expense. Bad economics.

Open-access resources. When it is impossible or very difficult to restrict access to an environmental resource—such as the atmosphere, fishing grounds, and regional watersheds—there are grounds to fear that that resource will be overused in ways that will result in what Garrett Hardin famously described as "a tragedy of the commons." The central insight is that even when a resource has been degraded by overuse in ways that threaten the interests of all users, any given user has an incentive to further deplete the resource, for he receives the immediate benefit of what is taken, while he shares the cost of the resource's depletion with all others. Inasmuch as he can predict that others will do the same, he would seem a fool not to seize what benefits he may while there are benefits left to seize, for he is surely bearing the costs of others doing the same.

Were the user of the resource able to exclude others' use, of course, the costs of depleting the resource would be entirely his, and he would, thereby, have incentives to conserve the resource so as to guarantee its long-term profitability. But the coal-mining industry does not own and cannot exclude others from all the environmental goods and services that it uses, and to that degree it does not have the conservation incentives that would guarantee the long-term stewardship of those resources. As such, the price of coal does not reflect the costs of depleting those goods and services. As the industry pollutes rivers with sulfuric acid and dissolved iron, it takes what it does not pay for—namely, the ability of downstream users to access clean water. As it levels mountains and fills valleys, it takes what it does not pay for—namely, the aesthetic and cultural enjoyment of those in the larger region who link their Appalachian identity to the rugged mountains of the area; the species in the region that depend for their survival on delicate ecosystems that are buried by surface-mining methods; and the coal itself, which, by virtue of being nonrenewable, is a resource that can be measured only by its opportunity costs, for each use today costs those who will not be able to use it tomorrow. The result, again, is cheap coal at others' expense. Bad economics.

Nonrival and nonexcludable public goods. A third and related reason for the market's failure to properly price environmental resources derives from the fact that, in many instances, such resources are public goods, the provision of which is both nonrival and nonexcludable. For example, climate stability and healthy air quality are not zero-sum goods; they are nonrival, in the sense that to achieve these goods in one place is not to diminish them in another. And these goods are nonexcludable, for efforts to prevent climate change and improve air quality accrue to the benefit of us all. Knowing this, each person has an incentive to deny or conceal his interest in these benefits so as to free ride on the carbon abatement and pollution-reduction efforts of others, the benefits of which will be as much his as theirs.

Inasmuch as the advantages of public goods extend beyond those who work to create or sustain them, the market prices of such goods tend not to reflect their true benefits. Others underinvest in such goods because they calculate that they will be able to enjoy such goods by free riding on the efforts of those who will produce or preserve them. As a result, the prices of public goods are not accurately reflected in the costs of activities that depend on them or adversely affect them. The price of coal thus fails to reflect the effects that coal mining has on the air quality, water quality, soil quality, and recreational and aesthetic values of local lands, for these are free for the taking, and coal companies can hope that those who have a passion for their revival will shoulder the burdens of restoration. The result: cheap coal at others' expense. Bad economics.

Information asymmetries. When parties to a transaction do not possess matching information about relevant costs and benefits, the transaction can produce results that fail to reflect the true preferences of the parties. Thus, for example, a purchaser of a used automobile might be sold a lemon by a dealer who well appreciates, but does not disclose, the car's accident history or hidden defects. And a buyer of insurance might succeed in purchasing a policy from an insurance agent who would not sell that policy if she knew of the buyer's well-concealed risk conditions.

One suspects that in many instances, the prices of products fail to reflect their environmental costs because consumers are ignorant of those costs and thus do not perceive that in purchasing such products they are complicit in contributing to environmental degradation. If consumers did not suffer from informational disadvantages, they would view such products as "moral lemons," because they would appreciate that such products fail to honor their own values and are thereby "morally defective." If those values were given expression, the prices of products would rise as their means of production were modified to honor morally responsive consumer preferences. Products would go "green" both in quality and in price as consumers learned of the advantages to themselves, to others, and to the planet of ensuring that products are made sustainably.

Of course, in many instances consumer ignorance appears willful, and, as such, one suspects that it does not disserve subjective consumer preferences. Those who do not want to know about the relationship between carbon emissions and climate instability precisely because they want to continue driving their SUVs and turning up their air conditioning without guilt can hardly be thought to be victimized by industries that sell them cheap fuel. But when consumer ignorance is a function of the invisibility of an industry's environmental degradation (as is clearly the case with regard to coal, the costs of which are visited on isolated regions and absorbed invisibly into the planet's atmosphere) or is a product of active efforts on the part of an industry to prevent the leakage of information (as is the case with the commercial meat industry, which anxiously excludes curious customers, journalists, and activists from the grisly conditions of factory farms and slaughterhouses), there is more reason to think that consumers are not making informed choices and that, if they could, the costs of products would increase as a reflection of consumer preferences for "greener" practices. The bottom line: our ignorance makes our markets an untrustworthy means of meeting our own preferences. Once again, bad economics.

Means of Fixing Market Failures

It is tempting to think that the sorts of market failures I have outlined might be cured through a combination of economic and political strategies. And in fact there is no question that we have at our disposal practical ways of better pricing nature's products within markets that already treat them as fungible commodities. We could fix quotas on forms of environmental degradation that could be enforced through tradable degradation permits (e.g., tradable emission permits, pollution permits, habitat-reduction permits). Such permit systems could be predicted to incentivize entrepreneurial efforts to reduce environmental degradation, for permit holders who adopted more sustainable practices could then trade unused permits to less innovative market players for a profit. We could revoke "dirty subsidies" that externalize the environmental costs of activities to taxpayers in ways that conceal the true costs of many goods and services. We could levy taxes on activities that capture some fraction of the value of the environmental services those activities use or degrade so that the prices of goods and services would better reflect not just their labor and materials costs but their environmental costs as well. And finally, we could continue to experiment with methods of privatizing nature's bounty in the hopes that, by giving identifiable parties clear property rights in environmental services, they would have incentives to protect and conserve those resources for long-term profit, and they would make market trades that would, over time, direct environmental goods to their highest and best (or at least more preferred) uses.

Given the extraordinary political clout possessed by the many industries whose product prices we might want to perfect, there are reasons to predict that implementing any of these market-fixing mechanisms would require more political will than our democratically elected leaders have ever managed to muster. But my interests here are not practical; they are philosophical. We have cause to wring our hands over the failure of government to derive means of keeping markets honest only when, and only if, markets would properly manage Earth's resources if they functioned without significant structural failures. But why would this be so? Not only does such a claim presuppose that markets can be cured of their imperfections so as to direct resources to those who most prefer them; it presupposes that people's preferences dictate the highest and best uses to which those resources can and should be put. That is, it presupposes that our collective preferences concerning the distribution and use of the planet's natural resources are dispositive of the question of how those resources ought to be managed. If markets can be perfected so as to ensure that their results are a fair reflection of consumer preferences, then on this account, the results of market transactions are moral by definition. But such a claim rests on the assumption that the value of the planet's resources—the value of individual animals, species, ecosystems, and biomes—is entirely derivative of the value we subjectively place on them (as measured by our behavior in the marketplace and the voting booth).

While there are surely many who are convinced that Earth's provisions are valuable only if, and only to the extent that, they are valuable to us, there are also many who are convinced otherwise but cannot say why. And lacking a credible account of the moral considerability of natural entities, such persons are left wondering how to dispute those who can credibly assign measurable human value to the destruction of things with natural value. If we believe that Mother Nature ought to be treated as an independent market player, whose resources ought to be priced within market transactions so as to reflect a value that is separate from the value we place on them, or if we believe that at least some of nature's goods ought to be treated as priceless—that is, as noncommodifiable, nontradable, inalienable *by us*—then we must probe the basis of these judgments. We must get straight about the philosophical promise of notions that nonhuman entities have moral considerability. We must ask what's wrong with cutting down a two-thousand-year-old sequoia (that can be predicted to live for thirty-two-hundred years!) just to hear it fall? What explains the common revulsion that people experience when they see, first person, enormous machines rapidly leveling mountains in Appalachia that were created 480 million years ago when plate collisions first formed the earliest foundations of the North American continent? Why do we morally wince at the thought of driving West African black rhinos and eastern gorillas to extinction for the sake of securing questionable aphrodisiacs? And why might it be morally illegitimate to use the Grand Canyon as a giant landfill if it could be proved that this would be in the best long-term interests of humankind? It is to these questions that I want to turn. If we can explain why nature matters enough that we cannot destroy it for no reason, or for a bad reason, perhaps we can then make progress in understanding what reasons (if any) entitle us to cut down forests, fill in wetlands, level mountains, pollute rivers, subject animals to painful treatment, and add greenhouse gases to the atmosphere.

The Moral Considerability of Nonhuman Entities

Can Nonhuman Entities Be Said to Have Welfare?

Suppose markets worked perfectly. Would that exhaust the questions of environmental ethics? That depends on the viability and the completeness of the normative theory underlying modern welfare economics. That theory is conventionally taken to be utilitarian in character. The classical utilitarian theory of the nineteenth century (advanced by Jeremy Bentham and John Stuart Mill) has two components.

The first component of utilitarianism is its theory of what is intrinsically good. Utilitarianism is a monistic theory, taking there to be one thing and one thing only that has intrinsic value or goodness. While many other things may be instrumentally good—good because they contribute to what is intrinsically good—a monistic theory isolates but one thing that is intrinsically good. For utilitarianism, that thing is welfare. This notion of welfare has competing definitions within the utilitarian tradition. Bentham's hedonic calculus equated welfare with the presence of pleasure and the absence of pain. Mill substituted the more general notions of happiness for pleasure and unhappiness for pain in his interpretation of welfare. Twentieth-century utilitarians (including welfare economists) usually substitute preference satisfaction for happiness and preference frustration for unhappiness. Such economists also usually follow Pareto in eschewing interpersonal comparisons of welfare on the basis that intensities of preferences cannot be measured cardinally; they can only be compared ordinally. In this sense of welfare, stable trade points in costless markets are then taken as constitutive of welfare-maximizing distributions. Lastly, welfare has sometimes been given an objective interpretation. On this interpretation, something may be good for someone, even if she does not prefer it and even if the thing does not make her happy or give her pleasure.

The second component of utilitarianism is its consequentialist principle. Some action or institution is right if and only if it maximizes welfare. The animating intuition is that if welfare is good, more of it is better, and the best is then achieved when acts or institutions produce the most welfare possible. So construed, welfare economics is rightly seen as a branch of utilitarian ethics. To the classical utilitarianism of Bentham one adds: (1) the substitution of preference satisfaction for happiness or pleasure as the measure of welfare; (2) the Paretian skepticism about cardinal measures of preference intensity; (3) the substitution of ordinal measures of preference maximization, namely, Pareto optimality and Pareto superiority; (4) the behavioral measure of the ordinal criteria in terms of stable trade points in hypothetically costless markets; and (5) the assumption that real markets can sometimes induce those idealized, stable trade points, and when they cannot (because of market failures), regulatory guesses at hypothetical market behavior can supply such stable trade points.

The problem for welfare economics does not lie in the failures of actual markets to deliver evidence of what would maximally satisfy human preferences. The problem lies in taking such maximally satisfied preferences to be the sole criterion of what is valuable. For notoriously, people can and do have evil preferences. With respect to the environment, for example, people demonstrably do not yet care enough not to foul their Earthly nest. And even maximally satisfied good, or allowable, preferences can fail to do justice to individuals. The deeper problem with markets, then, is not that they only imperfectly realize our preferences; the problem is that they perfectly realize our preferences as much as they do!

The deeper problem with the utilitarian standard of value is that it makes *human* preferences the touchstone of valuation. The domain of those whose welfare counts for a utilitarian unsurprisingly leads to a standard that overvalues the interests of those who count and undervalues the interests of those who do not. With regard to environmental issues, utilitarianism is thus about as plausible as it was about slavery when the preferences, pains, or welfare of slaves were not counted.

This suggests the plausibility of a utilitarian theory that enlarges the domain of those whose welfare counts. Could we expand the utilitarian calculus so that nonhuman welfare counted in computations of how to maximize welfare? If welfare were translated classically as pleasure and pain, this would at least expand the domain to include animals that are sentient. If welfare were construed as happiness, perhaps the same limited expansion could be justified, so long as happiness were treated as a mood or other psychological state. The same is true if welfare were taken to concern itself with preferences, for animals are plausibly thought to have at least simple desires. And, of course, if the domain of those whose welfare counts were extended to include members of future generations of humans and animals, then our welfare calculations might well dictate actions that protect and preserve species, ecosystems, and biomes that themselves may have no capacities for pleasure, happiness, or preference satisfaction.

Yet however expansive the domain of utilitarian concern, it remains clear that any brand of utilitarianism that correlates moral action with subjective satisfaction cannot vest intrinsic value in entities that do not have subjective experiences. As such, their fate is properly at the whim of those of us who can have preferences about them. The only means of answering this perceived shortcoming consistent with the commitments of utilitarianism would be to adopt an objective theory of welfare, a theory that uncouples welfare from subjective well-being. If one can think of something as good for another even if that other does not now think it good for himself and never will think it good, one might be able to insist that utilitarianism demands the maximization of all things that are good for entities that can have a good, including ones that cannot appreciate that they have a good because they have no subjective experiences at all. On such an account, to maximize welfare is to do what is good for all things that can have "goods"—bacteria, fungi, plants, trees, grasslands, coral reefs, for example.

I do not propose to explore this possibility further at this point, because it will turn on whether we can give an account of what it means for an entity to have a good. This will be akin to pursuing the question of when entities can be said to have interests, and I propose to explore that question when I take up the dominant theory of rights—namely, the "interest theory"—in the next section. Suffice it to say here that, if we can make sense of the notion that (some) entities that are not sentient might nevertheless have interests, then we will have the ability either to pursue the question of whether such entities have interest-based rights or to return to the promise of a utilitarian theory that seeks to maximize objective welfare in the hopes of extracting an account of why we must treat as valuable a great deal more than we, ourselves, value.

Can Nonhuman Entities Be Said to Possess Rights?

Bolivia made recent history with its announcement of legislation granting to all of nature rights equal to those possessed by humans. The Law of Mother Earth will establish eleven new rights for nature, including the right to life and to exist, the right to continue vital cycles and processes free from human alteration, the right to pure water and clean air, the right to balance, the right to not be polluted, the right to not have cellular structure modified or genetically altered, and the right "to not be affected by mega-infrastructure and development projects that affect the balance of ecosystems and the local inhabitant communities." Bolivia intends to establish a Ministry of Mother Earth and to appoint an ombudsman whose charge it is to speak for Pachamama, the Earth deity whose independent legal standing has now been established.

One can appreciate that rights rhetoric might have powerful instrumental advantages. Bolivia is struggling to cope with rising temperatures, melting glaciers, and more extreme weather events, including more frequent floods, droughts, frosts, and mudslides. As global temperatures rise and Bolivia's vast glaciers melt, Bolivian glaciologists anticipate that Bolivia will confront devastating water shortages and may be little more than a vast desert within a century. But while it may be rhetorically useful to claim that Mother Nature has rights, the question is, Does she? Or must we think that talking about the rights of nature is simply a sensationalist device to draw attention to environmental strategies that would be advantageous to humans?

There are two species of rights theories, and it must be admitted that neither makes obvious room for the rights of nonhuman entities. On versions of the "will theory," rights are means by which one may assert dominion over others' actions. Their possession provides one with sovereignty over the scope of others' duties. They are instruments of autonomy because they enable one to exercise authority or moral control over others in ways that expand one's opportunities of self-authorship. To have a right is (by definition, according to the will theory) to be able to waive it, to manipulate it, to dictate the terms of its satisfaction. Thus, to have a promissory right is to "own" the promised action; it is to be able to waive or annul or suspend the promisor's duty to honor the promise.

On the will theory of rights, there can be no nonwaivable rights. And there can be no rights holders who are not able to waive rights. The will theory thus disqualifies from the category of rights holders those who cannot make the kinds of choices that are at the core of exercising sovereignty. Those incapable of autonomy are incapable of having rights. And so, fetuses, infants, the senile, the insane, and the comatose are without rights. And it follows, a fortiori, that animals, plants, species, ecosystems, and biomes cannot be accorded rights, except metaphorically. On the will theory of rights, Bolivia's talk about Mother Nature having rights is just that: it cannot make it so, and it cannot be thought to reflect any discovery of what *is* so.

On the second theory of rights—the "interest theory"—rights reflect powerful interests, and they trigger obligations on the part of others because those whose interests they reflect are made (substantially) better off by the satisfaction of those interests. A right, on such a view, is what one has when one's interests in a matter become substantial enough that one's life will go appreciably better if those interests are served in an obligatory way. As Jeremy Waldron characterizes the interest theory (which he assigns to Joseph Raz): "A person may be said to have a right if and only if some aspect of his well-being (some interest of his) is sufficiently important in itself to justify holding some other person or persons to be under a duty."[1]

On this theory, only beings capable of having interests are capable of having rights; but one may have interests even if one is not an autonomous agent capable of exercising choice about others' actions. The question, of course, is whether nonhuman entities can have interests, and, if so, on what basis. To answer such a question is to advance a theory of interests—which is not something the interest theory of rights itself does.

It would seem philosophically feasible to advance the claim that animals have interests, and those who write about the moral status of animals have certainly provided ample vindication of this claim. Creatures that are sentient—creatures that have subjective perceptual experiences, or "qualia"—are capable of feeling pain and pleasure, and as such they are capable of living lives that are subjectively better or worse *for them*. If the avoidance of pain (beyond a de minimis threshold) is a significant interest—if it is, in Waldron's formulation, a sufficiently important aspect of well-being—then the interest theory of rights may demand the recognition that animals have rights, rights, at least, against those who are capable of modifying their behavior so as to avoid the causing of pain to such creatures. And so such theorists as Tom Regan and Gary Francione have argued.

What is more philosophically challenging is to make a claim that nonsentient entities might have interests that would support a Bolivian-style recognition of rights in the biosphere itself (the global ecological system that integrates all living beings with one another and with the elements of the lithosphere, hydrosphere, and atmosphere, metaphorically called "Mother Nature") or in individual nonsentient entities (particular trees, plants, fungi) or groupings of entities, such as species, ecosystems, or biomes (wetlands, tropical forests, tundra). Some have argued that, while things cannot matter *to* individual plants or *to* collectivities such as coral reefs, they can matter *for* them. As one theorist has put it, "Matters can be better or worse for the tree, and this amounts to saying that the tree on its own has its goods and harms."[2] What attributes must entities have in order for us to say of them that some things are good for them, and some things are bad? In von Wright's view, any being that "can meaningfully be said to be well or ill, to thrive, [or] to flourish" is a being of whose good it is meaningful to talk. Thus, as he maintains, "the question 'What kinds or species of being have a good?' is . . . broadly identical with the question 'What kinds or species of being have a life?' "[3] Von Wright's view is echoed by numerous environmental thinkers who are anxious to extend the class of beings who have interests beyond the class of beings who can suffer. In common to all such accounts is the notion that interests are possessed by entities that have teleological ends or are "goal directed."[4] Paul Taylor, for example, accords plants interests on the basis that they are "teleological centers of life";[5] Kenneth Goodpaster maintains that plants exhibit "self-sustaining organization and integration" worthy of moral concern;[6] Jay Kantor vests interests in plants by virtue of their "self-regulating and homeostatic functions";[7] and James Mish'alani derives the interests of living things from their possession of "self-ameliorative competence," that is, the "capacity of a living thing to adjust to its circumstances in a manner to enhance its survival and natural growth."[8] But these claims must answer several criticisms, two of which I shall flesh out here. First, by their terms, it would appear that these accounts vest interests in individual living creatures, not in collective entities, and certainly not in nonliving entities such as rivers, lakes, or mountains. Such an account thus falls short of promising to vindicate anything like the Bolivian effort to extend rights to ecosystems, biomes, or the biosphere as a whole. One might dispute this claim by arguing that it is perfectly intelligible to talk about goods for collective entities without such talk reducing to claims about goods for individual members of those groups. The good of a population of deer, for example, may require the death of a great many of its members, and the continued life of none in particular. But if collectivities can have interests, they will have to rest on claims other than the ones just canvassed. For while collectivities have tendencies, there is a good deal of consensus among scientists of evolution that species or populations are not "goal directed." In Elliott Sober's terms, "Darwinism rejects the idea that species, communities, and ecosystems have adaptations that exist for their own benefit. These higher-level entities are not conceptualized as goal-directed systems; what properties of organization they possess are viewed as artifacts of processes operating at lower levels of organization."[9] In short, claims about the interests of species or ecosystems can be nothing more than shorthand for claims about the interests of each of their members.

Second, while there may be things that are good for an entity, this does not mean that the entity is itself good or that it possesses a good. While there are conditions that enable a virus to do well—to thrive or to flourish—this does not, by itself, suggest that the virus has interests that are of a sort that properly commands the moral attention or concern of humans. Put differently, that things can be instrumentally good for an entity is not sufficient to infuse that entity with goodness and to thereby make its goods into interests that might cumulate to the point of constituting rights. One must not confuse what Holmes Rolston describes as an entity that is "value-able" (able to use things in the service of its own good)[10] with the notion that it is valuable. Or as John O'Neill puts the point:

> That Y is a good of X does not entail that Y should be realised unless we have a prior reason for believing that X is the sort of thing whose good ought to be promoted. While there is not a logical gap between facts and values, in that some value statements are factual, there is a logical gap between facts and "oughts. "Y is good" does not entail "Y ought to be realised."[11]

This hasty bit of hand waving should be sufficient to prove the philosophical complexities of employing the interest theory to vindicate the claim that nonhuman entities can be accorded rights. Perhaps we can assess the wisdom of further dwelling on such complexities by inquiring into the implications of recognizing nonhuman entities as rights holders. What would be the normative implications of concluding that individual living things, or collectivities of such things, have rights? Would we be stopped from peeling back Appalachian mountains in order to extract their seams of coal? From bulldozing tracts of forest for crop lands, grazing lands, or lumber? From damning rivers for hydroelectric power? From filling in wetlands for commercial developments? From using factory-farm techniques to produce meat? From culling populations of density-independent animals?

It might seem, at first blush at least, that the virility of rights turns on whether they create categorical obligations (under a deontological account) or can be sacrificed in the name of other rights (under a rights-consequentialist theory). For rights consequentialists, rights are normatively significant because they define the borders of legitimate utilitarian (or social welfare–based) justifications. Rights bar the ability of others to use the object of a right—one's life, liberty, or property, for example—as a resource for the advancement of their utility or welfare. For deontologists, in contrast, rights patrol the borders of legitimate consequentialist justifications. Not only can rights not be traded for increases in utility or social welfare, but they also cannot be traded to protect an even greater number of other (equally significant or more weighty) rights. Thus, for example, if I have a right not to be tortured, then others have a duty not to torture me, even if, by so doing, they could prevent many others from being tortured and many others from suffering other equal or greater rights violations.

Those who argue that animals have rights have never been crystal clear about whether they are rights consequentialists or deontologists. Tom Regan, for example, insists that inasmuch as animals are "subjects of a life," they each have an inherent worth that is the equal of that possessed by any human, and as such, they have rights "not to be treated as mere means to human ends."[12] Regan thus criticizes those who believe "that we are *sometimes* justified in causing nonhuman animals significant pain, in pursuit of institutionalised human interests," insisting that "animal rightists deny that we are ever justified in doing this."[13] As such, he maintains that animals may not be used for food, cosmetic testing, military research, sport hunting, fur and leather products, or recreation (rodeos, circuses, etc.). Yet he rather clearly leaves open the possibility of justifying the use of animals for life-saving medical research, and he famously insists that if four humans and a dog find themselves in a lifeboat that can hold only four, the humans are justified in casting the dog overboard.[14] He thus appears to stop short of suggesting that animals' lives cannot be traded for the lives of humans, and, as a result, one might plausibly believe that at the end of the day he is a rights consequentialist, not a deontologist.

Those who find it philosophically incredible to attribute rights to animals (and to other nonhuman entities, as well) will no doubt be relieved to recognize that rights consequentialism at least permits the sacrifice of such rights in the name of other, more weighty (human!) rights. For almost no one believes that plants cannot be harvested for food and that trees cannot be cut for necessary shelter or warmth; very few believe that species of harmful viruses, bacteria, and disease-carrying pests cannot be altogether eradicated; and the great majority (who eat meat, wear leather, and clamor for cheap electricity) clearly believe that animals can be killed and mountains can be leveled for relatively trivial human comforts. Those who might hope that an attribution of rights to nonhuman entities would put a stop to the use of such entities for (non-necessary) human purposes might thus conclude that rights consequentialism is a practical oxymoron. It allows humans to continue to insist that their rights justify the exploitation of natural entities (even if those entities are themselves assigned rights). Champions of environmental rights might thus insist that the rights of nature are of a deontological pedigree: they create categorical duties on the part of humans that cannot be violated in the name of other human rights (let alone increased human welfare).

It would be wrong, however, to believe that deontology does not permit a fair bit of moral wiggle room for those anxious to maximize good consequences at the expense of nature's bounty. While deontological duties may categorically prohibit the intentional causing of harm (to entities that can be harmed), and while some deontological duties may affirmatively require the prevention of harm or provision of benefits in special circumstances, there are reasons to think that the notions of intentionality, causation, action, and omission that define the content of such rights have built-in limitations that ultimately make these categorical duties less expansive and less onerous than they might first appear.

First, those who embrace the doctrine of double effect insist that the duty correlative of, say, the right to life precludes one from acting with the purpose of taking a life, but it does not prohibit one from doing an act that one simply knows will cause death. So long as a rights infringement is simply a known side consequence of an act done for a different purpose, that infringement is not a rights violation, and if it produces more good consequences than bad, it is not a wrong. If the distinction between purpose and knowledge can bear the moral weight assigned to it by the doctrine of double effect, one can imagine that it might permit a good deal of environmental damage, for that damage is often not intended; it is simply known to follow from various human activities. Thus, for example, the doctrine of double effect might permit the eradication of the Delhi Sands flower-loving fly, if its extinction is not intended, but is a known side consequence of converting the coastal sage scrub ecosystem of the Colton Dunes within the Los Angeles basin into shopping centers, golf courses, and housing developments, the collective benefits of which might be thought to outweigh the elimination of this species of fly. Second, some maintain, in a somewhat similar vein, that one can often permissibly risk what one cannot knowingly cause. Thus, when the balance of consequences speaks in its favor, one can risk another's death or injury (e.g., by driving to work, by raising children near a lake, by taking a friend skydiving) even as one could not justify doing the same act if one knew it would cause death. And even this claim requires modification, for we regularly take people to be justified in pursuing activities (building skyscrapers, blasting tunnels, and mining coal) that they know, as a statistical matter, will cause others' deaths when they do not know the specific identity of those on whom such harms will fall (so as to make them mere riskers vis-à-vis each possible victim). If rights protect their holders from being caused harm but not from being risked, then many activities that risk harm to natural entities, but do not knowingly cause such harm, may remain permissible. And this is particularly so if the rights possessed by natural entities are possessed by individuals, rather than groups, for it must be a frequent phenomenon for persons to know statistically that they will cause harm to classes of environmental entities (through water pollution, air pollution, toxic waste dumping, etc.) without knowing, and without being able to know, which individual entities, in particular, will be harmed. All this is to say that the precautionary principle (which holds that, in instances of doubt, persons must err on the side of caution and must thus refrain from pursuing activities whose environmental implications are unclear) may not follow from according environmental entities categorical rights—for caution (the avoidance of risks) is not, itself, morally obligatory and can thus be cast to the wind when a net gain in good consequences can be anticipated.

Third, it is a common intuition that, when the consequential balance favors it, one can permissibly accelerate a harm to a rights holder that is imminent and nonpreventable, even as one could not have knowingly set in motion the chain of events that put the rights holder in peril. At the root of this intuition is the judgment that one is not a full cause when one simply speeds up, but does not instigate, an inevitable harm. One who accelerates the death of someone who is "already dead" is not a killer in the full sense of the term. Thus, a climber can cut a rope that is connecting him to a down-rope climber whose fall is inevitable, and whose weight will otherwise eventually drag the up-rope climber off the mountain as well. Or in the textbook case of *Dudley and Stephens,* the men stranded on the lifeboat were thought to do no wrong when they ultimately used their last strength to kill and eat the languishing cabin boy, Richard Parker, who was sure to die before any rescue effort could save him.

If there is moral merit in this notion that good consequences can make deontologically permissible the acceleration of imminent and nonpreventable harms, then a number of implications may follow within the environmental context. For example, one might think that certain active efforts to control or stabilize population growth within a species might then be permissible. If in actively culling a population (of deer, elk, feral pigs, etc.), one is targeting animals that are themselves facing imminent death (through starvation brought on by overgrazing, for example), one may not, on this account, be violating any rights, even if rights are possessed by individual animals. More surprisingly (and more troublingly), if rights vest in species, rather than individuals, then perversely it may be permissible to accelerate the extinction of a critically endangered species, if so doing achieves a net gain in good consequences, for a critically endangered species might be thought to be "already dead." (Ironically, if rights vest in individual members of a species, and not in the species as a whole, the opposite might follow, for each individual member of a critically endangered species may still have ahead of it a full life and may not, itself, be in peril.)

Fourth, deontologists frequently place weight on the act-omission distinction, arguing that one can consequentially justify omissions to render life-saving aid when one could not so justify an active killing. One can thus fail to throw a rope to a drowning man in order to use that rope to save two others who are also drowning. But one could not forcibly drown the man, even if, by so doing, one could thereby save two others (who might then be able to use his life jacket for flotation). In the environmental context, this distinction proves its worth in answering the argument that anyone who would vest rights in animals, for example, must be committed to preventing their deaths by natural means. If one can morally defend the distinction between causing harm and omitting to prevent harm, one can explain why we need not affirmatively prevent natural predation even as we must avoid actions that cause the death of nonhuman entities through habitat loss, pollution, and global warming.

More troubling, however, is the thought that this distinction may allow many to take moral refuge in their environmental inaction. While it might be said that consumer behavior drives corporate behavior (and corporate behavior drives political behavior!), so that the environmental devastation caused by coal companies, oil companies, large-scale agricultural operations, and so forth, is, in fact, caused by the consumer choices we each individually make, such a claim founders on the fact that there are a great many intervening causes between a consumer's act of buying a product and an industry's responsive production of more such goods. On what I take to be the most promising theory of proximate causation (the so-called direct theory), "free, informed, voluntary actions" sever causal chains that would otherwise reach back to the actions of others, making those prior actions causally nonproximate. If those who operate the enormous machines that access veins of coal by clear cutting trees, shaving layers off mountains, and burying streambeds in "overburden" are sufficiently free and informed to count as responsible agents (as they surely are), then our best theories of proximate causation will declare them intervening causers. Those whose prior choices may have motivated their actions (consumers, politicians, family members, etc.) are thereby made nonproximate to the ensuing harm. If such prior actors are to be thought responsible for the harms they have inspired but not caused, it must be by virtue of our thinking that they are blameworthy for omitting to prevent that harm. But if, as a general matter, one violates no rights when one omits to enforce those rights, then our sense of blame will have to derive from some source other than the claim that environmental inaction is deontologically wrong.

Fifth, a somewhat different distinction would be needed to justify the active management of plant and animal populations through indirect means—say, by the (re)introduction of predator species into ecosystems that are unstable without them. To reintroduce wolves into a habitat overpopulated by deer is affirmatively to act in a manner that will cause the deaths of individual deer. To introduce biological controls (pathogens, parasitoids, predators, and weed feeders) so as to check the spread of pests or invasive plant species is to act in a manner that will eradicate those species from the habitat. If such an action is not a rights violation, it must be by virtue of finding moral merit in what theorists have called "nonomissive allowings." A nonomissive allowing is an act (not an omission) that allows nature to take its course. There are several kinds of nonomissive allowings, and I will not sketch here the various ways in which all of them might be employed by those who seek to employ consequential justifications in defense of actions that tread very close to violating categorical obligations toward natural entities.

Consider just one category, however—that of being an enabler of another's action. Many believe that one can consequentially justify an act that enables another to do a deed that one could not do oneself. Thus, for example, it is axiomatic for deontologists to insist that one is prohibited from killing an innocent person, even if so doing will motivate a killer to spare the lives of twenty others. But when asked whether one can simply hand the gun to the killer, who himself will pull the trigger, if by so enabling him to kill the one, twenty others will be saved, many agree that such an enabling would not constitute a violation of the rights of the one who is then executed by the killer (even as his execution at the hands of the killer is surely a rights violation by the killer). This intuition that one can enable what one cannot cause is surely at the root of America's willingness to outsource torture through the method of extraordinary rendition so as to gain intelligence through the efforts of others (e.g., Egyptian interrogators) that it could not itself extract. By so doing, we exploit the notion that those who perform the interrogations are themselves "free, informed, voluntary actors" who break the causal chain extending back to our extradition, making our actions nonproximate to the rights violations that ensue. If one does not violate another's rights unless one does so proximately, the distinction between enabling and causing creates room for consequentially justified enabling just as the distinction between omitting and causing creates room for consequentially justified inaction.

If enabling can be consequentially justified, then those who believe that nonhuman entities have rights may nevertheless be able to justify the positive introduction (or reintroduction) of predators and other biological controls in order to check, indirectly, the expansion of populations of plants and animals that themselves, either individually or collectively, have rights to life. Such methods reflect nonomissive allowings, for they involve actions that then allow nature to take its course. Of course, we do not normally think of animals, let alone insects or bacteria, as "free, informed, voluntary actors" who break causal chains, so it would surely take some innovative theorizing to adapt this deontological modification to justify the environmental analogue of extraordinary renditions. Still, I think that this notion that we can actively use nature to control nature, even as more direct methods of control may be impermissible, captures common intuitions among those who take natural entities to be properly protected by categorical rights.

This nonexhaustive outline of the various ways by which deontologists themselves blunt the protections afforded by rights suggests that those who look to environmental rights as trumps may find themselves disappointed by the enduring moral license that humans will have to trump nature even if nature is vested with deontological rights. They thus might conclude that the benefits of rights are not worth the costs of vindicating the contentious claim that nonhuman entities have rights, that is, that nonhuman entities have interests to begin with of a type and weight that generates obligations on our part. And even if nonhuman entities can be shown to satisfy the criteria of the interest theory of rights, and even if the strategies I've discussed to circumscribe the force of those rights can themselves be circumscribed, at the end of the day rights will not provide a promising means of arguing that nonliving entities that cannot be thought to have interests—mountains, rivers, canyons, and oceans—themselves possess moral considerability. One must thus confess that, while one might do wrong to humans or other living entities, one would do no wrong to Death Valley by trucking in loads of soil to raise its elevation above sea level; one would do no wrong to Mount Everest by removing its peak (so as to make K2 the highest mountain on Earth); one would do no wrong to the Grand Canyon by filling it with human garbage; one would do no wrong to the Moon by mining it; and we now do no wrong to the Appalachian mountains by doing in days what natural processes could do only in millennia. If we are to make sense of the common but philosophically uncomfortable notion that (at least some) nonliving environmental entities deserve protection for their own sake, then we will have to look beyond claims of right. But to what?

Can Nonhuman Entities Be Said to Be Objects of Our Virtue?

I have canvassed various means by which natural entities might be said to possess moral considerability on nonanthropocentric grounds, that is, by virtue of being valuable in themselves and not by virtue of our valuing them. And I have sought to reveal how the traditional schools of moral thought are systematically anthropocentric, and thus provide surprisingly limited means by which to give expression to deep-seated intuitions about the independent moral standing of natural entities. I want to close by examining the moral promise of a theory that explicitly concedes that "it's all about us," a theory that derives our obligations to prevent environmental degradation from considerations about *us*, but that does so in a manner that suggests that if we serve ourselves as morality demands, we will protect nonhuman entities for their own sake.

The theory I have in mind is an aretaic one, one that takes the morality of our relationships with the natural world to derive from our satisfaction of aretaic duties to cultivate virtuous character traits and suppress vicious ones. This account draws on the view that morality consists of both deontic and aretaic duties. Deontic duties (whatever the theory that underlies them, be it a rights-based or a utilitarian theory) concern actions that are, in particular circumstances, prohibited or required, while aretaic duties concern dispositions that must be cultivated or suppressed over the course of one's life in order to be thought a person of good character. The objects of deontic duties are commissions or omissions at razor points in time, while the objects of aretaic duties are traits of character, tendencies of thought and action that cumulatively define what sort of person a person is. A man does his deontic duty if he sustains his children in a material state that meets their essential physical and psychological needs, but he does not do his aretaic duty as a father unless he loves them, that is, unless he possesses that complex package of dispositional attitudes toward them that includes affection, empathy, identification, concern, pride, and so on. A woman does her deontic duty if she refrains from taking the property of others, but she cannot be thought to be an honest person if the only thing that keeps her from taking others' property is a fear of detection and punishment.

There is a significant literature on the question of whether aretaic duties can be collapsed into deontic duties or vice versa. Is one virtuous when, and only because, one does right actions? Or are one's actions right when, and only because, they are virtuous? I have argued in some detail that both of these hypotheses are wrong and that right action and virtuous character are quite independent of each other. After all, one can both be scrupulous in doing the right thing without being a person of good character (think of Javert in *Les Misérables*), and one can be a person of quite laudable character who at least sometimes, and perhaps often, fails to act rightly (think of the judge who indulges mercy too frequently and who thus fails to give offenders their just deserts or to treat like cases alike). It is, therefore, open to us to say that persons *aretaically ought* to cultivate certain character traits that will (by their nature) motivate actions that are not *deontically required* and as to which others have no *deontic rights.*

Indeed, inasmuch as virtuous character traits are psychological dispositions, they will often bleed over into circumstances in which they are not, on moral grounds, required. Character traits are habits of thought and action. They incline one toward beliefs, judgments, and decisions before reason has even had its say. They function as default responses, as first instincts. They define our essential selves because they assert themselves in moments of crisis, trauma, or excitement when our powers to think and act strategically have been suspended or impaired. They are responsible for the moral intuitions that we then use reason to articulate and rationalize, and, in that sense, they are at the core of our moral perceptions, beliefs, and judgments. For all of these reasons, character traits tend to be "overinclusive"; they tend to creep into circumstances in which reason would rightly exclude them. And so, deeply honest people tend to be honest to a fault; genuinely courageous people tend to be foolhardy about their own safety; generous people tend to be enablers of those who would fare better with a little tough love; and, in reverse, those who lie to protect their interests tend to lie even when it does not do so; those who indulge their appetites tend to overindulge them; those who enjoy the limelight tend toward narcissism; and so forth. I would even hazard that a person's character is often best revealed in circumstances in which his dispositions are in tension with his deontic rights and duties—when he reveals generosity toward one who is selfish (think of the benevolent Monsieur Myriel, the bishop of Digne, who gives Jean Valjean the candlesticks in order to cover for his theft in the opening scenes of *Les Misérables*), or when he desires to win an argument, even when nothing turns on it. To be a good person is to exhibit attributes of admirable character (kindness, generosity of judgment, courage, moderation, honesty, self-sacrifice, etc.) even toward those who cannot make a claim to deserving it.

One might plausibly think, then, that to be a virtuous person, one must possess a set of character traits that collectively motivates one to treat the environment *as if* it possessed intrinsic value, as if it possessed the independent moral considerability that one might be able to defend were one's philosophical tools less devotedly anthropocentric. What are these personal traits from which we can extract such a valuation of nature?

Put most broadly, it seems to me that to be virtuous is "to know one's place in the universe." It is to recognize that we are newcomers to a place long occupied by others. ("If you take the history of life as the length of your arm, then one stroke of a nail file erases human history.") It is thus to have a sense that we must make a place for ourselves among those whose physical stake in the planet far supersedes ours (even if we cannot force fit the notion that they have antecedently existing moral claims into our self-regarding moral theories). This notion that virtue resides, in part, in "knowing one's place in the universe" is surely not an easy one to unpack. It connotes a number of different judgments and attitudes, many of which smuggle back in notions of rights and interests that we have already found wanting. But, of course, as I have just argued, a virtuous person does just that: she brings, as psychological baggage, her respect for others' rights and her fear of shirking her own duties to arenas in which such concerns may be morally invalid. She thus feels (nonmoral) guilt, for example, even when she has done no moral wrong. And she resists praise (without it being a product of false modesty) even when she has done something genuinely supererogatory. So it should be no surprise that as we unpack the attitudes that a virtuous person has toward those whose claims to the planet's resources predate our own, we should talk in terms of "claims," when to do so is to do so loosely, or only metaphorically (if I was right in the previous sections).

First, to suggest that virtue requires that one know one's place in the universe is to suggest that one should honor notions of fairness and considerations of equality even before, and probably even after, one can establish with philosophical exactitude the degree to which others are entitled (as a matter of right or as a matter of other defensible moral criteria) to such treatment. On pain of violating the "first come, first served" and "finder's keeper" maxims that even a child learns and finds intuitive at an early age, one should be dispositionally reluctant to displace anything that has already come to rely for its existence upon its present circumstances. As a newcomer, one's first instincts should be to learn and adapt to existing arrangements, rather than to force the rearrangement of those circumstances for private gain. We take it to be definitional of a spoiled child that he does not appreciate that he must leave toys alone until others have finished playing with them (regardless of whose toys they are), and we are similarly offended at adults who do not appreciate that their demands will thwart others' reliance on the continuation of the status quo.

Second, to know one's place in the universe is to exhibit environmental humility. It is to appreciate how short our individual lives are in comparison to other living things (the oldest living plant on Earth is more than five thousand years old!) and to the geological formations that form the contours of our world. One who would cut down a two-thousand-year-old sequoia in less than an hour for lumber, or level a mountain within days that has been formed over millennia, or drive a species to extinction in order to build a shopping center, lacks the sort of perspective that one considers constitutive of a virtuous person. While it may be hard to attribute rights or interests to trees, rocks, lakes, and rivers, and while individual creatures and whole species may lack the attributes that demand sufficient moral consideration to compel their protection for their own sakes, it does not seem a stretch to suggest that we ought to conceive of ourselves as being connected to and dependent upon such entities so as to require that we act with humility when effecting the course that nature would otherwise dictate for them.

Third, a virtuous person is a generous person, one who bestows benefits on others even when they cannot be said to be entitled or deserving. Inasmuch as generosity crosses the boundaries of desert, one would also expect it to be indifferent to the boundaries between humans and animals, between animals and plants, and between species, ecosystems, and biospheres. One would expect that the virtuous person would take all things that could be made better to be worthy objects of generosity and to thus make sacrifices for the good of environmental entities in the same way (and for the same nonobligating reasons) that she makes sacrifices for other persons.

Finally, to be virtuous is not just to be morally modest; it is to be epistemically modest as well. It is to resist the arrogance of conquerors who destroy what is local before they even know its value. It is to take lessons from those of the past whose haughty haste to convert natural resources to human use deprived successive generations of remarkable species and altered the planet's terrain in irreparable ways. In the absence of full information about how our activities will impact upon delicate ecosystems, virtue would seem to require action in accordance with the precautionary principle, the principle that demands that we do not undertake risky ventures without real confidence that we can ensure the enduring health of those nonhuman entities with whom we share the planet.

Admittedly, all of these claims are vague and, in many ways, worrisome. There is much within these brief suggestions with which to find fault and much to be unpacked. Let me close with several examples that simply reveal the need for considerable further work. First, while our species is a relative newcomer to Earth as compared to other species, each individual living entity on Earth today is a comparative newcomer (although there is no question that we are each short-lived compared to individual members of many other species). Why are our virtues, as individuals, made relative to the longevity, history, and behavior of our species as a whole? As a general matter, we do not assign guilt to persons by virtue of their mere association with others who are guilty. So why would we think that the aretaic duties that persons have are properly responsive to the (short) history and past behavior of the species *Homo sapiens*?

Second, while one can appreciate, as an empirical matter, that virtue is sometimes (and maybe often) overinclusive relative to duty, so that virtues demonstrate themselves when they are often not required, we require an account of why this *should* be so before we can derive from virtue any moral hope that the environment will be a beneficiary of its promotion. For it is tempting to say, with Aristotle, that virtue becomes vice when taken to an extreme, that it ceases to be virtue at all when it is extended to unworthy objects, that one is guilty of tilting at windmills when one behaves virtuously in contexts in which it is inappropriate. Thus, while our own imperfections may prevent us from ever cabining virtue in its appropriate quarters, we should be wary of resting the fate of our environment on the promise that, if we cultivate virtue enough, we will cultivate it too much and only thereby ensure the protection of our planet. For while too much virtue is surely not a fear we need have anytime soon, we ought to be nervous about suggesting that we can protect our planet only if we effectively make a vice of virtue.

Finally, and most troublingly, I remain unconvinced that an aretaic theory of environmental care can properly explain the intuitions that many have concerning the moral standing of environmental entities. Such a theory is explicitly "all about us." It makes the value of the environment a function of the value of our own virtue. While real virtue may require devoted stewardship of the planet and its many entities, I remain unconvinced that the reason we are bound to engage in such stewardship is that *we* will be aretaically worse off if we do not. I take the moral significance of the Pacific Ocean to be independent of (and far greater than) the significance to be attached to the relative virtue of those who have an effect upon it. While it may be that if we, as citizens of the lands that border that ocean, were as virtuous of character as we ought to be, we would act to ensure that its fish populations were restored, its coral reefs protected, its whales made safe, and its currents unaffected by global warming. But even if we were so virtuous, I would not think that its value as an ocean lay in the value of our exhibited virtue.

Conclusion

And thus I end where I began. I worry that our best ethics are not up to the task of protecting the global environment from our worst economics. If we, as philosophers, cannot devise the theoretical means by which to give voice to deep-seated intuitions about the moral status of the natural world on which we depend, we surely cannot blame market players for failing to reflect the value of the natural world in their economic computations, and we cannot blame our political leaders for failing to keep our markets honest and for failing to exempt from market practices those aspects of the natural world that ought not to be commodified at all.

NOTES

1. Jeremy Waldron, *Liberal Rights: Collected Papers, 1981–1991* (Cambridge: Cambridge University Press, 1993), 204.

2. Holmes Rolston III, "Intrinsic Values on Earth: Nature and Nations," in *Environmental Ethics and International Policy,* ed. Henk A. M. J. ten Have (Paris: United Nations Educational, Scientific, and Cultural Organization, 2006), 54.

3. George Henrick von Wright, *The Varieties of Goodness,* The Gifford Lectures, 1958–1960 (London: Routledge and Kegan Paul, 1963). This is in answer to question 6, "What kinds or species of being have a good?" in chap. 3, "Utilitarian and Medical Goodness. The Beneficial and the Harmful. The Notions of Health and Illness."

4. For an excellent discussion and critique of accounts that rely on the goal directedness of interest holders, including the ones outlined later in the chapter, see Harley Cahen, "Against the Moral Considerability of Ecosystems," *Environmental Ethics* 10, no. 3 (1988), 195–216.

5. Paul Taylor, *Respect for Nature: A Theory of Environmental Ethics* (Princeton, NJ: Princeton University Press, 1986), 99.

6. Kenneth E. Goodpaster, "On Being Morally Considerable," *Journal of Philosophy* 75, no. 6 (1978), 308–325.

7. Jay Kantor, "The Interests of Natural Objects," *Environmental Ethics* 2 (1980), 169.

8. James K. Mish'alani, "The Limits of Moral Community and the Limits of Moral Thought," *Journal of Value Inquiry* 16 (1982), 138.

9. Elliot Sober, "Philosophical Problems of Environmentalism," in *The Preservation of Species,* ed. Bryan G. Norton (Princeton, NJ: Princeton University Press, 1986), 185. For more sustained criticism of the thesis that groups or species can have interests, see Cahen, "Against the Moral Considerability of Ecosystems."

10. Holmes Rolston III, "Naturalizing Values: Organisms and Species," in *Environmental Ethics: Readings in Theory and Application,* ed. Louis P. Pojman, 3rd ed. (Belmont, CA: Wadsworth Publishing/Thomson Learning, 2001), 78–89.

11. John O'Neill, "The Varieties of Intrinsic Value," *Monist* 75, no. 2 (April 1992), 119.

12. Tom Regan, *The Case for Animal Rights* (Berkeley: University of California Press, 1983), 243.

13. Tom Regan, *Defending Animal Rights* (Champaign: University of Illinois Press, 2001), 35.

14. Regan, *Case for Animal Rights,* 324.

The Visible and the Invisible 5

Rethinking Values and Justice from a Buddhist-Postmodern Perspective

Jin Y. Park

Values: The Human and the Inhuman

In his book *Small Is Beautiful* (1973), the economist E. F. Schumacher diagnosed the problem of value in the capitalist economic system and warned of its disastrous result if we did not change the way we understood economic growth and the development of human society. Schumacher asked, "What is the meaning of democracy, freedom, human dignity, standard of living, self-realization, fulfillment? Is it a matter of goods, or of people?"[1] As his book's subtitle, "Economics as if People Mattered," suggests, Schumacher's discussion of the meaning of economics and economic development focuses on their impacts on human beings, society, and environments and underlines how the abstraction of values in a capitalist economic system blinds us to human value. Although it was published four decades ago, the concerns expressed in Schumacher's book are even more relevant in the twenty-first century, as the postmodern world becomes more globally connected and economic development constantly challenges the theory of nongrowth. We live in a time when, in the midst of continued economic growth, poverty and hunger are the reality of the lives of many people. Poverty is not simply an issue for countries categorized as underdeveloped or individuals on the lowest rung of the ladder of gross national income. A recent survey reports that in the United States approximately one out of six people lives in poverty.[2] The reality of poverty in the midst of seeming affluence has attracted the attention of economists such as Amartya Sen, who begins his book on the meaning of development with the statement, "We live in a world of unprecedented opulence, of a kind that would have been hard even to imagine a century or two ago. . . . And yet we also live in a world with remarkable deprivation, destitution and oppression."[3] Observations by economists themselves, in addition to our own experience of living in a capitalist society, cause us to question the meaning of economic growth and development and consider more rigorously the question raised by Schumacher. What would it mean to think about an economics that gives consideration to people and to put a human face on our understanding of democracy, freedom, and human dignity? Here we encounter a moment that begs us to reconsider one of our most cherished, fundamental values: humanism.

Humanism in our society has been understood as a positive value because of its perceived advocacy of values fundamental to what it means to be human. But what we have frequently forgotten to ponder is the meaning of "human" in that value system. In diagnosing the nature of postmodern society, Jean-François Lyotard characterizes the postmodern worldview as "inhuman." Lyotard writes, "What if human beings, in humanism's sense, were in the process of, constrained into, becoming inhuman . . . ? And . . . what if what is 'proper' to humankind were to be inhabited by the inhuman?"[4] Unlike the common understanding of the inhuman as being purely negative, Lyotard here distinguishes two types of the inhuman. The first refers to dehumanizing situations in which human beings are treated as a means for supporting a system, be it an economic system in the name of development or a political system in the name of freedom and democracy. The second meaning of the inhuman points to the opposite of the first. Lyotard clarifies this distinction as follows: "The inhumanity of the system which is currently being consolidated under the name of development (among others) must not be confused with the infinitely secret one of which the soul is hostage." In this context, Lyotard cites a statement by the French poet Guillaume Apollinaire (1880–1918): "More than anything artists are men who want to become inhuman," and also Theodore Adorno's 1969 statement "Art remains loyal to humankind uniquely through its inhumanity in regard to it."[5] A certain signification of the expression "the inhuman" that Lyotard identifies as a characteristic of the postmodern worldview begins to emerge. And in an ironic way, inhumanity as a quality necessary to be a human converges with Schumacher's idea of thinking of economics, human rights, freedom, and democracy with a human face.

The modern conception of human history distinguishes the modern from the premodern by a shift in the tools of justification and legitimization of individual actions and social changes. In premodern society the source of justification and legitimation was theological, whereas in modern secular society, nontheological concepts serve that function.[6] The ideals that we cherish—such as equality, freedom, democracy, progress—lie at the center of modern secular society. Such concepts, however, cannot exist in and of themselves; they are claimed and exercised by some system, be it a government, the law, social mores, or an economic structure. To bring attention to that fact, however, is not to address the gap between the theory and practice as traditionally understood. It is also not about creating a perfect system to address the problems that human beings face. What I want to address here is the very nature of a system, any system, which is double-edged.

Since ideas and ideals cannot exist in and for themselves, it is inevitable that there be a system by which they can be put into practice in human society. Creation of a system is possible only through the process of condensation and unification. A system, as Jacques Derrida states, "constitutes itself by repressing what makes it possible, which is not systematic."[7] The existence of a system relies on the maintenance of order and consistency. Regardless of the degree of its success as a mechanism to maintain coherence and consistency, no system is created to demonstrate an impossibility of creating an order, and order is not possible without a coherent entity. Social apparatus are necessary to advance democracy, practice freedom, improve human dignity, and attain a higher standard of living, but exercise of such apparatus also accompanies suppression of some of the fundamental ideals for which the system was created. A belief in the value of the functional nature of a system dominates human society in our time. Diverse political and governmental bodies have been created and are still being created in order to install freedom and justice, and economic structures were supposed to do their service for the promotion of such ideals. The idea was that if the world is orderly and coherent by nature, humans would not have considered creating a system. The existence of a system is evidence that what makes a system possible and necessary is the unsystematic non-homogeneous reality of human existence. The modern period was the time when systems with their functionalism were promoted to the greatest extent and the functional efficiency of a system was given the highest value in human society. The result is that we have forgotten what made a system possible and necessary. Not only that, but we have come to view anything not part of the system as inferior and thus negligible. When we ignore the double-edged nature of a system and understand the system as a genuine representation of the ideas and ideals we promote, the system turns into a totalitarian agent that suppresses what makes the system possible.

Here we once again reflect on the meaning of Schumacher's call for thinking about democracy, freedom, and progress with a human face. To inscribe a human face on the fundamental values of our society and economic progress and to thereby reconceptualize our value system does not mean that we approach these values from a human-centered perspective. Instead, the meaning of the human face in this case is close to what Lyotard defines as the inhuman: an understanding of the nature of human existence as that which always defies any systematic presentation through a coherent structure, and thus an understanding of human existence in the milieu of heterogeneity.

The Buddhist understanding of the identity of a being takes a position that shares the fundamental ideas of Lyotard's inhuman humanism and Schumacher's vision of economics and values with a human face. Buddhist doctrine fundamentally denies the existence of an independent and permanent essence of a being. The Buddhist theory of no-self understands human existence as being possible through the "co-working" of impersonal categories. The same logic applies to every kind of being, in the sense that no being exists by virtue of its own independent essence, but through the dependently co-arising multiple elements that are involved in its existence each moment. Like a system, an individual's identity represents a relatively coherent conceptual entity. Contradictory elements might be found in one's identity, but an entity would consistently make an effort to create a coherent image of itself. Envisioning an identity based on the fundamental Buddhist worldview would mean that an entity is always already an open being, and the subject, to borrow Julia Kristeva's expression, is the subject in process/on trial (*le sujet en procès*).[8]

Huayan Buddhism, a school of Buddhism found in East Asia, offers a paradigm that explains the two sides of identity construction through two levels: the level of particularity (or phenomenon, Chinese *shi*) and the level of totality (noumenon, Chinese *li*). At the level of particularity, each entity is understood though its provisional separate identity, and at the level of totality, entities are understood through their fundamental openness or interrelatedness with others. The key to understanding the Buddhist construction of identity is the nondualities of individuality and totality. Although a separate identity exists at the level of individual events, this is provisional because heterogeneous contributors make individual existence possible. The idea that identity exists because of numerous diverse participants' working together challenges a vision of the world in which human beings and humanistic values occupy the central role. In this Buddhist world, both humans and nonhumans have the same rights by virtue of the openness of identity.

In this sense, the Korean Buddhist thinker Kim Iryŏp (1896–1971) stated, "The world of the Buddha is the world of absolute equality in which even a piece of a broken tile has the right to claim that it is a buddha." This vision of equality, in which humans and a piece of broken tile or a particle of sand claim the same rights, might be understood as negating the value of humans. Against such an understanding, Kim Iryŏp defines the goal of Buddhist practice as a search for true humanhood. She argues that "to attain buddhahood means to attain humanhood."[9] In her autobiographical book, *Reflections of a Zen Buddhist Nun* (*Ŏnŭ sudoin ŭi hoesang*), Kim Iryŏp wrote that when she joined the monastery, she was surprised by three facts:

> First I was shocked when I realized that I had lost my own self. Secondly, I was astonished to realize that the entire world consists of a group of people who had lost their selves; and thirdly, I was stunned to realize that even though the entire world is populated by people who have lost their selves, they are not aware of it, and, instead, each individual is deluded to think that they are smart people and pretend that they know everything. People act, but they do not even try to think about what it is that makes them act.[10]

Kim Iryŏp's grounds for the claim that the majority of people in her time had lost their selves is based on her simple observations of daily life, in which individuals constantly experience dissatisfaction and a sense of lack. Kim Iryŏp asks, "If we are in fact the owner of our own selves as we claim to be, why do we still feel lacking and discontented?" When individuals claim that they have something, Kim Iryŏp argues, it should indicate that they are in charge of their possessions. This means that if individuals own their selves, they should be fully in charge of them, and freedom and satisfaction should be their state of being. On the contrary, the daily life of an individual in our society is characterized by dissatisfaction and a sense of lack, which Kim Iryŏp contends is proof that people are not the true owners of their selves. The relationship between ownership and one's level of contentment as discussed by Kim Iryŏp might be contested, but the fundamentals of her reflection point to the fragility and even fictitious nature of one's concept of self. Kim Iryŏp calls this presumed self the "small-self," as opposed to the "great-self" that is to be recovered through the realization of the true nature of one's existence.

Kim Iryŏp's diagnosis of the imbalance between one's perception of self and the self's actual state in daily life aptly describes the blind spot of consumerism in a capitalist society, a phenomenon that pervades every shopping mall and dominates the lives of Americans. The fundamental logic of acquisition in a consumer society is based on the dualism of self and others. When the self is understood as a closed system, it is limited by the existence of others. In this understanding, the self exists in competition with other selves and comes to believe that its power increases as it acquires more elements that exist outside oneself. The logic of desire is a foundation that consolidates one's power in the competition with others. Only when one has an object of desire, either physically or mentally, do desires arise, and desire can be satisfied only through the conquest of another's territory. In a capitalist society, economic power is understood as being essential to the satisfaction of one's desire. Purchasing power, however, can never bring permanent satisfaction to the consumer, not because it does not have value as it is, but because the structure on which the logic is anchored cannot break the boundary of the self and others. Insofar as one understands one's self in competition with others, there will always be the object the subject needs to conquer in order to confirm the power of the self, and there will be no end of the process.

While identifying the constant sense of lack and dissatisfaction in the lives of modern individuals as a state of lost-self, Kim Iryŏp proposes a search for one's self as the fundamental goal of Buddhist practice. For her, the state in which the individual constantly needs to fill the lack is a bound state, one that lacks freedom. Freedom from this bound state does not come from enhancing the subject's power to control an object. Instead, the first step in finding the real self is to recognize the nature of one's self, which from the Buddhist perspective is to be realized by acknowledging the subject's fundamental interconnectedness with others.

Justice in Question

The influence of economic reality in a capitalist society is not limited to an individual's social position, consumerism, or the construction of a misled identity. Economics has the power to transform, overtly or covertly, various fundamental value systems, including society's notion of social justice. In his evaluation of criminal justice in American society, Jeffrey Reiman, in his book *The Rich Get Richer and the Poor Get Prison,* claims that "the criminal justice system fails in the fight against crime while making it look as if crime is the work of the poor. This conveys the map that the real danger to decent, law-abiding Americans comes from below them, rather than from above them, on the economic ladder." Reiman argues that studies in criminal justice "consistently showed the presence of significant bias against lower-class suspects at every stage of criminal justice processing from arrest on."[11] In fact, the bias against the poor begins even before an arrest is made, Reiman argues, if we consider how the definition of a crime in our society closely relates to one's economic status. Reiman supports his argument by drawing evidence from various materials, including legal cases and the presentation of criminal cases in American mass media. In one such example, Reiman discusses the deaths of ten miners that resulted from a methane explosion in Kentucky in 1993. After the explosion, the mining company pleaded guilty to "a pattern of safety misconduct." The company was fined $3.75 million, but "the acting foreman at the mine was the only individual charged by the federal government." This foreman received the minimum sentence, which meant "probation to six months in prison."[12] The *New York Times* reported the case as "the worst American mining accident in nearly a decade" and "the company's president expressed regret for the tragedy." Reiman compares this case with that of a "mass murder" that same year in which five passengers were killed by a 1.9 mm pistol fired by a man on a commuter train in Garden City, New York. Reiman asks, "Why do ten dead miners amount to an 'accident' and a 'tragedy' and five dead commuters a 'mass murder'? 'Murder' suggests a murderer, whereas 'accident' and 'tragedy' suggest the work of impersonal force."[13] Reiman claims that "the label 'crime' is not used in America to name all or the worst of the actions that cause misery and suffering to Americans. It is reserved primarily for the dangerous actions of the poor."[14] In such a context, Reiman invites his reader to conduct the following experiment:

> Think of a crime, any crime. Picture the first "crime" that comes into your mind. What do you see? The odds are you are not imagining a mining company execu-

> tive sitting at his desk, calculating the costs of proper safety precautions, and deciding not to invest in them. Probably what you do see with your mind's eye is one person attacking another physically or robbing something from another via the threat of physical attack. Look more closely. What does the attacker look like? It's a safe bet he (and it is a *he,* of course) is not wearing a suit and tie. In fact, my hunch is that you—like me, like almost anyone else in America—picture a young, tough, lower-class male when the thought of crime first pops into your head. You (we) picture someone like the Typical Criminal described above.[15]

As we have the image of the typical criminal, so we have the image of typical crime, Reiman argues, in which crime is understood as harm related to "physical injury, loss of something valuable, or both."[16] Excluded in this definition of crime is white-collar crime, discrimination, political corruption, exploitation of humans and of nature, and the list goes on. Employing various forms of documentation and reports by mass media, Reiman demonstrates the ways in which our society constantly regenerates the biased view of crime as a work of the poor. By contrast, according to his research, the public record on white-collar crime has consistently diminished for the past several decades. Reiman concludes that "the acts labeled crimes, instead of being all dangerous acts, were predominantly acts of the poor in society. And the dangerous acts not labeled crime were predominantly acts of the well-off."[17]

Reiman's demonstration of the correlation between the economic status of an individual and criminal justice is deeply disturbing. However, we might still consider this another version of the traditional claim that poverty is the source of crime, so there is nothing appalling in our envisioning of a typical criminal as a "young, lower-class male." Or we might want to understand the findings of Reiman's research as a confirmation of our conventional wisdom that the accumulation of wealth does not promote the cultivation of moral virtues but, instead, could be a source of injustice and unfairness. There is nothing new, then, about the manipulation of criminal justice by the rich in our society. And still, our moral vision, be it programmed by nature or planted through nurture, demands that we believe that there must exist some justice in our society and that human beings are capable of balancing material affluence with moral obligation for fellow human beings. This is the moment when material values and justice collide in an individual's mind. This clash of justice and material values tends to increase in our capitalist society. In contrast to increasing tension between economic reality and the practice of justice, our society tends to conceal, rather than face, the conflict. Ours is an age in which such a conflict between values and ambiguous justice becomes a part of daily life. However, we more readily suppress this conflict than allow it to evoke debate. A global market economy, accompanied by the globalization of culture, further facilitates the routine nature of this invisibility and expands Reiman's claim on the complicity between material power and justice to the global level.

On one level, the limits of the criminal justice system that Reiman reports here are related to the problems of a specific system, or its malfunctioning. At a deeper level, however, they are the limits of the system in general, as was discussed earlier. That is, a system, or an institution, comes to exist by suppressing diverse factors that made the system necessary. A fundamental question in this context is whether the authorship involved in the creation of a system is capable of maintaining absolute objectivity in the process of creating a system and of its functioning. When John Rawls proposes the "original position" as the basis of practicing justice as fairness, he seems to suggest one such possibility.

Jacques Derrida approaches the issue from a different perspective, attending to yet another aspect of the relationship between the idea and the apparatus. From Derrida's perspective, an apparatus that is created to practice an idea can never completely represent the idea because of the nature of a system. Not only does an apparatus always fall short of realizing the idea it represents, but also it functions to subvert the idea it represents. Derrida demonstrates this point through his discussion of the law in our society. The law is a social apparatus that is generated to practice justice. The law is there to protect citizens from violence. However, to exercise law, to "en-force" law, the exercise of force is required, which limits an individual's freedom. As much as law protects people from violence, law is also violence—legitimized violence. This double-edgedness makes possible the malfunctioning of the law reported by Reiman. The malfunctioning of a system, for Derrida, is not something that can be completely fixed through creation of a better law. The problem is related to the nature of the institution, any institution, by virtue of the fact that a system always implies authorship and thus implements selected perspectives. However comprehensive and objective an institution might be, the consolidation of power into a system becomes possible through exclusion and through promotion of what is included in the system. Its inherent nature makes the system susceptible to at least two different types of problems that would deter its proper functioning: the internal and external. When a system claims to be a self-sufficient structure without considering the elements excluded for its creation, the excluded party will eventually hinder the function of the system. On the other hand, when a system is blind to the factors excluded at its birth, the internal power would assume that its authority would allow insiders to manipulate the structure, which results in self-destructive forces. The external disturbance might take a longer time to become visible than internal disturbances because the excluded elements need to consolidate their own power to challenge the power of the existing system. Once the excluded factors are on the horizon, self-legitimation of a system is called into question, whether the system is an individual or a social apparatus.

Derrida thus asks, "Is it ever possible to say that an action is not only legal, but just?" . . . Is it ever possible to say, 'I know that I am just?' " Derrida claims that "such a confidence is essentially impossible."[18] Why is it not possible to say that one is just? Can one then say that one is correct? Can one say that one is right? When we find that our position is not supported by others, we defend ourselves with expressions like, "I'm right in my own sense," or "I'm correct in my own judgment," or we can even say, "I'm just operating from my own standard." When one claims that one is right or correct according to one's own standard or based on one's own perspective, does that person, in fact, claim that she or he is the sole source of the claim for rightness or correctness? Where, then, does the authority, legitimacy, and even authenticity of one's judgment come from? A foundation needs to be there, either implicitly or explicitly. If the foundation is found within oneself, as in the case of Cartesian modernist rationality, why is it that one is correct only in one's own judgment and not by the standard of all human beings who share the rational capacity of the human mind? If the foundation is anchored by the external source, such as divine power, how is it possible that one's judgment or action concurs with the judgment or action of the divine power when the divine power is, by definition, beyond human beings' calculation? At issue here is not that one cannot say one is just, correct, or right, but that it is impossible to put this concept into a closed system of definition despite our tendency to claim to be just, correct, or right. For Derrida, justice, understood in this manner, belongs to the realm of the incalculable.

To experience justice is to experience each and every case as a singular incident, as if there is no author or subject that defines what justice is. If not, justice would be subjectivized by that which (or the one who) declares a situation, an event, a person, or an action to be just. Since justice does not and cannot have the subject that provides the calculable definition of justice, it belongs to the realm of the incalculable, which evades definition. Does this mean that it is not possible to actually practice justice? What Derrida tries to bring out is not a claim that law always malfunctions or is tempered by those who have power, either economically or politically. Instead, the law, as a system recorded by the author—be it a ruler, a selected group, or the people of a nation—is constructed. By the nature of its birth, it is a system that becomes possible by interrupting the heterogeneous nature of existence. Derrida states, "Law is not justice. Law is the element of calculation, and it is just that there be law, but justice is incalculable, it demands that one calculate with the incalculable."[19] For Derrida, justice is the incalculable, the overflow or excess. The apparatus exists and functions by virtue of its consistency and coherence, which are both its power and utility function and its limitations. If justice is the incalculable, and the apparatus by which justice is practiced is calculable, and the gap between the two can never be closed, what actions need to be taken for an apparatus created at the level of the calculable to practice justice, which is at the level of the incalculable, to function properly?

Derrida's answer would be a constant deconstruction of the existing structure so that the structure will constantly be challenged against self-closure. The paradigm of the calculable and the incalculable in understanding the law and justice in particular, and an institution and the idea it represents in general, has a longer history in philosophical tradition. To look at Buddhist tradition, one finds a similar vision in the Huayan understanding of the relationship between individual existence—be it a human individual or a social institution—and its real nature.

Similar to Derrida's distinction of the calculable and the incalculable, Huayan Buddhism offers a hermeneutic device using the expressions *shi* and *li* in Chinese. As briefly mentioned earlier, *shi* refers to the individual event, or particularity, whereas *li* can be translated into principle, pattern. Individual events or beings exist through a calculable format: a being has a physical existence that is a closed form; an event has beginning and ending points. Understanding the existence of a being at the level of particularity, an individual being is characterized by its own independent identity. If one looks at it more closely, a being's existence is always related to other beings. Hence, the seemingly separate identity of a particular being is only provisional. A being then is both closed and open: it is a closed entity by virtue of its separation from other beings and at the same time is an open entity in the sense that a being does not exist without other elements that make contributions to its existence. By virtue of the multiplicity of the contributing factors in its number, one's existence is characterized by "excess" or "overflow."

One example that Huayan Buddhism provides to explain this dual nature of one's existence of separation and overflow is the identity of numbers in a numeric system of one through ten, with an assumption that the ten numbers represent the entirety of the numeric system that expands itself to infinity.[20] Using commonsense logic, each number in this scale has a distinctive identity. One is one and should not be confused with two. The same is true with the other nine numbers. However, this identity of one being different from the other nine numbers demonstrates only a partial reality of the number one. For the number one to function as the number one, the other nine numbers are necessary. The same is true with numbers two through ten. In the number one, all the other nine numbers are included. Furthermore, they are infinite because the ten numbers in this example indicate the entire numeric system. The infinite other, already within the individual, is the reality of an entity understood from the ultimate perspective. However, by virtue of its infinite nature, which is similar to the incalculableness of Derrida's justice, this infinite heterogeneity cannot demonstrate itself. The seventh century Huayan patriarch Fazang (643–712) described the nature of identity in this climate of multiple connections as "layers of inexhaustibility" (C. *chongchong wujin*). Even though each existence at its ultimate level is overflowing, inexhaustible, or in excess, it does not negate the separate identity of the individual existence of a particular being. This is the logic behind such Huayan hallmark statements as "it is possible to put the entire world into the follicle of a hair."[21]

The Huayan vision of existence, in which a follicle of hair can contain the entire universe, aptly challenges the human-centered worldview. By extension, it also challenges any form of centralized power to exert its self-sufficiency and demonstrates the limits of such power. Despite the fact that traditional Buddhist doctrine does not overtly offer a theory of justice in a manner similar to Western philosophical tradition, the Huayan Buddhist understanding of the nature of existence of a particular entity shares the Derridean notion of justice and its relation to an apparatus created to implement justice. This vision also brings our attention to the fact that visible reality cannot fully represent the reality of existence. When one's vision is limited by the visible, epistemological error is the inevitable result. From the Buddhist perspective, this is the cause of suffering. In a capitalist society, the visible reality of human existence becomes inflated, whereas the invisible aspects, which in fact are part of the identity of the visible, are consistently suppressed. Another aspect of the suppression of the invisible with an overemphasis on the visible takes the form of the deceptive reality of economic development in our time. Hunger and poverty become invisible behind the glitzy appearance of big cities and shopping malls filled with commodities, luring consumers of all ages and backgrounds. As Peter Hershock aptly points out, poverty does not refer simply to the lack of certain possessions or the absence of the means to obtain something that one needs. He argues that poverty also "occurs when either a person or an entire population is effectively blocked from contributing directly to the welfare of others."[22] Hershock proposes that alleviating poverty means to "foster increased capabilities-for (and commitments-to) giving appropriately to others."[23] His definition of poverty and poverty alleviation is also shared by the economist Amartya Sen, whose proposal views development as the enhancement of substantial freedom of societal members.[24] To understand poverty as capability deprivation emphasizes the diverse impact of individual actions on both the economic and noneconomic reality of one's existence. It also understands reality not only through the visible but also through the invisible aspects of the visible world.

The invisibility of hunger and poverty is different in nature from invisibility as discussed in the context of Derrida's justice as the incalculable, or the Huayan concept of *li,* principle. Invisibility in Derridean discussion and Huayan Buddhism refers to the state of existence itself, whereas the invisibility of poverty and hunger is a socially structured state of existence. Poverty and hunger are not the only forms of constructed invisibility in our society. Racism, gender discrimination, class conflict, and ethnic conflict have all been made invisible despite their existence in social reality. The nature of the invisibility in the case of hunger, poverty, racism, and so forth, and the nature of the invisibility of the "overflow" nature of our existence, are different. The failure, however, to see these seemingly invisible aspects of our life in both cases results in suffering to members of the community of beings, be it human or nonhuman. The main character in Ralph Ellison's novel *The Invisible Man* tells us that he is invisible, not because he does not exist or does not have substance, but "simply because people refuse to see [him]."[25] The denial of the existence of the other, or the turning of a blind eye to that which is not "I," is accelerated by the inflation of the visible world in our society. Just as there are different realms in what I have identified as the invisible in our lives, the visible world is also comprised of different layers. The natural world, with its grandeur of mountains, streams, flowers, and trees with foliage that changes colors, is visible. But do we really see the natural world when we see it? Do we see it as the source of our existence, as the earth on which we stand, the space in which we place our physical existence, and the air that we breathe each moment? The problem of the visible that I address here occurs when the visible world is constantly reified and identified in the form of commodities.

Maurice Merleau-Ponty advanced a convincing case about this in his discussion of visibility.[26] When one sees things, he proposes, the common understanding is that the subject sees the object. This understanding of visibility allows only one type of relationship between the subject and the object, which is a linear and causal movement from the subject to the object. Against this commonsense understanding, Merleau-Ponty proposes that visibility takes place in the chiasmic relationship between the subject and the object. In order for visibility to occur, not only does the subject see the object, but the subject is being seen by the subject. Only in this mutual seeing, Merleau-Ponty argues, can real visibility take place. What does this seemingly counterintuitive project on the relationship between the subject and the object propose? Ellison's Invisible Man is invisible because, even though a subject (the Invisible Man's other) sees him, that subject refuses to see him, the object, and this refusal deprives him of his own existence. In order for the subject to recognize and be aware of being seen by the object, the object needs to be accepted as a being at a level compatible with the subject. A dog on the street does not have much chance of being recognized by the passerby, unless the passerby is sympathetic to animals. On the other hand, not only would a dog as a precious pet within its owner's world be more likely to be seen by the owner, but the owner also would feel that he or she is being seen by the pet dog. The mutual recognition of the subject and the object in their understanding of each other is not just a matter whose scope is limited to seeing the other, but that which is related to the foundation in our life as a member of a community of beings. That is because the invisible realm of human existence is not trivial, nor can it be ignored in relation to the ontological, societal, or existential reality of existence. Both Buddhist and postmodern philosophers pay special attention to this invisible aspect of human existence. In doing so, they demand the reconceptualization of the relationship between visible existence and invisible reality. When the visible and the invisible are understood hierarchically, and the invisible is ignored, the dominance of the visible results in the creation of a totalitarian world. This power may be economic, as in a capitalist system, or socially generated, as in a patriarchal system, racism, sexism, or homophobia. These two sources generally work together, as demonstrated by Reiman's criminal justice research in America.

Philosophy and Responsibility

Evaluating his own research on criminal justice, Reiman emphasizes that a philosophical reflection on the nature of crime made it possible for him to see the problem innate in the practice of criminal justice.[27] A philosophical reflection on the nature of one's own existence also seems essential as we think about the role of philosophy in the context of today's economic reality. In his discussion of the September 11 attack on the Twin Towers in New York City, Derrida suggests that the event demands a new type of philosophy and suggests that we define philosophers as "those who, in the future, reflect in a responsible fashion on these questions [of international institutions and international law] and demand accountability from those in charge of public discourse, those responsible for the language and institutions of international laws."[28] International laws and institutions are emphasized here because the discussion was done in connection with September 11, but the realm for philosophers' engagement can be expanded to various societal issues. Likewise, Buddhist philosophers need to be vigilant and consistently confirm their position in relation to the real world in which individuals exist. Pŏpsŏng, a Korean Engaged Buddhist, challenges the understanding of Buddhism as an individualistic practice of the mind exclusively aiming for individual enlightenment and states that "Buddhism can be actualized in history and with people [the masses] through self-negation, but Buddhist self-negation should be guaranteed through a rigorous self-realization of Buddhist philosophy and Buddhist practice."[29] One needs to rigorously reconsider the traditional Buddhist practice in the context of current real-life situations. One such practice is implied in the Huayan idea of "cessation and contemplations,"[30] discussed in detail by the Huayan thinker Dushun (557–640). Cessation indicates stopping the subjective-oriented mode of thinking that anchors itself in the subject-object dualism. Contemplation means to see through phenomena so that one can be constantly reminded of the reality of things as they are instead of understanding them as isolated fragments.

As we emphasize the relational reality of existence and call for philosophy's responsibility for engaging itself with society, from where do we find the ground for such responsibility? On what basis do we argue for individuals' and philosophers' responsibility for our time? Here we once again refer to Derrida's proposal for understanding responsibility from the vantage point of an heir. Derrida writes, "To *be* . . . means . . . to inherit. All the questions on the subject of being or of what is to be (or not to be) are questions of inheritance." Derrida clarifies that inheritance in this case does not suggest that one has inherited specific assets that would enrich him or her materially. Instead, "the *being* of what we are *is* first of all inheritance, whether we like it or know it or not."[31] To put it in Buddhist terminology, one's existence is already dependent co-arising, which occurs both horizontally (through historical temporality) and vertically (in one's relationship with one's contemporaries).

Adding a modern twist to the classical Buddhist concept of dependent co-arising, a modern Korean Buddhist school known as Won Buddhism divides this interconnected setting of existence into four categories called the Four Beneficences. They are Beneficence of Heaven and Earth, Beneficence of Parents, Beneficence of Brethren, and Beneficence of Law.[32] Beneficence of Heaven and Earth refers to one's indebtedness to the environment. It is not difficult to connect this notion of one's dependence on nature with current global environmental concerns. Beneficence of Parents on the first level indicates indebtedness to one's parents as the immediate origin of existence. At the expanded level, this concept can be interpreted as a corporeal and biological reality of one's existence, including various genetic features and internal organs that make life possible. Beneficence of Brethren indicates the relationship of an individual to other human beings, and what one inherits by virtue of being part of the human race, history, and civilization. Finally, Beneficence of Law refers to an individual's relationship with various social institutions. This modern interpretation of the Buddhist dependent co-arising of Won Buddhism provides a more realistic look at the Huayan idea of *shi* (particular individual existence) and *li* (totality) in human existence and our earlier discussion of the visible and the invisible. A being's existence is then a combination of the natural, biological, human, and societal inheritance, as Derrida defines a being as inheritance. Like an heir who has received an inheritance and thus is responsible for taking care of that inheritance, each individual has inherited existence in this temporal and spatial reality of our time. If that is true, like an heir, one's existence is inseparable from responsibility. To exist means to be responsible.

NOTES

1. E. F. Schumacher, *Small Is Beautiful: Economics as if People Mattered* (Point Roberts, WA: Harley and Marks, 1999), 56.

2. *Income, Poverty, and Health Insurance Coverage in the United States 2010,* U.S. Bureau of the Census (Washington, DC, September 2011), http://www.census.gov/prod/2011pubs/p60-239.pdf, accessed September 14, 2011.

3. Amartya Sen, *Development as Freedom* (New York: Anchor Books, 1999), xi.

4. Jean-François Lyotard, *The Inhuman* (Stanford, CA: Stanford University Press, 1991), 2.

5. Ibid.

6. Jonathan I. Israel writes, "The basic difference between pre-modern revolts and upheavals and modern revolution, therefore is that, with the former, justification of social and political change invariably invoked theological *fundamenta,* customary law, and veneration of tradition while modern revolutions quintessentially legitimize themselves in terms of, and depend on, non-traditional, and newly introduced, fundamental concepts." Jonathan I. Israel, *Enlightenment Contested: Philosophy, Modernity, and the Emancipation of Man 1670–1752* (Oxford: Oxford University Press, 2006), 1.

7. Jacques Derrida, "I Have a Taste for the Secret," in *A Taste for the Secret* (Cambridge: Blackwell, 2001), 5–6.

8. Julia Kristeva, *Revolution in Poetic Language,* trans. Margaret Waller (New York: Columbia University Press, 1984), 22.

9. Kim Iryŏp, *Ŏnŭ sudoin ŭi hoesang* [Memoir of a practitioner] (Yesan, Korea: Sudŏksa, 1960), 22, 13. English translation by Jin Y. Park, *Reflections of a Zen Buddhist Nun: Essays by Zen Master Kim Iryŏp* (Honolulu: University of Hawai'i Press, 2014), 53, 42.

10. Ibid., 1. English translation, Park, 29.

11. Jeffrey Reiman, *The Rich Get Richer and the Poor Get Prison: Ideology, Class, and Criminal Justice* (Boston: Pearson, 2007), xiv–xv, 4.

12. Ibid., 60, 61.

13. Ibid., 61.

14. Ibid., 60. And more often than not, this lower class becomes identified as colored people, as Reiman cites, "I do know that it's true that if you wanted to reduce crime, you could—if that were your sole purpose—you could abort every black baby in this country, and your crime rate would go down" (cited in ibid., 63). The idea of defining the actions of an economically underprovided group in the society as crime and locking them up in a prison cell also has a common ground of judging the actions of the economically underprivileged as mentally disabled and locking them in a mental hospital, as elaborated in Jonathan M. Metzl, *The Protest Psychology: How Schizophrenia Became a Black Disease* (Boston: Beacon Press, 2009).

15. Reiman, *Rich Get Richer,* 70–71.

16. Ibid., 71.

17. Ibid., 244.

18. Jacques Derrida, "Force of Law," in *Acts of Religion,* ed. Gil Anidjar (New York and London: Routledge, 2002), 245.

19. Ibid., 244.

20. Fazang, *Huayan Wujiao zhang* [Treatise on the five teachings of Huayan], *Taishō shinshū daizōkyō,* ed. Takakusu Junjirō and Watanabe Kaikyoku, vol. 45.1866.477a–509a (Tokyo: Taishō Issaikyō Kankōkai, 1924–1932), 504b–504c.

21. Ibid., 703a.

22. Peter D. Hershock, *Buddhism in the Public Sphere: Reorienting Global Interdependence* (London: Routledge, 2006), 65.

23. Ibid.

24. See especially Sen, *Development as Freedom,* chap. 4.

25. Ralph Ellison, *The Invisible Man* (1947; New York: Vintage Books, 1972), 3.

26. Maurice Merleau-Ponty, *The Visible and the Invisible,* trans. Alphonso Lingis (Evanston, IL: Northwestern University Press, 1968); see esp. chap. 3, "The Intertwining–The Chiasm."

27. Reiman, *Rich Get Richer,* 244.

28. Quoted in Giovanna Borradori, *Philosophy in a Time of Terror: Dialogues with Jürgen Habermas and Jacques Derrida* (Chicago: University of Chicago Press, 2003), 106.

29. Pŏpsŏng, "Kkaedarŭm ŭi ilsangsŏng kwa hyŏngmyŏngsŏng-Han'guk Pulgyo tonjŏm nonjaeng e puch'ŏ" [The commonality and revolutionality of awakening: In relation to the sudden-gradual debate in Korean Buddhism], *Ch'angjak kwa pip'yŏng* 82 (Winter 1993), 329.

30. Dushun, *Huayan wujiao zhiguan* [Cessaion and contemplation of the five teachings of Huayan Buddhism], *Taishō shinshū daizōkyō*, ed. Takakusu Junjirō and Watanabe Kaikyoku, vol. 45.1867.509a–513c (Tokyo: Taishō Issaikyō Kankōkai, 1924–1932), 511b; English translation by Thomas Cleary, "Cessation and Contemplation in the Five Teachings of the Hua-yen," in *Entry into the Inconceivable: An Introduction to Hua-Yen Buddhism* (Honolulu: University of Hawai'i Press, 1994), 57.

31. Jacques Derrida, *Specters of Marx: The State of the Debt, the Work of Mourning, and the New International*, trans. Peggy Kamuf (New York: Routledge, 1994), 54; emphasis in original.

32. *Wŏnbulgyo chŏnsŏ* [Scripture of Wŏn Buddhism] (Chŏnbuk, Korea: Wŏnbulgyo ch'ulp'ansa, 1995). For an English translation of the sections related to the Four Beneficences, see Bongkil Chung, *The Scriptures of Won Buddhism with an Introduction* (Honolulu: University of Hawai'i Press, 2002), Canon, pt. 2, chap. 2.

"You Ought to Be Ashamed of Yourself!" 6

James Peterman

Recent financial scandals have raised questions about appropriate forms of punishment for white-collar crimes. Some commentators have argued that punishments for such crimes might need to be reduced from what they would otherwise be because white-collar criminals suffer shame from incarceration in a way that other criminals do not. It is, however, striking that some recent white-collar criminals, for example, Jeffrey Skilling of Enron fame, seem to express neither shame nor remorse at their crimes, but rather seek by all means to have their charges reversed legally. (His legal appeals, which have gone to the Supreme Court, continue as I write this sentence.) In effect, he has "lawyered up," claiming that his troubles are due to a faulty legal process. Of course, "lawyering up" as a practice excludes any public expression of shame because public expressions of shame might be used in court to count as an admission of guilt.

It is easy to have competing intuitions about what to make of white-collar criminals. It seems, on the one hand, a matter of regret that a person like Skilling, who, without feeling shame, remorse, or doubts about his involvement in the collapse of Enron, would have engaged in or overseen business practices that would have negatively impacted so many people, including company stockholders and employees, who lost their retirement savings and jobs. Expressing this feeling, communitarians, like Amitai Etzioni,[1] defend bringing shame back into the legal system. On the other hand, liberal critics of shaming, like Martha Nussbaum,[2] argue that shaming punishments violate our sense of human dignity. At one time, legal scholar Dan Kahan sided with the communitarians, but more recently, in his "What's Really Wrong with Shaming Sanctions,"[3] he poses a challenge to any attempt to generate a political consensus around even the mildest, most reasonable forms of shaming practices.

It would seem that classical texts of Confucianism could offer some insights about shame that would provide strategies for responding to Nussbaum's important critique. Specifically, we can ask, "What, if anything, does Confucianism, with its focus on learning ritual and developing from this a sense of shame (*Analects* 2.3),[4] contribute to this debate?" After all, Confucius indicates that those who practice ritual will have a sense of shame and will consequently be self-reforming. Several commentators, referring specifically to *Analects* 2.3, find in the *Analects* a spiritual home for restorative justice.[5] Although this point of view is initially plausible, I argue that this passage will not offer specific ways to respond to Nussbaum's and Kahan's challenges. The only thing it might do is *inspire* some response, for Confucius himself rejects any system of punishment, and the restorative justice movement develops a system of alternative punishment. Nonetheless, despite this difficulty, I argue that we can find in the *Analects* resources for diagnosing and influencing viewpoints of restorative justice critics. I argue that instead of looking to early Confucian statements of general principles expressing conceptual analysis, we should look instead to Confucius' strategies—with some help from D. Z. Phillips and Wittgenstein—of resolving deep ethical disagreement through ethical intervention.

Nussbaum's Critique

I begin with Nussbaum's basic argument. In her account of shame and other moral emotions, too complex to outline completely here, Nussbaum argues that there is an important distinction between primitive and healthy shame. Primitive shame, "closely connected to an infantile demand for omnipotence and the willingness to accept neediness—is, like disgust, a way of hiding from our humanity that is both irrational in the normative sense, embodying a wish to be a type of creature one is not, and unreliable in the practical sense, frequently bound up with narcissism and an unwillingness to recognize the rights and needs of others."[6] In contrast, healthy shame is defined in terms of awareness of one's failure to achieve, an ego ideal often associated with a moral ideal.[7]

The sense of the "primitive" here is twofold. First, this sort of shame manifests itself first in early childhood, when the child recognizes its finitude; and second, this sort of shame is "normatively unreliable in public life despite its potential for good."[8] In its unhealthy course of development, primitive shame gets associated with moral and mental failures: a sense of self-sufficiency and perfection that makes it impossible for a person to recognize both his needs or others' legitimate needs. As a result, those dominated by unresolved primitive shame fail to feel healthy moral shame at their own failures and, when exposed, wish instead to shame others.

Despite these problems Nussbaum associates with primitive shame, she admits that a healthy form of shame, when properly related to justifiable moral ideals, is a good thing. As she says,

> The immediate family is one very powerful agent of shame-development, whether healthy or unhealthy. But the surrounding society is another. In B's case, the explanation for his hypertrophy of shame lay primarily in his parents' behavior.

> But societies vary also in the type of developmental pattern they hold up as normal. What Winnicott prescribes is a form of life in which parents understand and present themselves as imperfect, and nourish in the child a sense of delight in the sort of "subtle interplay" that two equally incomplete figures can have.[9]

But Nussbaum also notes that, whereas healthy shame can be supported in the context of a healthy family, surrounding society might offer a different approach to shame.

In reviewing the work of legal scholar Dan Kahan on the positive role that shame can play in a legal context, Nussbaum acknowledges that "shame may at times play some of the good roles that Kahan ascribes to [it],"[10] such as "perceiving and condemning cruelty."[11] In general, she claims, Kahan likes shaming "because of its expressive power: no other mode of punishment as vividly surely expresses society's disapproval of the offender."[12] Despite this use of shame, which Kahan wishes to reserve for progressive ethical and political purposes, Nussbaum still rejects it. As she admits, "some forms of shame indeed have a positive ethical value; thus, if we criticize many roles shame plays in the law, as I think we should, it must be because those roles make appeal to a primitive or bad form of shame, or are *at risk* of doing so."[13] This point is telling. Even if the role of shame in the legal system does not make appeal to primitive shame, Nussbaum rejects its use in the law simply because of its "risk" of doing so. Since she never gives any actual examples of a legitimate role for shame in law, we might venture the hypothesis that she believes any shame used in the law is always at least at risk of being a primitive form of shame. Given her views, this might make sense. Insofar as it is often unclear whether an instance of shame is healthy or primitive, we should exclude all forms of shame from the legal system.

In developing this general argument in more detail, Nussbaum argues that her account of shame underpins the best recent reasons against use of shaming penalties.[14] I list them for convenience without much elaboration.

1. Shame penalties humiliate and so count as an offense against human dignity.
2. Shaming penalties involve a kind of mob justice.
3. Shame penalties are unreliable.
4. People who are humiliated become more alienated and troubled than before.
5. Shame penalties attempt to put an ever-widening net of people under their control.

All of these criticisms presuppose that shame penalties are penalties in which the guilty person is intentionally shamed or humiliated in punishment for his or her crime. That means that the guilty person is being shamed or humiliated by some legally designated agent of shame or humiliation. In this context, the shame is not self-generated shame. It is easy to see why someone might hold that such "active" shaming and humiliating of the guilty person violates the dignity of the person, fosters alienation, and thereby sustains the willingness of the guilty party to continue violating the law. But these criticisms have their limit. For Nussbaum's argument requires that she accept a role for healthy shame in the legal system if we could find one. What would such a role look like?

When Nussbaum discusses her preferred models of healthy shame outside of the law, she employs principles derived from John Stuart Mill's liberalism. Following Mill's general liberal framework, Nussbaum discusses examples of healthy shame that is purely self-controlled. As long as a person "invites herself" to feel shame, there is nothing unhealthy about it: "For adults, aspirational shame may be constructive, although it seems most appropriate that the *invitation* to feel shame come from oneself."[15] By extension, another person can invite someone else to feel shame. But it would be wrong for such a person to impose shame, thereby shaming or humiliating the person. This restriction leaves to a very few the range of cases where a person can be legitimately shamed in public. They are not hard to find, however; proposal of such legitimate forms of shame has been a central task of the restorative justice movement.

Nussbaum understands that the most noteworthy alternative uses of shame penalties that escape this list of criticisms are those defended in the restorative justice movement, among others, by John Braithwaite. Braithwaite defends the role of shame induction as a part of the process by which a victimizer, in the context of a restorative justice conference, comes to grips with the harm he has done his victim. In this conference, those with whom the victimizer has significant relations support him in his shame and at the same time help him use that sense of shame and its expression as a step toward apologizing, seeking forgiveness, committing to making amends, and restoring himself to the community. Nussbaum would have to accept this role for shame as acceptable provided that it (1) supports a positive moral ideal, (2) avoids active forms of primitive shaming and humiliation, and (3) avoids the risk of such shaming.

But despite adopting principles that would require her to accept this putatively healthy form of restorative shaming, Nussbaum rejects Braithwaite's account of shame as confused.[16] She maintains that he confuses two things: (1) being guilty of some specific legal norm and (2) being ashamed at such an act. As she says, "What is totally unclear is whether this [guilt and punishment] has anything to do with shame."[17] So despite the fact that shame in restorative justice is protected from her most serious criticisms aimed at "active," primitive shaming penalties, Nussbaum argues that shame should play no role in offering just penalties for a *guilty act* since the proper response to a guilty act is *guilt and appropriate punishment* attached to the *guilty act,* not *shame* attached to the person. On this basis, she claims that Braithwaite confuses guilt of the offender with his or her shame.

It is important to be clear that Nussbaum's criticism of restorative justice is quite limited. Provided that the restorative justice process is not forced on the guilty person and he or she knows well how the restorative conference works, the invitation to engage in the restorative justice will have been freely accepted. Those wishing to avoid the shaming encouraged in the conference can opt for more traditional forms of punishment. Assuming that an invitation to restorative justice mediation is sometimes freely accepted, given Nussbaum's argument, the only remaining problem is the alleged conceptual confusion in restorative justice theory. Can one of the spiritual roots of restorative justice, Confucianism, help resolve this issue?

A Confucian Interlude

It seems clear enough that Confucians will find Nussbaum's rejection of shame uncongenial. But it is less clear that there is much to be derived from the classical texts of Confucianism to directly address her criticism of restorative justice theory. I make my argument for this claim in terms of one key text alone, but assume that similar arguments might be possible for other passages in the *Analects.*

Take, for example, an argument that appeals to *Analects* 2.3:

> If a ruler rules people with edicts, straightens their conduct with punishments, the people will avoid crimes, but be without a sense of shame. If a ruler rules them with virtue, and straightens their conducts through practicing ritual, then people will have a sense of shame and, moreover, regulate themselves.

From this passage, we might construct the following response to Nussbaum's argument: Confucius holds that a system of punishment will bring about a deterrent effect but not the sort of moral sensitivity and self-reforming moral character he prefers. It would be better to have a population of people become sensitive to moral norms through the practice of ritual, and on that basis become self-regulating, than to have a population insensitive to moral norms and apt to avoid breaking rules out of a desire to escape punishment. How can this point, basic as it is to Confucianism, help us to argue against Nussbaum's critique of restorative justice theory?

Despite the initial plausibility of there being a connection between this passage and the restorative justice project, it is hard to get from Confucius' basic point to a specific critique of Nussbaum's points. Based on this and other passages in the *Analects,* we could, for example, say that we would rather have a system of social organization that develops and sustains moral sensitivity, involving a sense of shame, than have one that encourages people to see avoiding the punishments attached to edicts as their primary reason for conduct. But this basic principle is too vague and general to address the specific arguments against restorative justice that Nussbaum offers. Here I mention two. First, this general principle does not clearly bear on the question of how to structure penalties in a legal system. Indeed, it seems to offer an argument for not having a legal system with penalties in the first place. Second, the crucial distinction that Nussbaum draws in her criticism of Braithwaite between guilt from an act and shame from failing to achieve an ego ideal seems to be one that even a Confucian, using this passage, might wish to endorse. An *Analects*-style Confucian, appealing to *Analects* 2.3, might even wish to side with Nussbaum in her critique of Braithwaite's assimilation of guilt and shame. Guilt makes sense in a legal system that prohibits acts of a certain sort, and shame has its role in a system of ritual that fosters a sense of shame. On this view, arguably, the restorative justice system incoherently mixes restorative justice ritual with a system of legal penalties.[18]

Despite the fact that he acknowledges the *Analects* as a source for restorative justice thinking,[19] Braithwaite's responses to Nussbaum make no appeal to the *Analects*. For example, in their essay in *Taking Stock*,[20] Braithwaite and his co-authors, Eliza Ahmed and Valerie Braithwaite, while admitting that Nussbaum is right to criticize the use of punishment that shames by stigmatizing offenders, argue that their main point is that "societies that fail to communicate the idea that rape is shameful . . . will have a lot of rape."[21] Moreover, they explain, their notion of shame-guilt, which Nussbaum sees as incoherent, was motivated by empirical studies. They admit that their view requires further clarification. Their conceptual defense of their approach comes not from the Confucian tradition, however, but rather from the important work on shame of Bernard Williams.[22] What they wanted in their account, they say, was for the offenders to feel shame over what they *did*, but not over *themselves*. Now, based on Williams' analysis of the distinction between shame and guilt, they have altered their view.

In his important arguments about shame and guilt, Williams holds that guilt attaches primarily to acts, while shame attaches to the failure of the person to achieve an ideal. So Williams argues that while these orientations differ, they are both necessary for sustaining a moral framework. To have a sense that an act violates the law and one is guilty if one does that but not to have the additional sense that in being guilty one has failed as a person to live up to a moral ideal undermines the very possibility of a moral framework. This argument seems relevant to the Confucian view that we should prefer an approach to social organization that focuses on ritual and developing a sense of shame. But it is noteworthy that this view may conflict with *Analects* 2.3. For Williams argues for the mutual necessity of guilt and shame as features of a sustainable moral point of view, a view not clear in *Analects* 2.3.

Williams' argument is both complicated and theoretical. Williams argues in great detail that a shame orientation is both logically and psychologically distinct from guilt orientation.[23] Guilt is over an *act* that typically elicits in others feelings of anger, resentment, and indignation, and in the agent fear of punishment or desire for self-punishment. In contrast, shame is over *oneself* and elicits from others feelings of contempt and from the agent herself a lowering of self-respect and a wish to hide.[24] Based on his analysis of the "wiser" way the Greeks understand ethical emotions, Williams argues that guilt and shame are, despite these differences, interconnected, even for us: "We can feel both guilt and shame towards the same action."[25] He claims the feeling of guilt is connected to the fact that "we have let [others] down."[26] We feel shame because we have fallen short of "what we might have hoped of ourselves."[27] But for Williams, it is not just that a person can feel guilt and shame toward the same action. Shame has a primacy, for, as he argues, guilt separated from shame "cannot understand itself." In contrast, "shame can understand guilt."[28] We can understand guilt through the lens of shame better than through the lens of guilt insofar as contemporary conceptions of guilt cannot easily explain guilty harm done to others involuntarily.[29] Since our felt failure in having done such a thing cannot arise from knowing that we freely willed something bad, it must derive from a sense that we have failed to live up to a way of living with others that we embraced for ourselves. As Williams says, "This is the territory of shame."[30] Insofar as we wish to understand guilt, a preoccupation of modern morality, we must understand its relation to shame, something modern morality tends to reject.

In an important explication of the implications of this argument, Williams claims that a modern moral consciousness emphasizing guilt, and de-emphasizing shame, can help to focus an agent's attention on the damage he has happened to inflict on victims but cannot "help [the agent] understand one's relations to those happenings, or to rebuild the self that has done these things and the world in which that self has to live."[31]

Perhaps it is easy to surmise why Braithwaite and his coauthors turn to Williams rather than to the *Analects* to address Nussbaum's criticism. The *Analects* appears consistent with the view that a set of moral practices involving ritual and shame alone could be the whole of a moral point of view.[32] If this were the *Analects*' view, this position would offer no clear way for the restorative justice defenders to use it to respond to Nussbaum's critique. Indeed, the *Analects* might even provide some support for Nussbaum's criticism. Although *Analects*-style Confucianism would be comfortable thinking of specific violations of ritual norms as shameful, that does not itself count as a way to respond to restorative justice's problem of incoherence. For Confucius, as for Nussbaum, Braithwaite's approach to guilt and shame appears to rest on conceptual confusion, mixing the apples of legal guilt with the oranges of ritual shame.

Furthermore, Williams' argument offers restorative justice theorists a conceptual analysis of morality that responds directly to Nussbaum's argument that Braithwaite's view of guilt and shame is incoherent. Using Williams' analysis, we can argue that if laws embody norms that are socially enforced and motivating for those who live under them, then violations of laws need at some points, especially for saliently evil acts, to be publicly seen and treated as shameful, not just as guilty violations of law. The very same act can be seen as guilty from one point of view but shameful from another. Moreover, making sense of the guilt of some acts requires seeing the ways in which this guilt has to be explained in terms of its relation to shame.[33] More important than this, Williams' account of the relation of shame and guilt helps to explain the plausibility of the restorative justice model of mediation. Mediation is designed to help induce the victimizer to express publicly the shame that normally ought to accompany guilt, prompting the offender's acknowledgment of shame in public as a step toward becoming a restored, committed moral agent within his or her community, or as Williams says, helping the agent "to rebuild the self that has done these things and the world in which that self has to live."

It would seem, then, that to respond successfully to Nussbaum's critique, we need a more complex account of the necessary role of shame in taking communal stances against evil than what we find in the *Analects*. That is, we seemingly need an account of the necessity of shame in any moral framework that treats agents as guilty and an account of how shame can be structured so as to help to "rebuild [a victimizer's] self and his world."

If my argument about the limits of the contribution of Confucius' teaching works, it might seem that there is no obvious role for the *Analects* in this debate.[34] I will, however, argue that a possible role that the *Analects* points to in connection with this debate is one of ethical intervention to resolve deep disagreement. But before clarifying what that means, I turn to an analysis of why it is so difficult to get agreement about the use of shame in a system of *punishment*.

The Source of These Deep Disagreements

In "What's Really Wrong with Shaming Sanctions,"[35] Dan Kahan criticizes his earlier defense of the use of shaming penalties.[36] In an argument that is quite general and should give anyone reasons for cautious pessimism, Kahan offers the following analysis of the mistake of his shame penalty proposals.

> I emphasized that punishments, to be politically acceptable, must express authoritative moral condemnation. That's true, but incomplete. Members of society also expect punishments—and essentially all laws for that matter—to *affirm* the core values that animate their preferred ways of life. Modes of punishments that are equivalent in their power to convey moral disapproval might still convey radically conflicting messages about the nature of the ideal society. What's *really*

> wrong with shaming penalties, I believe, is that they are deeply partisan: when society picks them, it picks sides, aligning itself with those who subscribe to norms that give pride of place to community and social differentiation rather than to individuality and equality.[37]

In explaining this point, Kahan argues that in the sort of society we live in, we want to be *inclusive* in our approach toward fellow citizens. So we tend to opt for legal arrangements that do not exclude on philosophical and religious grounds. Any forms of legally sanctioned punishment that support shaming penalties would, he thinks, express support of the primacy of community over individuals and would thereby alienate liberal support, which sees shaming penalties as a violation of individual freedom and dignity.

Kahan argues that the distinctive advantage of incarceration is that such a system of punishment does not imply endorsement of either a liberal or communitarian view of the relation of community to individuals. Either of these orientations could justify on its own grounds incarceration as the basic form of punishment. As Kahan says,

> To fashion an acceptable alternative to imprisonment for minor forms of criminality, then, it is necessary to identify a form of punishment that not only condemns as forcefully as imprisonment but that also condemns as *ambiguously* as imprisonment does.[38]

Appealing to Wildavsky's[39] and Gusfield's[40] view of the role of cultural views in developing political consensus, Kahan offers an account of the failure of inclusiveness of his earlier views. Kahan summarizes Wildavsky's view as follows.

> Wildavsky systematizes these commitments using a scheme of culture types derived from the work of anthropologist Mary Douglas. The scheme characterizes preferred modes of social organization along two cross-cutting dimensions ("group" and "grid") that generate essentially four distinct cultural worldviews—hierocracy, egalitarianism, individualism, and solidarism or communitarianism.[41]

This account can be used to explain both the sources of entrenched political disagreement as well as the conditions under which it might be possible to achieve political consensus. For, as Kahan says, "Laws that manage to affirm diverse cultural worldviews simultaneously, then, are the ones most likely to overcome political conflict and generate broad scale support."[42] Based on this, we can see why politically acceptable punishment arrangements capable of producing consensus have been essentially ambiguous. Any scheme of punishment that prefers one cultural view to others will create a political backlash. A punishment scheme that appears to be neutral, however, will satisfy a necessary condition of becoming politically acceptable. Shaming penalties encode in the punishment scheme itself a meaning that embraces hierarchy and communitarianism. As Kahan says, "Beyond history (but likely related to it), the aesthetics of shame seem inescapably to conjure up the specter of hierarchy and coerced conformity."[43] As a result, we can predict that a system of shame penalties cannot easily become politically acceptable. And this account of the meaning of shame punishments contrasts unfavorably with the meanings available for incarceration:

> An immensely rich and ambiguous institution, imprisonment not only condemns, but condemns in a multiplicity of registers that make it simultaneously agreeable to persons of diverse cultural outlooks: hierarchists can see it as supplying a delicious form of debasement for those who resist their proper place in the social order; communitarians, a fitting gesture of banishment for those who wrongfully renounce social obligation; individualists, a reciprocal deprivation of liberty for those who fail to respect the liberty of others; and egalitarians, a uniquely democratic metric of punishment for persons who enjoy value by virtue of their capacity for autonomy.[44]

What does this analysis entail about the prospects for restorative justice, which brings in shame in the context of conferences of ritualized mediation designed to restore the offender to society? In his analysis, Kahan offers a very powerful reason for suspecting that even the restorative justice shaming project, despite its gentle, and noncoercive, use of rituals of shame, may not be capable of generating a political consensus. For Nussbaum and other liberals, any use of shaming will conjure up too many hierarchist and communitarian red flags to be acceptable. The argument that Nussbaum offers against restorative justice theorists is one way to protect the guilty from coerced communitarian meanings. To argue that guilt rests on shame is to undermine a fundamental tenet of liberalism, since it undermines that liberal demand that we preserve the dignity of individuals even when we punish them for acting in ways that we deem guilty. For liberals like Nussbaum, shaming is a greater violation of dignity than guilty incarceration.

Can we find any resources in the texts of early Confucianism for resolving this fundamental political problem with restorative justice? If Kahan is right, any Confucian use of the *Analects* and other texts of early Confucianism in defense of ritualized shame penalties would be persuasive only to members of like-minded cultural-political camps: Confucians or communitarians. In fact, Kahan's argument shows that his earlier attempts to defend shame penalties failed precisely because they lacked cultural and political neutrality. Traditional Confucian arguments in favor of ritualized shame punishments as a way to instantiate and support the moral ideal of *ren* (仁, moral goodness, authoritative personhood, humaneness), aligned with communitarian views of the human good, would, accordingly, undermine consensus. That being the case, it appears, once again, that Confucianism might need to be sidelined in this debate. Once again, how can an appeal to Confucianism help?

The Confucian Way

In response to this problem, I propose to take a hint from two sources: Fingarette's account of the goal of Confucius on cultural unification of Warring States China and D. Z. Phillips' Wittgenstein-inspired view of the need in philosophy for ethical intervention. I start with an overview of a key aspect of Fingarette's basic argument. Fingarette points out that one of Confucius' greatest achievements was to unify, around a secular-sacred view of the world, the warring states of his day. What Confucius succeeded in doing in the context of the Warring States period was to engage in various discussions designed to intervene in the lives of disciples and others in order to alter their practices and modes of reflection and understanding.[45] Having succeeded in doing this, he and his disciples were able to bring those practices and modes of reflection into political institutions. What form of intervention do we find Confucius engaging in?

Confucius' approach to conversation with his interlocutors, we might say, is more therapeutic than theoretical. The closest we get to an "ultimate" teaching, I would contend, is the invocation, without a detailed analysis, of those ideals that constitute *dao*. Along with such an invocation, Confucius offers suggestions of reform designed to draw his interlocutor toward *dao*-constituting ideals and practices. We can call these "interventions." I mean by "intervention" the attempt to get an interlocutor to understand better the ethical norms by recommending changes in his behavior in relation to an ethical ideal. I borrow this term from D. Z. Phillips, who uses the term in a different, but related way: according to Phillips, influenced as he is by the later Wittgenstein, interventions in ethics are often needed because of our deep-rooted tendency to theorize in ethics.[46] We want to give a general, theoretical account of the essence of morality. We search for this essence. The philosophical intervention we need, in that event, takes the form of reminders of possibilities, which the so-called essence cannot account for. Our trouble is not that we have failed to locate the real essence, but that we dogmatically assume that there is a real essence of morality to be found. We are rescued from the futile search for it by coming to pay attention to the heterogeneity of moral practices.[47]

There are, then, different sorts of intervention. The sort of "intervention" Phillips supports requires getting the philosopher to change her approach to philosophy by getting her to pay attention to and care about the heterogeneity of real and possible practices. This change in the philosopher's perspective as she pays attention to the diversity of practices gives rise to a change in her assumptions and in what seems interesting. In this way, the trouble about essences disappears. Confucius' interventions, of course, are different. He is not interested in undermining the interest in his interlocutors on the questions of the essence of any phenomenon; he is, rather, interested in getting them practically oriented to proper practices, which once implemented will make them better people.

This account of Confucian ethical intervention explains well why in the face of the various questions he is asked about *ren, xiao* (孝, filial piety), and the rest, Confucius typically offers different answers, answers that reflect his sense of how best to intervene and create a change of practice and reflection in his interlocutor. This strategy becomes crystal clear in *Analects* 11.20, in which Confucius clarifies why he offers two different answers to the question asked by two different interlocutors: "Should I put something I just learned into immediate practice?" Often commentators select one passage on, say, *ren,* over others as what Confucius thought, but they do so in tension with this meta-comment about his teaching in 11.20.[48] These passages, while offering important formulations in context, do not express Confucius' ultimate views.

I have already argued that it is not clear how the general approach to shame and punishment that we find in the *Analects* can directly address the problems offered by critics of restorative justice. This limitation may be the source of Braithwaite and his coauthors' appeal to Williams' argument about the relation of guilt to shame. But, as I will next argue, there is a problem with their appeal to Williams' argument, if, as it seems, we face a plurality of guilt-shame practices.

I offer a two-step response to these problems. D. Z. Phillips' ethical interventions can work in this case to draw attention to the fact of the heterogeneity of guilt-shame practices and relations between the concept of guilt and shame. Liberal claims that the guilt of guilty acts is logically and psychologically independent of the shame of falling below ideals shared by others in one's community is just wrong. Williams' arguments about the Greeks make it clear that the Greeks found a deep connection between guilt and shame. So we find here evidence of a counterexample to Nussbaum's analysis of guilt and shame. Williams also indicates that his analysis can help us to recognize features of our own moral psychology and relation between guilt and shame[49] that modern moral consciousness papers over.[50] His argument is, however, consistent with the heterogeneity of guilt-shame practices. At this point, we have identified at least two: a modern liberal separation of guilt and shame and the Greek connection of guilt and shame. Confucian shame might actually offer a third possibility.[51]

A Phillips-style intervention would attempt to undermine any conceptual argument about the relation of guilt to shame that, prior to examining the full range of actual and possible guilt-shame practices, claims to say what the conceptual relation between guilt and shame must be. Such an intervention, influenced as it is by Wittgenstein's later writings, is also consistent with inventing new possible practices and related conceptual relationships between guilt and shame.[52] This form of intervention, however, cuts two ways in this context. We can use Williams' account of the early Greek view of guilt and shame to undermine Nussbaum's claim to have discovered the only way to understand the guilt-shame relationship. But Williams suggests that the early Greek account shows us something about guilt and shame themselves.[53] Even if we suppose that he is right about this—and additional work would be required to show this—a Phillips-style intervention would require us to consider other possible guilt-shame practices and related conceptual relationships. Williams' account, even if it captures features of our life with guilt and shame, need not be the only possible form of life with guilt and shame. To make this point in a slightly different way—in terms of Kahan's analysis—the heterogeneity of political ideologies on punishment is related to the heterogeneity of punishment practices. Attempts to ground one ideology over the others will be subject to a Phillips-style intervention: when we are honest, we have to acknowledge that we find and understand different practices of guilt and shame along with different internally related claims about the relation of these concepts. Even if we are, as Williams suggests, like the Greeks, we can imagine other ways of orienting ourselves to guilt and shame.

This result is important for our evaluation of Braithwaite and his coauthors' appeal to Williams to respond to Nussbaum's critique. Williams' account of the relation of guilt to shame falls prey to the same problem we find in Nussbaum's account. Both seek to adopt a single view of the relation of guilt to shame. But using Phillips' interventionist strategy, we would need to reject both accounts as too limiting and as insufficiently attuned to diversity of guilt-shame practices, which are plural.

In the face of this heterogeneity, a liberal could, nevertheless, admit the diversity of approaches to the fundamental relationship between guilt and shame and still argue that some are better than others. Following Nussbaum, one could argue that one should protect an individual's dignity at all costs, even to the point of ensuring that the only justified shame—the only one consistent with human dignity—is shame one freely agrees to dwell in and respond to by oneself. Nussbaum offers an account of a liberal view of punishment that, I propose, evidences her grasp of tenets of liberalism as a mode of liberal common sense.[54] It is common sense to her that human dignity should be preserved and that its preservation excludes shaming, legal penalties, although it is common sense to her that human dignity is better preserved through a legal system that focuses on the guilt of acts distinct from shame, which is left to the individual. Even if we can find resources in Williams and Phillips to contest the narrowness of Nussbaum's conceptual argument, that argument still leaves us with the possibility of a clear reluctance to be open to alternatives that she and other liberals would reject as inferior even if they are forced to recognize them as coherent.[55] A Phillips-style intervention might not go as far as we need.

At this point, we might take a page out of the *Analects*' Confucian playbook. In the spirit of what I earlier called Confucian intervention, we could invite liberals to become involved in restorative justice practices, both as observers and as participants. By becoming familiar with their healthy practices of inviting individuals to engage in public expressions of shame, liberal critics might be able to view such expressions of shame as sustainers of the moral norms of mutual respect and dignity, not their enemy. And as they become more comfortable with such practices, they would come to better understand how guilty acts might be conceptually connected to feelings of shame. In the process, they might also better understand how a person's sense of self-respect can depend on the respect significant others feel for that person. These very connections would become manifest in the restorative justice process, which is a ritual designed—to use Williams' language—to "help one understand one's relations to those happenings (the guilty acts one has unintentionally done), or to rebuild the self that has done these things and the world in which that self has to live."[56]

This Confucian interventionist strategy rests firmly on Confucius' view, enunciated in *Analects* 2.15:

> If one merely learns how to do something but does not reflect on it, he will learn in vain. If one merely thinks about something, but does not learn how to do it, he will face trouble.

On this view, understanding follows practice. That being the case, only when liberals alter their practices, even as experiments in living, will they begin to understand alternative ways to live out and understand the relation of guilt to shame.

Of course, it might be difficult to get hard-core liberals to take up this invitation. But no one who advocated ethical interventions thought it would always work. Instead, their commitment was to the notion that some basic ethical disagreements are resolvable, if at all, through conversion to a new way of life. I have been arguing that the best way to use the *Analects* to address the liberal critique of restorative justice shame penalties is through its advocacy of intervention. If this is correct, restorative justice advocates need to follow Confucius' example and urge their liberal critics to participate in restorative justice interventions. Until that happens, we may wait a long time to see white-collar criminals stand up in public and, as they should, say, "I am ashamed of myself." But when arguments come to an end, and invitations to live and think differently are rejected, commitment to a moral view may express itself best in hope for a better day.

NOTES

1. Amitai Etzioni, *The Monochrome Society* (Princeton, NJ: Princeton University Press, 2001).

2. Martha Cravens Nussbaum, *Hiding from Humanity: Disgust, Shame, and the Law* (Princeton, NJ: Princeton University Press, 2004).

3. Dan M. Kahan, "What's Really Wrong with Shaming Sanctions," *Texas Law Review* 84 (2005), 2075–2095.

4. All references to *Analects* are to *A Concordance to the Analects of Confucius,* vol. 16, Harvard-Yenching Institute Sinological Index Series (Taipei, Taiwan: Ch'eng-wen Publishing, 1966). Translations are my own.

5. John Braithwaite, *Restorative Justice and Responsive Regulation* (Oxford: Oxford University Press, 2002); Edwin C. Hui and Kaijun Geng, "The Spirit and Practice of Restorative Justice in Chinese Culture," in *The Spiritual Roots of Restorative Justice,* ed. Michael Hadley (Albany: State University of New York Press, 2001); Christina Joseph, "Philosophical, Religious and Contemporary Ideas in the Evolution of Justice," *Restorative Justice Online* (2004), http://www.restorativejustice.org/articlesdb/authors/4329, accessed February 1, 2011; Jianhong Liu, "Philosophical Ideas of Confucius and Values of Restorative Justice," *Restorative Justice Online* (2004), http://www.restorativejustice.org, accessed February 26, 2011.

6. Nussbaum, *Hiding,* xx.

7. Bryan Van Norden, in his chapter "The Virtue of Righteousness in Mencius" (in *Confucian Ethics: A Comparative Study of Self, Autonomy, and Community,* ed. Kwong-loi Shun and David B. Wong [New York: Cambridge University Press, 2004], 162–164), argues that the early texts of Confucianism support a distinction between moral and conventional shame. While this is not exactly the same as Nussbaum's distinction, it may be related. If they were the same, then by Nussbaum's argument, all conventional shame would be primitive. I leave for another occasion the important question of whether this thesis might be true. Van Norden argues that conventional and moral shame are not easily separated.

8. Nussbaum, *Hiding,* 15.

9. Ibid., 193.

10. Ibid., 339–340.

11. Ibid., 74.

12. Ibid., 175.

13. Ibid., 176; emphasis mine.

14. Ibid., 230ff.

15. Ibid., 214; emphasis mine. The very idea of *inviting oneself* to feel shame seems odd. That a person can invite anyone to feel shame let alone invite oneself to feel shame seems odd. What form would it take: "Why don't I feel shame? No, thanks!"

16. Ibid., 241, 371.

17. Ibid., 371.

18. Third-century BCE Chinese Confucian philosopher Xunzi's approach differs from the *Analects,* but I reserve discussion of the details of his views for another occasion. Xunzi allows for punishment in the legal system, and this Confucian joint appeal to moral education combined with legal systems of punishment seems to dominate early Chinese legal systems. On this point, see Xinzhou Zhang, "A Restorative Justice Audit of the Chinese Criminal Justice System," *Restorative Justice Online* (2005), http://www.restorativejustice.org/editions/2005/oct05/china, accessed April 6, 2011.

19. Braithwaite, *Restorative Justice.*

20. John Braithwaite, Eliza Ahmed, and Valerie Braithwaite, "Shame, Restorative Justice and Crime," in *Taking Stock: The Status of Criminological Theory,* ed. Frances T. Cullen, John Paul Wright, and Kristie R. Blevins (New Brunswick, NJ: Transaction Publishers, 2006), 397–418.

21. Ibid., 398.

22. Bernard Arthur Owen Williams, *Shame and Necessity* (Berkeley: University of California Press, 1993), chap. 4.

23. Williams develops this argument in chapter 4 and also in the appendix of his *Shame and Necessity.*

24. Ibid., 89.

25. Ibid., 92.

26. Ibid.

27. Ibid.

28. Ibid.

29. Ibid., 93.

30. Ibid., 94.

31. Ibid.

32. I don't suggest that this is the final word about early Confucianism. But even if we find compelling accounts of ethics that can be used to resolve the specific criticism liberal critics offer to restorative justice shaming, we ought not with them or with the *Analects* fall into the fallacy of anachronism. We ought not to interpret these texts as offering responses to problems they were not aware of or especially interested in. On this general problem, see James Tully, *Meaning and Context: Quentin Skinner and His Critics* (Cambridge: Polity Press, 1988).

33. Williams does not argue that all forms of guilty acts must be understood as shameful violations of our sense of what we hope for ourselves. He argues for this thesis only in reference to unwilled bad acts. But once he can show that some forms of guilt are explainable in terms of shame, it might be a short step to entertain this as a possibility even in cases of willed guilty acts.

34. In making this claim, I am *not,* however, arguing that the Confucian *tradition* has no resources for addressing Nussbaum's criticism. Indeed, later Confucian thinkers, like Mencius, might have just the sort of resources necessary to address Nussbaum's worry. But how that would work in detail is by no means clear. In his essay "The Virtue of Righteousness in Mencius," in which he appeals to Williams' account of the relation of guilt to shame, Bryan Van Norden (see n. 7) argues Confucian shame is "always focused on the subject of the emotion rather than those whom the subject affects." Whether this notion of shame is able to do the work of showing a conceptual connection between guilt toward a victim and shame toward oneself is unclear to me.

35. Dan M. Kahan, "What's Really Wrong with Shaming Sanctions" (2006), Faculty Scholarship Series, paper 102, http://digitalcommons.law.yale.edu/fss_papers/102.

36. In his earlier work "What Do Alternative Sanctions Mean?" *University of Chicago Law Review* 63, no. 2 (Spring 1996), 591–653, Kahan argued that alternative punishments of shaming resolved a problem for the alternative punishment's movement, which often suggested use of punishments such as community service as an alternative to incarceration. But these sorts of alternative punishments, unlike incarceration, do not express the disapproval of society for crimes done. After all, community service is something many well-intentioned, upstanding citizens engage in all the time. Kahan's alternative proposal, designed to rectify this deficiency, was to offer shame punishments. This category of punishments runs the gamut from walking around with a placard saying "I shoplifted from this store" to cleaning the street with a toothbrush. Because these punishments expressed the societal sense of disapproval for the crime, Kahan argued, this was a form of alternative punishment we should be able to embrace.

37. Ibid., 3; emphasis in original.

38. Ibid.; emphasis in original.

39. Aaron Wildavsky, "Choosing Preferences by Constructing Institutions: A Cultural Theory of Preference Formation," *American Political Science Review* 81, no. 1 (1987), 4–21.

40. Joseph R. Gusfield, "On Legislating Morals: The Symbolic Process of Designating Deviance," *California Law Review* 56 (1968), 54–73.

41. Kahan, "What's Really Wrong," 10. As Kahan also notes, we can find these splits in a range of issues: "Gay marriage, flag desecration, the teaching of evolution in public schools, drug prohibition, and other 'symbolic' issues pit competing egalitarian and hierarchical, individualist and solidarist values against each other" (ibid., 1).

42. Ibid., 12.

43. Ibid., 18.

44. Ibid., 20.

45. Herbert Fingarette, *Confucius: The Secular as Sacred* (San Francisco: Harper and Row, 1972), 64.

46. I defend this view at length throughout my *Whose Tradition? Which Dao? Confucius and Wittgenstein on Moral Learning and Reflection* (Albany: State University of New York Press, forthcoming).

47. See D. Z. Phillips, *Interventions in Ethics* (London: Blackwell, 1992), viii.

48. Yang Xiao, "How Confucius Does Things with Words: Two Hermeneutic Paradigms in the *Analects* and Its Exegeses," *Journal of Asian Studies* 66, no. 2 (2007), 497–532.

49. Williams, *Shame,* 92, 94.

50. Ibid., 100–101.

51. See Van Norden's defense of a view of this sort in his "Virtue of Righteousness in Mencius."

52. Ludwig Wittgenstein, *Philosophical Investigations: The German Text, with a Revised English Translation,* trans. G. E. M. Anscombe, 3rd ed. (Malden, MA: Blackwell, 2003), sec. 122.

53. Williams, *Shame,* 92.

54. For an essay that does an excellent job of offering this account of the relation of Wittgenstein's *On Certainty* and his view of common sense there to ethical reflection, see Nigel Pleasants, "Wittgenstein, Ethics and Basic Moral Certainty," *Inquiry* 51, no. 3 (2008), 241–267.

55. Nussbaum in fact might very well reject these alternatives as coherent, but it is not how clear she could argue for that view in the face of Williams' powerful argument. My point here is just that even if she admits these alternatives as coherent possibilities, she could still reject them on political grounds.

56. Williams, *Shame,* 94.

Filial Piety and the Traditional Chinese Rural Community 7

An Alternative Ethical Paradigm for Modern Aging Societies

Yang Liuxin, Baoyan Cheng, and Xu Di

The Problem of Aging in Market-Oriented Societies and Its Ethical Predicaments

Developments in science, medicine, technology, and national economies have rapidly resulted in aging societies in both developed and developing countries around the world. The increasingly large number of elderly people has caused various problems to the political and economic systems of societies, including family structure, ethical relationships, lifestyles, and values, as well as to the emotional state of their members. Neither the spontaneous capitalistic market nor a state welfare system can easily resolve these issues. In a modern market economy ruled by the logic of capital and profit, elderly people, who, usually unemployed, are considered mere consumers, thus present a huge market for profit making. In the meantime, however, supporting the elderly becomes a real economic burden and a social problem. Herein lies a paradox: on the one hand, the market economy is making unprecedented profits from the aging population; on the other hand, the changes a market system brings—such as urbanization, mobility, separation of the family, and decreasing respect for the elderly—and a rising value on money have drastically changed the way the family, community, and society support the elderly, making the task much more challenging. In fact, problems around an aging society remain mostly unsolvable within the framework of a market economy because this framework is based on an ideology of capitalism, value of financial exchange, and individualism.

This predicament prompts one to reflect on the ethics of the existing market-based development paradigm, especially the limitations of a modern market economy and family system in terms of values and morality. We need to search for an alternative ethical paradigm to substitute for the existing one, which is based on individualism and value of financial exchange by exploiting the elderly in the current modern market economy and which is detrimental to families, community, and society. In order to address the current challenges, we examine in this essay the traditional Chinese value of filial piety and its practice in the rural community as a possible alternative paradigm for modern aging societies. We argue that the traditional Chinese rural community and its family-oriented lifestyle offer a different model that places higher value on the elderly than is the case in modern aging societies and that provides multigeneration support for elders and helps them negotiate the physical, emotional, and spiritual challenges that come as they age.

Filial Piety and Fraternal Duty in the Traditional Rural Community: The Ethical Significance of "Covering for One Another"

The ancient Chinese practices of filial piety and fraternal duty are embedded in the everyday life of the traditional Chinese rural community. This is illustrated by the following story from the *Analects*.

> The Governor of She in conversation with Confucius said, "In our village there is someone called 'True Goody.' When his father took a sheep on the sly, he reported him to the authorities."
>
> Confucius replied, "Those who are true in my village conduct themselves differently. A father covers for his son, and a son covers for his father. And being true lies in this."[1]

This story certainly demonstrates the son's filial piety toward his father and the father's benevolent affection toward his son. Confucius goes a step further, however, by highlighting his moral approval of those who are willing to protect the interest of family members above all. He then develops an ethical paradigm centered around filial piety and benevolent affection, and that is how the concept of *li* (propriety, 礼) came into being. This ethical paradigm, although entertaining the possibility of tolerating and even encouraging "illegal" behavior, takes the son's filial piety and the father's benevolent affections for granted. At the same time, this places such filial piety within a family above the social rules and regulations.

Filial conduct transcends official rules and regulations. While the governor of She in the anecdote describes following social norms and principles as "being true," a virtue in terms of society, what Confucius means by "being true" is the filial relation between a father and son through the bonding of a family. For Confucius, the higher value and more fundamental responsibility of the son is duty to his father rather than to society. If the case of the son's reporting of his father's conduct to the authority embodies procedural fairness in a legal sense, then the case of the son's covering for his father emphasizes the moral legitimacy of the blood tie and identity connection between the father and the son. In other words, it is only moral for the father and the son, as members of the same family community, to unconditionally accept their inherent connection to each other and possibly common destiny, even if it means violating the law. It is simply immoral not to accept this connection. The moral value of individual behaviors is not measured primarily by the legitimacy of those behaviors per se, but rather by whether they identify with and protect the family unit, which is the core of a society's formation and stability.

The case of the son covering for his father, as an example, demonstrates the morality of filial conduct. Mencius actually provided a case with an even more intense conflict between legal and moral principles. When asked what King Shun should do if his father committed the crime of killing someone, Mencius answered,

> Shun would have regarded abandoning the realm as he would abandoning an old shoe. Secretly, he would have taken his father on his back and fled, dwelling somewhere along the seacoast. There he would have happily remained to the end of his life, forgetting, in his delight, about the realm.[2]

He explains his thought-provoking reply and moral reasoning as follows:

> He [King Shun] thought that if he could not win the hearts of his parents, he could not be a human being, and that if he could not reach an accord with his parents, he could not be a son. Through Shun's fulfilling the Way of serving his parents, Gusou [Shun's father] came to be pleased, and when Gusou came to be pleased, the world was transformed. When Gusou came to be pleased, all the fathers and sons in the world became secure. This is called "great filiation."[3]

Not only are father and son part of a living community of family; the whole family, in fact, is an inherently connected community. The traditional rural community is composed of just such family communities, which are tightly bonded by blood ties. In these traditional communities the criteria for judging whether a moral principle or a custom is righteous are based on each family instead of each individual family member. It is on the basis of these kinds of criteria that people in these communities would consider a son's covering for his father a virtue of "being true." Obviously, the ethical system reflected in this kind of filial conduct is in conflict with, or even in opposition to, individual-based social moral values. This kind of family-oriented and family-based ethical system provides each member of the traditional rural community with a life of moral significance and dignity. In the case of the son covering for his father, the moral obligations and rights of each person are defined from the perspective of the family unit as a whole, not from the perspective of each individual. In fact, all individuals, as members of a living community of a family, need to overcome or transcend their legal obligations and rights based on social criteria and realize that their moral significance and dignity are accepted and determined by the filial criteria in the traditional rural community, even if it means the illegal behavior of covering for family members.

Further, the Confucian definition of "being true," as reflected in the case of the son covering for the father, contains the five virtues of benevolence, righteousness, propriety, wisdom, and trustworthiness. Benevolence (*ren,* 仁) could refer to the son's filial piety toward his father and the father's benevolent affection toward his son in the context of a family. It means that each member of the family has to identify with the family community he or she lives in and should try to protect it. The moral duty of family ties and relationship (*yi,* 义) reflected in the Confucian definition of "being true" has to do with each family member's family obligations toward other members. Confucius' approval and high praise of the son who covered for his father reflects the ethical criteria and consensus among the traditional rural community, which, instead of recognizing the individual, views the entire family as a unit. Therefore, the son's conduct, widely accepted by the members of the traditional rural community, conforms to the Confucian virtue of family relationship and is part of the core of propriety (*li*) in a traditional rural community. The wisdom (*zhi,* 智) of the Confucian definition of "being true" relies mainly on the morality that the basic living community of the family is the foundation of the society and its preservation and protection outweigh and transcend the rationality of legal principles. The essence of trustworthiness (*xin,* 信) is one's own sincerity and other people's trust. A son covering for his father is undoubtedly sincere and can be trusted by other family members. His filial behavior also serves to preserve his family's name and fate in the larger community. The Chinese traditional rural community believes that this kind of trustworthiness originates from a natural genetic connection and bonding and holds it in high esteem.

Through the previous case analysis of the son's covering for his father, we can see that the moral criteria of filial piety are based on the biological bonding of a family. Further, from the Confucian definition of "being true," we can assert that ancient China stressed filial piety as the primary foundation of community and society and that the traditional rural community is one instance in which bonds are made through filial conduct and behaviors. The Chinese traditional rural community approves and embraces such filial behaviors as moral principles and codes of conduct. By doing so, members of the community make filial piety a necessity of social life and personal identity. The moral reasoning of filial piety is that an individual's identity is the carrier of his family identity. That is to say, the father-son relationship is a symbiotic one, as the father's life overlaps and intertwines with the son's. All members of a family share a "core," or "essence," of the same family identity with their current family members and blood relatives and their living or deceased ancestors, as well as with the family members of future generations.

The objective of a Confucian society is to achieve harmony and balance, and having stable families is the way to accomplish this objective. The role of the family is to provide security, support, and cohesion for its members, and one of the key characteristics of a Confucian family is filial piety. It means that the responsibility of the offspring is to respect the authority of the father, and the father, in return, is obliged to take care of the family. Therefore, not informing on a family member is not really "covering up" the family member's "crimes," but fulfilling one's responsibility toward the family, thus maintaining its unity, stability, and continuity.

Confucius' moral premises and practices advocated maintaining the harmonious relations of family and community instead of making the wrongdoing public. Many may view this alarmingly or critically as an ethically compromised and corrupted teaching and practice, which are likely to promote nepotism and corruption. However, in the entire canon of Confucius' teaching, he taught morality and ethics of the highest order. At the same time, he addressed and applied the ethics in a pragmatic and relational manner. The private dealing with the ethical matters often provides an opportunity for the wrongdoer to make changes in a less humiliating manner and strengthens the family relation as the base of stability of the society. Here Confucius is consistent with his "middle of the road" approach, with the emphasis on the person, the family, the community, and the nation as one. To him, family relationships and ties are the most basic and profound foundations of all social, cultural, ethical, and political unity.

The Essence of Filial Piety and Fraternal Duty: Ethics among Family Members

The principle of filial piety reflects a unique understanding of the concept of what it means to be human, which is based on family roles and life experience around the family structure. This comprehensive value system of symbiosis and reciprocity holds family at its core, and all the social order orbits around this focal point. In the *Analects,* Confucius elaborates on his understanding of filial piety as follows:

> Meng Yizi asked about filial conduct (*xiao* 孝). The Master replied: "Do not act contrary." . . . The Master replied: "While they are living, serve them according to the observances of ritual propriety (*li* 礼); when they are dead, bury them and sacrifice to them according to the observances of ritual propriety."
>
> Meng Wubo asked about filial conduct (*xiao* 孝). The Master replied: "Give your mother and father nothing to worry about beyond your physical well-being."
>
> Ziyou asked about filial conduct (*xiao* 孝). The Master replied: "Those today who are filial are considered so because they are able to provide for their parents.

> But even dogs and horses are given that much care. If you do not respect your parents, what is the difference?"
>
> Zixia asked about filial conduct (*xiao* 孝). The Master replied: "It all lies in showing the proper countenance. As for the young contributing their energies when there is work to be done, and deferring to their elders when there is wine and food to be had—how can merely doing this be considered being filial?"[4]

Here Confucius interprets filial piety from three perspectives. First, he refers to the affectionate connection between parents and children. Second, the realization and expression of filial piety lie in the unity of sincere affection and respect as well as self-sacrifice that conforms to traditional propriety and customs. Third, filial piety involves both life and death, reflecting the infinite continuity of the intergenerational relationship within the interconnected family community.

The reality of human life is that human beings live together as a community; at the same time each human being has a relatively separate life as an individual. Confucianism always takes these two aspects of human existence into consideration when understanding the individual human being. Hence, in Confucianism, no person is understood as an abstract and autonomous individual with subjective freedom and equality; rather, each person is seen as an individual in the context of connected social relationships. The Confucian concept of humans is that they are active participants and members of a social community. The multiple roles each person plays in the pluralist social community to which he or she belongs are the key to defining and understanding that particular human being's conduct. Confucianism is concerned with each person who has an interdependent and symbiotic tie with other members of the social community and at the same time pays close attention to the actual living conditions and environment surrounding each individual. In a way, we may say that Confucianism does not acknowledge individuals as they are perceived in Western societies. A person in isolation from the community around him simply cannot attain his full potential as a human being.

To the Confucian a human being is first and foremost defined within the framework of a family. In *Focusing the Familiar* (*Zhongyong*), Confucius says, "Authoritative conduct means conducting oneself like a human being, wherein devotion to one's kin is most important."[5] In fact, Confucianism understands human relationships from an extended and broad sense of family. As Confucius states in chapter 12 of the *Analects*, "Since exemplary persons (*junzi* 君子) are respectful and impeccable in their conduct, are deferential to others, and observe ritual propriety (*li* 礼), everyone in the world is their brother. Why would exemplary persons worry over having no brothers?"[6] This concrete concept of human beings living within the framework of a family—in either a broad or narrow sense—is the core ethical "code" of Confucianism as well as the whole of classical, traditional Chinese culture. This means that a group in the typical form of a family as a basic unit of communal living and the individual person are merely two sides of the same coin. Chinese people in ancient times, when describing themselves, always looked back to the achievements of their ancestors. The reason is that the significance of any given person's life could be defined only by the continuity of one's family life and ancestral lineage. To use the common metaphor of a tree, in Confucianism the family is the root of an individual person's life, and the life of each person is the branch and leaf of the family. It is from this vantage point that a son's filial piety toward his father and a father's benevolent affection toward his son may be considered as conduct strengthening the connection between family members and their family roots. Thus, such behaviors possess significance, and they function as the cultivation of each person's life and his root connection with his lineage. Modern and Western individualism differs in its understanding of individuals from the Confucian view characterized by the concept of symbiotic unity. First, modern individualism separates the life of the family unit from that of the individual, thus dividing a holistic unity into two independent and separate entities. Second, it regards the abstract individual life as the primary and fundamental one and community life as merely a contractual and organizational form derived from individual lives. According to Confucian belief, such an understanding goes against the natural and actual life experience in relation to the community in which each person lives.

According to Confucianism, the living community of family contains three ethical relationships, namely, relationships between parents and children, relationships between siblings, and the relationship between husband and wife. The basic ethical principle of these relationships is loving one another, or benevolence (*ren*), which is embodied in parents' benevolent affection and children's filial piety, older siblings' caring and younger siblings' respect, and husband's righteousness and wife's subordination. The interpersonal dynamic among family members is stipulated by different rules of behavior, depending on the role and status of each family member. The order is that the younger subordinates to the older and the female subordinates to the male. Family members interact with one another out of sincere caring and benevolence, and those interactions and connections build a family into a harmonious community. Therefore, according to the Confucian view, the ethical order is one that sustains family life, is natural, and goes against the grain of the abstract and liberal principle of equality advocated by Western individualism. The reciprocal support among members of the traditional Chinese family is based not on individual contractual rights and legal obligations but on the natural process of gratitude and mutual caring in the context of shared identity.

The basis of filial piety is the natural and biological network and interlinking of human beings that connect intergenerational life experiences with blood ties and mutual affection. Here human beings are understood as participants in the living family community, and the traditional rural community may be considered the local extension of the family unit, or the "pan-family" living community. Human beings in this sense are not abstract or anonymous, autonomous individuals but members of an intricate family web. Each member of the family has his or her own identity and roles to fulfill. Each experiences birth, growth, marriage, and the birth of the next generation, and each enjoys his or her old age and leaves the world with the full support of the family. Following Chinese custom, descendants will cherish the memory and identity of their ancestors by regularly showing reverence and making ritual offerings to them, especially during Qing Ming, the annual Chinese holiday honoring those family members who have passed on into the other world.

The foundation of filial piety is the natural interdependence among family members defined by their biological blood ties. Even though the certitude of this natural relationship does not need to be sustained by religious belief, it does not necessarily exclude certain religious practices. In fact, ancestral worship has seeped into all aspects of family life. In Chinese culture, family has turned into an entity that embraces both the sacred and secular aspects of life. The understanding that Confucianism holds regarding the roots of the life of each individual family member is that the life of the family community to which a person belongs has infinite continuity and is connected with nature, or heaven (*tian*, 天), the cosmic and ultimate origin of all things (*wanwu*, 万物). Deceased ancestors live as deities in the same spiritual world with nature, and one may even say that the ancestral deities exist in a mysterious way with all the gods in nature or even with nature itself. Therefore, the communication with ancestral deities through rituals and services is a communication between human and deity, which serves to show descendants' respect for and gratitude to their forebears. At the same time, these practices are also a communication between human and nature through the medium of ancestral deities. In Confucianism, an individual person, his ancestors, and nature form an organic and integrated entity.

There are complex and profound physical, spiritual, and moral connections that naturally bond various family members with their ancestors and future generations. Because of the position of each person in the family genealogy, the family can deeply affect and influence his character development and the formation of his purpose in life. Each person plays multiple roles in his family, and these roles will gradually unfold and evolve as he grows and interacts with other family members throughout his life and along his journey. Although the multiple roles each person assumes are biologically predetermined, the ethical dimension of these roles is in a person's choice to take on his filial responsibilities and duties. In *The Great Learning*, Confucius thus praises King Wen: "As a son, he rested in filial piety. As a father, he rested in kindness."[7] It is only through such behaviors that the moral significance of the roles of the father and the son can be accomplished. From this perspective, one may say that family life is part of each person's life path, wherein one practices moral cultivation, fosters ethical development, and eventually achieves one's moral and ethical realization.

The concept of the human embedded in filial conduct reflects the human journey in its entirety throughout a person's life. A human life originates from the omnipresent and infinite source, *tian* (heaven or nature), and it eventually returns full circle and merges back into where it begins, *tian*. Along this journey, the concept of filial piety contextualizes the entire personal existence of a human being in the infinite continuation of the intergenerational life cycles of that family community. By doing so, the family provides a home for the person's physical being and an ethical establishment for his spiritual being. The fundamental ethical principle of filial piety is as follows: family is a living community where the lives of all its members interweave into one entity, and each family member seeks to be in harmony within this context, and maintains the peace for and with all its members. Not only does this internal harmony permeate the family within, but also, when it is properly and fully manifested in all families, this harmony extends to the entire nation, and even the whole universe. Confucius understands that under the sun, all belong to one family—a universal lineage and connection; thus, he equates filial piety with benevolence and morality in a general sense. Therefore, benevolence becomes the ethical norm of filial piety, which originates from the natural and biological bond among human beings in a family and may then be extended to all human beings and all beings in nature. In chapter 1 of the *Analects,* Master Youruo says, "Exemplary persons (*junzi* 君子) concentrate their efforts on the root, for the root having taken hold, the way (*dao* 道) will grow therefrom. As for filial and fraternal responsibility, it is, I suspect, the root of benevolence (*ren* 仁)."[8] For Confucius, filial conduct within a small family can be extended to a big family, such as a nation, or the whole universe. Thus, filial piety embodies and manifests the benevolence of caring for one another among all human beings.

From a Confucian perspective, the thought and practice of equating filial piety generally to benevolence and caring has always been in existence in Chinese culture and is a tradition with roots in the ancient times of King Yao and King Shun, prior to the Xia dynasty (twenty-first to sixteenth century BCE). The extension of the concept of filial piety beyond each family in a society promotes a universal norm of benevolence and evolves into a social filial piety of "respecting the elderly and caring for the young." As Mencius says,

> By treating the elders in one's own family as elders should be treated and extending this to the elders of other families, and by treating the young of one's own family as the young ought to be treated and extending this to the young of other people's families, the empire can be turned around on the palm of one's hand.[9]

From a practical point of view, one may say that the popularity of filial piety among traditional rural communities provides these communities with a special social value of caring and trusting relationships among their members. This is exactly what Confucius described as "neighborhoods of benevolence," exemplifying a social ambience with kindness, fairness, and a warm and harmonious interpersonal relationship within a family. It is in this context that Confucius' persistency in honoring family ties and relationship first and foremost begins to make sense in the larger relationship and connections with the community and the nation.

Governance of Filial Piety: A Utopian Ideal

Confucianism holds filial piety persistently as a utopian vision and advocates it as the primary governing principle in the family and the society. The *Book of Filial Piety* by Confucius makes it clear from the beginning that filial piety should be "the highest morality and the fundamental principle of governing states and the world." *Focusing the Familiar* contains the following statement:

> The sacrificial observances to *tian* 天 at the winter solstice in the southern suburbs of the capital and to the earth (*di* 地) at the summer solstice in the northern suburbs are ways of serving the high ancestors. Ritual observances performed in the ancestral temple are ways of making sacrifices to one's forebearers. For one who has a clear understanding of the sacrificial observances to *tian* and the earth, and the various ceremonies such as the Grand *di* sacrifice and autumnal *chang* sacrifice performed in the ancestral temple, the governing of the empire is as easy as placing something in the palm of one's hand.[10]

Even though Confucianism has the ideal of using filial piety as the governing principle, it seems that the exemplary practice of this ideal applauded by Confucianism is limited to only those ancient sage-kings such as Emperors Huang, Yao, Shun, and Yu, and Kings Wen, Wu, and Zhou, from approximately the thirtieth to tenth century BCE. Confucius and his followers are explicitly critical regarding the practices of those kings after the ancient sages and rulers mentioned previously in terms of their filial piety. In fact, the history thereafter is one in which feudal monarchs consolidated their royal power in the name of filial piety. This obvious approval of the ancient sage-kings and strong criticism of the kings thereafter are reflected in Mencius' comments: "The Way of Yao and Shun was that of filial and fraternal duty, that is all."[11] He also says, "Once Yao and Shun were no more, the Way of the sages declined, and oppressive rules arose one after another."[12] In fact, Confucians are not alone in this criticism; philosophers Laozi and Zhuangzi also voiced their strong disapproval of politicizing filial piety and using it as a ruling device.

Throughout history, the way that filial piety was practiced in the traditional rural community and the ancestral temples was very different from its practice in the imperial court. In the court, the feudal rulers exploited and distorted filial piety and used it as the excuse or justification for their autocratic and totalitarian power and as a tool to maintain their legitimacy. In contrast, among the traditional rural community, filial piety has kept its essential purity and sincerity in spite of various diluting factors. In Confucian theory, the principle of filial piety consists of two components that follow two reasoning paths, which are seemingly similar yet profoundly divergent in practice. The first is filial piety through benevolence, and the second is filial piety through loyalty. The former stresses that filial piety and responsibilities within a family are the roots of benevolence and that benevolence is an extension of filial piety, while the latter maintains that filial piety is the foundation of loyalty and that being filial is being loyal and being loyal to one's ruler is being filial at its best and highest. In order for the concept of filial piety to be applied to the relationship between a ruler and his subjects, it is necessary and essential to translate and equate such a relationship to a special bond of "a father and a son." Confucius articulated and described such transference from the family relationship to that of a ruler and subjects in his *Principles of Xiao* (*Xiaojing*): "It is only because exemplary persons (*junzi*, 君子) serve their parents with family reverence that this same feeling can be extended to their lord as loyalty (*zhong*, 忠)."[13] The classical Confucians believed that the principle of filial piety, as a utopian ideal, is a meaningful and feasible tool of governance in the world, even though they understood the difference between the logic of benevolent filial piety and that of loyal filial piety. They were also fully aware of the danger that the feudal rulers could use and distort the logic of filial piety to serve and enhance their imperial power. Therefore, Confucianism, out of idealistic aspiration, advocates that filial conduct is beneficial and amiable, and thus worth abiding by. As Mencius says, "If all people would love their parents and be respectful to their elders, the whole world would be at peace."[14]

In the political philosophy of pre-Qin Confucianism, the concept of "family" is a basic political unit and a basic model in the classical Chinese political system. Using family life experiences as the foundation, this political idea interprets each person and his or her multiple roles from the perspective of a family member: a father and a son, a husband or a wife, an older or younger brother, and so on. At the same time, following this model, each nation or state (*bang*, 邦) and the world are understood and viewed as an extended family (*jiating*, 家庭). Obviously, based on this political philosophy, a person is never an abstract, isolated, and autonomous being, nor is a nation or a state built on a legal and social contract among completely isolated or independent beings, or individuals with full rights as in Western society. We can even say that the family is the core of this political ideology because each person is defined by his roles and relationships in the family, and a nation or a state and the world are merely an extension of this family. Confucius considers filial piety demonstrated in daily life, even though commonplace, as the most significant component of politics, as illustrated by the following story in the *Analects.*

> Someone asked Confucius, "Why are you not employed in governing?" The Master replied, "The Book of Documents says: It is all in filial conduct (*xiao,* 孝)! Just being filial to your parents and befriending your brothers is carrying out the work of government. In doing this I am employed in governing. Why must I be 'employed in governing'?"[15]

As the Chinese people's basic principle for their daily life, filial piety is deeply rooted in human nature. It embodies benevolence and love, and its function is to ensure a shared destiny among family members and thus maintain indefinitely the continuity of the family lineage. The most important primary and natural practices of filial piety are caring and respecting elders as the essential human virtue. Evidence of the extreme significance of filial practices and behaviors is that the ancient dictionaries directly define filial piety according to such practices and behaviors. For instance, in *Definition and Explanation of Chinese Characters* (*Shuowen Jiezi*), it says, "Filial Piety is to treat one's parents kindly and benevolently."[16] Classical Confucianism emphasizes the social function of filial conduct mainly in the sense of caring for the elders. According to Confucianism, this includes both heartfelt respect for the parents and the elders and attentive caring for them in everyday life. Children should be considerate and sympathetic to their parents, and thus they should feel both joy and concern at the same time—joy because of the parents' good health and longevity, and concern due to their aging and needs. Confucius was quoted as saying, "Children must know the age of their father and mother. On one hand, it is a source of joy; on the other, of trepidation. . . . In serving your father and mother, remonstrate with them gently. On seeing that they do not heed your suggestions, remain respectful and do not act contrary. Although concerned, voice no resentment."[17]

In ancient China, caring for the elders is not only the social custom guided by filial ethics, but also the legal and institutional obligations of the nation. The institutionalized system for elder care is integrated with Chinese formal education, aiming to promote an ethical human relationship of respecting the old and caring for the elders. As Mencius says,

> Establish the *xiang,* the *xu,* the *xue* (学), and the *xiao* (校) so as to teach them. The *xiang* is for nourishing, the *xiao* for instruction, the *xu* is for archery, the Xia used the term *xiao;* the Yin used the term *xu;* the Zhou used the term *xiang.* All three used the term *xue.* And all were designed to clarify human relations.

> When human relations are clarified by those above, the little people will live in affection below.[18]

It is through such integrated and deliberate efforts that filial piety persistently served as the ethical, political, and practical principle of extreme importance in Chinese culture over thousands of years. It became the essential connector within family communities, micro and macro, among the various family members, their roles, and relations, and among all social beings at all levels in a village, a province, and the nation. As a result, it is also regarded as the ethical and moral yardstick that measures "the goodness" of a person, whether he be a commoner or an imperial ruler.

The Reconstruction of Filial Piety and the Traditional Rural Village Community: A Contemporary Challenge

Obviously, traditional Chinese ethics of filial piety and the lifestyle of a traditional rural community are distinctly different from the ethics and lifestyle of modern societies. The natural foundation of traditional ethics of filial piety is family, a natural, living community bonded by biological and blood ties. This is the "prototype" of the traditional Chinese feudal society. According to Confucianism, the traditional rural community, the nation or the state, and the whole world can all be understood as an extended family. Based on this understanding of family as a collective community, the Confucian interpretation of each human being differs greatly from that in a modern society, where each human being is an abstract, isolated, and autonomous individual. The starting point of Confucian ethics is a flesh-and-blood human being who has natural life experiences and biological ties. Each human being also plays a series of roles in the living community of the family and society. In addition, Chinese traditional ethics of filial piety and the traditional lifestyle in the rural community reveal a value system of mutual respect and caring, focusing on the harmony and well-being of all in the family or extended communities. Such emphasis offers social interactions and outcomes that are profoundly different from the modern concept of "financial value exchange" and "individualism."

Modern aging societies can gain various insights from the Chinese tradition of filial piety. First, the ethics of filial piety provides a counterpart and a reference for critically examining the individualistic ethics of modern societies. Second, it rekindles the hope of rejuvenating a lifestyle characterized by values such as caring and respect, thus enabling us to reconstruct mainstream values, which have been dominated and eroded by exchange values. Third, the ethics of filial piety makes it possible for us to revive the values of filial conduct and the customs and the order of the traditional rural community, which may prove to be the ultimate solution to the contemporary issue of caring for the elderly.

From a Confucian perspective, resolving the predicament faced by modern aging societies means that we need to restore our moral beliefs of honoring our ancestors, rebuild the customs and rituals of respecting the elders, reconstruct a family lifestyle based on the ethics of filial piety, and extend and expand healthy family relationships to the community. These reconstructions call for a series of reforms: first, human self-awareness needs to be transformed from individual centeredness to a collective consciousness, which, in turn, will lead to the restoration of the family ethics of filial piety and the full awakening of each family member regarding his or her relationship and connection with other members. Second, traditional customs and rituals such as village communal schools and paying respect to ancestors need to be brought back to life in the modern society. This means that the tradition will be preserved and creatively transformed according to the needs of modern times and local conditions. Third, education needs to undertake corresponding reforms, exploring, disseminating, and integrating the traditional and new values, ethical principles, moral ideas, and lifestyle.

However, in the world today, where the traditional villages are fast disappearing due to the process of urbanization, it is challenging to reconstruct a model that used to work in a primarily rural and agricultural society. While the traditional villages have given way to cities of millions of people around the globe, the new contemporary "villages" are created in the urban cities based on human needs and socialization. Some are families or villagers moving to work in the cities together. Others are a rainbow combination of former strangers and now a new *'ohana* (family) and community, supporting one another. The Chinatowns of the old and new have become a phenomenon, and they continue and expand the principles of filial piety and family ties as the migrant workers and immigrants establish themselves in new territories and countries. The grass roots of villages in the huge urban environments are critical for all levels of human connection, support, and development. They can serve as the foundations for social, emotional, ethical, and relational stability for the "villagers" as well as the entire city and the nation they reside in.

The ultimate goal of the recommended reforms is to integrate each unique person with the collective community he lives in, thus to promote the maximum potential of human nature in the context of a natural setting and with freedom and peace. While Confucius' teaching of filial piety may not offer a panacea for all the contemporary challenges and woes in a culturally diverse and philosophically pluralistic world, it does provide an alternative and insight, which beckon us to ponder and learn from the working solutions in the past to adapt and reform them for the present and the future.

NOTES

Thanks go to Norma Carlson for her assistance in proofreading the manuscript.

1. Roger T. Ames and Henry Rosemont Jr., *The Analects of Confucius: A Philosophical Translation* (New York: Ballantine Books, 1998), 167.
2. Irene Bloom, trans., *Mencius* (New York: Columbia University Press, 2009), 152.
3. Ibid., 85.
4. Ames and Rosemont, *Analects,* 77–78.
5. Roger T. Ames and David L. Hall, *Focusing the Familiar: A Translation and Philosophical Interpretation of the* Zhongyong (Honolulu: University of Hawai'i Press, 2001), 101.
6. Ames and Rosemont, *Analects,* 154.
7. James Legge, trans., *The Confucian Analects: The Great Learning and the Doctrine of the Mean* (New York: Cosimo, 2009), 362.
8. Ames and Rosemont, *Analects,* 71.
9. Bloom, *Mencius,* 9.
10. Ames and Hall, *Focusing the Familiar,* 99.
11. Bloom, *Mencius,* 133.
12. Ibid., 69.
13. Henry Rosemont Jr. and Roger T. Ames., *The Chinese Classic of Family Reverence: A Philosophical Translation of the Xiaojing* (Honolulu: University of Hawai'i Press, 2009), 113.
14. Bloom, *Mencius,* 80.
15. Ames and Rosemont, *Analects,* 80–81.
16. Xushen, *Shuowen Jiezi* (Beijing: Zhonghua Shuju, 1963), 173.
17. Ames and Rosemont, *Analects,* 93.
18. Bloom, *Mencius,* 53.

Doing Justice to Justice 8

SEEKING A MORE CAPACIOUS CONCEPTION OF JUSTICE FROM CONFUCIAN ROLE ETHICS

Roger T. Ames

Justice: A Case Study

A minimum standard of justice would seem to require that all U.S. children have equal access to U.S. educational institutions, and that any school admissions policy that would exclude a candidate on the basis of race or ethnicity is in clear violation of this principle. Such a basic standard has certainly been upheld by the judgment of the Supreme Court in lawsuits where it was contravened. But I want to argue that the Court in coming to such a decision not only might be failing to serve justice, but in fact would be compounding a grave injustice—at least in the case of Hawai‘i. I will contend that real justice needs to be served not only by the application of principle, but also by a panoramic and comprehensive survey of what are always particular situations.

It has been estimated that at the time of the first contact between Europeans and the indigenous people of Hawai‘i in 1778, the population in the islands was as great as 800,000. Princess Pauahi Bishop was the great-granddaughter of Kamehameha I, the warrior chief who united all the islands of Hawai‘i under his rule in 1810. By the time of Pauahi's birth in 1831, as a result of contagious and sexually transmitted diseases such as cholera, measles, mumps, whooping cough, smallpox, gonorrhea, and syphilis, the Hawaiian population had been reduced to 124,000, and by the time of her death in 1884, only 44,000 Hawaiians remained. The host culture of the islands at a fraction of its earlier numbers had been decimated by an invasive species—both physical and cultural—and its very survival was put at risk. Having experienced this unprecedented assault on her people in her own lifetime, Pauahi could, with a certain prescience, anticipate the ills that would continue to befall Hawaiians in the century that followed. In 1893 the Kingdom of Hawai‘i was illegally overthrown and then later formally annexed by a United States still committed to a policy of American exceptionalism and its manifest destiny. The native people over time were made increasingly desperate in their own home to the extent that today as many as 50 percent of the prison population in Hawai‘i are of Hawaiian descent.[1]

With foresight Pauahi left in her will a portion of her estate to establish the Kamehameha Schools as her vision for educating the brightest of the Hawaiian people and preserving their language and culture—a school system that in order to preserve the local culture has an admissions policy giving preference to children of Hawaiian blood.[2] Her endowment now supports what has become the largest independent prekindergarten-through-grade-twelve school system in the United States and an educational institution that at any one time serves some forty-eight hundred students throughout the state of Hawai'i.

In June 2000 a plaintiff identified as Jacob Doe filed a suit against Kamehameha Schools claiming that its admissions policy, in giving priority to students of Hawaiian ancestry, is unjust, being in violation of the constitutional rights guaranteed to the other children of the state of Hawai'i. Although Kamehameha is a private school and as such does not receive federal funding, it was still vulnerable in this suit because, without the tax-exempt status of its trust, which was put at risk in this lawsuit, it would be financially crippled.[3] The present disposition of this case still favors Kamehameha Schools, but it is a decision that has been gerrymandered and would undoubtedly be reversed if the case were ever brought to the Supreme Court again.[4]

For the courts to enforce the principle of equal access to education for all children regardless of race or ethnicity would seem consistent with its charge to uphold the principle of justice. But many of the people who live in Hawai'i—both people of Hawaiian descent as well as many of other races and ethnicities—are keenly aware of the many historical injustices that have been inflicted on the native people and, far from supporting a change in Kamehameha's preferential admissions policy for children of Hawaiian ancestry, might well credit this same policy, in part at least, for the contemporary renaissance in Hawaiian language and culture that we are presently enjoying in the islands.

Setting the Problem: Is Justice "in Principle" Actual Justice?

Justice has conventionally been understood as some antecedent moral principle that determines just conduct. It is a higher-order norm from which lower and more specific rules of behavior are derived. Justice is seen as that moral rightness or righteousness that is achieved by evaluating a situation and acting objectively and impartially by appeal to this principle. Indeed, it is the assumption that justice must function as an independent principle that has galvanized an intimate association between justice and the impartial rule of law that, in treating all human beings equally regardless of their particular histories or lived differences, serves as guarantor for the "upholding of justice." But does this assumption that justice is some kind of antecedent moral principle, either primordial or derived, that is to be applied to individuals impartially regardless of their differences really "do justice" to the complexity of the phenomenon?

There is a second understanding of justice that we might invoke as an alternative to this notion of upholding a principle of righteousness and rectitude. "To do justice" to something means to appreciate it fully and to respond to it in a way that respects its full worth. Indeed, this second, more holistic notion of justice references the complex, creative process of attempting to achieve what is optimally appropriate in the specific, usually inequitable relations and situations that locate us as always unique individuals within family and community. It is retrieving and exploring this second more robust sense of justice as an alternative to the clearer but less capacious notion of justice as principle that is the subject of this essay.

Sen's Attempt at a More Capacious *Idea of Justice*

Although John Rawls does not subscribe to either the mythology or the metaphysics of principled justice, his influential "theory of justice" with its "original position" and its "veil of ignorance" offers us an ambitious strategy for deriving a set of antecedent, fixed, objective, and impartial principles that are valid for all, independent of the personal, historical, and cultural context. And such principles can ostensibly be applied to do the same heavy lifting as the principle of justice described earlier. Amartya Sen is properly critical of many contemporary theorists of justice—his own teacher Rawls first among them—who, in presupposing that justice is to be found in the application of principle, take what Sen describes as a "transcendental" approach to the theorizing of justice. He describes such scholars as being "arrangement-focused" rather than "realization-focused." That is, these theorists are indeed theorists: they are concerned with defining institutional justice as a perfect, independent standard that can then be mechanically applied for fair adjudication without sufficient regard to the actualizing of justice in the lives of real people. At the end of the day, Sen is resistant to the universalistic, univocal, and exclusive claims that undergird such theories of justice.

Sen expresses a sincere appreciation of Rawls but at the same time makes several nuanced and sophisticated moves that are an attempt to establish a more comprehensive, pluralistic, and pragmatic understanding of justice—that is, in his language, a more capacious idea of justice. First, he introduces a distinction drawn from Indian philosophy between *nīti* (institutional justice) and *nyāya* (actual realized justice), insisting that any sufficiently robust idea of justice must include them both. He offers an "incomplete" notion of justice that abjures the need for a perfect standard before it can be applied, arguing that our starting point should be to proceed with urgency to right the obvious cases of grave injustice around the world upon which the world community can all agree.

Again, Sen worries over those "positional perspectives" and "objective illusions" that can compromise real impartiality. He appeals to Adam Smith in formulating his distinction between what he terms "closed" and "open" impartiality, underscoring the need to include the perspectives of indifferent spectators in the conversation that determines what is just as a counterbalance to entrenched tradition and custom and to vested interests. In so doing he opposes the Rawlsian contractarian approach to segregated original positions that limit the discussion to those directly involved in the decisions made.

Sen argues for the importance of discussion, dialogue, discourse, and communication as essential for the public reasoning that will produce a plurality of sustainable reasons in determining justice. He wants a permissive global perspective that allows for the "comparative questions" that emerge from different cultural values but that are at the same time exacting in being disciplined by public reason. He argues with conviction for an accommodation that allows for a plurality of defensible reasons for advocating what are ultimately incommensurable positions—as his specific example, those reasons that are marshaled to defend deontic, utilitarian, and virtue ethics.

In thinking through his strong commitment to liberty, Sen argues for capacity-based reasoning that is inclusive in allowing for differences among those conditions of particular persons that make a difference, and he further insists on including the *process* of choice as integral to comprehensive outcomes rather than simply depending on culminations. In many different ways, he is trying to formulate an idea of justice that is inclusive and accommodating. Sen eschews the means-end dichotomy in wanting to reinstate the relevance of human lives as lived (*nyaya*) for assessing how a society is doing as a complement to other economic indicators such as GNP and GDP.

But although Sen rejects what he calls "transcendental institutionalism" and argues for a more comprehensive, pluralistic, and pragmatic understanding of justice, he still shares many of the basic assumptions of the theorists whom he argues against. Most fundamentally, he wants to frame his idea (rather than ideal) of justice by appeal to the very same vocabulary that is invoked to define the liberal conception of person. For Sen as for these other theorists, individuals as the subjects of justice are to be characterized in the familiar language of individuality, equality, freedom and choice, rationality, autonomy, and objectivity or impartiality. Sen quite properly challenges a principled approach to justice on the grounds that such a mechanical application is insufficiently informed by the particular, lived circumstances of real people. But he then retains the liberal notion of the autonomous individual as an understanding of human agency that takes this generic conception of person to be the subject of justice without sufficient appreciation of personal and situational differences in the lives of real people.

Sen's Foundational Individualism

As I have observed, Sen in his critique of principled-based theories of justice appeals to the language of the Indian tradition in wanting to complement institutional thinking (*nīti*) with actual lived experience (*nyāya*). That is, Sen wants to avoid the separation and elevation of institutions from real-life experience by retaining the continuity between abstract generalities and the concrete detail of lived lives. He is seeking an idea of justice that takes as its warrant achieved equity in the lives of real people. I want to argue, however, that he vitiates his own deliberate strategy to achieve a more comprehensive model of justice when he reverts uncritically to the abstract notion of the discrete and autonomous individual as the subject of justice rather than starting from and ending with the shared lives of ordinary people as they are embedded in family and community. Said succinctly, both principles as independent objects and persons as autonomous subjects are simply the product of abstraction from lived relations. As Peter Hershock observes,

> What we take to be objects existing independently of ourselves are, in actuality, simply a function of habitual patterns of relationships. . . . This amounts to an ontological gestalt shift from taking independent and dependent actors to be first order realities and relations among them as second order, to seeing relationality as first order (or ultimate) reality and all individual actors as (conventionally) abstracted or derived from them.[5]

A. N. Whitehead calls foundational individualism a clear case of the "fallacy of simple location": that is, the familiar and yet fallacious claim that isolating, decontextualizing, and analyzing particulars is the best way to understand the content of our experience. The notion of the discrete individual that is assumed in much of liberal theorizing is a persistent example of this *deformation professionelle* and has serious consequences for Sen's attempt to formulate a coherent and practicable conception of justice.[6] Let us take just two examples of how a default individualism confounds the sought continuity between person and context in Sen's reformulation of the idea of justice.

In his discussion of rational choice theory—that is, the theory that people choose rationally if and only if they intelligently pursue their own self-interest—Sen wants to argue "that while rationality of choice can easily allow non-self-interested motivations, rationality does not on its own demand this. . . . Rationality as a characteristic of choice behaviour rules out neither the dedicated altruist, nor the reasoned seeker of personal gain."[7] For Sen, the putative "self" of both the self-abnegating altruist and the self-interested egoist is assumed to act in a way exclusive of the consequences that their conduct has for the quality of their relations with other people, and without regard for the personal growth for all concerned that emerges from cultivating such relations. But if we as persons are in fact constituted by our relations, the relationships then are primary and we as individual persons are abstractions from these relations. This being the case, we need to understand persons by virtue of their relationships with one another rather than by isolating them as individuals. And our transactional conduct either benefits both or neither of the parties in the relationship. A good teacher produces a good student, and a good student produces a good teacher; the better the student, the better the teacher. Otherwise, good persons might have a wayward child, but a good mother does not have a rotten daughter.

Of course, the irony is that if we are in fact relationally constituted persons rather than discrete selves, self-sacrificing altruists do not really benefit the object of their largesse, nor do self-interested egoists really benefit themselves.[8] Further, since Sen himself chooses to define rationality as choices based upon sustainable reasons,[9] we must ask the question: If the behavior of altruists and egoists benefits neither others nor themselves, respectively, can such conduct be considered rational according to Sen's own standard? Indeed, a scrutinizing Sen seems to doubt his ability to sustain his own reasons behind this claim when as an aside he himself questions "whether advantage-seeking, in either a direct or an indirect form, provides the only robust basis of reasonable behaviour in society." And he continues: "A related question is whether mutual benefit and reciprocity must be the foundations of all political reasonableness."[10] Although Sen does not answer this question for himself, I would contend that mutual benefit must be fundamental to all reasonableness, both personal and political (if there really is such a difference).

A second example of foundational individualism that I would argue leads Sen astray arises when he wants to interpret the Buddha's understanding of the motivation of a mother in helping her child as one to be explained by reference to power and obligation:

> The mother's reason for helping the child, in this line of thinking, is not guided by the rewards of cooperation, but precisely from her recognition that she can, asymmetrically, do things for the child that will make a huge difference to the child's life and which the child itself cannot do. The mother does not have to seek any mutual benefit—real or imagined—nor seek any "as if" contract to understand her obligation to the child. That is the point Gautama was making.[11]

Sen is certainly correct in dismissing contractarian thinking as being too gross to have any relevance for conventional family relations such as mother and child. But does any mother really think of her parenting, as Sen would suggest, in terms of power and obligation? Sen's interpretation of the words of the Buddha becomes implausible when he insinuates a liberal conception of the discrete individual and a doctrine of external relations into the mother-child relationship that effectively separates mother as benefactor and child as beneficiary.

If Sen were instead to appeal to a Buddhist relational understanding of person defined as it is in terms of *anattā*, a doctrine of "no-self" in the sense of no permanent, autonomous agency that is located in a cosmology of *pratītyasamutpāda* or dependent co-arising wherein persons are motivated by *karuṇā* and *mettā*—the desire to remove harm and suffering and to bring about well-being and happiness, respectively—the mother's reason (or perhaps better, motivation) for helping her child would be the motherly love that has mutual benefit in enriching not only the lives of both, but the lives of all. As we read in the *Sutta-Nipāta* that Sen himself is referencing:

> Just as a mother would protect her only child at the risk of her own life, even so, let him cultivate a boundless heart towards all beings. Let his thought of boundless love pervade the whole world: above, below and across without any obstruction, without any hatred, without any enmity.[12]

An important consideration here that I will return to later in the context of Confucian role ethics is the inadequacy of "reason" alone to account for or to justify the mother's conduct. A mother might well reason about *how* to help her child, but her motherly feelings would dispose her to be helpful in any case without having to find reasons for doing so.

Bernard Williams is properly concerned that moral problems be couched in concepts thick enough to apply to real features of the world so that they can be resolved objectively. Indeed, when it comes to giving reasons for justifying actions that entail intimate family members, Williams gives us the example of a person involved in a rescue situation having to choose between two people who will otherwise perish, a stranger and his wife. Williams observes that "it might have been hoped by some people (for instance, by his wife) that his motivating thought, fully spelled out, would be the thought that it was his wife, not that it was his wife and that in situations of this kind it is permissible to save one's wife."[13] Williams is suggesting that any system of morality that insists on some impersonal and impartial standard to justify a husband saving his wife is guilty of asking the husband to have "one thought too many." That is, the husband's action is really motivated and justified by appeal to the intimate, meaningful relationship he shares with this particular woman, and has nothing at all to do with the formulation of some general and reasoned principle of moral obligation.

Seeking Capaciousness from Confucian Role Ethics

In seeking to frame my conception of justice in a more pragmatic, holistic, and inclusive way, I will draw upon Confucian role ethics as an alternative to the liberal tradition. Confucian philosophy begins from a fundamentally relational and gerundive notion of unique persons that stands in stark contrast to a foundational individualism that still persists in Sen, and it culminates in insisting that any theorizing of the human experience must find its ultimate warrant empirically in the ordinary affairs of the day.

After offering my reasons for sharing the road with Sen in rejecting the transcendental principled approach to justice, I will turn to an alternative cluster of terms that might be appealed to in the canons of the Confucian tradition to shed light on an alternative conception of justice. This vocabulary used to express Confucian role ethics takes life as lived in the family as its point of entry.

Abjuring Transcendentalism

In order to formulate a truly capacious conception of justice that does justice to the phenomenon, we need both to begin and to end with the wholeness of the human experience. The abstract, principled approach to justice familiar among both classical and contemporary theorists ignores the fact that, as A. N. Whitehead contends, "we think in generalities, but we live in detail." As Sen has argued, a problem arises when we disengage our institutional strategies for realizing and sustaining order from the complexities of life itself. Such theorizing is fatally reductionist and suffers from what Whitehead has described as "the fallacy of misplaced concreteness" by equating the abstract and independent ideal with what is real while at the same time being insufficiently cognizant of the genuine connectedness of things in our ordinary experience. Justice as principle offers us a thin theory that does not have the capacity to strike the balance needed between generalities and detail. Indeed, Whitehead criticizes the classical Greek aesthetic sensibility on this same account for losing sight of the proper balance between the particular details and the harmony achieved in the totality of the effect:

> The enjoyment of Greek art is always haunted by a longing for the details to exhibit some rugged independence apart from the oppressive harmony. In the greatest examples of any form of art, a miraculous balance is achieved. The whole displays its component parts, each with its own value enhanced; and the parts lead up to a whole, which is beyond themselves, yet not destructive of themselves.[14]

The same issue arises when we turn to the high art of human flourishing. It is disclosure in the living of our unique relationships that makes this particular family and this particular community consummately meaningful. Any understanding of social harmony or justice that demands conformity to principle at the expense of a disclosing particularity does so at the cost of productive difference, and as such, is quite literally life threatening. As Whitehead observes:

> Our lives are passed in the experience of disclosure. As we lose this sense of disclosure, we are shedding that mode of functioning which is the soul. We are descending to mere conformity with the average of the past. Complete conformity means the loss of life. There remains the barren existence of inorganic nature.[15]

The thrust of what Whitehead is saying here is that a sense of social harmony achieved by optimizing relationships can emerge only out of the real, reciprocated experiences of always unique yet overlapping persons in their full connectivity. As such, the realization of justice will always be collateral rather than unilateral, correlative rather than univocal, and a matter of disclosure rather than closure. Justice is primarily concrete and local, and it is from real actualizations in the ordinary business of the day that it can be abstracted as a kind of functional ideal.

Reinstating Experience

In this essay, then, I want to try to formulate an understanding of justice that will aspire to appreciate and "do justice" to the full complexity of the human experience. To this end, I will begin from John Dewey, who, in asking after what human experience is, and what it means, introduces what he calls his postulate of immediate empiricism:

> Immediate empiricism postulates that things—anything, everything, in the ordinary or non-technical use of the term "thing"—are what they are experienced as. . . . If *any* experience, then a *determinate* experience; and this determinateness is the only, and is the adequate, principle of control, or "objectivity." . . . If you wish to find out what subjective, objective, physical, mental, cosmic, psychic, cause, substance, purpose, activity, evil, being, quality—any philosophic term, in short—means, go to experience and see what the thing is experienced *as*.[16]

We want to add "justice" to "subjectivity" and the other terms on the list of philosophical terms that Dewey insists can be adequately defined only by looking at how they are lived and what we experience them *as*.

A more recent advocate of a pragmatic approach to philosophy, Hilary Putnam, brings further clarity to this postulate of immediate empiricism not only by rejecting "view-from-nowhere" objectivism, but by further insisting that the subjective dimension of experience is integral to what the world really is. Putnam insists that:

> elements of what we call "language" or "mind" *penetrate so deeply into what we call "reality" that the very project of representing ourselves as being "mappers" of something "language-independent" is fatally compromised from the start.* Like Relativism, but in a different way, Realism is an impossible attempt to view the world from Nowhere.[17]

Putnam will not admit of any understanding of the real world that cleaves it off from its human participation and that does not accept our experience of it as what it *really* is:

> The heart of pragmatism, it seems to me—of James' and Dewey's pragmatism if not of Peirce's—was the supremacy of the agent point of view. If we find that we must take a certain point of view, use a certain "conceptual system," when engaged in a practical activity, in the widest sense of practical activity, then we must not simultaneously advance the claim that it is not really "the way things are in themselves."[18]

In arguing for the reality of experience itself, these Pragmatists see the familiar equation between knowledge and reality that has grounded classical epistemology—"reality as the self-luminous vision of the Absolute"[19]—as being a fundamental and persistent error. Simply put, experience is what it is, and it is all real.

Resourcing the Confucian Canons: Human Nature *as* Conduct

Confucian role ethics subscribes to neither the "fallacy of simple location" nor its familiar instantiations in the notion of the principle of justice and in a foundational individualism. The classical Confucian texts give us a Chinese instance of the postulate of immediate empiricism in that they appeal to a relatively straightforward account of our actual life experiences as the ultimate source of our abstracted entities. For Confucianism, the content of experience is in fact organic, relational, processual, and interdependent. In the growth of a friendship, the friendship itself is what is most concrete, and the individual friends are an abstraction from their friendship. The friends are best understood in their connectivity rather than in isolation, and they become distinctive as individuals because of the growth in this connectivity, not in spite of it. In this Confucian view, we are not individuals in the discrete sense of an Aristotelian *psyche,* but are rather interrelated persons living a multiplicity of roles that constitute who we are and that allow us to pursue a unique distinctiveness and virtuosity in our conduct. In other words, each of us is the sum of the roles we live in consonance with our fellows.

Confucian role ethics locates persons in appealing to their entire identity as it is achieved through embodied propriety (*ti,* 體) in their roles and relations (*li,* 禮) within the actual content of experience without a severe distinction between the habits of transactional agents and their aggregating conduct. *Ren* (仁) is at once persons and their conduct. As gerundive persons—that is, as erstwhile verbal nouns—we are what we do, and what we do, we do together.

Viewed critically from a Confucian perspective, we are inclined to make a miscalculation in thinking of human nature retrospectively as the potential "being" of human "beings" rather than prospectively as the evolving product of "becoming" human. From the perspective of this relational human *becoming*, then, we are committing *the* philosophical fallacy by making the product of an ongoing process antecedent to it and then ascribing to it a foundational and causal status.

In thinking of human nature, we are disposed to default to a retrospective causal or a teleological explanation rather than to provide a more holistic, prospective, contextual, and processive account of what it means to *become* human both individually and as a species. In so doing, we come to presuppose that human nature is either a given potential to be actualized or some preexisting ideal to be attained. It is believed by some scholars that notions such as free agency and moral responsibility require the isolation of individuals from their relationships by positing a definition of what it *is* to be a human being.[20] Ironically we would argue that such scholars in thus insisting upon a definition of some ready-made human *being* or some guiding teleological hand not only truncate any robust existential notion of agency or responsibility, but also, in asserting this kind of essential sameness among human beings, diminish the possibilities of productive difference.

Justice as a Relational Virtuosity

Turning from who we are to what we do: if a notion of a given human nature is problematic, so is the principle of justice conceived as an antecedent principle. In looking for guidance for our actions, we are inclined to presume, uncritically perhaps, that because we have a word, we have a "thing." As this reasoning goes, not only does "justice" have an immediate referent, but further, this referent is somehow independent of our actions and thus either has causal status as a given antecedent to what we do or has a teleological status as a predetermined goal for our actions.[21] To the extent that we think of justice as a *principle,* there is a strong sense of antecedence, of generality of application, and of derivation. Indeed, the word "principle" carries just such connotations: a basic source, an essence or determining characteristic, an original faculty or endowment, an originating or actuating or determining force, a higher-order norm from which lower and more specific rules of behavior are derived, a fixed or predetermined mode of action, an axiom of conduct.

But we can in fact argue from a Confucian perspective that, on reflection, if justice does indeed have a referent, it is primarily as a generalization derived from acting justly within our family and community relations. Rather than being fixed and retrospective, such a principle points most concretely to the unfolding of complex configurations of always-unique relations as they are informed by analogy with past experience. Justice is the deliberate and circumspect evaluation of the assignments of these students by this teacher. Putative principles are in fact a perceived virtuosity—a quality of efficacious and productive behavior attained when human transactions are informed by our best efforts at cultivation and personal growth.

When we turn to Confucian role ethics and its assumptions about living justly, it certainly offers guidelines for conduct, but more than appealing to *abstract* principles or values or virtues, it looks primarily to the contours of our concrete familial and social roles for guidance, roles that are existentially more instructive than such bald abstractions. We have real intuitive insight into the appropriate role of brother or daughter or friend from our lived experience. Role ethics offers guidance on how to behave most productively and provides an explanation for proper conduct that seeks to accommodate the inevitable complexity of human activities. In relying on what is most clearly empirical for guidance rather than appealing to abstract principles such as justice, courage, temperance, and so on, we find that there is a vital, felt sense of propriety in our concrete roles and relations that suggests to us quite specifically what we ought to do next in order to act justly.

Upholding Justice or Revering the Family

The fact that, in Confucian role ethics, relationally constituted persons and abstracted principles are understood by an appeal to concrete context can be readily demonstrated from passages in the canonical texts and by the relevance that these passages have for contemporary debates in ethics and political philosophy. Indeed, today as the Leviathan China continues to struggle on its long march to the rule of law, endemic corruption that arises from the privileging of personal relations over law has been one of its greatest challenges. It is thus not surprising that much ink has been spilled (and in our contemporary idiom, many blogs have been posted) over the last decade both within China and abroad in a debate over a passage from the *Analects* in which Confucius himself seems to privilege intimate family roles over the principle of justice:

> The Governor of She in conversation with Confucius said, "In our village there is someone called 'True Goody.' When his father took a sheep on the sly,[22] he reported him to the authorities."
>
> Confucius replied, "Those who are 'true' in my village conduct themselves differently. A father covers for his son, and a son covers for his father. And being 'true' lies in doing just this."[23]

The question here, succinctly put, has been: Do the intimate relations that are entailed in "family reverence" (*xiao*, 孝)—the ground of the Confucian vision of a moral life—lead inevitably to nepotism and cronyism and then, in turn, to political corruption? Or is the practice of *xiao* in the intimate relations of family a necessary condition for the cultivation of consummatory conduct (*ren*) and the flourishing community? Are intimate relations inimical to the principle of justice? Or is real justice to be found in the social harmony achieved through virtuosity in the intimate relations that constitute family and community?

In many ways, this example from the *Analects* returns us to the same point as the case of Kamehameha Schools cited earlier. That is, this anecdote brings into question the assumption that justice is best understood as a higher order and independent principle that can be applied through the impartial rule of law to treat all human beings equally, regardless of their particular histories or lived differences. And again we must ask: Does such an assumption really "do justice" to the complexity of the phenomenon?

I have read with interest and have gained insight from many of the recent articles proffered in response to this timely issue.[24] Liu Qingping and his supporters have mounted a well-reasoned attack on the position Confucius endorses that would seem to protect law-breaking family members from state retribution. Such an obstruction of justice would, by most anyone's definition of the term, seem to be a rather egregious form of corruption. To oversimplify somewhat, it is Liu's position that the culprit that ultimately produces corruption is *xiao*—those intimate feelings expressed as "family reverence."[25] That is, *xiao* as the privileging of personal relations over law is the source of immoral conduct.

Ably defending the Confucian tradition, on the other hand, is Guo Qiyong, along with others who claim that the proper priority given to family feeling does not necessarily lead to any untoward favoritism and hence should not be seen as leading inevitably to corruption. In the end, I, too, will offer a defense of the Confucian position. But I will do so by approaching the debate at least initially from a meta-ethical position. That is to say, I will argue that, to the extent that the classical Confucian texts are being interpreted in this debate against the background of modern Western moral theory, the debate provides neither an adequate account of the passages under scrutiny nor the vision needed for a way forward in moral thinking that they might otherwise yield. Indeed, I will attempt to show ways in which these ancient texts, taken on their own terms, offer a perspective on key moral (and political) issues that, in their departure from Western ethical theory, are worthy of our attention.

In the first instance we must be clear about what is at stake in the dispute as we see it. Within a (roughly) Confucian framework, the contributors to the debate so far seem to have structured the discussion around the question of whether it is "family reverence" (*xiao*) or "consummatory conduct" (*ren*) that should be taken as most fundamental for the Master. Liu and the critics claim that this emphasis on family is at the expense of *ren;* after all, consummatory human conduct can hardly be made to square with tolerating, or indeed abetting, illegal and immoral activity that will lead to corruption. Guo and the upholders of the

Confucian canons, on the other hand, claim not only that there is no inconsistency between the ways and the demands of *xiao* and *ren* as they are employed in the texts, but also that the priority of *xiao* is necessary for the achievement and maintenance of *ren*. That is, family feeling is a prior and necessary condition for extending and developing fellow feeling for all others in the community.

But rather than joining this debate, I would argue instead that concern about the respective priority of *xiao* and *ren* does not address the fundamental problem. In the case of "True Goody" that is referenced and analyzed here, it is clear that *xiao* is central: that is, Confucius is saying that we should protect our family members, even when they are wrongdoers. I believe that, although Guo Qiyong and the defenders of the canon are taking the argument in the right direction, they are missing a subtext to the debate on which the matter actually turns.

This subtext is discernible by noting that, for Confucius, familial loyalties trump loyalty not to *humanity* writ large (the community of people with whom one lives) as focusing on *ren* would require, but rather loyalty to the *state* (those who govern and the regulations they enforce). This is a crucial distinction. The charge of nepotism qua corruption carries little opprobrium if it is merely the favoritism I show my cousin in hiring her as the bookkeeper for my store. It only becomes an issue if my cousin is the less competent candidate for keeping the books in a district for whose financial concerns I am the responsible person appointed by the government.[26] And as far as the members of our families are concerned, and very probably our neighbors and friends as well, there are priorities in our response to problematic situations. Calling in the police is not what we would do *first,* but probably only as a last resort; initially at least we would almost surely try other, more imaginative means to remedy the difficulty.

And we must not overlook the fact that built into the Confucian position here is the imperative of making the situation right for all members of the community who are affected. What sheds light on this case, while at the same time making the situation somewhat more complex, is the internal demand in Confucian role ethics to pursue optimal appropriateness in any particular situation (*yi,* 義). To this end, "remonstrance" (*jian,* 諫)—that is, the obligation that a child has to protest against and to rectify the conduct of an erring parent—has a prominent and crucial role in the Confucian literature on family reverence (*xiao*). Such remonstrance is not an option, but a strict obligation. With this in mind, we would have to assume that the expectation of Confucius in his evaluation of this case would be that the concerned son in "covering for his father" must necessarily do his best to set the ledger right with any members of the community who had suffered loss on account of the conduct of his parent, and further, would do what is needed to return his father to the straight and narrow—that is, to optimally appropriate conduct (*yi*).

Loyalty to Family or State in the Western Narrative

It is perhaps a distinguishing characteristic of the Western philosophical narrative: *no* later thinker has answered the question of divided loyalties between family and state at all satisfactorily, and indeed, for most of the past two and a half centuries, none of our philosophers have even asked it. The reasons for this neglect are, I believe, instructive for everyone participating in the debate on the relationship between *xiao*, corruption, and *ren*.

Throughout the story of Western philosophy evolving with the discovery of the immortal soul by Pythagoras and the classical Greeks, the dominant view of human beings has tended to be that of abstract, individuated selves: autonomous, rational, free, and (usually) self-interested. Reinforced by Augustine and the perceived necessity for an individuated moral will for one to qualify as a moral agent, this view of what it is to be human has been pretty much unquestioned from the time of Locke and had become thoroughly entrenched as an unannounced presupposition by the time of Hume and Kant. Indeed, a foundational individualism is the Enlightenment model of humanity and has been a key motivating factor in those populist revolutions instigated to curb the excesses of authoritarian governments. At the same time, appeal to the institution of family as a source and model of moral order has, with few oblique exceptions (such as Aristotle, Rousseau, and Hegel), been markedly absent from the Western philosophical tradition.

If we conceive of what it means to be human in this individualistic manner, it would seem to follow that in thinking about how we ought to deal morally with our fellows, we should seek as abstract and general a viewpoint as possible. If the dignity of *everyone* is derived from the (highly valued) qualities associated with this individualism—autonomy, equality, rationality, freedom—then it is just these qualities we must respect at all times, and hence gender, age, ethnic background, religion, skin color, and so on should play no significant role in our decisions about how to interact with others.

Universalism in Ethics and the Negation of Family Considerations

With this persistent assumption of a foundational individualism, it is thus incumbent upon us to seek universal principles and values applicable to all peoples at all times. Otherwise the hope of a world at peace, devoid of group conflicts, racism, sexism, homophobia, and ethnocentrism, will never be realized. Moreover, the best way to arrive at these universal principles is to transcend our own spatiotemporal location and cultural tradition—to overcome, that is, our personal prejudices, hopes, fears, likes and dislikes—and on the basis of impersonal reason alone ascertain beliefs and principles that should be compelling to all other rational persons equally committed to transcending their specific locations, backgrounds, and biases. Our differing heritages, personalities, sexual orientations, religious beliefs, and much more that divide us are all sources of possible conflict. But normal human beings have the capacity to reason that thus unites us and consequently offers a greater hope for a less violent human future than has been the case in the past and is the case at present.

This emphasis on reason, objectivity, impartiality, and abstraction has provided a strong impetus for seeking universalism in ethics. Many people, and most Western philosophers, have been influenced by this perspective, and not unreasonably so; it is complete with a vision of peace, freedom, and equality. From this position, the rare challenges to it heard within the corridors of the Western academy seem either hopelessly relativistic or authoritarian, or both.

The two dominant universalistic ethical theories, grounded in the concept of the foundational individual we have just outlined, reflect this orientation: deontological ethics, emphasizing our moral duties, and utilitarianism, attending to the consequences of what we do in the moral sphere. While the participants in the current *xiao* debate are no doubt familiar with these theories, I want to rehearse them briefly in order to make sure that they are not what are at issue in the discussion, and also to make clear how I would contextualize them in the tradition of moral philosophy.

The deontological theory is associated with Immanuel Kant, whose fundamental moral principle, the Categorical Imperative, is roughly "Always act on a maxim you could will to become a universal law." Kant sought to establish a certain, universally valid basis for human moral behavior that could withstand relativistic and skeptical challenges. That is, he believed he had structured the logic of moral arguments such that they would reveal our unconditional moral obligations without reference to historical experience, inclination, or personal values. The substance of our autonomy, for Kant, is thus an inner rational faculty uncorrupted by external circumstances, enabling us to develop and then exercise a pure moral will in compliance with such imperatives. Autonomy thus defined is devoid of our particularities as unique individuals living in a specific time, place, and culture and is grounded only in the principle of noncontradiction.[27]

Utilitarianism was developed by Jeremy Bentham and John Stuart Mill three-quarters of a century after Kant, and its most fundamental principle is to act so as to maximize the utility or happiness of the greatest number of people (with the minimal disutility and unhappiness for the rest). For Kant, logic reigns, the primary focus being on compliance and consistency more than on consequences; for Bentham and Mill the situation is more nearly—but not quite—reversed, since inductive probabilities instead of deductive certainties must weigh heavily in a moral agent's calculations about the consequences of his or her actions in accordance with the principle of utility. For Bentham and Mill, calculating benefits or happiness is the proper employment of reason as applied in our moral deliberations. Like Kant's Categorical Imperative, however, the principle of utility is universal, being based on reason alone, and is applicable to any and all moral situations wherein each individual counts for one, and no one counts for more than one. It is only by ignoring individual particularities—again, time, place, and culture—that utilitarians believe true justice and equality can be achieved.[28]

Both of these universalistic ethical theories have had, and continue to have, numerous champions in philosophy, theology, and political theory, and they have had, and continue to have, a great deal of influence in other circles as well. In general, the influence of Kant can be seen fairly clearly in the courts of the United States, where consistency and precedent are prized, even if at times the consequences of the decision are untoward (witness famous cases such as *Dred Scott* or *Miranda*). Legislators, on the other hand, typically look to consequences when enacting laws and find no problem in repealing a law when the consequences of the law appear to become adverse (for example, the repeal of prohibition and the draft).

If my summaries of these positions and issues have merit, we can begin to see not only why questions of family versus state loyalties cannot be answered by these prominent Western moral theories but also why they cannot even be asked. Indeed, *no* moral questions concerning the family can even be framed for examination because, by definition, family members are not abstract, autonomous individuals, parts of the public, but are flesh and blood, highly specific, young and old, male and female fellow human beings related to ourselves in highly private and intimate ways. Thus, all moral questions pertaining to family matters have been swept under the conceptual rug of a "private" realm that involves personal matters of taste, orientation, and religious belief—a realm wherein moral and political philosophy do not properly enter.

Only by divesting persons of any uniquely individuating characteristics can we begin to think of developing a theory of moral principles that will hold in all instances. With respect to family, this is precisely what we cannot do if we are even to attempt to formulate in a coherent way the relevant moral questions about loyalties and obligations, for as soon as we use the expression "my mother" in a moral question, we are not dealing with an abstract, autonomous individual, but one who carried us, brought us into this world, nurtured and comforted us, and has given of herself extraordinarily for our benefit.

Just as Kant, Bentham, and Mill endeavor to be universalistic, Confucianism is paradigmatically and resolutely particularistic. Thus, to search for a universalistic moral principle of some sort in the Confucian writings is to try to square the circle. To seek a principled ground for moral judgments in the classical Chinese texts is, to my mind, like expecting a Kantian to take specific cultural differences into account as conditions that qualify his Categorical Imperative when in fact the Categorical Imperative is the very test for a principle as an unconditional universal law. Stated succinctly, we cannot appeal to Western moral theory to adjudicate the decidedly Confucian problem of family loyalty versus loyalty to the state.[29]

Invoking Confucian Role Ethics

Against this meta-ethical background, I should like now to advance some arguments that suggest that the *Analects* offers insights into our manifold moral and political predicaments that Kant, Bentham, and Mill (and John Rawls, for that matter) cannot provide. If this be true, then an understanding of the Confucian persuasion is important not only for the Chinese world today, but for everyone.

In order to make these arguments, we will have to understand the passages from the Confucian canons that focus this debate from within their own interpretive context. I will argue that, taken on their own terms, such classical Confucian texts appeal to a relatively straightforward account of our actual life experience rather than abstract principle, and in so doing provide a justification for reinstating the intimacy of family feeling as the concrete ground of an always emergent moral order. I will argue further that there is a real difference between Western ethical theories that are directed at best at enabling people to think and talk more coherently about ethics, and a Confucian vision of a moral life that seeks to inspire people to be better persons. I refer to this Confucian vision as a *role ethics*. But I do not intend to advance role ethics as an alternative moral *theory* so much as a vision of human flourishing, one that integrates the social, political, economic, aesthetic, moral, *and religious* dimensions of our lives.[30] In this view, we are not individuals in the discrete sense, but rather are interrelated persons living—not "playing"—a multiplicity of roles that constitute who we are and allow us to pursue a unique distinctiveness and virtuosity in our conduct. Relationships are primary, and discrete persons are an abstraction from them.

The central message of the seminal texts of classical Confucianism, the *Four Books*, is that while familial, social, political, aesthetic, and cosmic (religious) cultivation is ultimately coterminous and mutually entailing, still it must always begin from the Confucian project of personal cultivation. We become morally competent not by divesting ourselves of our particular roles and relationships in order to apprehend those universal principles that provide moral justification but, on the contrary, by cultivating these same unique roles that constitute each of us into "meaningful" relations as the ultimate source of moral meaning. Each person is a unique window on family, community, polity, and so on, and through a process of personal articulation and growth, he or she is able with resolve to bring the resolution of his or her relationships into clearer and more meaningful focus. That is, the production of meaning is both radial, beginning from one's own roles and relations, and collateral in always resourcing and having consequences for the contextualizing others. Cultivating one's own person grows and adds meaning to the cosmos, and, in turn, this meaningful cosmos provides a fertile context for the project of one's personal cultivation.

Another way of putting this point is to say that personal cultivation is what we should see as the basic spiritual discipline in Confucianism, coming to a deepening and broadening sense of *belonging,* a strong feeling of being a part of something larger and more enduring than ourselves, a feeling that begins in and with the family (*xiao*) and, with increasing effort, can culminate in a sense of close affinity with all fellow human beings, dead and alive, as well as with the cosmos. But the family must clearly be the basis of this discipline.[31]

Such personal cultivation is prerequisite not only for one's own personal life and family, however, but also for the development of a better world. This is the fundamental message of the *Great Learning.* This shortest of texts asserts unambiguously that it is only by committing oneself to a regimen of personal cultivation that one can achieve the quality of intellectual and moral understanding necessary to change oneself and the world for the better. In this singularly important respect, we must get our priorities right. And the priority is that the cultivated person is constituted first and foremost by intimate family relations. Far from being in competition with the state, family is the root of effective governance and, as such, must be properly tended to in order to sustain a healthy political canopy. This continuity between family and state is clear in the concluding paragraph of the *Great Learning.*

> From the emperor down to the common folk, everything is rooted in personal cultivation. There can be no healthy branches when the root is rotten, and it would never do for priorities to be reversed between what should be invested with importance and what should be treated more lightly. This is called both the root and the height of wisdom.[32]

It is significant that the text appeals to the metaphor of "root," where the assumption is that, although healthy growth in the root and a luxurious canopy are coterminous and mutually entailing, the horticultural process begins with tending to and securing what is incipient. With these same priorities in mind, Confucius insists that moral order starts here and goes there: "I study what is near at hand and aspire to what is lofty,"[33] and again he is adamant that becoming consummate as a person must be self-originating.[34] It is this local nature of the source of consummate conduct that makes any moral guidelines not *principles,* but *generalizations* made from particular situations. In the *Analects,* Youzi claims that becoming *ren* begins at home. That is, the ground of our consummate humanity is family feeling.

> Exemplary persons (*junzi* 君子) concentrate their efforts on the root, for the root having taken hold, the way will grow therefrom. As for family reverence (*xiao*) and fraternal responsibility (*ti* 弟), it is, I suspect, the root of becoming consummate in one's conduct (*ren*).[35]

Since family feeling is the ground of Confucian role ethics, and since polity in this tradition is a direct extension of the family—literally "country-family" (*guojia,* 國家)—Confucius can further claim that being a responsible and productive member of one's family is tantamount to governing the country.

> Someone asked Confucius, "Why are you not employed in governing?" The Master replied, "*The Book of Documents* says: 'It is all in family reverence! Just being reverent to your parents and a friend to your brothers is carrying out the work of government.' In doing this I am employed in governing. Why must I be 'employed in governing'?"[36]

This passage can be easily misunderstood as minimalist—each one of us in our families makes our own small contribution to the greater political order. Confucius' point, however, is quite the opposite. Most of our political lives are lived out close to home. If we ask after the relative importance of the state and the family in effecting cosmic harmony, we must allow that family is the ultimate ground and locus of political order, and without it, political order is a sham. It is for this reason that any formal pretense to democracy independent of the flourishing community is hollow. And taken one step further, any discussion of a flourishing community without reference to a robust family life is again an empty abstraction.[37]

Returning to the Case of "True Goody"

To take the example of "True Goody" cited earlier: the Confucian question is not a legal one: "Is it just for a son to cover for a father who has committed a crime?" It is rather a matter of priorities: what the *Great Learning* describes metaphorically as setting the roots as a precondition for a luxurious canopy. Indeed, the focus in this passage is not on the father as a discrete, autonomous individual perpetrating a crime against the state, but rather on how the mutually constitutive father-son relationship can be "trued" when strained by circumstances. How should one behave to best recover and sustain the quantum of equilibrium, focus, and harmony within the existing configuration of roles and relations that constitute this family and this community and, by extension, this state? The assumption here would be that endorsing a litigious course of action on the part of a son as the appropriate way to act in such cases not only would be anathema to the ultimate interests of familial and communal harmony, but ultimately would be detrimental to the prospects of a prosperous state.

The Confucian tradition is preemptive in trying to establish a social fabric that would reduce the possibility of crime rather than being preoccupied with adjudicating hard cases after the fact. We might be better off trying to create a community that does not give rise to spousal abuse rather than struggling to find a fail-safe procedure for retribution after the victim has been injured or worse—all the more so since the preponderance of evidence shows that the threat of retribution is not an effective deterrent against criminal activity.

In *Analects* 1.13 we read, "Making good on one's word (*xin* 信) gets one close to being optimally appropriate (*yi* 義) because then what one says will bear repeating." When we ask after the source of moral meaning, the answer might lie in exhorting the community to embrace uprightness as a way of life rather than in a post hoc auditing procedure for weeding out corruption. In the Confucian tradition, it is the fabric woven of strong family bonds rather than inviolate laws that enables the community to thrive. In fact, appeal to law is perceived broadly as a dehumanizing (although unfortunately sometimes necessary) last resort. In this Confucian world, invoking the law is a clear admission of communal failure.

In setting priorities, then, the initial response in Confucian role ethics is to appeal to the moral resources within our family and community to reestablish a communal harmony that has been diminished by sometimes thoughtless conduct. The challenge is how to draw upon these resources most imaginatively to make the best of the situation and to restore its moral prosperity. Family reverence (*xiao*), far from being the source of corruption, is our best hope in avoiding it by serving as the ground for consummate human conduct and is the best hope for a social and political order much more humane than those in which we currently live.

In the Confucian tradition, real freedom is concrete: it is the opportunity to realize oneself fully within the roles and relations that constitute one, first, in the family, and then, by extension, within the world more broadly construed. Freedom is maximizing personal growth as it is determined by full participation in and enjoyment of one's family and community relations. The main theme of the *Zhongyong,* the most inspirational of the *Four Books,* which we have translated as *Focusing the Familiar,* is a celebration of this creative participation in world making.

Of course there are trade-offs in surrendering the individual autonomy that undergirds much of Western ethical and religious thinking. This way of thinking about the human experience brings with it much that we hold in high regard: a quality of individual freedom and independence, equality, privacy, rights and entitlements, personal integrity, and indeed the sacredness of human life are for most of us good things. However, it must be seen that when we give these qualities pride of place in prioritizing our values, we do so at an important cost. Individualism can bring with it a diminished sense of shame and responsibility and a reduced appreciation of our interdependence. Each of us has a moral obligation to respect the civil and political rights of all others. Governments have often been remiss, and worse, in granting such respect, but for persons, it is very easy, for we can fully respect those rights simply by ignoring the others. You surely have the right to speak, for example, but not to have us listen. Indeed, individualism in its extremes can precipitate feelings of alienation, depression, and selfishness, and a continuing tendency to "blame the victim" when confronted with gross social injustice, despite the absurdity of the denial of community responsibility. Too much freedom becomes license, too much independence becomes loneliness, too much autonomy becomes moral autism, and too much sacralizing of the human being comes at the cost of massive species extinction.

My overall argument here is simple. A careful consideration of Confucian role ethics prompts us to ask after the benefits that come with an increased awareness of the centrality of family feeling. What do we get in exchange—ethically, socially, politically, and religiously—for what we have to give up when we surrender in degree our emotive attachment to personal autonomy and all that it entails? And is the trade-off worth it?

NOTES

1. The 2000 U.S. census has only about 22.3 percent of the prison population as being of Hawaiian descent, but the calculation of this figure is much contested.

2. Although the will does not explicitly state the contested admissions policy, at least Pauahi's husband believed that this was the spirit of the document. See the Founders' Day speech by Pauahi's widower, Charles Reed Bishop, in *Handicraft* 1, no. 1 (January 1889). "Bernice Pauahi Bishop . . . intended to establish institutions which should be of lasting benefit to her country. . . . The founder of these schools was a true Hawaiian. She knew the advantages of education and well directed industry. . . . Her heart was heavy, when she saw the rapid diminution of the Hawaiian people going on decade after decade and felt it was largely the result of ignorance. . . . The hope that there would come a turning point, when, through enlightenment, the adoption of regular habits and Christian ways of living, the natives would not only hold their numbers, but would increase again. . . . And so, in order that her own people might have the opportunity for fitting themselves for such competition, and be able to hold their own in a manly and friendly way, without asking any favors which they were not likely to receive, these schools were provided for, in which Hawaiians have the preference, and which she hoped would value and take the advantages of as fully as possible."

3. I am grateful to our late colleague Jon Van Dyke for the following information. Regarding the challenge to the admissions policies of the Kamehameha Schools (*Doe v. Kamehameha Schools*), after the Ninth Circuit's en banc 8–7 decision finding the Kamehameha's admissions policies to be constitutional, Doe filed for certiorari from the U.S. Supreme Court. The Court, for several weeks, did not seem able to make a decision whether to grant the petition and kept putting it off to the future. During that delay, the parties reached a settlement whereby the schools paid an amount (reputed to be about $7 million) to Doe to settle the case, after which the petition for certiorari was withdrawn and

no further decision was issued. The result is that the Ninth Circuit's 8–7 ruling is the law of the case. The press reported that Doe's attorneys engaged in disputes about how the money was to be divided.

4. Eric Grant, a Sacramento attorney and the lead counsel for the plaintiff, Jacob Doe, has written a hypothetical Supreme Court opinion entitled "*Doe v. Kamehameha Schools:* The Undiscovered Opinion," published in the *University of Hawai'i Law Review* 30 (Summer 2008), 355, that makes a compelling case for judgment against Kamehameha Schools were this case ever to be heard.

5. Peter Hershock, *Buddhism in the Public Sphere: Reorienting Global Interdependence* (New York: Routledge, 2006), 140, 147.

6. Whitehead observes: "This presupposition of individual independence is what I have elsewhere called, the 'fallacy of simple location.'" A. N. Whitehead, *Process and Reality* (New York: Macmillan, 1929, 208; corrected ed., New York, Free Press, 1978, 137). Charles Hartshorne elaborates: "As Whitehead has most clearly seen—individuals generally are not simply outside each other (the fallacy of 'simple location') but in each other, and God's inclusion of all things is merely the extreme or super-case of the social relativity or mutual immanence of individuals." *A History of Philosophical Systems* (New York: Philosophical Library, 1950), 443.

7. Amartya Sen, *The Idea of Justice* (Cambridge, MA: Harvard University Press, 2009), 194–195.

8. In a footnote, Sen seems to be aware of this problem when he observes, "Paul would have to take note, among other considerations, of the fact that a no-nonsense pursuit of self-love may adversely affect his relations with others, which could be a loss even for self-interested reasons." *Idea of Justice*, 195.

9. Ibid., 180–181.

10. Ibid., 205.

11. Ibid., 205–206.

12. *The Sutta-Nipāta,* trans. H. Saddhatissa (London: Curzon Press, 1985), 16.

13. Bernard Williams, *Moral Luck* (Cambridge: Cambridge University Press, 1981), 18.

14. A. N. Whitehead, *Modes of Thought* (New York: Macmillan, 1938), 62.

15. Ibid.

16. John Dewey, *The Essential Dewey,* ed. Larry Hickman and Thomas Alexander (Bloomington: Indiana University Press, 1998), 1:115, 117, 118; emphasis in original.

17. Hilary Putnam, *Realism with a Human Face* (Cambridge, MA: Harvard University Press, 1990), 28; emphasis in original.

18. Hilary Putnam, *The Many Faces of Realism* (La Salle, IL: Open Court, 1987), 83.

19. Dewey, *Essential Dewey,* 117.

20. This seems to be a major concern for May Sim in her reading of Confucius. See May Sim, *Remastering Morals with Aristotle and Confucius* (Cambridge: Cambridge University Press, 2007), 13: "The Confucian self . . . is so relationalistic that it is difficult to see how it could function as a source of agency or locus of responsibility as Confucian ethics demands."

21. For example, in her seminal essay that has underwritten much more recent work in Aristotelian naturalism, "Modern Moral Philosophy," Elizabeth Anscombe suggests that "just as *man* has so many teeth . . . so perhaps the species *man,* regarded not just biologically, but from the point of view of the activity of thought and choice in regard to the various departments of life . . . 'has' such-and-such virtues." In *The Collected Philosophical Papers of G.E.M. Anscombe,* vol. 3, *Ethics, Religion and Politics* (Minneapolis: University of Minnesota Press, 1981), 38.

22. This passage goes to the centrality of both family reverence and moral imagination in Confucian role ethics. On Zhu Xi's reading, the father is in dire straits—*rang* (攘) means "to steal when in difficult straits"—and thus purloins the sheep out of abject need. But on

such a reading, the putative "crime" of the father evaporates, and the son is just rotten. Perhaps Confucius has a more serious situation in mind: indeed, a hard case.

23. *Analects* 13.18. See interesting and amusing developments of this anecdote in *Hanfeizi* (韓非子) 49.9.2 (*Hanfeizi suoyin,* 韓非子索引 [Beijing: Zhonghua shuju, 1982]); *Lüshichunqiu* (呂氏春秋) (Xu Weiyu, 許維遹 [Beijing: Wenxue guji kanxingshe, 1955]), 449; and *Huainanzi* (淮南子) 13/125/14 (*Huainanzi zhuzisuoyin,* 淮南子逐字索引 [Hong Kong: Commercial Press, 1992]). Here and throughout this essay all translations from the *Analects* are based on Roger T. Ames and Henry Rosemont Jr., trans., *The Analects of Confucius: A Philosophical Translation* (New York: Random House/Ballantine Books, 1998).

24. Articles by Liu Qingping (劉清平) and Guo Qiyong (郭齊勇) have been published in *Dao: A Journal of Comparative Philosophy* 6, no. 1 (March 2007). Additional articles by them and others in the debate, in English translation, can be found in a special issue of *Contemporary Chinese Thought* 39, no. 1 (Fall 2007) on "Filial Piety: The Root of Morality or the Source of Corruption?" with an introduction by guest editor Huang Yong. Guo Qiyong has published a summary collection of articles in *Rujia lunlixue zhengmingji: yiqinqin huyin weizhongxin* (儒家倫理爭鳴集：以親親互隱為中心) [Debates on Confucian ethics: The mutual concealment among family members] (Wuhan: Wuhan Education Press, 2004). There is a collection of the articles in this debate at www.confucius2000.com.

25. *Xiao* (孝) has conventionally been rendered "filial piety" in English, but we translate it as "family reverence," or "family feeling," to avoid the close Christian associations with the word "piety" today. For details of our semantic and philosophical analysis of this term, see Henry Rosemont Jr. and Roger T. Ames, trans., introduction to *The Chinese Classic of Family Reverence: A Philosophical Translation of the* Xiaojing 孝經 (Honolulu: University of Hawai'i Press, 2009).

26. It might be argued that Liu Qingping and his pro-*ren* colleagues would claim that the alternative to the family is the community (other persons) rather than the state. The two—the community and the state—may indeed be distinguished. But the moral issue in the passages under discussion remains one between the family and the government representing the community rather than the community of persons itself, whether that community be local, state, or national. What else is the state besides the impersonal enforcer of community norms? What else could it be?

27. The locus classicus for Kant's views here is *The Groundwork for the Metaphysics of Morals,* various editions.

28. The locus classicus is Mill's *Utilitarianism,* various editions.

29. As we will note later in the chapter, it is of course possible to derive generalizations from the Confucian canon, but these are a long way from claims about universal "principles," because the latter can be refuted by a single counterexample. Generalizations, however, are defeated not by a counterexample—or even several of them—but rather by incorporating the counterexample to make a better generalization; we should not be thinking of English "all" so much as "many," or "most." Some might wish to claim that the "negative golden rule" found in *Analects* 5.12, 12.2, and 15.24 is paradigmatically a universal principle. I believe it is more correctly and incisively seen as a rough generalization about an attitude one should have for determining what is most appropriate in one's relations with others that does not presume to know from the beginning what is right for everyone. We cultivate a sense of deference (*shu,* 恕) initially in our family relations and then extend this sensibility with imagination to those who are much different from us as our lives unfold. Indeed, far from being an argument *for* universalism in ethics, *shu* as deference is a compelling argument *against* it.

30. Many if not most contemporary comparative philosophers, especially in the English-speaking world, are now portraying Confucianism as a "virtue ethics," more or less on the model of Aristotle and his contemporary champions. My own view is that Confucianism no more fits a Western "virtue" model of ethics than a deontological or

consequentialist one and, indeed, that it is not a "moral theory" in the Western sense. For discussion of this point, and for an extended argument on how Confucian role ethics differs from a classical Aristotelian model of virtue ethics, see the Rosemont and Ames translation and commentary on the *Xiaojing* cited earlier.

31. Whether speaking cosmologically (the cosmos), or religiously (a sense of felt worth and belonging), I want to make it clear that I am referencing *this* world, the world in which our family ties are bound, the only world there is in classical Confucianism. There is no transcendental realm in the Judaic-Christian sense of something on which our world is utterly and wholly dependent, but which is in no way dependent on us. For the cosmological side, see David L. Hall and Roger T. Ames, *Thinking through Confucius* (Albany: State University of New York Press, 1987). For the religious implications, see Henry Rosemont Jr., *Rationality and Religious Experience* (La Salle, IL: Open Court Publishing, 2001); and Roger T. Ames, chap. 5, "Human-Centered Religiousness," in *Confucian Role Ethics: A Vocabulary* (Hong Kong: Chinese University Press; Honolulu: University of Hawai'i Press, 2011).

32. Zhu Xi (1969) 2b, Zhu Xi (朱熹), *Sishujizhu* (四書集註) [Collected commentaries on the four books] (Taipei: Yiwen yinshuguan, 1969).

33. *Analects* 14.35.

34. *Analects* 12.1.

35. *Analects* 1.2.

36. *Analects* 2.21.

37. There is a similar point to be made with respect to the attitude expressed in the *Analects* toward religiousness. Confucius, in being asked by Zilu about how we best serve the spirits and gods and about what happens after we pass from this life, returns the discussion to our life in this world and our service to other human beings (11.12). Indeed, when he is asked by Fan Chi about wisdom, he replies, "To devote yourself to what is most appropriate for the people, and to show respect for the ghosts and spirits while keeping them at a distance can be called wisdom" (6.22). Some interpreters read this focus on this life and this world as reflecting a kind of secular humanism, while I would suggest that Confucius sees our immediate relationships as the ultimate source of a human-centered religiousness.

PART II

DYNAMISM AND CONTEXTUALITY

Moral Equivalents 9

Kathleen M. Higgins

In his essay "The Moral Equivalent of War" (1910), William James observes that despite its obvious destructiveness, war has long had its defenders, who stress the important role that wartime military service has traditionally served in developing discipline, toughness, and character in young men. Although himself motivated by the desire for a peaceful world, James concedes that "militarism is the great preserver of our ideals of hardihood, and human life with no use for hardihood would be contemptible."[1] Given the harms that come from war, he argues that we need a "moral equivalent" of war, a nonviolent alternative to cultivating the desirable character traits associated with army discipline. His proposal is that young men be drafted to a national service that would work as "an army enlisted against *Nature*."

> To coal and iron mines, to freight trains, to fishing fleets in December, to dishwashing, clothes-washing, and window-washing, to road-building and tunnel-making, to foundries and stoke-holes, and to the frames of sky-scrapers, would our gilded youths be drafted off, according to their choice, to get the childishness knocked out of them, and to come back into society with healthier sympathies and soberer ideas. They would have paid their blood-tax, done their own part in the immemorial human warfare against nature.[2]

By "nature" James seems to mean whatever conditions would prevail without human endeavors to improve things.

The idea of a moral equivalence between wartime military service and conscripted labor for peaceful projects is startling. The moral character of the two is exactly what seems *unequal,* and if they were truly equivalent, James would hardly claim, as he does, that his idea is utopian. He uses the term "moral equivalents" in reference to the beneficial effects on character produced by military service and by his proposed alternative. The shock value of James' concept is reduced if we recognize the limited nature of the equivalence he has in mind. We might diminish it further by stressing the "moral" in moral equivalent. Given that war is of dubious morality at least much of the time, the national service

James recommends would be relatively *moral,* though equivalent in accomplishing the desired building of character.

Yet the notion of equivalence in James' formula is what makes the idea topical in the context of discussing value and values. "Equivalence" suggests the arena of market exchange and deal making. James is calling for a reevaluation of our institutions in terms of costs and benefits. His essay implicitly raises a number of questions: How much are specific institutions that yield benefits really worth? How might we achieve morally desirable goals without paying the cost of our current arrangements, particularly when it is excessive? How can we as a society make better deals for ourselves?

This last question points to what is at stake in James' proposal: although offering an alleged moral equivalent, he is really aiming at a trade-up. If we abandon war, which many see as valuable despite its toll, we can opt for something that has similar advantages but greater net value. Insofar as James refers to equivalence but actually seeks a trade-up, his reasoning resembles the logic of capitalism. The trader's aim in a capitalist economy is to exchange what is supposedly equal (e.g., money and a product of purportedly comparable value) in such a way that the capitalist procures a good deal, ideally a better deal than that secured by the trading partner. The logic of capitalist exchange requires each party involved in a transaction to seek the best deal.

James makes a good case for thinking that required national service would be a better deal than war. My purpose in drawing attention to his essay is not to argue for his specific utopian plan, however. I want to propose that we use the idea of moral equivalents to consider how we might change our ways of operating so as to confront some of our practical problems. Like James, we might analyze our current problematic strategies to achieve desirable outcomes and to contemplate alternative mechanisms that would generate these results less harmfully.

I will suggest two contemporary tendencies that have harmful impacts for which we might seek moral equivalents. In keeping with James' idea, I will label them provocatively. I will be discussing the moral equivalent of sacrifice for the common good and (at the other end of the spectrum) the moral equivalent of conspicuous consumption. The point here, as in James' essay, is to acknowledge realities about our psychology that have the potential to result in calamities but that might be channeled in ways that lead to more advantageous results. I will focus on psychological orientations that result in damage to the environment. My discussion will indicate some of the emotional obstacles to dealing with this problem.

The Moral Equivalent of Sacrifice for the Common Good

One common ploy in campaigns to save the planet is to encourage self-denial. Reducing our carbon footprints seems a desirable aim, and one that can be monitored. I hardly want to argue against the goal of lessening our damaging impact on the environment. But I will be arguing that promoting self-denial is an ineffective means for furthering that end. Instead, we should seek a moral equivalent of sacrifice for the common good.

Of course, to call for such a moral equivalent is an overly polemical way of putting my point. There are situations in which sacrifice for the common good is virtuous and even obligatory. In order to address our environmental problems, however, we need to win the hearts and minds of the body politic, and we fail in this aim if we rely on calls for large-scale asceticism. What we need instead is a campaign to market environmentalism.

That environmentalists were attempting to promote their aims by encouraging asceticism was brought home to me over a decade ago when I took a visiting friend to a store and she bought a board game for her children. The box for the game advertised it as "environment friendly," and so it appeared to be. Except for a small bit of plastic on the spinner, the other parts of the game were made entirely of corrugated, undyed cardboard. The problem with the game was that its appeal seemed to be entirely based on a prospective buyer's concern to be a good environmental citizen. The game did not seem particularly entertaining or clever, and no aesthetic appeals seemed to compensate for the unalleviated brown of the presentation. A child who had already developed a sense of environmental citizenship might feel noble in choosing to play a game like this one. But I am certain that most children who had the choice between this game and one that was more colorful, possibly featuring favorite cartoon or movie characters, would not opt for the environment-friendly choice.

This game may be an atypical example. Over the past decade, environmentally friendly wares have become much more inviting. It is now possible, for example, to buy glossy and colorful wrapping paper made from recycled paper (though one might still question whether the inks and dyes involved cause harmful environmental effects). What interests me about the cardboard game is not its typicality in the current context, but the mind-set that it expresses. This mind-set is that enough right-minded people will seek out less attractive but more earth-friendly options, and this will make a significant impact on the problem of environmental degradation. No doubt there are people who will forgo greater sensory pleasure in order to be good environmental citizens in their buying habits. Yuriko Saito has observed that a special "green aesthetic" promoting qualities contrary to popular taste has a certain following. The difficulty, she rightly contends, is that such a specialized aesthetic will appeal only to a self-selecting few and will not draw others into more environmental consciousness.[3]

One basis for resistance to adopting more ecologically conscientious behavior is the fear that this choice would lead to a dreary future. Surely this is a more likely scenario if we don't develop sustainable lifestyles than if we do, but the fear that taking environmentalism seriously would result in a world of corrugated cardboard games encourages the "eat, drink, and be merry" attitude that is so common in the United States. In this context, environmentalism will become part of the general cultural fabric only if people are convinced that good environmental choices do not require the adoption of an ascetic lifestyle.

Let me reiterate that I do think that sacrifice for the common good is sometimes warranted. In the short run, appeals to sacrifice for the sake of societal survival can inspire heroic efforts. Winston Churchill, though offering only "blood, sweat, and tears," was able to rally his countrymen by appealing to their sense of patriotic obligation at a time of crisis: "Let us therefore brace ourselves to our duties, and so bear ourselves, that if the British Empire and its Commonwealth last for a thousand years, men will still say, This was their finest hour." Churchill's constituents heeded his request, demonstrating that at least in some circumstances populations are willing to rise to the occasion.

However, in order to rise to the occasion, there needs to be an occasion. People will sometimes do surprisingly admirable things when the situation calls for it, but the situation needs to be sufficiently circumscribed that they can see it as an occasion. In the case of our current environmental situation, however, we face problems without clear temporal boundaries. Proposed solutions, too, lack specificity. The effects of environmental action will become evident only gradually, and then only if efforts are sustained. The critical moment—the point at which environmental degradation is irreversible, as is sometimes prognosticated about climate change—is not identifiable in advance except as an outcome of theoretical constructions. This is why Al Gore uses so many charts and theoretical explanations in *An Inconvenient Truth*. When there is no evident end in sight, as is the case with the vague and growing environmental crisis, it is hard to see how people will be motivated to sacrifice. This is the first problem I see with calling for a spirit of sacrifice—as a long-term solution, it is unmotivating.

A second problem is that, if adopted as a long-term tendency, this ascetic orientation is typically debilitating. This is, I think, one of the chief problems with Peter Singer's 1979 argument that the affluent should devote all their resources to combating absolute poverty beyond what is required to satisfy their own needs of comparable moral significance.[4] Certainly there are other problems with Singer's proposal beyond its impact on motivation. If actualized on a wide scale, such a plan would have extreme consequences for the economy, undercutting businesses that deal in products that are not of comparable moral worth to those of reducing poverty (resulting, one would expect, in job loss and, thus, in greater need). Any trade or product that simply made life more commodious would seemingly fail to be morally legitimate, by Singer's standards. Moreover, nothing in his proposal would resolve the current challenge of ensuring that all charitable donations actually reached those who are supposed to be their beneficiaries, although Singer's response is to turn this problem back on donors, insisting that they have the responsibility to make sure that their money reaches the poor.

The problematic feature of Singer's case that I want to emphasize here is the leveling aim of his entire argument. According to his argument, if my standard of living exceeds what would be subsistence for the absolutely poor, I have no right to this excess. I fulfill my moral obligation only if I give all of my wealth beyond subsistence to combat world poverty. The goal of Singer's proposal seems to be the achievement of equal subsistence for all. But this ideal is not motivating, particularly for the people to whom it is directed. It does not inspire people who are not deeply poor to work hard to redistribute the wealth to the point that they are on the verge of deep poverty. Instead, it encourages them to feel guilty for whatever they have beyond the bare minimum. It treats any motivation to work that stems from desire for some material good as a pursuit of ill-gotten gain. At the very least, the working member of an affluent society would likely be demoralized should he or she adopt Singer's worldview. By Singer's standards, a very generous person would justly feel a moral failure for yielding to even minor consumerist desires.

The self-vilification that would result from endorsing Singer's picture would further damage motivation. As Nietzsche argues, asceticism and self-vilification go hand in hand, and both are spiritually impoverishing. They wear down the potential for eros-driven generosity, for they reduce one's energies. I think the same is true of Singer's 1979 proposal. Calling for extreme self-denial, it fails to tap into the most reliable sources of munificence toward the poor: what Nietzsche would call overflowing eros and a confident sense that one has sufficient resources to be generous.

The psychology of Singer's early approach does not work. I suspect that he has concluded this himself, since he is now urging members of affluent societies (assuming they are not themselves deeply impoverished) to give 20 percent of their income to the poor. This latter approach is much more likely to be effective than his previous one. The current approach allows for striving to achieve benefits for oneself while also resulting in benefits for the poor of the world.

Advocates of environmentalism would do well to shift their appeals in a similar direction. Encouraging people to recognize the value of nonmarket goods and to shift their sense of priorities accordingly is appropriate and warranted, but the idea that they should lower what they commonly perceive to be their hard-won standard of living is dispiriting. Whatever appeal is made to encourage more environmentally responsible citizenship will be effective only if it is consistent with people's notions of thriving. When it is a self-motivated choice, self-denial can yield a sense of self-control and self-mastery; but when it is called for as a long-term political agenda, it is disempowering.[5]

None of this should be construed as an argument against coercion in the form of laws to protect the environment. Laws are necessary to confront two further emotional bases for resistance to adopting more environmentally conscious lifestyles: economic worries (coupled with the impression that environmentalism is expensive) and the sense that one's efforts will have no impact because not enough people are taking similar steps. Laws should intervene to make environmentalism more affordable (by offering rebates for greater energy efficiency, for example) and by requiring all corporations doing business in the United States to adhere to certain standards regarding environmental impact (to minimize the free-rider problem at the corporate level). Businesses will not voluntarily spend the money to make their operations less environmentally harmful if this puts their competitors at a financial advantage. Laws requiring companies to reduce environmental damage caused by their operations or their products are virtually essential for getting positive environmental results.

As far as individual citizens are concerned, I think laws can also be used effectively to incentivize participation in eco-friendly efforts. This would minimize fears that one's measures have no impact because others are not taking similar steps. Using laws to incentivize is likely to be more effective than coercive measures. No matter how much the public supports the aims in view, coercion inevitably inspires resistance. This insight led Confucius to argue that ritual, which encouraged voluntary civic participation, was more effective than coercive law.

> The Master said, Govern the people by regulations, keep order among them by chastisements, and they will flee from you, and lose all self-respect. Govern them by moral force, keep order among them by ritual and they will keep their self-respect and come to you of their own accord.[6]

This point is apt for our environmental situation. When catalytic converters were required in new cars, many U.S. citizens sabotaged these devices in order to get better gas mileage. I would defend the law that mandates catalytic converters as standard equipment, but the resistance of many car buyers indicates the continued relevance of Confucius' point. Ideally, policy should incentivize voluntary adoption of ecologically sound practices. For this to happen on a broad scale, such choices need to be attractive, both aesthetically and economically. This being so, certain incentive-oriented laws can encourage the sense that one's efforts are not nullified by others' less environmentally helpful choices. The plastic bag tax in Ireland, begun in March 2002, is a good example of such a successful legal intervention. Shoppers are charged approximately fifteen cents for each plastic bag they get from stores. CNN reported that, before this new tax was in effect, Irish stores were distributing about 1.2 billion plastic bags each year. Five months later, the stores involved had cut this number by 90 percent. The money raised by the new tax—3.5 million euros (then $3.4 million) after the first five months—is directed into environmental programs.[7]

The effectiveness of this strategy depends on consumers' interpreting the decision to go without plastic bags as a "smart shopper" option. Even the financially well off usually want to think their purchasing choices are intelligent.

Particular cases should be analyzed carefully, however, to avoid strategies that backfire. I suspect that the plastic bag tax has had better results by being associated with smart consumerism than it would have had if the emphasis had been on forgoing convenience for the greater good. In cases where a desired environmentally sensitive behavior might have various spins attached, advertising—marketing of a direct sort—has an important role to play. In any case, the Irish approach to resolving the plastic bag problem is an instance of the incentivizing approach that serves as a moral equivalent of self-sacrifice for the common good. A common good has been achieved while people feel they are making intelligent choices for their own benefit.

The Moral Equivalent of Conspicuous Consumption

One of the tendencies of American behavior that has been criticized as contributing to our environmental problems is our high level of consumption, particularly of nonrenewable resources and nonbiodegradable products that end up in landfills. Presumably lessened consumption would be a constructive step toward combating our environmental problems. But if Thorstein Veblen is right, our consumption habits express deep-seated psychological needs. According to Veblen, conspicuous consumption is a strategy adopted from a desire to assert one's social status. "The basis on which good repute in any highly organized industrial community ultimately rests is pecuniary strength; and the means of showing pecuniary strength, and so of gaining or retaining a good name, are leisure and a conspicuous consumption of goods."[8] Possessions and wealth are markers of being esteemed in one's community, and "in order to be reputable it must be wasteful."[9] Obviously, this ideal of being wasteful is at odds with the orientation environmentalists want to encourage. If Veblen is right, however, a deep-seated desire for social recognition and esteem is operating at cross-purposes with ecological responsibility.

We need not look far to find conspicuous consumption run amok in American society. Dental grillz—the gold-plated and diamond-studded teeth popularized by some hip-hop musicians—would certainly be an instance of this. But so would extremely large houses of the sort that have become popular in the United States and that contributed to the boom and bust of the housing market in the first decade of the twenty-first century. Terms such as "rampant consumerism," "shopaholic," and "credit card addiction," the existence of an organization called Debtors Anonymous, and a pervasive advertising agenda that promotes the ideology "You are what you own" all testify to efforts to conspicuously consume on a grand (if pathetic) scale.[10]

Many accounts might be given to explain the self-sabotaging motives of the shopping addict. Veblen's account provides one explanation, and it coheres with the "You are what you own" mentality that advertisers promote. If conspicuous consumption is rooted in a desire to assert one's high status and respectability, perhaps we can find moral equivalents that would achieve these things without the environmental degradation that results from the agenda of consuming resources for the sake of displaying wastefulness. To do this we need not shun the desire for status in itself. While perhaps not redolent of the highest form of spiritual consciousness, this motive can and does inspire many admirable undertakings along with more questionable ventures. The desire for individual advancement is often cited as essential to the capitalist spirit, and capitalist motivations have been associated with virtues, much as military service was characterized by James' promilitary interlocutors. Adam Smith argued that commercial ventures, though motivated by self-interest, encourage people to concern themselves with one another's needs and wants. Voltaire and Schumpeter both argued that capitalistic enterprises promote a greater sense of tolerance (since it is in one's own interest to develop good relations with very different sorts of people as a way of widening one's base of trading partners), as well as encouraging a sense of self-reliance. Schumpeter also argued that capitalism has encouraged people's belief that society can change and improve.[11] Whether or not one agrees with these thinkers' sanguine views of the capitalist system and the desire for upward mobility, the system encourages aspiration, willingness to defer gratification, and conscientious effort—desirable character traits.

Accordingly, I am not arguing against the desire for social status as such in proposing a moral equivalent of conspicuous consumption. I am inclined to agree with Veblen that our motivations to seek recognition from one another and to demonstrate our respectability are deep-seated. I am not targeting the "conspicuous" part of conspicuous consumption when I suggest that we seek a moral equivalent for it. Instead, it is the wasteful *consumption* that I think we would do well to replace.

We need to explore possibilities for establishing an association between status and environmental citizenship. One possibility is that the moral equivalent of conspicuous consumption can be achieved by conspicuous choices of environmentally sound options. Unfortunately, many environmentally sensitive goods and services are beyond the means of much of the population. But the high cost of green choices could be exploited on behalf of environmentalism, even while efforts are made to drive down the costs of many eco-friendly options. Members of the social elite opting for environmentally conscious designs in their homes and cars, for example, can do much to popularize environmentally benign choices.

Saito has rightly suggested that it is important that those with social status adopt environmentalism as a value.[12] A key problem in winning hearts over to the environmentalist program is the pervasive tendency to associate waste with social status and wealth. To counter this tendency, we need prominent citizens to model lifestyles of waste-free elegance. How will such individuals be persuaded? Here is a case in which ingenious design could make a tremendous difference. Inroads are apparently already being made in this direction. The Tesla electric roadster is one example. Green luxury homes are also becoming more common and more widely publicized than only a short while ago, and awards for green design can help to make them even more visible. As Tara Loader Wilkinson, writing in the *Wall Street Journal,* reports,

> The luxury carbon-neutral home concept . . . has been labeled "a conscience salve," "greenwashing" and "a complete misnomer" by critics. Despite that skepticism, developers are hoping to turn a seemingly contradictory phrase into a 21st-century success story, laying plans for prime deluxe carbon-neutral property all over Europe. New homes in the U.K., Portugal, Italy, Morocco and Switzerland are being marketed to wealthy individuals around the world, with developers reporting strong demand.[13]

Japanese history furnishes an example of a new aesthetic becoming widely accepted because of its adoption by the social elite. Saito, in her work on Japanese aesthetics, points out that in the sixteenth century Japanese tea huts underwent a change of style with the upper class leading the way. By contrast with the often lavish structures that had previously been in vogue, an aesthetics of insufficiency came to dominate among members of the upper class, who often spent vast amounts of money on tea huts that exhibited *wabi* (modesty). Saito observes that statesman Ii Naosuke (1815–1860) wrote an essay applauding the social value of the tea ceremony in such settings for encouraging satisfaction with one's lot.[14] Whether less affluent people actually did feel greater satisfaction as a result of the popular adoption of this aesthetic, the fact is that shunning lavish displays of wealth did become a status symbol. This example illustrates a change of the relation of social status to conspicuous consumption of the sort that I am suggesting.

I might be inclined to consider my proposal as utopian as James apparently did his, except for the fact that some exceedingly wealthy individuals seem to be pursuing something along the same lines. What I have in mind is the Giving Pledge initiated by Warren Buffett and Bill Gates. Buffett and Gates urged other billionaires to follow their lead by committing themselves to giving the majority of their wealth to philanthropy. The Giving Pledge is a means by which these well-off individuals conspicuously demonstrate their status in a way that abstains from consuming (i.e., using up resources).[15] Philanthropy in general involves many arrangements that enhance donors' status. Large donors are given prominence, with their names installed on buildings, scholarship funds, colleges, and the like. Smaller contributors, too, often achieve some visibility in this way, sometimes with their names on bricks that are used in building projects to which they have donated, but often at least with their names on lists of donors and "sustainers." Such displays of wealth and resultant gains in prestige are acknowledged by economic theorists as being among the private benefits that accrue to charitable donors, and empirical evidence supports these as important factors that motivate giving.[16]

The Giving Pledge, however, sets a new bar for displaying high status. If people have a tendency (fortunate or unfortunate) to look up to those with wealth, the wealthy are in a position to model and popularize responsible choices while maintaining their social prestige. The Giving Pledge suggests that many are, in fact, willing to do exactly that. Although I am concerned about the danger of a new plutocracy practically displacing democracy in the United States, I am happy to acknowledge the de facto aristocrats in our society as admirable to the extent that they recognize the tradition of noblesse oblige.

The Giving Pledge represents an instance of the moral equivalent of conspicuous consumption. To make the Giving Pledge is a gesture that attracts notice and might inspire envy. The pledge is an equivalent to conspicuous consumption in being a badge of extremely high status, displaying the message "I have resources to burn." Indeed, Peter Singer has suggested that making donations to charity quite publicly can have the desirable effect of motivating others to give and help to shift social norms so that giving a significant part of one's income to charity comes to be considered de rigueur.[17] The Giving Pledge amounts to a mark of combined moral and financial aristocracy that foregoes wasteful consumption (of more than half of the wealth of those pledging) in favor of making an impact. Surely it is a trade-up on traditional conspicuous consumption and thus a moral equivalent of the sort James describes.

The Moral Equivalent of Capitalism?

Like many of James' ideas, his notion of the moral equivalent of war is akin to one of Friedrich Nietzsche's themes, the revaluation of values. Nietzsche contended that we should reconsider values that we have taken for granted and the institutions that are constructed upon them, with the ultimate aim of recalibrating our values to achieve better outcomes. This idea is often construed as being aimed at a single historical revaluation, and Nietzsche's texts offer grounds for this interpretation. The values he was most interested in revaluing were the moral values that he associated with Christianity, and this focus predominates in his work. The idea of revaluing values, however, can productively and justifiably be read as an ongoing project of trading up toward better, more functional values.[18] In this respect, James' idea of seeking a moral equivalent for war is a revaluation of the sort that Nietzsche promoted, even though the latter was himself one of the advocates of martial virtue to whom James is responding.

I have already suggested that the idea of seeking moral equivalents follows a logic that is evident in capitalism itself. The idea is to seek more efficient ways of achieving certain ends with fewer negative side effects. If Nietzsche is right that our basic values should be subjected to reassessment, this would seem to apply to our economic values as well our moral ones. If that is the case, we should consider reassessing the values enshrined in capitalism as we now practice it.

The history of capitalism has demonstrated that our institutions—even those termed "capitalistic"—are capable of evolution. In the last century, we witnessed the growth of more welfare-oriented capitalistic arrangements, on the one hand, and gargantuan multinational ventures that resist political controls, on the other. Both developments suggest evolution in accordance with revaluations of economic values. But this evolution is not necessarily consistent in its direction. This opens the possibility of proposing various moral equivalents of a particular form of capitalism that may have better consequences while preserving its benefits.

Contemporary visions of capitalism vary, and some are atavistic. Significantly, most have defenders on moral grounds. Even defenders of the cutthroat type of capitalism epitomized by Gordon Gecko, the antagonist in Oliver Stone's film *Wall Street,* appeal to the "goodness" of their version of capitalism. "Greed is good," says Gecko, because it motivates in a way that results in efficiency and prosperity.[19] Gecko's argument is not the final word, however. Efficiency and prosperity are good goals, but most of us would hope for a moral equivalent to his kind of capitalism in which these goods are achieved without the economic damage to others that Gecko routinely inflicts.

Another moral equivalent might be offered as an alternative to the overheated economy model that is endemic to contemporary capitalism. Modern economics operates on the assumption that economy is not a zero-sum game, overthrowing a conception that held sway for millennia before that. This seems to be a morally beneficial idea, in keeping with Socrates' notion that self-interest is best served when one is part of a flourishing community in which the interests of others as well as one's own are well served. However, we need to ask ourselves whether we haven't taken this idea to absurd conclusions when we imagine that economic growth can escalate indefinitely. We should also ask what "growth" even amounts to. Are we measuring the right things if our growth as people, able to enjoy our lives and our interactions, is precluded by our frenetic pursuit of growth by our economic measures—or if our growth in this sense is shrinking the potential to sustain our species on the planet? This is the question that Bhutan's King Jigme Singye Wangchuck raises with his proposal that gross national happiness take precedence over gross national product. He is, in effect, calling for a moral equivalent to capitalism as most people conceive of it at present.

James' notion of moral equivalents is consistent with holding that it is apposite to have maintained the name "capitalism" through capitalism's vicissitudes.

After all, he proposed as an alternative to actual war a "war against nature." At the same time, James' idea draws our attention to the desirability of rearranging our institutions with the logic of trading up in mind. If we discover that capitalism is not serving our needs with respect to the environment or other aspects of our lives, James' notion offers us a tool for asking whether we should seek a replacement for capitalism, at least in its current form. By trading up, in line with James' idea, we would be enacting a moral equivalent of capitalism even while moving beyond our present sense of it. Like capitalism itself, James' notion encourages us to always be on the lookout for ways that we can make a better deal. And as Nietzsche reminds us, asking ourselves how we might do that is the most important question we can ask ourselves about value and values.

NOTES

1. William James, "The Moral Equivalent of War," in *The Writings of William James,* ed. John J. McDermott (New York: Random House, 1967), 664.

2. Ibid., 669.

3. Yuriko Saito makes this claim in "The Role of Aesthetics in Ecological Design" (paper presented at the national meeting of the American Society for Aesthetics, Coral Gables, Florida, October 31, 2002). See also Daniel Harris, *Cute, Quaint, Hungry and Romantic: The Aesthetics of Consumerism* (Cambridge, MA: Da Capo Press, 2001), 181–184.

4. See Peter Singer, *Practical Ethics* (Cambridge: Cambridge University Press, 1979), 157–181.

5. For a more detailed analysis of our environmental crisis and the failure of efforts that advocate self-denial, see Ted Nordhaus and Michael Shellenberger, *Break Through: From the Death of Environmentalism to the Politics of Possibility* (Boston: Houghton Mifflin, 2007).

6. *The Analects of Confucius,* trans. Burton Watson (New York: Random House, 1989), 2:3, 88.

7. See Elisabeth Rosenthal, "By 'Bagging It,' Ireland Rids Itself of a Plastic Nuisance," *New York Times,* January 31, 2008, http://www.nytimes.com/2008/01/31/world/europe/31iht-bags.4.9650382.html?pagewanted=1. Rosenthal reports that, within a few weeks of the plastic bag tax, the use of plastic bags in Ireland had dropped by 94 percent and that the use of plastic bags is no longer considered socially acceptable. One might imagine that in the United States, as phobic as the population is about the word "tax," such a strategy would have to be differently described to be effective. The word "surcharge" would probably work as well.

8. Thorstein Veblen, *The Theory of the Leisure Class: An Economic Study of Institutions* (New York: Macmillan, 1902), 84.

9. Ibid., 96.

10. For a discussion of advertising's "You are what you own" ideology, see John Waide, "The Making of Self and World in Advertising," *Journal of Business Ethics* 6 (1987), 73–79.

11. For a discussion of these and other theorists' assessments of the virtues and vices of capitalism, see Jerry Z. Muller, *The Mind and the Market: Capitalism in Western Thought* (New York: Random House, 2002).

12. Saito, "Role of Aesthetics in Ecological Design."

13. Tara Loader Wilkinson, "The Green, Green Luxury of Home," *Wall Street Journal,* January 7, 2011, http://online.wsj.com/article/SB10001424052748704278404576037910799329784.html.

14. Yuriko Saito, "The Japanese Aesthetics of Imperfection and Insufficiency," *Journal of Aesthetics and Art Criticism* 55, no. 4 (1997), 380–381. See also Yuriko Saito, "Japanese Aesthetics: Historical Overview," in *Encyclopedia of Aesthetics,* ed. Michael Kelly (New York: Oxford University Press, 1998), 2:549–550.

15. Other initiatives, too, enable participants to achieve distinction by means of exemplary philanthropy, including the 50% League, which one joins by giving 50 percent of one's income or assets to charity. See Peter Singer, "Look Who's Being Generous!" *Guardian,* June 22, 2008, http://www.theguardian.com/money/2008/jun/22/charitablegiving. Not all who are part of the 50% League are wealthy, but surmounting its high bar establishes one's membership in an elite group, elite in this case for one's extreme commitment to generosity. Interestingly, the less wealthy members may be more noteworthy for giving to an extent that impacts their lifestyles, while the wealthier members are more conspicuous by virtue of the size of their donations.

16. See Lise Vesterlund, "Why Do People Give?" in *The Nonprofit Sector: A Research Handbook,* ed. Walter W. Powell and Richard Steinberg, 2nd ed. (New Haven, CT: Yale University Press, 2006), 573. See also ibid., 578, where Vesterlund points out that a charitable organization's public announcement of who has donated previously and the amount of their contributions results in greater contributions. This suggests that public display may figure in the motivations of those who give to charity, at least to the extent that it may affect how much they give. Vesterlund contends, however, that the impact on the size of donations is due in even greater degree to the tendency of subsequent donors to follow the example of those donors whose significant contributions in some previous round of giving have been publicly announced. She does not think that prestige is the only motive in subsequent giving by others, but claims that a large donation by an initial donor is also an indication that the charity itself is high quality, which can motivate prospective donors to contribute to it. She notes, however, that "there is ample anecdotal evidence . . . that actual donors are influenced by concerns for status" (580).

17. See Singer, "Look Who's Being Generous!"

18. Nietzsche sometimes refers to the revaluation of *all* values. See, for example, Friedrich Nietzsche, *Ecce Homo,* trans. Walter Kaufmann (together with *On the Genealogy of Morals,* trans. Walter Kaufmann and R. J. Hollingdale) (New York: Random House, 1967), 4.1, 326. See also Friedrich Nietzsche, *The Gay Science,* trans. Walter Kaufmann (New York: Random House, 1974), §269, 219.

19. Oliver Stone and Stanley Weiser, *Wall Street* (screenplay), produced in the film of the same name, directed by Oliver Stone (Los Angeles: Twentieth Century Fox, 1987).

A Critique of Economic Reason 10

Between Tradition and Postcoloniality

Purushottama Bilimoria

It is my intention in this essay to problematize the relationship between economics and ethics. The route I will take is an unconventional one—though not so unconventional if we consider Amartya Sen's original position on capabilities and his radical revision of the Rawlsian theory of justice. Sen's thinking is informed by his deep-rooted awareness of alternative possibilities within the heterogeneous—especially given his own argumentative Indian mind—Asian/Indian traditions. My case will be argued through a critique of *models*—those that have worked and those that have not, or are on the road to extinction; inevitably, the analytical discussion of economic models that economists are so enamored of in their works will be interspersed with narratives of case studies I present, much in the spirit of narrative ethics, to which economists such as Sen, Dasgupta, and Bardhan make frequent recourse in their own studies, especially of non-Western scenarios. Bland theorizing risks being empty without such exemplifications.

I begin here with the ancient *Arthaśāstra* corpus,[1] with some reference to Buddhist governance practices (notably, those of Aśoka) and an economic system balanced against the imperatives of welfare and just and fair treatment of citizens in all aspects of their lives, needs, and entitlements. I will also be alluding to some contemporary works, notably those of Daya Krishna on the *Puruśārthas,* Arvind Sharma's *The Hindu Scriptural Value System and India's Economic Development,* Amartya Sen's, of course, and Pranab Bardhan and Partha Dasgupta's on rethinking how "wealth" and "well-being" are measured, as well as some Indian constitutional directives on economic rights. I will be looking for resourcefulness of *thinking* about economics in consonance with the Kantian kingdom of ends of moral and spiritual enlightenment rather than purely in the terms of that mainstay of modernity, instrumental reason. The latter, it may be argued, turns into economic rationalism, the unrestricted market economy that involves foreign investment strategies, global free trade, trade-offs between supply and demand, control over export/import, tariff barriers and protectionism, payment of national debts and (defaulting on) excessive borrowing, profit-driven enterprise and entrepreneurship, strategies of power over capital, the unsavory pressures of corporatism, even globalism and universalization of avarice, all of which manifest as commodity fetishism (or commodification) and a consumer *mentalité*, what Dasgupta calls in an underdetermined way the "tyranny of free-market."[2]

India's recent reemergence into the global economy—and even before that the success in both economic and technological terms of the 3-million-strong Indian diaspora—has caused the global pundits to sit up and look afresh at the rhetoric about India's long history of poverty and inability to rise to the economic standards of the West (read "capitalist economy") as Karl Marx and Max Weber indeed lamented. Hitherto, as Milton Singer observed, agreement was much easier to obtain "on the negative thesis that India's traditional ideals and values—asceticism, fatalism, the cyclical view of time, the low value put on manual labor, the village-centered caste society, and so on—are major obstacles to economic development, than on the positive cultural conditions for such development."[3] It was in consonance with this widely held thesis that James Mills and John Mills sought to help alleviate the precivilizational ailment and rampant feudalism afflicting the Indian populace by prescribing Benthamite utilitarianism via the machinations of the colonial East India Company. Modern India initiated the nonalignment movement veering toward the Soviet model, which did not help to mitigate this adverse imaginary. Into the 1980s, India's financial performance remained in the doldrums,[4] a condition largely ignored by its galaxy of brilliant economists, who instead helped beef up the economic think tanks of the West. Liberalization policies of the 1990s helped lift the steel curtain, as it were, and things began to change on the Indian economic front, or rather the *attitudinal* landscape shifted (because people, not economists, change the world). No lesser players in this shift have been the well-educated business and skilled labor migrants who, though scattered in the diaspora, have retained strong links with Mother India under the Indian government's fervently promoted scheme known as Pravasi Bharatiya (citizens of Indian origin abroad) incentives, or more colloquially "NRIs (non-resident Indians) bring it all back home."[5]

Little attention, however, is paid to the extent to which "the cultural imaginings of India's spiritual values"[6] are linked to this renascence. By "India's spiritual" I do not mean only Hindu; rather, I use this term inclusively to underscore equally Jain, Buddhist, Parsi, Christian, Muslim, Sikh, Gandhian, and quasi-secularist forays that have contributed to, if you will, the "gross economic wisdom"—GEW—of the subcontinent (comparable to the Bhutan government's index of GNH, gross national happiness). The recently deceased guru Sri Sathya Sai Baba, a towering, though controversial by modern standards, figure, drew on the immense wealth of the Indian diaspora, members of the business and middle classes within India and Sri Lanka, and international philanthropists to fund an array of good works, among them all-free, super-specialty hospitals, clinics, and hospices; water-harvesting-cum-rural-distribution plants; and schools and colleges. Sai Baba's organizations have helped build and operate such social service facilities in poverty-stricken regions to the tune of an estimated $9 billion, supplemented with a lot of volunteer labor and donated time. In India alone there are some thirteen thousand institutes thus supported, and the Indian model is emulated with human values curricula across 136 countries. The head monk of the Sera Jhe (Tibetan Buddhist) monastery in Bylakuppe near Mysore, the Venerable Gyumed Khensur Rinpoche Lobsang Jampa, in a eulogy, compared Sai Baba's enterprising work to that of Emperor Aśoka's state-managed, almost Fabian-style welfare system.[7] What this demonstrates perhaps is the implementation of the *bhakti,* or devotional-style caring-for-the-other ethos, with the utilization of trust, trusteeship, and dedication. Trust is an undervalued moral good that grows with use and conversely decays with disuse or abuse.[8] This approach to welfare and well-being harks back to the organic model of society prevalent in traditional India, with its emphasis on trust, compassion, hospitality, and sensitivity to the distress of others, along with a host of personal and social virtues. Gandhi raised this ideal to a practicable-institutional level and called it *sarvodaya.* And this heuristically serves as the analogue to the Heideggerean principle of *Sorge* writ large. In this model, the virtue of thrift is active in place of and as a corrective to instrumentalist reason, or "self-confirming rational beliefs," as Dasgupta puts it,[9] or rationalization in the Weberian sense, as the basis of the normative universality of Western modernity, that is, the differentiation of different spheres of life, the rise of capitalism, liberal democracy, and the nation-state.[10] Keeping in mind the Weberian thesis of the Protestant ethic for progressive development and the stagnation caused by the traditional structures of caste and otherworldliness of Hindu society, Milton Singer once again offers a valuable insight. In looking for new spiritual incentives to help modernize India's economy,[11] he commented—in contradistinction to a purely materialistic and instrumental rationale for economic development—"In their indigenous 'materialism,' as well as in their philosophy of renunciation, interpreted by Gandhi as a discipline of action in the service of others, and in their quest for spiritual salvation under the guidance of gurus who have already achieved self-realization, may reside the psychological and moral motive forces needed for a democratic and nonviolent industrial development of India."[12]

Singer notwithstanding, for a long while it was believed that Indian religions were a temperamental hindrance to economic growth, fostering a kind of "Indo-lence," to coin a term. This attitude harkened back to the well-worn Orientalist-Indologists' prejudice of their times that Hinduistic otherworldliness resulted in an "emptying," not unlike the Confucian "distancing," of consciousness.[13] Weber proposed that the spiritual and cultural values of a people determined their economic ideology. (Of course, the converse could be the case as well, as we know from the global impact of latter-day secular capitalism.) For Weber the best propellant for economic growth was Protestant-work-ethic laissez-faire capitalism.[14] It could be argued, however, that the real "Indolence" that hamstrung India was due to any one or a combination of other factors: the colonial intervention, the Moghul interlude, the collapse of the Navadvipa-Nalanda and Mithila philosophical-ethical-juridical schools,[15] or the stridently persistent caste system with its inequities. Overall, this medieval aberration accounted for what Bimal K. Matilal called India's "Dark Period."[16] Speculation regarding causation aside, India came to be perceived, as Gandhi acknowledged, as a nation of weak-kneed, lazy, effeminate self-forgetters. This is certainly not how Aristotle and his commodore Alexander the Great beheld the giant rival to their Macedonian imperial designs.

The current, rather clichéd "elephantine," "gargantuan" Indian rate of economic growth belies some of that prejudice as well as real-term indolence. The changes, however, as I remarked just previously, have a broader compass and ramification. Consider what brought about the huge shift in the Gupta period (320–550 CE) that spontaneously propelled a new religious ideology that almost overturned the Brāhmaṇic hegemony. Greg Bailey and Ian Mabbett have argued that rapid urbanization and state formation destabilized society such that the middle (merchant and agricultural) classes sought to reconcile the Brāhmaṇic quasi-materialistic pressures with the inwardly unsustainable deeper sense of "lack," the ascetic otherworldly calling of Jain and *śrāmaṇic* (yoga-steeped) monks: both held out their temptations. There emerged not just a Buddha but a new hermeneutic of dharma—the principle that names the universal law, and the normative ethics that sustains social order that no longer required meticulous observation of sacrifices and rituals and dedication of offerings to the gods or their earthly patrons, the Brahmins. What emerged, rather, was a code of moral conduct and a business-mercantile ethic that straddled the two tempting and tempestuous world possibilities. The economy of the late Gupta period thrived in ways it never had before. By the time of Emperor Aśoka, a Gupta warrior king turned benevolent sovereign, the spiritual edge of the dharma teachings had been eclipsed by the end game of the hugely urbanized economy. Aśoka set about rectifying the situation by reinjecting spiritual vision into the larger structural reorganization of society, paying keen attention to the welfare and well-being of every citizen. The reason that Buddhism found greater success for its egalitarian economic template outside India than within was probably the same reason Gandhi had expressed the hope that his teachings of nonviolence, *swadeshi* (self-reliance), and *satyāgraha* (truth-force) would find speedier realization and application outside than within the caste and priestly hierarchized society that India had become.

But consider the Jains, who hail from the non-Brāhmaṇic forest-dwelling ascetic (*śrāmaṇic*) tradition and from whom Gandhi drew various of his insights. As Banias (business clans), Jains were the most successful commercial conglomerate in the subcontinent until the arrival of the Persian-Parsis and European traders, who were initially dependent on the goodwill of the Jains and with whom they had to liaise and compete. While the Jains lost their commercial preeminence in the subcontinent, they have remained successful in other British colonies where they followed Indian indentured laborers and have been no less successful in the diaspora. After the missionaries left the subcontinent, Jains built and ran large numbers of subsidized hospitals and colleges all across India. Such altruism surely stems not from an ascetic disposition but from engagement with the community as fellow sufferers and seekers. The Sikhs have not been far behind in this regard. In the 1980s they spearheaded the green revolution with an intensely socially engaged reform initiative platform. This initiative lasted until Indira Gandhi, desirous of a larger federal share of the Panjabi success story, intruded in Sikh affairs. The resultant havoc, which cost Gandhi her life, delayed nationwide economic reform toward which the country's best economic advisers were subtly guiding the Nehru dynasty.

Coincidentally, the Nehruvian license-privileged socialism was being eroded by a liberal economic ethos. Then came the collapse of the Soviet Union and the rise of the Chinese model, with its huge market-based/bilateral trading relations with just about every nation of the globe, the largest concentration being with the United States. "*Chalo chalo Amrika!*" (Let us, let us take off for America!) became the refrain. One could almost hear in the ensuing lines of this Bollywood song a subtext declaring: "The Japanese conquered the West with their quaint camera; after TM and yoga, and Deepak Chopra, we will conquer Amerika first and then other nations with our I-Techi-suave software, outsourcing, 7–Elevens, Dinky Donuts, exported CEOs; we'll 'buy 'em up' giant steel mills, pharmaceutical industries, Jaguar car plants, HMOs, and eventually the big banks as well; Citibank is already on the local corruption list." No mistaking, this is the new Indian entrepreneurship. But it threatens to end up being the same old game of "dollars, dollars, and more karma-cola dollars," chasing the lures of economic dominance across the globe. Even as India's global outreach brings its economic growth rate to close to 9.3 percent (in 2010, though pegging at 7 to 8 percent in early 2012, and with declining rupee value against the dollar and euro, to a meager 4.8 percent by August 2013, further downgraded by the IMF to 3.7 percent come 2014), billions of dollars lie fallow because of the lack of adequate infrastructure for the money's proper redistribution and utilization for microsocial programs and empowerment for the disadvantaged. Much of the funding directed toward those ends vanishes, mostly diverted into the pockets of members of an arcane, unwieldy bureaucracy given to excessive red tape, or of middle-management agencies such as the

Reddys in Hyderabad, who have close links to megalithic Japanese and Korean mining companies operating more freely with all the payouts (*bakshis*) on a golden platter this entails in the Indian rural context, than the helpless farmers (who have been taking themselves in droves to suicide), the stepping-in women farmers, or the powerless vegetable vendor in the local market.[17] As Pranab Bardhan points out,[18] this is India's postcolonial tragedy, in contrast to China's much better organized infrastructure and distribution systems (even if Chinese welfare reforms have not lived up to expectations).

Statistics and the stark reality on the ground aside, one does not have to be a Hegelian historicist or a subaltern scholar of colonialism to trace the antecedents to the conditions. I wish now to focus on the link between ethically cogent economic growth and religio-cultural factors. First, think of the Buddhist-Shintoist management style pursued more recently by Japan and South Korea as part of the East Asian emerging economies.[19] The Buddhist ideal for a practical economics begins with the recognition of the centrality of family values and interdependent social ethics. Both Pāli and Mahāyāna texts stress that several interrelated, interactive, and interdependent aspects of living, singly and collectively, "demand that its stakeholders strictly adhere to the ethical and moral norms (*dhamma*) laid down by the Buddha if they are to achieve the expected material well-being and moral happiness while winning as lay people both this world and the next world."[20] G. A. Somaratne urges that the ethical framework (*dhamma*) of this family economic plan should the respect "the rights of all living beings to live and make a living, as its foundation. As such, it invites its stakeholders to adjust their lifestyles and economic goals to the norm of 'moderation' while practicing the rules of law and discipline (*dhamma*) that are grounded on such universally accepted good principles (*dhamma*) as simplicity, truthfulness, nonviolence, friendship, compassion, social justice, and equality."[21] Shinto practices of economic well-being are consistent with the Buddhist wisdom in all significant respects, and they have reinforced, indeed supplement and work in unison with each other, in East Asian regions.

To the Buddhist-Shinto model, we may add the indigenous Confucian management ethos pursued in East Asian countries like the republics of China, Singapore, and Hong Kong, and other emerging economies of Southeast Asia, such as Thailand, have not gone unnoticed among the Indian diaspora and Indian economist-philosophers, Sen included. Second, as Arvind Sharma showed long ago, certain economic virtues are inherent in Hinduism as an *operational* system.[22] I quote here from some important reportage by a fellow Australian, Thomas Birtchnell.

> "Business Excellence Enshrined in Vedic (Hindu) Philosophy" by Anil Sharma and Balvir Talwar develops a counterpoint to the popular Japanese interpretation of Deming's model of Total Quality Management (TQM), envisioning the concepts

this larger order. As Gandhi stressed, "Economics is untrue which disregards moral values. This extension of the law of nonviolence in the domain of economics means nothing less than the introduction of moral values. I use the adjective moral as synonymous with spiritual."[29] What is interesting about the Gandhian model of economics is that in this ideology, exploitation is replaced by service, acquisitiveness by renunciation or minimalism, local by global, and self-regulation by centralization. "The economic system, politically nonviolent and democratic, should be cooperative and constructive instead of [being] exclusive, competitive and militant."[30] This does not, however, preclude public utilities on larger-scale plans nor centralized and capital-intensive public services for other needs, provided there is a measure of balance with small-scale, labor-intensive, decentralized, and village- or rather community-based service portals that provide for the diverse needs of human beings and animals in a protected ecological environment. Gandhi eschewed reliance on luxurious and superfluous goods and the entertainment fetishism that provides no moral or intellectual succor and does not help with the development of character.

Poverty in the Age of Plenty

I will return now to some depressing statistics. Taking the case of India as symptomatic of Third World societies, malnutrition among children, infant morbidity (feticide being one factor accounting for the imbalance in the male-female ratio), illiteracy, lack of access to basic amenities and capabilities-engendering resources, and gender inequality (the question of women as a disadvantaged minority, along with the deplorable marginalization of Dalits, Christians, and Muslims), are proportionately higher than in some comparable African countries. Yet in the West the disparities are equally glaring on the obverse side: the four hundred highest income earners in the United States make as much money in a year as the entire population of twenty African nations, or more than 300 million people. The richest 10 percent of the world population's income is roughly 117 times higher than the poorest 10 percent, which is a huge increase over the ratio in 1980, when it was about 79 times higher than the poorest 10 percent.[31] There are other gaps besides those measured by income. The supposed "knowledge revolution" has also served to accentuate old differences and create new inequalities. In 2004, less than three out of every one hundred Africans had access to the internet, compared with an average of one out of every two inhabitants of the G8 countries (Canada, France, Germany, Italy, Japan, Russia, the United Kingdom, and the United States).[32] More internet users reside in the G8 countries than in the rest of the world combined.

Moreover, real GDP per capita in the United States has grown thirty times in size in two hundred years, implying that the average annual growth rate of income per person there has been about 1.7 percent. Contrast this with, say, income in Ethiopia, where GDP remains where it was two hundred years ago (a little over $700 per year in today's terms). People in so-called developing countries live on a subsistence level of $2 per day, partly accounting for the recent shift in political consciousness in the Middle East.

Of course, as many enlightened minds remind us and the United Nations Development Program has accordingly revised its yardstick for evaluating human flourishing, the standard of living is not most optimally measured by the size of a nation's GDP/GNP, or the ready access to the internet, and so on, but by an index that combines GDP per capita, along with life expectancy at birth, literacy, and aesthetic cultivations—all of which would not be there without empowering capabilities and engendering individual and collective virtues and obligations, rights, and entitlements, as discussed earlier.

While classical economists continue to believe in the myth of economic growth, increasingly in the postindustrial, secular age, experts such as Amartya Sen would argue that GDP by itself should not be the sole measure of economic and social well-being. As Partha Dasgupta points out,

> No economist has ever claimed that there is a single driving force behind economic growth. . . . In the contemporary world, an accumulation of, say, manufactured goods raises real GDP, other things being equal. This enables societies to set aside more of their incomes for education and health, triggering a reduction in both fertility and child mortality. Education increases GDP further . . . while reduced fertility and child mortality typically lower population growth; which, taken together enable societies to set aside more of their incomes for the production of new ideas.[33]

Likewise, the Nobel Laureate in Economics and Bharat Ratna (India's highest national Award of Distinction), Amartya Sen, is even more strongly of the view that actual physical growth and economic development that are intrinsically aligned to engendering welfare capabilities, but not GDP or GNP alone, are the real measure of the *quality* of life, which encompasses respect for human rights and human dignity along with advocacy, education, gender equity, ecological sensitivity, and activism or social engagement, all of which enable actual human and other sentient capabilities. Sen has been critical of the model held up in India by the success stories of the current chief minister of Gujarat, Narendra Modi, who is acknowledged as having single-handedly raised the economic productivity and created a clean administration for business culture, mostly through foreign investment and facilitating industrial initiatives with local reinvestments, in his state, which had long lingered in poverty and communal strife.[34] Sen's complaint has been that while Modi has done well in terms of material growth, that is, building a massive infrastructure for a burgeoning industrial renascence in his state, he has done badly in the social sector in terms of uplifting the disadvantaged and involving the teeming population of Gujarat, especially among the deprived minority communities and the female community, in the benefits of education, health, and capability building. Rather, Sen argues, Modi may have exacerbated these deficiencies, and neglected gender inequality also, by his one-sided purchase on the national policy of economic liberalization and decentralization of economic control, hitherto known as the "license-permit raj."

Sen, in turn, has been severely criticized by his rival Indian economists from Columbia and Yale Universities, namely, Jagdish Bhagwati and Arvind Panagariya, for, as it were, putting the cart before the horse, or being misled by what they call the Track-2-over-Track-1 model.[35] Sen is attributed in this debate as believing that the starting point for achieving the desired goal of eliminating poverty, illiteracy, failing health, and other deprivations must be an immediate massive attack on these ills of the society, which would bring about (physical) growth because the citizens that make up the workforce would be healthier and more literate, which in turn would feed back toward the campaign against the social conditions of inequity and injustices inherent therein. The adversarial duo, who, too, like Sen have been advisers to successive Indian governments (central and local) on the virtues of the new economic turn, argue instead that it is Track 1 reforms that provide the true starting point for any poor country: on the one hand, rapid growth empowers the citizens through increased incomes with which they can purchase high-quality education and health in the marketplace; and on the other hand, it provides the government with ever-rising revenues to further enhance public expenditure on health and education.[36] Sen is unrepentant, arguing that no amount of huge economic reform and growth measured in terms of GNP or GDP would be insufficient where a nation is lacking in substantive policies and commitment to achieve something worthwhile with the short-term results of such progressive moves. He cites countries such as Brazil, Mexico, Thailand, Singapore, Taiwan, Korea, and China, where the state began with education and health care reforms right away without waiting for its citizens to become rich enough to "buy" education and health care[37]—a practice, needless to say, that has brought the United States to a standstill over President Barack Obama's attempt to instate universal state-supported health care, or something close to it, despite the crunchingly unprecedented debt crisis in the United States. Sen is adamant that the view that calls for an enlightened vision on the part of the government and national leaders is not new, rather, that this was advocated by Kauṭilya in his *Arthaśāstras* (as we saw earlier), by the Buddhist emperor Aśoka, by the Mogul ruler Akbar, and indeed by Adam Smith in his *Wealth of Nations* (1776), underscoring essentially the importance of growth to human capabilities, which makes a difference to the kind of life one leads but also enhances one's ability to be a productive part of society and not merely a dispensable cog in the wheel of the modern times.

Following on the coattails of Sen's argument, Martha Nussbaum adds that GNP doesn't address the actual distribution of wealth but rather promotes an "overall social good in ways that may in effect use some people as means to the enrichment of others,"[38] as against "adaptive preferences," through which a society or culture dictates what people can do and should want while ignoring actual capabilities such as a good life, health, freedom, and integrity, and thereby placing restrictions on access to social goods and development strategies. Furthermore, Thomas Pogge asserts that poverty results indirectly from a lack of basic social and economic rights, sometimes called welfare rights,[39] and directly from a lack of civil and political rights. These deprivations lead to devastating levels of poverty, such as food and water insecurities, as are found in Third World countries. And yet the World Trade Organization, which has acceded to the free-trade ideology championed by the United States to boost its own global economic imperialism, permits wealthy nations to favor their companies through traffic tariff reliefs, quotas, subsidies, and the like. First World powers encourage the proliferation hegemonies through complicitous neocolonial regimes, global corporatism, and imposed chaos, including famine and civil wars.

While China, by liberalizing its erstwhile tight hold on citizens' economic rights and spearheading the fastest economic growth rate after the United States during the cold war period, succeeded in reducing its people in poverty by 220 million between 1978 and 1994, India reduced its number of poor from a glaring 407 million to 269 million between 2004–2005 and 2011–2012 not by an equitable distribution of wealth and capability development but by redefining poverty and the concomitant line of poverty in rupee terms rather than in terms of the availability of health care and education, and so on. This explains why the government-passed Women Farmers Entitlement Bill (2011) and, significantly, the Food Security Bill (2012) promise to cover 67 percent of the population, but the latter especially includes leakages to the nonpoor and fixing the subsidy to the poor at an alarming subsistence rate of just over $2 per day ($2 per day being the moderate poverty line by learned Indian estimate in the Northwest!). By titling the equilibrium and widening the gap between the growing middle class and the unprecedented cloisters of the unfealty billionaires, it in effect serves to disempower the poor sufficient to render them invisible from the landscape.[40] This process is tantamount to the colonial Australian Lockean ploy of *terra nullius* (land being empty of inhabitants despite the presence of its native aborigines for more than sixty thousand years) in the eighteenth century, or a slow genocide of the undesirables and presumed unproductive of a society by some method of social engineering and communal strangulation, or by stagnating the economy, shutting it down, and depending almost exclusively on handouts and credit borrowings from wealthier nations (as with Cuba's reliance on Venezuela). Modi, whom we mentioned earlier, while (and still remains after four contested elections) Gujarat's chief minister, with his obliging cohorts, including the state's public agencies, is said to have chanced upon a pogrom in the 2002–2003 statewide riots between Muslims and Hindus to eliminate the poverty-stricken sectors of the Muslim community in his state by unleashing or instigating public communal violence, called "After Godhra." This was found to be so in the judgment of a Special Commission of Inquiry on the Gujarat Riots within the High (Apex) Court; however, no sentence or action ensued from or by the powers that be for the hopeful chief minister, whose stature paradoxically has grown in even greater proportion on account of the "economic success narrative," deafeningly broadcasted from Gujarati in the media across India for the endearment and luring aggrandizement of the middle class. So much so that the Hannibal Lecter, the twinkle of the right-wing sophisticates, and the most re-deconstructed economic politician of modernity's India now has been elevated to its singular preferred prime ministerial candidate in the upcoming federal elections by the reactionary Bharitya Janata Party of India (against the wisdom of ante-quotidian traditionalists such as the leader of the opposition in the Indian government and a BJP whip, L. K. Advani). India, then, is poised to follow the economic model of Gujarat, whose chief adviser has been none other than the Columbian Distinguished Professor of Economics, Jagdish Bhagwati of Track 1 fame, applauding its consistent 8.4 percent growth rate record over two decades.[41] And yet, malnutrition and illiteracy afflict 47 percent of Gujarat's younger and aging population. So much, then, for unbridled growth for growth's sake.

Hence, adequate levels of agency, self-sufficiency, and morally defined basic rights, and valuable capabilities along with individual and collective duties for everyone, regardless of nationality, ethnicity, religion, age, gender, or sexual preference, would seem to be a part of the solution, though not the panacea for the economic woes of the globe. Changes in institutional arrangements and social attitudes, rather than simply effected through legislation or universal charters, are needed if these rights are to be delivered and to be maximally realized.

Through his critique of conventional contractarian ideals and John Rawls' theory of justice and its defective implications for economic justice, Sen deploys the comparative approach, in which he argues for a greater space for public reasoning, and that, too, in a pluralist or heterogeneous modality. First, he sees the need to point to "the prevalence of unreason in the world and to the unrealism involved in assuming that the world will go in the way reason dictates."[42] The alternative kinds of reason he has in mind are those of—his own example—Mary Wollstonecraft, who argued against the establishment for its perpetration of inequities suffered by not only women but other deprived people, such as slaves in the United States. Sen is not averse to plurality of reasons either. "Judgments about justice have to take on board the task of accommodating different kinds of reasons and evaluative concerns." Sen is perhaps alluding here to Rawls' parochial abhorrence of including what he, Rawls, calls "comprehensive views" and competing concerns that come from outside of mainstream liberal views, such as feminist, racial, and religious.[43] For Sen, each person's experience matters, citing Martin Luther King Jr., who reminded us that "injustice anywhere is a threat to justice everywhere."[44] And indeed, neither King nor the plight of the African Americans and their demand for civil and economic rights on a par with the white majority is something Rawls engaged with, even though this consideration would be entailed by his principle of reflective equilibrium.

A final word on money: here is a possible scenario, suggested counterfactually, for the author argues precisely against his better judgment, being an economist:

> Imagine a world where everyone is known to be utterly trustworthy; where people don't incur any cost in computing, remembering, and recognizing people; and where every transaction—whether here and now, or across time, space, and uncertain contingencies—can be carried out costlessly. In that world people would be able to do business with one another merely on the basis of their word. There would be no need of money.[45]

An unconventional suggestion I wish to canvass in concluding this essay is whether, in all possible worlds, there could be an economic system where there are no sellers and no buyers but rather only givers and receivers, no market or store managers and customers or clients but *atithis,* guests and gifting welfarers. The worth and value of the flourishing of the community at the end of the day is here measured qualitatively in terms of how much one and all are able to give or gift (thus lessening the burden of karma, as of state taxes and poll taxes), while beholding a glowing happiness in the face of the infinite other.

NOTES

1. Purushottama Bilimoria, "Kauṭilya [*Arthaśāstra*]" (fl. ca. 321–ca. 296 BCE), in *Encyclopaedia of Philosophy,* ed. Edward Craig (London: Routledge, 1998), 220–222.
2. Partha Dasgupta, *Economics: A Very Short Introduction* (Oxford: Oxford University Press, 2007), 83.
3. Milton Singer, "Cultural Values in India's Economic Development," *American Academy of Political and Social Sciences* 305 (May 1956), 81.
4. Thomas Birtchnell, "From 'Hindolence' to 'Spirinomics': Discourse, Practice and the Myth of Indian Enterprise," *South Asia: Journal of South Asian Studies* 32, no. 2 (2009), 252.
5. "Pravasi Bharatiya Divas," Ministry of Overseas Indian Affairs, n.d., http://moia.gov.in/services.aspx?id1=25&id=m1&idp=25&mainid=23.
6. Birtchnell, "From 'Hindolence' to 'Spirinomics,'" 251.
7. "Dalai Lama Mourns Sathya Sai Baba's Death," *World News,* April 25, 2011, http://article.wn.com/view/2011/04/25/Dalai_Lama_mourns_Sathya_Sai_Babas_death/.
8. Dasgupta, *Economics,* 68.
9. Ibid.

10. Joseph Prabhu with P. Bilimoria, "Reflections on Moral Ideals and Modernity: Gandhi and Nonviolence," in *Indian Ethics,* vol. 1, *Classical Traditions and Contemporary Challenges,* ed. P. Bilimoria, Joseph Prabhu, and Renuka Sharma (Aldershot, UK: Ashgate Publishing, 2007; New Delhi: Oxford University Press, 2008), 330.

11. Milton Singer, "Religion and Social Change in India: The Max Weber Thesis, Phase Three," *Economic Development and Cultural Change* 14, no. 4 (July 1966), 497.

12. Singer, "Cultural Values in India's Economic Development," 91.

13. Pratap Bhanu Mehta, "The Ethical Irrationality of the World: Weber and Hindu Ethics," in *Indian Ethics,* ed. Bilimoria, Prabhu, and Sharma, 370–371.

14. Purushottama Bilimoria, "Protestant Work Ethic and Hindu Dharma," in *The Contemporary Essays on the Bhagavadgita,* ed. Braj Sinha (Delhi: Siddharta Publications, 1995); Bilimoria, "Kauṭilya [*Arthaśāstra*]," 36, 53.

15. Jonardon Ganeri, *The Lost Age of Reason: Philosophy in Early Modern India, 1450–1700* (Oxford: Oxford University Press, 2011).

16. Bimal K. Matilal, *A History of Indian Literature,* vol. 6, fasc. 2, *Nyāya-Vaiśeṣika Literature* (Wiesbaden: Otto Harrassowitz, 1977), 59.

17. "CBI Checks out Jagan's Palatial Hyderabad House," *World News,* July 22, 2011, http://article.wn.com/view/2011/07/22/CBI_checks_out_Jagans_palatial_Hyderabad_house/.

18. Pranab Bardhan, "What Makes a Miracle: Some Myths about the Rise of China and India," http://bostonreview.net/BR33.1/bardhan.php, accessed September 11, 2011. See also more detailed discussion in his *Awakening Giants, Feet of Clay: Assessing the Economic Rise of China and India* (Princeton, NJ: Princeton University Press, 2010).

19. Birtchnell, "From 'Hindolence' to 'Spirinomics,'" 263; Tu Wei-Ming, "The Mirror of Modernity and Spiritual Resources for the Global Community," *Sophia* 34, no. 1 (April 1995), 79–91.

20. G. A. Somaratne, "Moral Framework (*Dhamma*) for Family Economics" (address to International Buddhist College, 2012; courtesy of Padmasiri de Silva).

21. Ibid.

22. Arvind Sharma, *The Hindu Scriptural Value System and India's Economic Development* (Delhi: Heritage, 1980), 88–100.

23. Birtchnell, "From 'Hindolence' to 'Spirinomics,'" 264.

24. Lawina Melwani, "Deepak Chopra: Vedantic Evangelist," *Hinduism Today,* n.d., http://www.hinduismtoday.com/modules/smartsection/item.php?itemid=4199.

25. Birtchnell, "From 'Hindolence' to 'Spirinomics,'" 265.

26. Ibid., 266.

27. Daya Krishna (paper presented at the Sixth East-West Philosophers' Conference, Honolulu, Hawai'i, 1989).

28. Daya Krishna, "The Myth of the Ethics of *Puruṣārtha* or Humanity's Life-Goals," in *Indian Ethics,* ed. Bilimoria, Prabhu, and Sharma, 114–115.

29. Srimati Kamala, *Mahatma Gandhi: An American Profile* (Washington, DC: Mahatma Gandhi Memorial Foundation, 1987), 61.

30. Ibid.

31. Robert Weissman, "Grotesque Inequality: Corporate Globalization and the Global Gap between Rich and Poor," *Multinational Monitor* 24, nos. 7–8 (July–August 2003), 9.

32. Devaki Jain, "Morals in Politics—the Gandhian Touch," *Man in India* 90, nos. 1–2 (2010), 47–60.

33. Dasgupta, *Economics,* 22.

34. Since writing this paper Mr. Modi has been elected at the ballots with a significant majority vote against the rival Congress Party candidate to serve as the new Prime Minister of India.

35. Arvind Panagariya, "What Amartya Sen Doesn't See: Growth-Orientated Reforms Provide the True Starting Point for a Poor Country," *Times of India,* Of Ideas column, July 27, 2013, 22.

36. Ibid.

37. See "Interview with Amartya Sen," *India Today,* August 5, 2013, 35–37, where Sen responds to Bhagawati's article in *The Economist* that accuses Sen of belatedly learning to pay lip service to growth; Sen rebukes this by confessing that he was never in favor of the license-permit raj and that he also gave positive advice to Manmohan Singh, the architect of India's liberalized economic reforms, in the 1990s in favor of liberalization and globalization, and also had discussions with Modi in the early 2000s; "Deep Focus Interviews: Amarya Sen," *Sunday Times of India,* July 28, 2013, 5.

38. Martha Craven Nussbaum, *Frontiers of Justice: Disability, Nationality, Species Membership* (Cambridge, MA: Belknap Press of Harvard University, 2006), 71.

39. Amartya Sen, *The Idea of Justice* (Cambridge, MA: Belknap Press of Harvard University, 2009), 379.

40. This critique is from one of the major contributors on economics in India's vibrant democracy, Swaminathan S. Anklesaria Aiyar, "Why No Applause for 138 Million Exiting Poverty?" *Times of India,* July 21, 2013.

41. Panagariya, "What Amartya Sen Doesn't See."

42. Ibid., xvii.

43. Ibid., 394.

44. Ibid., 403.

45. Dasgupta, *Economics,* 54.

Economies of Scarcity and Acquisition, Economies of Gift and Thanksgiving 11

Lessons from Cultural Anthropology

Kenneth W. Stikkers

So much of the now-stale debate between capitalism and socialism, begun already in the early nineteenth century, hinged on contradictory claims about human nature. Is it competitive, or is it cooperative? Acquisitive or sharing? Egoistic or altruistic? Indeed, it was out of this debate and a desire to settle empirically once and for all what had largely been a battle of opposing, merely speculative assertions that the science of cultural anthropology in large measure was born.

Contemporary cultural anthropologists largely consider the debate over "human nature" a red herring. Humans have no simple, single "nature" but from infancy exhibit complex, conflicting biological impulses and tendencies, and so the real issues are: Which tendencies will be encouraged and reinforced and which will be discouraged by the society? In what contexts, if any, is competition to be encouraged? What limits is the culture to place upon it? The debate that undergirds the capitalist-communist divide, though, is no simple empirical matter; it is an ethical one. Which of the competing tendencies found in humans *ought* the culture nurture and in what circumstances? Which tendencies *ought* it discourage and when?

Mainstream economics has long prided itself on being not only an empirical science but even the most empirical and most scientifically rigorous of the social sciences. Yet it continues to assert and assume unequivocally, as some of its most foundational premises, anthropological claims, especially regarding human nature, that are flatly contradicted by more than a century of empirical findings by cultural anthropology and other social sciences. Karl Polanyi made this point more than sixty years ago and is widely hailed as the founder of economic anthropology, that subdiscipline that critically examines the empirical anthropological claims and presuppositions underlying economic theories. He boldly concluded:

> The nineteenth century attempted to establish a self-regulating economic system on the motive of individual gain. We maintain that such a venture was in the very nature of things impossible. Here we are merely concerned with the distorted

> view of life and society implied in such an approach. Nineteenth-century thinkers assumed, for instance, that to behave like a trader in the market was "natural," and any other mode of behavior being artificial economic behavior—the result of interferences with human instincts; that markets would spontaneously arise, if only men were let alone; that whatever the desirability of such a society on moral grounds, its practicality, at least, was founded on the immutable characteristics of the race, and so on. Almost exactly the opposite of these assertions is implied in the testimony of modern research in various fields of social science such as social anthropology, primitive economics, the history of early civilization, and general economic history. *Indeed, there is hardly an anthropological or sociological assumption—whether explicit or implicit—contained in the philosophy of economic liberalism that has not been [empirically] refuted.*[1]

Other anthropological assumptions that Polanyi identifies as commonly held by orthodox economists but refuted by empirical anthropological evidence include the notions that the motive of personal gain is "natural," that people "naturally" expect payment for labor, and that people "naturally" seek "to restrict labor to the unavoidable minimum."

I contend in this essay that empirical studies in economic anthropology, such as Polanyi's, do much to challenge the philosophical assumptions that undergird orthodox economic theory and thereby open a space wherein economy can be thought anew, beyond the stale false dichotomies assumed by professional economists and public policy makers alike and that currently stifle economic thinking and hence undermine our ability to address pressing economic issues in fresh and creative ways.

Numerous more recent studies have confirmed the conclusions in Polanyi's pioneer work. Marshall Sahlins, for one, in his now classic *Stone Age Economics,* proves wrong virtually all of the assumptions that had been made, particularly by economists, about hunter-gatherer economies, especially as they are contrasted unfavorably to modern market economies. For example, economists commonly and unquestioningly have followed Thomas Hobbes in characterizing Stone Age life as one of unrelenting toil. Furthermore, anthropologists and economists alike simply assumed, prior to Sahlins' study, that hunting and gathering peoples did not stockpile food to safeguard against the presumably constant threat of starvation because they lacked the necessary technological know-how. That lack was then cited as evidence of the hunter-gatherers' primitiveness. Sahlins' research, and research following it, reveals, however, that Stone Age people did not stockpile because they generally had no need for doing so. Hunger among such societies was a great rarity rather than the norm, in contrast to the prolonged sort of food deprivation that so many experience in our world today. Furthermore, such people enjoyed significant amounts of leisure time, more than do most in modern industrial societies. Indeed, Sahlins terms them "the original affluent society."[2] Robert Heilbroner, too, drawing from the findings of economic anthropologists, demonstrates how the so-called universal laws of the market that mainstream economists presume pertain to only a very small slice of human history and cultures; the bulk of economic production takes place according to patterns of custom and tradition and structures of command, and market systems are always embedded in such patterns and structures.[3] In these and so many other ways, the empirical findings of economic anthropologists flat-out contradict the presuppositions of orthodox economists about human and social behavior.

A sound philosophical anthropology, that is, a coherent theory of human nature and fulfillment and an account of what Hannah Arendt termed "the human condition," informed by the most current empirical findings of cultural anthropology, is prerequisite for sound economic theory and a healthy economy. Indeed, no economic theory can be any more sound than the philosophical assumptions upon which it rests. Economic theories based on a "distorted view of [human] life and society"[4] cannot succeed in contributing much of lasting value to human learning, life, and society, and an economy resting on a twisted understanding of human nature, fulfillment, and society can promote only twisted human beings and societies. The importance of sound philosophical anthropology for economic theory can perhaps best be seen in what are two of the most fundamental premises of modern economics, the second one following from the first. First is the assumption that desire for unlimited material gain is natural, and second is that the human condition to be addressed by economics and economic institutions is irreducibly one of scarcity. Such scarcity then, in turn, is part of the basis for assuming competition to be constitutive of the human condition.

Indeed, economics textbooks, following Lionel Robbins, commonly include scarcity in their definitions of the discipline. They describe scarcity as *the* problem of economics and define economics as the management of scarcity, the study of the production and distribution of goods and services under conditions of scarcity.[5] As Sahlins puts it, "Modern capitalist societies, however richly endowed, dedicate themselves to the proposition of scarcity. Inadequacy of economic means is the first principle of the world's wealthiest people."[6] "Scarcity," though, has both an absolute and relative use. Classical and neoclassical economic theorists often describe the necessities of life, in what they imagine as the state of nature, as absolutely scarce. As in Hobbes' famous account, the human state of nature is imagined as pre-social, "solitary, poor, nasty, brutish, and short." In 1930 John Maynard Keynes imagined at least the industrial West, despite its impending Great Depression, to be on the verge of solving at last the problem of absolute scarcity: "The *economic problem* may be solved, or at least in sight of solution, within a hundred years," he boldly and optimistically proclaimed.[7]

Largely in light of modern affluence, which for some confirms Keynes' prediction, orthodox economists tend to describe scarcity as relative to what they unquestioningly take to be unlimited human desires: the problem of scarcity will never be solved, they claim, because human desires, being unlimited, will always run ahead of an economy's ability to provide. As Sahlins writes, the modern West "erected a shrine to the Unattainable: *Infinite Needs*,"[8] and it is before this shrine that modern economists kneel in worship. The logical response to such presumed scarcity is to acquire and amass competitively as much as possible without waste as a bulwark against insecurity—the more, the better. According to Harvard economist Stephen Marglin, "In mainstream economics, it is axiomatic that wants are unbounded. Unbounded wants are the root of scarcity, and scarcity is the keystone of economics. Scarcity in turn causes rivalry—division of the [economic] pies is normally treated as my blood or thine rather than as a moral issue."[9] In Marglin's observation we see how scarcity forms part of the wedge that divides economics from ethics: in a world of cutthroat competition over scarce goods, morality appears as a luxury that we cannot afford. Such, however, would be the case under only absolute, not relative, scarcity, because, after all, would it not be possible for someone to learn to moderate his or her superfluous wants in order to provide for another's necessities? But there is, of course, much more to the story.

In his 1932 *Essay on the Nature and Significance of Economic Science*, Robbins rejected the then common definition of economics as the study of wealth, its creation and distribution—what he termed the "materialist" definition—in favor of a scarcity one, citing Carl Menger and Ludwig von Mises: "Economics is the science which studies human behaviour as a relationship between ends and scarce means which have alternative uses."[10] Economics is thus reduced to the study of opportunity costs, a science purely of means divorced from any concern for ends, which Robbins took as merely subjective, hence arbitrary, and thus outside the domain of science. It becomes, in effect, the efficient manager of misery. Economists, according to Robbins, should thus stop concerning themselves with wealth altogether, because wealth is merely relative to subjective, arbitrary human ends. Moreover, Robbins' definition transforms economy from one domain of human activity into a universal feature encompassing *all* human life. After all, does not every human action entail opportunity costs, the preferring of one thing over another, the forgoing of something in order to do something else?

> Here we are, sentient creatures with bundles of desires and aspirations, with masses of instinctive tendencies all urging us in different ways to action. But the time in which these tendencies can be expressed is limited. The external world does not offer full opportunities for their complete achievement. Life is short. Nature is niggardly.[11]

Robbins thus enshrined scarcity as the most foundational principle of economy and economics.

If it is the task of modern economies, with modern technologies as their handmaidens, to extract from a begrudging, "niggardly" nature the means to satisfy human desires—consumer demand, again, assumed to be unlimited—then the task is an impossible one. Modern theories of property, such as John Locke's, take it as the natural right of humans to appropriate from nature whatever they find useful in satisfying their personal wants, and Adam Smith illustrates how deeply entrenched is the assumption that the satisfaction of consumer wants is the principal aim of economic activity.

> Consumption is the sole end and purpose of all production; and the interest of the producer ought to be attended to, only so far as it may be necessary for promoting that of the economy. The maxim is so perfectly self-evident that it would be absurd to attempt to prove it.[12]

Keynes wholeheartedly concurs: "All production is for the purpose of ultimately satisfying a consumer."[13] That the aim of economy is to satisfy consumer wants, assumed to be unlimited and thus creating the condition of at least relative scarcity, is a central dogma of most modern economics, capitalist and socialist alike. What follows from such an assumption is that the exchange of goods and services occurs only so that individuals can more effectually satisfy their own desires. As Smith famously asserts, "It is not from the benevolence of the butcher, the brewer, or the baker, that we expect our dinner, but from their regard to their own interests."[14] He goes on to assume that the desire for acquisition is the universal basis for the distribution of goods, underlying the supply-and-demand principles of the "invisible hand."

Standing in sharp contrast to modern Western economics' assumptions regarding the unlimited character of human desire to consume and the scarcity of nature are those economies based on opposite assumptions of gift and thanksgiving. Many, perhaps the great majority of human cultures throughout history, have experienced nature not as niggardly but as abundant and overflowing, and such a feeling for the world moderates one's desires. If one experiences nature as bountiful and generous, it would be difficult to bemoan that one does not enjoy more. As a Native American elder expressed to me, "Today is a gift. Who am I to begrudge the fact that I might not have tomorrow?" Archaic peoples tend to see as bizarre Western economists' description of human wants as unlimited. They simply do not recognize the supposedly universal human condition assumed by mainstream economics. The problem of economy for them is not what is to be done about our natural condition of scarcity, but what is the proper response to nature's, or her creator's, generosity and abundance. The most obvious response might be to express gratitude and to honor the giver—nature, the Great Spirit, the gods—by in turn acting generously toward others, not only other members of one's community but also strangers, and not endlessly and selfishly to demand and acquire more.

Marcel Mauss' classic study, *The Gift,* well demonstrates how goods and services in archaic economies effectively circulate according to principles of giving rather than of acquisition, and thus complements Polanyi's work in radically questioning modern economy's assumptions about the self-interestedness and acquisitiveness of human nature. Through giving, one participates in and celebrates the sacred. By the "sacred" we mean here the organic interconnectedness of all creation and of the bountifulness of being, or, as Georges Bataille, following Mauss, describes it, "the sense of . . . divine continuity of living beings with the world,"[15] which engenders a feeling of the plentitude, the bountifulness of being, of life constantly overflowing itself—"excess energy, translated into the effervescence of life."[16] Mauss describes the matter thus: "Everything is there for passing on. . . . Everything passes to and fro as if there were a constant exchange of spiritual matter."[17] The Navajo characterize this circulating spiritual matter as a "Holy Wind," or *nilch'i,* which, "suffusing all of nature, . . . gives life, thought, speech, and the power of motion to all living things, and serves as the means of communication between all elements of the living world. . . . By this concept the Navajo Soul is linked to the immanent powers of the universe."[18]

Exchanges of gifts might resemble, when viewed from the outside, the buying and selling of goods found in modern market economies, but, Mauss cautions, exchanges of "presents do not serve the same purpose as commerce and exchange in [modern economies]. The goal is above all a moral one, the object being to foster friendly feelings between the two persons in question,"[19] rather than the mutual optimization of personal utility. The taking and consuming of goods, for example, food, is not the mere utilitarian satisfaction of some want but participation in the cosmic circulation of spiritual energy that binds together the whole of creation—human and nonhuman, present and past generations alike—and engenders a profound sense of gratitude for being. Mauss' study focuses largely on the Trobriand Islanders and the tribes of Pacific Northwest America, but historian Nathan Huggins well illustrates Mauss' point in his descriptions of traditional African communities, thereby demonstrating the extensiveness of this primal feeling of abundance and gratitude throughout a wide array of archaic economies.[20]

The *value* of goods in archaic economies thus comes not simply from the utility derived by personal consumption, as modern economic theories tend to assume, but foremost from how goods solidify relationships through their circulation. Food not only provides nourishment for the individual but, even more important, when generously shared, promotes friendly feelings, necessary for food's continued cooperative procurement. Without strong communal solidarity, nurtured by sharing and generosity, food cannot be effectively produced. Indeed, once objects become removed from sacred circulation, becoming, through selfishness or greed, objects of private possession and hence divisiveness rather than for sharing and the strengthening of relationships, they cease to be "goods" but now become "evils" or "poison," and might even need to be destroyed. Traditional African and Native American cultures provide abundant examples of this relationalist notion of value, but Mauss offers an especially pointed example from traditional Hindu economy.

> It is in the nature of food to be shared out. Not to share it with others is "to kill its essence," it is to destroy it both for oneself and for others. . . . Wealth is made to be given away. If there were to be no Brahmins to receive it, "vain would be the riches of the rich." "He who eats without knowledge [of this need to share] kills the food, and once it is eaten, it kills him." Avarice breaks the circle of the law; rewards and foods are perpetually reborn from one another.[21]

For gift economies, as this passage illustrates, wealth does not consist in the amassment of riches but in the strength of relationships fostered by the circulation of goods. Selfishness and greed cut off that circulation, destroy the value of objects, and threaten the health of both the individual and the community. Affluence stems from the steady, unimpeded circulation of spiritual matter, which nurtures communal relationships. Nature remains bountiful and no one starves so long as such circulation remains unobstructed by avarice and relationships are thereby continuously fed. As Mauss observes, "To refuse to give, to fail to invite, just as to refuse to accept, is tantamount to declaring war; it is to reject the bond of alliance and communality."[22] When acquisitiveness and greed disrupt this flow, friendships become broken, cooperative activity becomes impossible, and scarcity reigns.

Tribal communities commonly view the desire for acquisition as evidence of one's dependence on external goods and hence a sign of one's inner weakness and slavish character and a mark against one's social standing. In the lavish giving of gifts one celebrates simultaneously the bountifulness of nature and one's own vital-spiritual strength and fitness, one's ability to live with minimal dependency upon external goods, one's inner freedom and plentitude. Among the Trobriand Islanders, for example, the aim of the exchange of gifts, Mauss observes, "is to display generosity, freedom, and autonomous action, as well as greatness."[23]

The Native American tribes of North America illustrate especially well the extensiveness of gift economies among non-Western peoples and many of the gift economy's central features, particularly Mauss' point about the giving of gifts as a celebration of strength, autonomy, and greatness. Historian David Stannard warns against generalizing about Native American tribes, noting vast differences among them. He nevertheless observes that "one characteristic of America's indigenous peoples that does seem almost universal, transcending the great diversity of other cultural traits, was an extraordinary capacity for hospitality," a pervasively strong ethic of generosity, extending to tribal members as well as to strangers.[24] Indeed, without the generosity of the indigenous people, early settlements, such as those in Virginia and Massachusetts Bay, would have failed. Historian Edmund S. Morgan describes just such a situation, with respect to Virginia in the 1580s. "Wingina [the local chief] welcomed the visitors, and the Indians gave freely of their supplies to the English, who had lost most of their own when [their ship] the *Tyger* grounded."[25] Morgan then notes, "The Indians . . . could have done the English in simply by deserting them,"[26] and Stannard adds, "They did not desert them, however, and in that act they sealed their fate. The same was true throughout the Americas: the cultural traits and the material achievements of the native people were turned against them once the European invasion began. Indian openness and generosity were met with European stealth and greed."[27] In the conquest of America we thus see a violent collision of the two forms of economy. The Lakota took gift giving as the natural order of things, such that when they encountered European settlers and their tendencies to acquire and hoard for themselves, they questioned the latter's very humanity. As Native American anthropologist Ella Deloria notes, "The giving system certainly was not for enriching oneself at the expense of others. A man who showed that tendency was suspect, as if he were not quite human."[28] Ironically, the British considered it "unnatural" for indigenous peoples to be so generous with their possessions, took such generosity as evidence that Native Americans were not fully human, and banned the potlatch celebrations in the Pacific Northwest for many years.

Lakota philosopher Robert Bunge indicates how gift economies entail a radically different understanding of security than the one entailed in the acquisitive economies of the modern West. He notes, first, that the Lakota understanding of security is rooted in an acceptance of "insecurity as the ground of any appreciation of and zest for life."[29] As the Buddha taught in his First Noble Truth, human existence is ontologically disastrous. Ultimately nothing—no amount of wealth, no amount of planning—will secure one against suffering and death. Although one might certainly try to avoid unnecessary suffering, at some point the desire to secure oneself against pain and death also inhibits one's ability to feel the joy of living, to feel fully alive, to feel gratitude for the gift of life, and hence to give in turn as a show of such gratitude. As Bunge writes, "For the Native American, this was a very good world despite its terrors and insecurity—an insecurity which he, in his wisdom, would not end if he could because all the color, excitement, urgency, meaning and value of life were grounded therein."[30] Huggins similarly notes how, in traditional African culture, where an economy of gift and thanksgiving reinforced a powerful sense of interrelationship, "Death mattered not. . . . Life was of the person, and the person of life—all a continuum—so that the forces of life ebbed and flowed through him, making him a conduit of the life force."[31]

By contrast, modern Western peoples tend to bemoan the shortness, the finitude of life. As I argue elsewhere,[32] the emergence of the notion of scarcity in modern economics coincides with what French sociologist Philippe Aries famously describes as the West's growing denial of death.[33] Since the Middle Ages death increasingly appears as an intrusion into one's right to happiness,[34] by contrast to both the Lakota and earlier Western sense that acceptance of death is a condition for happiness. Increasingly unable to face their own mortality, modern Western peoples have projected on nature their own finitude. It is not so much that we are finite creatures, born inevitably to die, as it is that nature fails to provide what we need for life eternal and happiness without end. If only nature were not so stingy, if only the problem of economic scarcity could be solved, then we might secure ourselves once and for all against suffering and death—or so Western peoples commonly imagine. By contrast, the Lakota hold no such illusions. From childhood they are taught that suffering and death are natural and inevitable phases in the cycle of life, and as a result, Bunge suggests, they experience a fullness of and gratitude for life little known in the modern West. Attitudes toward wealth and economy are thus fundamentally tied to attitudes toward death. In the modern West, wealth is viewed as a bulwark against the vicissitudes of life, and the aim of economy is seen as one of increasingly providing such wealth, of fortifying the bulwark. Among the Lakota, and many others, by contrast, acceptance of suffering and death frees and empowers one to participate in the great circulatory economy of being, to breathe in and to partake of Holy Wind, and thus to emulate the generosity of the Great Spirit.

The second feature of the Lakota sense of security that Bunge identifies is that it is based in interpersonal relationships rather than upon things. "Non-Indian society," he observes, "hedges against insecurity by ringing itself with material goods—*with things.*" By contrast,

> *The Lakota knew that security does not arise from matter and then spread to the soul. It arises, if . . . at all, in the soul to begin with and has its ultimate basis in the insecurity of life itself* [as we described earlier]. . . . True, the Indian valued security too, but he did not attempt to build a rampart against life's vicissitudes with *possessions;* he built his rampart with *people.* People and what they *were* were what made life secure, not how much they *had.*[35]

We note in this passage from Bunge a distinction, commonly credited to Karl Marx[36] but developed also by existentialists such as Gabriel Marcel[37] and Erich Fromm,[38] between "having" and "being." "Having" characterizes alienated existence: it is a mode of living whereby one seeks identity and meaning through what is external to oneself, through what one *has,* or owns. "Being," by contrast, characterizes nonalienated living; it is a mode of existence whereby identity and meaning emerge from one's own inner creativity, resources, and character—who one *is.* Deloria's analysis of the Lakota sense of security complements Bunge's, and in it she contrasts sharply Native American practices of gift giving to modern European tendencies toward acquisitiveness and possessiveness: "The two systems . . . are irreconcilable," she proclaims.

> They go counter to each other. One says in effect: "Get, get, get now; all you can, as you can, for yourself, and so insure security for yourself. If all will do this, then everyone will be safe." And it depends upon things, primarily.
>
> The other said: "Give, give, give to others. Let gifts flow freely out and they will flow back to you again. In the universal and endless stream of giving this is bound to be so." And that system depended on human beings—friends.[39]

Gift giving among the Lakota is especially significant, too, because it illustrates an older form of gift economy that Mauss fails to consider. Mauss focuses on specific, reciprocal exchanges of gifts, that is, gift giving that imposes a direct obligation on the recipient to reciprocate. By imposing such obligation, the giver exerts power over the recipient, placing the recipient in his debt. Mauss describes how South Pacific islanders and Northwest Native American tribes would lavish gifts on neighboring tribes as a strategy for placing the latter in their debt, thereby holding potential rivals at bay and commanding power over them. Such displays of power through gift giving that expects return are not far removed from modern market exchanges, wherein one gives to the merchant in order to get what one wants, as Smith described, and served historically as bridges to economies of acquisition. But the expectation of return is absent among the Lakota. Rather, the Lakota practice a form of general exchange. That is, they expect no immediate return directly from the recipient of a gift that they have given, but rather they trust that in the general cycle of energy and matter, which, as we saw, characterizes the sacredness of the cosmos, good things will return to the giver, all in due time, if unimpeded by greed. Another Lakota author, Charles Alexander Eastman, writes, "It is common to give to the point of utter impoverishment. The Indian in his simplicity literally gives all that he has, to relatives, to guests of another tribe or clan, but above all to the poor and aged from whom he can hope for no return."[40] All are under the general obligation to emulate the generosity of the Great Spirit through generosity with one another: as the Great Spirit has been generous with us, by giving us life and all that abounds, so we are to do likewise, to emulate the generosity of the Great Spirit, without expectation for immediate return.

An unnamed Lakota elder illustrates the principle of general economy, operative in the Lakota community, as well as what has been said about the Lakota sense of security, in his advice to the young.

> My children, never skimp. Give adequately in a manner worthy of yourselves, or not at all. Give abundantly and with glorious abandon. Better not to honor someone than dishonor him by doing it haltingly and calculatingly. Pity the coward who gives half holding back, timid for his own private security because he does not put faith in men but in mere chattel.

> My children, it is better to give and have nothing left, if need be, than to appear stingy. Property always flow back in due time to those who let it flow freely forth. In the endless process of giving, that is bound to be so.[41]

We notice, too, in this passage, that the aim of gift giving is definitely not to place the recipient in one's debt but to honor him or her. Moreover, in giving, as noted earlier, one demonstrates and celebrates one's own vital strength and courage: the more one gives, without expectation of immediate return, the more one becomes and the more one's social status grows. Indeed, as Bunge describes,[42] and as I have experienced firsthand, when a Lakota tribal member dies, the family honors and celebrates the generosity of the deceased by giving away, often with abandon, not only the deceased person's possessions but their own as well—clothing, tools, furniture, appliances, rifles, pickup trucks. Conversely, the more possessive one appears and the less able one is to let go of what one possesses in order to give, the weaker one appears, the more one is to be pitied, and the lower becomes one's social status. As Eastman confirms,

> It was our belief that the love of possessions is a weakness to be overcome. Its appeal is to the material part, and if allowed its way it will in time disturb the spiritual balance of the man. Therefore the child must early learn the beauty of generosity. He is taught to give what he prizes most. . . . If a child is inclined to be grasping, legends are related to him, telling of the contempt and disgrace falling upon the ungenerous and mean man.[43]

(We note here what was observed at the beginning of this chapter, namely, how the empirical question of human nature distracts us from the more important, ethical question: What impulses and tendencies in a person, especially a child, *ought* the community encourage, and which *ought* it discourage?)

Such traditions stand in sharp contrast to modern Western economies of acquisition, wherein social status generally increases in accord with one's ability to amass possessions. For example, Bill Gates is admired and envied generally more for the billions he has acquired for himself than for the billions he has given to charity. Moreover, we see in the economies of gift how wealth—money and goods—through their sharing and circulation, entwine persons in the order of the world, in the great web of being. By contrast, in economies of acquisition, as we find in the modern West, wealth serves as a marker of distinction and separation, a wall of difference, a fortification against life's precariousness. Such differences are invariably hierarchical, that is, indicators of "better" or "lesser," "upper-class" or "lower-class" standing. Such is perhaps most clearly seen, as Max Weber showed in *The Protestant Ethics and Spirit of Capitalism,* in later Calvinism, where wealth became interpreted as a sign of election, marking those whom God sovereignly chose for salvation from those left for eternal damnation. Later still, through the influence of social Darwinists such as Herbert Spencer, a more secularized spirit of capitalism would see wealth as a sign that someone is among the "fittest" of the species.

Michel Foucault observes that, with the rise of modern Western economy, "a sensibility was born, which had drawn a line and laid a cornerstone, and which chose—only to banish."[44] Specifically with regard to matters of poverty and wealth, Foucault claims, the modern binary logic of sameness and difference "organizes into a complex unity a new sensibility to poverty and to the duties of assistance, new forms of reaction to the economic problems of unemployment and idleness, a new ethic of work."[45] The West has thus come to view wealth less and less as something whose circulation within the order of things entwines persons in webs of community, in the order of being itself, and instead sees it increasingly as a marker of hierarchical difference. In other words, economy has ceased to be a force that draws together into community, as we saw in economies of gift, and has become instead what Foucault terms a "dividing practice," a force that separates, confines, isolates, and banishes.

The aim of this essay, then, has been neither to romanticize the past nor to suggest that we need to recreate archaic forms of economy, as though that could even be done. Rather, the aim has been to illustrate, first, that sound economic theory must rest on sound philosophical anthropology and, second, that cultural anthropology is highly useful to economic theorizing. Cultural anthropology challenges fundamental assumptions found in conventional economic wisdom, especially regarding human nature, and it thereby opens up possibilities for thinking that orthodox economics tends to exclude a priori. It frees our imaginations to think differently about both economy in general and our current economic problems in particular. According to mainstream Western economies, which I have characterized in terms of scarcity and acquisition, humans are viewed as naturally egoistic and acquisitive, and human well-being is assumed to come from the satisfaction of individual desires. By contrast, gift economies invite us to consider other definitions of wealth and prosperity than those that have dominated Western thinking since the advent of modernity. They challenge us to consider whether the prevailing utilitarian notion of wealth that Western economies use to measure themselves and others and in support of their self-proclaimed progress and superiority—economies whose current impending decline instills such anxiety and insecurity—may not have been fools' gold all along. The question I hope to have raised here is definitely *not* how might we recreate economies of gift and thanksgiving. A better question might be about what we can learn from such economies. But an even better one is what possibilities for economy a study of archaic economies enables us to imagine that orthodox economics tends to preclude a priori. Our study of gift economies suggests that an important measure of economic well-being is the strength of relationships that modes of production, distribution, and consumption strengthen or undermine, something altogether ignored by contemporary mainstream measures of economy, most notably the pervasive use of utilitarian per capita gross domestic product.[46]

In presenting some of my reflections discussed earlier to orthodox economists, I have come to expect their a priori rejection of the suggestion that archaic peoples might have something to teach us in the modern West about economy. (Heilbroner reports similar experiences.[47]) In this regard I am reminded of the famous story that Benjamin Franklin told about the missionary who, after preaching the Christian gospel, from Adam and Eve through the resurrection of Jesus, refused to hear the Native American's story of creation, claiming, "What I delivered to you were sacred Truths; but what you tell me is mere Fable, Fiction & Falsehood."[48] Similarly, missionaries of the gospel of the free market tell their sacred "scientific" Truth about how an invisible power, operating throughout the universe through two great and powerful spirits, Supply and Demand, miraculously cleanses us of our sins, magically transforming human greed and selfishness into social good and abundance, but reject out of hand the "unscientific" fables, fictions, and falsehoods stemming from various world cultural traditions, such as those concerning the generosity of Holy Wind or the Great Spirit.

NOTES

1. Karl Polanyi, *Great Transformation: The Political and Economic Origins of Our Time* (Boston: Beacon Press, 1944), 269–273; Karl Polanyi, *Primitive, Archaic and Modern Economies,* ed. George Dalton (Garden City, NY: Anchor Books, 1968), 19–21; emphasis added.

2. Marshall Sahlins, *Stone Age Economics* (Hawthorne, NY: Aldine de Gruyter, 1972), 1–39.

3. Robert Heilbroner, *Behind the Veil of Economics: Essays in the Worldly Philosophy* (New York: W. W. Norton, 1988), 15–17.

4. Hannah Arendt, *The Human Condition* (Chicago: University of Chicago Press, 1958).

5. Lionel Robbins, *An Essay on the Nature and Significance of Economic Science,* 2nd ed. (London: Macmillan, 1935). Hilary Putnam, too, notes Robbins' profound influence on mainstream economics in this regard. See Putman's *Collapse of the Fact-Value Dichotomy, and Other Essays* (Cambridge, MA: Harvard University Press, 2002), 54, 60, 74.

6. Sahlins, *Stone Age Economics,* 3.

7. John Maynard Keynes, "Economic Possibilities for Our Grandchildren," in *Essays in Persuasion* (Hampshire, England: Palgrave Macmillan, 2010), 331; emphasis in original.

8. Sahlins, *Stone Age Economics,* 39; emphasis in original. Benjamin Franklin had already observed of the Native Americans, "Almost all their Wants are supplied by the spontaneous Productions of Nature, with the addition of very little labour, if hunting and fishing may indeed be called labour when Game is so plenty. . . . They have few but natural wants, and these easily supplied." By contrast, "With us are infinite Artificial wants, no less craving than those of Nature, and much more difficult to satisfy." See Franklin's letter to

Peter Collinson, May 9, 1753, in *Benjamin Franklin: Writings,* ed. J. A. Leo Lemay (New York: Library of America, 1987), 470–471.

9. Stephen A. Marglin, *The Dismal Science: How Thinking Like an Economist Undermines Community* (Cambridge, MA: Harvard University Press, 2010), 200.

10. Robbins, *Nature and Significance of Economic Science,* 16.

11. Ibid., 13.

12. Adam Smith, *An Inquiry in to the Nature and Causes of the Wealth of Nations* (1776), ed. Edwin Cannan (Chicago: University of Chicago Press, 1976), II:179.

13. John Maynard Keynes, *The General Theory of Employment, Interest, and Money* (New York: Harcourt, Brace, 1936), 46.

14. Smith, *Wealth of Nations,* I:118.

15. Georges Bataille, *Theory of Religion,* trans. Robert Hurley (New York: Zone Books, 1992), 35.

16. Georges Bataille, *The Accursed Share,* trans. Robert Hurley (New York: Zone Books, 1989), 1:10.

17. Marcel Mauss, *The Gift: The Form and Reason for Exchange in Archaic Societies,* trans. W. D. Halls (New York: W. W. Norton, 1990), 14.

18. James Kale McNeley, *Holy Wind in Navajo Philosophy* (Tucson: University of Arizona Press, 1988), 1.

19. Brown, as quoted in Mauss, *The Gift,* 19.

20. Nathan Huggins, *Black Odyssey: The African-American Ordeal in Slavery* (New York: Vintage Books, 1990), 14.

21. Mauss, *The Gift,* 57.

22. Ibid., 13.

23. Ibid., 23.

24. David Stannard, *American Holocaust: Columbus and the Conquest of the New World* (New York: Oxford University Press, 1992), 52.

25. Edmund S. Morgan, *American Slavery, American Freedom: The Ordeal of Colonial Virginia* (New York: W. W. Norton, 1975), 39.

26. Ibid., 40.

27. Stannard, *American Holocaust,* 53.

28. Ella Deloria, *Speaking of Indians* (Vermillion: University of South Dakota Press, 1979), 50.

29. Robert Pierce Bunge, *An American* Urphilosophie*: American Philosophy BP (Before Pragmatism)* (Lanham, MD: University Press of America, 1984), 126.

30. Ibid., 131.

31. Huggins, *Black Odyssey,* 13.

32. Kenneth W. Stikkers, "Phenomenology and Economic Science," in *Descriptions,* ed. Don Inde and Hugh J. Silverman (Albany: State University of New York Press, 1985), 212–214.

33. Philippe Aries, *Western Attitudes toward Death from the Middle Ages to the Present,* trans. Patricia M. Ranum (Baltimore, MD: Johns Hopkins University Press, 1974), 85–103.

34. Ibid., 93–95.

35. Bunge, *American* Urphilosophie, 129; emphasis in the original.

36. Karl Marx, *The Economic and Philosophic Manuscripts of 1844,* trans. Martin Milligan, ed. Dirk J. Struik (New York: International Publishers, 1964), 138–139.

37. Gabriel Marcel, *Being and Having: An Existentialist Diary,* trans. Katherine Farrer (New York: Harper and Row, 1965).

38. Erich Fromm, *To Have or to Be?* (New York: Harper and Row, 1976).

39. Deloria, *Speaking of Indians,* 77.

40. Charles Alexander Eastman, *The Soul of the Indian* (Lincoln: University of Nebraska Press, 1980), 101.

41. As quoted by Deloria, *Speaking of Indians,* 45.

42. Robert Pierce Bunge, "The Sense of Community among the Traditional Teton Sioux" (paper presented to the Society for the Advancement of American Philosophy, Boston, March 1984).

43. Eastman, *Soul of the Indian,* 99–100.

44. Michel Foucault, *Madness and Civilization: A History of Insanity in the Age of Reason,* trans. Richard Howard (New York: Pantheon Books, 1965), 64.

45. Ibid., 46.

46. The recent *Report by the Commission on the Measurement of Economic Performance and Social Progress,* commissioned by French president Nicolas Sarkozy and coauthored by Nobel Laureates Joseph E. Stiglitz and Amartya Sen, along with Jean-Paul Fitsoussi, *Mismeasuring Our Lives,* offers strong evidence that leading economists are discontent with conventional economic measures and are in search of alternatives.

47. Robert Heilbroner, "Putting Economics in Its Place" (Coss Lecture, Society for the Advancement of American Philosophy, Boston, March 1995).

48. Franklin, "Remarks Concerning the Savages," in *Benjamin Franklin: Writings,* ed. J. A. Leo Lemay (New York: Library of America, 1987), 972.

12 John Dewey, Institutional Economics, and Confucian Democracies

Larry A. Hickman

For some economists, institutional theories offer an attractive alternative, or perhaps better put, attractive supplements, to conservative approaches based on the work of free-market theorists such as Milton Friedman and Friedrich Hayek, as well as liberal theories based on the work of John Maynard Keynes, which taken together form the central doctrines of what has been called the "neoclassical synthesis."[1] According to one noted conservative economist, neoclassical economic theory is based on several fundamental assumptions, including the following: "1. People have rational preferences among outcomes. 2. Individuals maximize utility and firms maximize profits. 3. People act independently on the basis of full and relevant information."[2]

There are several things worth noting about this economist's list and his accompanying commentary. First, he claims that these assumptions are not open to discussion among neoclassical economists, since they are so widely shared. Second, after listing several alternative metatheoretical frameworks, including institutional economics, he compares their proponents to flat-earthers in departments of geography and suggests that it would be better that they keep their views to themselves, at least until such time that they receive tenure. Third, and perhaps most important, he cheerfully acknowledges that the basic models of neoclassical economics are at base beholden to the language of mid-nineteenth-century physics. "Agents were like atoms; utility was like energy; utility maximization was like the minimization of potential energy, and so forth."[3] Once this linkage was in place, "to challenge the neoclassical approach was to seem to challenge science and progress and modernity." Finally, he points out that all participants in economically based decisions—and he pointedly includes environmentalists—now speak the language of neoclassical economics.

Well, perhaps—but not quite. There have been and still are alternatives, or perhaps supplements, that are worth considering. In his now famous essay "Why Is Economics Not an Evolutionary Science?," for example, published in 1898, Thorstein Veblen argued that some of these unquestioned assumptions of neoclassical economics are not only questionable but in fact deeply flawed.

He proposed supplanting the older economic models, based as they are on nineteenth-century physics (and metaphysics), with newer ones that are rooted in the evolutionary models of the biological sciences. He argued that neoclassical economic theory was in need of reconstruction because of its reliance on pre-Darwinian assumptions and outlooks.[4]

Veblen's principal criticism of neoclassical economics, conveyed in his luxuriant prose, was that it portrays the economic man (and woman) "as a lightening calculator of pleasures and pains, who oscillates like a homogeneous globule of desire of happiness under the impulse of stimuli that shift him about the area, but leave him intact. . . . He is an isolated definitive human datum, in stable equilibrium except for the buffets of the impinging forces that displace him in one direction or another."[5]

Veblen thus drills down beneath the stated assumptions of neoclassical economic theory[6] to reveal several of its even deeper unstated *metaphysical* assumptions, all of which he regards as outmoded and therefore defective. First, there is the idea of a Cartesian self with a fixed essence: *the rational man (and woman).* But of course William James had all but demolished this idea eight years earlier with the publication of his *Principles of Psychology*.

Second, there is the idea that this Cartesian self floats free as an atomic economic entity, independent and with scant regard for institutional context. Dewey, of course, thought otherwise. He charged this notion of economic individualism with impeding the progress of science and technology. "For the most part," he wrote, "economic individualism interpreted as energy and enterprise devoted to private profit, has been an adjunct, often a parasitical one, to the movement of technical and scientific forces."[7]

Third, there is the idea that pleasures and pains impinge on *Homo economicus* in ways that are specifiable, quantifiable, and calculable. Dewey had already addressed this issue, charging the utilitarians and their heirs with being hedonists committed to an unredeemable subjectivism. "The hedonists," he wrote in 1894, ". . . have appealed to feeling, and to feeling they must go for judgment. And feeling exists only as it is felt and only to him who feels it."[8] He recognized that there had been attempts to reform the earlier hedonistic theory by the introduction of "marginal utility," but he thought that the problem of subjectivism remained and still had not been dealt with adequately.[9]

Simply put, values and valuations must be part of a much larger inquiriential context. "Only where reflection occurs with a view to choice," Dewey writes, "is there comparison, and this comparison places each want in a system of activities, from its place in which each want derives its character, its degree and rank."[10] Here once again Dewey is emphasizing context, and moreover, context that is much larger than tends to be accounted for by doctrines of marginal utility. Lionel Robbins was later to move in this direction in *An Essay on the Nature and Significance of Economic Science*, in which he defined economics as "the science which studies human behavior as a relationship between ends and scarce means which have alternative uses."[11]

Elaborating on this point, Dewey summarized the fallacy of the neoclassical argument in the following way. "The essential fallacy is that the theory assumes that original and natural wants determine the economic phenomena of production and exchange. In fact, before they become economic wants—effective demands—they are reshaped by the existing distributive-exchange system. The market and business determine wants, not the reverse; the argument moves in a vicious circle." He then pointed out that the argument contains a logical mistake. There is an ambiguous middle term: "want" as psychological and "want" as actual demand are conflated.[12] Dewey's point is that putative fixes, such as the distinction between "absolute" demand and "effectual" demand, merely fine-tune the problem of hedonism. They do not fix it.

For his part, Veblen charges neoclassical economists with holding a type of behaviorism that relies on an antiquated model of the reflex arc that, he doubtless knew, had been thoroughly discredited by Dewey two years earlier in Dewey's now classic 1896 essay "The Reflex Arc Concept in Psychology."[13] One of the effects of this reconstruction of the traditional reflex arc model, of course, is a new emphasis on the formation and cultivation of selective interest among individuals through the activities of institutions, including social groups.

Dewey's and Veblen's alternative offered economists an image of an embodied and socially contexted human being who is "a coherent structure of propensities and habits which seeks realization and expression in an unfolding activity."[14] This alternative to the neoclassical version *Homo economicus* would not be isolated and autonomous, but situated and conditioned within the context of formative institutions of many and various types.

In other words, an evolutionary economic theory would take into account the history and present tendencies of the institutions that are instrumental to the formation of individuals and communities. The idea of a more or less static economic entity pushed and pulled by various forces but regularly returning to equilibrium would be replaced by a post-Darwinian model in which changing circumstances create newly informed and reconfigured individuals who are continually required to seek new ways of recalibrating their situation within those changing environments. Some cognitive neuroscientists working within the field of dynamic systems theory have designated these continually adjusting and readjusting matrices of organism/environment as "basins of attraction," and some of them, such as W. Teed Rockwell, have liberally acknowledged the influence of Dewey's groundbreaking "Reflex Arc" essay, published more than one hundred years ago.[15]

For Dewey, of course, the most important of these formative institutions are the ones charged with the task of education. Dewey continually stressed the importance of context (and especially the contextual role of educational institutions) in the formation of habits of action, including those involving economic behavior. He thought that even though most people are aware of an economic system in much the same way that they are aware of the weather, when the educational factor is introduced, when consciousness of the economic system is brought into the foreground, then it is possible to see their economic situation "as it is reflected in the imagination; in desire, hope, fear, intention to support or to change. In short, the contention is not in the least that our will, the body of our desires and purposes, is subservient to social conditions, but that the latter are incorporated into our attitudes, and our attitudes into social conditions, to such an extent that to maintain one is to maintain the other, to change one is to change the other."[16]

Institutionalism in economic theory thus received an early articulation in the work of Veblen, who was John Dewey's colleague at the University of Chicago during the 1890s. Institutionalism was further advanced during the 1930s and 1940s by John R. Commons, in his 1934 work *Institutional Economics,* and also by Clarence Ayres, who developed a rich synthesis of the insights of Veblen and Dewey. From Veblen, Ayres borrowed the distinction between instrumentalist and ceremonial (or institutional) values. From Dewey he adopted an instrumentalist theory of inquiry and an avoidance of underlying dualisms of all sorts. Ayres argued that whereas economists have tended to think of their field as primarily concerned with the science of prices, economics has more properly to do with the ways in which we can allocate goods so that there will continually be more to allocate. He thus follows Dewey in turning away from the idea of value as a predetermined essence to the idea that *valuing* (and not just *values*) is itself generally inchoate and thus in need of reconstruction by means of processes of evaluation that involve institutional factors.[17] There are many other, more recent contributions to institutionalism, of course, that I will not have the time to mention.

To recap, mainstream or neoclassical economics can now fairly be defined as the study of prices, or to put the matter more bluntly, "the study of choice in the face of scarcity." Moreover, "the agents who do the choosing are assumed to be rational, autonomous, self-interested, with preferences given in advance."[18] One of the primary methods of mainstream economics tends to be econometrics, or the application of mathematical and statistical models to economic data.

Schools of institutional economics tend to offer a broader purview. Especially in its newer forms they do not so much eschew mathematical analysis as argue that our understanding of economic conditions requires that we take fuller account of the cultural contexts within which mathematical and statistical models operate. Institutionalists are thus highly critical of some of the "unquestioned" assumptions of the classical synthesis, such as most versions of "rational choice theory" and what they regard as subjectivist accounts of "utility."

Dewey regarded the type of "unquestioned assumptions" of the classical synthesis that I have cited as an instance of what he termed "vicious intellectualism," on a par with the mythical social contract theories of the seventeenth and eighteenth centuries and the notion advanced by some utilitarian philosophers that there are pleasure units that can enter into a rational calculus. As I have already noted, he argued that there is a profound and debilitating subjectivism inherent in some of the assumptions of the neoclassical synthesis (i.e., that "individuals maximize utility" and that "people act independently on the basis of full and relevant information"). How, we can almost hear Dewey asking in his master work *Democracy and Education,* can it be claimed that "people can act independently on the basis of full and relevant information" in the absence of consideration of background institutions that support the type of socialization that binds them as individuals to communities at the same time that it provides them with ever broader vistas of the possible courses of action that will be required for the reconstruction of those institutions?

Dewey's rejection of some of the key assumptions of neoclassical economics was thus not simply advanced on the grounds that those assumptions tend too much toward laissez-faire, although that was in fact a part of his critique. It is a fairly simple matter to demonstrate the difficulties of hard-line libertarian economic ideas, since they are reductionistic on their face. As I write, for example, an economic study of lighthouses and autopsies has crossed my desk.[19] Lighthouses, of course, are public goods. They are something that we all need. Without them, much of our commerce would be impaired. But the market does not provide for lighthouses. The same is true of autopsies. Autopsies can provide important indicators of public health that are of potential benefit to all of us as a community. But free-market economic conditions do not support autopsies. The person being autopsied clearly has no interest in them. Under ordinary circumstances, families and relatives have little or no incentive to pay for them. And physicians, perhaps fearing malpractice suits, have a positive incentive to avoid them. Absent intervention into market forces by institutions of various types, how will these common goods be paid for?

It might be objected that these cases are trivial, or that in any event a pure free-market system is a mythical entity and that everyone agrees on the necessity of mechanisms of some sort or other to address market shortcomings and irregularities. Even though Friedrich Hayek is regarded in some circles as one of the patron saints of libertarian economists, for example, even he argued that an affluent state has the obligation to establish a viable set of safety nets, including some form of social security. And as John Kenneth Galbraith famously pointed out, citing a U.S. Department of Commerce brochure that promoted a "lemon aid stand" depiction of unregulated markets as the genius of the American system, there seems to be an "approved contradiction" between accounts of the way the American system is said to work, as a "lemon aid stand"–type market, and the way it works in practice, with its many regulations, tax loopholes, earmarks, and corporate bailouts.[20]

I should not leave this issue, however, without reporting that, during my years on the faculty at Texas A&M University, more than one of the members of the Department of Economics, a department whose faculty were heavily influenced by the Chicago School of economics and that at one point included future U.S. senator Phil Gramm, argued that the Great Depression of the 1930s was *caused* by government intervention into the free market and that left to its own devices the market would rapidly have corrected the situation. In short, it does not quite seem to be the case that "everyone" agrees that there need to be mechanisms of some sort or other available to address market shortcomings and irregularities, even during periods such as the Great Depression of the 1930s.

Examples of lighthouses and autopsies may be fresh, but the argument they are used to support in this particular case is hardly novel. Garrett Hardin's now famous 1968 essay, "The Tragedy of the Commons," for example, provided a clear demonstration of the kind of thinking that honors the subjective utility of the old individualism at the expense of community values, and he draws out some of the debilitating consequences for communal life.[21] Given the current, almost criminal neglect of the infrastructure of the United States, including its educational programs and facilities as well as its roads and bridges, it is perhaps time to encourage its public officials to revisit Hardin's argument.

What, then, can we say more specifically about the connections between institutionalism and discussions about democracy and economic development in Confucian societies, alluded to in my title?

First, the institutionalist insistence on cultural context fits nicely with arguments by sociologist Daniel A. Bell and others that the Chinese Communist Party will need to manage the country's economic development in ways that acknowledge and honor its Confucian traditions. In his 2008 book *China's New Confucianism,* for example, Bell argued that the government's emphasis on Confucian values would need to continue and that there is a high probability that it will.[22] "It is not entirely fanciful to surmise," he wrote, "that the Chinese Communist Party will be relabeled the Chinese Confucian Party in the next couple of decades." But, he added, "relabeling won't suffice if the government really plans to adopt Confucianism. The government needs to change the way it does things."[23] Bell then proceeds to argue that some aspects of Western-style liberal democracies may not be applicable to China's Confucian society, that it is arguable that there are currently more, and more interesting, experiments in democracy taking place in China than anywhere else in the world, and that there is a high probability that China's future will involve a system in which political leaders will be selected by examinations. "Performance on an exam, rather than party loyalty," he suggests, "would determine who occupies what government post."[24]

In short, he thinks that China's economic development will need to be embedded in a Confucian cultural-institutional context.

In one sense, Bell's analysis appears to be consistent with that of Veblen, who argued that the individual "enters into each successful action as a whole, although the specific end sought in a given action may be sought avowedly on the basis of a particular interest; as e.g., the economic, aesthetic, sexual, humanitarian, devotional interests. . . . There is, therefore, no neatly isolable range of cultural phenomena that can be rigorously set apart under the head of economic institutions, although a category of 'economic institutions' may be of service as a convenient caption."[25] In other words, economic activity is inevitably embedded in cultural traditions, whether acknowledged as such or not. Simply put, to ignore those traditions inevitably deforms analyses of economic activity, effectively leaving them as exercises on a drawing board, isolated from the flux of real-world events. As I write, U.S. congressman Paul Ryan and his Republican colleagues in the House of Representatives are rapidly learning that their attempts to end Medicare are colliding with some very insistent real-world events.

In this connection it should not be forgotten that even though Confucianism emphasizes the importance of institutions, those institutions have historically tended to be hierarchical in nature and to ossify over time. Dewey took note of this. Recognizing the fact that the Chinese tend to be quite pragmatic, he called for a new, more fluid form of Confucianism to be built on that institutional base. I shall say something more about this matter in a moment.

The case of another Confucian society, South Korea, may also prove instructive. Economist J. Barkley Rosser Jr. calls South Korea the "most Confucianist" of the three major Confucian states of China, Korea, and Japan. He describes what he terms "new institutional economics" as an attempt to reconcile the old institutional economics with conventional neoclassical economic theory. Drawing on the work of Karl Polanyi and others, he identifies a "new traditional economy," that is, an economy in which market forces "become at least somewhat embedded within some traditional structure, most likely based on a traditional religion, but also usually emphasizing [what he terms] familistic groupism."[26] New traditional economies thus employ modern forms of technology and are integrated into the world economy. The Confucian version of the new traditional economy (the Islamic version would be another one) emphasizes harmony and hierarchy, with emphasis on reciprocity within the hierarchy.

In the case of Korean Confucianism in general, according to Rosser, there has been a move away from the notion of hierarchy to a stronger emphasis on the importance of education and the central role of the family. But Rosser also finds a pattern within Korea of industrial firms that are designed for "a minimization of transaction costs within a hierarchically organized entity that runs itself along traditional Confucian lines within a technologically advanced economy integrated into the world economy."[27] The upside of this type of economic arrangement is that it does in fact take account of institutional contexts. The downside is that it is prone to crony capitalism.

This move away from hierarchy, coupled with a stronger emphasis on education,[28] and the role of the family as socializing force, fits nicely with Dewey's contention that scientific methods and the methods of democracy are intimately connected. As I have already noted, Dewey was well-informed about the cultural influence of Confucian values. He spent twenty-seven months in China, from May 1919 to August 1921, and he was deeply impressed by what he found there. In her 1999 book *John Dewey in China,* Jessica Ching-Sze Wang analyzed some of the subtle changes in Dewey's acute understanding of social institutions that appear in his post-1921 publications.[29] She attributed them to Dewey's observation of Chinese culture. She has done a great deal to illuminate the extent to which Dewey was not only teaching during those years, but learning as well. She has made a cogent case that what Dewey learned in China affected his later work, especially his thinking about democracy, in significant ways.

So Dewey understood and appreciated the pervasiveness of Confucian ideas and practices within Chinese culture, and he identified those ideas and practices, at their best, with the type of grassroots democracy that he thought laudatory. At the same time, however, he was critical of what he termed the old "petrified" expressions of Confucianism, which he thought were neither appropriate to modern conditions nor consistent with core Confucian values themselves. "The breakdown in Chinese national life," he wrote, "is proof of their inefficacy according to the standard of Confucianism itself. And Confucian education had become aristocratic, for the few only. Hence the need for a new culture, in which what is best in western thought is to be freely adopted—but adapted to Chinese conditions, employed as an instrumentality in building up a rejuvenated Chinese culture."[30] In short, Dewey called for a birth of a new Confucianism, a form of Confucianism that would better express the values that he identified as the profoundest cultural values of the Chinese people. The new Confucianism would not exhibit blind reliance on custom. It would avoid rigid hierarchies. It would be a culture of thought and intellectual influence.[31] This would be the institutional context, the cultural context, the new Confucian matrix, in which local development of science and technology would become embedded.

Dewey was particularly impressed with the Confucian emphasis on education, which, he noted, "created that extraordinary reverence for the teacher, that conviction of his abiding influence upon the life as well as the learning of pupils, which is so remarkable a trait of Chinese life, and which helps to explain the tendency of the Chinese to rely upon pacific reason rather than upon brawling force for settlement of troubles. Is there any other people," he wrote, "that has persistently believed that the influence of the teacher is in the end the most powerful of all social forces? What other nations are there whose heroes are moral teachers rather than revealers of supernatural affairs, priests, generals, statesmen?"[32]

It is also worth noting in this connection that Dewey rejected two sorts of arguments regarding the relationship of traditional cultures to science and technology. On one side, he rejected the claims of those who argued for the putative superiority of European culture on grounds that science and technology were "Western" in nature. On the other side, he argued against those who claimed that, because science and technology were uniquely "Western" in nature, their methods were inapplicable to non-Western cultures. More generally, he had little patience with claims that science and technology were uniquely Western, in any event. He thought that the methods of scientific thinking that had begun to be developed during the European seventeenth century were only accidentally European in origin. He thought it demonstrable that the methods of the techno-sciences have been proven to be effective across cultures. But he also thought that the expression of those methods would, and should, vary from one culture to another.

Major contributions to understanding the connections between Dewey's version of Pragmatism and the new Confucianism can of course be found in the work of David L. Hall and Roger T. Ames. Viewed in the context of the foregoing discussion, their analysis provides avenues whereby democratic practices in Confucian societies can be understood in terms of Pragmatism, and conversely. In their classic work *Democracy of the Dead,* published in 1999, for example, they discuss several features held in common by the two traditions. They include: (1) ethnocentrism and the importance of narrative, (2) social engagement, (3) self-cultivation, (4) the duty of remonstrance, (5) the importance of tradition, and (6) a democratic vision.[33]

Regarding the first point, Hall and Ames view what they term a "benign ethnocentrism" at work in both Pragmatism and Confucianism. This would involve a rejection of fixed essences such as the essentialist Cartesian self that is assumed by neoclassical economics and that I discussed earlier, as well as essentialist treatments of abstract political categories such as "democracy," "socialism," and so on. On the pragmatist side, William James put it very well: essences are teleological weapons of the mind. On the Confucian side, this involves an appreciation of the importance of cultural narratives. Here are Hall and Ames: "Universal laws of nature, scientific principles or logical categories do not best serve to define us at the levels of personal, social, and political existence."[34]

Given the current debates regarding the possibility of "universal values," it is important to be as clear as possible about this issue. According to a September 30, 2010, article in the *Economist,* Qin Xiao, recently retired chairman of China Merchants, the country's sixth-largest bank, set off a flurry of debate when he urged the graduates of one of China's leading business schools to "resist the lure of worldly things and to pursue 'universal values' such as freedom and democracy." According to Mr. Qin, discussions of universal values are anything but abstract: "Universal values tell us that government serves the people, that assets belong to the public and that urbanization is for the sake of people's happiness." He suggested that supporters of the "China Model" "believe the opposite: that people should obey the government, the state should control assets and the interests of individuals are subordinate to those of local development."[35]

Mr. Qin's statement about universal values is highly relevant to the theme of this presentation, since he seems to have put his finger on a deep fissure within the policies of the Chinese government. On one side, there appears to be an eagerness to capitalize on traditional Confucian values in order to promote harmony within a diverse, rapidly developing country. On the other side, the leaders seem to have allowed the values of the neoclassical economists to penetrate rather too deeply into that cultural context, with the consequence that the very cultural values that are being praised are also the ones that are most threatened. In short, Mr. Qin has illuminated the debate within government circles, and he has come down on the side of the institutionalists by appealing to the government to honor its own stated cultural commitments.

With respect to Confucianism more specifically, the Chinese government seems unable, so far, to make up its mind. It seems to want to counter the growing appeal of religious organizations and the diminished faith in communist utopian ideals by utilizing the Confucian card to maintain social unity and harmony. On the other side, however, it appears that the government is wary of *too much* Confucianism and so keeps a close eye on meetings in Confucius' hometown, fearing that Confucianism may take on the role of a new religion in competition with the party. Especially in China, then, among the main Confucian cultures, the current situation appears to be quite fluid. There is consequently much more that could be said about the role of institutional economic theory in the context of traditional cultures.

I will close, however, by pointing out that there are now strong indications that some of the new projects in institutional economics are beginning to get some traction. I call your attention, for example, to several essays produced by the Political Economy Program at the National Bureau of Economic Research, authored or coauthored by Alberto F. Alesina. Alesina writes of the increasing difficulty of fitting the various complexities of contemporary societies into the "traditional model of economic policy in which benevolent social planners maximize the utility of a representative individual." Some economists, he reports, have "started exploring how political forces affected the choice of policies, paying special attention to the distributive conflicts and political institutions, which are absent in representative agent models."[36]

If we add analysis of underlying ethical issues to this, we get something very much like John Dewey's analysis of desiderata for projects in economics. And if we add the specifics of institutional influences in traditionally Confucian societies, I suggest, then we get important resources to bring to the continuing discussions about the future of democratic forms of life in those societies.

NOTES

I am grateful to Kenneth Stikkers and Sun Ning for their helpful comments on an earlier draft of this essay.

1. Paul Samuelson, among others, emphasized the continuity between neoclassical microeconomics and Keynesian macroeconomics.

2. See E. Roy Weintraub, "Neoclassical Economics," *Concise Encyclopedia of Economics,* http://www.econlib.org/library/Encl/NeoclassicalEconomics.html, accessed September 8, 2011.

3. Ibid.

4. My colleague Kenneth Stikkers reminds me that neoclassical economists now claim that, even if their anthropology may be a bit off, their position nevertheless has strong predictive value.

5. Thorstein Veblen, "Why Is Economics Not an Evolutionary Science?" *Quarterly Journal of Economics* 12, no. 4 (1898), 389.

6. Veblen was apparently one of the first, if not the first, to employ the term "neoclassical economics." See his essay "The Preconceptions of Economic Science," *Quarterly Journal of Economics* 14, no. 2 (February 1900), 240–269. He uses the term on page 261.

7. John Dewey, *Later Works,* 5.85.

8. John Dewey, *Early Works,* 3.272.

9. John Dewey, *Middle Works,* 15.264. "Marginal utility" is usually defined as the utility gained (or lost) as a result of an increase (or decrease) in the consumption of a good or service.

10. Dewey, *Middle Works,* 15.265.

11. Lionel Robbins, *An Essay on the Nature and Significance of Economic Science* (London: Macmillan, 1932), 15.

12. Dewey, *Later Works,* 15.264. Economists in the nineteenth century distinguished between "absolute demand" and "effectual demand." In fine, the difference is between "I want *x*" and "I want *x* so much that I am willing to sacrifice *y*." Dewey's response is that this distinction does not fix the hedonism problem.

13. Dewey, *Early Works,* 5.96–109.

14. Veblen, "Why Is Economics Not an Evolutionary Science?" 390.

15. See W. Teed Rockwell, *Neither Brain nor Ghost* (Cambridge, MA: MIT Press, 2005).

16. Dewey, *Later Works,* 7.342.

17. Other influential institutional economists have included J. Fagg Foster, Marc R. Tool, and James Webb.

18. Julie A. Nelson, "Value as Rationality: Feminist, Pragmatist, and Process Thought Meet Economics," *Journal of Speculative Philosophy* 15, no. 2 (2001), 139.

19. David Kestenbaum, "What Should the Government Pay For? Autopsies and Lighthouses!" NPR Planet Money Blog, http://www.npr.org/blogs/money/2010/12/10/131784161/what-should-the-government-pay-for-autopsies-lighthouses, accessed September 7, 2011.

20. John Kenneth Galbraith, *The New Industrial State,* 4th ed. (New York: Houghton Mifflin, 1985), 27.

21. See Garrett Hardin, "The Tragedy of the Commons," *Garrett Hardin Society,* http://www.garretthardinsociety.org/articles/art_tragedy_of_the_commons.html, accessed September 8, 2011 (previously published in *Science,* December 13, 1968).

22. Daniel A. Bell, *China's New Confucianism: Politics and Everyday Life in a Changing Society* (Princeton, NJ: Princeton University Press, 2008), 13.

23. Ibid., 12–13.

24. Ibid., 13.

25. Veblen, "Why Is Economics Not an Evolutionary Science?" 393.

26. J. Barkley Rosser Jr. and Marina V. Rosser, "The New Institutional Economy and the New Traditional Economy in Korea: Does the Confucian Tradition Give It a Competitive Edge," 8, http://cob.jmu.edu/rosserjb/THE%20NEW%20INSTITUTIONAL%20ECONOMY%20AND%20THE%20NEW%20TRADITIONAL%20ECONOMY%20IN%20KOREA.doc, accessed September 8, 2011.

27. Rosser, "New Institutional Economy," 15.

28. The caveat here is that education in some Asian societies tends to emphasize "cramming."

29. Jessica Ching-Sze Wang, *John Dewey in China* (Albany: State University of New York Press, 2007).

30. Dewey, *Middle Works,* 13.114.

31. Dewey, *Middle Works,* 13.256.

32. Dewey, *Middle Works,* 13.224–225.

33. Roger T. Ames and David L. Hall, *Democracy of the Dead: Dewey, Confucius, and the Hope for Democracy in China* (Chicago: Open Court, 1999), 150–162.

34. Ibid., 151.

35. "The Debate over Universal Values," *Economist,* September 30, 2010, http://www.economist.com/node/17150224.

36. Alberto F. Alesina, "Program Report," *NBER Reporter* 3 (2007), http://www.nber.org/programs/pol/pol.html, accessed September 9, 2011.

The Responsible Society as Social Harmony

13

Walter G. Muelder's Communitarian Social Ethics as a Bridge Tradition for Confucian Economics

Robert Smid

The question of what would constitute a "Confucian" economics for the twenty-first century is a decidedly unsettled one. Drawing back to the places and times in which the Confucian tradition held significant sway over such questions, it is fair to say that it resulted in nothing much like the two economic systems—communism and capitalism—that have dominated the twentieth century (any minor similarities notwithstanding). At the same time, however, the powerful influence of these two systems requires that any consideration of new economic directions, Confucian or otherwise, proceed in conversation with at least one—or, ideally, both—of these systems.

Contemporary China is, of course, a case in point. While it has roughly two thousand years of Confucian influence informing its development, the last sixty—the most influential sixty on the present—have been informed primarily by its embrace of communism. So strong has the latter influence been that, even in the case of China's experimentation with capitalism, such experiments are better understood against the backdrop of its communist history than against its earlier Confucian commitments. As the source and historical mainstay of the Confucian tradition, China could achieve powerful and game-changing results in its economic organization if it were able to draw productively on the strengths of that tradition, but it will be able to do so only if it can bring Confucianism into dialogue with both communism and capitalism.

The obvious question at the beginning of any such inquiry is simple: Why bother? Confucianism may represent an interesting part of China's history, but what is there about the tradition to suggest that it has anything to offer a twenty-first-century economy—Chinese or otherwise? The argument for exploring the contemporary application of Confucianism, I believe, stems less from its own inherent advantages and more from the evident shortcomings of existing systems. That is, it is unlikely that Confucianism will be able to provide a full-fledged economic system that is a viable alternative to communism or capitalism, something made clear by the fact that every country in its sphere of influence has embraced one or the other of the alternatives. This notwithstanding, it can still make an important contribution to economic theory—both in its own sphere and worldwide—if it can provide a helpful corrective to one or both of those alternatives.

As communism and capitalism reach increasingly higher levels of refinement, they become not only more effective at delivering on their strengths but also more exposed in their weaknesses. Communism may have already revealed its weaknesses—not least of which is its tendency toward unchecked tyranny at the highest levels—which has contributed in part to the continued success of capitalism; but capitalism, too, seems to be reaching its apex, as demonstrated by its increasingly evident inability to foster the very conditions that sustain it (e.g., honesty, loyalty, and equality of opportunity, to name a few). These are not mere "inefficiencies" within these economic systems, such as could be addressed by more stringent application of their basic commitments; instead, they reveal problems that these systems were never meant to address, but which turn out to be of importance not only to their viability in particular but also to the quality and stability of broader societies in which they are located.

In this essay, I argue that Confucianism has within it the resources to launch a constructive critique of both economic theories. Certainly, one need not look very far to find a well-grounded moral critique that can apply to either system; however, a mere critique is not enough. In order to be taken seriously in the global marketplace of ideas, any such critique must be followed by a promising and practicable alternative. This will be somewhat more challenging for Confucianism, insofar as its failure to present a viable alternative to communism and capitalism has also largely prevented it from developing a more modest and constructive corrective to those systems.

To help the Confucian tradition meet this challenge, I propose the employment of a bridge tradition as a medium between it and the two economic systems. The idea for such a medium is adapted from the work of David Hall and Roger Ames, who recognized that it is often easier to understand the dominant tradition in another culture when meaningful lines of connection can be drawn by analogy to similar, albeit recessive traditions in one's own culture. For their comparative work, this meant taking their cues "from the manner in which the intellectual activity in classical China *most analogous to* our first problematic has been addressed."[1] Whereas Hall and Ames employed bridge traditions to facilitate cross-cultural hermeneutics, however, I propose employing them to facilitate cross-cultural theory construction. While the Confucian tradition fared poorly in the twentieth century as a conversation partner for economic systems, other traditions from very different cultural contexts have been able to develop a much richer discourse as critical yet constructive correctives for these systems. If meaningful lines of connection can be drawn by analogy between these traditions and the underlying commitments and concerns of the Confucian tradition, they could serve as a springboard for contemporary Confucians to more ably develop their own critical constructive discourse in economics.

Rather than scouring the later Confucian tradition for the most insightful critiques of communism and capitalism, then, I will draw attention to one of the core values of the Confucian tradition—namely, the ideal of harmony (*he*, 和)—and demonstrate how it informs classical Chinese economic considerations. I will then move to consider a largely sidelined Western tradition, Walter G. Muelder's communitarian social ethics, which I believe both presents an incisive critique of communism and capitalism and also bears significant similarities with Confucian concerns. Specifically, I will draw attention to how his understanding of property rights in the context of a "responsible society" bears significant similarities to the Confucian ideal of harmony as understood in a social context. Finally, in light of the analogous, cross-cultural connection between these two traditions, I will consider how a Confucian critique of these economic systems might be informed by Muelder's thought and offer some thoughts about what the resulting discourse might look like.[2]

Economic Values from Classical Confucians

The difficulty in trying to identify the core values that would inform Confucian economics derives from the fact that the classical Confucians never laid out a coherent economic system of their own; instead, their contributions tend to stem from critiques of initiatives undertaken by other ruling parties. The most promising approach to identifying these values, then, is to start with core Confucian values and find out which ones find consistent embodiment in those critiques. Of the many values that Confucians champion, I have found the ideal of harmony to be not only one of the most pervasive and influential but also the most consistently embodied in economic discourse.[3]

The Chinese word for harmony has an interesting history that helps explain the underlying meaning of the term, having roots in at least two different but related veins of Chinese history and culture. The first of these can be found in the etymology of the component graphs themselves, 和, which—stemming back to early bronze inscriptions—represent a plant and a mouth;[4] as suggested by several Zhou dynasty texts, this is often taken to represent the need to balance a variety of diverse flavors to create a tasty dish.[5] The second root pertains to traditional singing practices in ancient China. Quoting the *Shuowen jiezi* (Explanation of words and characters), which states that "'harmony' is one replying to another" (2a, *kou bu,* 32a), Zhang Dainian explains that the term reflects the way in which one singer would respond to another in traditional musical form.[6] Harmony, in this context, is thus the bringing together of otherwise disparate voices into a common refrain.[7]

Although the contexts of these two roots are different, they share a common concern. This connection is made clear in the *Zuo zhuan* (Zuo's commentary) when Yanzi (Yan Ying) argues that harmony is different from mere assent.

> As the early kings established the doctrine of the five tastes, so they made the harmony of the five notes, to make their minds equable and to perfect their government. There is an analogy between sounds and flavors. . . . If you would try to give water a flavor with water, who would care to partake of the result? If lutes were to be confined to one note, who would be able to listen to them? Such is the insufficiency of mere assent.[8]

Harmony, he insists, may require that things be brought together into a unity, but one cannot do this without also acknowledging and embracing their diversity. True harmony integrates diverse elements in a way that does not diminish variety or eliminate opposition, but rather reconciles them in a new way within a broader context.[9]

For Confucians, this notion of harmony finds application in at least three contexts: within individual human beings, among fellow human beings in society, and between Heaven and human beings (bringing their respective orders in continuity with one another). These contexts are taken to be fundamentally interrelated, such that harmony in one context can inspire, inform, or reflect harmony in the others. Seminal texts like the *Zhongyong* link these contexts explicitly, and those connections reverberate through the mainstay of Confucian accounts of harmony. Accordingly, any account of harmony must pay attention to all three contexts, even if one is of particular concern and relevance. I will examine each one in turn, paying particular attention to how each applies to economic considerations.

Understood within the context of individual human beings, Confucians typically use the term "harmony" to refer to the proper ordering and expression of feelings and emotions. Feelings and emotions are taken to be natural in their own right, but their naturalness does not justify their unregulated expression; rather, being civilized requires a careful ordering and/or nurturing of these natural drives. Understood in an individual context, this is equivalent to moral self-cultivation, a process that can be both inspired and reinforced by the consistent practice of appropriate rituals.

As applied to economics, this is perhaps best exemplified in discussions pertaining to the desire for personal profit. Confucius himself doesn't seem to discuss the issue in great detail, but he does make two comments in the *Lunyu* that set the stage for all subsequent discourse within the tradition. "The noble person is concerned with rightness," he states; "the small person is concerned with profit."[10] Likewise, he notes that "wealth and honor are what people desire, but one should not abide in them if it cannot be done in accordance with the Way."[11] From these passages, it is clear that he gives moral considerations a higher standing than economic ones; what the passages fail to address, however, is what value economic considerations have in their own right.

To find further clarification, we must look to Mencius, who was able to develop several of Confucius' basic ideas in much more detail. Indeed, Mencius proves himself to be particularly concerned with the relative importance of material well-being. For example, the opening passage of the *Mencius* recounts a conversation he had with King Hui of Liang, in which the king asked him how the wandering teacher could profit his state. "Why must the king speak of profit?" Mencius replied. "There are humaneness and rightness, that is all."[12] He goes on to explain that concerning oneself with profit only encourages others to do likewise, thus leading eventually to a society in which each person is concerned only with his or her own advantage—in other words, hardly a society at all. "When rightness is subordinated to profit," he warns, "the urge to lay claim to more becomes irresistible."[13] What this suggests is that the desire for profit is not bad in its own right but becomes destructive when it is left unbounded and not circumscribed by humaneness and rightness.

This reading is reinforced by Mencius' more general discussion of moral beginnings, or "sprouts." Beyond the famous discussion of the "four beginnings,"[14] Mencius uses the discourse of beginnings as a strategy for encouraging moral development in his interlocutors. When he meets with another king who claims a love of wealth as one of his weaknesses, Mencius turns the tables and points out how such love is, at its most basic, a source of enjoyment and a good to that extent. The love of wealth becomes problematic only when it is not enjoyed in the context of socially appropriate forms (i.e., rituals). The challenge for the king, then, is not to give up his love of wealth, but to learn how to extend the enjoyment it entails to his people as well.[15] Such an action not only would order the king's desires appropriately, but also would create favorable conditions under which his subjects could cultivate their own morality. In this context, then, material well-being is not the impediment to moral development, but the catalyst for it—if only ordered appropriately.

As should be evident, attending to harmony in the individual has inevitable social connotations, so it provides a smooth transition into the social dimensions of harmony. As Xinzhong Yao writes, social harmony is

> the result of an appropriate accommodation of one's own needs to the requirements of others. Confucianism holds that a human is by nature a social being, who knows innately, or can be taught to know, how to relate to others and how to treat others properly. To be a human, therefore, is not merely to look after one's own interests and satisfy one's own desires.[16]

Rather, to be human is to be concerned with the interests of all human beings and with how to coordinate their often conflicting desires in such a way that serves the best interests of everyone in the community. As in the individual sphere, the Confucian solution to moderating these conflicting interests (i.e., achieving social harmony) has typically been the careful observation of proper rituals, although Confucian scholars have not hesitated to critique specific practices and propose eminently practical solutions.

Within a social context, economic considerations have applied primarily to questions concerning fair standards of the distribution of wealth. For example, the well-field system championed—or, in his terms, revived—by Mencius attempts to set up a tax structure that provides an adequate income to the government while both moderating the tax burden on any individual and ensuring equality of that burden among individuals.[17] The idea behind this arrangement was that it properly balanced the competing needs of individuals and the state and was thus able to provide the framework for a harmonious society. Likewise, the Confucian position in the Salt and Iron Debates[18] was premised in large part on the undue hardship that state monopolies placed on the rest of the population, both through price gouging and by exacerbating the growing gap between rich and poor. Both examples share a set of basic underlying convictions: first, that, while the government must be able to secure the material means for its own survival, the people need to be able to do the same; and second, that any economic considerations beyond this should be structured in such a way as to benefit the whole.

The implications of whether or not one achieves this harmony on a social level are played out in the third context: namely, the harmony between human beings and Heaven. As Yao notes, while Confucians are most vocal about the need for harmony on this level, they are also the most divided about what such harmony entails.[19] Such differences notwithstanding, the economic repercussions are clear: the extent to which harmony is achieved on an individual and social level both reflects and feeds into the broader harmony that exists in the cosmos as a whole. If a ruler tends only to his own personal gain, he can expect his kingdom to suffer for it; likewise, if he fails to moderate the conflicting needs and desires of his people, he can expect the same. If left untended long enough, a ruler can expect to lose the mandate of Heaven; stated differently, if disorder is allowed to reach a certain magnitude, the mandate will naturally gravitate toward a new center that can restore the harmonious balance modeled by Heaven. What this reveals is that, while Confucians acknowledge that there is sufficient moral reason to be concerned with the plight of the poor and a fair distribution of resources, there is a very practical reason to be so concerned as well. The stability of civilization itself depends on the ruler's ability to maintain harmonious relationships within society.

Given the nearly limitless effects of governing well or poorly, it is not surprising to find that Confucians have seldom hesitated to propose sweeping changes when such changes are seen as necessary for establishing or maintaining harmony. This is nowhere better exemplified than in the well-field system mentioned earlier—championed by Mencius but revived at various points throughout the Confucian tradition. Adopting this system would have required the king to redistribute all land under his control, not only relocating all those who worked the land but also redefining their communities. To Mencius, such a revolutionary change was worthwhile because of the equitable distribution of workload and tax burden that it placed on people—a distribution that he considered otherwise impossible in the social and economic arrangements of his time. Moreover, he argued, it was the economic arrangement (supposedly) adopted by the ancient sage-kings, which should provide additional confidence not only that it was the best possible arrangement but also that it was possible to implement. Mencius' arguments notwithstanding, it is arguably the radical nature of his proposed changes that prevented them from being adopted not only in his own time but in any time thereafter, despite its continued support by several later Confucians.

The success of the well-field system (or lack thereof) notwithstanding, the point is not that Confucians have been known to make radical propositions, but rather that they have been willing to fundamentally reconsider any aspect of existing arrangements, economic and otherwise. Because all such arrangements are human constructions, they are all subject to review; to not make a choice, in such cases, is still to make a choice. Accordingly, Confucians have felt no compunction to apply any talk of individual rights into economic considerations; as the well-field system makes clear, any claim that an individual might make to any resource is itself a social arrangement, and one that can be modified at the discretion of those responsible for ordering that society. Indeed, this conviction is at the heart of all Confucian discussions about taxation.

Before moving on, it is worth noting one last point about the role of harmony in Confucian discourse: although it consists of the reconciliation of conflicts within a broader context, there is nothing in the discussion of harmony to suggest that the ultimate goal is the elimination of such conflicts. Conflict is taken to be a natural part of the world, such that trying to eliminate it would be as futile as trying to eliminate desire. A successful implementation of harmony is instead one that can recognize conflicts as they emerge and reconcile them in short order. In other words, harmony is best exemplified not in the *reconciliation* of conflicts but in *reconciling* them. What this means is that there can be no "Confucian economics" in any static sense; rather, any such economics must be defined primarily by its readiness to adjust as necessary to bring about the greatest harmony in each new situation. As Yao writes, "harmony is not considered a static identity, in which everything holds to its status quo and nothing is to be changed. Rather, harmony is regarded as a result of constant changes and reconciliation of conflict."[20] In this respect, it is reflective of the Dao itself: always changing, and having a character definable only in terms of the constancy of those changes. It may be that the Confucian tradition is ill equipped to launch a full-scale economic theory and is better suited to critiquing existing economic systems in light of the disharmonious features of a given context.

Walter G. Muelder and the "Responsible Society"

Walter Muelder was not a Confucian. While he took seriously the contributions of non-Western intellectual traditions and maintained an active interest in their relevance to Western ideas,[21] he was primarily a Christian theologian, personalist philosopher, and social ethicist. In fact, according to Gary Dorrien, he was "the leading personalist of his generation"[22] and "one of the mid-century's four leading proponents of social ethics as a discipline, along with Niebuhr, Bennett, and James Luther Adams."[23] In addition, he was also a Social Gospeler, a pacifist, and a socialist, who, by virtue of his prominent standing as the dean of Boston University's School of Theology, was able to exert tremendous influence on the social issues of his day. But Muelder was not a Confucian—Boston or otherwise—and I will make no attempt to dress him up as such.

The reason for focusing on Muelder, then, is because his commitments bear some striking similarities to those of classical Confucians, which provides reason to believe that his work might help to inform the development of a constructive Confucian critique of contemporary economics.[24] Standing outside of the mainstream allowed Muelder to attain some critical distance from the assumptions that typically dominate Western discourse. For example, his commitment to socialism makes him critical of both communism and capitalism, placing him in much the same constructive space as Confucians in trying to forge a constructive critique of both systems. Moreover, his willingness to critique the social arrangements of his time is reminiscent of that of the classical Confucians, even if Muelder's specific commitments—which consisted of strong support for women's rights and a prominent role in fighting against racial segregation—are quite far removed from those of most Confucians.

Most important, however, are the similarities that his communitarian social ethics seem to bear with Confucian commitments.[25] Communitarianism is based on the conviction that, because human beings are social by nature, it is not necessarily inappropriate to subordinate individuals to social institutions. Social institutions can serve an important—and, at points, indispensable—role in enabling human flourishing (including individual self-realization, the strengthening of social bonds, and organization toward common ends), and such institutions should be accorded power over individuals proportionate to the requirements of their task (i.e., relative to the responsibilities placed on them). This is not to say that individuals should always be subordinated to institutions but that in some cases this may be the most appropriate arrangement.

Given his simultaneous commitment to the Social Gospel, Muelder may seem an unlikely candidate for linkage with a Confucian vision for economics. The Social Gospel is well-known for its emphasis on the social and structural dimensions of economic and other related forms of exploitation, which seems to run counter to a Confucian tradition that has looked primarily to social structures as the means for dispensing and preserving morally appropriate economic and other relations. As aware as he was of the potential evils of social institutions, however, Muelder also recognized their positive potential and did not hesitate to make them a central part of the solutions he posed to the most pressing problems of his day. A fair rendering of his position on social institutions is that he remained keenly aware of both their promise and their peril and sought to make careful and informed judgments about the conditions under which they should be given power over individual interests.

Muelder's commitment to this "mixed-economy" model—wherein some economic problems were solved privately and others by the government, each determined in accordance with the particular context of the problem—helps to locate him between laissez-faire capitalism and communism and thus to maintain some critical distance from both. Certainly, he tended more toward socialism than most of his contemporaries in America—hence, his moniker as the "Red Dean" of Boston University—but, as his student J. Philip Wogaman notes, his commitment to a mixed-economy model was not itself outside of the mainstream in the economic discussions of his day.[26]

The standard that Muelder used to navigate judicious support for social institutions was *responsibility,* a virtue that plays a central role in all of his work. Responsibility, for Muelder, entails the willingness of people both as individuals and as a social whole to attend not only to their material interests but also to the ethical claims that they have on one another. At a basic minimum, it includes "ideas of human dignity, moral obligation, freedom, values, social goals, participation and interpersonal solidarity."[27] Within the context of economic concerns, responsibility entails recognizing the social implications of any set of economic arrangements, and bringing the related ethical claims to bear on those arrangements.

It is not enough to recognize those claims, however; responsibility also requires action, and action requires realistic possibilities. Muelder writes that "responsibility must go beyond both accommodation and negative moral protest. Ideal possibilities alone do not suffice; responsible possibilities must be in principle practicable."[28] In some cases, it may be possible to achieve responsible ends through individual means, while in other cases an institutional solution is required. In any case, a responsible society is one in which the economic interests are not treated in isolation from social ethical claims, and in which solutions—individual or institutional—are applied in accordance with the general welfare of the whole.

Responsibility is thus, for Muelder, "a thoroughly constructive idea."[29] It does not propose a static economic framework along the lines of communism or capitalism, but rather argues for a flexibility that preserves both economic interests and ethical claims, a delicate balance that is likely to differ in different contexts. It is also an ultimately productive idea: it is, in the end, better for the general welfare to allow government interaction at various points. He writes:

> Left to itself, private economic activity will fluctuate, and when it contracts it is inevitable that there will be intervention of some sort. Thus, it is no longer a question of government versus no government; it is a question of the community accepting responsibility for the general welfare.[30]

If the government can (and must) intervene for reasons of economic stability, then there is no reason why it should not be able to do so for ethical reasons as well; such interventions, if undertaken responsibly, will improve the general welfare. Certainly, there may be some who do not benefit from such interventions, but if government—as a social construction—is supposed to be concerned with protecting the general welfare, then this should always trump the interests of individuals.

A good example of how such an idea can be applied practically is found in Muelder's treatment of the concept of property. The dominant assumption in Western traditions of economics, he notes, is that the idea of "property" consists of a supposed relation between persons and things. This understanding is not only wrongheaded, he argues; it is also baseless. It is impossible to guarantee that all existing property has been fairly and legitimately distributed, and it is equally impossible to guarantee that such fairness and legitimacy are maintained in any ongoing exchanges. Such problems as theft are not eliminated by such a system, but rather masked and perpetuated. In such a model, any existing arrangement of property distribution can be accounted for only in terms of arbitrary happenstance, defended only in terms of the insistence by the supposed owners of property of their rightful claim, and maintained only by the power of property owners to enforce their claims.

The problem with this account of property, he argues, is that it rests on a misunderstanding of the fundamental relationship underlying it. Property is not a relationship between persons and things, but rather a relationship among persons within a community with respect to goods available within that community. It thus reflects an agreement within a community that some person or group of persons is granted use of a certain set of goods and that that claim to those goods is validated and enforced by the community. Understood in this respect, property can still be bought and sold, but such transactions pertain to claims rather than things. The community therefore remains relevant to any such transactions, insofar as it is only the community that can validate—or, if necessary, invalidate—such claims.

Such an understanding of property is much more capable of supporting and defending the distribution of property. Whatever the history behind the accumulation of property and however transactions of property have been enacted, the existing distribution is always the expression of the will of the community. Even when the community abrogates its responsibility—as, if Muelder is right, it typically does in laissez-faire capitalism—the existing arrangements still represent its tacit approval. This is evidenced from the fact that, if the community refused to acknowledge the claims of any given property holder, that claim would effectively become meaningless.

It is important to take note at this point that, when Muelder refers to "the community," he has in mind communities as they exist within a democratic context—namely, where the community is the ultimate source of political power. Yet, arguably, the case can be extended to veritably any form of government (except in the most extreme cases), as government itself is meaningless apart from the consent of the governed. For Muelder's account of property to work, therefore, the only requisite feature of government is that its laws reflect in some way the will of the community.

What this means is that the government has a profound mix of latitude and responsibility in ordering the property relations that exist among its people. The latitude stems from the fact that all claims to property are subject to reconsideration by the government, insofar as it represents the legal enforcement of the will of the community. Certainly, stability is of utmost importance to responsible management, since frequent and frivolous changes to any claim to property undermine the value of all claims to property. However, it also reminds property holders that their claims are not eternal and absolute but rather part of a complex and ongoing set of negotiations within the community.

The responsibility, in turn, stems from the requirement that, in any transactions pertaining to property, the government always represent the best interests of the community as a whole. This account of the government's responsibility requires some further explanation on three points. First, there may be, by virtue (or vice) of the current political arrangements, some gap between what a community wants and what is in its best interests. In representative democracies, for example, leaders are elected not primarily on their willingness to do whatever the community wants but rather on their ability to make sound decisions that represent the best interests of the people. Similarly, in constitutional monarchies, rulers are bestowed with the trust—albeit somewhat guarded—that they will act in the best interests of the community. All of this notwithstanding the fact that communities often don't know what their interests are (best or otherwise) or are too fragmented or disorganized to manifest a united voice. To be sure, Muelder, as a communitarian, argues that strengthening the role of community within government will allow for a more agreeable distribution of property, but the fact is that his theory of property can be applied in noncommunitarian settings with positive results so long as the government can be understood to be working in the best interests of the community.

Second, in attempting to represent the will of the community, the government must actively and consciously distinguish between the best interests of some (including many or most) of the community and those of the community as a whole (i.e., the community itself). Communities are not like joint shareholders, where the ones with the most property and/or the loudest voices are the ones who should have the most influence. Instead, all decisions should be made in the best interests of the community qua community. This may result in a disproportionate distribution of property among members, and it may not; these are decisions that the government will have to make, either reflective of or otherwise on behalf of the community's best interests.

Finally, this understanding of property does not obviate talk of property rights. Rights continue to be important, although they are understood in terms of moral claims rather than contractual ones. Muelder writes that

> a right is a moral claim of the person on the community for some value which is essential to the . . . satisfaction of some common need in human nature. Property rights, then, have to do with moral claims of members of a community on each other, or of groups of persons on other groups, with respect to scarce instrumental values.[31]

Property rights, then, constitute the moral claim made by one part of a community to a set of goods that is otherwise open to the whole community and that is affirmed in turn by the rest of the community. While this does not prevent that claim from being rescinded by the community, it should provide them with an added level of security and stability insofar as they represent concessions from the community. In other words, property rights are not inviolate, but they should be taken seriously.

Cross-Cultural Connections

As should be clear from the explications of the Confucian value of harmony (*he*) and Muelder's concept of the "responsible society," there are some strong points of convergence between the two. Although neither represents a full-fledged economic system, both have been active as critics of the prevailing systems of their day. Furthermore, if one considers Confucianism in its contemporary context, both strive to develop a critical voice in contrast to both communism and capitalism. Most important, however, both seek to develop this voice within the context of a social vision that integrates economic interests with social ethical concerns, on the conviction that such integration best serves the general welfare. Indeed, the two even share a similar vision with respect to what values should inform a good society—embodied responsibility turns out not to be so different from social harmony after all. While they might not champion all the same values (e.g., Confucians have typically placed much less emphasis on freedom and democratic participation), Confucians would find it quite natural to lend support to the other values Muelder uses to describe the responsible society: human dignity, moral obligation, social goals, and interpersonal solidarity.[32]

Take, for example, the similarities between Muelder's account of property and Mencius' advocacy for the well-field system. Evidently, both are willing to reconceive even the most fundamental rules of how society is organized if it will ultimately result in a more appropriate—responsible or harmonious—ordering of the needs and desires of the members of that society. Moreover, their rationale for such a reordering seems to stem from a common conviction that, because human beings are fundamentally social, it is not necessarily inappropriate to give priority to the interests of the general welfare even over those of specific individuals. Finally, the intended result of each reorganization is a strengthening of society as a whole, expressed through themes of social integration, fairness (through at least rough equality), and encouragement of general human flourishing. Thus, it is hard not to hear a certain Boston personalist resonating in a strikingly similar key when Irene Bloom writes the following:

> In his discussion of the well-field system Mencius harks back to a time in the past when, according to tradition, landholding among the common people had been generally equal and village life had been cooperative. Whether the well-field system actually pertained in the past, as Mencius claims, or represented an idealization that gained reality through a process of recreation of the historical past, his recalling it suggests that *equality of landholding and mutual cooperation among the people represented themes of considerable antiquity and moral resonance.*[33]

Again, the point here is not to argue that Muelder's commitments are the same as those of the Confucian tradition; rather, it is to argue that they are sufficiently analogous as to provide a productive conversation partner for the Confucian tradition as it develops its own critical constructive position with respect to contemporary economic systems.

The advantage that Muelder's communitarianism has over traditional Confucian engagements with economics is that it is eminently more practicable. Looking back to the well-field system, for example, the large-scale and immediate changes that it would have required—redistributing all land, relocating families, redefining communities, and so on—make it little mystery that it was never successfully implemented in China for any significant period of time. Muelder's account, by contrast, carries with it the same readiness to redefine property relations in light of social ethical concerns, but it requires no radical redistribution up front; rather, property claims are renegotiated as conflicts arise, allowing for a more gradual—and less risky—implementation.

Certainly, Confucians have proposed less revolutionary economic arrangements over the course of their history, but because they have more often than not represented the status quo, they have often had difficulty productively engaging new economic developments. This can be seen in the resistance evident in most classical Confucians in coming to terms with the emerging mercantile economy (see, e.g., the agrarian foundations of the well-field system and the distrust of merchants in the Salt and Iron Debates), a tendency that contributed to the downfall of Confucianism as China rushed to enter the modern world. The end result is a tradition that doesn't have ready at hand the necessary resources for engaging the complexities of contemporary global economics in an informed and compelling way.

Muelder's communitarianism, by contrast, emerged out of the contemporary context and is informed by a penetrating critique of prevailing economic systems founded in concrete experience of their shortcomings. As a result, it is able to forge ahead with progressive proposals for the revision of existing economic systems. Now that it has been stripped of the imperial patronage that it had enjoyed—for the most part—for over two millennia, Confucianism can no longer assume the conservative perspective it maintained during its tenure; to be relevant, it must make a critical contribution to the existing system, and in this respect it must take on a progressive voice, something that it can learn to do quickly by taking its lead from communitarianism.

Moreover, communitarianism carries with it a well-developed language for critiquing those systems and more specifically for doing so in a way that can integrate social ethical concerns with informed economic analysis. By drawing on this language, the Confucian tradition can circumvent the difficult process of identifying the weaknesses of these systems and proceed with a means for addressing them in a manner that is already congenial to its own commitments.

For example, it can draw on the carefully argued critiques of the fact/value distinction, a distinction that is far less pronounced in traditionally Confucian contexts but that dominates economic considerations in laissez-faire capitalism. If Confucianism is going to be taken seriously as a conversation partner in economic matters, it must be able to more than insist on the central relevance of values in economic life; it must demonstrate that relevance in a compelling way. At the same time, however, if it is to avoid the weaknesses of communism, it must demonstrate that it is possible to maintain those values in a way that does not ultimately sacrifice economic interests and incentives, in other words, that ultimately best serves the general welfare. Again, this is an idea central to Confucianism but that must find expression in twenty-first-century dialogue to be taken seriously.

One might object that, however more feasible or otherwise attractive Muelder's account may seem, it has fared no better than the well-field system in actually getting implemented. That is, it hardly helps a tradition struggling to find its voice to draw on a tradition that has had such difficulty having its voice heard. The answer to this lies in the notion of a bridge tradition itself. Earlier, I mentioned that Hall and Ames drew on traditions marginalized in one culture for the sake of understanding analogous traditions in another culture. Here, the same question could be asked: Why bother learning about classical Chinese thought if it is similar to a tradition that has largely been dismissed in the West? The answer is that the authors don't believe that either the bridge tradition or the tradition to which it is analogous has been given its fair due, and there is much to be gained by paying these traditions proper attention.

Similarly, I think that both Muelder's communitarianism and the Confucian tradition have an important contribution to make to contemporary economics, their mutual lack of success in realizing that contribution notwithstanding. Especially in the wake of the flurry of scandals that have plagued Western economics of late—WorldCom, Enron, Lehman Brothers, Bernie Madoff, to name just a few—I find the need for an account of economics that can integrate social ethical concerns in an informed way to be almost palpable. Contemporary economic systems have failed to take seriously the nonquantitative factors of social life and so have failed to provide a sufficiently robust and realistic economic theory. The failure of these systems, in other words, is not economic (as if it were a problem of efficient employment of the system). The cause, rather, is that they collapse under the weight of all of the noneconomic factors they have consistently failed to acknowledge and address.

I point Confucianism toward communitarianism only because I believe that the latter is much better positioned at present to make that contribution successfully. Muelder's critique is only a half century old, so I think it would be premature to start writing it off just yet. One must remember that, in accounting for his own success in challenging the racist social structures of his day, Martin Luther King Jr. credited Muelder's work as one of the primary sources of his inspiration. When asking the question of where genuine reform can come from in a system choked by its own self-perpetuating forces, Muelder's distinctive variety of social ethics has already demonstrated that it has the potential to bring about profound change in even the most unlikely of circumstances.

Drawing on traditions like Muelder's communitarianism, then, may be the difference between the Confucian tradition having something interesting yet wistfully idealistic to say in the economic sphere (of the "but I have a fiduciary responsibility to my shareholders" variety) and developing a penetrating and forceful discourse concerning the ideal organization of that sphere (of the "social responsibilities are real and have a direct impact on the economic health of a society" variety). It is already rooted deep in the heart of a Chinese economy that has already demonstrated repeatedly that it is not limited by many of the stagnating forces of more traditional Western economies (e.g., in the pursuit of green technologies) and that it can often set the conditions by which global trends proceed (e.g., in the stabilization of the U.S. dollar). If the Confucian tradition can effectively recover the social ethical dimensions of earlier Chinese economic sensibilities, it may determine the difference between China as an economic also-ran—a rough facsimile of Western economies—and one that brings about profound economic change in even the most unlikely of circumstances.

To conclude, I believe that both communitarianism and Confucianism have an important contribution to make to contemporary economics, that this contribution is similar in several important respects, and that that contribution is more likely to be realized effectively if the two traditions can draw on each other productively in its development. While Confucianism need not maintain its connection with communitarianism in the long run—since, ultimately, there are important differences between the two—forging an early connection may facilitate and strengthen its entry into the contemporary debate.

NOTES

1. David L. Hall and Roger Ames, *Anticipating China: Thinking through the Narratives of Chinese and Western Culture* (Albany: State University of New York Press, 1995), xix. By "first problematic," Hall and Ames mean the Western tradition of analogical thinking that, although largely sublimated, spans from the sophists through the American pragmatists and postmoderns.

2. I am aware of the Chinese communist ideal of the "harmonious society" (*hexie shehui*) championed at least since the 1980s (and most recently in the Beijing Olympic Games in 2008). As should become clear, however, while there are affinities between the communist vision of harmony and that described by the early Confucians, this is by no means the only possible rendering of that ideal. Furthermore, as I will argue, developing that ideal in light of its connections to Muelder's notion of the "responsible society" can do more to recapture a viable alternative to the prevailing capitalist and communist options. One notable difference, for example, entails the relation of harmony to the right to protest or even revolt against such things as social injustice. See, e.g., Lin Yuan, "Exploring Conflict and Harmony: Hong Kong and Macao," trans. Lin Yuan and Chan U. Chan, in *Peace Studies in the Chinese Century: International Perspectives,* ed. Alan Hunter (Burlington, VT: Ashgate Publishing, 2006), 165–169, which is something about which even the early Confucians were admittedly divided.

3. This is consistently reinforced by passages such as the following one from the *Chunqiu fanlu yizheng* (Interpretation of the luxuriant gems of the spring and autumn annals), which states that "centrality is that by which Heaven and Earth start and end, harmony is that by which Heaven and Earth produce [the myriad things]. Therefore, of all the virtues the highest is harmony." Quoted in Xinzhong Yao, *An Introduction to Confucianism* (New York: Cambridge University Press, 2000), 172.

4. Ibid., 170.

5. Fung Yu-lan, *A History of Chinese Philosophy,* trans. Derk Bodde (Princeton, NJ: Princeton University Press, 1952), 1:35–36; Zhang Dainian, *Key Terms in Chinese Philosophy,* trans. and ed. Edmund Ryden (New Haven, CT: Yale University Press, 2002), 270–272.

6. Zhang, *Key Terms in Chinese Philosophy,* 270. Zhang is quoting from a Chinese-only edition of the text (*Shuowen jiezi* [Beijing: Zhonghua Shuju, 1963]), and the translation appears to be his own.

7. It is worth noting that this does not require the sublimation of one voice to another as it typically does in Western accounts of harmony, whereby one voice sings the melody that would persist even without a harmony, while a second voice finds ways to complement that leading voice with tones of agreeable proportion. Insofar as it doesn't emphasize simultaneity, the Chinese account is not pressed to privilege one voice over the other and can thus allow for a mutuality and equality often lost in Western accounts of harmony. While this difference may have bearing on the way that the concept has developed within each context, I do not think it should be overemphasized.

8. James Legge, *The Chinese Classics,* vol. 5, pt. 2, *The* Ch'un ts'ew, *with the* Tso chuen (Oxford: Clarendon Press, 1893; reprint, Taibei, Southern Materials Centre, 1985), 679. Although Legge's translation is surely dated, it remains a viable translation when considering passages for which no more recent translation is readily available. In this case, I have followed Fung, *History of Chinese Philosophy,* and Zhang, *Key Terms in Chinese Philosophy,* in using Legge's translation because the relevant passage does not appear in Watson's more recent but abridged translation. See Burton Watson, *The* Tso chuan: *Selections from China's Oldest Narrative History* (New York: Columbia University Press, 1989).

9. Zhang does an excellent job of supporting this understanding of harmony with passages from late Zhou dynasty texts, including the *Analects* (*Lunyu*), the *Sayings of the States* (*Guo yu*), and *Zuo's Commentary* (*Zuo zhuan*). See Zhang, *Key Terms in Chinese Philosophy,* 270–272, for more information.

10. *Lunyu,* 4:16; Wm. Theodore de Bary and Irene Bloom, *Sources of Chinese Tradition: From Earliest Times to 1600,* 2nd ed. (New York: Columbia University Press, 1999), 1:49. All passages from the *Lunyu* are translated by Irene Bloom.

11. *Lunyu,* 4:5; de Bary and Bloom, *Sources of Chinese Tradition,* 48.

12. *Mencius,* 1A:1; de Bary and Bloom, *Sources of Chinese Tradition,* 116. All passages from the *Mencius* are translated by Irene Bloom.

13. *Mencius,* 1A:1; de Bary and Bloom, *Sources,* 117.

14. *Mencius,* 2A:6.

15. *Mencius,* 1B:5.

16. Yao, *Introduction to Confucianism,* 179.

17. *Mencius,* 3A:3.

18. The Salt and Iron Debates, which took place during the early Han dynasty, considered whether or not to continue the late emperor Wu's controversial policy of establishing state monopolies on the production of salt and iron. These were not only vital industries (in many respects) but extremely lucrative ones as well. The debates pitted a major source of government revenue against the well-being of the broader population.

19. Yao, *Introduction to Confucianism,* 173.

20. Ibid., 178.

21. See, e.g., Muelder's introduction to Swami Akhilananda, *Hindu View of Christ* (Boston: Branden Press, 1949).

22. Gary Dorrien, *Social Ethics in the Making: Interpreting an American Tradition* (Malden, MA: Wiley-Blackwell, 2009), 308.

23. Ibid., 306.

24. Certainly there is plenty to be found in Muelder's work that is of no use to Confucianism—most notably his commitments to Christianity and personalism—but the argument I am making is that there are enough lines of connection between Muelder and the classical Confucians to make drawing on him for the development of a Confucian economics a worthwhile endeavor.

25. It should be noted that, in using the term "communitarian" to describe Muelder, I do not mean to associate him with the usage of the term that became popular toward the end of the twentieth century. That more recent usage is used to describe the critique of the strong individualism apparent in John Rawls' *Theory of Justice* (Cambridge, MA: Harvard University Press, 1971), which limited the role of government to the distribution of the basic materials that individuals need to lead free and secure lives; see, e.g., Michael J. Sandel, *Liberalism and the Limits of Justice* (Cambridge: Cambridge University Press, 1998); and Robert D. Putnam, *Bowling Alone: The Collapse and Revival of American Community* (New York: Simon and Schuster, 2000). It is sometimes used to describe an appreciation for the role of civil society more generally. By contrast, Muelder used the term in the 1950s to describe the strong social emphasis that he brought to an otherwise individualistic personalism that emphasized the importance of social institutions for cultivating the full potential of "persons-in-society" (Muelder's term for the combined individual and social nature of the individual).

26. J. Philip Wogaman, *Christian Perspectives on Politics,* rev. and exp. ed. (Louisville, KY: Westminster John Knox Press, 2000), 278.

27. Walter George Muelder, *Religion and Economic Responsibility* (New York: Charles Scribner's Sons, 1953), xi.

28. Ibid.

29. Ibid.

30. Ibid., 169.

31. Ibid., 135–136.

32. Ibid., xi.

33. de Bary and Bloom, *Sources of Chinese Tradition,* 130; emphasis mine.

Swaraj and *Swadeshi* 14

Gandhi and Tagore on Ethics, Development, and Freedom

Nalini Bhushan and Jay L. Garfield

"*Svaraj* in Ideas," Ideas about *Swaraj*

Gandhi introduced the terms *swaraj* and *swadeshi* to colonial Indian discourse, and while many academics and activists adopted these terms in their framings of the Indian independence struggle, consensus on their interpretation was hard to come by. The debate between Tagore and Gandhi is often taken as crucial in the contest over the meanings of these terms, but the interpretation of that debate is itself contested. We would like to reexamine that well-known debate as it is refracted through the lens of an epistemological predicament articulated by K. C. Bhattacharyya. This will allow us to see more clearly points of both agreement and disagreement between Tagore and Gandhi and to show why Tagore regarded Gandhi's ideology as not only shortsighted but incoherent.

In his lecture "*Svaraj* in Ideas" Bhattacharyya articulates for his students the kind of *swaraj* worth fighting for. At a moment when the desire for political freedom was at center stage, Bhattacharyya focuses instead on a form of subjugation at the same time more subtle and more powerful than political colonialism, a form so subtle as to be phenomenologically invisible.

> We speak today of Svaraj or self-determination in politics. Man's domination over man is felt in the most tangible form in the political sphere. There is however a subtler domination exercised in the sphere of ideas by one culture on another, a domination all the more serious in the consequence, because it is not ordinarily felt. Political subjection primarily means restraint on the outer life of a people and although it tends gradually to sink into the inner life of the soul, the fact that one is conscious of it operates against the tendency. So long as one is conscious of a restraint, it is possible to resist it or to bear it as a necessary evil and to keep free in spirit. Slavery begins when one ceases to feel the evil and it deepens when the evil is accepted as a good. Cultural subjection is ordinarily of an unconscious character and it implies slavery from the very start. When I speak of cultural subjection, I do not mean the assimilation of an alien culture. That assimilation need not be an evil; it may be positively necessary for healthy progress and in any case

> it does not mean a lapse of freedom. There is cultural subjection only when one's traditional cast of ideas and sentiments is superseded without comparison or competition by a new cast representing an alien culture which possesses one like a ghost.[1]

This is the subjugation constituted by immersion from a very early age in a cultural, conceptual, and evaluative framework that is not one's own. This immersion, effected by education and public discourse as well as by political and commercial institutions, is so total that one comes to inhabit the foreign values and ideology without any awareness, thereby unconsciously accepting one's own ideological imprisonment, indeed, experiencing it as freedom.

In the case of colonial India, this subjugation was facilitated by the adoption of broadly Western cultural norms, ways of seeing, values, and habits of mind, all ingested through the English language, the medium of instruction at the premier Indian schools and universities, including the one at which Bhattacharyya was a professor. As a consequence of this linguistic and cultural hegemony, the deliberate policy since Thomas Macaulay's "Minute on Indian Education" (1835), all ideas, from abstract physics to notions of nation, self, and culture, were inevitably articulated from an orientation that promotes itself as neutral, self-evidently objective, and universal, despite its particularity. Immersion in that conceptual scheme leads those subjected to it to adopt those practices and perspectives as their own in their own quest for neutral, objective, universalist maturity. This intellectual certainty in the face of a freely chosen realm of ideas and practices is reinforced phenomenologically in the degree of felt comfort and familiarity with which one inhabits it. But this very certainty, argues Bhattacharyya, is illusory, and represents the deepest form of false consciousness.

> We ourselves asked for this education, and we feel, and perhaps rightly, that it has been a blessing in certain ways. I mean only that it has not generally been assimilated by us in an open-eyed way with our old-world Indian mind. That Indian mind has simply lapsed in most cases for our educated men, and has subsided below the conscious level of culture.[2]

As Swami Vivekananda would put it, "This, too, is *māya* [illusion]."

Bhattacharyya argues instead that this education was something no Indian could confidently claim as his or her own.[3] According to his profound diagnosis of the epistemological predicament of the colonial Indian subject, this educational system alienated Indians from the norms, ways of seeing, and habits of mind necessary for "an authentic intellectual life."[4] Thus, what was taken to be genuine cultural progress during that time was a sham, or in Bhattacharyya's words, "imaginary progressiveness."[5] What was taken to be genuine reform was rote imitation, and imitation is the very antithesis of freedom, as it stands in the way of creativity and of fresh thinking, which must always be particular, contextually grounded, and differentiated.

Bhattacharyya's point here is that this loss of creativity is structurally and institutionally grounded. Its restoration, therefore, while not impossible, would require a radical restructuring of the way we approach knowledge. Bhattacharyya envisions this restructuring in terms of an expansion and a critique of the foundations and norms taken for granted, rather than their wholesale elimination and replacement. For instance, multiple languages would be taught and utilized; India's ancient philosophy, religion, and ways of life would be introduced as part of the valuational background, generating opportunities for multiple perspectives and orientations. Such immersion in multiple literatures and practices would enable both a genuine appraisal of all values in play and, significantly, the development of a doubt that is deep and rich. For Bhattacharyya, doubt is the epistemic attitude that renders an authentic life possible. Doubt fosters the cultivation of a skeptical sensibility that brings a person or a nation into serious confrontation with the ideas and values that it takes for granted. This kind of internal confrontation—whether within an individual or a nation—is the surest guarantor of the genuinely free life.

Bhattacharyya's educational and cultural goal is not a "hybridisation" of ideas.[6] The route to an authentic intellectual, social, and political life is a product not of free mixing but of hard critical thinking. This in turn is made possible only by accessing that which in the colonial context remains hidden: one's own traditions, forms of reflections, and habits of mind and heart. Such access is made possible by explicit exposure in the first instance and by critical reasoning, reflection, doubt, and serious comparison in the second. Nor does Bhattacharyya advocate the rejection of one set of ideas—Western and modern—and the preservation and restoration to a privileged position of Indian ideas. In the end, he hopes for a renaissance of authenticity and creativity in the Indian context grounded in a reorientation of the mind.

It is in philosophy, or by philosophizing, in the sense described previously that Bhattacharyya sees the route to an authentic self-understanding and hence the route to freedom from "cultural subjection" and a "slavery of the spirit."[7] The kind of *swadeshi* that is worth having, then, for Bhattacharyya, is one that trades in *desi* (local, belonging to one's own country) ideas. These are ideas that have been subject to doubt, to searching critical appraisal in light of multiple perspectives and orientations, and then found to be worth keeping. Ideas that are the result of such scrutiny, whatever their historical or cultural origin, would be one's own, *swadesh*. As we will see, this view of the nature of *swaraj* and *swadeshi* as fundamentally epistemic links Bhattacharyya to Gandhi, who is also taken with an epistemological predicament that besets colonial India; but Bhattacharyya's more cosmopolitan outlook and his solution are more akin to those of Tagore.

The Juggernaut of Modernity: Problem or Promise

Gandhi's real target was modernity, and he saw British colonial rule of India as merely a natural outgrowth of that process. He therefore argued not for liberation from the British nor for a liberation that would permit India to enter the modern world order as an equal. Rather, he argued for liberation from modernity itself and for renunciation of what he saw as its irretrievably immoral consequences. Gandhi saw modernity as an inextricably linked web of political, industrial, economic, and social institutions that posed a direct threat both to the individual and to the nation, a threat always disguised as a promise. For many, particularly those subject to colonial domination, the promise of modernity was undeniable. Modernity brought the freedom represented by liberal democracy; the economic development, availability of consumer goods, and social mobility made possible by capitalism and industrialization; the liberation of thought attendant on the march of secularism; and the medical and other technical benefits made possible by science.

To many in the colonial era, including Tagore, B. K. Sarkar, and even J. Nehru, modernization and the kind of liberation it entailed were part and parcel of the anticolonial struggle, providing the ideological basis for the critique of foreign domination, the technical and material basis of national prosperity, and the mode of entry as a fully equal partner in a global community of nations. The great promise of modernization was an independent and prosperous India, an India that would contribute to, and benefit from, intercourse with other free, prosperous nations.

Gandhi took all of this hope to be a fraud, arguing that these baubles were but the lures tempting a grand and fundamentally morally sound culture to its own destruction, ensuring the moral degradation and economic and spiritual enslavement of its citizens. His critique was grounded not on the claim that the benefits of modernity are outweighed by its harms, but rather on the conviction that its putative benefits, when seen properly, are themselves harms.

How does this deep moral critique go? Modernity, Gandhi thought, could not support, only erode, national identity by virtue of the homogeneity of culture it entails. Cultural homogeneity is ensured by the importation into Indian culture of social institutions, values, and even modes of dress and conduct made inevitable by the commodification and sale of all that is profitable and associated with progress. The adoption of the English language, of Western dress and taste, of English administrative and political institutions, and of capitalist modes of production were the immediate symptoms of moral decline in colonial India. Contemporary global popular culture and global corporate culture, he would say today, are the modern confirmation of this prescient indictment, apocalyptic, paranoid, and parochial as it might have seemed a century ago.

Modernity, Gandhi argues, is immoral at its core. Individual liberty is eroded, not enhanced, by modern society, its promise of choice in fact coercive, forcing individuals into a limited range of consumer options or into interchangeable jobs as cogs in a single machine. Modernity vests real control only in those who control capital. Capitalism demands colonialism and a mutually reinforcing regime of production, commodification, violence, and inequality of wealth. In Gandhi's view, to participate in the institutions of modernity is, hence, to paraphrase Marx, to be complicit in one's own moral degradation.

But Gandhi's critique of modernity is not unqualified. After all, his rhetoric of *swaraj*—although delivered in cadences borrowed from the *Bhagavad Gītā* as well as from Tolstoy and Thoreau—is also grounded in a call for liberty and political autonomy whose intellectual roots are in Kant and Mill, and a critique of the colonial project that is indebted to Jefferson and Marx. Gandhi criticizes colonial rule and capitalism in part for their deprivation of the very fundamental rights and liberties articulated by the social contract tradition and for their abrogation of the rights of individuals and collectives to choose their own political leaders that is the heritage of the French and American revolutions. This tension runs through his political and moral work, a tension to which we return in the next section.

Tagore and Gandhi on Ethics and Economics

Gandhi's twin terms *swaraj* and *swadeshi* encapsulate both his ethical/political theory and his approach to a new economics of postcolonial life. *Swaraj* means *self-mastery* or *self-rule,* and both the *swa* and the *raj* are nicely ambiguous. The first can denote either the individual or the national subject; the second either spiritual self-control (that is, autonomy) or political rule (that is, autonomy). Gandhi was happy to play on this ambiguity and to argue that *swaraj* in the political sense is subordinate to and dependent on *swaraj* in the personal sense.

Swadeshi is also a nicely polysemic notion. The *swa* remains ambiguous in the familiar way. But how could *deshi* be read? Its obvious primary sense involves the products of one's own land—a kind of "buy Indian" campaign—and indeed, that was a large component of *swadeshi.* The most prominent example concerns the campaign to buy Indian *khadi* (cotton clothing) instead of clothing from Manchester. But as with *swaraj,* there is a temporal and spiritual side to *swadeshi.* A commitment to valorizing and practicing one's own traditions, languages, ideologies, and forms of life is also a part of *swadeshi,* and in part—but only in part—motivates the material side (which after all has as its most direct goal the protection of the welfare of native industries, handicrafts, and livelihoods, though also, importantly, the forms of social organization they entail). For Gandhi, this commitment to valorize also entails a commitment to resist—to resist traditions, languages, ideologies, and forms of life alien to one's own culture. Resistance becomes a way of preserving one's own culture and a way of preserving oneself from cultural heteronomy.

Bhattacharyya's account of *swaraj* incorporates the positive side of Gandhi's account of *swadeshi*—that is, an insistence on the creative engagement with one's own ideas and tradition. He is not, however, closed to the ideas and traditions of others. He worries only about their becoming unconsciously hegemonic. We will see a similar selective adherence to the positive, but not the negative side of Gandhian *swadeshi* in the thought of Tagore.

It should be clear that Gandhi's *swaraj-swadeshi* complex involves both ethical/political and economic dimensions. Ethically and politically, Gandhi calls for a kind of spiritual self-mastery and for a materially self-sufficient social order governed at home according to authentically national principles. Given the critique of modernity and capitalism that grounds this position, and by virtue of the impossibility of achieving either *swaraj* or *swadeshi* in the framework of modernity, this also demands, according to Gandhi, a premodern mode of production, consumption, and economic order. We will explore the deeper motivations for this position later in the chapter.

It is widely known that Tagore and Gandhi disagreed about *swadeshi*. It is less widely appreciated that their disagreement—fundamental as it was—was grounded in even more fundamental agreement about general principles. Tagore agrees with Gandhi that national unity and freedom are *spiritual*, rather than *political* goals. He also agrees that a substantial engagement with the specifically Indian philosophical, religious, artistic, and social traditions is the essential vehicle for the recovery of personal and political freedom. For each, this set of commitments is the basis for their critique of British rule, not the mere fact that the British are not Indian. But whereas this spiritual understanding of independence unites them, they are divided by the conclusions they draw from this understanding.

Tagore, like Bhattacharyya, rejects the negative side of Gandhi's *swadeshi*. Whereas Gandhi adopts an essentially parochial reading of values and institutions, with its rejection of all things foreign, and an essentially conservative view of identity, Tagore is instinctively cosmopolitan and indeed progressive. A great deal of his critique of Gandhi's views of development rests on his view that Gandhi never took economic considerations seriously as being ethical—as having value in their own right. The critique has two points. In the first place, Tagore regards it as a duty of the nation to promote the material well-being of its citizens, and to the degree that this requires the adoption of new, modern, or even foreign methods or forms of organization, this at least prima facie legitimizes those interventions. While Gandhi dons the mantle of poverty as a virtue, for Tagore poverty is by itself a problem. Second, Tagore regards ideas and values as transnational: he appreciated Japanese art, English poetry, Chinese calligraphy. In his view, national growth requires not insulation from the world, but integration into it—not the adoption wholesale of a foreign imposition, but the willingness to import what is worthwhile and to export one's own values in return. In order to understand the Gandhi-Tagore debate more fully, it will be necessary to return to Gandhi and to his first principles of *swaraj* and *swadeshi.*

Transparency and Opacity

In *Hind Swaraj,* Gandhi rails against such apparently innocuous targets as doctors, lawyers, and ordinary household machines. Many contemporary readers of these screeds react with shock and surprise, seeing this as a wholesale attack on anything new and suspecting that Gandhi may have been nothing more than a slightly cracked Luddite. Why reject the good offices of those who might cure disease or protect one from tyranny? Gandhi's critique does not, as one might be inclined to think, rely on the fact that these people take fees. He supports the right to earn a livelihood. Nor is this a wholesale rejection of anything mechanical. He rails, for example, against the power loom but encourages the use of another machine, the spinning wheel, and against railroads but not bullock carts. What, then, is the fundamental principle that guides Gandhi's critique?

When Gandhi approaches machinery and technicians, he does so with an eye to the way that they organize life, how they occlude that process of organization, and especially to the degree to which they make life opaque to those who live it. Consider the power loom or the locomotive engine. Gandhi emphasizes that each *regulates* the lives of those who live in their context. Their very production requires armies of regimented labor, concentration of capital, and the minimization of expenses through a competitive labor market pitting workers against one another. Each requires labor to attend and operate the machine on regular cycles, regimenting the lives of those who use them. Each contributes in turn to the maintenance and intensification of the socio-economic order that gives it birth.[8]

> Machinery has begun to desolate Europe. Ruination is now knocking at the English gates. Machinery is the chief symbol of modern civilization. It is a great sin.
>
> The workers in the mills of Bombay have become slaves. . . . It would be folly to assume that an Indian Rockefeller would be better than the American Rockefeller. Impoverished India can become free, but it will be hard for an India made rich through immorality to regain its freedom.[9]

Moreover, these processes of regimentation are taken for granted, accepted as natural, and fade into the background of consciousness, just as K. C. Bhattacharyya argued that the regimentation of thought by foreign education fades into the background. There is hence a tacit, but inevitable process of occlusion of the social violence done by this machinery, machinery that arrives with the promise of liberation from toil. Finally, the machinery itself is opaque to those who use it. Nobody who drives a locomotive, rides a train, sells railway tickets, works at a power loom, or buys textiles made by industrialized factories in Manchester has a clue about how these machines actually work. That is the province of distant experts. The abstraction of the knowledge essential to production and its alienation from those most immediately involved in that production is complete.

The situation is very different for the person involved with a bullock cart or a spinning wheel. These can be produced by ordinary people on their own time from locally available resources, using knowledge freely available in the communities in which the machines function. They can be used by individuals on their own time, with their own ends. And those who use them can simply see how they work. There is no abstraction, no alienation, and no reordering of society or redistribution of wealth and power built into these technologies, technologies though they may be.[10] Gandhi's critique is hence not a critique of the machine per se, but of the opacity and alienation built into the modern incarnation of machinery.

This makes sense of the otherwise bizarre attacks on doctors and lawyers. For the modern incarnations of these professions, as opposed to their premodern antecedents—*ayurvedic* healers and *panchayat* elders—trade on specialized knowledge and enframing structures of power akin to those induced by power machinery. The medical establishment, with its bureaucratic machinery of public health officials, hospitals, and medical boards, regiments not only the production of doctors and their practice but also access to medicine and to knowledge about illness and cure. The practice of medicine becomes opaque to patients, and the knowledge required for the maintenance of health becomes increasingly abstracted and inaccessible.

> Doctors have almost unhinged us. . . . Their business is really to rid the body of diseases that might afflict it . . . I over-eat, I have indigestion, I go to a doctor, he gives me medicine, I am cured. I over-eat again, and I take his pills again. . . . A continuance of a course of a medicine must, therefore, result in loss of control over the mind. . . . Hospitals are institutions for propagating sin. Men take less care of their bodies, and immorality increases.[11]

The legal establishment mystifies and regulates conflict and relations not only between individuals and the governments that structure their lives, but also between private individuals. Lawyers replace dialogue with lawsuit, infraction with crime, justice with punishment.

> Lawyers, as a rule, advance quarrels, instead of repressing them. Moreover, men take up that profession, not in order to help others out of their miseries, but to enrich themselves.[12]
>
> It is wrong to consider that courts are established for the benefit of the people. Those who want to perpetuate their power do so through the courts. If people were to settle their own quarrels, a third party would not be able to exercise any

> authority over them. . . . The parties alone know who is right. We, in our simplicity and ignorance, imagine that a stranger, by taking our money, gives us justice.[13]

Whether it be a doctor or a lawyer, a mediator who arrives as an ally in fact alienates the patient or client from his or her own life and interests.

This focus on alienation and opacity also illuminates Gandhi's apparently simple and straightforwardly romantic attachment to the village as the appropriate forum for human relationships. One might wonder what is wrong with a city, per se. After all, cities offer so much. Once again, regardless of how it might appear, Gandhi is not simply rejecting whatever is new. He saw that cities, like certain machines and certain professions, implicitly and inexorably regiment life. Cities as well occlude from ordinary individuals the processes that structure their lives; cities render the levers of control over one's life inaccessible, even invisible; and in the end, cities make life itself incomprehensible.

> If we are to do without the railways, we shall have to do without the tram-cars. Machinery is like a snake-hole which may contain from one to a hundred snakes. Where there is machinery there are large cities; and where there are large cities, there are tram-cars and railways; and there only does one see electric light. . . . I cannot recall a single good point in connection with machinery.[14]

For Gandhi, then, the problem with modernity is neither strictly political nor economic. As would Bhattacharyya, he sees the real problem as epistemological and phenomenological. Modernity and the gifts it promises inevitably alienate us from our own lives and our own fellows and hide that very alienation with the ribbons and bows of efficiency, rationality, wealth, and progress. The problem of modernity is therefore a moral problem only in a derivative sense. In seeking the self-mastery and freedom modernity promised, we lost the self-mastery and freedom once available to us, articulated in such profound texts as the *Gītā*, a mastery and freedom grounded in real *jñāna* (knowledge) and rendered impossible in the modern context.

Gandhi's Freedom, Tagore's Freedom

We have in Tagore and Gandhi two distinct conceptions of freedom. Gandhi's freedom, which is at its core self-mastery, involves a renunciation of the material and political attractions of modernity, as well as global entanglement, and the adoption of a simpler, more local, agrarian life. Tagore's freedom is entirely different. Tagore is after freedom *from* poverty and isolation, freedom *to* engage with others and other cultures, freedom to create. Whereas Gandhi sees modernity as antithetical to freedom, Tagore sees it as a vehicle to that goal.

Recall that Gandhi's primary concern was epistemological, about opacity in the modern world. Opacity and its deleterious consequences were exacerbated in the Indian colonial context by the wholesale imposition of Western cultural practices, languages, and norms, themselves constituting additional opaque layers. The goal for Gandhi was to replace that opacity with transparency. In practical terms this entails a shift from the complex specialized and regimented life of modernity to a simpler, premodern life. The renunciation of modernity is therefore mandatory if any kind of a meaningful, autonomous life is to be recovered.

Tagore, on the other hand, does not see opacity, per se, as a problem for colonial India. Certainly, opacity is *sometimes* problematic. For instance, the opacity of a folk or classical tradition to the young who have been alienated from it is a problem. But in this context it is the alienation, not the opacity, that is at stake. Tagore's deepest concern is not an epistemological gap but a material lack. Tagore cares in the first instance about poverty and the absence of choice it engenders. An adequate standard of living and personal liberty and the opportunity for creativity are for Tagore fundamental human rights. Once poverty is eliminated, the citizenry can be trusted to choose their own lives, to create their own future, supported by trust in one another, in a government that respects their individuality, and presumably in a progressive economic order that facilitates material, social, and artistic development.

> In America national habits and traditions have not had time to spread their clutching roots round your hearts. . . . But in this present age of transition, when a new era of civilization is sending its trumpet call to all peoples of the world across an unlimited future, this very freedom of detachment will enable you to accept its invitation and to achieve the goal for which Europe began her journey but lost herself midway. . . . So much for the social and the political regeneration of India. Now we come to her industries, and I am very often asked whether there is in India any industrial regeneration since the advent of the British Government. It must be remembered that at the beginning of the British rule in India our industries were suppressed and since then we have not met with any real help or encouragement to enable us to make a stand against the monster commercial organizations of the world. The nations have decreed that we must remain purely an agricultural people, even forgetting the use of arms for all time to come. Thus India is being turned into so many predigested morsels of food ready to be swallowed at any moment by any nation which has even the most rudimentary set of teeth in its head. India, therefore has very little outlet for her industrial genius.[15]

Tagore's own romantic vision is that of a nation working in harmony, creatively united not by an abstract nationalism but by the concrete individual interests and goals of materially secure, freely developing individuals. For Tagore, then, specialization and expertise, and the division of labor modernity occasions, do not necessarily lead to alienation or to an incomprehensibly complex life. Instead, the developments such a social order makes possible can in fact lead to a simpler life. It is a life that facilitates greater understanding and contemplation of that which is worth understanding precisely because one need not be concerned with, for instance, how one's sewing machine or medicine works. These matters can be entrusted to the relevant experts, whose expertise frees one to write poetry, to paint, to read or to write philosophy or even to play cricket.

> Let our life be simple in its outer aspect and rich in its inner gain. Let our civilization take its firm stand upon its basis of social cooperation and not upon that of economic exploitation and conflict. How to do it in the teeth of the drainage of our life-blood by the economic dragons is the task set before the thinkers of all oriental nations who have faith in the human soul. It is a sign of laziness and impotency to accept conditions imposed upon us by others who have other ideals than ours. We should actively try to adapt the world powers to guide our history to its own perfect end.[16]

Tagore therefore sees *swaraj* in terms of human rights as we would recognize them today and, like Bhattacharyya, *swadeshi* in terms of a healthy respect for one's own cultural traditions and heritage in the context of global interchange. Gandhi, on the other hand, sees *swaraj* in terms of spiritual or yogic discipline and *swadeshi* as an isolation from that interchange. This is one way of putting the disagreement between Tagore and Gandhi.

We can put Tagore's point in another way, though, and putting it this way identifies a real tension in Gandhi's view, one to which we adverted earlier. This is a tension that, if faced, may indicate that the view is ultimately unstable, or even incoherent. We can look at this from the standpoint of *swaraj* first. Gandhi must be able to argue for *swaraj* as an ideal. His argument for its importance rests on fundamental claims about human beings as free, as self-determining. And these are conceptions of human beings that derive not from the *Gītā,* but from Rousseau and Locke. These ideals of freedom are ideals of *opportunity for self-development,* and indeed a great deal of Gandhi's own antimodernist rhetoric, paradoxically, concerns the way the mechanization of life and abstraction of knowledge into the hands of experts impedes self-development for most of us. This is indeed one of Gandhi's deepest insights and reflects his kinship with Tolstoy and Ruskin.

But in the end, Gandhi's rural utopia, as Tagore points out, sabotages the kinds of development many would most desire. For many of us, self-development is not found in cleaning toilets or spinning cloth; many of us want more for our children than rural poverty; and many of us think that what is distinctive about the human community is the possibility of intercultural communication and discussion, such as that in which we are engaged in this volume. What is one to do who finds as her calling medicine or the study of French literature? Or philosophy? Tagore and Bhattacharyya urge one to follow that calling, Gandhi to renounce it. Which kind of freedom do we want?

This is the difference between K. C. Bhattacharyya's and Gandhi's conceptions of *swaraj* and the reason that Bhattacharyya is more aligned with Tagore than he is with Gandhi. Bhattacharyya, as we have seen, neither takes *swaraj* to be the extreme rejection of all ideas from outside nor *swadeshi* to be cultural isolationism. Rather, each involves critical engagement with all possible ideas and the embrace of the possibility of progress grounded in one's own culture and values but open to the appreciation of the cultures and values of others.

> It is wrong not to accept an ideal . . . simply because it hails from a foreign country. To reject it would be to insist on individuality for the sake of individuality and would be a form of national conceit and obscurantism.[17]

But equally,

> The form of practical life in which an ideal has to be translated, has to be decided by ourselves according to the genius of our own community. A synthesis of our ideals with Western ideals is not demanded in every case. Where it is demanded, the foreign ideal is to be assimilated to our ideal and not the other way.[18]

On this account, self-mastery is the ability to imagine, not to restrict, a range of possible futures for oneself; nationalism is the commitment to develop, not to isolate, one's own country, to advance its culture in dialogue with, not as an alternative to, the ideas and products of others.

This alternative approach to *swaraj* and *swadeshi* makes room for material development but also for genuine human development, insofar as human development is facilitated, rather than impeded, by open cultural exchange. It recognizes, as does Tagore in *Home and the World,* that Gandhian *swadeshi* comes with enormous costs, and that, just as Gandhi argued that freedom is not material but spiritual, these costs are not only material but spiritual as well. Gandhian *swaraj* and *swadeshi* together involve the stultifying of intellectual, artistic, and material development for anyone who seriously buys into them.

It is central to Gandhi's conception of *swaraj* and *swadeshi* that each represents the realization of fundamental human rights. The problem is that it is hard to get a discourse of human rights off the ground without the individualism, universalism, and progressivism that characterize modernity. Gandhi seems to have sawn off the branch on which he needs to stand.

Flushing the Toilets

At the end of *Untouchable,* which is at its core a novel about freedom, Mulk Raj Anand raises Tagore's question to Gandhi. Anand's protagonist, Bakha, is leaving a rally just addressed by the mahatma. Our hero considers the three solutions he has encountered to the problem of untouchability. One possibility, he muses, is conversion, the adoption of the alien Christian religion. A second is the Gandhian solution of *swaraj* for the untouchable within the bounds of the

Indian context. Gandhi would not abandon the untouchable's degrading work of cleaning toilets. He would instead cultivate respect for such work. But there is a third route to freedom: that of the poet (whatever poet it was that Anand had in mind): import the flush toilet.

We close with Mulk Raj Anand:

> As the brief Indian twilight came and went, a sudden impulse shot through the transformations of space and time, and gathered all the elements that were dispersed in the stream of his [Bakha's] soul into a tentative decision: "I shall go and tell father all that Gandhi said about us," he whispered to himself, "and all that that poet said. Perhaps I can find the poet some day and ask him about his machine." And he proceeded homewards.[19]

NOTES

1. K. C. Bhattacharyya, "*Svaraj* in Ideas," in *Indian Philosophy in English from Renaissance to Independence,* ed. Nalani Bhushan and Jay L. Garfield (New York: Oxford University Press, 2011), 103.
2. Ibid., 104.
3. Ibid., 386.
4. K. J. Shah, "In Search of Development," *Indian Philosophical Quarterly* 11, no. 1, 473.
5. Bhattacharyya, "*Svaraj* in Ideas," 105.
6. Ibid., 106.
7. Ibid., 103.
8. For a similar analysis see S. Sahasrabudhey, "The Machine," in *Gandhi's Challenge to Modern Science,* ed. S. Sahasrabudhey (Goa: Other Indian Press, 2002), 176–177, 179–191.
9. M. K. Gandhi, *Hind Swaraj* (Cambridge: Cambridge University Press, 1909/1997), 102–108.
10. Sahasrabudhey, "The Machine," 180–181.
11. Gandhi, *Hind Swaraj,* 63–64.
12. Ibid., 59.
13. Ibid., 61.
14. Ibid., 110.
15. R. Tagore, "Nationalism," in *Indian Philosophy in English, from Renaissance to Independence,* ed. Nalani Bhushan and Jay L. Garfield (New York: Oxford University Press, 2011), 33–35.
16. Ibid., 35.
17. Ibid., 108.
18. Ibid., 107.
19. M. R. Anand, *Untouchable* (London: Penguin, 1935), 157.

Economics and Religion or Economics versus Religion

15

The Concept of an Islamic Economics

Oliver Leaman

There are two contrasting images of Islamic economics that are often evoked today, and both are wrong. One is that Islamic finance has done well in the banking crises that began in the twenty-first century, the implication being that it is more solidly based and less speculative. Opposed to that is the image of Islam as an obstacle to the flourishing of the economies of the Islamic world because it is so restrictive as to what can be done with money and how property can be passed down to the next generation. Yet the fact is that Islamic banks have had their problems in the recent monetary crisis as well as their fair share of scandals and controversies. On the other hand, there is no evidence that Islam has impeded trade and enterprise. To cite one example, the traveler flying from Lahore to Dubai is exposed to two kinds of airport shop, both largely staffed and owned by Pakistanis. In Lahore the shops are few, dusty, and dark, containing nothing that anyone would want to buy. In Dubai the reverse is the case. Yet both airports are in Islamic countries. Two contrasting points can be drawn from these examples about the concept of Islamic economics. One is very positive and suggests that God established rules for human beings in the conduct of their everyday commercial affairs; for Muslims those rules are expressed in the Qur'an and other canonical texts and their appropriate interpretations. This is opposed by the view that any attempt to implicate Islam in economics is misguided because establishing a precise set of rules is casuistic. That is, the distinction between acceptable and unacceptable economic relations is both personal and fairly arbitrary. So, while there are indeed general ideas about what is acceptable in our relationships with one another, and some of these will be commercial, a religion cannot get into the detail of economics in any definitive manner.

Islamic Economics

What are the main criteria of Islamic economics? According to much of the literature, it is based on the principles of justice, equality, and the desire to increase wealth throughout the region, emphasizing honesty and fairness in our dealings with one another. The claim is made that Islam not only is a system of beliefs, but also involves a whole way of life, as though this were unique to Islam. In fact, virtually all religions share this feature: few religions say to their followers that they should believe in a set of propositions but can do whatever they like in terms of their personal behavior. One of the distinctive features of Islam perhaps is that its leading figure, the Prophet Muhammad, was himself initially a trader and came from a thoroughly commercial background, as did his first wife. Much of the opposition to him from his own community may well have been motivated by the concern that a new form of worship would interfere with their monopolization of the pilgrimage trade to Mecca. It is perhaps not coincidental that Islam very quickly came to institutionalize that trade as part of its core beliefs, and presumably that form of commercial life as a consequence continued to the mutual profit of all involved. There are a number of significant direct references to commerce in the Qur'an, but as always in religion these are merely the initial comments on which a vast amount of legislation is constructed, with reliance on other, often more explicit religious sources. In Islam these sources vary depending on the sort of Muslim one is. They can include the hadith, the sayings of the Prophet, the works of jurisprudence that represent the ideas of the main legal authorities, and for the Shiʿi the pronouncements of the imam and/or those close to or representing him. The sayings of the Prophet are significant in part since the *sunnah,* the way of life followed by the Prophet, and what comments he had to make to his companions and others, including the comments made by those otherwise close to him, are taken to represent how everyone ought to live.

Let us look at some of the leading points of what is often taken to be Islamic banking. Islamic law, or *shariʿah,* is critical of financial interest, often taken to be a translation of *ribah.* It is also critical of speculation (*maysir*) and its link with uncertainty (*gharah*). The banks are supposed to be more than just commercial institutions; they are enjoined by *shariʿah* to concern themselves with social responsibility. Many consumers of banking in the Islamic world say they are keen on using Islamic banks, but their motivation is unclear, since many of the qualities they associate with such banks have nothing to do with religion but relate rather to service and reliability. All Islamic banks have an advisory board that ensures their compliance with *shariʿah.* It has been argued that, since board members are paid to carry out their oversight function, they are often motivated to be happy with what they find, like financial regulators in a variety of countries. Because the rules are indeterminate, there is wide scope for individual decision about what makes a bank an Islamic bank, and one does not have to be unduly cynical to wonder how strict an advisory board is in its regulation. In any case, all banks have to exist in competition with other banking systems, a fact that presumably limits how much they might differ from one another. And, because most Muslims have a choice of where they put their money, Islamic banks have to be rather similar to other banking institutions if they are to attract their fair share of business. One can expect idealism to go only so far.

It is possible to interpret Islamic economics as ruling out all sorts of activities. Wasteful spending on unnecessary things through special price offers, for example, is against the teachings of Islam if one takes seriously its advocacy of moderation both in spending and in saving. Does that mean, however, that Muslims should not use price to encourage consumers to buy their products? Price discounts offered by retailers that save consumers money are encouraged. It is stated in the Qur'an, "Those who, when they spend, are not extravagant and not niggardly, but hold a just [balance] between those [extremes]" (25:67). So there is nothing wrong with getting a bargain, nor in representing one's products in that way, provided they really are a bargain. Islam sees itself very much as a religion in the middle, between the asceticism of Christianity and the materialism of Judaism. Muslims are to divert resources to charity (*zakat*) and pray, of course, but they are encouraged to play a committed commercial role as well. Yet this moderation is difficult to define. For example, it is possible to buy TVs with both very large and very small screens, and one wonders what the moderate choice is here. Although presumably it would be a TV with neither a very small nor a very large screen, would it not be a shame to inhibit the choice of those who are TV enthusiasts and would (appropriately) prefer a large screen? This preference does not imply that they are extravagant on the whole, just in one aspect of their lives that for them is important. Since we all differ in our enthusiasms, it seems appropriate to allocate our spending accordingly, albeit within the bounds of what is reasonable.

The Qur'an links businessmen, and in particular those who travel for the purpose of trade, with the mujahideen (those who strive in the cause of God) (73:20). In other places in the text, God praises the equipment used to promote trade (35:12). It should be understood from these passages that Islam does not oppose activities aimed at promoting business and industry. But these activities are to be undertaken with great sensitivity to the ethical rules specified by the Qur'an and the *sunnah* (way) of the Prophet. Accordingly, the annual hajj pilgrimage serves to encourage international trade and business (Qur'an 22:27–28, 2:198). There is nothing wrong with promoting sales or enhancing one's business by selling during conferences, times of pilgrimage, or trade fairs, insofar as such activity does not compromise purity of intention and justice. The rector of al-Azhar in 2002 was called on to express a judgment on the practice of prespecifying profits on an investment, and he referred to Qur'an 4:29, where the injunction is not to devour the property of others in impermissible ways and to carry out trade by mutual consent.[1] Mutual consent is clearly present when an agreement is made on how much the investor will get back at the end of a period, say, and when the conditions of the agreement are mutually agreeable.

Commerce can, however, be a rather cruel affair. A modern legal thinker, Yusuf al-Qaradawi, comments that Islam forbids trade where someone's gain is another's loss; he at the same time advocates free-market principles. His ringing defense of free trade and competition is difficult to reconcile with his claim that one person's gain should not involve another person's loss. If I am a more skillful shopkeeper than someone else, I will prosper perhaps at his expense, and he may go out of business. Mr. Ali may benefit from Mrs. Khan's going out of business, since local customers may then have no recourse but to all shop at his store. But if Mr. Ali's store is cleaner, cheaper, better stocked, and so on, this is all to the good. Of course, once Mrs. Khan is out of action he can jack up his prices and not clean his store so assiduously, and here the general desirability of competition might usefully limit the deterioration of the service he provides. Transactions do often result in losses for one party without being unfair. In the long run perhaps the community as a whole gains through competition, but there are surely casualties along the way. Not everyone can compete. In fact, al-Qaradawi's book is typical of many of the more popular texts on the topic in its incoherence. It is far more about producing ringing declarations of how wonderful it would be for Islam to be the main organizing principle of economics than about providing any detail whatsoever on how to reconcile the obvious difficulties that arise when the commercial sector is regulated by the very general and vague principles of any religion.

Islamic Economies

If we examine some recent studies of the different economies in the Middle East and North Africa, it is important to note not only the variety of economies that exist within the area but also some remarkable similarities. One theme that is difficult to avoid is the overactive government sector in many of the economies. This is surprising since there is nothing dirigiste about the description of the economy in either the Qur'an or the hadith literature. There is a stress on the significance of charity, but it is a bit of a stretch to get from there to the sorts of highly state-directed economies of the current Middle East, which have, in the view of many, played a large part in the current unrest there. One of the problems with such economies is that they have been very poor in providing employment, the state having such a dominating effect on society that individual risk taking and enterprise are elbowed out. What is particularly interesting, though, is that for most countries in the Islamic world we do not need to know anything about Islam to understand their economies. There is, furthermore, no reason to believe that there might be something different about the economies of this area due to the preponderant religious orientation toward Islam. The term "Islam" does not even appear in the index of a recent work on monetary policy in the Middle East and North Africa.[2] Since the theme is money and banking, it is perhaps surprising that Islamic banking is totally ignored, unless, that is, there is nothing very different about this form of finance. What makes religion irrelevant here is that, even where there are Islamic banks—banks that do not charge interest—they nevertheless structure their financial instruments in line with current interest rates and must do so to complete with banks that, having no need to comply with Islamic law, offer a rate of interest on money deposited. A good example of this can be found in the Islamic Interbank Benchmark Rate, established in November 2012, which establishes the rate at which Islamic banks will lend to one another. It is based on money flows between banks as investments that depend on the performance of underlying assets, by contrast with interest-bearing loans. This is certainly a very different way of regarding the benchmark as compared, for instance, with LIBOR, the London Interbank Offered Rate, which is purely a rate of interest and therefore contrary to Islamic law. Yet in practice the two rates are usually uncannily close to each other, for obvious reasons. Banks can go elsewhere if the rate they are offered is unsatisfactory; if the rate is too generous, then anyone could take advantage of it and resell cheaper funds at higher prices. Similarly for the issuance of Islamic corporate and sovereign bonds, they are based on the real nature of the assets they represent, and yet, of course, they closely mirror the bond market in general, since otherwise they could not attract and hold investors.

Rasem Khayed and Muhammad Hassan have done a study of Islamic entrepreneurship that looks at business attitudes in Saudi Arabia with respect to the sorts of ideas and ambitions that those setting up and promoting commercial enterprises possess.[3] The authors establish plausibly from the start that there is nothing incompatible between commerce and Islam, and they delve into the history of the Prophet and the early years of Islam to make this point. The hadith literature is particularly helpful here. Of course the Islamic world has long been a center of commercial activity. It could be said that the way that Islam has spread around the world has often been influenced by traders and their activities and that Muslims are enjoined to carry out business in a particular manner, one that embodies the principles of Islam. By that reasoning, there should exist specific Islamic institutions such as banks that operate in accordance with those principles and that avoid any kind of commercial arrangement that is illegitimate from a religious point of view. The research presented by Khayed and Hassan, though, suggests that, while many respondents express the desire to use Islamic banks, few do and even fewer know what such banks do. Further, the main issues that were singled out by Saudi entrepreneurs as contrary to Islam were not about banking or partnership arrangements, but were rather related to marketing practices such as advertising, promotion, and deception, issues that are common to all economies.

Islamic Law

By the time we have read the two books discussed previously, we might wonder whether there is really an effective and distinctive role for Islam in the economics of the modern world. This is a topic taken up by Maha-Hanaan Balala, who makes the interesting argument that the best way for Islamic economic law to adapt to modernity is through a common-law process.[4] She uses this approach to explore various controversial issues in Islamic law, including securitization, interest, risk, the sale of debt, and the operation of a dual banking system with Islamic and other kinds of banks within one jurisdiction. She has Malaysia in mind here. It is the basis of her approach, not the detail, that is so intriguing, though. She takes for granted that no one really understands precisely what Islamic finance is, since apart from the name widely bandied about, there is no general agreement on what if any reality accords with it. The solution she puts forth is to adopt a common-law approach, using precedent and significant examples to exemplify the principles of justice that lie at the basis of Islamic finance and to work out from there which practices are acceptable and which are not. She is alert to the danger of what she calls "re-characterization," whereby a familiar financial vehicle that is objectionable on religious grounds is redescribed in such a way as to make it apparently acceptable. There is, with re-characterization, the suggestion that a sleight of hand has taken place and what is now being described is not really in accord with Islamic law. She does not say so, but the implication is that a legal system in which authorities are perhaps able to receive some sort of reward for characterizing an arrangement as halal, that is, permissible, is not likely to operate without blemish.

The most flexible of the Sunni schools of law is undoubtedly the Hanafi (the most popular of the legal approaches to Islam), and Balala bases herself firmly on it, and in particular its application of general principles of welfare, in making sense of how to interpret scripture when it seems to impose difficulties on people. As she rightly points out, Islamic law is intended for everyone, not Muslims alone. When God revealed the Qur'an he presented a message for the whole world, and the economic arrangements he advocated are the best for everyone, not just the Muslim community. Given that not everyone is a Muslim, on the principle of welfare, allowances and arrangements must allow a variety of ways of doing things, ways that can nevertheless be based on the principle of welfare. In that regard, Balala suggests that a common-law approach is helpful, since it enables us to work from the general principle and some other legal practices that are both in accordance with the law and yet also not onerous to observe.

This latter point is significant, since the role of law in Islam is not to make things harder for people but easier, according as it does with what it is in their interests as a whole to do anyway. So while interest and speculation are forbidden, the *salam* system is accepted, according to which it is all right for someone who is not yet in possession of a product to borrow money on the basis of its eventual appearance. This is clearly a useful device for farmers, among others, who need money to cover their needs until their crops come in, and the person who provides the funds will expect to do so at a discount to the final value of the product. This may seem rather similar to a rate of interest and to speculation, but Balala argues that there is a significant difference.

Now, one could cynically say, as always with religious law, that the techniques for making legal what is already in practice look very artificial. This is especially so if one follows, as most Sunni Muslims do, the Hanafi legal school, which emphasizes general principles such as welfare and the idea that the law should not be burdensome. This approach often leads to what look like sleights of hand, a form of words or way of doing things where not much changes in terms of what is done but much is changed in how what is done is described. I agree with Balala here in calling for a common-law approach, since in that case-by-case methodology one can build up a series of examples, instances, and ways of doing things that are more like what is said to be clearly halal than otherwise, and where it is generally accepted that what lawyers have to deal with is not so much a halal/haram (allowed/forbidden) dichotomy as a continuum of legality and illegality. For religious enthusiasts this might seem to disparage the clarity and purity of the Qur'an and what stems from it, but religious law is based not only on God's will but also on human behavior, with all its complications and imperfections. In any case, our grasp of God's will and how it should be carried out is itself often imperfect. It is common law with its careful and piecemeal approach that represents how we ought to understand Islamic financial law and how it will develop and extend its influence globally.

This seems a plausible direction in which to go. Judges in religious courts do obviously refer to the particular case in front of them by referring to other similar cases and the judgments that are reached in those cases. One of the conceptual tools that makes this sort of argument more plausible is the existence of some *Grundnorm,* or general organizing principle, that lies behind the approach to law. In the Hanafi tradition, this is the principle of *istihsan,* the principle of general well-being, which can obviously and quite easily moderate the harshest interpretation of Islamic law. So, for example, according to this principle, *riba,* or what is often taken to be interest, might be regarded not as interest per se but as illegitimate interest, a rate of interest so high as to defeat the point of borrowing money, since repayment is well-nigh impossible. The general well-being might be regarded as best served by having moderate levels of interest, if this is not directly forbidden by the canonical texts, and in fact of course the profit-sharing arrangements that exist in explicitly *shari'ah*-structured financial instruments are rather like interest but in another form. The assumption is that riskier enterprises would attract a demand by investors for higher rates of profit sharing and that this rate would fluctuate also with the rate of interest in the economy as a whole, since investors have available to them the non-Islamic banking sector. In any case, from a moral point of view, is an investor not entitled to receive more of a return for putting money into a riskier prospect? Islam is critical of speculation, but here again the term can be interpreted in a variety of ways, and a company that is developing a new product, or better put, trying to develop a new product, can be seen either as objectionably speculative (if it fails) or as farsighted and innovative (if it succeeds).

Again we are faced with one of those unsavory choices in talking about religion and economics of either stressing the distinctness of the religion's teachings on economics, at the cost of making it look implausible, or accepting that the religion acknowledged the desirability of the main aspects of economic life, thus making the religion look vague. If Islam genuinely forbids interest, and anything that resembles interest, then it really is a radical approach to human commercial interaction, and an entirely new sort of economy is envisaged. The fact that we have been cynical about present-day Islamic banking arrangements may be largely due to the fact that in an environment in which there are non-Islamic alternatives—interest, in other words—it is difficult for other forms of banking without some interest equivalent to exist. Or so it would seem. On the other hand, Islam also advocates sexual modesty and marriage as the appropriate place for sexual relations; yet in a culture where it is possible to stray, the existence of this possibility does not excuse those who do so. Nor does it suggest that such rules are implausible or unrealistic. If, however, Islam merely advocates more of a commitment by people to charity and social justice, that seems quite easy to accept, and there is no reason why almost any economic system should not share that commitment, at least nominally. There is throughout the Qur'an a passionate demand for justice and charity within the context of free trade, and there is no suggestion that there is anything wrong with such forms of commerce, provided that appropriate measures are taken to help those who have been unfortunate and who do not do well in society. There is nothing in the Qur'an or the hadith to upset the reader of the *Wall Street Journal*, who also probably is in favor of helping the poor and not concentrating ceaselessly on wealth creation as though this were the only aim that has significance. Who could argue with that? But if this is what Islamic economics is all about, it is hardly very interesting.

A more plausible but even vaguer suggestion is this: people living in a society and genuinely trying to base their lives on the directions of God and his Messenger would produce a harmonious and prosperous polity. After all, religion comes from God, who, having created us, knows what sorts of creatures we are. He instructs us to live in certain ways that are in accordance with what he knows is best for us. If we do so, we flourish; if we fail to do so, we suffer. A society in which people really are interested in regulating their lives in accordance with God's will is going to be well prepared for an economic system that will not only produce wealth but also distribute it in a reasonable and just manner. This is a theme of the Qur'an, and the fact that most Muslim societies, if not all of them, do not live up to their ideal is perhaps an indication that they are not really Muslim societies in the view of many observers. Most people do not really think about what God wishes them to do before acting and so give charity grudgingly and unwillingly and seek to hold on to as much of their earnings as they possibly can, perhaps by concealing them from the tax authorities. People do not always treat their employees with respect or even pay them their due if they can get away with it, and working conditions are often grim and exploitative. The fact that on the whole there is mass emigration from Islamic-majority countries to the rest of the world suggests that the situation in those countries is far from ideal. It is not just that they are often poor, although they are, but also that the ways in which people live and treat one another are lacking in the sort of respect that all religions regard as significant. This is very much one of the themes of the recent unrest in the Arab world and suggests that, although countries often call themselves Muslim, they are not experienced as being so by many of their inhabitants, if Islam is understood to be more than just rituals and prayers.

The Way Forward

Is there here scope for being less negative in postulating what an Islamic economics would turn out to be? Clearly the main principles of being moderate in one's dealings with saving and spending are not going to be easy to specify. The principle of devoting adequate resources to charity is also not something that has an easy answer; it will rather have to be discussed and worked out depending on the vagaries of a particular situation and those within it. What sort of interest is burdensome is hardly obvious either. In the state of Kentucky, where I live, a bill was recently presented to the legislature to regulate more closely the many check-cashing services that exist and can charge enormous rates of interest. The owners of these businesses defend their practices by pointing out that they are handing out money with no security whatsoever and therefore reasonably expecting a high rate of failure to repay. They also pointed out that the conditions of the agreement with their customers are clear, and that they offer the convenience of cash at very short notice. Was it not reasonable, they suggested, for customers to pay a premium for such services, since without the high interest rates the service could not be offered? I will not comment on the validity of this argument, but it is not on the face of it a bad argument, and one can see how it could be made to justify what might otherwise seem to be egregious interest rates, the sort that the Qur'an describes so nicely as devouring those involved with them. As we know, someone who merely makes the periodic minimum payment will eventually be paying huge rates of interest. But, as the check-cashing businesses argued, the borrowers consented to the arrangement, and it is not the duty of those carrying out such trade to insist that customers be prudent. The Qur'an seems to contemplate a free-market economy, a system in which some will be foolish and others cautious, and naturally not everyone will be able to establish for themselves a middle position between the extremes, something that the Qur'an constantly demands.

As mentioned earlier, this middle position is difficult to determine. We do need to leave scope for risk takers, and they may abandon the idea of a middle position while they are pursuing their plans. This kind of behavior may be ruled out as speculation, but it is difficult to determine what is speculation and what is not. Suppose that I think that the price of a raw material that I use in my business is going to go up a good deal, and as a consequence I spend everything I can, and more, on buying stockpiles of the item. If I am wrong and the price suddenly drops, I am left with far more expensive material than my competitors and presumably will suffer as a result. They can price their goods below my price and still make a profit. If I am right, however, my action looks prudent. Yet I had no guarantee of the success of my strategy, and it could have undone my commercial operations entirely. Is the middle position to buy some extra material but not a lot? Not necessarily, since we are not talking about buying lottery tickets here, which surely would be banned by Islam as speculation. A business owner can use his or her own intelligence to try to work out the future and take decisions on that basis accordingly. Farmers have been doing this ever since markets existed. Sometimes they get it right and sometimes not, and surely when the Qur'an urges moderate behavior it does not mean that one should never take risks.

The problem of trying to find a religious interpretation of economics is that one goes either too far or not far enough. The normal ways in which markets operate are on some interpretations unaffected by the religion, in which case it looks like the religion has made little difference. By contrast, through the injection of religion into the market, the market could be transformed entirely into something different, and probably unworkable, in which case the religion looks like it has had too much influence, making things a lot worse than they were before. If we avoid this way of characterizing the basic economic rules of the religion, we are back to presenting a system that is not substantially different from that without the religion. We do not have to be so dismissive, however. Islam, like many other religions, calls for a moral revolution in our lives intended to bring about a new way of commercial life. Putting commerce in its place by giving an appropriate role to charity would not transform the nature of commerce, but it would change the nature of society, perhaps for the better. If believers were to put commerce in a more subsidiary place in their lives by contrast with religion, then both commercial life and what it led to might be an improvement on the present situation. This brings out something significant about the impact of religion on economics: it is not a quick fix. It is not like a new regulation to make markets work better; it is about a gradual change in the moral consciousness of the individual and the society that also has economic implications.

NOTES

1. Translated in Rauf Azhar, *Economics of an Islamic Economy* (Leiden: Brill, 2010), 415–417.
2. See David Cobham and Ghassam Dibeh, eds., *Money in the Middle East and North Africa: Monetary Policy Frameworks and Strategies* (London: Routledge, 2011).
3. Rasem Khayed and Muhammad Hassan, *Islamic Entrepreneurship* (London: Routledge, 2011).
4. See Maha-Hanaan Balala, *Islamic Finance and Law: Theory and Practice in a Globalized World* (London: I. B. Tauris, 2011).

Two Challenges to Market Daoism

16

James Behuniak Jr.

Libertarians and free-market theorists routinely claim Laozi as one of their own. David Boaz, for instance, in his reader on libertarianism, features selections "from Lao-tzu to Milton Friedman," reflecting his belief that Laozi was the "first known libertarian."[1] Such claims are based on the perception that notions of nonintervention and spontaneity in the *Daodejing* are identical to those of laissez-faire and spontaneous order in the thought of Adam Smith and Friedrich Hayek. Ken McCormick, for instance, treats such notions as equivalent. In his article, "The Tao of Laissez-Faire," he writes:

> *Laissez-faire* is simply an extension of *wu-wei* to government policy. Harmonizing with the Tao, which is universal and whose power extends everywhere, even to the social realm, allows a beneficent natural order to emerge. Moreover, this natural order is superior to any order which human beings could create because human knowledge is partial and fragmented. In order to take advantage of this natural order, the ruler must seek stillness. By following a course of non-action, the natural order will emerge on its own, with beneficial results for the society.[2]

To illustrate that Laozi's advocacy of laissez-faire is explicit, McCormick quotes chapter 57 of the *Daodejing*. The chapter reads:

> I take no action and the people are transformed of themselves. I prefer stillness and the people are rectified of themselves. I am not meddlesome and the people prosper of themselves.[3]

From here, the logic proceeds as follows. Daoists advocate nonintervention in the form of *wuwei*. Capitalists advocate that government interference in the free market be reduced to a bare minimum: laissez-faire. The two ideas (*wuwei* and laissez-faire) are identical. Therefore, Daoism provides further philosophical justification for free-market capitalism. McCormick finds it very exciting that laissez-faire was, as he sees it, "independently developed in China, in such a different culture, time, and place."[4] This, he says, enables free-market advocates to "call upon another, quite powerful, philosophical tradition for help" in promoting their economic vision. He continues:

> Taoism has existed for more than two millennia, and it is not a philosophy that can be easily dismissed. . . . It is a tradition which is unmistakably different from Classical Liberalism, but on the very important subject of the propriety of a policy of *laissez-faire,* there is complete agreement.[5]

McCormick interprets free-market reforms in China accordingly. Such reforms are "not so much [an] importation of a foreign ideology, but [rather the] reawakening of a home-grown concept."[6] James Dorn, vice president for academic affairs at the Cato Institute, echoes McCormick's enthusiasm in his own article, "China's Future: Market Socialism or Market Taoism?" As Dorn sees it:

> The market-liberal vision is not new to China; it was inherent in the Taoist doctrine of *wu-wei* developed by Lao Tzu and his disciples. China's leaders need only let the Chinese people return to their roots to see the wisdom of letting the spontaneous market process organize economic life, while limiting government to the protection of life, liberty, and prosperity."[7]

Based on the perceived equivalence of *wuwei* and laissez-faire, "market Daoism" assumes that the former, like the latter, must lend support to market liberalism. Such a brisk inference, however, bypasses some important questions. Was *wuwei* originally connected to an economic ideal in early Daoism? If so, was that ideal one of market liberalism? If not, were there features of that ideal that would preclude market liberalism? Coming at Daoism as they invariably do, not as scholars of Chinese thought but as free-market advocates, "market Daoists" seldom ask such questions. They do need to be asked, however, if Daoism is to be legitimately enlisted on behalf of market capitalism.

In this essay, I offer two challenges to "market Daoism." First, I assess the suggestion that Laozi himself endorsed market-friendly policies. Given the socio-economic ideal provided in the *Daodejing* and other historical evidence, I maintain that he did not. Next, I assess the suggestion that the *Daodejing* is philosophically consistent with and supportive of free-market capitalism. I argue that its teachings are clearly not, and assertions made to the contrary are in plain disregard of Daoist philosophy. In short, I argue that market Daoism does little justice to the *Daodejing* historically or philosophically.

The Historical Challenge

We begin by considering the ideal society envisioned in chapter 80 of the *Daodejing*. It is hardly a scene of robust commercial activity. Rather, it is a society in which people will

> find relish in their food. And beauty in their clothes.
> Will be content in their abode. And happy in the way they live.
>
> Adjoining states are within sight of one another, and the sounds of dogs barking and cocks crowing in one state can be heard in another, yet the people of one state will grow old and die without having had any dealings with those of another.

The absence of contact with adjoining states does not preclude basic economic activity within the confines of a state. However, as economic historians such as Karl Polanyi argue, primitive localism of the type envisioned here does not suggest activities consistent with the emergence of full-scale market mechanisms. Contrary to the logic of classical economic theory, Polanyi argues that markets are not institutions "functioning mainly within" economies, but rather among economies.[8] Markets, he argues, are primarily and originally the result of distance contact. Even if markets are understood instead as the result of an innate desire to trade, as they are in classical liberal theory,[9] the vision in chapter 80 is one in which such desire is ignored. Thus, it is not at all clear that Laozi's ideal community is consistent with even the most rudimentary notion of a market, let alone free-market capitalism.

Be that as it may, there were of course markets in ancient China. Trade was an indispensible and closely monitored component of social life. The *advent* of market exchange, like the advent of every social innovation in China, was attributed not to the essence of "nature," nor to some innate impulse. Rather, it traced its origin to the ingenuity of the historical sages. According to the cultural history sketched in *Dazhuan,* it was Shen Nong who first inaugurated markets. According to this account:

> [Shen Nong] made it such that markets were held at midday. He brought it about that all the people would assemble their goods, exchange them, and withdraw, each securing that which they obtained.[10]

Noteworthy in this passage are the active verbs. The market system was something that was originally "done" (為, *wei*) by Shen Nong. It was something "brought about" (致, *zhi*) by the policies of the sage. In other words, markets did not pop up spontaneously. Once markets gained momentum in early China, they were carefully regulated by the state. During the Western Zhou, market frequency, location, hours of operation, the arrangement of goods, products made available, and prices were all subject to state control.[11] As the quality of handicrafts gradually improved, the market economy expanded, and the strictly controlled markets of the Western Zhou gave way to freer systems of exchange. This process eventually gave birth to an independent merchant class.

Merchants have historically been held in rather low esteem in China. In the social hierarchy, they occupied a place below the royal, the civil, the military, the intellectual, the agricultural, and the artisan classes. As Romeyn Taylor explains, this new class was immediately regarded as a threat.

> Although the orthodox social order comfortably accommodated the concept of economy as livelihood, the emergence of an autonomous market system on a significant scale in the late Zhou and Han presented a fundamental threat in the form of a flourishing merchant class ambitious for higher status. In the former Han the battle was joined. Merchants were forbidden by law to buy land or hold office and, continuing Zhou practice, trade was confined to officially administered urban markets. Government monopolies were established in some commodities in order to divert commercial profits from private to public hands.[12]

Confucians taught that it was important for wealth not to accumulate in the hands of any elite group, neither state nor commercial. The Confucian ideal of governing was to govern as a "Parent of the People" (民之父母, *minzhifumu*). As the *Daxue* explains, this required that virtue be prioritized over profit and that wealth be widely distributed. The text explains:

> Virtue is primary. Getting rich is secondary. If virtue becomes an afterthought and getting rich is foremost, [the ruler] will compete with the people and engage in theft. Hence, to gather riches is to scatter the people. To scatter wealth is to draw the people to you.[13]

While most of the prescriptions in the *Daxue* are addressed to rulers rather than private citizens, its principles regarding the accumulation of wealth applied across all social classes. As the text observes, "head of a state or head of a household, anyone devoted to wealth and its use must be under the influence of a petty person."[14]

Then as now, the primary source of income for the early Chinese state was tax revenue, and a common grievance among people was lavish state spending. Mozi represents the populist sentiment in this regard. He advocated for moderation in state expenditures, and identified and criticized the insufficient production of such basic goods as housing, clothing, food, and transportation—production that needed to be met if the population of a kingdom was to increase. Mencius was also interested in expanding the size of the kingdom, and he pushed for broad-based tax reductions: the elimination of duties at border stations, the remittance of property tax on local merchants, and relief for those working public lands into production.[15] Before Mencius gets branded the first Tea Party activist, we should recognize that he endorsed a standard set of limited stimulus measures. These measures—the elimination of duties at border stations, the remittance of property tax on local merchants, and relief for those working public lands into production—are outlined in the "Monthly Government Orders" ("Yueling," 月令) chapter of the *Liji* as well as in the *Lüshi chunqiu*. Rather than being prescribed as general government policy, these measures were understood to be only periodically appropriate: specifically, for the second month of autumn and in some cases the first month of summer.[16] The permanent elimination of taxes and border tariffs is not endorsed in the ancient records. Rather, what is advised is the periodic "modification" (易 *yi*) of taxes and border tariffs. Such adjustments are indicative of continued state control, and there is nothing to indicate that Mencius was unorthodox in this respect. Certainly, Mencius had no inherent bias against taxing the merchants. It is in the *Mencius,* after all, that we learn of the original rationale for doing so. The *Mencius* relates:

> In ancient times, markets were instituted so that people could exchange what they had for what they did not have. Officials were there just to keep order. But then came some despicable people who sought out a "high mound" and scaled it. They looked left and right and monopolized the market profits. The people all recognized them as despicable, so they went ahead and taxed them. The practice of taxing merchants originated with such despicable people.[17]

There were good reasons for Chinese thinkers to be wary of the merchant class. One of the primary economic concerns in early China was that heightened commercial activity would have a detrimental effect on the production of basic necessities, especially food. Xunzi recommended that the state "keep statistical records to reduce the number of merchants and traders" in order to prevent farmers and craftspeople from abandoning their vocations in pursuit of greater profits.[18] Xunzi described such restrictions as "allowing the people a generous living through the exercise of government."[19] Across the board, Chinese philosophers advised government intervention to limit the expansion of market activity and to avert its ill effect as they perceived it.

The proponents of market Daoism would have us believe that Laozi was profoundly different in this regard. For Murray Rothbard, cofounder of the Cato Institute, Laozi was the "first political economist to discern the systemic effects of government intervention."[20] The early Daoists ("the world's first libertarians," in his estimation) advocated "virtually no interference by the state in economy or society."[21] There is, however, zero textual evidence that Laozi envisioned *wuwei* as applicable to economies specifically. Instead, a careful reading of the *Daodejing* suggests similar concerns, if not the advocacy of similar policies, current in the period. Like Xunzi, the *Daodejing* is concerned that certain vocations might become too profitable and have a detrimental impact on vital industries. As Laozi says, when there are "robbers" possessed of too much wealth, the fields become overgrown with weeds and granaries stand empty.[22] Like Mencius, the *Daodejing* is concerned with despicable agents who thrive where profits are easily made. As Laozi says, "discard profit" and thereby get rid of thieves and bandits.[23] Like Mozi, the *Daodejing* is concerned that profligate state spending (especially military) misallocates treasure. As Laozi says, when Dao prevails in the land, the best horses are found working the field rather than being diverted by the state for military use.[24] And like everyone, the *Daodejing* is interested in targeted tax relief. As Laozi says, people are hungry because those in power eat up too much in taxes.[25]

One might extrapolate from this a "Daoist" economic theory—or not. This is not the point. The point is that, in respect to economic concerns, the *Daodejing* is not *so* very different from other Chinese philosophical schools. We see the same general themes here as elsewhere: a distrust of the profit motive and concerns over vital industries, unfair taxation, and the misallocation of state treasure. There is, however, one *key* difference between Laozi and the others. Laozi never appeals to the standard list of market-friendly policies outlined in the *Yueling* and elsewhere. Why? Because the lowering of border tariffs, the remittance of taxes on merchants, and the incentives for commercial development were motivated by the desire to *increase the size of the kingdom.* But unlike other philosophers, Laozi did not wish to increase the size of the kingdom. As he plainly states: "Reduce the size and population of the state (*guo*)."[26] As he saw it, the best way to survive amid warring states was to maintain a low demographic profile. The growth of the kingdom, the only goal that ever motivated early Chinese thinkers to adopt pro-market policies, was something that Laozi wished to avoid. He did not want to facilitate economic growth, and he had no interest in developing interstate commerce. This being so, to casually assert as Dorn and others do that Laozi represents the "market-liberal vision" in early China is not only unsubstantiated, it is positively contradicted by the facts.

The Philosophical Challenge

Turning to philosophical considerations, we again find market Daoism disregarding important dimensions of its subject. Daoist teachings on human desire and human nature are largely ignored in market Daoist treatments. Not surprisingly, proponents of market Daoism approach Daoism already committed to theories of human nature that support their capitalist views. As if by reflex, when they encounter appeals to "nature" in the *Daodejing,* such preferences inform their interpretations of the text. Flagrant omissions, equivocations, and distortions result. McCormick, for instance, regards Adam Smith and Daoism as identical in that both maintain "that we must not interfere with the natural order of things," and both believe "[that] it is not proper to *force* people to oppose their own natural inclinations."[27] He never once considers that a view of "nature" might imply something other than a free-market system. Dorn is equally neglectful in this regard. He asserts that alternative economic systems are "contrary to human nature" and that if people are simply left alone to find their way (i.e., *wuwei*), "a spontaneous market order will arise."[28] It never enters his mind that Daoism might have its own theory of "human nature" and that this theory might be antithetical to the emergence of a market order.[29] Such oversights need to be addressed.

It is true that Laozi advocates *wuwei* as a strategy for governance. Chapter 57 of the *Daodejing* is a clear illustration of this, and it is the darling passage of "market Daoism." It is noteworthy, however, that in the works of Rothberg, McCormick, and Dorn its concluding line is consistently edited out. The full passage reads as follows:

> I take no action and the people are transformed of themselves. I prefer stillness and the people are rectified of themselves. I am not meddlesome and the people prosper of themselves. *I am free from desire and the people of themselves become simple like the un-carved block.*

"Market Daoists" regard Laozi's teachings on desire, here restored, to be irrelevant to his teachings on *wuwei;* hence their systematic removal of the last line. Rothbard, for instance, suggests that it was only after "seeing no hope for a mass movement" in support of laissez-faire that Laozi turned to "[counseling] the now familiar Taoist path of withdrawal, retreat, and limitations of one's desires."[30] This is pure speculation on Rothbard's part, a wild guess. McCormick is more explicit in arguing that the topic of desire *should* be severed from *wuwei* for philosophical reasons. As he sees it, "one must not confound [Daoist] moral arguments regarding proper individual behavior with [its] policy recommendations."[31] For McCormick, Daoist teachings on desire operate on a different level from its teachings on *wuwei.* His argument:

> The fact that [Daoists] do not think that wealth brings contentment does not change the fact that [they do not advocate] a policy to stop people from pursuing what they want. Wise people will learn on their own that riches do not bring contentment. The fact that other people may not understand this does not justify economic restrictions. One cannot force people to be virtuous.[32]

This is a classic red herring. The question is not whether one can force another to be virtuous. The question is whether desire is a good thing according to Daoism. McCormick's premise here is false anyway. The *Daodejing* does not expect us to "learn on our own" that rampant desire and the accumulation of material goods do not bring contentment. To the contrary, the text tells us so over and over again. Let chapter 46 suffice:

> There is no crime greater than having too many desires.
> There is no disaster greater than not being content.
> There is no misfortune greater than being covetous.
> Hence, in being content, one will always have enough.

However market Daoism tries to reconcile or hide the issue,[33] the fact remains that *wuwei* and desire are closely related topics in the *Daodejing.* In fact, the widespread reduction of desire is precisely the type of transformation that government by *wuwei* is intended to effect. In chapter 37, the outcome of such governing is presented in terms of desire explicitly:

> The myriad creatures will be transformed of their own accord. After they are transformed, should desire raise its head, I shall press it down with the weight of the nameless un-carved block. The nameless un-carved block is freedom from desire. And if I cease to desire and remain still, the empire will be at peace of its own accord.

"Market Daoists" feel safe ignoring the link between *wuwei* and desire for the simple reason that the European idea of laissez-faire has nothing to do with the psychology of desire. McCormick argues exactly that. At precisely this juncture, however, a more critical scholar would pause to inquire into the differences between *wuwei* and laissez-faire. McCormick does not do this. Perhaps better scholarship can help clarify the issue. In his work on *wuwei,* Edward Slingerland explains that the term *wei* (為) has a broad semantic range in classical Chinese. The term *wuwei,* in addition to meaning "not doing," also means "not taking" things to be a certain way. It means "not regarding" things to be such or so.[34] To be "without regard" (*wuwei*) or "non-regarding" (*wuyiwei,* 無以為) is to resist attributing undue worth to things.[35] It means "not making" things into what they are not, and not thereby being motivated by erroneous estimations of worth. Such "non-regarding" is a central theme in the *Daodejing*. Slingerland explains:

> [In] Laozi's view desire is merely a symptom of a deeper malaise: knowledge, or the "regarding" (為 *wei*) that springs from knowledge. "Regarding" in the sense that is criticized by Laozi refers to making normative, not merely definitional, distinctions—to hold something in (high) regard. Such regarding causes a person to value one thing over another, and therefore provides ulterior motives for action.[36]

Such "ulterior motives," in the form of desires, can lead to misguided government policy, and this illuminates an important dimension of Laozi's advocacy of *wuwei*. Chapter 75 of the *Daodejing* explains that difficulties in governing emerge when those in power "have regard" (*youwei,* 有為). Lau's translation, however, offers a different gloss. He suggests that such difficulties result from government action itself. His rendition: "The people are difficult to govern. It is because those in authority are too fond of action [*wei*] that the people are difficult to govern." Relying on such a translation, market Daoism seizes on this passage. It appears to advocate for European-style laissez-faire. But *pace* Lau, the *wei* spoken of in this passage is something that rulers "have" (*you,* 有). It is not something that they "do," nor is it something they are unusually "fond" of doing. Slingerland's understanding of *wei* as "regard" is a more adequate translation of the term in this instance.[37] With such an adjustment, the meaning of the passage might be glossed as follows: "Difficulties in governing are a result of those in charge having special regard for some particular outcome or interest."[38] Such an observation does not lead to a prescription for doing literally nothing, laissez-faire. Rather, it advises that those in government not subordinate the actual process of governing to a fixed end that is held in higher regard. This means that governing should remain intelligent, flexible, and patient: like "cooking a small fish."[39]

The Daoist ideal, accordingly, is one in which government does not hastily impose its own design on the social order. This much market Daoism recognizes. What it fails to recognize, however, is that such "non-regard" (*wuwei*) is both a means and an end to the ideal social order. As chapter 37 relates, the aim of governing "without regard" (*wuwei*) is that people return to the state of the "uncarved block," free from desire themselves. As Lau explains, the uncarved block is "a symbol for the original state of man before desire is produced in him by artificial means."[40] Here it becomes important to recognize the difference between "nature" as conceived in Daoism and "human nature" as conceived in classical liberal economics. For Daoism, the human being is not primordially driven by the desire to profit, to acquire, to barter, or to trade. Such desires are the result of a "regard" (*wei*) for things that comes not from nature but from its perversion. Government may instigate such inclinations by acting perversely itself, desiring to grow the kingdom beyond its natural limits and wanting to acquire the goods of its neighbor. Such perversion was commonplace in the Warring States period. The ideal Daoist state was posited as an antidote to this. It rejects economic expansion and interstate commerce, both of which increase the desire for material goods and trigger an unremitting cycle of acquisition and exchange. According to the logic of Daoism, this is precisely the spiraling dynamic that makes populations difficult to manage. Thus, to have "as few desires as possible" is the aim of Daoism, both individually and communally.[41] Only with the reduction of desire will "peace of its own accord" be achieved.[42] Thus, early Daoism was, as Jichuang Hu observes, "indifferent to, if not disdainful of human economic activities."[43] If anything, market activities would make society *more* difficult to govern according to the logic of Daoism.

This is where contemporary market Daoism fails to recognize its own self-refutation: the very antipathy between *markets* and *Daoism*. This fatal error becomes all the more egregious as their argument is mobilized in support of modern consumer capitalism. After all, in modern parlance, the word "market" is a verb as well as a noun. Hundreds of billions of dollars are spent each year on advertising worldwide. In such a hypercommercial environment, attention itself becomes a commodity. Gimmicks are developed to excite and absorb attention, and then markets are created to redistribute it for the sole purpose of creating desire where desire does not exist. Hans-Georg Moeller recognizes straightaway the manner in which such a system is utterly out of synch with classical Daoism. He observes:

> Obviously [Laozi] did not envision a capitalist market economy with its culture of creating demand and desires through advertising and a public ideal of ever-increasing prosperity. The early Daoists, it seems, were not interested in "heating up" the economy by stimulating the acquiring of goods and possessions. Consumption was meant to remain rather basic.[44]

As D. C. Lau observes, there is "no doubt" that an early Daoist would recognize advertising as one of the "banes of modern life," a practice that "creates new desires for objects [that] no one would have missed if they had not been invented."[45] Nothing is more antithetical to Daoism than the creation of such desires. The degree to which market Daoism ignores this fact is stunning. In "The Case for Market Taoism," Dorn claims that the good Daoist government (i.e., one by *wuwei*) acts "in harmony with each person's desire to prosper and to expand the range of choice."[46] Positively omitted in his reasoning is that Daoism is totally opposed to feeding such desire and expanding the range of choice. As the *Daodejing* teaches:

> The five colors blind the eyes. The five tones deafen the ears.
> The five flavors destroy the palate. Racing and hunting make a mind wild and crazy.
> Rare and expensive things make people lose their way.[47]

Such colossal oversights are the result of two philosophical errors. The first is the severing of *wuwei* from the topic of desire. This results in a distortion of the meaning of *wuwei* and thus a failure to recognize its psychological dimension. The second error is ignoring the fact that Daoism has a conception of "nature" distinct from that of classical liberalism. At crucial junctures, market Daoism conflates the teachings of Daoism with liberalism, thus failing to detect the relevant and distinguishing features of Daoist philosophy. Taken together, these two errors leave market Daoism with little philosophical credence.

Concluding Thoughts

According to McCormick, Daoism "is not a philosophy that can be easily dismissed." The truth of that statement is what prompts the present essay. Market Daoism too easily dismisses aspects of Daoist philosophy that are in tension with capitalism, and too hastily amplifies aspects that appear congruent. In the process, Daoism is distorted both historically and philosophically. In the final analysis, the most generous thing that can be said about market Daoism is that it is poor scholarship. In its defense, it might be argued that any attempt to make an ancient tradition applicable to modern institutions is prone to the sort of omissions and oversights characteristic of the argument for market Daoism. Applying Daoism to modern economic institutions is anachronistic by its very nature; some aspects of the tradition are bound to be omitted, and others foregrounded, if sense is to be made in such an application. This may be the case, but legitimate criticism then focuses on the adequacy of the teachings reconstructed for such a purpose. To neglect Daoism's teachings on the reduction of desire, and to altogether ignore its own economic ideal, results in an unacceptably truncated version of Daoism. Such features are too important to bracket out. The result is not Daoism.

Even with better scholarship, we should not expect to find Daoism univocally endorsing or disavowing our modern economic practices. The historical divergences are too wide, and the contemporary world is too complex. Consider again the ideal Daoist society. Here, adjoining states are "within sight of one another," hearing "the sounds of dogs barking and cocks crowing," yet their populations have no substantive dealings with one another. Such a vision is patently naive in our globalized world. El Paso and Juárez are technically neighboring cities separated by national borders, but they are integrated by a larger global system creating relationships that cannot be ignored.[48] In such instances, primitive localism of the type advocated by Laozi does not speak cogently to our current situation. There are, however, other modern practices the intelligence of which can be directly challenged in Daoist terms. Our desire for "rare and expensive things," for instance, today creates markets for exotic fruits and vegetables in all seasons and in defiance of any natural geographical limits. The result is modern industrial agriculture, along with its attending problems of resource depletion, unfair labor practices, and nutritional degradation. Here, it seems that Daoist teachings can speak quite cogently to the situation in which we find ourselves. We desire too much, and we fail to recognize how such inflated desires are ruining us.

In any case, inquiry into what Daoism can teach us about our economic practices strikes me as a rich area for research, one deserving of serious scholarly work. In comparison with such work, responding to market Daoism is a modest assignment. Still, it seems a necessary task given the profound misguidedness of this particular reading.

NOTES

1. See David Boaz, *The Libertarian Reader: Classic and Contemporary Writings from Lao-tzu to Milton Friedman* (New York: Free Press, 1997). Quote is from David Boaz, *Libertarianism: A Primer* (New York: Free Press, 1997), 27.

2. Ken McCormick, "The Tao of Laissez-Faire," *Eastern Economic Journal* 25, no. 3 (1999), 334.

3. Ibid. McCormick uses D. C. Lau's translation of the *Daodejing*. For the sake of consistency, I will do the same.

4. McCormick, "The Tao of Laissez-Faire," 339.

5. Ibid.

6. Ibid.

7. James A. Dorn, "China's Future: Market Socialism or Market Taoism?" *Cato Journal* 18, no. 1 (1989), 144.

8. Karl Polanyi, *The Great Transformation: The Political and Economic Origins of Our Time* (Boston: Beacon Press, 1944), 61.

9. Such as Adam Smith's postulation in *Wealth of Nations* (part 1.ii.1) of the human being's innate "propensity to truck, barter, and exchange one thing for another."

10. *Dazhuan,* 2.4. See Richard Wilhelm, *The I Ching or Book of Changes* (Princeton, NJ: Princeton University Press, 1977), 331.

11. Jichuang Hu, *A Concise History of Chinese Economic Thought* (Beijing: Foreign Languages Press, 1988), 7–10.

12. Romeyn Taylor, "Chinese Hierarchy in Comparative Perspective," *Journal of Asian Studies* 48, no. 3 (1989), 500.

13. *Daxue,* chap. 10. See Wing-Tsit Chan, *A Sourcebook in Chinese Philosophy* (Princeton, NJ: Princeton University Press, 1963), 92–93.

14. *Daxue,* chap. 10. See Chan, *A Sourcebook in Chinese Philosophy,* 94.

15. *Mencius,* 2A:5.

16. See James Legge, *Li Chi Book of Rites* (New Hyde Park, NY: University Books, 1967), 1:274, 289; and John Knoblock and Jeffrey Riegal, *The Annals of Lü Buwei* (Stanford, CA: Stanford University Press, 2000), 134, 192.

17. *Mencius,* 2B:10.

18. See John Knoblock, *Xunzi: A Translation and Study of the Complete Works* (Stanford, CA: Stanford University Press, 1990), 2:123.

19. Ibid.

20. Murray N. Rothbard, *Economic Thought before Adam Smith,* vol. 1, *An Austrian Perspective on the History of Economic Thought* (Cheltenham, UK: Edward Elgar, 1995), 23.

21. Ibid.

22. *Daodejing,* chap. 53.

23. *Daodejing,* chap. 19.

24. *Daodejing,* chap. 46.

25. *Daodejing,* chap. 75.

26. *Daodejing,* chap. 80.

27. McCormick, "The Tao of Laissez-Faire," 338–339.

28. Dorn, "China's Future," 143, 135.

29. Dorn repeats this error in his article "The Primacy of Property in a Liberal Constitutional Order: Lessons for China," *Independent Review* 7, no. 4 (2003), 492–493.

30. Rothbard, *Economic Thought before Adam Smith,* 23.

31. McCormick, "The Tao of Laissez-Faire," 339.

32. Ibid., 338.

33. Dorn simply suppresses the evidence.

34. Edward Slingerland, *Effortless Action: Wu-Wei as a Conceptual Metaphor and Spiritual Ideal in Early China* (Oxford: Oxford University Press, 2003), 78–84; see also 303n4.

35. The latter construction appears in *Daodejing,* chap. 38, as a description of those of highest accomplishment.

36. Slingerland, *Effortless Action,* 79.

37. In addition to its grammatical advantages, this rendition is more thematically consistent with the chapter's subsequent, parallel discussion of "regard" (為, *wei*) for life (*yishengwei*, 以生為).

38. Or, as in John C. H. Wu's rendition, the people are difficult to govern "because those above them are fussy and have private ends to serve."

39. *Daodejing*, chap. 60.

40. D. C. Lau, *Lao Tzu Tao Te Ching* (London: Penguin Classics, 1963), xxxii.

41. *Daodejing*, chap. 19.

42. *Daodejing*, chap. 37.

43. Hu, *Concise History of Chinese Economic Thought*, 209.

44. Hans-Georg Moeller, *The Philosophy of the* Daodejing (New York: Columbia University Press, 2006), 91.

45. Lau, *Lao Tzu Tao Te Ching*, xxxi.

46. James Dorn, "The Case for Market Taoism," *American Spectator*, September 24, 2007, http://spectator.org/archives/2007/09/24/the-case-for-market-taoism#.

47. *Daodejing*, chap. 12.

48. I thank Danny Coyle for this vivid example.

Buddhist, Western, and Hybrid Perspectives on Liberty Rights and Economic Rights 17

Gordon Davis

There has been a lively debate among contemporary Buddhist philosophers and commentators on Buddhist ethics as to whether a robust conception of human rights can be justified within any major Buddhist tradition. This debate echoes similar debates over the past twenty years about the prospects for defenses of human rights in various non-Western traditions of ethical reflection. In this essay, I show that recent defenses offered by Buddhist philosophers share an important feature: they are all based on the indirect and contingent benefits of institutionalized rights rather than the direct or intrinsic moral value of rights. I will argue, though, that this sort of defense may offer the soundest moral reasoning when it comes to justifying the majority of putative human rights. The indirect justification that seems to represent something of a consensus among Buddhist ethicists might be the most sensible one, both practically and theoretically. I hope to show that one advantage of this sort of justification is that it supports economic rights as much as liberty rights. Rather than merely assuming that economic rights are defensible and valuable, however, I appeal to some views of Western provenance to make a case for this, and I defend such rights against two major objections. One objection is based on the potential for unresolvable conflicts between economic rights and other, supposedly more important, rights. The second objection is based on worries about which values and which rights are likely to be recognized universally across cultures—the objection being that economic rights cannot garner the same degree of transcultural agreement as liberty rights. Both objections are often overstated and can in any case be preempted; indeed, Buddhist ethics can help us to do this. In the course of exploring these issues, we will see how much is to be gained from the distinctively teleological emphasis of Buddhist ethics, and how much we can learn about ethics itself from convergences and divergences between Buddhist and modern Western reflections on personhood, law, morality, and the public sphere.

Consequentialist and Teleological Tendencies in Buddhist Ethics

In a recent survey of both primary and secondary sources on Buddhist ethical ideas, Robert Florida argues that there is little evidence of any conception of human rights in classical Buddhist texts and traditions.[1] His conclusion applies to scriptures originating in both the Theravada and Mahāyāna traditions—and, construed in terms of any strict understanding of rights language, that conclusion seems correct, though in some ways unsurprising.[2] As well as drawing on his knowledge of classical Buddhist scripture, Florida cites numerous scholars who have reached the same conclusion, such as David Chappell and Donald Swearer,[3] and several contributors to a landmark volume on Buddhism and human rights, including Kenneth Inada, Craig Ihara, and Peter Junger.[4]

Among these writers, however, opinions differ on whether the general spirit of Buddhist ethics would encourage or discourage appeals to human rights discourse as an expedient method of advancing the primary goals of Buddhist ethics and Buddhist spiritual practice. Ihara and Junger, uneasy with what they see as an unhealthy individualism in rights discourse, argue that Buddhist ethics should direct its ideals and efforts elsewhere—and meanwhile stay true to the values explicit in Buddhist scripture. Chappell, Inada, and Swearer, on the other hand, see human rights discourse as a potentially valuable partner in advancing the goals of Buddhist ethics. Florida echoes the tentativeness of this latter perspective, concluding:

> It cannot be claimed that traditional Buddhist scripture and ethical thought directly support human rights concepts; and, in both theory and practice, the assertive individualism of much of human rights advocacy goes against the spirit and teachings of *buddhadharma*. But to hold too tightly to doctrinal formulations—such as the rejection of rights language—may also go against the spirit and teachings of *buddhadharma*. As long as it is kept clearly in mind that rights are transient human constructs and . . . should not be reified into absolutes, it would be safe enough for Buddhists to invoke them. . . . In light of the [modern] efficacy of human rights claims, it could even be an example of Buddhist skillful means to defend the oppressed by using the rhetoric of human rights.[5]

In acknowledging the potential value of the "rhetoric" of human rights, Florida appears far from offering a ringing endorsement of rights discourse. Two other Buddhist philosophers, by contrast, seem to go much further in their defense of human rights ideals. In separate, and quite different, contributions to the debate, Jay Garfield and Damien Keown strongly support the human rights movement and the role of "engaged" Buddhists in advancing the cause of human rights in Asia and elsewhere. They do not treat the ideal of universal rights as a mere device to be strategically deployed at some times and not others. However, they do describe the ultimate value of human rights in ways that displace them from their proximity to values traditionally connected to rights, such as dignity and justice.

One common response of ethicists encountering the ideas of Buddhist ethics is to praise the role of compassion and generosity in Buddhism while feeling that Buddhists may have overlooked the correct foundation for such values. Garfield turns this reaction on its head. Westerners have had the right idea, he says, regarding human rights, at least at the engaged level that operates at the interface of morality, politics, and law; but they have generally mistaken their moral foundation—that is, what explains the value of rights. In his view, compassion explains the importance of human rights, rather than the other way around. For his part, Damien Keown also eschews human rights qua moral foundation; but in his case, he emphasizes the normative foci of the third and fourth noble truths, that is, the importance of nirvanic or *jhanic* spiritual goals, and the importance of enabling individuals to pursue those goals in peace and security. On this foundation, he believes we can justify a central role for human rights in the theory and practice of social reform.

However the attitudes among these various writers may vary, we should consider whether there is ultimately much difference philosophically in their understanding of the ethical justification of such social ideals as human rights and social justice. The approaches of Inada, Chappell, Swearer, and Florida clearly qualify as *instrumentalist:* for them, human rights have no intrinsic value (let alone intrinsic existence), but rather have instrumental value in relation to the goals of reducing suffering and promoting spiritual development. Meanwhile, the approaches of Garfield and Keown are less focused on expedience; and yet, perhaps they are more instrumentalist than they seem. If social reforms that enhance individual rights are justified by values that are quite different from dignity and justice, it follows that successful reforms ultimately serve those other values, and this again invokes an instrumental relationship between rights and those broader goals. Perhaps reflecting the centrality of "skillful means" in Buddhist ethics (noted by Florida in the passage earlier), all of the ethicists cited previously really share the same general approach.[6]

Instrumentalism about certain ethical values need not be either dangerous or unsound, or at any rate not unless it is part of a generalized instrumentalism about all values.[7] In one form, it enters into moral consequentialism, which is both a defensible view and a notable interpretation of the foundations of Buddhist ethical thought. Some who share the views summarized earlier might prefer to call themselves "consequentialists" about human rights, but I will reserve the term "consequentialism" for the view that all evaluative focal points (though not all values) should be assessed in terms of results, not just the granting of rights or other acts and institutions relating to justice. For present purposes, and for the sake of brevity, I will refer to the approaches mentioned previously as *instrumentalist,* without implying that they are either consequentialist or instrumentalist about value in general.

However, it is worth comparing their instrumentalism about human rights to other views on a spectrum, at one end of which is a consequentialism applied to all focal points—actions, rules, laws, virtues, ideals, institutions—and at the other end a much more restricted endorsement of instrumental considerations. (The consensus view of the Buddhist ethicists discussed previously might be close to the consequentialism end of the spectrum, but we cannot assume that they would instrumentalize virtues and ideals in the way that they might instrumentalize provisions for human rights; indeed, some would not.[8]) At the more restricted end of the spectrum would be views that would not instrumentalize human rights only to achieve something unrelated to rights (such as happiness or spiritual liberation) and that, while perhaps instrumentalizing the workings of a system of rights protections, would do this in order to achieve something more than mere respect for rights, such as autonomy or dignity. In this context, we can assume that the degree of autonomy or dignity one enjoys is more than just contingently related to the rights one enjoys, so on the latter view, human rights are not dispensable so long as (for example) autonomy is considered good for its own sake. Despite the differences, all these approaches share what is often called a *teleological* orientation. On the latter view, autonomy is not to be understood in a Kantian way, as an all-or-nothing formal condition of freedom, but rather as a component of a good life, something we can refine and enhance but also sometimes trade off when values conflict. Autonomy can be a telos, just as much as virtue or happiness can. I will call this third view a form of *modest teleology,* since it does not presume to say whether we should trade off all values in an overall maximizing, that is consequentialist, way.

Before introducing the theme of economic rights in particular, I should preview a claim I will be defending later, namely that all of these approaches have strong connections with various traditions of Buddhist ethics.[9] If the instrumentalist view allows beliefs and practices of human rights to be used to make progress toward the highest form of happiness (*ariyasukha* rather than mere *sukha*), this brings it within the orbit of several common understandings of Buddhist ideals. This is illustrated in the works of many of the writers noted previously, even if many of them tend to speak in terms of reduction of suffering rather than of promoting happiness. Meanwhile, I noted that a consequentialist framework is sometimes used to sum up the core of Buddhist ethics. This has been attempted most recently by Charles Goodman, who draws mainly on Mahāyāna sources to develop a complex form of consequentialism, wherein rights, rules, and spiritual practices can and ought to be tailored to serve ends that include not only collective happiness but also achievements and refinements of personal virtue.[10] As for the modest teleological approach, I will suggest in section 3 later in this chapter that some ancient Buddhist scriptures support an approach along these lines.

I do not propose to resolve the question of which of these forms of teleology might best capture the foundational structure of Buddhist ethics (if there can be such a thing).[11] But it is notable that in each of them, economic rights would be just as important as liberty rights—a point that seems to have been neglected by most participants in the debate over the place of human rights in Buddhist ethics. A right to certain material provisions may not be a precondition for possessing formal liberty rights, but it is a precondition for having any confidence that one can experience a meaningfully and rewardingly autonomous life. (I discuss later how this basic point is unaffected by nuances in Buddhist views that relate to differences in the needs of laypersons and monks.) Such a right would be seen as crucial not only from the perspective of modest teleology but also further along the teleological spectrum. Economic rights—not necessarily including a right to equality of resources or outcomes, but at least rights to a minimum provision of resources and opportunities—would greatly assist the social and spiritual progress envisioned by instrumentalists and consequentialists. In fact, putting this in terms of a *minimum* shows that the importance of such rights is at least as universally recognizable as the importance of more classical, and allegedly more universal, liberty rights. Arguably, cultures not accustomed to the language of rights would recognize the need for a material minimum (even in the specific case of its relation to cultivating autonomy) more readily than they would recognize the importance of some of the liberty rights that are seen as fundamental in Western societies. I will return to the question of whether conflicts between these two kinds of entitlement are made more unresolvable when the economic entitlements are construed as "rights." But first, I turn to a moral justification of human rights that adds some detail to the notion of a "modest" teleological approach, so that we can compare some specific features of Buddhist texts with that approach.

A Western Teleological Perspective: James Griffin's Defense of Human Rights

In contemporary debates concerning universalism about human rights, it is often assumed that the Western—and putatively universal—conception is characterized by a focus on the inviolability of the individual. The standard Western view is presumed to highlight a primary set of individual rights, some of which are absolute (ethically and—as proponents envisage—legally as well), and the rest of which have at least a very high threshold for being overridden by other interests of society. Nuanced variations, such as Will Kymlicka's famous inclusion of group rights, often still fall within this standard conception, insofar as certain individual rights remain *primary*.[12] Seeing this prioritization of individual liberty rights in many other contemporary political theorists, and with legally minded thinkers such as John Locke and Thomas Jefferson looming large in images of Western thought, many infer that belief in the priority and absoluteness of such rights characterizes the *standard* Western view.

There is a curious blind spot involved in characterizing things this way, however, made all the more curious by the fact that if what is at stake is the *universal validity* of human rights, this puts defenders of human rights in the position of having to address moral rather than merely political or legal considerations. Many Western moral philosophers have argued both that there is something universal about the values at the heart of human rights discourse and that, nonetheless, the rights themselves are not absolute, in either a legal or a broader deontological sense. Human rights advocates and theorists who work mainly within the Western tradition of moral and political thought should consider whether Western landmarks in moral philosophy are as beholden to a deontology of individual inviolability as the image described earlier presumes. If we scrutinize the dominant long-term trends in modern Western ethics, in fact, we find that utilitarianism and other consequentialist views have been at least as central as the kinds of deontology that defend absolute human rights. (Of course, even if a survey showed that most Western thinkers were and are really consequentialists of one kind or another, that would not by itself vindicate consequentialism—as a theory, let alone a guide to policy—and moreover, it could be that both consequentialists and deontologists are fundamentally mistaken about moral truth; universalism in the abstract might hold even though perhaps the entire Western tradition has been built on a variety of moral errors.[13]) There are admittedly many figures who are difficult to categorize—perhaps most notably John Stuart Mill, associated as he is with both utilitarianism and spirited defenses of individual rights. But it seems clear that Mill's utilitarianism was normatively fundamental in his outlook, so that he could not have been an absolutist about human rights. Meanwhile, it is even safer to say that protections of individual rights have been considered to have instrumental value rather than intrinsic value (let alone absolute priority), in the views of Hume, Helvétius, Bentham, Hegel, Sidgwick, G. E. Moore, and R. M. Hare—down to Derek Parfit and Peter Singer in the present day.

We can hardly assume, then, that the teleological emphasis of Buddhist defenses of human rights marks a divergence from Western values (for better or worse). In fact, we can reinforce the contrary conclusion by considering a contemporary "Western" perspective that, while not as plainly consequentialist as the tradition that stretches from Hume to Singer, and not even as consequentialist as John Stuart Mill's, is in some ways like Mill's—and in any case, just as typically "Western." In his recent book *On Human Rights,* James Griffin offers such a perspective on human rights, one that he himself calls "teleological," but not "consequentialist."[14] As we have seen, Buddhist ethics is sometimes interpreted as consequentialist, and if that interpretation is correct, it overlaps with one—if not the—major tradition of modern Western ethics; but by considering Griffin's more nuanced approach, we will see that important parts of Buddhist ethics overlap with this approach as well. This will also help us to see how economic rights can be derived from key Buddhist values.

Starting from a premise that may initially seem foreign to any Buddhist perspective, Griffin claims that one of our deepest values is the value of personhood, the value of having and developing a capacity to lead a life that is sensitive to what is genuinely worthwhile in any life but that also expresses one's distinctive, lifelong response to the challenge of judging what is worth pursuing and achieving in one's particular case. What is at stake here is not the metaphysics of personhood, but the *value* of personhood—in fact, the value of a kind of cumulative experience.[15] What the prospect of such personal development requires, in Griffin's view, is autonomy, liberty, and welfare: autonomy, to enable one to form plans and priorities and to make well-informed choices between and within them; liberty, to disable or else stay clear of obstacles that are not themselves reasonable constraints based on others' rights and needs; and welfare, to enable one to carry through at least some of the reasonable plans one might adopt.[16]

More so than liberty and welfare, autonomy is partly constitutive of personhood.[17] Personhood and autonomy are intrinsically, but not supremely, good. That is, like certain kinds of pleasure, they are good for their own sake but do not have any sort of categorical or absolute priority over other goals and interests. As Griffin puts it:

> [The] way to understand the value of personhood is to see the exercise of our personhood as an end the realization of which enhances the value of life. It would clearly be a highly important such feature, but none the less not, in principle, immune to trade-off with other things that make a life good, such as accomplishment, certain kinds of understanding, deep personal relations, and so on.[18]

The goods that Griffin lists here—along with the more hedonic value of what he calls "enjoyment"—are among those he has elsewhere[19] presented as the primary components of a good life (or "prudential values").[20] It is notable, perhaps, that the three other goods mentioned here, which must be balanced along with personhood and autonomy, can be seen as overlapping with the aim of buddhahood (the highest form of "accomplishment" in Buddhism), the value of *dhamma/dharma* (corresponding to what Griffin calls "understanding," though more precisely in this context, what is worth understanding), and the value of *sangha* (corresponding to "personal relations")—in other words, the three refuges of Buddhism. These are perhaps best seen as placeholders, to be fleshed out in terms of spiritual states, wisdom, and virtue, respectively, in the Buddhist context; but the key point is that Griffin's mundane and perhaps Western-sounding values are deeper and more general than they might first appear.

The list of three refuges is not generally intended as an exhaustive account of ethical, prudential, or even soteriological values, and in fact, part of the value of each refuge (as this term suggests) is instrumental in relation to the pursuit of enlightenment. When Griffin claims that one of the other intrinsic goods is autonomy, he is not imposing a "side-constraint" on such pursuits. Griffin's teleological ideal, defended in his various writings, involves helping people to realize as many of these goods as possible, without any absolute constraints on how to find the optimal mix.[21] His theory of human rights, meanwhile, addresses the practicalities and social requirements for just one of these goods (personhood/autonomy), but it remains teleological in two key respects. First of all, the relation between the specific rights themselves and autonomy is an instrumental one, both prudentially and in terms of society-wide promotion of autonomy. Second, the goal of autonomy has intrinsic value—at least in practical terms[22]—but the higher-order telos of an overall good life entails that personally, socially, and politically we must sometimes limit autonomy in the interest of giving due attention to other values. Unlike in the instrumentalist framework shared by the contemporary Buddhist writers cited earlier, limitations to autonomy are not assessed purely in terms of how such limitations can help reduce suffering or promote compassion or advance our collective spiritual progress—that is, at this level, autonomy and its limits are not assessed only instrumentally. Any prospective limitations to autonomy must be assessed partly in light of what would be lost in terms of the intrinsic value of autonomy itself.

Given all these teleological considerations, as well as Griffin's own inclusion of welfare alongside autonomy and liberty as essential to the good that rights promote, it is clear that economic rights will be fundamental within this approach. In the form of a right to a provision of resources that is the minimum required for autonomy and liberty, Griffin endorses this. Before saying more about the form such rights might take, we can note finally that this general approach permits a morally coherent response to the second of the two problems most often cited in connection with conceiving of economic assistance as a form of respect for the "rights" of recipients. The first of these problems concerned the allegedly dubious transcultural universality of such rights (which was addressed in section 1); the second concerns the prospect of economic rights requiring levels of taxation that might conflict with the enjoyment of liberty. Conflicts of rights may be inevitable, but, libertarian critics stress, introducing economic rights seems to lead to such deep stalemates as to undermine the overall coherence of any normative ideal centered on human rights.

In response, we can point out that while taxation may feel like an infringement of *liberty*, it is unlikely ever to be so extreme as to threaten *autonomy*.[23]

Since liberty rights are primarily valuable in relation to promoting autonomy, this greatly reduces the *moral* cost, so to speak, of welfare-state levels of taxation. In any case, the teleological structure of the view we are considering makes it easier to weigh conflicting claims and to justify favoring one kind of claim (e.g., to liberty rights) in some circumstances while favoring another kind (e.g., a claim to economic rights) in other circumstances. It is above all an approach like Kant's deontology that finds it unacceptable to resolve conflicts in favor of different rights or duties at different times. By contrast, John Stuart Mill frequently stressed that an advantage of his brand of teleology (i.e., utilitarianism) was its ability to apply a kind of cost-benefit criterion to every case where the duties of justice appeared to conflict. A similar, though perhaps less clear-cut, advantage can be claimed by most forms of modest teleology, and the contextualism made possible by such Buddhist virtues as skillful means likewise loosens the paralysis such conflicts so often seem to entail.

The Preconditions of Buddhist Autonomy: Liberty Rights and Economic Rights

Once we locate the value of mutual respect for shared rights in a notion of autonomy as a good that we can aim at having more or less of (ideally more, but subject to trade-offs), we may see new parallels between famous passages of Buddhist scripture and intuitions about the value of human rights. Said another way, if we play down claims about the nature of individuals as bearers of certain fixed liberty rights, and if we play down the formal aspects of rights declarations and legal protections (e.g., the Kantian attempt to favor the formal constraints of rights and duties over any possible contribution to the good life), we can pay more attention to what autonomy and respect for autonomy may contribute to worthwhile activities, whether lay focused or more strictly spiritual. And we can see new links to themes of rights and autonomy within Buddhist scriptures that discuss the dangers of domination, manipulation, and arbitrary authority.

Three passages in the Pali Canon may serve as examples of how these themes were important to the Buddha as depicted there. (1) In the *Mahaparinibbana Sutta,* the Buddha as he is nearing death warns his followers not to accept uncritically what a monk in a position of institutional authority might say about the *dhamma;* those who would become Buddhists must rely on their own wisdom to choose what to believe.[24] (2) In a section of the *Vinaya* highlighted by Richard Gombrich, the Buddha stressed that students should be at liberty to disagree with their teachers. As Gombrich remarks, "That . . . has few parallels in world history" (and if this can be construed as taking the form of a right against indoctrination, its taking that form might have even fewer parallels in premodern history).[25] (3) In the *Samaññaphala Sutta* of the *Digha Nikāya,* the

Buddha describes to a king a slave who considers it unjust that his master is free while he is not, and the king agrees that the slave deserves at least the choice of becoming a monk; it is later made clear that the slave gains not merely by entering the monastic life, but also by being liberated from slavery; still later, the monk's eventual enlightenment is metaphorically compared to liberation from slavery.[26]

With the possible exception of the last remark, these passages may not perfectly match the kind of teleological emphasis we saw in Griffin's account of autonomy. That is, we might not feel sure that the kinds of autonomy described here are treated as having intrinsic value rather than mere instrumental value. Someone might object, for example, that only enlightenment has intrinsic value and that each of these endorsements of autonomy is an endorsement of something that will instrumentally conduce to enlightenment. What this objection overlooks, however, is how closely autonomy and enlightenment are themselves intertwined.

It is worth noting here what Griffin sees as the "enemies of autonomy": "indoctrination, brain-washing, domination, manipulation, conformity, conventionality, false consciousness [and] certain forms of immaturity."[27] To overcome any of these is not merely a step in the direction of some higher good; each overcoming *itself* has intrinsic value, according to Griffin, since each overcoming ipso facto realizes one's autonomy. Moreover, we might add that to overcome the most psychologically tenacious forms of such heteronomy is something close to enlightenment itself. We may feel safest in saying this about Mahāyāna conceptions of enlightenment, which consider the main obstacle to enlightenment to be ignorance rather than craving, and some of which recognize forms of enlightenment that are within reach of ordinary reflective people (especially if we consider such notions as beginner's *bodhicitta* or sudden insight into Buddha-nature as forms of enlightenment). But the point might be generalizable beyond Mahāyāna contexts. It is familiar enough to hear it said, in connection with Theravada texts, that enlightenment is the realization of a certain kind of autonomy.[28]

This is all far from saying that a form of human rights discourse is apparent in ancient Buddhist texts. But this may not matter, perhaps not even to those who have engaged in the human rights debates I mentioned at the outset of this chapter. If what is at issue is the normative validity of human rights, then the required kind of defense is one that identifies a universal value that for its realization requires respect for rights as a practical necessity. That is, what really matters is the case for that value's being a universal value, while the importance of rights follows as a practical corollary. In a context where the transmitters of Buddhism were mostly members of monastic communities, the corollary about rights as socio-political entitlements—which would primarily be claimed vis-à-vis governments—may never have seemed relevant to those who wrote or edited works of Buddhist philosophy. Conversely, if a philosopher like Griffin had ignored this corollary, someone else could easily have derived it from his theory of autonomy, and yet Griffin himself would still have made a contribution to the theoretical debate about the universal validity of human rights. There is at least some scope for thinking that a tradition such as that of Buddhist ethics may find itself in the same position.

The potential contribution of classical Buddhist ethical ideas to a defense of *economic* rights would admittedly be even more indirect, and perhaps more dubious as a result. There is, nonetheless, at least one key concept in Buddhist ethics that has a bearing on Griffin's notion of minimum provision of material resources. This is the concept of the Middle Way, which in its ethical (rather than metaphysical) manifestation prescribes a way of life that avoids crippling asceticism as much as it avoids harmful sensual indulgence. What is needed to correct any ascetic excesses in the midst of renunciation is simply a minimum provision of food and shelter. That minimum provision is as significant to the monk's autonomy, however, as Griffin's more extensive conception of minimum provision is to a layperson's autonomy.

Nevertheless, we face again the fact that no connection between "autonomy" and economic "rights" is drawn in Buddhist scripture itself. But here too the considerations discussed earlier apply. Does it matter that ancient and medieval Buddhist texts say so little about economic justice, let alone economic rights? In this context, it might help to compare two writers concerned with justice and well-being to see that the spirit of an ethical view can matter much more than the letter, even when it comes to working out valuable applications of such a view to modern life and modern society. The comparison I have in mind puts John Stuart Mill in a favorable light compared to Karl Marx. Marx stressed the actual economic needs and interests of workers, whereas Mill mainly stressed other things, such as the capitalist system as a means to prosperity and such goods as pleasure, culture, and education as components of that prosperity. As such, economic rights seem less *explicit* in Mill's approach.[29] Yet Mill's view might provide a more solid justification of economic rights, precisely because it is a more robustly normative—in the sense of being a more ethically grounded—view. And just as rights of (for example) internet access could be derived from Mill's general views on freedom of expression and communication (to take a starker example of a kind of right he did not anticipate), economic rights that are not explicitly noted by Mill may be clear implications of his ethics and normative political philosophy. By the same token, the absence of discussions of economic rights from the ancient Buddhist tradition does not disqualify the ethical parts of that tradition from providing a valuable defense, or part of a comprehensive defense, of economic rights.

By way of conclusion, it may be worthwhile to respond to two sources of concern that are likely to be felt by many who are skeptical about allegedly deep connections between Buddhist values and human rights discourse. One of these sources of concern would seize on the sense of historical and cultural artificiality that might remain even after one considers the passages cited previously from the Pali Canon, and even after my pleas have been considered, to the effect that the absence of specific overlap in Western and Buddhist traditions (regarding human rights) should not deter us from making the connection. The second source of concern would relate to core Buddhist values: Could these be so deontological or so individual-centered as to accommodate normative notions of autonomy and human rights?

Rather than repeating my argument that it may not matter if early Buddhist ideas and human rights discourse are far apart, I will respond here in a different way to the first source of concern. Buddhism has modern as well as ancient incarnations. Some modern incarnations are so traditionally oriented that few doubt their qualifications to claim to be genuinely Buddhist; meanwhile, others are sometimes regarded as marginally Buddhist, if Buddhist at all. In between, there are some modern movements whose growth and integration into wider spheres of Buddhist discussion have been so extensive that they can claim at least some degree of authenticity. One example, arguably, is B. R. Ambedkar's *Navayana* Buddhism in India. Ambedkar's overall conception was based on Buddhist scripture—in some detail, even if a few details were exegetically and ethically innovative.[30] But it also focused on human rights and justice as natural extensions of traditional ideals in Buddhist ethics.[31] In light of the guiding ideals of movements like this one, denying a role for human rights discourse in Buddhist ethics risks relegating these movements to the status of pseudo-Buddhism.

The second concern prompts us to ask whether Buddhist ethics could be so individualistic as to place human rights among the core values of Buddhism. This concern is well-founded, and since I share the favorable attitude to moral consequentialism that we saw to be widespread among Buddhist ethicists in the first section of this chapter, I have reservations about importing any kind of normative individualism into systems of belief that have succeeded in overcoming it, at least within their ideals. But if we turn to one of the most fundamental distinctions in all traditions of Buddhism, the distinction between ultimate and conventional truth, we might find further support for the sort of synthesis developed here, in sections 2 and 3. As well as some ideals having ultimate value, it is inevitable that some will have only conventional value. (The latter may even hold for the basic moral precepts of Buddhism.[32]) Placing human rights among conventional values need not result in the narrower sorts of instrumentalism discussed earlier, and need not disqualify them as core Buddhist values, or at least core *modern* Buddhist values.

This approach may enable us to reconcile a "personhood" account of autonomy and rights (such as Griffin's) and a reductionist analysis of selfhood based on the truth of anatta or anatman (no-self/non-self). Apart from a few

Mahāyāna subtraditions, most Buddhists regard the latter truth as an ultimate truth, and as such it is consistent with a different, "conventional" truth about individual personhood as a natural and useful focus of practical concern.[33] This need not imply that all beliefs about intrinsic value in ethics merely reflect conventional truths. There may be ultimate truths in soteriology, which are not just about the metaphysics of anatman and the transcendence of samsara, but also about the normative status of nirvana, *nirodha,* and/or the *pāramitās* (perfections/virtues). These would be truths, in other words, about what has intrinsic value[34]—and such insights would be ethical insofar as they are invoked to guide our decisions and actions. Nonetheless, there may be other, less veridical beliefs about what has intrinsic value, which, if true in any sense, would be true conventionally, and yet these beliefs might be psychologically or conceptually inescapable, and thus universal. This might be true of beliefs about all the goods in life that require us, for at least certain stretches of our lives, to see ourselves as authors of our own life plans. A prime example would be belief in the intrinsic value of autonomy. Knowledge of the ultimate truth about value might supersede this belief, but in practice, ethics has no choice but to combine ultimate and conventional considerations.

If any Buddhist or hybrid approach must qualify its commitment to the value of autonomy in this way, that might weaken its ability to vindicate absolute rights based on autonomy. But as we saw, absolutism is opposed by many Western ethicists, and by Griffin in particular.[35] What teleological approaches offer, both in Buddhist and Western guises, are defeasible human rights, whose normative weight is not rendered insignificant by considerations of ultimate intrinsic value but is to be weighed against both conventional and ultimate conceptions of what has intrinsic value. While the legal and political frameworks surrounding human rights may have been Western contributions, the meta-ethical distinction I have appealed to here (between conventional and ultimate truth) is a Buddhist contribution. Both may be contributions toward an understanding of ethical value that is at least a candidate for what might emerge via a reasoned convergence among members of otherwise very different cultures and religions.

NOTES

I would like to thank David Loy, Matthew McKenzie, and Mark Siderits for their comments; and Christopher Framarin, Stephen Harris, Ethan Mills, and Gino Signoracci for many memorable discussions of related themes.

1. R. E. Florida, *Human Rights and the World's Major Religions,* vol. 5, *The Buddhist Tradition* (Westport, CT: Praeger, 2005).

2. Unsurprising, considering that the *language* of rights is also absent from ancient ethical and political writing in the European tradition (i.e., Greek and Roman writers). If

one considers underlying concepts—such as dignity, justice, or autonomy—to be more important than the terminology of "rights," then the situation in both traditions is less clear. I will be highlighting some ethical concepts connected to the notion of autonomy, which I believe can form a bridge between these traditions, despite the potential for tension with some conceptions of anatta/anatman (which I address at the end of the essay).

3. D. Chappell, "Buddhist Peace Principles," in *Buddhist Peacework: Creating Cultures of Peace*, ed. D. Chappell (Boston: Wisdom Publications, 1999); D. Swearer, "'Rights' Because of Intrinsic Nature or 'Responsibilities' Because of Mutual Interdependence?" in *Buddhist Perspectives on the Earth Charter*, ed. A. Morgante (Boston: Boston Research Center for the 21st Century, 1997).

4. K. Inada, "A Buddhist Response to the Nature of Human Rights," P. Junger, "Why the Buddha Has No Rights," and C. Ihara, "Why There Are No Rights in Buddhism: A Reply to Damien Keown," all in *Buddhism and Human Rights*, ed. D. Keown, C. Prebish, and W. Husted (Surrey, UK: Curzon, 1998).

5. Florida, *Human Rights*, 49.

6. The concept of skillful means (*upāya*) is mainly identified with Mahāyāna ethics, but a similar emphasis on broadly strategic considerations can be found in all Buddhist traditions (cf. J. W. Schroeder, *Skillful Means: The Heart of Buddhist Compassion* [Honolulu: University of Hawai'i Press, 2001]). Meanwhile, I mean to include Ihara and Junger in what I say in the text, as it would appear that they are opposed in practice rather than in principle to a reliance on human rights discourse—i.e., they are equally instrumentalist; it is just that they make different practical judgments in this area.

7. A generalized instrumentalism would be a form of moral skepticism, whereas localized forms of instrumentalism need not be (e.g., Aristotle might have seen certain virtues as only instrumentally valuable, while affirming the intrinsic value of others, as part of an overall moral realist picture); and moral consequentialism is not, because the maximized good at which it aims can, it claims, be assessed as an end and not merely a means. Though we should not simply assume that moral skepticism is ruled out, it would be, at best, an awkward partner for *any* of the views discussed here.

8. A case in point would be Keown—who would not wish to instrumentalize virtues, at least.

9. They are not the only three candidates, of course, for refining or condensing Buddhist ethics into a core set of principles or values. Even when it comes specifically to Buddhist defenses of human rights, there are other approaches. For instance, Anton Luis Sevilla has argued that the Mahāyāna notion of *tathāgathagarbha* (the Buddha-nature that each person has) affords a strong basis for individual rights, which could potentially justify a more deontological understanding of the respect owed to individuals (A. L. Sevilla, "Founding Human Rights within Buddhism: Exploring Buddha-Nature as an Ethical Foundation," *Journal of Buddhist Ethics* 17 [2010], 214–252).

10. Despite these complexities, Goodman's favored view closely resembles utilitarianism (C. Goodman, *Consequences of Compassion: An Interpretation and Defense of Buddhist Ethics* [Oxford: Oxford University Press, 2009]), and several philosophers in the Theravada tradition, as he notes, do endorse utilitarianism specifically. One theorist who is skeptical of any consequentialist interpretation is Damien Keown (*The Nature of Buddhist Ethics*, 2nd ed. [New York: Palgrave, 2001]); in fact, his view is akin to what I am calling "modest teleology," but it is focused on a teleology of virtue rather than a teleology of autonomy, so I will not be discussing it in this chapter.

11. I return to the question of "foundations," and the related question of ultimate truth in ethics, at the end of the chapter.

12. W. Kymlicka, *Multicultural Citizenship* (Oxford: Oxford University Press, 1995).

13. If there are universal truths in ethics, or universally applicable values, they cannot be made normatively legitimate just by their cultural or civilizational provenance (or by

majority opinion within a particular culture). Thus, Western champions of human rights, if they are genuine universalists in the sense that would require some form of moral cognitivism or realism, must admit that any tradition—including all those under the Western umbrella—*might* be mistaken. Accepting universalism in the abstract leaves it open as to which world tradition (if any) has got things right. Buddhists of many stripes can easily accept both this generic universalism as well as agnosticism about the ultimate foundations of moral and axiological truth. Agnosticism is not relativism. Since Buddhist views on the pervasiveness of moral ignorance suggest that Buddhists might indeed agree, Buddhist ethics may be even further (than Western human rights discourse) from the sort of cultural relativism that proponents of "Asian values" are sometimes presumed to hold.

14. J. Griffin, *On Human Rights* (Oxford: Oxford University Press, 2008), 57.

15. Ibid., 29–37; 149ff. This way of putting it may disarm at least some of the skepticism that the reductionist analysis of selfhood would dispose many Buddhists to feel, on hearing some of the previous formulations of Griffin's view.

16. Ibid., chaps. 8–10.

17. At the end of this chapter I return to the question of how the insight of anatta/anatman might modify—but not undermine—the evaluative claims that Griffin bases on this connection between personhood and autonomy.

18. Griffin, *On Human Rights,* 57.

19. J. Griffin, *Value Judgement: Improving Our Ethical Beliefs* (Oxford: Clarendon, 1996).

20. The same list is favored by Hooker (*Ideal Code, Real World* [Oxford: Clarendon, 2000]), and nearly the same list was offered, as part of the first "objective list theory of the good," by Parfit (*Reasons and Persons* [Oxford: Clarendon Press, 1984]). The general outlines of this theory of value have been defended in a Buddhist context by Goodman in his *Consequences of Compassion.*

21. A consequentialist version of this ideal would add "to help as many people as possible, to the greatest extent possible." Griffin stops short of claiming the moral necessity of maximizing the aggregate good. Aggregate considerations do matter within his modest teleology, but in his view they need not take over at the precise point that they first seem to impersonally outweigh one's own interests and one's rights-derived duties. Buddhists who see the appeal of Griffin's value theory may, however, wish to part with Griffin on this point, and they could combine the value theory with consequentialism. Unlike utilitarians, they might aim to maximize a good that includes some of the nonhedonic elements just mentioned, as well as autonomy, provided it is seen as part of a good life (like the pleasures that remain part of the equation) and not a deep metaphysical reality (again, like the nature of pleasure).

22. At the end of this chapter, I consider a distinction between intrinsic value of a practical (or conventional) kind and a metaphysically loaded conception of intrinsic value. Some might prefer to call the former not "intrinsic" but rather "final" value, in the sense that things like understanding, accomplishment, and autonomy could be desirable for their own sake (each only to some extent). Griffin's conception of ethics is quite practically oriented, such that he is content to have an account of the good life be guided by deep reasons for *believing* that certain things have intrinsic value (while not closing the question of whether they might indeed *have* a metaphysically real kind of value). I will return to the role such reasons can have in Buddhist ethics with reference to the ultimate/conventional distinction.

23. Griffin makes the latter point about liberty itself (*On Human Rights,* 179).

24. T. W. R. Davids, trans., *Dialogues of the Buddha,* vol. 1, *Digha Nikāya[0], Sutta* (London: Oxford University Press, 1899–1921), 16.

25. R. Gombrich, in *What the Buddha Thought* (London: Equinox, 2009), 15–16, citing *Vinaya,* I:46 and I:49. As Gombrich relates it, however, a student cannot disagree as he pleases; rather, he can *correct* his teacher—which admittedly introduces duties as well as rights.

26. Davids, *Dialogues of the Buddha,* vol. 1, *Digha Nikāya[0], Sutta* 2. Cf. Florida, *Human Rights,* 112.

27. Griffin, *On Human Rights,* 151.

28. A famous image sometimes invoked in this connection is that of the solitary rhinoceros, in the Pali Canon, as a symbol of the arhat who has achieved independence from social norms and pressures.

29. The qualification about "seeming" relates more to Marx than to Mill. Doubts have often been expressed about whether Marx had a place for rights or justice in his system (see, e.g., A. Wood, "Marx against Morality," in *A Companion to Ethics,* ed. P. Singer [Oxford: Blackwell, 1991]). Nonetheless, we can safely say that the economic *claims* of workers are more fully articulated in Marx than in Mill.

30. See A. Fiske and C. Emmrich, "The Use of Buddhist Scriptures in B. R. Ambedkar's *The Buddha and His Dhamma,*" and C. Queen, "Ambedkar's Dhamma: Source and Method in the Construction of Engaged Buddhism," both in *Reconstructing the World: B. R. Ambedkar and Buddhism in India,* ed. S. Jondhale and J. Beltz (Delhi: Oxford University Press, 2004), as well as his own exposition, in Ambedkar, *The Buddha and His Dhamma* (Mumbai: Maharashtra Department of Education, 1957).

31. Ambedkar published detailed comparisons of ideas from the Buddha and ideas from Karl Marx, and unlike Marx, he had a striking ability to cast his ethical conclusions in the language of rights and justice (see Ambedkar, *The Essential Writings of B. R. Ambedkar,* ed. V. Rodrigues [Delhi: Oxford University Press, 2002]). Despite putting great emphasis on economic rights, it seems undeniable that Ambedkar's normative reflections were much closer to Buddhist than to Marxian approaches. Nonetheless, one notable feature of Ambedkar's Buddhism was his application of its highest ideals to the concerns of laypersons, and conversely, his elevation of the economic life of the layperson to a status that required an extension of Buddhist notion(s) of moral and spiritual worth.

32. Cf. Goodman's discussions of the precepts, and transcendence of them, in Goodman, *Consequences of Compassion.*

33. Cf. M. Siderits, "Buddhist Reductionism and the Structure of Buddhist Ethics," in *Indian Ethics: Classical and Contemporary Challenges,* ed. P. Bilimoria, J. Prabhu, and R. Sharma (Aldershot, UK: Ashgate, 2006).

34. Assuming, here, that intrinsic value need not be grounded in any of the kinds of (putative) *svabhava* that turn out to be illusory from the ultimate point of view.

35. Western and Buddhist ethicists might agree that dangerous forms of clinging (*upādāna*) can arise when rights (or, for that matter, autonomy) are thought of as absolute side-constraints. It must be admitted, though, that accounts of what makes this dangerous will often diverge; a source of disagreement could be the question of whether clinging is of direct or indirect disvalue—i.e., whether overcoming it is intrinsically or only instrumentally valuable. I am grateful to Matthew McKenzie for drawing my attention to concerns about *upādāna* in this context.

The Conversation of Justice 18

Rawls, Sandel, Cavell, and Education for Political Literacy

Naoko Saito

> I hardly need refer now to the laborers in our Southern States who produce the staple exports of this country, and are themselves a staple production of the South. But to confine myself to those who are said to be in *moderate* circumstances.
>
> —*Henry D. Thoreau, Walden*

In the introduction to this collection, Roger Ames and Peter Hershock draw attention to the need, in the context of contemporary global dynamics, for a conversation between economics and ethics. The issues of fairness and justice cannot be separated from our "senses of what is good" and from "how and why we live as we do." As a characterization of the kind of conversation between economics and ethics that they have in mind, Ames and Hershock suggest the necessity of diversity, inclusiveness, and particularity. This would be a conversation that involved "multiple voices" so that "different disciplines and cultures come into significant and sustained interaction." "Comparative philosophy," they say, is a site for such interaction. From within such conversation, diverse responses are produced across "cultural and national boundaries." Conventional concepts in the Western tradition such as autonomy and the individual agent are then to be destabilized. An attempt at such a conversation is demonstrated in Michael Sandel's approach to justice—a conversation of justice across cultural and national boundaries.

In May 2010, Michael Sandel's *Justice: What's the Right Thing to Do?* was published in Japanese with a title whose literal translation would be *Let's Discuss "Justice" from Now On: Philosophy for Surviving the Present.* The book quickly became a best seller.[1] In August 2010 Sandel traveled to Japan and gave a lecture at the University of Tokyo. By September 2010 the book was in its sixty-third printing. Go to any major bookstore in Japan, and the book is piled high in the main section. The fact that a political philosophy book on justice should become a best seller in Japan is a kind of miracle. In a country where modernization came so late, and where democracy as a political form was not established until the end of World War II, the concept of justice (*seigi*) is not a part of everyday vocabulary but rather is part of the lexicon of certain academics and politicians. Sandel's book, however, has dramatically changed this. Not only has "*seigi*" suddenly become a popular word in the minds of ordinary Japanese; the book has created a real interest in philosophical conversation on politics and democracy and has involved the wider public in conversations about justice. Of course, other factors have aided this national phenomenon. For one, when there is a change in government, people typically start to ask critical questions about political issues in relation to how they impact the day-to-day lives of ordinary people. Sales of the book were also helped by the fact that Sandel's original lecture at Harvard University was broadcast on NHK, Japan's national broadcasting channel.[2] However it became a best seller, it is not too much to say that the "Sandel boom" has had an enlightening effect on the minds of the Japanese people. The phenomenon itself demonstrates the fact that people outside academia have been awaiting philosophical conversation on political issues.

Sandel's project and the Sandel boom itself have created an occasion for scholars to rethink the role of the humanities in higher education and have raised fundamental questions for philosophers and philosophers of education. How should we respond to the public call for a philosophical conversation on justice? What should be the nature of the language used in philosophical conversations about justice and democracy? And how should philosophers and philosophers of education speak to a wider public? These questions are relevant to the conversation between economics and ethics that Ames and Hershock call for.

In order to elucidate the nature of conversation that is required today in the pursuit of justice in global economics, and yet without simply relying on the familiar discourse of diversity, inclusiveness, and sharing, I shall try to respond indirectly to the questions I have just presented: I shall conduct a critique of Sandel's criticism of John Rawls, but in a way that does not side with Rawls. My position on Rawls derives from Stanley Cavell's criticism of Rawls, which he phrases in terms of the *conversation of justice*. The philosophical stances taken by Sandel and Cavell share some common ground insofar as both are engaged in critical dialogue with Rawls' liberal concept of justice, and, by implication, they both take the view that philosophical dialogue on justice cannot be separated from moral questions. The point of having these American philosophers engaged in critical dialogue, however, is not simply to compare the substance of their arguments. The focus is rather on *how* they use the language of justice and *how* their respective critiques of Rawls reveal different concepts of what the role of philosophy should be in awakening our common political consciousness. In developing this line of argument, three contrasting stances will be presented: (1) Rawls' approach to conversation about justice; (2) Sandel's to conversation about justice; and (3) Cavell's to the conversation *of* justice. The double genitive in Cavell's preferred phrase distinguishes his position from the other two in that the conversation that is to take place is not only our conversation *about* justice, for justice is to speak to us, to you and me. I shall try to show that Cavell's critical framework (in conjunction with his reading of Emersonian perfectionism and Wittgensteinian ordinary language philosophy) elucidates what is missing not only from Rawls' but also from Sandel's accounts; it reminds us of an alternative and richer view on conversation of justice. In conclusion, I shall present Cavell's perfectionist vision of education for political literacy from within, as a way of bridging the private and the public. My hope is to show, through a Cavellian perspective, an alternative vision of the conversation of justice, one that cannot have been contained in the principle of exchange and mutual recognition, and by so doing, to explore an alternative horizon of economy—an economy of living, to borrow the phrase used by Cavell and Thoreau.

Sandel's Conversation about Justice

> What would a more morally engaged public discourse look like, and how would it differ from the kind of political argument to which we've become accustomed? These are not merely philosophical questions. They lie at the heart of an attempt to reinvigorate political discourse and renew our civic life.
>
> —*Michael J. Sandel, Justice*[3]

The book jacket blurb on the Japanese translation of Sandel's *Justice* is written by a famous Japanese sociologist, Shinji Miyadai: "Justice tends to be interpreted in the context of liberalism, but it should be reinterpreted in the context of communitarianism. In such reinterpretation, a way towards the regaining of community is necessary, even at the risk of taking a paternal standpoint. This is Sandel's position as a communitarian."[4] Miyadai captures tersely and yet powerfully the gist of Sandel's position. As a communitarian, Sandel presents the idea that we are "encumbered selves, open to moral claims we have not willed" and that we are constrained by "communal encumbrances."[5] At the back of this claim lies his criticism of the Kantian-Rawlsian liberal concept of the "unencumbered self."[6] He is opposed to Rawls' liberal idea of justice, which takes it that "our duties and rights should be neutral with respect to competing conceptions of the good life." Instead, "to achieve a just society we have to reason together about the meaning of the good life, and to create a public culture hospitable to the disagreements that will inevitably arise." This he calls the "politics of the common good." He encourages "moral disagreements" within public discourse, as it is disagreements that offer "a stronger, not a weaker, basis for mutual respect." He names this whole procedure a "politics of moral engagement," taking it as a promising "basis for a just society."[7]

Substantial and significant though this staking out of his communitarian position undoubtedly is, what is also important is the fact that *Justice* is a book that exemplifies the conversation about justice. In his earlier writing (originally published in 1984), Sandel says, "Philosophy inhabits the world from the start; our practices and institutes are embodiments of theory. To engage in a political practice is already to stand in relation to theory."[8] *Justice* is a book that puts into practice his earlier theory. Paying attention to the nature of the conversation about justice and to the language used, it is possible to discern some distinctive characteristics of the way he achieves this. First, philosophy's language is bridged to ordinary language: the theoretical language of past philosophers (Aristotle, Kant, Mill, and Rawls) is translated into the terms of everyday practice. Whoever reads this book is struck by how accessible the language is. Second, the book is filled with concrete examples of the kinds of moral questions we encounter in our ordinary lives. Third, as he says, the book is "a journey beyond the bounds of liberal public reason," and it is through this that he engages people in the process of "reasoning together" by raising "hard moral questions" ("What would you do if . . . ?") and by setting up the realistic moral dilemmas the common cannot simply stay "normal" or "typical." Through these methods, Sandel succeeds in involving people in conversation; he gives life to philosophical language.

At the same time, however, the book may cause uneasiness in some readers—the traditional liberal against whom Sandel's communitarian criticism is directed, but also the more conventional philosopher, who is on the side of *theoria* against *praxis* and who is engaged in, in Sandel's term, "merely philosophical questions." In addition to these expected reactions, however, there may be some who do not belong to any political camp but who feel alienated by the very accessibility of the language and the public nature of the conversation: those who cannot or perhaps choose not to participate in "the common spaces of a shared democratic citizenship."[9] These are, in Thoreau's words, that "mass of men" who "lead lives of quiet desperation."[10] These are people who see no immediate need to be engaged in the political and moral questions illustrated in the book, and hence, who lead an apparently comfortable life of withdrawal. Yet they are still faced with personal, domestic, existential, or interpersonal questions that arise in their daily lives. And so are we to say that such questions relate only to our private lives and, hence, have no public import? Can there be, as Sandel envisions, conversation based on the politics of moral engagement that will create the space for disagreement? Does conversation *about* justice, in the mode of "reasoning together"—in a language that is articulate, open, and rationally discursive, a language that *positions* "competing conceptions of the right way of valuing goods"[11]—enable us to answer fully the question concerning human freedom raised by Sandel himself: "How can we see ourselves as situated and yet free?"[12] Despite the claim of disagreement and diversity, it sounds as if *the choices of my position were already given.*

This issue of positioning is also related to the question of the subject of conversation about justice: Who takes the position and with whom? In this conversation about justice, readers are constantly confronted with the author's questions: What kind of position would you take when . . . ? The subject who answers is constructed as "we." It is we who need to take responsibility for moral questions, but who we are is pre-given. If there is moral disagreement, the line of difference is drawn between different communities, and communities here are "communities we inhabit." In criticism of the "language of moral individualism,"[13] there is no space for the "I" as the subject of conversation: "no language for freedom except that its concern is directed to the whole."[14]

Where does conversation about justice start? Who is the subject of the conversation? With whom are you engaged in conversation about justice? In answering these questions, Sandel's conversation about justice does not go beyond the limitations of the conversation-about conducted by Rawls.

Cavell and the Conversation of Justice

> Philosophical problems are not solved polemically, which etymologically says, not by taking sides. . . . Philosophical arguments must not be won (philosophy does not conquer by victimization); political arguments must not be lost (the conversation of justice must not be lost, or else the political becomes a realm of victimization).
>
> —*Stanley Cavell, Cities of Words*[15]

Critique of Rawls in the Light of Emersonian Moral Perfectionism

It is Stanley Cavell who invites us beyond the limits of conversation *about* justice to a realm of moral life that precedes those political questions raised by competing positions. Like Sandel, Cavell criticizes Rawls, but from the position of neither liberalism nor communitarianism—and this destabilizes the common ground of their polemical argument.

He is engaged in dialogue with Rawls from the perspective of American transcendentalist Ralph W. Emerson. Cavell entrusts his hope for American democracy in what he calls "Emersonian moral perfectionism." It is in terms of this idea of perfection that Cavell initiates his conversation with Rawls. The issue of perfectionism arises most clearly in paragraph 50 of *A Theory of Justice*, where Rawls argues that Nietzsche's version is inherently elitist.[16] In response, and on the strength of ample evidence of Emerson's influence on Nietzsche, Cavell finds in their work a common spirit of perfectionism and argues that Rawls misreads Nietzsche.[17] Emersonian moral perfectionism raises a "different concern at a different point in the system," different from "the image of justice's sword."[18] Cavell's attempt is to revive the "public importance" of Emersonian "personal conversation."[19] It is not so much to belittle the significance of the conversation of justice as he finds it in Rawls—a conversation I have referred to as a conversation-about—as to reconstruct from the Emersonian perspective its meaning and its place in democracy.

A major difference between Cavell and Rawls is that, for the former, conversation in the name of democracy begins "at the end of the conversation of justice, when moral justifications come to an end and something is to be shown."[20] Here is the suggestion of another dimension of the moral life, in which Rawls' analogy between games and morality loses its purchase, for "no rule can function in the moral life as the three strike rule functions in its game."[21] The sense that our moral life begins when justifications come to an end and that philosophy begins in loss permeates Cavell's Emersonian moral perfectionism. An analytically minded person might understandably respond: "If this is where morality begins, as you say, then what happens in conversation-about is not morality at all." But this is not Cavell's view. What happens after justifications come to an end casts its light back over the whole, and hence conditions the kind of deliberation that takes place in conversations-about. If not, the latter are worthless, just games. And he would also say that it casts its light back over our very acquisition of language. A major difference between Cavell and Sandel is that whereas for Sandel moral disagreement comes at the end of reasoning (together), such that we then have to appeal to the principle of mutual respect, for Cavell, respect does not bring us sufficiently close to the source of our despair and disappointment. Rather it is the avoidance of philosophy. To enter this uncertain, fragile, and unforeseen territory of the moral life is the point of continuing the conversation of justice. *Philosophy begins after political debate is over.*

Even in the course of moral debate between the elevation of society and its misery, and between moral disagreement and the ascertaining of the common good, people in "*moderate* circumstances" can subside too easily into self-indulgent mediocrity and the "mendacity of public discourse."[22] This is, in light of Emersonian perfectionism, the debased state of conformity, our "shrinking participation in democracy."[23] Here the sense of distance created between one's own self and society cannot be simply measured by "justice's sword," or by the degree of disagreement measured by reason's scale. What is at stake in Emersonian moral perfectionism is representativeness, that is, democracy's hope that the "voice I lend in recognizing a society as mine, as speaking for me, is my voice, my own."[24] It is the task of the conversation of justice to give expression to such hope, and simultaneously to the sense of shame that one's own voice is forgotten, suppressed, or, worse, violated. Faced with the "political emotions" of depression, cynicism and irony, the conversation of justice calls for more than " 'cooperation' as the general state of social interaction,"[25] *and* more than a face-to-face dialectic of moral engagement.

It is here that Cavell introduces the Emersonian idea of "moral encounter."[26] What matters for Cavell is how each of us confronts ourselves, which simultaneously means how we confront others. In moral relationships of confrontation, our positioning is jeopardized.[27] My position is not established but is something to be found—perhaps always still to be found.[28] We cannot remain (pretend to be) ignorant of the ambiguous and uncertain realm of human knowledge, "the opacity, or non-transparence, of the present state of our interactions."[29] Confronting loss and uncertainty, however, is not the negation of reason or acquiescence in irrationality. "What makes [reasons'] use rational is their relevance to the person confronted, and the legitimacy your position gives you to confront him or her in the mode you take responsibility for."[30] In contrast to conversation about justice, the conversation *of* justice involves the "I" *as the subject of speech*. How can this "I" be distinguished from the autonomous individual of Rawls' conversation about justice?

Ordinary Language Philosophy

Chronologically speaking, the conversation of justice, in Cavell's view, begins *after* polemical debate and moral argument are over. This is, as we saw, however, just one side of the story. When you speak, you are already involved, however ineptly, in the conversation of justice. In this sense the conversation of justice begins *before* political debate. If the conversation's emergence after debate is highlighted in Cavell's Emersonian perfectionism, its presence in the very acquisition of language is elaborated more fully in his Wittgensteinianism.

Cavell's reinterpretation, in *The Claim of Reason,* of Wittgenstein's *Philosophical Investigations,* touches most sensitively on the present discussion in its holding of two thoughts in tension: Wittgenstein asks in effect what we should do when we are at a "crossroads," for "if the disagreement persists, there is no appeal beyond us, or if beyond us two, then not beyond some eventual us";[31] yet he is intrigued by "the astonishing fact of the astonishing extent to which we *do* agree in judgment; eliciting criteria goes to show therefore that our judgments *are* public, that is, shared."[32]

In Sandel, the plural subject, the "we," is the main carrier of the conversation. Similarly, in Cavell's conversation of justice, which involves also questions of self-knowledge and commitment to others, the "we" is as crucial as the "I."

But the nature of the "we" is different. For Cavell, the voice of the "I" is exposed to the test of language community of the "we."

> The authority one has, or assumes, in expressing statements of initiation, in saying "We," is related to the authority one has in expressing or declaring one's promises or intentions. Such declarations cannot be countered by evidence because they are not supported by evidence. . . . An expression of intention is not a specific claim about the world, but an utterance (outer-ance) of oneself.[33]

There is no choice other than to be political: our language is inevitably political, though of course most of us are asleep, and the political is repressed. Therefore, *becoming* political requires reeducation of one's relation to common language, and hence, to one's human nature. The division between the private and the public is not drawn a priori. You cannot simply talk "privately," as your words are already part of a language community. Hence, the task of philosophy, if we are to become political, is the reacquisition of language, and relearning to speak in the first-person voice of the "I" in relation to the "we." The utterance of words involves the search for the neighbor. "Who these other are, for whom you speak and by whom you are spoken for, is not known a priori, though it is in practice generally treated as given."[34]

While in Sandel the common is pre-given, the common for Cavell is always to be achieved. "Common things, merely not held in common."[35] The common can never be presented as some*thing* the self and the other share as a bond (something solid in solidarity). Rather the common, and indeed community itself, already entails internally the element of deviation.

> Dissent is not the undoing of consent but a dispute about its content, a dispute within it over whether a present arrangement is faithful to it. The alternative to speaking for yourself politically is not: speaking for yourself privately. . . . The alternative is having nothing (political) to say.[36]

This echoes Cavell's approach to skepticism: to live *the truth of skepticism*. Skepticism is never fully overcome, the self is never fully exhausted by reasons, and therefore one's answerability to the other is never ended. This is to recognize that "we may already be as outside, in community, as we can be."[37] If the sense of being outside is already inside community, the common cannot simply stay "normal, typical, average, unexceptional."[38] The common is in this sense to be rediscovered and, indeed, to be achieved as uncommon: the ordinary as extraordinary. Thoreau and Wittgenstein, Cavell says, both hope "to be ordinary, preaching the everyday as the locale of the sublime."[39] *We are already uncommon in the common life*. The phrase "common people" then does not refer to people whose lives can be measured against the scale of justice as fairness, from the average standpoint. The conversation of justice is directed neither at the identification of a common standard nor at some measure of deviation. The "position of the self's averageness is itself one to which I relate myself, one upon which *I must take a stand, perhaps an average stand.*"[40]

Education for Political Literacy: *Becoming* Political from Within

> Direct your eye right inward, and you'll find
> A thousand regions in your mind
> Yet undiscovered.
>
> —William Habbington quoted by Thoreau, *Walden*[41]

This exploration of Cavell's conversation of justice has revealed what is missing from the start in Sandel's conversation about justice, and it has clarified the source of anxiety over his manner of expression—his accessible, easy-to-understand language. Self-examination is the task of philosophy, and it is at the heart of political education.[42] The public is to be achieved from within the private, from the inmost to the outmost.[43] The conversation of justice in this sense responds to the "perfectionist's call . . . for freedom," being an ongoing process of achieving a further self (in one's self and others) as a next step toward one's freedom.[44] Here the autonomy of the self is replaced by a *singularity* of the self, and solidarity by *separateness*. Justice calls upon us not to lose our partiality, but to become representative of human partiality. The conversation of justice is also the process of learning to be neighbors: learning to be a neighbor to your own self, without identification and "embracing immigrancy within yourself."[45] Cavell is as communitarian as Sandel to the extent that both search for the good life as the precondition of justice, and such a good life requires one's participation in community. They differ, however, in terms of what they mean by "community" and of how this is to be achieved through conversation. And such difference is reflected in the different prepositions "about" and "of."

The conversation of justice is in itself the process of education for political literacy—learning to relate oneself to one's common language, to find an average point in yourself as a matter of "authorship,"[46] which means to regain "authority in speech."[47] The mode of conversation of justice is not, however, authoritarian: its virtue is "listening, the responsiveness to difference, the willingness for change,"[48] risking "your understanding of the other as of yourself."[49] For justice to speak, another kind of political literacy is called for—one that points us to an alternative mode of speech, beyond the language of *polemos*. The kind of language uttered in the conversation of justice is passionate as it regains the pathos for life, awakening in "those who are said to be in *moderate* circumstances" the sense of the extraordinary. The language of the "I" uttered and tested in the language community of the "we" is also prophetic in that it explores the uncertain realm of the moral life that extends beyond political debate, after that debate is over. It should be "extra-vagant," in order "to speak somewhere without bounds; like a man in a waking moment, to men in their waking moments."[50] To reengage with one's common language is not to speak one's mother tongue smoothly; it necessarily initiates us into a more complicated relationship to language, what Thoreau calls the relationship to the father tongue, something that, in the name of shared language, is merely covered over by "Easy Reading."[51]

Education for political literacy will follow different courses, depending on the mode of conversation over justice. Sandel calls for the creation of a common, public space for the cultivation of civic virtue. Cavell, in refocusing on the idea of the common, calls for the creation of what Thoreau names "uncommon schools"—through which we relearn our common language "when we begin to be men and women."[52] Such learning would not enable us to locate our identity as "we." Rather it would bring us to utopian "cities of words," toward which we are invited in every corner of our moral life, in every word we utter in moral encounters. The political literacy realized in such uncommon schooling would not trap us in the dichotomous choice between participation and withdrawal; rather, it would encourage withdrawal as a form of participation, a crucial condition of our becoming political. It would not start by solidifying the ground of conversation in the name of solidarity, or for that matter, of diversity, inclusiveness, or sharing; instead it would understand "education for citizenship" as "education for isolation"[53]—call it *citizenship without inclusion* as a third vision of a democratic community beyond liberalism and communitarianism. This is a broader sense of political education, which invites us to a dimension of the moral life that is obscured by the veil of knowledge. This will be an alternative horizon of economy—one that enables us to rethink the relationship between economics and ethics, and even to destabilize this categorization itself.

NOTES

Epigraph. Henry D. Thoreau, *Walden,* in *Walden and Resistance to Civil Government,* ed. William Rossi (New York: W. W. Norton, 1992), 24.

1. Michael J. Sandel, *Justice: What's the Right Thing to Do?* (London: Penguin Books, 2010); *Korekara no seigi no hanashi o shiyo: Ima o ikinobiru tameno tetsugaku,* trans. Shinobu Onizawa (Tokyo: Hayakawa Shobo, 2010).
2. The original lecture also became the germ of the series delivered as the Reith Lectures for the BBC.
3. Sandel, *Justice,* 243.
4. Shinji Miyadai, blurb for Sandel's *Korekara no Seigi;* my translation.

5. Sandel, *Justice,* 220, 221.

6. Michael J. Sandel, "The Procedural Republic and the Unencumbered Self," in *Blackwell Guide to Political Philosophy* (Oxford: Blackwell, 2010), 240.

7. Sandel, *Justice,* 242, 261, 263, 268, 269.

8. Sandel, "The Procedural Republic," 239.

9. Ibid., 267.

10. Henry D. Thoreau, *Walden,* in *Walden and Resistance to Civil Government,* ed. William Rossi (New York: W.W. Norton, 1992), 5.

11. Sandel, *Justice,* 265.

12. Ibid., 221.

13. Ibid., 241.

14. Ibid., 263.

15. Stanley Cavell, *Cities of Words: Pedagogical Letters of a Register of the Moral Life* (Cambridge, MA: Belknap Press of Harvard University Press, 2004), 185–186.

16. John Rawls, *A Theory of Justice,* rev. ed. (Cambridge, MA: Belknap Press of Harvard University Press, 1999), 212.

17. Cavell, *Cities of Words,* 248.

18. Ibid., 172.

19. Stanley Cavell, *Conditions Handsome and Unhandsome: The Constitution of Emersonian Perfectionism* (Chicago: University of Chicago Press, 1990), 102.

20. Ibid., 124.

21. Ibid., 113.

22. Cavell, *Cities of Words,* 189.

23. Cavell, *Conditions Handsome and Unhandsome,* 51.

24. Ibid., 27.

25. Cavell, *Cities of Words,* 125, 173.

26. Cavell, *Conditions Handsome and Unhandsome,* 112, 117; Cavell, *Cities of Words,* 187.

27. Cavell, *Cities of Words,* 235.

28. Stanley Cavell, *The Claim of Reason: Wittgenstein, Skepticism, Morality, and Tragedy* (Oxford: Oxford University Press, 1979), 326.

29. Cavell, *Cities of Words,* 173.

30. Cavell, *Claim of Reason,* 323.

31. Ibid., 19.

32. Ibid., 31.

33. Ibid., 179–180.

34. Ibid., 27.

35. Ibid., 384.

36. Ibid., 28.

37. Ibid., 447.

38. *Oxford Thesaurus of English.*

39. Cavell, *Claim of Reason,* 463.

40. Ibid., 386; emphasis mine.

41. Thoreau, *Walden,* 213.

42. Cavell, *Claim of Reason,* 25.

43. Ralph Waldo Emerson, *The Essential Writings of Ralph Waldo Emerson,* ed. Brooks Atkinson (New York: Modern Library, 2000), 132.

44. Cavell, *Conditions Handsome and Unhandsome,* 117, 118, 125.

45. Stanley Cavell, *The Senses of Walden* (Chicago: University of Chicago Press, 1992), 158.

46. Cavell, *Conditions Handsome and Unhandsome,* 19.

47. Cavell, *Cities of Words,* 203.

48. Ibid., 174.
49. Ibid., 235.
50. Thoreau, *Walden,* 216.
51. Ibid., 72.
52. Ibid, 74. See further: Paul Standish, "Uncommon Schools: Stanley Cavell and the Teaching of *Walden,*" *Studies in Philosophy and Education* 25, nos. 1–2 (2006), 145–157.
53. Cavell, *Senses of Walden,* 85.

Social Justice and the Occident 19

Paul Standish

"Social justice" is a phrase that recurs with some force in contemporary political and academic discussion, and in many respects this is understandable. One can scarcely imagine a form of human life for which justice does not remain a question, and the effects of the adjective point up the particular pressures to which that question is exposed in an overcrowded and, in some ways, environmentally depleted world. How are we to live together in justice, in our own countries and continents, and in the world as a whole?

But we can move too quickly with the phrase, and it does bear some critical examination. My discussion begins by examining social justice in terms of the ways that as an idea it has become influential in educational research and related fields (section 1). It goes on to show how, in global terms, this influence cannot be separated from the global dominance of English (section 2). This is related in turn to questions of translation (section 3). The particular pertinence of this is then emphasized by turning to a topic that, although it may seem a digression, goes to the heart of thinking in philosophy and social science: the nature of subjectivity, in translation (section 4). And finally a return is made to aspects of social justice considered in section 1 in order to unsettle some of the dominant patterns of influence and to open the way toward a different kind of thinking (section 5).

1. Concept, Ideology, Narrative

In the first place, let us look more closely at what the adjective "social" in "social justice" adds. As justice is necessarily justice among people, it is inevitably understood in relation to a social world. What other kind of justice can there be? In this respect the adjective does indeed seem to be redundant.

But the question "How are we to live together *fairly*?" in fact points to a better defense of the expression, because it cannot be taken for granted that "justice" means "fairness." Thus, a feudal or caste-based society, in which one's station in life is limited by birth or marriage, may be regarded as aligned with some sense of the right ordering of things, just as it is not *incoherent* to understand as just a society, such as an extreme communist one, in which the individual is but a part of the organic whole of the state—however objectionable we may find such arrangements today. To accept that "justice" means "fairness," by contrast, is to take a step toward a commitment to equality and to the kind of universalism that that implies: we are all equal qua human beings.

There is still, however, scope for a divergence of views, for justice as fairness is compatible with commitments to equality of outcome and equality of opportunity, to egalitarianism and to meritocracy. Nor does the principle take us far in solving, for example, such a practical question as whether inheritance tax is fair. In view of this it is right to see politicians and thinkers from across much of the spectrum as committed to justice in this way. Hence, if the addition of the adjective "social" is taken to imply the specific idea of justice as fairness, this may save it from the charge of redundancy, but the purchase of the expression remains very broad.

The most concerted contemporary attempt to reason through these differences is undoubtedly to be found in the work of John Rawls, and his writings have in many respects set the agenda for (at least Anglophone) political philosophy these past four decades. In response to the question of in what sense citizens of a democracy can be free, Rawls writes:

> One can try to deal with this question by viewing political society in a certain way, namely, as a fair system of cooperation over time from one generation to the next, where those engaged in cooperation are viewed as free and equal citizens and normal cooperating members of society over a complete life. We can then try to formulate principles of political justice such that if the basic structure of society—the main political and social institutions and the way they fit together as one scheme of cooperation—satisfies those principles, then we can say without pretense and fakery that citizens are indeed free and equal.[1]

Rawls is alert here and elsewhere in his writings to the ways in which justice as fairness can itself become too easy a slogan, propping up the status quo and in the process becoming ideological. One way in which he resists this is in his emphasis on the pluralism of democracy and hence its difference from community insofar as the members of the latter share a comprehensive conception of the good. The central organizing idea of cooperation is then understood to have three essential features. First, cooperation is not merely a matter of socially coordinated activity but is guided by publicly recognized rules and procedures that those involved accept as appropriate. Second, fair terms of cooperation, the terms that participants may, and sometimes should, reasonably accept, are characterized by a reciprocity or mutuality of benefit. And third, cooperation includes the idea of rational advantage to participants from the standpoint of their own good.

With regard to the provision of education in a democracy, there is no doubt that these principles have enormous power, and they have guided reflection and policy on such matters as educational opportunity, institutional diversity, and funding. Here and in political philosophy more generally, such discussions can appear as "footnotes to Rawls," and this is testimony to the importance of his achievement. Let me trail the thought here, however, that the consistency and assurance of this discourse may reinforce a certain conception of the human subject, perhaps foreclosing approaches to social justice via different avenues of thought. Nevertheless, given that the term "social justice" has acquired particular prominence in educational research, I take this Rawlsian philosophical understanding to be one of the two principal ways in which it is currently interpreted and received.

The other set of associations the term carries is more emotive in kind. It relates to the various ways in which campaigns for social justice have sought both to redress inequalities and, in what has become known as the politics of recognition, to acknowledge the forms of human diversity. Thus, it combines elements of neo-Marxism and classic egalitarianism with a more recent sensitization to difference. Critical pedagogy can be taken as a prominent expression of such streams of thought.

What I would like to emphasize is the extent to which these two principal elaborations of social justice are apt discursively to determine educational thought about these matters. That is, they provide the textual reference points, the vocabulary, and the rhetorical codes in which discussion takes place. There is a danger, then, that they become ideological, in the Marxist sense to which Rawls refers.

In the light of this, it is worth pondering the following point. It is not uncommon for an education or social science department in a university to style its work in terms of "social justice," whether as the name of its research focus or the title of one of its courses: this becomes part of its "narrative" of itself. Today, as never before, departments are required to have a narrative, and the coherence, plausibility, and political marketability of this may be critical to their success, even to their survival. It is no rejection of those underlying values with which the term has reasonably been associated to acknowledge now the rhetorical force that "social justice" has acquired. In this ideological degeneration it risks becoming little more than a marketing or makeover term. But in fact it is part of the contemporary, globalized, cultural context, and a facet of neoliberalism, that any term, no matter how noble its associations, risks becoming a facile slogan or vacuous cliché, and hence a barrier to responsible thought. Let us pursue this further.

2. Policy Borrowing and the Hegemony of English

To see how this works has entailed paying some attention to the nature of the language itself, and inevitably here this means attending to the English language. This is not simply because it is an English term we are dealing with, but because of the effects on academic research of the global hegemony of English. The coincidence of the supremacy of the British and American empires with spectacular technological change has given English prominence as a language in a way that is unprecedented, that is seemingly self-reinforcing and self-perpetuating, and that, especially in the post-1989 global settlement, we have been inclined to accept as irreversible. It may be that this has a special importance in education because academic research in this field is typically under pressure from a number of sources. Not only is it rightly understood to pursue the questions where they lead and, hence, as with more traditional disciplines, to engage in a form of inquiry that transcends national boundaries; it is also expected, quite reasonably once again, to contribute practically to the society in which it is located, through, for example, the training of teachers and the undertaking of research to guide or support national policy. That policy context has now, however, been drastically altered by changes on a global scale. Three factors in this stand out. In the first place, institutions such as the Organization for Economic Cooperation and Development's Program for International Student Assessment mean that countries are exposed to international comparisons in a way that is hard to avoid and that has important internal political consequences. In the second, for many countries policy is constrained because of dependence on international organizations such as the World Bank. And in the third, there are the more general and pervasive aspects of globalization: the mass media, the internet, and travel mean that the lives of people generally are inevitably less self-contained, more exposed, more invaded than was the case even in the comparatively recent past. None of these facts seems set to change, and in all of them English is dominant.

In such circumstances it is inevitable that English expressions carry a certain authority. This has two facets to it. First, they have *practical* authority through being understood more widely than any other in international contexts. Second, they have added *perceived* authority because of the economic power and cultural prestige associated with Anglophone—that is, especially, American—culture. These points are all the more telling in the light of the sheer scale of educational research in North America—witness the size of the annual American Educational Research Association meeting (about fourteen thousand attendees). Add to this the fact that there has been an extraordinary growth in publication in educational research and that this is predominantly in English. And add to this the fact that measures of research quality typically give priority to publication in English. And, once again, add to this the fact that Anglophone researchers then have an obvious advantage in this process.

Certainly, within Taiwan, for example, there has been some consideration of the significance of these matters as part of the discussion of "policy borrowing." Thus, for example, Yang Shen-Keng has examined Taiwan's following of the global trend toward deregulation, has (most significantly for present purposes) identified this as the "motto" of its education reform, and has drawn attention to the imbalances that have ensued between competition and social justice.[2] With similar concerns but in relation to German influence, Liu Wei-Zhi has analyzed the dissemination of German pedagogy in China and Japan from 1928 to 1983 and the attempts of four educationalists to develop a pedagogy that combined German and Taiwanese elements.[3] And Chen Wen-Yan has considered different types of policy transfer research, including its historical study, its prospective evaluation, theory-building on its basis, and most important the various critiques of it that have been developed.[4] My knowledge of these papers is regrettably confined to their abstracts, but I take it that there is some evidence here of a growing questioning of the dynamics of policy borrowing—as the related terms "policy traveling" and "policy transplant" perhaps more obviously indicate. While it is entirely prudent for nations to be ready to look at practice abroad and to seek to emulate or adapt or learn from this in various ways, it seems inevitable that, at least as far as the relationship with Anglophone countries is concerned, the traffic is likely to be one-way. In fact this raises questions about comparative education as a field of study: whereas, in many countries where this thrives, its aims are couched partly in terms of the mutual benefits of learning of differences in practice, in the United States, especially, comparative study is likely to be undertaken out of purely academic interest.

3. Social Justice in Translation

But my purpose here is not to consider policy borrowing only in its most literal sense, for there are larger issues that constitute the background to these more specific matters. My remarks about language in section 2 have been woven around questions concerning the adoption of the term "social justice." I want now to speculate further about the experience of, for example, the Taiwanese researcher when the term arises. In the first place, insofar as the term is encountered in Anglophone contexts—say, in journals and books or at conferences in the English-speaking world—it is likely to be embedded in cultural circumstances that are alien in various ways and where there are chains of connection that will be only partly understood. Second, in international contexts where there is no shared language—involving participants from, say, Korea and Italy—the default means of communication will most likely be English; or, to be more precise, it will be English as a foreign language. It is English of this functional but culturally anodyne kind that has become the world language. Third, even in circumstances that involve only native speakers of Chinese, where English is not being used, it is likely that certain academic kudos will attach to the command of key terms in English—very much in the way that the incorporation of the occasional German or French or ancient Greek word into academic English can give the native speaker of English an air of sophistication; indeed because of the power and importance of English it may be hard to avoid these terms. I understand that when social justice is the topic of research in Japan, the katakana *sosharu jasutisu* is sometimes used instead of the authentic *shakai seigi.*

Beyond these factors, however, there is a more complex point. Where "social justice" is translated and a corresponding expression in Chinese is used (社會正義), it is likely that the respective terms will have different connotations, opening different chains of association. A Chinese speaker who is sensitive to this will experience a difference between semantic fields. By contrast, for the native speaker of English, who encounters only the English term, this will not be the case. In both cases the presence and power of English will have its effects, totally and directly in the case of the English speaker, partially and indirectly in that of the speaker of Chinese.

This is partly to make the familiar point that different languages divide up the world in different ways, engendering diverse patterns of conceptual connection and different possibilities of thought. I say that this point is familiar, but it is also for many of us an uncomfortable matter: it is convenient, especially for native English speakers, to play down or dismiss its importance. This dismissal then leads to the complacent assumption that this is just a matter of translation, that translation is primarily a technical matter, and that differences between languages are merely to be overcome.[5] Think of this as a suppression of thought, of which the monolingual person may be unaware.

4. Changing the Subject

To illustrate more fully the significance of translation, I turn now to a set of terms that is of central importance to the social sciences and the humanities and that has been addressed systematically and more richly. These concern the notions of subjectivity and the self. To do this I draw especially on the work of Sakai Naoki, a graduate of Tokyo University who pursued doctoral studies, following ten years in business, at the University of Chicago, since when he has been a professor at Cornell.

Sakai is plainly influenced by Foucauldian notions of subjectivation and of technologies of the self—that is, that we become subjects or selves through the discursive regimes in which we find ourselves and that these are historical and diverse. Sakai finds a specific point of departure in Suzuki Akira's examination in the early nineteenth century of the idea of foreign-language learning. Writing during the period of Japan's closure to the outside world (1600–1868), Suzuki understood such learning in terms of the acquisition of an ancient language, of China or Japan. But the crucial thing for present purposes is that this process was understood to involve an absorption of the textures of a social and political reality different from one's own; it was, in addition, through this that there would be a "co-figuring" of each. Hence, learning of this kind (and the relation to literature and language that it implies) is of an order somewhat different from that of "literature" or "foreign-language learning" in their current familiar forms: whereas the contemporary study of literature might be conceived in terms of, say, a literary-critical approach, and a language might be studied for instrumental reasons, in Suzuki's account learning is closer to the experience of the novice monk, where one becomes absorbed in the content and textual practices of the language in question, including its characteristic disciplining of the body, and commits or submits oneself to its ethos. Such an account of literature is overtly related to the construction of subjectivity, with all the ethical richness that that implies. Sakai takes this to be "an ecstatic project, a project of moving away from and getting out of the self-same that the figure of a foreign language solicits me to venture into. It is a project of transforming me into that which is not familiar rather than a project of returning to the authentic self."[6] Hence, this encounter with the foreign language realizes a possibility of subjectivity on both fronts (the "home" language and the foreign language), and this is transformative in kind.

He explains this in terms of divergent conceptions of subjectivity, realized in two possible translations of the word "subject," a term notoriously problematic for Japanese and Chinese translators. Part of the background to the distinction he draws is found in the ethics and anthropology of Watsuji Tetsurō, developed in the 1930s and 1940s. Watsuji himself relates his account to Marx's dissatisfactions with eighteenth-century materialism, a metaphysics that divided the world into objects of knowledge, on the one hand, and epistemological subjects, on the other. It was against this that Marx emphasized the idea of praxis, where the subject is understood as (bodily) engaged in activities and hence socially and historically located. In the light of this distinction, Watsuji identifies the epistemological subject as *shukan* and the subject of practice as *shutai*. Thus:

主観	主体
shukan	*shutai*
epistemological subject	subject of praxis

(The conceptual field of, and the relation between, the equivalent terms in Chinese—*zhuguan* and *zhuti*—is, I understand, slightly different, and in what follows I shall follow Sakai in using the Japanese.) If I have understood this correctly, the popular connotations may be somewhat different from their more philosophical ones. It should be remembered also that their more philosophical use in Japanese is recent: philosophy as an academic form of study was "imported" only with the ending of Japan's period of closure in the late nineteenth century. Thus, in popular terms *shukan* can have negative associations related to a kind of lack of objectivity, to being too subjective in one's consideration of things, or perhaps to being egotistical. When Nishi Amane (1829–1927), in the late nineteenth century, introduced philosophy into Japan and created a name for it, *tetsugaku* (哲学), he gave *shukan* more positive connotations by preferring it as the equivalent of "epistemological subject." According to Sakai, Nishi was not alone at the time in deploring the absence of systematic reasoning in Japan, and the emphasis on *shukan* was presumably intended to answer to this lack. *Shutai* by contrast, a term less visible in philosophy as it was then established in Japan, can imply a kind of independence of thought, or perhaps better a self-reliance or resourcefulness, such that one is not too easily influenced by others. The second part of the Chinese written expression (体) refers to the body, blurring the boundaries of epistemology and ethics, and this helps to show the way that it turns us back to notions of practical engagement and hence brings us closer to Marx.

Sakai's usage of these terms retains some of these connotations, but he attempts to give them more precision. In particular he formulates a distinction between what he calls *shukan-teki* technology and *shutai-teki* technology: the former expression connotes a more conventional conception of technology, wherein the subject "manipulates and transforms the object for a predetermined objective," while the latter suggests an understanding of technology as involving also the subject's manufacturing and production of itself.[7] In this he is not alone. Nishida Kitarō (1870–1945), for example, makes a distinction along similar lines.

> One may automatically assume that poiesis or technology is immediately *shukan-teki*. But . . . what may appear simply technological, such as the building of a house, is possible only upon the relevant historical substratum, whereas what may appear unrelated to technology, such as language, must in fact be constituted technologically. It goes without saying that society cannot exist without language. Hence, our dialogue here and now is already a historical manufacturing act, and it therefore is a matter of technology. . . . Technology requires dexterity. Dexterity means the historical formation of the individual's habits. However, the habits are not formed by the individual's subjective [*shukan-teki*] act: they are formed as historical manufacturing acts. Otherwise, we would never be able to manufacture anything by those habits. Our habits, therefore, are the habits of the historical world.[8]

While the anticipation of Foucault is evident here, what also needs to be registered is the proximity of these reflections of subjectivity to notions of identity. To make things clearer, let us touch on Sakai's critique of Watsuji.

While it may seem, as Watsuji implies, that *shukan* is the mode of subjectivity of "the West" and *shutai* that of "the East," Sakai is eager to show that the Japanese are also *shukan-teki* in their construction of the West.[9] Thus, the "interiority called Japan" in Watsuji's anthropology ends up being thoroughly "Western"—the grafting of an image of Japan on Japan determined by Western notions of identity.[10] In the same way subjects are apt to become *shukan* in confronting cultural difference insofar as, in this process, the other is objectified. To identify *shutai* as the *defining characteristic* of subjectivity in the East is ironically self-defeating. So these are questions about what can be understood by identity itself. Sakai's response to this implies that the wrong kind of emphasis on identity here involves "a repression of the singular eventhood of historicity, of what cannot be arrested in the phenomenality of the representable within the economy of chronological temporality."[11] It is important then that these terms are asymmetrical: there is a difference between what can be accommodated in a general economy of universality and particularity, and what flees as soon as any attempt is made to arrest it. "By *shutai,* therefore," he continues, "I like to suggest the impossibility of full saturation of any identity and, particularly, of the agent of action, as well as an undecidability that underwrites the possibility of social and ethical action. Yet the *shutai* is not the agent of action possessing free choice as it is understood in liberal humanism because freedom is neither owned by it nor in it."[12] The resistance here is, I take it, against the idea of freedom as either a possession of a subject or as internal to an ego, and the reason for this is that freedom is "out there," in the engagement of ethical action and with the absence of any final settlement. Plainly the metaphysics implied by Sakai's remarks here is at odds with assumptions that pervade the Rawlsian discourse of rational choosers, and plainly then this must have its bearing on ways in which social justice is conceived and realized.

It was said earlier that the word "subject" presents problems for translators, and this exploration of *shukan* and *shutai* helps to show why this is so. Inevitably in philosophy and social science, not to mention practical politics, this is a peculiarly pivotal term, and so the cross-cultural consequences of this translational problem should be plain enough. But in fact this exemplifies a more general difficulty. The translator normally confronts a gap between meanings for which there is no ultimately satisfactory resolution. As a result the translator experiences the space for judgment—precisely that space where there is no rule to resolve the difficulty she faces. There is then an inherent openness and "ab-solution"[13] in what she does. Thus, translation, as Sakai claims, is a *shutai-teki* technology par excellence.[14] In this respect the monolingual may be morally blind.

The fact that subjects become *shukan-teki* in the objectification of the other, and that this can happen at an intercultural level, is amply evident in the familiar forms of Orientalism. Sakai exposes, in his account of Japan's response to the West, what might be called a corresponding Occidentalism, and it would seem then that this reciprocates with the West in the process of co-figuring that

Sakai describes. But in my view there remains a difference. The West's Orientalism is born out of a sense of superiority coupled to an (ethnocentric) universalist metaphysics. While Japan has its own sense of superiority, even if this falters at times, there is a crucial difference in that its Occidentalism is not derived from an indigenous universalist metaphysics. Of course, Occidentalism is not confined to Japan, and this latter point applies also, I believe, to its manifestations elsewhere.

I confess that I do not know quite what to make of this, if it is true, but it does strike me that whereas Orientalism may be a "natural," though objectionable outgrowth of Western ways of thinking, Occidentalism has the character of a double grafting: it is grafted on a borrowed notion of subjectivity and of identity.[15]

This, I think, reinforces the bad aspects of policy borrowing and reduces the possibilities of exchange between countries. At the same time it foregrounds *shukan-teki* ways of thinking and being at the expense of the greater openness and possibility of the *shutai-teki*.

5. Toward a New Conversation

Of course, I want to bring together my exposure of the problems of monolingualism with my critique of dominant conceptions of social justice and the way these play out in educational research. The experience of translation, which has been illustrated with reference to *shukan* and *shutai,* does not occur only between languages: as has been widely recognized, it occurs also in an intralingual way.[16]

My frustration or disappointment with the familiar expressions of social justice that I identified in section 1 has two aspects. First, I think there is a continuing need to be sensitized to the rhetorical inflation of this and similar terms, as found, for example, in critical pedagogy, in statements of policy, and in mobilizations of "narrative." Second, while I do not doubt the worthiness and value of much of the work undertaken in the wake of Rawls, research that addresses questions concerning, say, the fair distribution of educational opportunity, I find that this tradition of thought has less to say about certain central aspects of education—that is, about the substance of teaching and learning, and about its transformative place in human life—and that its discourse is apt to hide the importance of these matters. The dominance of *shukan-teki* ways of thinking suggests that there is much to be learned from the different semantic fields that Japanese and Chinese open.

My reaction in this respect has a parallel in Stanley Cavell's criticism of Rawls' emphasis on cooperation, a central democratic virtue at the heart of justice. In a comparatively recent iteration of this, he writes:

> "Cooperation," as a general state of social interaction, suggests the idea of society as a whole either as having a project or, at the other extreme, as being a neutral field in which each can pursue his or her own projects. Intuitively these extremes are analogous to aspects of the interesting institution of competitive games. . . .
> The idea of "conversation," in contrast, emphasizes neither a given social project nor a field of fairness for individual projects. (Nor, as I have insisted, does it deny the importance of these ideas.)

Conversation is, then, the field within which I might discover what my projects might be. Cavell continues:

> What it emphasizes is, I might say, the opacity, or non-transparence, of the present state of our interactions, cooperative or antagonistic—the present seen as the outcome of our history as the realization of attempts to reform ourselves in the direction of compliance with the principles of justice. The virtues most in request here are those of listening, the responsiveness to difference, the willingness for change. The issue is not whether there is a choice between the virtues of cooperation and of conversation. God forbid. The issue is what their relation is, whether one of them discourages the other.[17]

My issue, then, is that the dominance of particular kinds of discourse, in critical pedagogy and political liberalism, perpetuates monolingualism of a kind. A better idiom for educational thought requires the release of language, and this can be realized in both interlingual and intralingual ways.

Cavell finds in the second syllable of "conversation" ("vers"—cf. reversal, diversion, averse) the suggestion of a turning of thought such that it cannot proceed solely, and in many respects does not proceed best, when it travels along straight, systematic lines: openness to conversation, a readiness to be turned (to be shaped, fashioned, sometimes diverted, sometimes rebuffed), requires that I do not seek to shore up my own identity but rather am ready for new possibilities—that is, ready to become.

Plainly this is to take conversation not as just any kind of verbal exchange between people but to idealize it as something to be aspired to. And plainly, given that Emerson is never far from Cavell's account, the readiness to be fashioned cannot be an acquiescence in conformity. Emerson says of conversation that its laws are "analogous to the laws of society" and that it is the "first office of friendship,"[18] where the friend is not someone who merely reinforces my identity, who secures me where I am, but rather someone ready to challenge me toward my next, best possibility. Transformative rather than informative, conversation requires a listening through which, as Branka Arsić puts this, I forget "the texts, codes, and judgments that constitute the conversing 'I'; it happens only as self-abandonment."[19] The interruption that the friend in conversation represents has the character of "the singular eventhood of historicity," in Sakai's phrase. It is in this spirit that Emerson advocates a kind of self-reliance, not as individualistic autonomy but as the receptivity, openness, and resourcefulness that is achieved in the act of abandonment.[20]

There is nothing arbitrary about turning to Emerson here, for he was deeply influenced by East Asian thought. Hence, this nineteenth-century American philosophy, in partial reaction against Europe, finds some company with the East. Ancient Confucian teaching emphasizes the necessity of the growth of moral sensibility within the student. That the Chinese character for *shutai* incorporates the symbol for the body (体), and that this body cannot be understood in terms of any oppressive mind-body dualism, emphasizes practical engagement: hence, far from being an immunization against the turbulence of the world, this is the realization of conduct that remains appropriately earthed—call this developing resourcefulness a conducting of the energies of experience.

But it is not surprising, then, that this aspect of Emerson's work is itself repressed: he is more conveniently championed and contained as the prophet of American individualism. I am drawn by the thought that the parallels between this repression and that of *shutai* extend to symmetries between them in respect of resourcefulness and self-reliance. Repression of this kind is itself a distortion of the possibilities of social justice, even its violation, as well as of the possibilities of learning from one another. Does academic research in education in some way collude in this?

NOTES

I should like to thank Kang Tsui-Ting, Kawaguchi Yukiko, Saito Naoko, and Wang Chia-Ling for help in the preparation of this essay. Onō Fumiō is thanked for encouraging some of my thoughts in this direction.

1. J. Rawls, *Justice as Fairness: A Restatement* (Cambridge, MA: Belknap Press of Harvard University Press, 2001), 4.
2. Yang S.-K., "Education Reform Facing the New Millennium—Methodological Reflection and International Comparison," *Bulletin of Educational Research* 44 (2000), 1–34.
3. Liu W.-Z., "A Historical Review on Dissemination of German Pedagogy in China and Taiwan (1928–1983)," *Bulletin of Educational Research* 54, no. 4 (2008), 19–51.
4. Chen W.-Y., "Policy Transfer Research: Retrospects and Prospects," *Journal of Educational Research and Development* 5, no. 93 (2009), 73–94.
5. See, for example, P. Standish, "One Language, One World: The Common Measure of Education," *Philosophy of Education Yearbook, 2011,* http://ojs.ed.uiuc.edu/index.php/pes/article/viewFile/3057/1132, accessed March 14, 2012.
6. N. Sakai, *Translation and Subjectivity: On "Japan" and Cultural Nationalism* (Minneapolis: University of Minnesota Press, 1997), 33.
7. Ibid., 24.
8. K. Nishida, "Poieshisu to Parakushisu," in *Nishida Kitarō Zenshu* (Tokyo: Iwanami Shoten, 1965), 10:135, in Sakai, *Translation and Subjectivity,* 198–199n10; Sakai's translation (originally published in *Shisō* 223 [December 1940]).

9. It should be obvious that these terms are used in a discussion such as this as shorthand expressions. There is no suggestion that countries in East Asia and countries in Europe or North America divide in such clear-cut ways. And of course so much of what is referred to as "the West" permeates the East, just as countries and people in the West are affected by influences from "the East" in multiple ways.

10. Watsuji's latent Sinophobia is said to bear the features of a certain anti-Semitism, indicative of a repression of anxiety, an anxiety over identity. This is a repression, Sakai claims, from which Asian studies has never entirely been free (Sakai, *Translation and Subjectivity,* 151), and I venture to suggest that it is a potential threat more generally to comparative education.

11. Ibid., 149.

12. Ibid., 150.

13. Sakai's term here has multiple senses, but at the least it should indicate that the task she faces cannot be understood in any simple logic of problem *solving*. The difficulty she faces is irreducible, although she still must exercise judgment and act.

14. Sakai, *Translation and Subjectivity,* 198n10.

15. In other words, the East's construction of the West is grafted on a Western construction of the East, but the origin of such identity construction is in Western forms of representation and objectification, and Western notions of identity.

16. This is readily evident in the writings of, for example, Mikhail Bakhtin, Paul Ricoeur, and Jacques Derrida (see Standish, "One Language, One World").

17. S. Cavell, *Cities of Words: Pedagogical Letters on the Moral Life* (Cambridge, MA: Belknap Press of Harvard University Press, 2004), 173–174.

18. R. W. Emerson, *The Early Lectures of Ralph Waldo Emerson,* ed. S. E. Whicher, R. E. Spiller, and W. E. Williams (Cambridge, MA: Harvard University Press, 1961), 2:292.

19. B. Arsić, *On Leaving* (Cambridge, MA: Harvard University Press, 2010), 196.

20. See, for example, N. Saito, *The Gleam of Light: Moral Perfection and Education in Dewey and Emerson* (New York: Fordham University Press, 2005), 147.

Three-Level Eco-Humanism in Japanese Confucianism 20

Combining Environmental with Humanist Social Ethics

T. Yamauchi

> In many indigenous cultures nature was represented as inspirited or divine (the ancient Japanese *kami* are a leading example)—and therefore the direct object of respect or of reverence.
>
> —*J. B. Callicott, "Toward a Global Environmental Ethic"*

> In the Confucian tradition, moral ideas are much more than social norms. In the case of *Chung-yung* [*Zhongyong*], the ultimate manifestation of morality transcends social ethics and reaches its ultimacy in the unity of Heaven and man.
>
> —*Tu Wei-ming, Centrality and Commonality*

> A Confucian ethics might be described as a form of social ecology because a key component is relationality in the human order against the background of the natural order. A profound sense of interconnectedness of the human with one another and with nature is central to Confucian thinking. The individual is never seen as an isolated entity but always as a person in relation to another and the cosmos.
>
> —*M. E. Tucker, "Ecological Themes in Taoism and Confucianism"*

The scholars quoted here are referring to Edo-period Japan (1603–1867), a time when people valued and enriched the natural environment, and, thereby, a green, sustainable society nourished about 30 million people in small island communities. In today's Japan a so-called scientific technologic culture has become bloated and the cause of deterioration of the natural environment. The secret of Edo Japan's success in achieving and maintaining sustainability for more than three hundred years is, I think, in its environmental policies. Those policies were based on *an eco-holistic environmental ethics*, which had its source in Japanese Confucianism. There have been attempts to shed new light on Edo society, defining it as the "Edo model," in hopes of finding a solution to today's environmental distress.[1] Yet the gap between the two societies of old and new

Japan is so deep and wide that it is difficult to identify green wisdom in the Edo model without criticizing the ethical attitude underlying our current civilization. The environmental ethic articulated in this essay is an attempt to reconcile the organismic view of nature in Edo society and the mechanistic view of nature in contemporary Japan, a recommended course of action that can, hopefully, put restrictions on today's materialistic economy and politics.

In order to compare Edo and today's "modernized" society, let us first take up Platonic philosophy, which (along with Christianity) is the source of modern Western thought. Because Platonic cosmology has profoundly influenced Western thought about the environment, it is worth examining its ethical framework and comparing it with Japanese Confucian cosmology. By introducing the idea of "distinction of levels," I will try to find a way of reconciling both philosophies, East and West. Such a reconciliation is important because contemporary Japan must, as it surely will, remain a part of the international community and the global economy. Just as surely, the international community and the global economy will look for guidance and inspiration to the intellectual heritage and resources of both the West and the East, as China, India, and Japan equally and eventually promise to exceed the United States and Europe in economic, political, and cultural influence as the twenty-first century unfolds. Therefore, I will attempt to synthesize both social and environmental ethics, which are problematically separated into different disciplines in the mainstream of today's Western environmental ethics. Finally, applying the distinction of levels, I will search for the wisdom for engendering a sustainable society.

Platonic Cosmology and the Organismic View of Nature

According to the Platonic myth recounted in *Timaeus,* the cosmos was composed by the demiurge. The *maker* made this *cosmos* using the eternally existing *paradigm* (*paradeigma*) of Forms (*eidos*) as its model, and this world of generation (i.e., *cosmos*) is only an image or copy (*eikôn*) of these Forms.[2] An important implication here is that Plato considered this cosmos an eternally *living* being that is a perfect *organism* (*zôon*).[3] The cosmos is therefore not a machine, nor is it an aggregate of materials or objects; it is, so to speak, an integrated, stable, and beautiful living being. The Platonic view is in one respect very similar to the Christian view in that it presupposes the maker or the creator as an agent or efficient cause. But it is very different from the Christian view in another respect: in Christian theology God created the universe from nothing, ex nihilo. Yet, if the maker of the cosmos is a transcendent Christian God or a transcendent Platonic demiurge, then humans have nothing to do with creation because humans can take no role as *moral agents* in that creation.

Plato's social and personal ethics appears to be uninformed by his cosmology, for why else was environmental thought not part of his philosophy given his organismic view of cosmic nature? While a maker is usually assumed to make something artificial, in the organismic view it would usually be considered that an organ is autogenetic. There are, thus, two different tendencies mixed in Platonic cosmology: the artificial moment on the one hand and the organismic moment on the other. The organismic view had in Western Europe disappeared after the age of the Scientific Revolution, and all that remained was the view of nature as an artifact.[4]

Platonic social ethics was also organismic, deepening the mystery of the absence of an environmental philosophy in the Platonic corpus. For Plato, social happiness takes precedence over the interests of individual persons. In the Platonic ideal state, the pursuit of social happiness is based on, and limited by, the organismic view of the (macro)cosmos and social (micro)cosmos precisely so that society can be sustainable. One of the central themes of Plato's *Republic* is moral education. The point of his personal ethics is for reason (*nous* or *logistikon*) to regulate desire (*epithymia* or *epithymetikon*) with the aid of the spirit (*thymos* or *thymoeides*); analogously the point of his politics is for the rulers to regulate common people with the aid of their guardians. Therefore, the essence of the Platonic organismic state lies in the regulation of superfluous human desires—such as the desire for money, power, fame, and luxury—in the interest of achieving the good of the social whole, which is of much greater value than the (questionable) "values" that would be gained by the satisfaction of the superfluous desires of individual persons.

While the mechanistic view of nature held sway in Western Europe after the Scientific Revolution began in the sixteenth century, was consummated in the seventeenth, and was enculturated in the eighteenth, organismic views of nature prevailed until recently in the traditional societies of the East. In the anthropocentric view of nature in the modern West, humans take the role of maker rather than God being the creator; and after the Industrial Revolution, Western people pursued their personal interests at the expense of the organic welfare of both society and nature. Thus, the idea of dominion over nature, which is considered the basic cause of today's environmental crisis, triumphed. The decisive moment that divides the modern mechanist worldview from traditional organismic worldviews is that, in the former, human moral agents treat nature like a huge machine instead of a living organism. Whereas a machine may be tinkered with and reengineered to better serve its human designers, an organism must be nourished, protected, and cared for in order to sustain its healthy state of being.

Human beings can now use or misuse, protect or destroy, the natural environment. Although most people today treat nature like a lifeless machine, they could treat it, if they wished, like a living organism. Human beings as free moral agents can now make the world better or worse and are morally responsible for a course of civilization that devastates nature and thus makes society unsustainable. A most crucial indictment of the modern mechanistic worldview is that cossetting human self-interest results in sacrificing the welfare of both nature and society. The problem, which is not only in the increase of the human population but also in the free reign of human desires, has become too overwhelming to be controlled in advanced, wealthy countries. Because people have long been accustomed to the neglect of nature, they have realized too late that there is a crisis. In this situation, one of the most important and urgent dilemmas is how to reconcile human-centered mechanistic views with ecological, or rather organismic, views of nature. Before going into this problem, let us explore how it is seen through the lens of Japanese Confucianism.

Social and Environmental Ethics in Traditional Japanese Confucianism

In Edo-era Japan, there appeared distinguished Japanese Confucian philosophers who contributed to the development of environmental thought. Their philosophy was in the tradition of Chinese neo-Confucianism represented by Zhu Xi (1130–1200) and Wang Yangming (1472–1529), which they indigenized (i.e., Japanized) so that it blended with traditional Japanese thought, which was a mixture of Taoism and Japanized Buddhism grounded in Shintoism. One of the reasons why neo-Confucianism was so well accepted by Japanese philosophers was that it was originally a nature-oriented philosophy much influenced by Daoism and Chinese Buddhism, and that indigenous Japanese thought was similarly nature oriented.

The focus of Japanese Confucianism is the organismic view of nature. Japanese Confucians considered the whole of nature (that is, the cosmos) as a huge living organism; it was referred to as the Great Father and Mother that brought forth everything. According to Kaibara Ekken (1630–1714), a leading voice in the development of Japanese Confucianism, “Heaven and Earth are the Great Father and Mother.” The virtue of heaven and earth is in “life and production.” Heaven and earth, in this view, have brought forth and nourished everything, including human beings. Humans therefore owe a debt (恩, *on*) to these cosmic parents and therefore have a basic duty (or a Categorical Imperative, to use the term of modern ethics) to repay that debt (報恩, *houon*). In Confucianism, filial piety (孝, *kō*) is the central duty among duties originating from human relationships. It follows that filial piety to the cosmic parents must have been considered as preexisting duty to human parents. Ekken writes as follows:

> Heaven (*ten* 天) and Earth (*chi* 地) give birth to and nourish all things, but the deep compassion with which they treat humans is different from [the way they

> nourish] birds and beasts, trees and plants. Therefore, among all things only humans are the children of the universe. Thus, humans have heaven as their father and earth as their mother and receive their great kindness. Because of this, always to serve heaven and earth is the Human way. What is the Way by which we should serve heaven and earth? Humans have a heart of heaven and earth, namely, the heart of compassion, which gives birth to and nurtures all things. This heart is called humaneness (仁: C. *jen* or *ren;* J. *jin*), humaneness is the original nature implanted by heaven in the human heart.[5]

Thus, human beings could, according to Ekken, become moral agents serving the natural environment even as they remain members of a "land community" (to borrow a term from Leopold's land ethic). Humans, then, are moral agents *apart from* nature and moral patients as *a part of* nature at the same time. This idea, because it posits the moral agency of humans, makes it possible for them to manage the human-nature relationship (in accordance with environmental ethics), on the one hand, and human-human relationships (in accordance with social ethics), on the other. If one compares Japanese Confucianism, from an environmental ethical viewpoint, with Platonic cosmology and Judeo-Christian stewardship ethics, one will find that in Japanese Confucianism, nature, not transcendental Forms or God, comes first. This situates Japanese Confucianism between Platonism and Christianity in the sense that it shares the organismic view of nature with Platonism and the stewardship ethics with Christianity.

Ogyū Sorai (荻生徂徠, 1666–1728), an influential philosopher of the Edo era, argued, criticizing Zhu Xi's philosophy of heavenly reason (天理、, *ten-ri*), that Confucian social morality (especially the teachings of ritual, music, the legal system, and politics) (禮楽刑政, *rai-kagu-kei-sei*) is not a set of heaven-given precepts but rather a collection of artificial institutions created by the ancient sage-kings for the welfare of people.[6] This means that the Confucian institutions, legal systems, teachings, dogmas, and so on were created by human leaders for the purpose of *social happiness* (安民 安天下, *anmin-antenka*) and therefore subject to change when they were no longer useful for the original purpose of social happiness. Thus, Sorai divided moral thinking into two aspects (or levels or dimensions): the basic happiness principle (that pursues social happiness) on one hand, and the secondary or derivative principles that are useful means for the purpose of the happiness principle on the other hand. This maneuver reminds us of today's two-level utilitarianism propagated by Hare and Singer. (It is with that in mind that Sorai criticized some aspects of the feudalistic class society of the Tokugawa shogunate.)[7] Zhu Xi's philosophy distinguishes *principle* (理, *li,* or reason) and *vital force* (気, *qi*) in its metaphysics. Principle, on the one hand, becomes heavenly reason, which is a transcendental, objective value (in the terms of Western ethics) like the Platonic Forms; vital force, on the other hand, becomes humanly desire, which should be eliminated as a morally destructive force. The motto "the preservation of the heavenly principle and the elimination of human desires" (存天理去人欲) was the central moral precept of Zhu Xi's ethics.[8] Sorai's opposition to this motto means that he considered the universe, or nature ("heaven-earth-nature" according to the Japanese Confucian term, 天地自然, *ten-chi-sizen*), to be everything; there is no need to suppose the existence of the transcendent heavenly reason of Zhu Xi. Hare also agreed with J. Mackie that "there is no objective value," which is a shibboleth among today's utilitarian thinkers. Hare denied the existence of the Platonic Forms or Christian God from which moral precepts for humans are said to originate, just as Sorai denied the existence of Zhu Xi's principle of heaven three hundred years before Hare. Both philosophers pulled morality from heaven down to earthly human happiness.

My own method is to place Hare's and Singer's two-level utilitarian ethics on a more basic, holistic level. My interpretation of the Soraian ethics originates from Hare's division of moral thinking into two levels: the intuitive level (where people obey simple moral principles in everyday moral thinking) and the critical level (where people must critically think and choose simple moral principles for everyday moral life and moral education).[9] Now, let me explain Hare's solution of moral conflict. We have, in everyday moral life and for educating our children, very simple and general moral principles, customary morality, or social norms that are accepted in each society. These include "don't lie," "be kind to others," and "respect your parents." And a society where people obey these principles is one that is nicer and more comfortable to live within than otherwise. To teach such sound principles to our children is also important for the creation of a sense of conscience in their minds. However, it sometimes happens that these principles cause conflict. The moral principle "to be honest," for instance, sometimes conflicts with another principle, "to be kind to other people." Hare's device for resolving such conflicts is to separate the levels of moral thinking into two; that is, when conflict occurs at the level of our intuitive moral thinking, we must shelve these intuitive moral principles and shift moral thinking to the critical level, where we think critically about which course of action will lead to a better conclusion, balancing and weighing the interests or preference-satisfaction that two alternative courses will bring. Hare's method is to balance and weigh the interests (or preference-satisfaction) of two alternative courses of action for all the participants. And when the conflict is resolved, the intuitive principles are revived for everyday moral use as usual. In this way Hare solved the problem of moral conflict, a solution so clear and fine, in my view, as to be applicable for solving the difficult moral dilemma people today confront: that is, the dilemma of how to balance the pursuit of the general interests/happiness of people with the preservation of the natural environment. My solution for this problem is inspired by Hare's two-level utilitarianism. As mentioned previously, Soraian social ethics of dividing levels of moral thinking corresponds well, according to our interpretation, with Hare's two-level utilitarianism.

Sorai considered, furthermore, that heaven (which symbolizes nature) should be the object of worship on the basis of agnosticism, the whole universe being in principle unknowable to the human intellect. It is this respect for heaven as the basis of social ethics that distinguishes Sorai's Confucian ethics from Western modern social ethics. In this respect, Sorai has admitted, in our interpretation, a third level of moral thinking on which his social ethics should be based. This means that the same moral agent can, or must, pursue social happiness, respect nature, and take care of and serve the welfare of the eco-social whole, including all humans and nature.

Thus, Sorai's ethical framework could be interpreted as consisting of both a holistic environmental ethics and a holistic social ethics (that is based on his environmental ethics). Soraian environmental ethics is on a different, third level from Hare's two levels of social ethics. It could be situated on another even more basic level than Hare's intuitive and critical levels, which could be called *the eco-holistic level.* The focus in the Soraian social ethics is on social happiness that corresponds well to Hare's utilitarian social happiness in his *critical level* of moral thinking. If Sorai's representations of rituals, music, the legal system, and politics are considered, as he originally intended, not as heaven-endowed moral teachings or precepts, but man-made, artificial moral principles for the purpose of social happiness, then his teachings correspond to Hare's moral principles of the *intuitive level* of moral thinking. In Hare's case, moral principles, teachings for moral education, customary moralities, and even social justice and human rights are located on the intuitive level; and so, too, should be Sorai's teachings on rituals, music, the legal system, and politics. (Sorai's social ethics could be located in what Hare called the "critical level," a term somewhat at odds with Sorai's terminology.) Therefore, let me tentatively call Hare's intuitive level *the institutional level* in Sorai's case and Hare's critical level *the social ethical level* (or *the separated level* in the sense that humans and nature are separated on this level), contrary to the eco-holistic level.[10]

Level 1 in the table may be called the *eco-holist level,* level 2, the *social happiness (or separated) level* (because humans are here separated from nature), and level 3, the *institutional level.* In this schema, one and the same human moral agent can, and must, pursue, first, the welfare of the whole land-community, including human interest and nature's welfare in the eco-holist level (level 1); second, social happiness in the social happiness level (level 2); and third, moral principles (originated for the purpose of both eco-holistic welfare and social happiness) in the institutional level (level 3).

These three levels of moral thinking—institutional, social-happiness, and eco-holist—originated from the notion that human society should be founded on a sound and healthy base of Earth as a totality. Human society and the Earth might be *ontologically* different objects of scientific research, but both can be *ethically* the same object of consideration, since the moral agents who pursue

Sorai's Three-Level Ethics

Level	Sorai's Teachings	Hare's Levels
1	Eco-holism (the welfare of the whole of humanity and nature)	
2	Social happiness ethics	Critical level
3	Institutions and teachings	Intuitive level

both social and environmental welfare can be the same moral agents. By setting up the eco-holist level (level 1), one can now clearly distinguish humanism from anthropocentrism. The pursuit of human interest is in itself a good thing, but if it goes to such excessive lengths as to degrade and destroy the welfare of nature, it is an evil thing that will bring disaster to human society. When human self-interest clashes with the welfare of nature in the separated level (level 2), it could be adjusted by the critical thinking of the eco-holist level—by restricting human interest from the viewpoint of the integrated welfare of humans and nature. Accordingly, one can define anthropocentrism as the excessive pursuit of human self-interest over natural welfare, and humanism as the adjusted and balanced pursuit of human interest with appropriate regard for nature's welfare.

Sontoku's Experiments in Farming

Ninomiya Sontoku (二宮尊徳, 1787–1856), known as the "farmer saint," was regarded in industrial and political circles of prewar Japan as the most influential thinker and practitioner in the field of moral education. Today, his influence reaches as far as Chinese academic circles, and as recently as 2004 the International Ninomiya Sontoku Association was founded.[11] Sontoku separates the "human way" (人道, humanism) from "heaven's way" (天道).

> If one leaves the matter to heaven's-way, all nature will turn into wilderness and return to the original beginning of the world, since this is the course of nature (i.e., "the way of heaven-reason-nature," 天理自然の道 *ten-ri-sizen-no-michi*). There is no distinction between good and evil in heaven (i.e., nature); therefore heaven makes no distinction between rice and weeds, let everything that has seeds grow, and let everything that is alive be generated. Although the human-way obeys heaven-reason, the human way makes distinctions; as it considers

> weeds to be evil, rice and wheat to be good, so that people consider everything convenient to humans as good, and everything inconvenient to humans as evil. The human way, being different from heaven's way, is artificial things set up by humans. The human way is like cuisines, created by the ancient sage kings and their wise subjects.[12]

Here one can see that Sorai's distinction of three levels is also operative in Sontoku's thought. Nature brings forth everything, but nature itself doesn't consider or treat human beings as something special; humans, on the other hand, order nature for the purpose of human profit. In this sense, Sontoku separates human interest from the welfare of nature. To increase human interest is one thing; to let nature take its own course is another. (The former might be called *anthropocentrism* and the latter *eco-centrism* in today's environmental ethical terms.) What this division of morality will cause is the moral dilemma between the pursuit of ever-increasing self-interest on the part of people and the imperative of nature to increase indiscriminately. This is the crucial moral quandary in the field of environmental ethics, the solution to which I think can be found in Sontoku's practical ethics.

Sontoku inherited the Soraian theme that human morality is a man-made, artificial institution of principles, laws, and teachings, not heaven-given justice, rights, universal moral laws, and the like apart from nature. Ethical efforts for humans should not be in the pursuit of heavenly laws or precepts, but in the furthering of human interest. Yet the increase of human interest should not result in the domination of nature; it should lead rather to human beings helping and supporting nature to increase its productivity. Sontoku's ethics is not for the pursuit of human interest alone, nor is it concerned solely with the welfare of nature. It is rather interested in the pursuit of both at the same time specifically through farming. Sontoku is said to have saved a large number of villagers from starvation by encouraging despairing people to take up agrarian labor. The increased yield of rice and vegetables didn't deplete nature; it enriched nature. People were at that time demi-vegetarians (meat-eating being illegal at that time) and did not use in their farming any pollution-causing products. Sontoku helped the lord of his domain to rebuild the local economy and, later in life, to reclaim land via drainage. His actions exemplify the saying that in Edo society there was *industrious* revolution instead of an *industrial* revolution.

As in Platonic ethics, Japanese Buddhist and Confucian education made a virtue of the regulation of surplus desires. This ethical position made it easier for government to create an ecology-oriented sustainable society in which people could have a poor, simple, and yet contented lifestyle, accepting disease and natural calamities as their fate and eschewing needless, surplus desires and greed. Sontoku was neither a scientist nor a learned scholar; he claimed only that he read the unwritten "Sutra of Heaven and Earth." For

Sontoku, the classics were written in nature; his farming, financial accounting, and control of water were all learned from nature. In this sense, nature was the laboratory where he gleaned everything he needed to advance his career and ideas.

No human being is capable of knowing the entire universe, a fact that Sontoku surely recognized, which is why he expressed his ideas about the whole of humans and nature by means of similes, parables, sayings, or proverbs. So when he talks about "Heaven and Earth as great Father and Mother," he doesn't intend the phrase to encapsulate the entire universe or express a scientific fact. If the whole is unknown to humans, the views of nature, whether mechanistic, ecological, or organismic—insofar as they intend to express the whole of nature—are only hypotheses. However, each such hypothesis may offer a partially accurate and exact piece of scientific knowledge. The success of Sontoku's farming and finance techniques testifies to the efficacy of his method of assisting nature's productive process. The aim of his method could be expressed in today's environmental ethical terms as follows: to pursue the increase (and to prevent the deterioration) of the welfare of the whole (of both humans and nature) by the actions of humans as moral agents.

Sontoku's farming increased the benefit to human beings by helping nature produce, that is, by "*assisting in the transforming and nourishing process of Heaven and Earth* (賛天地之化育) *Zhongyong* (*The Doctrine of the Mean* 中庸)."[13] This may be interpreted as the way in which human moral agents, instead of a Platonic demiurge, take care of the Platonic organismic nature as a cosmic living being. The ethical structure of Japanese Confucianism, in which the human moral agent helps the whole of nature (including humans), so thoroughly permeated Edo-era ethico-politics that here the Confucian ideal was, though only on a small scale, realized: "*cultivate oneself, regulate the family, order the state, and bring the world peace* (「修身、斉家、治国、平天下」, *Great Learning*)."[14]

Separating the Levels of Moral Thinking and Eclecticism

If humanity is to survive, we will have to change the direction of the prevailing course of our civilization. One of the most effective ways to accomplish this would be to use the environmental ethics born in the advanced Western countries to shed fresh light on traditional Eastern environmental thought. Today's Western ethics seems to be separated, contrarily so from the perspective of Edo-era Japanese Confucian ethics, into two camps: newly emerged environmental ethics as represented by Aldo Leopold, Arne Naess, J. Baird Callicott, and others, on the one hand, and the humanistic social ethics represented by thinkers such as John Rawls, R. M. Hare, and Peter Singer, on the other hand.

Insofar as the two camps take into account the survival of humanity, which cannot endure without a well-functioning natural environment, there may be hope for a manner of moral thinking that will combine both ethical camps. Let me explain my own method of combining some Eastern and Western environmental ethics into a coherent framework.

In Japanese Confucianism, the concern for the welfare of nature comes first, followed by the social welfare ethics of human beings. Such an ethic is quite parallel to the ethics of Plato, in which the ideal of the world of Form (*eidos*) comes before a concern with social and individual human happiness in the phenomenal world of genesis. Therefore, if one considers nature rather than Platonic Forms as the basis of society, one would find an ethics that somewhat resembles Japanese Confucian ethics.

An Example of Eco-holistic Society

Imagine a group of people living on a small, remote island where survival depends on preservation of the natural environment. Some islanders are interested only in human welfare and begin to damage the natural environment, having forgotten the benefits nature had brought them. In such a situation, where people blindly choose the satisfaction of human interests over the welfare of nature, nature will be an easy victim—to the point where there will be no future for the human inhabitants. At this point, hopefully, our islanders will consult with one another and their leaders to try to solve the problem, lest the welfare of the whole community (including both humans and nature) should decay. The perspective of people who see it as a case of the welfare of the whole differs completely from that of people who value only human interest or only the welfare of nature. The separation of human welfare from the welfare of nature creates a clash of interests, whereas the synoptic view on the eco-holistic level (level 1 in our table earlier) has the potential to bring about a solution to that conflict. Let me next apply Sontoku's solution as I understand it.

Imagine that some of our islanders propose to convert the forest to farmland in order to prevent starvation of people. Those whose lives depend on the forest will obviously oppose such an action. Disputes between people who argue for human interest and those who wish to protect nature are unresolvable. For one cannot weigh the relative merits and demerits of each course of action when there are no common criteria by which to compare them: there is no common valuing, estimation, or priority between human interest and the welfare of nature.

Yet there is hope of finding a method of weighing and balancing the two in the eco-holist level of moral thinking. Returning to the problem of converting our small island's forest to farmland, one can begin by comparing the present situation of the land with the situation fifty years ago, when people led simpler lives as part of a smaller population in a rich environment. In comparing the choice of the present situation to that of the past, one can factor in the expected future situation of the island with a larger population. When judged by this eco-holistic standard, the scale will tilt toward preserving the forest over converting it to farmland. Prudent leaders might persuade people to curb their excessive, unnecessary desires and might educate them so that they embrace a simpler lifestyle. While in this situation, leaders could choose the best course for the welfare of the whole, restricting the population, allocating farms, forests, mountains, lakes, and residential places to promote a balance between satisfying human interests and the welfare of nature. Once the framework of a division of labor, based on eco-holistic ethico-politics, is decided, people can, in their everyday routines, lead simple lives without constantly calculating which course of action would lead to increasing the welfare of the whole. If eco-holism were the prevailing ethic, a clash of human interest with the welfare of nature would be unlikely to occur because the islanders would not hold an anthropocentric worldview.

This is reminiscent of the *land community* of Leopold's land ethic. The welfare of the whole land (including all people and the natural environment) must have been their supreme imperative.

Indeed, people could compare Edo-period and present-day Japan, present-day and future Japan, since the Edo-period Japanese had, seeing the whole land as an organism, a sufficiently eco-holistic view. For example, if a forest grew and its animal populations increased, people knew how to protect their farms from animal invasions by making a long defensive stone wall against deer and wild pigs, or by killing such animals and eating their meat. When the human population increased, they knew how to reduce the population by birth control, recommending celibacy, or sometimes by infanticide (called "thinning out"). This approach is different from so-called eco-fascism, for eco-fascism occurs when the human-centered view clashes with the eco-centric view in the separated level of moral thinking. Eco-fascism or anthropo-fascism, if it occurs, is a problem caused by the separation of humans and nature in the separated level, not in the *eco-holist* level. When some moral dilemma occurred, they could weigh and balance, in the eco-holist way, the present situation with possible alternative courses of action.

Many might consider today's Japanese as being much happier than the Japanese of the feudalistic class society ruled by despotic rulers. In order to increase natural welfare, people in the past had to sacrifice their interests, living in poor, simple, situations. However, it is nearly impossible to compare the state of well-being of Edo-era Japanese with that of today's Japanese because of contemporary Japan's involvement, politically, militarily, and economically, in international relationships. Japanese people have become much richer, leading much more liberated, convenient lifestyles, because of Japan's participation in global economics. But it is important to remember that today's economic prosperity is based on the exploitation of the Third World and a deteriorating global environment. If one compares today's situation with that of the old days, one must take into account the welfare of the entire planet, with the totality of its human population and natural environment, that is, seeing our planet as a whole, as a huge land community or an organism. To see the whole Earth as an organism, like a global village, is, however, not an easy task in today's advanced scientific and technological society characterized by international capitalism, liberalism, individualism, and so on. If we imagine the future generations who will suffer from environmental catastrophe, we can only conclude that today's crisis is too serious to be neglected.

NOTES

My thanks to J. B. Callicott, whose help made this essay clearer and more elegant. In translating Professor Callicott's *Earth's Insights* into Japanese, I learned much about the Western way of thinking. I believe that collaborations such as this with a distinguished Western environmental philosopher are most necessary in today's philosophical environment. My thanks are also due to Professor James McRae, who helped me to prepare the conference paper on which this chapter is based. In the following notes, the place of publication for Japanese sources is Tokyo unless otherwise indicated.

Epigraphs. J. B. Callicott, "Toward a Global Environmental Ethic," in *Worldviews and Ecology: Religion, Philosophy, and the Environment,* ed. M. E. Tucker and J. A. Grim (Maryknoll, NY: Orbis Books, 1994), 32. Tu Wei-ming, *Centrality and Commonality: An Essay on Confucian Religiousness* (Albany: State University of New York Press, 1989), 67. M. E. Tucker, "Ecological Themes in Taoism and Confucianism," in Tucker and Grim, *Worldviews and Ecology,* 157.

1. See Tsuchida Atsushi, *Entropy and Ecology: The Science That Questions Life and Lifestyle* (in Japanese) (Daiamondo-sha, 1986).
2. *Timaeus,* 28c ff.
3. *Timaeus,* 30b ff.
4. See C. Merchant, *The Death of Nature: Women, Ecology and the Scientific Revolution* (San Francisco: Harper San Francisco, 1980), 105, 125.
5. M. E. Tucker, *Moral and Spiritual Cultivation in Japanese Neo-Confucianism: The Life and Thought of Kaibara Ekken* (Albany: State University of New York Press, 1989), 136. See also T. Yamauchi, "Kaibara Ekken: The Founder of Japanese Neo-Confucianism," *Memoirs of Osaka Kyoiku University,* ser. 1, *Humanities* 59, no. 2 (2011).
6. See T. Yamauchi, "The Confucian Environmental Ethics of Ogyū Sorai," in *Environmental Philosophy in the Asian Traditions of Thought,* ed. J. Baird Callicott and James McRae (Albany: State University of New York Press, 2014).
7. See Ogyū Sorai, *Talks on Politics,* in *Ogyū Sorai,* ed. Bitou Masahide (Chūkō-backs, 1983). See R. M. Hare, *Moral Thinking: Its Levels, Method and Point* (Oxford: Oxford University Press, 1981).

8. Tu Wei-ming, *Confucian Thought: Selfhood as Creative Transformation* (Albany: State University of New York Press, 1985), 30.

9. See Hare, *Moral Thinking,* part 1, "Levels"; and Peter Singer, *Practical Ethics,* 2nd ed. (Cambridge: Cambridge University Press, 1993), 92ff.

10. See Yamauchi, "Confucian Environmental Ethics of Ogyū Sorai."

11. See T. Yamauchi, "Sontoku's Environmental Ethics," *Hotoku Studies* 1 (2004).

12. Kodama Kota, ed., *Ninomiya Sontoku* (Chūkō-backs, 1984), 208.

13. See Tu Wei-ming, *Centrality and Commonality,* 78ff.

14. See Tu Wei-ming, *Confucian Thought,* 17.

Economic Growth, Human Well-Being, and the Environment 21

Workineh Kelbessa

The cleavage between developed and developing countries in contemporary discourse is misleading. In today's world, the older, modern terms of "North and South," "West and East," "First World and Third World," "developed and underdeveloped," seem intrinsically obsolete. The current context of increasing differentiation between countries encapsulated under these terms, the virtual disappearance of the so-called Second World, and problematic modernist connotations of such terms make their use questionable. The limitations notwithstanding, I will use them interchangeably throughout this chapter for lack of better terms. Their continued use, it has been argued, encourages a rethinking of patterns of inequality and power relations that the terms convey, rather than neglect or denial of their continuing significance under the guise of plurality and difference.

For early theorists and practitioners, development is a straightforward economic problem that should be studied by economists. They have focused on technical examination of mobilizing resources forcefully and efficiently so as to promote growth. They have, in the process, failed to examine critically societal value changes and environmental issues. Although some development ethicists have argued that development should involve normative and descriptive aspects and have correctly stated that development is ethical in character and should aim to promote human flourishing and reduce poverty, they have not paid attention to the environmental dimensions of development. In this chapter, I regard as sound the notion that development empowers people and involves economic well-being and accept the relevance of environmental care and social concerns. As Nigel Dower notes, "A form of development might be sustainable while being undemocratic, socially unjust or cruel to animals."[1] Accordingly, the term "environmentally sound development" is used here to refer to environmentally, socially, and economically justified development. This form of development also involves environmentally friendly indigenous knowledge and practices and promotes people-centered development.

Three-fourths of humanity lives in the Third World countries. Of these populations, 80 percent live in rural areas and depend largely on agricultural activities for their daily subsistence. Development as conceived by its founding fathers has not changed the living conditions of the majority of the people in the world. It has not only not overcome poverty; in some cases it has actually led to poverty, malnutrition, high rates of infant mortality, low life expectancy, high rates of morbidity, low rates of health care, low average productivity, and environmental degradation. While development is conceived both as the process of moving away from these evils to more satisfactory levels of life expectancy, health, literacy, and productivity, and the condition of a society that has largely attained satisfactory levels, the reality on the ground contradicts such expectations.

The environmental consequences of destructive development have begun to show signs of massive degradation in almost all natural resource sectors, with serious implications for food production, famine, and increasing poverty. Moreover, the rate of environmental exploitation has been aggravated by pressure from developed nations of the West that, while in the minority, consume 80 percent of the world's carrying capacity, thereby rapidly depleting available resources to sustain their industrial development. Paul Hawken has explained this fact as follows: "The cornucopia of resources that are being extracted, mined, and harvested is so poorly distributed that 20 percent of the earth's people are chronically hungry or starving, while the top 20 percent of the population, largely in the north, control and consume 80 percent of the world's wealth."[2] Some Northern countries have harmed the environment in the South through such direct acts as the dumping of hazardous wastes and the relocation of polluting industries. In this chapter, therefore, I aim at examining how and why development theory and practice have failed to make a difference and try to show the interconnections among economic growth, human well-being, and the natural environment.

Development Theory and Practice

Different schools of development theory have approached the economic problems of the so-called Third World countries in various ways. Among others, growth theory was popular from the late 1940s to mid-1950s. Growth theorists attacked the orthodox classical theory of development for being static and ignoring the structural rigidities that prevented markets from responding to price changes in developing countries. They favored the Keynesian interventionist school because they believed that the structural transformation of a society is impossible without state intervention. For them economic growth is a unilinear process and identical with development. Economic growth is the central feature of the dominant paradigm of development. The proponents of this view seem to believe that all social problems are fundamentally economic. In spite of its failure to address the socio-economic and political problems of Third World countries, growth theory has influenced subsequent development theories associated with the modernization approach. According to John Brohman, "In many ways modernization theory represented a deepening and extension of the basic conceptual apparatus of growth theory."[3]

The international economic order established after the Second World War and the competition between the superpowers led to the rise of modernization theory. The United States and the Organization for Economic Cooperation and Development countries endeavored to influence countries in the South by offering "capitalist growth and modernization to counter the Soviet Union's proposal for socialist development."[4] Thus, the development era began after the Second World War. It should be noted that it was President Harry Truman who, on January 20, 1949, for the first time designated countries in the South as "underdeveloped areas." "Suddenly, a seemingly indelible concept was established, cramming the immeasurable diversity of the South into one single category—the underdeveloped."[5] Truman and modernization theorists believed that all countries were moving along the same track, and Third World countries should participate in the development race, catching up with the lead runners by avoiding old ways of living, patterns of work, and modes of knowing, webs of loyalties, and rules of governance.[6]

In spite of the drawbacks of colonialism in non-European countries, modernization theorists have considered development as the transfer of the technological fruits of science to developing countries. They argue that modern values will be diffused through education and technology transfer to the elites of the Third World countries. They have suggested that the backwardness of the South, Africa, for example, was an "original" backwardness, something primeval that could be overcome through Western know-how and capital.[7] The dominant paradigm thus aims to reduce the gap between rich and poor countries and thereby tackle absolute poverty in the developing world. However, rather than alleviating the so-called developing countries from the shackles of backwardness and poverty, modernization as practice has led to further subordination of these countries at the global economic level and increased poverty and deprivation. Development policies based on modernization theory have damaged the environment and people's health.

There are some development theorists who advocate a modification of that dominant paradigm. They maintain that some kind of intervention or direction from central institutions such as governments is required to facilitate the reduction of poverty. "Modifications (within mainstream development economics/studies) of this economic growth model included 'growth with equity' (i.e., growth with mechanisms, generally state-directed ones, to redistribute wealth in favor of the poor), and 'basic needs' theories, again targeting the poor with programs designed to meet basic needs."[8] Dependency theory, on the other hand, which began as a radical challenge to the optimism of the old established theories, inverted many of the assumptions of modernization theory.

Many dependency writers think that dependency is applicable to all the Third World countries. Most agree that development and underdevelopment are two aspects of the same economic process in the sense that the expansion of capitalism leads to the development of metropolises and the underdevelopment of satellites. Some dependency writers argue that so-called developed countries took the normal path of capitalist development while Third World countries were forced to be integrated into the capitalist economy on an inherently unequal basis. Consequently, Third World countries became the producers of primary products and raw materials. In order to explain the general pattern of dependency, there are some dependency theorists who employed the model of the metropolis-satellite or center-periphery relationship. In this model, the center represents all advanced countries, whereas the periphery encompasses all poor countries. The center exploits the periphery by extracting surplus through foreign investment, trade (unequal exchange), foreign aid and loans, and technology transfers. Moreover, within the peripheral regions, local elites align themselves with the center and exploit the rural population.[9] Some dependency writers cite external factors as the cause of the underdevelopment of Third World countries. They stress that the historical heritage of colonialism and the perpetuation of the unequal international division of labor are the main causes of underdevelopment. Theotonio dos Santos, Osvaldo Sunkel, and Celso Furtado emphasize the interaction between internal and external factors of underdevelopment. In particular, Fernando Henrique Cardoso gives due attention to the role of internal factors.[10] Early dependency writers restrict themselves to the analysis of economic conditions. They see dependency as the result of the flow of economic surplus from the periphery to the center. They underline that, with the continual flow of surplus from the periphery to the center, genuine capitalist development is unthinkable. Hence, according to them, dependency and development are incompatible. Cardoso and Enzo Faletto argue to the contrary that dependency and development can go together. Cardoso, for instance, proposes that a dependent capitalist or associated dependent capitalist is possible in the periphery.

Dependency writers have put forward different proposals to solve the problems faced by underdeveloped countries. A considerable number of them suggest that radical structural change should take place so as to eradicate the structure of the metropolis-satellite relation. A delinking of ties with imperialism, they think, will enable underdeveloped countries to promote genuine autocentric economic development and accumulation and prevent surplus transfer from the periphery to the metropolitan countries. They argue that without replacing the neocolonial state by a revolutionary state, the chances for delinking from the capitalist framework will be blocked and whatever development there is will remain dependent development. In order to avoid the unequal relationship between Third World countries and advanced capitalist countries, they argue, the links between developed and underdeveloped countries should be broken. Dependency theorists think that, through socialist revolution, peripheral countries will be able to build free and independent societies. Socialist revolution is also the means of avoiding the old ruling elites, who previously favored foreigners. Thus, subordinate classes in underdeveloped countries will be the leaders of the revolution. Although most of them advocate social revolution as an effective means to reduce economic disparities in the world system, their proposals differ from Marxism, because they believe that industrialization is not a prerequisite for a liberating revolution. They argue against internationalism and support the process of delinking from the capitalist framework.[11] They therefore advised peripheral countries to disassociate themselves from the world market and capitalist countries and strive for self-reliance. They do not in fact mean self-reliance to be complete isolation from other peripheral countries; they recommend cooperation with other peripheral and socialist countries.

While dependency theory appealed to many Third World countries, it received severe criticism at the theoretical level and was undermined by the success of the newly industrialized countries. For instance, following Cardoso's analysis, G. Palma contends that the thesis that capitalist development in Latin America is impossible and other related ideas of dependency writers are erroneous.[12] These critics thus propose that dependency and development can go together. According to So, "Countries such as Canada are 'dependent' in the sense that their economies have been penetrated by foreign-owned subsidiaries, yet Canada exhibits a standard of living higher than that of most Third World Countries."[13]

There are those who have stressed that the policy recommendations of dependency theorists cannot help Third World countries to address the problems of development. The Tanzanian experience in the 1970s is regarded as an example of the failure of dependency theory. After independence, Tanzanian leaders and intellectuals tried to translate the recommendations of dependency theorists into practical policies. They made valiant attempts to revitalize traditional African socialism. Regrettably, however, the new experiment did not generate positive results. The country experienced economic crises during the mid-1970s. "Thus . . . we might say that the Tanzanian experience during the 1970s once again proved that the real world is far more complex than the dependency school figured it to be."[14]

In spite of these drawbacks, the dependency school has had a considerable impact on development theory and practice. Among others, the works of dependency theorists have paved the way for the serious study of development problems in Third World countries.[15] They have provided a catalyst for further research into industrialization, state-society relations, class formation, ideology, and the like. The influence of dependency theory is reflected in the politicization of development at international, national, and grassroots levels. Third World countries, for instance, formed different groups, such as the nonaligned movement, so as to challenge the influence of developed countries. Dependency theory also influenced the proponents of the notion of empowerment.[16] Many anti-imperialist and anticolonial movements employed in their struggles the theoretical and political theories of dependency writers.[17] It has been found as well that the dependency writers' analysis of the terms of trade and unequal exchange is sound.[18] Dependency theorists also have challenged the doctrine of comparative advantage, arguing that the technological and financial imbalance between developed and developing countries has harmful consequences. I think such a view still reflects the present economic conditions of underdeveloped countries. The state of underdevelopment of the so-called Third World persists and becomes even more entrenched. Furthermore, the gap between advanced and underdeveloped countries, instead of narrowing, has been widening.

Marxist theory emphasizes the importance of economic planning and state intervention in the process of development. In most cases, Marxist theory approaches the market's private initiative as a component of exploitation. Experience, however, has shown that orthodox socialism as perceived by Marxist-Leninist scholars and politicians has failed to produce economic development that is superior to capitalism. In fact, socialism as a development model began to be challenged in the 1980s and early 1990s. By the turn of the 1990s, the winds of change had destroyed the former Soviet Union and other socialist countries. Consequently, we witnessed the resurgence of the neoclassical theory of development. Neoliberals stress that market institutions, if only they are left alone, would promote economic growth.[19] Some of the former socialist countries and the Third World countries have introduced systemic reforms that involve privatization and significant liberalization.

The proponents of free trade and capitalism argue that it is poor government practice, rootless businessmen, corruption, and lack of knowledge in Third World countries that are mainly responsible for global environmental crises. They keep saying that noncapitalist countries have more problems than capitalist countries do. In particular, neoliberals proclaim that capitalism is capable of controlling environmental problems. However, the neoliberal development model, which has been practiced for decades in many countries, has aggravated the condition of poorer people and has led to the concentration of power and wealth in a few unaccountable transnational corporations.

Powerful capitalist countries have created various multilateral international trade instruments and have continued to exploit powerless Third World countries and the natural environment. Third World countries are too poor and powerless to challenge these countries. Environmental laws and principles are required to be subservient to international trade treaties. And the General Agreement on Tariffs and Trade (GATT) has challenged governmental export controls. The exponents of GATT argue that "A government trying to conserve scarce resources by restricting their export will violate GATT."[20] Also, under GATT, national governments are required to remove foreign investment requirements, export quotas, local procurements, and technology specifications. Thus, free trade has very little to contribute to environmental protection. In global free trade, what is valuable is decided by money. Big companies have been able to externalize environmental and social costs.

The economic pressures in the Third World countries and the desire to earn foreign exchange have forced them to export their natural resources to First World countries. Hence, resources have flooded up from the poor to the rich. Furthermore, some countries have allowed unaccountable transnational corporations to carry on an unregulated exploitation of natural forests. The decline in commodity prices has further aggravated the economic situation in Third World countries.

Many Third World countries were forced to borrow heavily in the late 1970s and early 1980s. The conservation strategies of the Third World countries have been influenced by World Bank and International Monetary Fund (IMF) development policies. These institutions have suggested minimalist state intervention in the economies of the Third World. As a result, the vast majority of state enterprises were sold off to private companies. The governments of these countries reduced public spending on health, education, and social services. Local elites and foreign transnationals have been the main beneficiaries of these measures. Third World governments are being forced by the World Bank and the IMF to redirect spending away from public services and publicly owned enterprises into servicing debt.

The foregoing discussion indicates that, contrary to the expectations of Western capitalist countries and some development theorists, sixty years of development experience reveals a yawning gap between theory and practice. The sole beneficiaries of development are the global middle and upper classes in the North and small groups of elites in the South. At the same time, development-era and foreign-sponsored conservation programs have led to irreversible destruction of the regenerative powers of nature and the underdevelopment of hundreds of millions of people.[21] Donor governments and agencies as well as national governments in the global South encouraged environmentally destructive approaches to agriculture in the name of modernization.

Denis Goulet notes that development is a two-edged sword, simultaneously a creator and destroyer of values.[22] It brings material and technological gains and new freedoms but also breeds injustice, destroys cultures, damages environments, and generalizes *anomie*. He adds, "By thrusting the rural poor into mass impersonal urban settings and competitive monetary circuits, development destroys solidarity systems—extended families, caste associations, village and ethnic networks—founded on principles of reciprocal obligations."[23] In fact, it is also true that in the traditional "solidarity system," people were also often, poor, illiterate, and suffering from different problems.

The development measures of conventional approaches are also flawed. Gross domestic product fails to measure products consumed within the family and services exchanged informally, as it only "measures that part of production sold for a price in a formal market." Accordingly, "conventional" accounting procedures ignore or underestimate a major portion of the economic activity in many Third World countries.[24] This led Peet and Hartwick to conclude that "all conventional economic theories of growth and development are hopelessly flawed because economics harbors deeply within its structure an unrealistic and biased view of the world."[25] Critics of conventional development theories call for a thorough revision. In the words of Peet and Hartwick, "Conventional thinking about modernity, growth, and development, so defined, is hopelessly, dangerously, and perversely blind to its structural deficiencies and devoid of real alternatives taken seriously in the centers of power. The future existence of the world's people depends on breaking this utterly deficient style of developmental thought."[26]

In the 1990s, the United Nations Development Program *Human Development Reports* seemed to have looked at development from a different angle. From this perspective, human development is the end and economic development the means.[27] As stated earlier, development has conventionally been defined as a process of change aimed at attaining economic growth (a rapid and sustained rise in real output per capita). Such a definition, however, does not give sufficient attention to human and social transformation. A high economic growth rate does not necessarily suggest higher levels of human development. This gap between income and human development (for instance, levels of life expectancy and literacy) is manifested in many countries, both developed and developing. In these instances, economic growth has improved the status of the already wealthy people while undermining the basis of survival for the poor. The so-called trickle-down effect—where eventually everyone benefits from growth as income trickles down from the rich—does not work. Recently, however, some development theorists and the United Nations Development Program in its *Human Development Reports* have questioned this approach and paid attention to the role of human development.[28] There is a growing recognition that human development is intended to promote human well-being. The main parameters of human well-being include health, literacy, life expectancy, community, rule of law, liberty, and the exercise of choice or control over one's life.[29]

As can be judged from the discussion so far, genuine development is often to be contrasted with the policies of the IMF, World Bank, and the like. Genuine development requires a restructuring of the international economic system, as Paul Ekins argues.[30] Without an appreciation or recognition of the causes of previous failures of development strategies, hegemonic forces will never be able to contribute to workable solutions for development problems.

Economic Growth, Human Well-Being, and the Environment

The theory about a good life is not new. The difference between a good life and material possessions was conceptualized in ancient Greece. Some philosophers stressed that the fullness of human good and the possession of many goods are not the same. For Aristotle, "the amount of property which is needed for a good life is not unlimited."[31] Although he recognized the importance of property for human beings to live temperately and liberally, he made the following observation: "It should not be thought that the man who is to be happy will need many or great possessions, merely because it is not possible to be blessed without external goods."[32] Moreover, Aristotle offers normative guidance to economists:

> The economist ought to possess four qualities in relation to wealth. He ought to be able to acquire it and to guard it; otherwise there is no advantage in acquiring it, but it is a case of drawing water with a sieve, or the proverbial jar with a hole in it. Further, he ought to be able to order his possessions aright and make a proper use of them; for it is for these purposes that we require wealth.[33]

This idea might be in sharp contradiction to his belief that slaves and non-Greeks should be treated as "animals." It was not clear whether he gave this advice to Alexander the Great. Fifteen centuries later Thomas Aquinas cites Aristotle with approval, saying "It is better to pursue wisdom than riches, though riches are more useful when you are in need."[34]

Before the emergence of development ethics, individuals who analyzed development in value terms include the Frenchman L. J. Lebret and Swedish economist Gunnar Myrdal.[35] According to Lebret, "Societies are more human or more developed, not when men and women 'have more' but when they are enabled 'to be more.' "[36] From this perspective development should be judged on the basis of qualitative human enrichment rather than on the basis of increased production or material well-being alone. Similarly, Placide Tempels stresses that the manner in which the human person is treated is more important than material prowess. He raises the following questions: Do the improvements of the material conditions of life "constitute 'civilization'? Is not civilization, above all else, progress in human personality?"[37] Tempels is of the opinion that, for all its material achievements, the West neglects human beings. Thus, Tempels criticizes the West for its excessive immersion in material pursuits and comforts. Barry Lopez, a student of Native American societies, echoes this view, defining wealth as follows: "Some native ideas could serve us well in this historical moment: that a concept of wealth should be founded in physical health and spiritual well-being, not material possessions; that to be 'poor' is to be without family, without a tribe—without people who care deeply for you."[38] There are, as well, some development ethicists who have criticized the mainstream development discourse. They define wealth differently and emphasize the role of development ethics in resolving the moral quandaries raised by development policies and practice. Development ethics examines normative and value questions around the analysis of competing models of the good life, the just society, theories of human need, strategies for social change, and so on.

Denis Goulet, considered the father and initiator of development ethics, reflected on the relationship between ethics and development from the 1960s and has influenced scholars, international financial institutions, and practitioners. On the basis of his academic training in philosophy, political science, and social planning as well as grassroots or project experience in numerous countries, Goulet tries to address "the ethical and value questions posed by development theory, planning and practice."[39] According to Goulet, conventional images of development are ethically deficient in several ways. In the first place, he characterizes the image of a mass consumption paradise as a cruel illusion because it cannot be attained by all, given limited resources. Moreover, the growth paradigm of development failed to pay sufficient attention to equity in the distribution of aggregate gross national product by assigning priority to its quantitative development. Development professionals talk about development in purely descriptive terms by ignoring a normative view of development. They describe a certain quantitative level of performance, a certain gross national product, a certain investment ratio, a certain level of trading activity, a certain structure of employment. The growth paradigm paves the way for the destruction of cultural values, local institutions, and networks of solidarity because it favors modernity and undermines local and national self-reliance and perpetuates relationships of dependency. At the same time, growth-oriented strategies have proven to be both wasteful of resources and environmentally destructive because they have concentrated on aggregate gains in industrial output, export trade, and financial earnings without paying sufficient attention to environmental issues.[40]

"Development is above all else a question of values and human attitudes, self-defined goals, and criteria for determining what are tolerable costs to be borne in the course of change."[41] Like David Pollock, Goulet suggests that transcendental values should be one of the essential components of development. Pollock writes:

> Let us assume that a country's economic pie increases. Let us further assume that there is a heightened degree of equity in the way the fruits of that economic pie are distributed. Let us, finally, assume that decisions affecting production and consumption of the economic pie—nationally and internationally—involve the full participation of all affected parties. Is that the end of the matter? Does man live by GNP alone? Perhaps the latter has been the prevailing line of thought throughout the postwar period since, in the short-run, policy makers must focus primarily upon the pressing issue of increased incomes for the masses; particularly for those below the poverty line. But, despite the obvious importance of such short-run objectives, we should also be asking ourselves other, more uplifting questions. Should we not take advantage of our longer-term vision and ask what kind of person Latin America may wish to evolve by the end of this century? What are the transcendental values—cultural, ethical, artistic, religious, moral—that extended beyond the current workings of the purely economic and social system? How to appeal to youth, who so often seek nourishment in dreams, as well as in bread? What, in short, should be the new face of the Latin American Society in the future, and what human values should lie behind the new countenance.[42]

Goulet characterized those who reduced development to the pursuit of material well-being and ignored political and religio-cultural components as "one-eyed giants."[43] He laments:

> They analyze, prescribe, and act as if humans could live by bread alone, as if human destiny could be stripped down to its material dimensions alone. High indices of suicide in developed countries hint at the truth that material abundance may be less essential—even for survival—than is the presence of *meaning*. In order to survive one must want to survive, but how can one want to survive unless one's life has a meaning? Indeed, having a meaningful existence may well be the most basic of all human needs.[44]

According to Goulet, qualitative human enrichment rather than growth in production or material well-being is the true indicator of development, although he concedes that there is a need for quantitative increases in goods and services.[45] A good life does not necessarily mean having an abundance of goods, although possession of enough goods is important. "Abundance of goods and fullness of goods are not synonymous: one may *have* much and be mediocre or *have* little and *be* rich. Nevertheless, we need to have a certain quantity of goods in order to be fully human, and certain kinds of goods enhance our being more than others."[46] Goulet stresses that being should come before having. Having is not the essence of being. He defended his view by appealing to the views of the "great masters of living":

> Yet the great masters of Living have made the alternative between having and being a central issue of their respective systems. The Buddha teaches that in order to arrive at the highest stage of human development, we must not crave possessions. Jesus teaches: "For whosoever will save his life shall lose it; but whosoever will lose his life for my sake, the same shall save it. For what is a man advantaged, if he gain the whole world, and lose himself, or be cast away?" (Luke 9:24–25) Master Eckhart taught that to have nothing and make oneself open and "empty," not to let one's ego stand in one's way, is the condition for achieving spiritual wealth and strength. Marx taught that luxury is as much a vice as poverty and that our goal should be to be much, not to have much. (I refer here to the real Marx, the radical humanist, not to the vulgar forgery presented by Soviet communism.)[47]

What has been discussed so far suggests that we should avoid the extreme positions of materialism and anti-materialism that have different attitudes toward the acquisition and possession of commodities and human well-being. For materialism, well-being is based on worldly goods, especially those that bring comfort and convenience.[48] Anti-materialism, on the other hand, emphasizes the freedom from all attachments to material goods, although some more moderate forms of anti-materialism recognize the importance of both material and nonmaterial realities.[49]

As David Crocker notes, neither approach enables us to promote well-being. On the one hand, commodities *by themselves* cannot give meaning to life. On the other hand, certain goods and services are important to the physical aspects of human well-being. It is true that humans need economic growth to lead a good life, to have choices, to have more control over their environment than if they remained poor, and to avoid economic depression, unemployment, human suffering, poverty, and misery. But the question is: In order to become more, how much is enough? One may suggest that the goods that satisfy the basic biological needs of humans can be enough. Goulet proposes that, because of the fact that human life is more than mere survival, a full stomach, or a warm body, goods that enable humans to meet the goals of development that all individuals and societies desire, namely, optimal life sustenance, esteem, and freedom, can be considered enough.[50] The quality of life can be dehumanized by both the absolute insufficiency of goods and relative excess.[51] Crocker also suggests that "We must seek to replace materialism and anti-materialism with a balanced and stable conception of the sources and meaning of well-being."[52]

It is important to note that most people in developing countries still derive their primary source of meaning from religious beliefs, symbols, practices, and mysteries.[53] According to Goulet:

> in rich and poor countries alike, a growing chorus of voices proclaims that full human development is not possible without regard for essential religious values. They assert that achievements in political, social, economic, technical, artistic, and scientific realms do not exhaust the creativity, beauty, or triumphs of which

human beings are capable. Development thus appears both as a grandiose historical task and as a summons—or an opening—to transcendence.[54]

Thus, development agents should not treat religious and other indigenous values in a purely instrumental fashion. A noninstrumental treatment of traditional values shows that they harbor within them a latent dynamism, which, when properly respected, can serve as the springboard for modes of development that are more humane than those derived from outside paradigms. When development builds on indigenous values, it exacts lower social costs and imposes less human suffering and cultural destruction than when it copies outside models.[55]

However, traditional ideas alone cannot be the basis for action. What is required is a critical re-examination of old values in the light of modern diagnoses of human needs for a better life. According to Goulet, the central task of development ethics is to provide wise normative guidance in order to choose between producing a decent sufficiency of essential goods for everyone or adopting incentive systems that allow a few to have more while the masses are left without enough.[56] Development ethics is required in order to "diagnose value conflicts, to assess policies (actual and possible), and to validate or refute valuations placed on development performance."[57] The instrumental treatment of values alone is not sufficient for development ethicists to discharge their function. They need to subject development critically to "the values tests of justice, human enhancement, spiritual liberation, and reciprocal relations. It is these values that judge development, not vice versa."[58] Goulet also contends that the primary mission of development ethics is "to keep hope alive."[59]

Other Western philosophers for their part have shown the link between economic growth and human well-being, emphasizing that human well-being should be the goal of development.[60] Dower, for instance, states that progress in human well-being/flourishing should be the central concern of development and stresses that economic growth and industrialization are only means to certain ends, not ends in themselves.[61] Paul Streeten and Amartya Sen have also emphasized the ethical dimensions of development. According to Sen, the goal of development is not economic growth, industrialization, or modernization but rather expansion of people's "valuable capabilities and functionings," "what people can or cannot do, e.g., whether they can live long, escape avoidable morbidity, be well nourished, be able to read and write and communicate, take part in literacy and scientific pursuits, and so forth."[62] Sen stresses that development is required to enhance capability (i.e., a person's ability to do valuable acts or reach valuable states of being). So, for him commodities or opulence, utilitarian happiness or preference satisfaction, are not the major elements of a standard of living. Instead, human well-being should be explained in terms of certain valuable human functionings and capabilities. "If we value the capability to function, then that is what we do value, and the possession of goods with the corresponding characteristics is only instrumentally valued and that again only to the extent that it helps in the achievement of the things that we do value (namely, capabilities)."[63] Accordingly, in the capability approach, we are not required to value only *desire fulfillment* and happiness, as the state of being happy is one among several objects of value. Sen also recognizes the importance of "material capabilities" in judging the standard of living of people in poor countries. The following questions need to be answered in order to judge the standard of living of people: "Are they well nourished? Are they free from avoidable morbidity? Do they live long? Can they read and write? Can they count?"[64]

Sen's "capability approach" leads us to look at the range of life options that people have (their "capabilities set") and the actual things they do and achieve (their "functionings"), rather than just looking at their incomes or their declared state of satisfaction, which can by themselves be missing. In this way, he urges us to consider development as an extension of the range of attainable and worthwhile life options that people have.

Martha C. Nussbaum, for her part, favors what she calls the "capabilities approach." According to her, central human functional capabilities include life, bodily health and integrity, pleasure and pain, senses, imagination, thought, emotions, practical reason, affiliation, other species, play, separateness, and strong separateness.[65] In her view, the "capabilities approach" claims that "a life that lacks any one of these capabilities, no matter what else it has, will fall short of being a good human life."[66] Relying on Aristotle's ethic of human flourishing and the works of Sen and Nussbaum, Crocker identified four kinds of valuable capabilities (and functionings): physical well-being, mental well-being, social well-being, and what Nussbaum calls "separateness." Crocker stresses that to lead a good life, we need to promote balance and harmony among the four kinds of valuable capabilities (and functionings). "Too much or too little of a good thing in one dimension may decrease our overall well-being in one or more of the others."[67]

Since 1987 the International Development Ethics Association (IDEA) has also questioned the mainstream development paradigm by encouraging systematic research and publication in development ethics. The major aims of IDEA are

- to apply ethical reflection to development goals and strategies and to relations between the (developed) North and (under- or undeveloped) South;

- to effect ethically sound development policies, institutions, and practices;

- to promote solidarity, mutual support, and interchange among those development theorists and practitioners throughout the world who are seeking to implement ethically better development and strategies.[68]

Some development ethicists, however, have not sufficiently shown the interlinkage between economic growth, human well-being, and the natural environment. They have focused on the link between normative and descriptive aspects of development. They stress that development ethics originated as the "ethics of Third World development" and that development ethicists should be committed to understanding and reducing human deprivation and misery in poor countries. In his later work David Crocker seems, in fact, to consider all societies as developing. He writes, "International development ethics is moral reflection on the ends and means of societal and global change."[69]

Development ethicists do not agree among themselves whether the focus of development ethics should be Third World, international, or global. The founding fathers of development, it should be stressed, argue that development is only the problem of the Third World or developing countries. In the same way, for most Western development ethicists, development ethics deals exclusively with the development conditions of poor countries, as if advanced countries do not need any development. Unlike development ethicists who assert that international development ethics is ethical reflection on the ends and means of socioeconomic change in poor countries and regions, I would suggest that development ethics should also look at the impact of global powers on the people and the planet Earth. Development ethics should deal with development issues in all countries, including rich countries. As Goulet persuasively notes:

> No nation is fully developed in all respects, for no nation adequately meets the real needs of all its members, and in no society are all essential relationships organised satisfactorily. Not surprisingly, therefore, many who enjoy material ease, in rich and poor countries alike, complain that their life or work does not seem fulfilling, and that they feel no sense of community around them. Their laments suggest the need for a normative, and not a purely descriptive, conception of development.[70]

Unlike some development ethicists, Goulet stresses the interlinkage between development and nature. He suggests that humans should balance human freedom and nature and consider them as relative values:

> Sound development enjoins and practices ecological wisdom, just as ecological wisdom (integrally and comprehensively understood) promotes sound and harmonious human development. What is urged here is not some passive stance in which no human interventions will be made upon nature to promote some sort of economic growth. Rather, the scope and content of that growth will be redefined and renegotiated to assure just and adequate access to essential goods by all, and to protect biosystematic sustainability.[71]

Although different groups give priority to either nature or freedom, Goulet suggests that different values:

> ought to enjoy parity of moral status because any long-term, sustainable equity-enhancing combat against poverty requires wisdom in the exploitation of resources, just as the preservation of species cannot persuasively be held out as a priority goal if the human species is threatened with degrading poverty or extinction. Nature itself is diminished when its human members are kept "underdeveloped"; reciprocally, human members cannot become truly "developed" if their supportive nature is violated.[72]

There are, on the other hand, some organizations and writers who have discussed the basic features of sustainability in order to show the relationship between environmental and developmental issues. The International Union for the Conservation of Nature used the concept of sustainable development in its report in 1980. This concept was given more emphasis in the Brundtland Report, which suggests that the international community should work toward sustainable development.[73] The idea of sustainable development was designed to accommodate economic development and environmental concerns and assumed that environmental capacity can satisfy human needs. A new development path was conceived that aims to relieve poverty and sustain environmental capacity. Thus, the principle of sustainable development is formulated as follows: "development that meets the needs of the present without compromising the ability of future generations to meet their own needs."[74]

It should be noted that in the 1980s, countries in the South gave priority to development so as to overcome poverty and reverse global inequalities. In contrast, countries in the North gave priority to nature. The United Nations Conference on Environment and Development, held in Rio de Janeiro in 1992, embraced the idea of sustainable development, as it appears to accommodate the concerns of developed countries, which favor environmental protection, as well as developing countries, which suspected that the former tried to limit development progress in the South by denying access to methods used by Northern countries in their industrialization processes. The authors of the Brundtland Report and delegates at the Rio conference believed that the concept "sustainable development" could address both development and environment concerns in an integrated manner at global, national, and local levels. They emphasized that the preservation of the natural resource base is the foundation of economic and social progress. Although the Brundtland Report links issues of intragenerational equity with those of intergenerational equity, it does not have a clear proposal for environmental protection.[75]

Sustainable development, according to Alan Holland, proceeds from the connection between human well-being and states of the natural world. He writes that "there are conceptions of the human good that make a concern for nature for its own sake a contributing or even constitutive factor in human well-being. In this way human interest and ecological integrity do not just happen to coincide, but exhibit an interlocking conceptual relationship."[76] Goulet for his part emphasizes a fivefold need for sustainability:

> Sustainability is needed in five domains: economic, political, social, cultural, and environmental. Long-term economic and environmental viability requires using resources in a way which does not irreversibly deplete them. Political viability rests on creating for all members of society a stake in its survival: this cannot be achieved unless all enjoy freedom and inviolable personal rights and believe that the political system within which they live pursues some common good and not mere particular interests. Finally, if development is to be socially and culturally sustainable, the foundations of community and symbolic meaning systems must be protected. Otherwise, they will be steam-rolled into oblivion under the pretext of submitting to the requirements of scientific and technological "rationality."[77]

Holland laments that the transition to environmental sustainability and redistributive social and economic policies has been hampered by certain characteristics of the present global economy, for example, the mobility of labor and capital and the centralization of knowledge and power.[78] Following other writers, Robin Attfield contends that sustainable development depends on the transformation of the structures of international aid, trade, and debt and the cooperation of the countries in the South to preserve their biodiversity and to research pathways for biotechnical development. It might also depend, he suggests, on superseding international capitalism or subjecting it to global regulation to curtail its inherent tendencies to unsustainability.[79] In Attfield's opinion, global resources can be protected through international treaties complemented by global citizenship, as embodied in transnational groups and groupings, international peace groups, and federations of trade unions, minorities, and ethnic groups such as the Environmental Justice Movement.

The facts on the ground, however, do not bear out Attfield's faith. Neither international organizations, including the United Nations, nor popular movements have so far been able to compel transnational corporations and capitalism to be environmentally friendly and to respect international treaties. Powerful industrialized countries can ignore regional and global environmental and developmental treaties and continue to destroy the environment. Although there exist economic policy instruments intended to compel environmental action, environmentalists and like-minded countries have no real power to force compliance with environmental laws. In the end, power seizes knowledge for its own ends and marginalizes ethics.

The fact is that developmental and environmental issues are not simply ethical questions that are resolvable merely by moral persuasion. Political power must be taken into account. In order to address global problems there have to be major changes at both the political and ethical levels.

There are those who believe that the idea of sustainable growth is not feasible because there is a limit to growth. Ecological economists like Herman Daly argue that economic growth cannot continue indefinitely:

> Even "green growth" is not sustainable. There is a limit to the population of trees the earth can support, just as there is a limit to the populations of humans and of automobiles. To delude ourselves into believing that growth is still possible and desirable if only we label it "sustainable" or color it "green" will justly delay the inevitable transition and make it more painful.[80]

He suggests that the current use of the term "sustainable development" as a synonym for the oxymoronic "sustainable growth" must be abandoned. "Sustainable development" should, rather, be understood as " 'development without growth,'—i.e., qualitative improvement of a physical economic base that is maintained in a steady state by a throughput of matter-energy that is within the regenerative and assimilative capacities of the ecosystem. . . . Sustainable development must be development without growth—but with population control and wealth redistribution—if it is to be a serious attack on poverty."[81] For Daly, development refers to qualitative improvement, which is the goal of human life.

However, for mainstream economists such as James Tobin, Robert Solow, and William B. Nordhaus, there is no limit to economic growth set by nature.[82] They argue to the contrary that human intelligence and ingenuity enable people to satisfy their preferences using alternatives to strained natural resources. For mainstream economists the only limits to economic expansion are those of human knowledge. Citing evidence that shows the potential conversion of sunlight to electricity, the use of water, wind, and biomass as the sources of energy, the prospects of "nonsolar alternatives, such as tidal power, which captures gravitational energy, and geothermal power, which employs heat coming from the earth's core," and the contingent relationship between economic growth and environmental degradation, Mark Sagoff questions the arguments of ecological economists. He notes that in some instances absence of economic growth rather than its presence can lead to environmental degradation. In other words, destitution is far worse for the environment than economic development because it can force people to overexploit their environment. He writes,

> No one believes that economic growth is likely to lead automatically to environmental protection. We have found no reason to agree with the contention of ecological economics, however, that growth in the sense of greater gross domestic product is unsustainable because it necessarily strains natural limits and leads automatically to resource depletion and ecological demise.[83]

Sagoff stresses that there is no necessary relationship between economic growth and environmental stress. Some Scandinavian countries with big gross domestic products have not devastated their environments. Instead, they have been protecting nature and supporting countries with smaller economies, like Poland, in their efforts to clean up the environmental mess. In agreement with mainstream economists, Sagoff asserts that "Ecological economists are unable to point to a single scarcity of natural capital that knowledge and ingenuity are unlikely to alleviate."[84]

While it may be true that there is no necessary connection between economic growth and environmental stress, I do not agree that knowledge and ingenuity can always solve developmental and environmental problems. Science and technology have not yet enabled human beings to address all environmental issues. At the current level of our knowledge, it is difficult to see how we can maintain sustainable development that is compatible with a high material standard of living, as presently defined, for all human populations. Accordingly, both capitalist and noncapitalist countries must acknowledge that unlimited growth for an indefinite period is simply not possible. They cannot have economic growth, and growth in consumption and pollution, indefinitely. Unabated accelerated misuse of the natural environment will lead to an array of long-term negative consequences—the decline of agriculture and of individual and community income, poverty, increased competition for scarce resources, loss of forest products, and the like—that will endanger the survival of present and future generations of human and nonhuman species. We already face global ecological problems, including rising sea levels, the melting of the polar icecaps, shortage of freshwater, and ozone layer depletion, that make clear the need to reexamine our worldviews and change our attitudes toward growth and natural resources. Ethics comes into it in helping us frame our ultimate goal from the point of view of some ideal or vision. There are grave imbalances in the current global system that must be addressed, and a necessary condition for addressing them is ethical clarification and rectification. Environmental philosophers and development ethicists have tried to stress these points and thereby encourage people to promote environmentally and socially sustainable development.

Conclusion

The problems faced by development theories illustrate the ambiguities surrounding the whole idea of development. Mainstream development discourse not only is produced in and by industrialized countries but is also enforced by the same hegemonic actors. Little attention is given to what is happening on the ground in developing countries. Development is thus currently a site of contestation where many scholars question not only how development has been practiced in the Third World but also how the discourse of development has been deployed to inform development practice.

Many writers have been preoccupied with social and economic concerns and have ignored human and environmental well-being. Development has been equated with economic growth. It has been argued, on the other hand, that development be distinguished from growth as measured simply by gross national product, which registers much economic activity not conducive to development and which takes no account of economic activity where no money changes hands. Development is "more than the sheer accumulation of worldly goods." I have suggested in this chapter the need for a consideration of the moral dimension of development theory and practice. Besides social and economic concerns, quality of life, cultural and environmental impact, and individual rights and freedoms need to be addressed. Development conceived simply as aggregate economic growth does not appear to have a future because various environmental and social problems make it unsustainable.

Development as conceptualized by the "founding fathers" has become a vehicle of disempowerment and bondage. In the development era, the people have not been sufficiently consulted regarding their environment and development issues. Modern scientists and donors have tried to impose their own theories of what constitutes development on the rural poor. The promotion of Western development models at the expense of indigenous knowledge and practice has long-term negative consequences for the former. Such models have very little to do with local realities or the wishes of the people on the land. International institutions of development assistance such as the World Bank and the IMF along with trade regimes such as that being negotiated within the World Trade Organization tend to promote large, in effect monocultural, projects. In agriculture, for example, this leads to a limited number of uniform crop varieties gaining dominance, with the production of same limited to highly specialized plant breeding and seed production institutions. This trend imposes serious limitations on farmers' abilities to develop and produce their own seeds and exchange them with other farmers, thereby limiting or eliminating the protection of farmer-bred varieties that are competitive in the market. Development and the solution of development problems should be grounded in people's cultural heritage and institutions, which enable them to live together in permanent harmony, develop agriculture and society, and utilize the natural resources of their local environment in an ecologically sustainable manner. We cannot apply development theory in exactly the same way in Ethiopia as in Europe. Development strategies should reflect the values, interests, concerns, and worldviews of the concerned people.

I have further suggested in this chapter that, in order to change the position of the poor and promote their interests in the current world order, global and multilateral institutions should be more inclusive, democratic, and equitable in terms of representation and voice. Accordingly, what are needed are fundamental democratic changes in the structures of global power such that the "weaker" countries that represent the vast majority of humanity are no longer weak and the "powerful" countries that represent a tiny minority of humanity—and perhaps have no one's real long-term interests at heart—are no longer powerful. What is undeniable to any rational and informed human being is that humanity as a whole must develop alternative attitudes toward the current world order. This imperative suggests that, even if only within the framework of a minimal utilitarian justificatory scheme, the global community has ethical obligations to assist the Third World countries to rid themselves of oppressive and exploitative global structures. Thus, instead of searching for short-term profits or looking only for immediate gratification, transnational corporations and other powerful players in the current world order should be forced to respect the knowledge, needs, aspirations, and voices of Third World nations.

Development ethics can help guide development policy and practice in both developing and developed countries. Development ethics should focus on ethical dimensions of development theory and planning and grassroots development projects and practice all the world over. It should examine the impact of global powers on the health of the planet Earth—international trade, capital flows, migration, environmental pacts, military intervention, and responses to human rights violations committed by prior regimes—as well as the moral responsibilities of transnational corporations and their host governments, and should address human deprivation in both developing and developed countries. If development ethics broadens its scope and addresses the injustice done to the majority of the people and to nonhuman species, it will have a paramount role in creating awareness within countries and globally about the actions of transnational corporations, irresponsible capitalist countries, and local industries that damage the environment. The efforts of the many may one day bring change in favor of the majority of the people, nonhuman species, and planet Earth. There are grounds for hope, but there is still a formidable distance to travel.

NOTES

This chapter is based on my article "Rethinking Development: The Need for Ethics in Development Theory and Practice" published in CIÊNCIA and TRÓPICO in 2011. I would like to thank David Chapple for his valuable comments on the earlier draft. I also benefited from the comments and suggestions made by the other East-West Philosophers' Conference participants in Honolulu, in May 2011, and the editors of the conference volume.

1. Nigel Dower, "Human Development—Friend or Foe to Environmental Ethics?" *Environmental Values* 9, no. 1 (2000), 44.

2. Paul Hawken, "A Declaration of Sustainability," in *Environmental Philosophy from Animal Rights to Radical Ecology,* 4th ed., ed. M. E. Zimmerman et al. (Upper Saddle River, NJ: Prentice Hall, 2005), 420.

3. John Brohman, *Popular Development: Rethinking the Theory and Practice of Development* (Oxford: Blackwell Publishers, 1996), 15.

4. Ibid., 11.

5. W. Sachs, "Global Ecology and the Shadow of 'Development,'" in *Deep Ecology for the Twenty-First Century,* ed. G. Sessions (Boston: Shambhala, 1995), 429.

6. Ibid., 429–430.

7. C. Leys, *The Rise and Fall of Development Theory* (Nairobi: EAEP, 1996), 9–11, 111.

8. N. Dower, "Development Ethics," in *Encyclopedia of Applied Ethics,* ed. R. Chadwick (London: Academic Press, 1998), 1:758.

9. Magnus Blomström and Björn Hettne, *Development Theory in Transition: The Dependency Debate and Beyond* (London: Zed Books, 1984); and K. Gardner and D. Lewis, *Anthropology, Development and the Post-Modern Challenge* (London: Pluto Press, 1996).

10. See Blomström and Hettne, *Development Theory in Transition,* 72.

11. Ibid.

12. G. Palma, "Dependency: A Formal Theory of Underdevelopment or a Methodology for the Analysis of Concrete Situations of Underdevelopment," *World Development* 6 (1978): 903–904.

13. Alvin Y. So, *Social Change and Development: Modernization, Dependency and World-System Theories* (London: Sage, 1990), 134.

14. Blomström and Hettne, *Development Theory in Transition,* 155.

15. Ibid., 195.

16. Gardner and Lewis, *Anthropology, Development and the Post-Modern Challenge,* 18–19.

17. Howard Nicholas, "Dependency: A Critical Assessment," *Upanathi* (1987), 143.

18. C. Kay, "The Latin American Contribution to Development Theory" (ISS Working Paper Series, no. 82, 1990), 22.

19. Colin Leys, *The Rise and Fall of Development Theory* (Nairobi: EAEP, 1996), 17–19.

20. P. Hawken, *The Ecology of Commerce* (New York: Harper Business, 1993), 100.

21. D. Goulet, "Development Ethics and Ecological Wisdom," in *Ethics of Environment and Development,* ed. J. R. Engel and J. G. Engel (London: Belhaven Press, 1990), 36.

22. D. Goulet, "Development: Creator and Destroyer of Values," *World Development* 20, no. 3 (1992), 467–475.

23. D. Goulet, "Development Ethics: A New Discipline," *International Journal of Social Economics* 24, no. 11 (1997), 491.

24. R. Peet and E. Hartwick, *Theories of Development: Contentions, Arguments, Alternatives,* 2nd ed. (New York: Guilford Press, 2009), 10.

25. Ibid., 15.

26. Ibid., 278; see also G. Esteva, "Development," in *The Development Dictionary,* ed. W. Sachs (London: Zed Books, 1992), 6–25; S. Amin, *Africa and the Challenge of Development: Essays by Samir Amin,* ed. C. Uroh (Ibadan: Hope Publishers, 1998).

27. United Nations Development Program, *Human Development Reports* (New York: United Nations, 1994).

28. See ibid.; Dower, "Human Development."

29. Dower, "Human Development," 40–41.

30. P. Ekins, "Making Development Sustainable," in *Global Ecology,* ed. W. Sachs (London: Zed Books, 1993), 91–103.

31. W. D. Ross, quoted in D. Goulet, "What Is a Just Economy in a Globalized World?" *International Journal of Social Economics* 29, nos. 1–2 (2002), 11.

32. R. Bambrough, quoted in ibid., 11.
33. W. D. Ross, quoted in ibid., 11.
34. Thomas Aquinas, quoted in ibid., 11.
35. For details see Goulet, "Development Ethics."
36. D. Goulet, *Development Ethics: A Guide to Theory and Practice* (New York: Apex Press, 1995), 6–7.
37. Placide Tempels, quoted in M. Kebede, *Africa's Quest for the Philosophy of Decolonization* (Amsterdam: Rodopi, 2004), 44.
38. Barry Lopez, quoted in Goulet, *Development Ethics,* 129.
39. D. Goulet, *The Uncertain Promise: Value Conflicts in Technology Transfer* (New York: IDOC/North America, 1977), 5.
40. For details see D. Goulet, "Culture and Traditional Values in Development," in *The Ethics of Development: The Pacific in the 21st Century,* ed. S. Stratigos and P. J. Hughes (Port Moresby: University of New Guinea Press, 1987), 171.
41. D. Goulet, *The Cruel Choice* (New York: Athenaeum, 1971).
42. Quoted in D. Goulet, "Doing Ethics in Development Arenas," *Journal of Regional Policy* 11, nos. 3–4 (1991), 604.
43. D. Goulet, "Development Experts: The One-Eyed Giants," *World Development,* nos. 7–8 (July–August 1980), 481–489.
44. D. Goulet, "Development: Historical Task or Opening to Transcendence?" *Cross Currents* 46, no. 2 (1996), 221–222.
45. Goulet, "Development Ethics," 1168; Goulet, "What Is a Just Economy," 22.
46. Goulet, *Development Ethics,* 53.
47. D. Goulet, "On Culture, Religion, and Development," in *Reclaiming Democracy: The Social Justice and Political Economy of Gregory Baum and Kari Polanyi Levitt,* ed. M. Mendell (Montreal: McGill-Queen's University Press, 2005), 28.
48. D. Crocker, "Consumption, Well-Being, and Capability," in *Ethics of Consumption: The Good Life, Justice, and Global Stewardship,* ed. D. A. Crocker and T. Linden (Lanham, MD: Rowman and Littlefield, 1998), 368.
49. Ibid., 369.
50. Goulet, *Development Ethics,* 55.
51. Ibid., 62.
52. Crocker, "Consumption, Well-Being, and Capability," 371.
53. Jeff Haynes, cited in Goulet, "Development: Historical Task," 222.
54. Ibid., 229.
55. Ibid., 225.
56. D. Goulet, "The Challenge of Development Economics," *Communications and Development Review* 2, no. 1 (1978): 18–23.
57. Goulet, "Development Ethics," 1168.
58. D. Goulet, *Incentives for Development: The Key to Equity* (New York: New Horizon Press, 1989), 94.
59. Goulet, "Development Ethics."
60. See D. Crocker, "Toward Development Ethics," *World Development* 19, no. 5 (1991), 457–483; Dower, "Development Ethics"; D. Gasper, *The Ethics of Development: From Economism to Human Development* (Edinburgh: Edinburgh University Press, 2004).
61. Dower, "Development Ethics," 758.
62. A. Sen, *Resources, Values and Development* (Oxford: Basil Blackwell, 1984), 497.
63. A. Sen, "The Living Standard," in *Ethics of Consumption: The Good Life, Justice, and Global Stewardship,* ed. D. A. Crocker and T. Linden (Lanham, MD: Rowman and Littlefield, 1998), 294.
64. Ibid., 295.

65. For details see M. C. Nussbaum, "The Good as Discipline, the Good as Freedom," in *Ethics of Consumption: The Good Life, Justice, and Global Stewardship,* ed. D. A. Crocker and T. Linden (Lanham, MD: Rowman and Littlefield, 1998), 318–321.

66. Ibid., 320.

67. Crocker, "Consumption, Well-Being, and Capability," 374.

68. See International Development Ethics Association, "About: History of IDEA" (n.d.), http://developmentethics.org/about-2/.

69. D. Crocker, "Insiders and Outsiders in International Development," *Ethics and International Affairs* 5 (1991), 149.

70. Goulet, "Culture and Traditional Values," 170.

71. Goulet, *Development Ethics,* 126.

72. Ibid., 122.

73. United Nations World Commission on Environment and Development, *Our Common Future* (New York: Oxford University Press, 1987).

74. Ibid., 8.

75. A. Holland, "Sustainability," in *A Companion to Environmental Philosophy,* ed. D. Jamieson (Malden, MA: Blackwell Publishing, 2001), 391.

76. Ibid., 394.

77. Goulet, "On Culture, Religion, and Development," 29.

78. Holland, "Sustainability," 399.

79. R. Attfield, *The Ethics of Global Environment* (Edinburgh: Edinburgh University Press, 1999), 112.

80. H. E. Daly, "Sustainable Growth: An Impossibility Theorem," in *Environmental Ethics: Concepts, Policy, and Theory,* ed. J. Desjardins (Mountain View, CA: Mayfield, 1999), 424.

81. Ibid., 424–425.

82. M. Sagoff, "Carrying Capacity and Ecological Economics," in *Ethics of Consumption: The Good Life, Justice, and Global Stewardship,* ed. D. A. Crocker and T. Linden (Lanham, MD: Rowman and Littlefield, 1998), 29.

83. Ibid., 38.

84. Ibid., 8, 45.

PART III

EQUITY AND DIVERSITY

The Moral Necessity of Socialism 22

Karsten J. Struhl

In the classical Marxist tradition, socialism was often understood as a historical necessity. Both the Frankfurt School and the Althusserian reformulation of classical Marxism made the very idea of historical necessity problematic, as have the failed attempts to construct socialism in the twentieth century. I argue in this essay that socialism, while not a historical necessity, is, perhaps more than ever, a *moral* necessity. This is not to say simply that socialism is morally preferable to capitalism but that it has become, at this historical juncture, a moral imperative for humanity.

Concept of Moral Necessity

To say that something is necessary is always to say that it is necessary relative to certain purposes and conditions. If I have pneumonia, it is necessary that I take certain antibiotics. If I want to become a lawyer, a doctor, or a philosophy professor, I am required to undertake a certain course of study. If I want to organize a revolution, I have to engage with others to develop a strategy that can reasonably be put into effect. Of course, if a new form of homeopathic remedy turns out to be effective in eliminating pneumonia, I don't need antibiotics. If I don't care about being a lawyer, a doctor, or a philosophy professor, it is not necessary for me to engage in the courses of study that are relevant to those fields. And if I am not interested in radically changing society, I don't need to develop a revolutionary strategy.

What is morally necessary is also relative to certain purposes and certain conditions. Human morality is relative to the needs and purposes of the human species and to the historical conditions and problems that confront us. This is not to deny that certain groups have different and often antagonistic interests. For example, Engels in the *Anti-Dühring* correctly notes that morality has historically represented class interests, that moral concepts like equality and freedom take on a different meaning depending on which class uses them. Still, even

Engels is ambivalent. While he insists that neither the bourgeois nor the proletariat morality have an "absolute finality,"[1] he nonetheless insists that the proletariat morality represents the communist future in which there will ultimately be a "really human morality, which stands above class antagonisms."[2] Marx in his *Contribution to the Critique of Hegel's Philosophy of Right: An Introduction* asserts that revolutionary criticism rests on "the *categorical imperative to overthrow all those conditions* in which man is a degraded, enslaved, neglected, contemptible being."[3] In this same work, Marx deduces the necessity of the proletariat as the revolutionary class, because the proletariat is the class that represents "the *complete loss* of humanity and can only redeem itself through the *total redemption of humanity*."[4] Thus, both the early Marx and the later Engels can simultaneously insist on the relativity of morality to class interests *and* the possibility of a morality that transcends class interest—a "truly human morality." My point here is not to defend the specific Marxist conception of morality but to show how it is possible to recognize the way in which morality can be relative to the interests of certain groups, to allow that these groups may have interests that are antagonistic to one another, and still to insist that there can be a morality for the species as a whole. In the case of Marx and Engels, such a universal human morality is placed in the communist future. However, if there are certain problems that we can recognize as facing every human being at this present historical juncture, then a universal human morality can be constructed in relation to the interests of our species as a whole. In other words, while the practice of a universal human morality may be in the future, it can, at least in general terms, be formulated now. That is, if there are certain values that are necessary for our species to survive or at least to survive in a way that we would consider a reasonable human existence, then those values can be formulated as universal moral values. Thus, if we are confronted with problems that either threaten the existence of our species or that, if not solved, would so thoroughly degrade human existence as to render it inhumane by any reasonable standard, then whatever would be necessary to solve those problems would be a moral necessity. If we confront social, political, or economic institutions that engender behavior that threatens the extinction of our species or that thoroughly degrades us as human beings, it becomes morally necessary to radically change those institutions.

Nevertheless, while it is possible to formulate a human morality that is universal in its scope, such a morality will still have a historical dimension. What action is morally necessary for human beings to solve their common problems at one historical moment may be different in another historical moment. We face two problems at this historical conjuncture. The first is that our global culture approximates what Norman Geras calls "the contract of mutual indifference," a state that fundamentally degrades us and undermines our sense of what it means to be human. The second is the ecological crisis that threatens the survival of our own and many other species. I want to argue that these two problems are interrelated and that they cannot be solved within the parameters of global capitalism. I shall further argue that only socialism, understood as a fundamental moral project, can begin to address these problems.[5] It is in this sense that I claim that socialism is a moral necessity.

The Contract of Mutual Indifference and the Need for a New Moral Culture

In 1972, Colin Turnbull published *The Mountain People*,[6] which describes the Ik, a small ethnic group living in in the mountains of northeast Uganda. The Ik, originally hunter-gatherers, were pushed out of their ancient territory, which the government turned into a national park and game preserve. Forbidden to hunt, they were forced to support themselves as subsistence farmers on unproductive land with disastrous result. They soon found themselves on the edge of survival. Parents were unable to take care of their children, who were often expelled from the parental hut by the age of three or four to fend for themselves. The elderly were left to starve. The Ik were not only uncaring about one another's suffering but often got pleasure from one another's misfortunes. They were deliberately cruel to one another. Turnbull tells of one child who stood out from the others in that she seemed to have retained some sense of empathy and familial loyalty. She brought food to her parents, who refused her shelter and laughed at her hunger. Her peers tormented her and beat her. And her parents eventually locked her in a hut and left her to starve to death. The Ik seemed to have lost all sense of community. As Turnbull relates one horrifying example after another, the Ik come to seem almost inhuman. Except, of course, that they are human beings, human beings who show us what can happen to our species under certain extreme conditions. Are the Ik the exception, or do they portend a possible fate for all of us?

One billion people in the world are hungry. Eight million die from hunger and lack of nutrition every year. Twenty-two thousand children under the age of five die each day as a result of poverty. One billion one hundred thousand people in developing countries lack access to adequate water supplies. Fifteen percent of the world's population lack access to health services. In other words, a large part of the world's population is in a state of permanent emergency. We are not yet like the Ik in deriving joy from their suffering. However, that so little is done to alleviate these conditions suggests that most people are relatively indifferent to this suffering.

Norman Geras addresses just this question in *The Contract of Mutual Indifference: Political Philosophy after the Holocaust*.[7] The book is in part an indictment of much of contemporary political philosophy, which, with few exceptions, has refused to take into account a disturbing social phenomenon manifested dramatically by the experience of the Holocaust. For Geras, the phenomenon that political philosophy needs especially to confront is not simply the cruelty and pathology of the Nazis but the indifference of the bystanders, without which the Nazis could not have carried out their atrocities. Geras quotes Ian Kershaw, who in his book *Popular Opinion and Political Dissent in the Third Reich* puts the problem of the Holocaust this way: "The road to Auschwitz was built on hate, but paved with indifference."[8] A man who lived next to the Treblinka concentration camp is interviewed in Claude Lansmann's film *Shoa*. He saw many of the inmates who arrived at the camp. When asked what he thought, he said, "Well. It is this way. If I cut my finger, it doesn't hurt him."[9] Geras suggests the following general description of the situation: "All over Germany, prisoners are marched back and forward: from the station to the concentration camp, from the camp to the work site, back to the camp, to the station for another camp. They see the outside world, see people. These people raise their fists against them. Or they spit, look the other way, turn their backs. Or *they* somehow do not 'see.' . . . Or they do see but look on with indifference."[10] A woman tells of having felt pity for a particular Jew but then describes her amusement at his "incongruous gait—'like a circus horse'—[which] was forced upon this man by the pain in his bare feet and the whipping of the guards." Then, she says, "I'm happy when I hear nothing and see nothing of it. As far as I am concerned they aren't interned. That's it. Over. It does not interest me at all."[11] What can we say about these good German citizens? But the more important question is what we should say about ourselves, or, if we think we are an exception, what of so many people in the United States and on this planet, people who seem indifferent to those who are impoverished and hungry, indifferent to torture and to sexual slavery, to genocide and to other war crimes. They may love their families and be kind to their friends, but when someone outside of their circle of concern bleeds, it does not hurt them. They are happiest when they hear nothing and see nothing.

Geras argues that the moral significance of this bystander phenomenon might best be described as "a contract of mutual indifference." It is as though most, if not all, of us have tacitly agreed not to come to one another's aid, even and perhaps especially in cases of emergency. Geras writes:

> Here is the core idea. If you do not come to the aid of others who are under grave assault, in acute danger or crying need, you cannot reasonably expect others to come to your aid in a similar emergency; you cannot consider them so obligated to you. Other people, equally unmoved by the emergencies of others, cannot reasonably be expected to be helped in deep trouble themselves, or consider others obligated to help them. I call this *the contract of mutual indifference*.[12]

Geras asks us to imagine a world in which everyone acts like this, behaves, in effect, like a global manifestation of the society of the Ik. Our world is not exactly like this, perhaps, but it is close enough to say that something is fundamentally wrong.[13] Kant claims that we could not will such a world, and he is, in one sense, right. We could not will it as rational moral agents, for in such a world we would all be in grave danger, since we cannot reasonably expect others to come to our aid. However, as Geras observes, it is still possible to will something that conflicts with our future needs as long as it does not conflict with our present needs. Irrational as it is in the long run, most of us act as though we do, in fact, will such a world. If Geras is correct, and I think he is, then the contract of mutual indifference is close enough to our real world to say that something is fundamentally wrong with our global culture and that it is morally necessary that this be changed. Here I would add that to change this culture is not merely a morally good thing, not merely something morally preferable. Rather, it is a fundamental moral necessity that the culture that underlies the contract of mutual indifference be changed. As Geras puts it,

> The moral reality I attempt to encapsulate in the contract of mutual indifference is . . . *unbearable*. The mechanisms of denial themselves say it. It is unbearable that people should be made to suffer in terrible ways. So it gets shut out. But if it is unbearable that they should be made to, it is unbearable also that they are left to.[14]

To change *the contract of mutual indifference,* we must create a new moral culture, a culture in which human beings feel responsible for one another, even if they are strangers, even if they belong to other ethnicities and nationalities or are at great geographical remove from us. It would be a culture in which the duty to aid others would be given priority and in which we could substitute for *the contract of mutual indifference* a *contract of mutual concern and aid.* Geras posits that such a culture of mutual concern would be grounded in a "vision of a global community in which an obligation to come to the assistance of others in danger or distress was widely felt as among the most powerful of imperatives."[15]

The Socialist Ethic and the Contract of Mutual Concern and Aid

What is the political and economic significance of this? Geras, argues, and I would agree, that such a contract of mutual concern and aid is a fundamental component of the socialist ethic. "A serious-minded view of socialism today . . . is dependent for its consistency and realism on the centrality of the imperative of mutual concern."[16] The capitalist ethic, in contrast, is an ethic of self-interest and competition. It promotes a culture of everyone for him- or herself. Since the primary right entailed by the capitalist ethic is the right to be free to enter the marketplace and to compete freely with others, it entails the duty not to interfere with this right. Insofar as it is conjoined with a liberal ethic, it puts emphasis on the right to speak freely, to practice one's religion of choice, to associate with others, to live as one wishes as long as one does not directly cause harm to others, and so on, and on the duty not to interfere with these rights as exercised by others. It does not, however, very much concern itself with the fate of those who do not prosper in the marketplace, and it says little about the duty to aid others. It certainly does not insist that this duty have central importance.

The socialist ethic is based on a different conception of freedom, a positive and not merely a negative freedom, which is the freedom to fully develop our potentials and our capacities.[17] Saint-Simon envisioned a socialist society as one in which all of its members had "the greatest possible opportunities for the development of their faculties."[18] This, in turn, entails that we be able to collectively control the social, economic, and political conditions that would limit or enhance those potentials and capacities, in effect that we collectively control the institutions of social life that impact our lives. Thus, socialism entails the extension of democracy from the strictly political realm to the economic realm and, indeed, to every level of society.[19] It also would promote a substantive equality between the participants, on both the political and economic levels. None of this is possible without a sense of mutual concern, a sense of community, what is often termed "solidarity." And this sense of mutuality entails the internalization of the duty to aid one another. The logic of this is as follows: If we each have a right to the fullest development of our capacities, then we all have a duty to one another to create conditions so that each of us can fully develop our capacities. Marx and Engels stated this ideal succinctly when, in *The Communist Manifesto*, they declared, "We shall have an association in which the free development of each is the condition for the free development of all."[20]

Thus, the socialist ethic presents the duty to aid one another as a central duty. It therefore presents a challenge to liberalism's emphasis on negative duties and to the capitalist ethic of individual self-interest and competition. However, the idea of socialism is not simply an ethical ideal. It also entails a political and economic organization of society as a means by which socialist values can be realized. The basis of this organization is that ownership is essentially social, not individual, that, at the very least, the major means of production, of distribution, and of finance are collectively owned and democratically controlled by the population at large.[21]

In other words, a socialist ethic requires for its realization socialist institutions that would promote and support that ethic. However, conversely, while such institutions are necessary, they are not by themselves sufficient. These socialist economic and political institutions need to be animated by a socialist ethic. They can function effectively only if there is a culture of mutual concern and mutual aid, and a culture of mutual concern and mutual aid is not an automatic result of socialist economic and political institutions. In other words, the creation of democratic socialist institutions, while a necessary condition for a culture of mutual concern and aid, does not guarantee such a culture. The moral necessity is to overcome global capitalism, which generates the contract of mutual indifference, but it is also morally necessary that the socialism that would take its place genuinely embody a new contract of mutual concern and aid.

The Ecological Crisis

This brings me to the second reason that socialism is a moral necessity. In the ecological crisis, we face not only a degraded human existence but also the possible extinction of our species as well as a great number of other living species. The ecological crisis is, in fact, a set of interrelated crises. From 1972 (when the Club of Rome issued *The Limits of Growth*) to 2000 (the date of *Earth Day 2000*), oil consumption increased from 46 million to 73 million barrels a day. Currently, one-half of the world's forests have disappeared. The hole in the ozone layer has dramatically increased so that it is now three times the size of the United States. Human carbon emissions have increased from 3.9 million metric tons per year to 6.4 million. We are losing six species per hour, fifty thousand species per year. In fifty years, at the current rate, one-half of the earth's species will die off—the greatest mass extinction since the dinosaurs. The problem of global warming is now a climate emergency. In 2007, the Intergovernmental Panel on Climate Emergency issued a report that described some of the events that would ensue if carbon gas emissions were not reduced: an increase of major storms and floods and deadly heat waves; the collapse of agriculture in many regions of the world and expansion of the world's deserts; hundreds of millions suffering from water shortages and famine; the rapid melting of the earth's ice sheets; and oceans swallowing the world's coastlines, including cities like New York, Calcutta, Shanghai, Mumbai, Tokyo, Hong Kong, Singapore, and London. The world's temperature is already one degree centigrade above average. A two- to three-centigrade increase would mean no arctic sea ice and perhaps a seven- to twelve-foot rise in sea levels. A three- to four-degree increase would mean a loss of perhaps 70 percent of the world's snow and glacial areas.

Furthermore, the problems of global warming and other forms of ecological destruction have a variety of feedback and multiplying effects. Ecosystems are internally related and the results are therefore nonlinear, chaotic, and unpredictable. For example, the burning of the tropical rain forest causes 25 percent of all carbon gas emissions. The melting of the sea ice releases huge amounts of methane, which is a more aggressive greenhouse gas than carbon dioxide. The melting of the polar ice eliminates the albedo effect (wherein solar energy is reflected from the ice). The result is a greater absorption of solar energy and an even greater increase in global temperature. The melting of the frozen tundra also releases methane. Ocean acidification caused, in part, by oil extraction and spills means that the ocean has less ability to absorb carbon and therefore contributes to more global warming. Finally, changes in climate zones, as a result of global warming, result in the collapse of ecosystems and the extinction of species dependent on them, which results in the collapse of more ecosystems and the extinction of more species. The result of all this is that we may be reaching the tipping point where our own species will be threatened, if not with extinction then surely with a horribly degraded existence.

> It is beyond debate that the ecology of Earth—including the life support systems on which humans and all other species depend—is under sustained and severe attack by human activities. It is also clear that if we don't radically change our ways, the results will be devastating. The multifaceted, complex, and rapidly accelerating character of the planetary environmental crisis is traceable to a single systematic cause: the economic and social order in which we live.[22]

The economic and social order underlying this ecological crisis is global capitalism, and there are several reasons that this crisis cannot be solved within the parameters of capitalism.

The first reason is the imperative of profit accumulation. Capitalism changes C-M-C into M-C-M′. What this means is that what distinguishes capitalism from simply commodity exchange is that money (M) is no longer essentially a means to exchange commodities (C), no longer simply an intermediary between commodities (C-M-C). With capitalism money has the commanding role and commodities are the intermediaries (M-C-M′). The money at the end of the exchange must be more than the money at the beginning. The goal of capitalism is to use money to create commodities in order to produce more money, which is to say, to produce a value beyond its original value, a surplus value. The circuit cannot be continued unless it generates surplus value, and this requires both the exploitation of labor and the domination and exploitation of nature. It requires exponential growth without limits. As Marx wrote in the *Grundrisse,* "Capital is the Endless and limitless drive to go beyond its limiting barrier. Every boundary is and has to be a barrier for it. Else it would cease to be capital—money as self-reproductive."[23] The second reason why capitalism cannot address the crisis is that globalization has as its basic mission to convert the entire world to the accumulation process. It must, therefore, penetrate every life world in order to foster accumulation. The whole of nature is simply a resource for this process. Any CEO of a corporation who wants to remain a CEO must disregard that which is not profitable, but *capital,* in any case, selects persons who are self-seeking and ruthless. The third reason is, to quote Michael Parenti, that "pollution pays, while ecology costs. Every dollar a company spends on environmental protections is one less dollar in earnings. It is more profitable to treat the environment like a septic tank, to externalize corporate diseconomies by dumping raw industrial effluent into the atmosphere, rivers, and bays, turning waterways into open sewers."[24] The fourth reason is that the commodity form puts exchange value over use value, which has its culmination in financial capital. Financial capital is an even more abstract/pure capital—more liquid, requiring more need for immediate rewards (short-term profitability). With Wall Street as command central, pure financial capital becomes a self-expanding machine that must constantly seek ways to overcome any limits that nature might impose. Finally, as capital can never be satisfied, it forces a constant sense of lack, creating conditions that foster greed (for profit), attachment (to consumer objects and money), and a variety of cravings and artificial needs. Hence, capitalism creates a consumer society in need of a constant infusion of energy and resources to satisfy it.[25] Thus, in order to solve the ecological crisis, it is morally necessary to overcome capitalism.

It is not immediately clear, however, that socialism can overcome the ecological crisis. The problem here is not just what has been called "really existing socialism" in the twentieth century,[26] the most notable examples being the Soviet Union and China, which were ecological disasters, but also the anthropocentric, Promethean, and productivist assumptions that were built into classical socialist thinking. The anthropocentric and Promethean assumptions imply that human beings have a privileged position vis-à-vis the rest of nature and have, therefore, the right to exploit and change nature to their advantage. The productivist assumption is that production must be unlimited if we are to go from the "kingdom of necessity" to the "realm of freedom." Nature, then, remains a resource to be controlled and dominated. Here, for example, is Trotsky in an essay in *Literature and Revolution:* "Through the machine, man in Socialist society will command nature in its entirety. . . . He will point out places for mountains and passes. He will change the course of rivers, and he will lay down rules for the ocean."[27] The socialism that is morally necessary must give up these assumptions. It must embrace an ethic of mutual concern and mutual aid that includes other species. In other words, the answer to both the contract of mutual indifference and the ecological crisis is a socialist ethic of compassion that embraces a sense of our interdependence with humanity and with the whole of nature.

Socialism as a Global Ethic

Socialism, then, is a fundamental moral as well as political project that addresses the crises of our historical epoch. Socialism, in fact, has always been a moral project. From the initial use of the term in the nineteenth century,[28] it has been a protest against injustice, exploitation, and immiseration, and an insistence that we go beyond negative rights to the positive rights of self-development. It entails a duty to create the conditions by which each of us can develop to our full potentials, to create institutions that replace private ownership of the means of production and control of economic life with social ownership and control. It is, therefore, also an ethic of solidarity, an ethic of cooperation and mutuality, which entails a duty to aid one another. As I have argued in the previous section, the socialist ethic must today include a sense of interdependence not only with other human beings but also with other species. I now want to add two additional components of the socialist ethic. First, there is a more intimate connection between mutual concern and aid *and* the development of individual potentials. It is not merely that by creating certain conditions and by mutual aid we can help one another advance to our fullest potentials. There is, in addition, the recognition that as social animals we can advance to our full potentials only through our sociality, which is to say, through our mutual aid and concern. In other words, nurturing a concern for one another is in itself fundamental to the development of our potentialities. Second, as these crises have a global dimension, the socialist ethic must become a global ethic.

Much has been written about the possibility of a global ethic and what a global ethic would entail. In September 1993, representatives of 120 of the world's religions assembled in Chicago to convene a Parliament of the Worlds Religions. Their task was to discuss a draft of a global ethic written by Hans Küng, a well-respected ecumenical German theologian. The final draft, entitled *Declaration toward a Global Ethic*,[29] argued that within the religions of the world there is a "common core set of values" and that this core consensus provides the basis of a global ethic that not only all religions but all persons of reasonable ethical sensibilities could affirm. Among the key principles of this global ethic was the idea that "every human being must be treated humanely," a principle that, the document asserts, can be derived from the golden rule: "What you do not wish to be done to yourself, do not do to others. . . . What you wish done to yourself, do to others." Following from this basic principle are several more specific guidelines, among which are a "commitment to a culture of non-violence and respect for life," not only for human but also for non-human animals and plants, and a "commitment to a culture of solidarity and a just economic order." In 1997, UNESCO initiated the Universal Ethics Project, which brought together philosophers and theologians representing a variety of ethical traditions and cultures in order to develop a universal ethic that would provide the philosophical principles from which the rights indicated in the UN Declaration of Human Rights could be derived.[30] The underlying assumption of these and other attempts to formulate a global ethic[31] is that this consensus must be more than a very general statement of agreement. It must be capable of generating norms that can address the problems that humanity confronts at this historical juncture. In other words, this minimal consensus must be capable of constructing a substantive ethic that can address these problems. I am skeptical of the ability of such a minimal consensus to do this and even of the ability to develop such a minimal consensus within these contexts.

In an article published in 2005,[32] I pointed to what I see as the problems with an attempt to discover a minimal consensus on ethical norms. The first is the problem of how to decide who participates in the dialogue to reach such a minimal consensus and how the dialogue is to be conducted. If a global ethic is to represent a consensus among the world's religions, who should speak for each of the religious traditions? The Parliament of the World's Religions' version of the global ethic at best represents a consensus among the liberal progressive wings of the world's religions. What about the fundamentalists? Should they also be party to the dialogue? Furthermore, even if we could somehow arrive at a consensus among all sectors within the world's religions, we are still left with the problem of how we could extend that consensus beyond the world's religions. Who will represent the different cultures of the world? It is hardly likely that there is a consensus even among people within a given culture that would yield anything like the principles suggested by the *Declaration toward a Global Ethic*. Should we, then, use the majority of the culture as a standard or look only to progressives within the culture? There is a second problem: however we delimit the scope of the participants, we can anticipate that there would be some significant disagreements, and it is by no means clear how these disagreements could be reconciled. This leads to a third problem with the attempt to develop even a minimal moral consensus, which is that it is somewhat doubtful that we can find a genuine moral consensus among even the world's religions.[33]

One attempt to solve this last problem is to appeal to the golden rule. However, while it is true that each religion and indeed each culture has some version of the golden rule, there is a problem of specificity. George Bernard Shaw is said to have remarked, "Do not do unto others what you would have others do unto you. Others may have different tastes." Liberal cultures would insist that each person has the right to pursue his or her own interests as long as they do not result in harm to others. However, many cultures would insist that there are forms of sexuality that individuals might want that, even if they do not directly harm another, are a violation of God's commandments, intrinsically unhealthy, or harmful to the community as a whole. Furthermore, exactly how to define what is harmful has no clear consensus even among liberal intellectuals. A second difficulty with the appeal to the golden rule as the basis for even a minimal ethical consensus arises with respect to the scope of the concern. "Do not do unto others." But which others? Conquistadors like Balboa and Cortés and members of the clergy who took slavery to be morally legitimate did not see their actions as contradicting the golden rule. While most of the world's people now hold slavery to be immoral, large numbers of people in a variety of cultures continue to harbor, often in overt and aggressive forms, assumptions that are racist, colonial, and imperialist. Even where there is an explicit rejection of racism and colonialism, these assumptions persist in a more subtle form. The suffering of those in other nations and in other cultures and religions is accorded a lesser place than the suffering of those in one's own nation or who belong to one's own religion or culture. This helps to perpetuate the contract of mutual indifference on a global scale. Furthermore, perhaps the majority of the human population in the West excludes nonhuman animals from the golden rule.

Even if we could formulate such a minimal consensus through dialogue among the world's religions and cultures, it is unlikely that we could derive from it a substantial enough global ethic to address the global problems we currently confront. The possibility of a more substantial global ethic, one that could help to reorganize our economic and political institutions, that could address the problems of the contract of mutual indifference and the ecological crisis, requires not simply dialogue but political struggle, a struggle for a new global order. This is a tall order, but the good news is that such a struggle is already beginning to take place.

The early stages of this struggle began at the close of the twentieth century and the dawn of the twenty-first century. In late November 1999 a diverse coalition of international social forces converged in Seattle, Washington, for a series of demonstrations against the World Trade Organization. Since then, millions of people with many different ideologies, specific agendas, and social priorities have engaged in a struggle against the institutions of international trade and finance. They have organized massive demonstrations in Washington, D.C., Quebec City, Genoa, and Prague and have organized international social forums that have brought together hundreds of thousands of social activists from almost every corner of the globe. They have met in Porto Alegre, Brazil; Mumbai, India; Caracas, Venezuela; Bamako, Mali; Karachi, Pakistan; and Nairobi, Kenya. The participants in these social forums were ideologically diverse and had many different social priorities. They were ecologically concerned citizens, feminists, consumer advocates, AIDS activists protesting the high costs of drugs, indigenous peoples protesting the exploitation of their tribal lands, landless peasants from the less developed world. They were rank-and-file workers protesting such international trade agreements as NAFTA and struggling for an internationally recognized code of labor rights, representatives of Third World groups opposing the structural adjustment policies of the International Monetary Fund and the World Bank, activists for global justice demanding the cancelation of debts owed by the world's poorest countries and in opposition to global sweatshops, advocates of small farmers, human rights groups, and peace groups, among others. These various interest groups discussed how best to network with one another and to support one another's projects. Much of this networking and support continues to this day. Even though these social activists were and are ideologically diverse, they shared and continue to "share an opposition to transnational corporations and to the neoliberal government policies which enable them to flourish."[34] They are often referred to collectively as the "anti-globalization movement," but they are not, for the most part, against globalization as such.[35] They have, rather, begun to think about ways in which it is possible to delink the technological and cultural integrative forces from the existing financial and corporate capitalist forces. In short, however they may disagree on particulars, they have begun to conceive of the possibility of an alternative form of globalization; hence, they are less an anti-globalization movement than an alter-globalization movement. They are a movement of globalization from below seeking to counter the prevailing globalization from above. They see themselves as beginning to organize a global civil society, one with a vision of an ethical order that can address the various problems and crises we confront today as a species. Insofar as these struggles support one another's agendas, they already embody a sense of mutual aid and concern. They also envision a global order that can organize production in a rational way to meet human need and to avoid ecological catastrophe. Thus, they represent a new global ethic in the making, one that, while not fully formed, guides their struggles and that could help to create the construction of a new socialist global society.

The second stage of the struggle for a new social order is of a more recent vintage. In 2011 a new set of struggles and movements from different parts of the world inspired and often collaborated with one another.[36] They were preceded by a number of struggles throughout Europe that were in reaction to the austerity measures imposed as a response to the global financial crisis of 2007–2008. There were huge protests in Italy, France, and Germany and massive demonstrations and general strikes in Greece. On May 15, 2011, a group of activists who became known as the *indignados* occupied the Puerta del Sol in Madrid calling for "real democracy now." They remained there until they were evicted by the national police on August 2, after which they sent out a call to continue occupations in other ways and mobilized to stop evictions. Occupations also occurred in Barcelona and Seville. The *indignados* in Spain not only were an outgrowth of the movements against austerity in Europe but were in large part inspired by the Arab Spring.

What is called the Arab Spring began in Tunisia on December 17, 2010, when Mohammed Bouazizi set himself on fire as a protest against police corruption and brutality and against the dictatorship of Zine el-Abidine Ben Ali. Bouazizi's action was the spark that set fire to such massive nonviolent resistance that by January 14, 2011, Ben Ali fled the country and the dictatorship was overthrown. The events in Tunisia, in turn, inspired resistance in Egypt, where on January 25, more than fifty thousand protesters in Cairo occupied Tahrir Square, remaining there for eighteen days until, on February 11, the Egyptian army removed Hosni Mubarak from power. In July, activists concerned with the slow pace of the transition and fearing that the army would hold on to power reoccupied Tahrir Square for three weeks. Inspired by the Tunisian and Egyptian examples, the resistance to autocratic regimes spread to Libya, where the government was overthrown and Muammar Gaddhafi killed, and to Yemen, Bahrain, and Syria. Major protests have also occurred in Morocco, Kuwait, and Jordan.

The occupy movement came to the United States first in Madison, Wisconsin, in February 2011, where more than one hundred thousand people protested Governor Scott Walker's proposed legislation to eliminate collective bargaining rights for public employees. Many remained and physically occupied the public spaces around the state capital building for several weeks. On September 17, thousands of people took over Zuccotti Park, which is located in the Wall Street area of Manhattan. They quickly renamed the park "Liberty Square," a conscious nod to Egypt's Tahrir Square, since *tahrir* means "liberty." This group referred to itself as Occupy Wall Street (OWS), and its slogan was "We are the 99%," a reference to the growing inequality that exists in the United States between the top 1 percent and everyone else, where 1 percent of the population has 23 percent of the income and 34 percent of the country's total wealth, more wealth than the bottom 90 percent of the population.

> OWS presented a competing narrative that resonated with millions of people: corporate power and greed got us into this mess, the only way out is for the 99% to stand together to demand equality, justice and fairness. It is that broad perspective, narrative or worldview—as opposed to a laundry list of demands—that helped change the political debate.[37]

While there was no definitive list of demands, it is clear that the occupy movement, like the movement for globalization from below, has galvanized the energies of hundreds of thousands and perhaps millions of people throughout the world. While still in its infancy, it is already a global movement. In the United States, OWS has generated occupation encampments in as many as fourteen hundred cities, including Occupy Oakland, which shut down the Port of Oakland, Occupy San Diego, Occupy Boston, Occupy Chicago, Occupy Seattle, Occupy Pittsburg, Occupy Minnesota, Occupy Birmingham, Occupy Phoenix, Occupy Denver, Occupy New Haven, Occupy Atlanta, Occupy Des Moines, Occupy Greensboro, Occupy Milwaukee, Occupy San Juan, Occupy Fairbanks, and Occupy Honolulu. Outside the United States, occupations have taken place in close to one hundred cities in eighty-two countries, including London, Edinburgh, Belfast, Dublin, Paris, Rome, Zurich, Frankfurt, Berlin, Ontario,

Montreal, Halifax, Vancouver, Sidney, Melbourne, Brussels, Copenhagen, Oslo, Zurich, Hong Kong, Tel Aviv, Auckland, Seoul, and Mexico City. The "occupiers" in these different cities have a profound awareness and sense of solidarity with one another. "Occupy Wall Street was unequivocally influenced by the Egyptian uprising, but yesterday the citizens in Tahrir Square flipped the script: a group of protesters, dismayed by the police brutality California protesters were met with this week, marched in solidarity with Occupy Oakland."[38]

In these occupations, there is no central committee. Instead, there are general assemblies that, at least in OWS, function on a consensus basis and are open to whoever wants to attend. Yet, somehow they do function. Like the movement for globalization from below, these occupy movements attempt to prefigure a world to come, which is to say that they function not only to change the world but to change themselves.

> Perhaps the most critical component of OWS is its creation of alternative communities which reflect the egalitarian, democratic world that its activists seek for the future. Sometimes referred to as "pre-figurative politics," this perspective seeks to create in microcosm the alternative models that reflect the future world that the activists support, while at the same time using those institutions to engage in direct action to change the current reality. By creating a community dedicated to solidarity, consensus decision-making, everyone's participation, respect for everyone's opinion, and equality, OWS attempted to demonstrate that another world is possible, not in theory but in practice.[39]

One of the organizers of OWS, Yotam Marom, says, "We're creating alternative models of the world we want to live in while also using those new institutions as a staging ground to fight for that world—that's what's radical and cool about the occupations."[40] Thus, like the movement for globalization from below, the occupy movement represents a new global ethic in the making. The occupation of public space is an attempt to create a commons. As a global movement it prefigures the creation of a global commons. As an opposition to the inequality of wealth and the 1 percent of the population who control the global economy, it poses a fundamental challenge to global capitalism. This nascent global ethic could become a global socialist ethic. As one of the invited speakers to Zuccotti Park, Richard Wolff, said,

> To achieve the goals of this renewed movement, we must finally change the organization of production that sustains and reproduces inequality and injustice. We need to replace the failed structure of our corporate enterprises that now deliver profits to so few, pollute the environment we all depend on, and corrupt our political system. . . . We can bring democracy to our enterprises—by transforming them into cooperatives owned, operated and governed by democratic assemblies composed of all who work in them and all the residents of the communities who are interdependent with them.[41]

OWS was evicted from Zuccotti Park in mid-November 2011, but they continue to hold general assemblies, organize political actions, and network with occupy groups throughout the world.[42] It is important to add that, while I have referred to it as a second stage for a new global order, the occupy movement is not separate from the first stage. The movement for globalization from below is still active, and many of its participants are now involved in the occupy movement. In other words, the occupy movement does not replace the movement for globalization from below but continues it in a different form. The two struggles interpenetrate and will, we can assume, eventually give birth to still a new kind of movement. What will happen to the occupy movement as such and what new forms may emerge is uncertain, but the ideal of "another world is possible" is not going to disappear. We can anticipate that the struggle for a new global order will continue, that new movements will emerge, and that perhaps the global ethic in the making may develop a more explicitly socialist form.

Buddhism and the Moral Necessity of Socialism

One of the participants in OWS told a journalist that what appealed to her about this movement was that it is "beyond political" and that it is "spiritual and philosophical."[43] Having just discussed the political side of the socialist ethic, I now want to consider its spiritual side. I have argued that the moral necessity of socialism rests on the recognition that both the contract of mutual indifference and the ecological crisis are intimately bound up with the imperatives of capitalism. I have argued that the socialism that is morally necessary must be a socialism that can embrace an ethic of mutual aid and concern that includes other species and that acknowledges our interdependence not only with global humanity but with the whole of the biosphere. I have also argued that there is a global ethic in the making, a global ethic that is emerging out of the struggles of the twenty-first century and that could lay the groundwork for a new global socialist ethic. There are, however, two impediments to the realization of such a global socialist ethic. The first is the problem that I mentioned in the earlier discussion of the golden rule: the scope of the circle of concern. Do unto others as you would have them do unto you, but which others? A global socialist ethic must develop a compassion that counters those feelings and desires fostered by capitalism that narrow the circle of concern to individual, corporate, and national self-interest. It must also develop a sense of compassion that transcends species self-interest. Furthermore, it must counter the problem of our emotional attachment to the commodity form, to the capital accumulation process and its attendant consumerism. Buddhism is well positioned to address both of these issues. Its critique of desire, craving, and attachment addresses both the assumptions that ground consumerism and the continual quest for profit accumulation. Its critique of the self goes to the heart of the problem of selfishness and greed that is the ideology of capitalism. Finally, Buddhism is not merely an intellectual critique but a practice of mindfulness that can see how various forms of craving and attachment arise and that, therefore, can help to break the habit formations that attach us to the commodity form. In addition, through the development of mindfulness, the attachment to the illusion of self can be reduced and perhaps ultimately extinguished, allowing for the development of wisdom and compassion.

How far can compassion extend? How far can we extend the circle of concern? It all depends on the boundaries of the self. Each boundary creates a form of self-interest to what is inside the boundary and disinterestedness, if not animosity, to what is on the other side of the boundary. Each form of social identity creates new self-boundaries, sometimes expanding the circle of concern—identification with the family, the ethnic or religious group, and the nation. But each of these entails lack of concern for those who are not my family, my ethnic or religious group, or my nation. It is these social identities that allow us to ignore the suffering of those on the other side of the boundary (or to exploit or kill them). One possible solution is to expand the boundaries of the self further through the development of a sense of human identity, thus expanding the boundaries of the self to include the species. But such a species self still needs to place something on the other side of the boundary. This still leaves us with an anthropocentric self-interest that places nonhumans and the rest of nature outside the circle of concern. In addition, it also allows us to put certain human beings outside the circle by defining them as not quite human. The solution needs to be more radical—to dissolve the circle, to dissolve the boundaries of the self. That is why the doctrine of no-self is at the heart of the Buddhist perspective. All self-constructions are illusions. Since all self-constructions are illusions, universal compassion can be fully affirmed only through the recognition that there is no self. The solution to the problem of how to widen the circle is to extinguish the boundaries that form the circle itself, which can then open to a boundless compassion for all living beings. There is no longer self-interest because there is no longer self. As a result, there is no longer national self-centeredness; no ethnic, religious, racial, or gender self-centeredness; no ideological self-centeredness; no anthropocentric self-centeredness. In short, nonattachment to the illusion of the self is also nonattachment to our social identities, and it is this nonattachment that allows for the development of a universal compassion. Here is the way a twentieth-century Buddhist in the Tibetan tradition expresses this idea:

> He who wants to follow the Path of the Buddha must give up all thoughts of "I" and "mine." But this giving up does not make us poorer . . . because what we

> renounce and destroy are the walls that kept us imprisoned; and what we gain is that supreme freedom according to which every individual is essentially connected to all that exists, thus embracing all living beings in his own mind, taking part in their deepest experience, sharing sorrow and joy.[44]

The idea of transcending the self and developing a sense of universal compassion can be developed outside the Buddhist context. Here is the way Albert Einstein, who, to my knowledge, was not influenced by Buddhism, expresses the same idea:

> A human being is a part of the whole called by us the "universe," a part limited in time and space. He experiences himself, his thoughts and feeling as something separated from the rest—a kind of optical delusion of his consciousness. The delusion is a kind of prison for us, restricting us to personal desires and to affection for a few persons nearest us. Our task must be to free ourselves from this prison by widening our circle of compassion to embrace all living creatures and the whole of nature in its beauty.[45]

I have two specific reasons for juxtaposing these two quotes. The first is to suggest that the Buddhist insight that the self is an illusion and that the transcendence of that illusion opens us to a wider compassion can be developed within the context of Western philosophical and scientific thought. The second is to make clear that I am not claiming that Buddhism is the only resource available to address the subjective/spiritual side of the problem. There are many possible resources that we can use to transcend self-interest and to break our attachment to the commodity form and its attendant consumerism. The building of a global community in the struggle to challenge corporate and financial capitalist globalization may itself foster a new kind of global consciousness. And, of course, there are spiritual disciplines other than Buddhism that can address these issues. What I am claiming is simply that Buddhism, given its specific analysis and its meditative practice, is well positioned to aid this process.

Troubles in Samsara

Still, even among those who have tasted the boundless, few can exist there for very long. The pulls of self-construction and social identification are strong. It is hard to know how to navigate the problems of ordinary life without them. Furthermore, social identities seem to be necessary to oppose oppression and exploitation. Groups that would initiate social change need, it would seem, to come together on the basis of a shared identity. How can we oppose capitalist exploitation and its attendant inequality without a shared class identity, if only to say, "We are the 99%." By the same reasoning, women need to develop a specific feminist gender identity, oppressed people of color a revolutionary racial identity, and so on for gay and lesbian identities, transsexual identities, various cultural, religious, and even national identities. If we want a globalization from below, we must form an identity that opposes those who would impose a globalization from above.

There is yet another problem. If ethics is relative to certain purposes and if the moral necessity of socialism is a morality for our species as a whole, then what does it mean to develop a global ecological socialist ethic that transcends our species' self-interest? In other words, if we transcend species interest, then on what basis is socialism a moral necessity for our species? Don't we, in some sense, have to prioritize human interests in constructing such a socialist ethic?

A global socialist ethic and socialist institutions can, of course, be constructed only by human beings. To do this, we need social identities and a concern for the survival of our species. Nonetheless, it is these social identities that draw the boundaries of self and limit the circle of concern. It is our species identity that fosters the anthropocentric and Promethean assumptions that, along with productivist assumption, have infected previous socialist projects. Social identities that struggle against oppression may promise a liberation transcending that social identity. A species identity may motivate us to create a new socialist global order. But the process of forming even emancipatory social identities constructs boundaries that close off compassion and often create pathways to new forms of oppression. How do we free ourselves from what Einstein called this "optical delusion of consciousness" and still act effectively in the social world? How do we combine the praxis of compassion with the praxis of political action?

There are, in my mind, no simple answers to these questions.

It may be the case that in real history we can never dispense with certain kinds of social identities. We cannot reside permanently in nirvana if we wish to change the world.[46] The problem, it seems to me, is not so much that we have these social identities but that we are attached to them. It is not these identities as such that allow us to ignore the suffering of those who are not included but rather the impermeable boundaries that we form around these identities through attachment. In other words, to see that these social identities are ultimately empty is not necessarily to dissolve them but to release our self-centered attachments to them.

A global ecological socialist ethic and socialist institutions can be constructed only by members of our species. Yet there is no reason that the interests of *our* species cannot include a moral concern for the interests of other species. In fact, the recognition of the ecological interdependence of the various species within the biosphere entails that we cannot ignore the interests of other species if we wish to survive. Thus, creating a global ecological socialist ethic is compatible with recognizing that the lives of the members of other species have not only a value for us but perhaps an intrinsic value. Perhaps, in the last analysis, we may need practically to give some priority to the interest of our species. At the moment, however, this is not the problem, as the economic and political forces threatening our species are the same forces threatening the existence of other species. The moral necessity of socialism is the moral necessity of overcoming a global capitalism that threatens our species with ecological disaster *and* the need to construct a socialist ethic and socialist institutions that foster mutual concern for members of our own species and a concern and sense of mutual interdependence with other species and, indeed, with the whole of the biosphere.

NOTES

I would like to thank John Pittman, John L. Hammond, and Igor Krupnik for their insightful criticisms and comments, which led to a number of revisions of the paper I presented at the East-West Philosophy Conference in Hawai'i.

1. Friedrich Engels, excerpt from *Anti-Dühring,* in *The Marx-Engels Reader,* 2nd ed., ed. Robert C. Tucker (New York: W. W. Norton, 1978), 726.

2. Ibid., 726–727.

3. Karl Marx, *Contribution to the Critique of Hegel's Philosophy of Right: An Introduction,* in *Karl Marx: Selected Writings,* ed. Lawrence H. Simon (Indianapolis: Hackett Publishing, 1994), 34.

4. Ibid., 38.

5. I am not claiming, as I shall make clear later, that socialism is *only* a moral project. I am, however, claiming that the moral dimension is a necessary and crucial part of the socialist project.

6. Colin M. Turnbull, *The Mountain People* (New York: Simon and Schuster, 1972).

7. Norman Geras, *The Contract of Mutual Indifference: Political Philosophy after the Holocaust* (New York: Verso Press, 1998).

8. Ibid., 18.

9. Ibid., 3.

10. Ibid., 5.

11. Ibid., 6.

12. Ibid., 28. Geras does not explicitly explain in what sense this is a "contract." It clearly is not an actual contract that people have made with one another. It can, however, be construed as a hypothetical construct implicit in our actual behavior. It is *as though* we have said to one another, "Don't expect me to help you and, you, in turn, have no obligation to help me."

13. Geras considers several possible objections to his thesis that our contemporary world approximates the contract of mutual indifference. For example, there are certainly people who dedicate much of their time to aiding others. Geras responds that, while this is certainly true and may serve as a nucleus of what might someday become an alternative moral universe, the contract of mutual indifference "still captures a moral reality, the dominant pattern of relationships, even once the qualifications are taken into account. . . . It captures . . . a brutal moral reality." Geras, *Contract of Mutual Indifference,* 45.

14. Ibid., 46.

15. Ibid., 57.

16. Ibid., 60.

17. This is not to deny the importance of certain liberal freedoms. However, socialism would directly challenge at least one freedom that is central to the capitalist ethic: the freedom of the capitalists to own the major means of production and to control and organize the work of the society. As Kai Nielsen puts it, "Socialism would indeed prohibit capitalist acts between consenting adults; the capitalist class would lose its freedom to buy and sell and to control the labor market." Kai Nielsen, "A Moral Case for Socialism," *Critical Review* 3, nos. 3–4 (Summer–Fall 1989), 546.

18. Quoted in Michael A. Lebowitz, *The Socialist Alternative* (New York: Monthly Review Press, 2010), 7.

19. Here it is important to emphasize that without democracy there can be no socialism. If there is to be genuine social control of economic life, then such control cannot be dictated from above. The attempt to identify socialism simply with state ownership and control of the means of production misses an important point. If the state owns and controls the means of production but the people in the society do not control the state, then the society does not, in any real sense, own the means of production or control economic life. Even if socialism is defined as the "dictatorship of the proletariat," if a small group of people constituting what in the former Soviet Union was called a *nomenklatura* (top party officials and a bureaucratic and managerial elite) control the mechanisms of economic activity, then we do not have a dictatorship *of* the proletariat but rather a dictatorship *over* the proletariat.

20. Karl Marx and Friedrich Engels, *The Communist Manifesto,* in Simon, *Karl Marx: Selected Writings,* 176. Lebowitz suggests that there is an essential connection between mutual cooperative activity and the development of our human capacities. The socialist insight, he writes, is that "the development of human capacities can occur only through practice and . . . thus points to our need to be able to develop through democratic, participatory, and protagonist activity in every aspect of our lives." Lebowitz, *Socialist Alternative,* 22.

21. This is a minimal conception of socialism. Michael Lebowitz suggests what he calls a "socialist triangle" in which (a) general social ownership of the means of production would be conjoined with (b) social production organized by workers within the various enterprises, what is often termed "self-management," and (c) a "solidarean society" that would give priority to production for communal needs and the satisfaction of social needs. Ibid., 31–81.

22. Fred Magdoff and John Bellamy Foster, *What Every Environmentalist Needs to Know about Capitalism* (New York: Monthly Review Press, 2011), 25.

23. Karl Marx, *Grundrisse,* trans. and ed. Martin Nicolas (London: Penguin Books, 1973), 334.

24. Michael Parenti, "Why the Corporate Rich Oppose Environmentalism," ZNET, August 4, 2005, http://www.zmag.org/sustainers/content/2005–08/04parenti.cfm.

25. For these arguments, I am especially indebted to Joel Kovel, *The Enemy of Nature: The End of Capitalism or the End of the World?* (New York: Zed Books, 2007).

26. To those who claim that the collapse of "really existing socialism" in Eastern Europe and the Soviet Union proves that socialism is now dead, Daniel Singer replied, "To have died you must have lived, and what we have known so far is *really inexisting socialism*"; italics mine. Daniel Singer, "Prometheus Rebound?" *Monthly Review* 42, no. 3 (July–August 1990), 75.

27. Leon Trotksy, from *Literature and Revolution,* in *The Marxists,* ed. C. Wright Mills (New York: Dell Publishing, 1962), 287.

28. Raymond Williams points out that the first recorded political use of the term in French was in 1833 and that it was not until the 1860s that the term became more generally used. See his entry on "Socialism" in Raymond Williams, *Key Words: A Vocabulary of*

Culture and Society (New York: Oxford University Press, 1983), 286–291. Of course, the values intended by the term have a much longer historical pedigree.

29. The full text of the final draft can be found in Hans Küng, ed., *Yes to a Global Ethic* (New York: Continuum Publishing, 1966). This book also has comments on the Parliament's declaration from a variety of internationally known persons, among them Lev Kopelev, Rigoberta Menchú, Patriarch Bartholomew I, Crown Prince Hassan bin Talil, Yehudi Menuhin, Elie Wiesel, Desmond Tutu, and Aung San Suu Kyi.

30. The discussion of the Universal Ethics Project can be found at http://unesdoc.unesco.org/images/0011/001176/117622eo.pdf.

31. In the same year that the Parliament of the World's Religions discussed Küng's draft, Leonard Swidler, a colleague of Küng's, wrote his own draft of a global ethic. Swidler's draft, which is entitled "A Universal Declaration of a Global Ethic," can be found at http://globalethic.org/Center/declarel.htm.

32. Karsten J. Struhl, "Is a Global Ethic Possible?" in *Planetary Politics: Human Rights, Terror, and Global Society,* ed. Stephen Eric Bronner (New York: Rowman and Littlefield, 2005), 173–190.

33. For example, there is a very different understanding of the meaning of violence within Islam and Buddhism. Of course, one can draw from certain passages in Islam a preference for nonviolence over violence, but, given Islam's affirmation of jihad as an obligation of Muslims (granted there are different interpretations of what this means), it is hard to see how this is compatible with Buddhism's fundamental commitment to nonharm (*ahimsa*) as a general principle of nonviolence.

34. Barbara Epstein, "Anarchism and Anti-Globalization," *Monthly Review* 53, no. 4 (September 2001), 10. Epstein's article is an excellent overview of the ideological tendencies within the movement and especially of its anarchist tendencies.

35. In fact, it is precisely globalization that creates the preconditions for this international networking, e.g., the use of the internet to provide critical coverage of events that are inadequately reported in the mainstream media and to organize various forms of global resistance.

36. While it is yet too soon to make a judgment, the year 2011 may, from the vantage point of a future perspective, be seen as a world historical year of global protests in the same way that we today think of the year 1968.

37. Jules Lobel, "The Future of the Occupy Movement," *Jurist,* Forum, December 6, 2011, http://jurist.org/forum/2011/12/jules-lobel-occupy-movement.php.

38. Julianne Escobedo Shepherd, "Egyptian Protesters March in Support of Occupy Oakland," *AlterNet,* October 29, 2011, http://www.alternet.org/newsandviews/article/687291/egyptian_protesters_march_in_support_of_occupy_oakland.

39. Lobel, "Future of the Occupy Movement."

40. Quoted in Richard Kim, "The Audacity of Occupy Wall Street," *Nation* 293, no. 21 (November 21, 2011), 18.

41. Richard Wolff, "Occupy Wall Street Ends Capitalism's Alibi," *Guardian,* October 4, 2011, http://www.guardian.co.uk/commentisfree/cifamerica/2011/oct/04/occupy-wall-street-new-york.

42. After the eviction, the police put barricades around Zuccotti Park, and individuals were allowed to enter only through two checkpoints and were not allowed to sleep in the park. On January 10, as a response to a complaint by the New York Civil Liberties Union, the barricades were removed. They were subsequently reinstated, removed again, and then reinstated. Zuccotti Park could no longer be a center of OWS activity.

43. Quoted in Kim, "The Audacity of Occupy Wall Street," 20.

44. Lama Anagarika Govinda, quoted in Nolan Pliny Jacobson, *Buddhism and the Contemporary World* (Carbondale: Southern Illinois University Press), 85.

45. Albert Einstein, quoted in Michael N. Nagler, *The Search for a Nonviolent Future* (San Francisco: Inner Ocean Publishing, 2004), 156. According to Max Jammer, "Einstein never showed any interest in Far Eastern philosophy and never expressed any sympathy with Oriental religious thought or mysticism." Max Jammer, *Einstein and Religion* (Princeton, NJ: Princeton University Press, 1999), 236.

46. We might, however, find a way to reside simultaneously within the contemplative perspective of nirvana and still engage in active political struggle in samsara.

Invaluable Justice 23

Heidegger, Derrida, and Daoism Thinking on Values and Justice

Steven Burik

What can comparative philosophy contribute to thinking about values, economics, and justice? Can we directly apply philosophy in general, and comparative philosophy in particular, to these problems? Martin Heidegger, one of the protagonists of this essay, has on occasion made it clear that philosophy is literally "useless,"[1] and so let me start with one of my favorite Heidegger quotes, to give an indication of what I will argue in this essay: "Philosophy . . . cannot be directly applied, or judged by its usefulness in the manner of economic or other professional knowledge. But what is useless can still be a force, perhaps the only real force."[2]

Values and justice are concepts central to ethics. It is often argued that Heidegger, Derrida, and the Daoist classics are inadequate in terms of ethical systems. In short, it is said that because they challenge the standard theories of ethics and philosophy, there is little or no ethics to be found in Heidegger, Derrida, and Daoism, and that, therefore, they display a kind of nihilist or relativist thinking best avoided. In this essay I will argue otherwise through an exploration of how Heidegger, Derrida, Zhuangzi, and Laozi think about values and justice. It will become clear that their thinking of values challenges preconceived notions of value and indeed challenges the importance of thinking in terms of value at all.

Heidegger and Derrida challenge the metaphysical history of Western thought. This metaphysical history tends to think in dualist, hierarchical structures by positing values and is still firmly entrenched as the dominant discourse. I will focus on how Heidegger, Derrida, and Daoism, all in their different ways, challenge a long-standing characteristic of metaphysical thought,[3] that is, the separation of *Sein* and *Sollen*, is and ought. They would argue that somehow, is and ought, although not identical, are nevertheless inseparable. This challenge to the perceived separation of is and ought amounts to a revaluation of the idea of value and, with it, of justice. Since the connection between justice and value is a close one, the values we hold are in an important way those that determine how we think of justice. And since Heidegger, Derrida, and the Daoists challenge these values, or at least challenge thinking in terms of values, they also challenge standard ideas of justice.

Following and comparing Heidegger, Derrida, and Daoism, the leading idea of this essay is that thinking in values leads to a hierarchy or form of duality that is inimical to justice. Traditionally justice has been understood as somehow based on equality, or equity, and the idea of valuation is based on making artificial and hierarchical distinctions between opposing structures. Against this normal sense of value, we will see in comparing our protagonists that they are really talking about the value of inclusion or relationality, or interdependence. Although they do this in different ways, it will be argued that there is an overall tendency in our protagonists toward a more inclusive way of thinking. But this will not translate into justice based on equality or sameness or equity, but rather justice based on difference or otherness.

Heidegger

Since most of Heidegger's thinking on values revolves around his treatment of Nietzsche's *Umwertung aller Werte,* the revaluation of all values, I would like to start there. Heidegger argues that the concept of value arises as soon as man is set as a subject opposed to an object. According to Heidegger, Nietzsche, as the last metaphysician, necessarily stays within the confines of metaphysical thought with his revaluation, since Nietzsche does not question the concept or idea of "value" but is rather concerned only with replacing the old set of values with something else. Heidegger therefore sees Nietzsche's *Umwertung* remaining within the influence of the metaphysical foundation in which subject and object are opposed. Nietzsche abolished the afterworld and relocated value in this world, under the will to power.[4] According to Heidegger, Nietzsche sees value in terms of justice as *Richtigkeit.* This *Richtigkeit* means what is appropriate, right, fitting, yet appropriateness must be understood here as according to life as Nietzsche sees it. The will to power then becomes *the* principle of valuation, which the subject uses to enhance life. In Heidegger's words, "Will to power manifests itself as the subjectivity that is characterized by value thinking."[5] And this is exactly where Heidegger's objection arises, since he thinks that "every metaphysics is a 'system of value-estimations.'"[6] Because Heidegger wants to overcome this metaphysical way of thought, he must think against the system of valuation, against "value thinking." In the "Letter on Humanism" Heidegger phrases it in the most succinct way:

> To think against "values" is not to maintain that everything interpreted as "a value"—"culture," "art," "science," "human dignity," "world," and "God"—is valueless. Rather, it is important finally to realize that precisely through the characterization of something as "a value" what is so valued is robbed of its worth.

> That is to say, by the assessment of something as a value what is valued is admitted only as an object for man's estimation. But what a thing is in its Being is not exhausted by its being an object, particularly when objectivity takes the form of value. Every valuing, even where it values positively, is a subjectivizing. It does not let beings: be. Rather, valuing lets beings: be valid—solely as the objects of its doing. . . . To think against values . . . means rather to bring the clearing of the truth of Being before thinking, as against subjectivizing beings into mere objects.[7]

What Heidegger (and I will claim that Derrida and the Daoists try to do something similar) wants is to think before or beyond this distinction of subject and object. Heidegger does not want to posit new values (or like Nietzsche, depose, revalue, or devalue values); he rather asks for a receptive attitude in terms of *Gelassenheit* that accepts value rather than trying to create it.

But if Heidegger tries to think beyond values, does that mean that he does not recognize any "value"? Of all of the philosophies around, surely relativism and nihilism, denying certain values, have the least to offer us here in our quest to contribute to questions of economics and justice. Is Heidegger a relativist or a nihilist? Yes and no. The main idea to understand is that Heidegger thinks that relativism and nihilism remain within the system of valuation under discussion. Only from *within* this system can one speak of relativism and nihilism. The question for Heidegger, rather, is not to seek to mend the shortcomings of the system within the system but to undo the shortcomings by stepping outside of the system, again something that I think Derrida and Daoism also try to do, albeit differently. Heidegger says we should go *through* the current nihilism not by returning to previous values or positing new ones but by overcoming them. For example, in *Zur Seinsfrage* Heidegger explains how relativism and nihilism are the last phases of metaphysics and how it is important to understand them as such in order to even conceive of crossing the line to another kind of thinking.[8]

Thinking in values denies something, loses something essential. If there is something left for the term "value," if value still has some meaning, it should be sought not in terms of economics, technology, human resources, *Gestell,* or any other human making or doing. From technology to economics, the scientific and metaphysical worldview sees the world in terms of resources, objects, value. Heidegger's *Gestell,* or "enframing," is a good word for this.[9] We have framed the world in such a way that it appears only within these artificial frames, as objects before a subject.[10]

Heidegger's well-known polemic against the philosophy behind modern technology (which he qualifies as thinking in values, calculation, goal and means, instrumentality) argues that this kind of thinking has pervaded metaphysics. Heidegger argues for a different way of existing, of being in the world. This different way can best be described as a deep or broad relationality.

Two terms, among others, come to mind when thinking of this Heideggerian form of relationality.[11] The first is *Auseinandersetzung*, usually translated as "con-frontation" or "setting-apart-together" or even as "conversation." All these translations are supposed to underscore the idea that *Auseinandersetzung* brings together what is different in an exposition of these differences. The second term is *Gelassenheit*, usually translated as "releasement." None of the translations are really satisfactory.

Let us take a closer look at these terms and what Heidegger tries to say with them, starting with *Auseinandersetzung*. *Auseinandersetzung*, or con-frontation, is what takes place in between differences. Opposites, differences, are always already connected in an essential way. Importantly, the "intimacy" or unity of the differences does not exist anywhere else but in the interplay of the differences. As such, there is no objective or dialectic third vantage point from which to judge the differences or into which they get dissolved, and thus no way to value any side of oppositional structures higher or lower than the other side.

Heidegger's famous reinterpretation of Heraclitus' fragment about war being the father of all things concludes that con-frontation, as *Auseinandersetzung*, is the begetter and keeper of all things. In this context Heidegger even explicitly names *polemos* (Heidegger's Greek basis for *Auseinandersetzung*) as "*die Lichtung*"[12] (the clearing). In other, very Heideggerian words, "Clearing [*Lichtung*] is never the empty, but the most originary thorough swaying [*Wesen*] of en-owning [*Ereignis*] as the settlement of the countering and strife—the 'in-between' held unto the ab-ground [*Abgrund*]."[13]

We must now ask how all of this relates to the concepts of value and justice. Con-frontation is a keeping apart in togetherness, or a thoughtful appropriation (*Ereignis*) that leaves the other as it is itself, to let things show themselves as they are of themselves, to loosely quote the motto of phenomenology, at least Heidegger's version of it. This means that *Auseinandersetzung* is largely focused around alterity, otherness, or foreignness. To con-front is to set apart in difference what belongs together exactly because of this difference. To become an authentic self includes a realization of this otherness, and such a realization literally implies the task to let this otherness, the other, be itself. As Heidegger puts it, "The appropriation of one's own *is* only as the encounter [*Auseinandersetzung*] and guest-like dialogue with the foreign."[14] For Heidegger, then, it seems that the only value there is, is the value of letting things be themselves, of showing and taking an interest in how things are, of not subjecting things to our human wants and frames, but leaving things their otherness. It is in this way that Heidegger's thinking beyond value becomes the condition for justice. Justice would be letting things be.

But before we make hasty decisions here regarding justice, let us see what Heidegger has to say about justice. As we saw, in the *Nietzsche* volume Heidegger considers Nietzsche's version of justice of to be that which enhances life, as given by the dictates of the will to power. But this kind of "appropriateness" is not exactly how Heidegger himself sees justice. In order to discover Heidegger's own views, we need to go to "The Anaximander Fragment."[15] In its minimal form, the fragment runs like this: "χατὰ τὸ χρεών. Διδόναι γὰρ αὐτὰ δίχην χαὶ τίσιν ἀλλήλοις τῆς ἀδιχίας" (*kata to kreon. Didonai gar auta diken kai tisin allelois tes adikias*). Traditionally the fragment gets translated along the lines of "out of necessity . . . ; for they suffer punishment and make reparation to one another for their injustice according to the order of time."[16] Heidegger, however, offers a different translation of this part, including a reinterpretation of *dike* and *adike*. Heidegger first of all does not want to restrict the meaning of the word *dike* to its usual translations of "justice" or "right," as he finds these translations too narrow. He focuses on three words in this fragment and says: "The words *δίχη*, *ἀδιχία* and *τίσις* have a broad significance which cannot be enclosed within the boundaries of particular disciplines. 'Broad' does not mean here extensive, in the sense of something flattened or thinned out, but rather far-reaching, rich, containing much thought."[17] Heidegger accordingly translates *dike* with *Fug, die Fuge,* in English, "what is fitting," "what is joined," "enjoined," "jointure."[18] "What is" fits itself in presencing between having come and going away. It would then seem that this is "fitting" in the sense of "appropriate," *in der Fuge*. Heidegger wonders why the fragment speaks of "what is" as being out of joint, *aus der Fuge*. His answer is that "it" is out of joint in that "what is" seems to insist on permanent being: "That which lingers perseveres in its presencing. In this way it extricates itself from its transitory while. It strikes the wilful pose of persistence [*den Eigensinn des Beharrens*], no longer concerning itself with whatever else is present. It stiffens—as if this were the way to linger—and aims solely for continuance and subsistence."[19] What we can gather from this Heideggerian jargon is that the "injustice" of things present lies in them seeking to remain present. This is not the "just" way of being or being present, as the "right" way is to linger (*weilen*), which does not consist in insisting on staying but in coming from nowhere and going to nowhere at its own time; what lingers traverses the passage. "The disjunction (*Unfuge, adikia*) consists in the fact that whatever lingers awhile seeks to win for itself a while based solely on the model of continuance. Lingering as persisting, considered with respect to the jointure of the while, is an insurrection on behalf of sheer endurance."[20] Yet *das Anwesende,* "what is," is and is not *aus der Fuge. Dike,* justice, *die Fuge,* rather pertains when

> whatever lingers awhile in presence comes to presence insofar as it lingers; all the while, emerging and passing away, and the jointure of the transition from approach to withdrawal, continue. This lingering endurance of the transition is the enjoined continuance of what is present. The enjoined continuance does not at all insist upon sheer persistence.[21]

To put it in ordinary language, injustice is insisting on staying the same, this being unnatural or rather against Being, and justice is going with the flow. Injustice is insisting on keeping the current system going where it has outlived its usefulness, has fossilized, and is now a hindrance rather than a help; justice is letting it go and starting to think differently.

Yet what exactly does Heidegger mean with this *Fug*? The most obvious translation tells us something already. It is "jointure" (things belonging together) or enjoining. But Heidegger gives the answer himself a bit later when he focuses on the rest of the fragment and especially on the third important word: *τίσις* (*tisis*). Heidegger plays with the possible translations of "consideration," "heeding," and "esteeming," but settles on *Ruch* (reck) and connects this with *geruhen* (to deign, to respect), *Rücksicht* (consideration, regard, thoughtfulness) and *Sorge* (care).[22] In short, what is right or just, appropriate, is consideration of other things, a giving room or letting things belong or be what they inherently are. And this Heidegger connects with the first part of the fragment, χατὰ τὸ χρεών (*kata to kreon*). Translating *kreon* with *Brauch,* "usage," sounds like a return to the notion of value. Things that are present are for usage; they have use-value. But this would be a complete misunderstanding of what Heidegger is trying to say. As with other words, Heidegger does not mean usage in this sense but rather as enjoyment of what is as it is, making usage in tune with *Sorge* (care) and *Ruch* (reck). To explain this I would like to introduce the word "reckoning" as a possible translation for *Ruch* or reck. This will have the advantage of doing two things: First, it gives us instead of Heideggerian jargon an English word we can all understand and relate to, and, second, it will show exactly how words like this are reinterpreted by Heidegger. To "reckon" is connected in our modern minds to verbs like to "calculate," "account for," "estimate," "weigh up." These words show clearly the metaphysical or scientistic attitude that Heidegger wants to argue against with his polemic against values. Yet at the same time, going back to what Heidegger would call a more "originary" meaning, the word "reckoning" can be seen as "consideration," "thoughtfulness," "attentiveness," and even "value," as long as it is clear now that value is thought of differently.

Based on all this it is fair to conclude that the order of things, appropriateness (*dike*), seems to demand that second of Heidegger's key ideas: *Gelassenheit.* As mentioned earlier, it seems that for Heidegger justice is *Gelassenheit.* This releasement is not a passive detachment but an attitude that lies beyond the opposition passive versus active. Releasement is keeping an open mind about the mystery of the world and existence. It is aimed at creating an openness toward otherness in which things can "be" what they are; it is a letting-things-be as they are and not, as in dualistic philosophy, to oppose or try to master them and see them as something usable or valuable. Since in this Heideggerian kind of relational thought it is understood that self and other are essentially connected, there naturally arises a feeling of care or concern for (*Sorge*) and reckoning with (which is *not* calculation) the world that we inhabit. If we must speak of value here, the only value is intrinsic value in and of itself and not for something else.

Heidegger thinks that with the history of metaphysics things have been increasingly "out of joint." To counter this, as Heidegger thinks we should, we must overcome "value thinking" and learn to be in tune with the *Ereignis,* or "event of appropriation," by thinking the jointure and by reckoning, in short by practicing *Gelassenheit.* In "The Anaximander Fragment" it is said that justice gives *(didonai diken) Fuge gibt.*[23] But it can give, offer, or be given only when we are attentive to it. This happens only if we become aware of the relationality of ourselves with the rest of the world, which in turn creates a form of justice as "letting things be."

Derrida

In *Specters of Marx* Derrida begins with a quote from Shakespeare's *Hamlet,* where Hamlet declares that "the time is out of joint."[24] Derrida uses this quote to question Heidegger on this so-called Gift of Justice. As Heidegger himself had already noted, this gift is problematic because it seems impossible for something that is "out of joint" to give jointure. Derrida notices that Heidegger indeed seems to argue that justice is "the jointure of the accord: the proper jointure to the other given by one who does not have it. Injustice would be the disjointure or disjoining."[25] Derrida questions the privilege Heidegger seems to give to jointure over and against disjointure, and rhetorically asks:

> Does not justice as a relation to the other suppose on the contrary the irreducible excess of a disjointure or an anachrony, some *Unfuge,* some "out of joint" dislocation in Being and in time itself, a disjointure that, in always risking the evil, expropriation, and injustice (*adikia*) against which there is no calculable insurance, would alone be able to *do justice* or to *render justice* to the other as other?[26]

For Derrida, then, the asymmetry of the disjointure, rather than the jointure, is the condition on which justice is founded. This disjointure is understood by Derrida as the irreducible difference of each singular other, much in the sense understood by Levinas. Derrida's justice is literally induced by otherness. In Simon Critchley's words, "It is the demand provoked by the other's decision in me that calls forth political invention, that provokes me into inventing a norm and taking a decision. The *singularity* of the context in which the demand arises provokes an act of invention whose criterion is *universal.*"[27] The other *gives* us the decision to make, yet this decision is not based on any higher principle, as it was in Kant's Categorical Imperative, but as a direct result of the other's difference.

Derrida is suggesting that the other or difference, although always singular and always irreducibly different, is also always already inserted into any form of identity, be it cultural, individual, or otherwise. There is no self without other, no jointure without disjointure, and what is other is constitutive for what is considered a self or identity. The play of *différance* at work here suggests that there are no pure identities; there is rather pure relationality of which identities are at best useful heuristic functions. This is how the "universal" in the previous quote from Critchley should be understood. The demand is universal, since it comes from the singularity of *every* other and since this alterity is *always* part of identity. And in this way justice is seen by Derrida as a direct outcome of this relationality. This demand of the other, this decision of the other, is incalculable, does not work according to any preset principle. In *Negotiations* Derrida puts it in the following way:

> The decision . . . is never certain. If one were sure of the calculation, it would not be an action or a decision; it would be programming. There must be decision, there must be absolute risk, and there must be the undecidable. There is no decision without the undecidable. If there are no undecidables, there is no decision. There is simply programming, calculation. There must be political, ethical decisions, but these decisions are possible only in situations where the undecidable is a necessary dilemma.[28]

As usual, Derrida is talking about a double bind. One must make decisions, yet these decisions seem impossible since, if they only follow reasons, calculations, and values, they are nothing more than program following and hence not real decisions. There is no real foundation for real decisions. One might go so far as to say that the undecidability of the decision is the foundation. Derrida again, this time in *Politics of Friendship:*

> The instant of decision must remain heterogeneous to all knowledge as such, to all theoretical or reportive determination, even if it may and must be preceded by all possible science and conscience. The latter are unable to determine the leap of decision without transforming it into the irresponsible application of a programme, hence without depriving it of what makes it a sovereign and free decision—in a word, of what makes it a decision, if there is one.[29]

This means that this decision making can be done only in direct response to the situation. This is probably why Derrida prefers to talk about singular others, about singular deconstructions instead of deconstruction as a programme. There is an interesting passage in *Limited Inc.* that could make us fully understand and appreciate this profound relationality in Derrida's thinking. Expounding on the infamous "There is no outside of the text," Derrida explains that what he was really saying is "that nothing exists outside context . . . , but also that the limit of the frame or the border of the context always entails a clause of non-closure. The outside penetrates and thus determines the inside."[30] This contextuality itself is constitutive of any identity, and as context it can never be closed off; it is structurally and inherently open, since it is nothing more or less than "the entire 'real-history-of-the-world.' "[31]

Derrida's extreme openness toward alterity and the importance of alterity, otherness and difference, is not to be seen as a relativism. Things are not complete and full unto themselves, but the fact that Derrida criticizes this fullness or completeness does not mean we are left with meaninglessness per se. The complication to which Derrida's thinking points is not a pure rejection of value or meaning, but it thinks differently, relationally, on these subjects. This then is the similarity between Heidegger and Derrida. Both seek to convey the idea that the traditional or metaphysical way of thought on which our economic and justice systems is based is incapable of thinking this relationality, since it is stuck in the subject-object distinction. Both want to convey the idea that, thinking of values and justice, we need to go beyond this metaphysical way of thought, to include otherness in our considerations in a different, more fundamental way than does the calculation of modernity.

Derrida makes a clear distinction between law (*droit*) and justice. Law belongs to the realm of calculation. Law is measurable, rule following, whereas justice is exactly that which goes beyond such rule following. In his own words, "Law is the element of calculation, and it is just that there be law, but justice is incalculable, it requires us to calculate with the incalculable."[32] Derrida says that we should deal (or maybe reckon) with this kind of *aporia* in the area of justice, since the experience of justice, and its foundation, can never be assessed with the same criteria as law. Man-made values such as law are always based on what Derrida calls a "violent" or "mystical" foundation, meaning that they themselves require something to found them, but this something is itself beyond the idea of foundation. We would like to find a foundation for justice, but we realize that we cannot or that all the attempts and suggestions, like equality, are seriously problematic. We must then acknowledge that justice as such *is* the foundation for which there is no further ground. As such, Derrida can say, "Justice in itself, if such a thing exists, outside or beyond law, is not deconstructible. No more than deconstruction itself, if such a thing exists. Deconstruction is justice."[33]

The singularity of every previously highlighted other makes every other constitutive for our self and irreplaceable, and, as such, we are responsible for it. Derrida establishes this by extending the notion of responsiveness to the other toward that of responsibility. What is other is something that must come of its own, but as Derrida says, "it is necessary to prepare for it; for to allow the coming of the entirely other, passivity, a certain kind of resigned passivity for which everything comes down to the same, is not suitable. Letting the other come is not inertia opening to anything whatever."[34] With this Derrida is arguing for a position similar to Heidegger's *Gelassenheit* (releasement).

Heidegger and Derrida were very much proponents of an ethical way of life, yet it is hard to establish where *Gelassenheit* or the decision to responsibility leads in actual societies. Derrida's ethical ideas stem largely from Levinas' notion of the other, whereby otherness is always perceived as singular. Ethics arises as a direct consequence of an opening toward what is other, both in Heidegger and in Derrida. Since what is other is always inserted into the self, and thus constitutive of it, it becomes impossible not to acknowledge the other, and that means a responsiveness that entails a responsibility. This responsibility is direct, not derived from some greater source or origin but purely as a consequence of the relationality to alterity or difference. There is thus, I would claim, as in Heidegger, also a direct relation between is and ought in Derrida, which he has also described as a philosophy of "affirmation" consonant with the "decision to justice."

So where does this leave the idea of value in Derrida? Although Derrida does not speak much about value itself, we can at least say that it should be turned away from the calculation that is economical value. Bartering, exchange in value, in economic exchange remains calculation. We should see value as something else, something that cannot be calculated. The relationship between value and justice should at the very least be turned around. It is not that value comes first and justice the calculated outcome of values, but rather that justice is the incalculable origin of values. Justice is undecidable, incalculable through other things such as values. A philosophy of affirmation such as that of Derrida and Daoism is called for. All societies and all contracts already presuppose one affirmation, and this must be tied to justice. Yet this affirmation is a moment of injustice and violence; it is not itself supported by anything else.[35] Thus the double bind, and the "time out of joint." This affirmation should also not be seen as a moment "before" the (just) society arises, but as a constant reminder of the necessity to negotiate between the incalculable foundation of justice (which lies in the demand of the other) and the practical application of the law.[36]

Daoism

As a preliminary to my claim that the distinction between is and ought does not feature prominently in Daoism, I would first like to look at the seat of thought, *xin* (心). Thinking and feeling are related through the character *xin*. In the words of Roger Ames and David Hall, "in this classical Chinese worldview broadly conceived, the mind cannot be divorced from the heart. There are not altogether rational thoughts devoid of feelings, not any raw feelings altogether lacking in cognitive content. . . . The prejudice to which Daoism is resolutely resistant is the dichotomy between the cognitive and the affective that would privilege knowing as some separate cognitive activity."[37] The nondistinction of thinking and feeling, of the so-called objective reason and subjective affections, leads one to at least suspect that in Daoism thinking would have an ethical component.

To understand how Daoism sees values and valuation, let us consult the *Daodejing*, especially those chapters that attack Confucianism as an artificial valuation system. It then immediately becomes clear that this valuation system, and its values, are intimately connected with, and the result of, "doing" (*wei,* 為) and "discrimination" or "disputation" (*pian,* 辨). Although Confucius makes it look as if his system is natural, the chapters in the *Daodejing* that directly attack Confucianism show that it is not. The *wu* forms, especially *wuwei* (無為), so prominent in Daoism, are obviously directed against such a way of doing and discriminating.[38] It is therefore that chapters such as 3, 5, and 12 promote an attitude against hierarchical valuation. And especially in chapters 18, 19, and 38, where Confucianism and its artificial values are directly targeted, we see that it is only when *dao* (道) is lost that we get what are usually seen as values. Only when *dao* is lost do we value certain things over others, which *is* the core of valuation in the first place: valuation makes things relative to one another and immediately places an unacceptable artificial value on certain things *over* other things. Only then does an artificial and human-centred moral system arise, where knowledge (*zhi,* 知) discriminates between different humans and between humans and the rest of the world, thus distinguishing humans in the process of introducing values. As is said in chapter 2 of the *Daodejing:* "As soon as everyone in the world knows that the beautiful are beautiful, there is already ugliness. As soon as everyone knows the able, there is ineptness."[39] Or in chapter 5: "The heavens and earth are not partial to institutionalized morality."[40] And finally in chapter 18: "It is only when grand way-making [*dao*] is abandoned, that authoritative conduct (*ren*) and appropriateness (*yi*) appear."[41] Many other passages of the *Daodejing* convey a similar message.

In the words of Ames and Hall, Daoist knowing is something completely opposite to the Confucian way: Daoist "knowledge, as unprincipled knowing, is the acceptance of the world on its own terms without recourse to rules of discrimination that separate one sort of thing from another."[42] Further on, in the commentary on chapter 38, they argue that "technical morality, imposed from without, is no more than a record of steady moral deterioration. The more elaborate the terms of such norms, the clearer is the indication that morality has slipped from what we do spontaneously and unconsciously."[43]

Discrimination is valuation, and setting values is the beginning of the end. The extreme perspectivism of the *Daodejing* conveys a relational understanding of the world, whereby it becomes impossible to differentiate hierarchically between things or even between oneself and other things, and, as such, the *Daodejing* goes directly against the very idea of valuation, hierarchy. It is much better to at least try to stay as close as possible to "the uncarved block of wood," where such discriminations and valuations are not yet prominent. In fact, returning to the uncarved block is imperative to undo the damage of the artificial Confucian value system. In chapter 28: "When unworked wood is split, it is made into utensils. When the sages are employed, they are made into head officials. There is no cutting, however, in the very best tailoring."[44]

Similar ideas are found in Zhuangzi, who argues that thinking in values is a sign of "chop logic,"[45] whereby, in the system of "discriminations," preferences are given to one thing rather than another, which goes against *dao*. In Zhuangzi's words: "To 'discriminate between alternatives' is to fail to see something."[46] Making artificial distinctions, which seems to be the key idea of valuation in the first place, leads one to value some things over others, where the Daoist tries to get beyond that distinction. This process of valuation as a departure from *dao* is described in chapter 2 of the *Zhuangzi:*

> The understanding of the men of ancient times went a long way. How far did it go? To the point where some of them believed that things have never existed—so far, to the end, where nothing can be added. Those at the next stage thought that things exist but recognized no boundaries among them. Those at the next stage thought there were boundaries but recognized no right and wrong. Because right and wrong appeared, the Way was injured.[47]

The fact that the ancient Daoists recognized no boundaries between themselves and the rest of the world is an indication that they thought in terms of relationality, where one's self is considered as continuous with others and other things. Consequently they saw morality as arising spontaneously, as a direct result of our being in the world with others and everything around us, and in that sense Daoism shows a proximity to Heidegger's *Gelassenheit* and to Derrida's decision without ground.

Staying with the *Zhuangzi,* we must also look at the usefulness of being useless. Zhuangzi says in chapter 4, "All men know the uses of the useful, but no one knows the uses of the useless."[48] Stories of this uselessness and its usefulness for those who are useless abound in the *Zhuangzi.* Most of these passages praise uselessness, but one passage in the *Zhuangzi* is ambivalent: the story of the good-for-nothing goose that gets killed,[49] where there seems to be a different approach to this uselessness. I think this rests on a mistaken conflation of two ways of using language in the concept of usefulness and uselessness. The tree in a previous story is useless, so it is spared. The goose is useless, so it dies. Because the tree is totally useless to humans, it is left alone. The goose, however, is not as useless as it seems. Although it cannot cackle, it has not lost its use-value as food to humans. So it is killed rather for being useful than for being useless. Even the cackling goose will not escape this fate. With that I think we can still hold on to the idea of the use of uselessness in Zhuangzi. I do not wish to absolutize uselessness in Zhuangzi's perspectivist thought, but I do think that he displays a general mistrust of usefulness and in that sense is definitely defending the idea that, once something or someone becomes useful or valuable, there is a good chance things will go wrong and depart from *dao.*

Having value or thinking in terms of values and discriminations can then be seen as being denied the possibility of possessing *dao*. Being valuable means you are stuck, like Confucius (who admits so himself according to Zhuangzi in chapter 6),[50] in an arbitrary and artificial system. This does not mean that the Daoist is totally against all values or norms. One needs provisional values, but we should take care to see these in the same way as the Daoists see language. Language is not to be discarded totally, but should be used sparingly with full awareness of its provisional status. Laozi recognizes this in chapter 32: "When we start to regulate the world we introduce names. But once names have been assigned, we must also know when to stop. Knowing when to stop is how to avoid danger."[51] In a way that might be seen as similar to Derrida, Laozi recognizes the unavoidability of naming and calculating, yet stays aware of the unnameable and incalculable (non-)foundation of this.

Turning again to the *Zhuangzi,* according to Graham, even Zhuangzi the relativist does indeed recognize two kinds of value as worthy of his consideration: filial piety and the duty of minister to ruler.[52] The first duty is, for Zhuangzi, a natural one. The second, although it is a duty, is best avoided by not taking office, only coming into play when taking office is unavoidable. These duties or values arise naturally out of the direct context of what we are and are not imposed by some principle that would stand outside of these contexts. Aside from these two, Zhuangzi does not accept the other values common to the traditional Chinese world, such as status, ritual, and bodily intactness. The thing to do is not to set value by conventional standards, but to value all alike without prejudice. In Zhuangzi, we can say that either everything has value, or nothing has value over anything else. In either case, introducing a hierarchy in value is something that Zhuangzi is against. *Lun* (論), the sorting and grading that is part of the title of the second chapter, is highly spoken of by Zhuangzi. Yet, as the title of this chapter suggests, Zhuangzi's *lun* is "the sorting which evens things out."[53] Zhuangzi finds as much value in trees, skulls, cripples, and the like, as in the human world. In the *Zhuangzi* there is a dismissal of any value judgment that thinks of values in terms of hierarchy.

Yet how else *can* we think of value? The only possible answer here would be as all-inclusive. When the inquirer in the "Autumn Floods" chapter, bewildered by Zhuangzi's insistent attack on the idea of value, asks what the value of *dao* is, the answer is simple. Having *dao* means you are aware of the patterns and intricacies of the world, and as such you will be able to see clearly and act accordingly: "Whoever knows the Way is sure of penetrating the patterns, whoever penetrates the patterns is sure to be clear-headed in weighing things, whoever is clear-headed in weighing things will not use other things to his own harm."[54] Not using other things to his own harm must be understood here in the light of what the *Zhuangzi* says elsewhere: "The utmost man uses the heart like a mirror; he does not escort things as they go or welcome them as they come, he responds and does not store."[55] This sounds like the sage does not care much about things, but that would be the wrong way to see this. Since value is inherent in everything, and the Daoist sage recognizes this inherent value in all things because they are all valuable from some point of view, the sage responds to things by letting them be what their nature intends. This is the basis for justice as the letting be of others, as giving space to diversity. This is indeed the way of the sage and is consistent with the Daoist version of a *wuwei* government: do not interfere with the natural inclination of things; let them run their course without artificially, and hierarchically, valuing them. Note, however, that this view is not metaphysical in any way. The wider, encompassing view of the sage is not one from outside of the world, but one that accepts all viewpoints and sees as necessary the patterns by which the world works.

Bringing Heidegger, Derrida, and Daoism Together

On the ethical level, notions of letting things take their natural course are readily found both in Heidegger and in Daoism. And, together with Derrida's idea of responsiveness, all three advocate an attitude of openness to things unfamiliar, a letting be of difference. This is in response to the perceived artificiality of the ideas current in their respective times. Thus the Daoists argue against the artificial Confucian standards, which they see as an obstacle to the development of natural or unmediated morality. Morality in this unmediated sense will develop of itself; it is *ziran* (自然), or spontaneous, without the artificial imposition of rules and regulations. Heidegger argues against the "they" (*Man*) attitude of social conventions and tries to establish how *Gelassenheit* could help us overcome this artificial approach. Derrida searches for ways to affirm otherness and to criticize the dominance of certain power systems and the metaphysical way of seeing things. With this he seeks to establish a natural responsiveness to others that is certainly ethical. I therefore see a definite ethical dimension to Heidegger, Derrida, and Daoism.

Zhuangzi's sages respond spontaneously, and this responding is comparable to Derrida's responsiveness as responsibility, since in a similar move Zhuangzi is not interested in an emotional, or passionate, responding to things (as would the Romanticist), but rather in an "impersonal calm,"[56] where responding means to let things take their own course. It is this kind of justice and responsibility that must be thought of as the indeconstructible source of our thought and of our coexistence (with everything) in the world. In this way responsiveness does lead to responsibility. Thus, contrary to popular opinion, I reject the notion that there is no ethical dimension to this view. One would assume that a so-called objective, bird's-eye (think of Peng) view tends for Westerners to be equated with the dichotomy of is and ought, where, accordingly, objectivity is understood to be "valueless" seeing. Such an objective view would see how things *are* but would not be able to see how they should be. Yet this idea of objectivity is rejected in Heidegger, Derrida, and Laozi and Zhuangzi, who all claim (maybe in different but compatible ways) that their views, in the form of a spontaneous responsiveness to the world that does not go by conventional standards, lead to a responsibility to stand up for the natural way things are, that is, to safeguard, to let be, and thus to deny the kind of objectivity functioning at the basis of the is-ought distinction.

According to Heidegger, *Gelassenheit* is not negative or passive, but an attitude that entails an abandoning of the subjective self to the primacy of the event, the *Ereignis*. Similarly, *wuwei* as nonassertive action does not mean one should not speak or act, but that one will speak and behave in a way that does not unnaturally restrict others. The ethical implications of this are obvious: the self should act in a way that recognizes the spontaneity of the other and does not impose conventional expectations and restrictions thereon. The similarity between *ziran* and *wuwei* and *Gelassenheit* is that there is recognition of the primacy of the relationality, of the spontaneity of the other. Karyn Lai puts it in the following way:

> If *ziran* is understood as spontaneity and we are to foster it, we must, in simple terms, refrain from interference: allowing for the spontaneity of an individual requires us not to impose unnecessary constraints on this individual. . . . In other words, it is to practice *wuwei*.[57]

So *Gelassenheit*, responsiveness as responsibility, *ziran*, and *wuwei* entail a realization of the uniqueness and spontaneity of each situation, of each response to the other. And this should be the ground, or rather nonground, for justice. The focus is not on the other as an oppositional figure, an object for a subject, but on the realization of the other. And here I mean realization in both senses of the word, as a necessary complement to the self and its development and as something that naturally causes some kind of feeling of responsibility for its well-being, at least through not interfering with its natural inclinations.

Conclusion

Morality in such an unmediated sense as described previously will develop of itself; it is spontaneous, without the artificial imposition of rules and regulations. As such it can be said to deny the dichotomy of is and ought. Thinking beyond values or use for Heidegger, Derrida, and Daoism can thus seem "useless" from the perspective of thought that maintains this dichotomy. I suggest that currently some of the best efforts at contributing to questions of values, economics, and justice still seem to be entrenched in a system of philosophy incapable of challenging its own presuppositions. And these presuppositions reflect themselves in (or are the reflections of) the wider system of thought in economics whereby the Western way of doing things is being transplanted globally. Based on what I have argued here, I think that what we need in the end is not this kind of philosophy's contribution to a sustainable economic growth, since that system of growth seems to be exactly what causes the problems. I don't think that equality will continue to function meaningfully as the basis of justice in the same way it has, since in our plural, multicultural societies it is increasingly the differences we are concerned with, differences we recognize and want to keep. Different cultures, different people, have different values, and although it is extremely useful to see where our similarities lie, it seems far more useful to see how we can make those differences productive, and for that I do think we need to drastically change our notion of values. There needs to be a paradigm shift from the artificial ways of thinking about values and justice to an alternative way of thought that perceives them as spontaneously arising from what our situation *is,* instead of trying to artificially impose them on this situation. I hope to have shown that there are resources in Heidegger, Derrida, and Daoism that can contribute to this.

NOTES

1. Martin Heidegger, *Beiträge zur Philosophie (vom Ereignis),* GA 65 (Frankfurt am Main: Klostermann, 2003), 36, 43.
2. Martin Heidegger, *An Introduction to Metaphysics,* trans. R. Manheim (New Haven, CT: Yale University Press, 1959), 8.
3. I say this reservedly, as of course the classical Daoists were not arguing against such a metaphysical system but were more arguing against the Confucian values and worldviews of their own time. Yet it is fruitful to see how their arguments can be understood as implicitly challenging metaphysics in this area.
4. I will not go into the question here of whether Heidegger's interpretation of Nietzsche is correct. At various places Derrida, for instance, has questioned Heidegger's often compelling, but indeed sometimes maybe one-sided interpretation of Nietzsche.
5. Martin Heidegger, *Nietzsche,* trans. D. Farrell Krell, 4 vols. (San Francisco: Harper and Row, 1979–1987), 3:200.
6. Ibid., 3:202.
7. Martin Heidegger, *Basic Writings,* trans. D. Farrell Krell (London: Routledge and Kegan Paul, 1978), 251.
8. See Martin Heidegger, *Wegmarken* (Frankfurt am Main: Klostermann, 1996), 421–425.
9. See Heidegger, *Basic Writings,* 325.
10. See ibid., 321, where Heidegger illustrates this by pointing to the different approaches to the river Rhine in the hydroelectric plant (use-value) and in Hölderlin's poem "The Rhine" to explain why thinking in values loses the "essence" of thinking of Being.

11. I have argued for this kind of relationality in Heidegger, Derrida, and Daoism elsewhere. See my "Thinking on the Edge: Heidegger, Derrida and the Daoist Gateway (*men* 門)," *Philosophy East and West* 60, no. 4 (October 2010).

12. Martin Heidegger, *Early Greek Thinking,* trans. D. Farrell Krell and F. Capuzzi (New York: Harper and Row, 1975), 119.

13. Martin Heidegger, *Mindfulness,* trans. Parvis Emad and Thomas Kalary (London: Continuum International, 2006), 90. *Ereignis* is usually and more clearly translated as "appropriation" or "event of appropriation," which must not be thought in terms of a subject appropriating an object, but more as a process or event which keeps the differences between subject and object while at the same time relating them; or rather *Ereignis* tries to overcome the subject-object way of thinking entirely. *Abgrund* is usually translated as "abyss" and is a word Heidegger uses to highlight the nonmetaphysical approach of his thought, being "without ground."

14. Martin Heidegger, *Hölderlin's Hymn "The Ister,"* trans. W. McNeill and J. Davis (Bloomington: Indiana University Press, 1996), 142; emphasis in original.

15. In Heidegger, *Early Greek Thinking,* 13–58. Anaximander was one of the earliest known Greek thinkers. Pre-Socratic thought in general was a great influence on Heidegger, and he reinterpreted many of the ancient Greek philosophers' ideas.

16. Translation adapted from Milton C. Nahm, *Selections from Early Greek Philosophy* (Englewood Cliffs, NJ: Prentice Hall, 1964), 39–40.

17. Heidegger, *Early Greek Thinking,* 21–22.

18. Note that these words are also used in German for masonry and carpentry/woodwork and refer to the "seam" or cement that joins the different parts together. They thus combine the different elements to one connected whole.

19. Heidegger, *Early Greek Thinking,* 42.

20. Ibid., 43.

21. Ibid., 43–44.

22. Ibid., 46–47.

23. Ibid., 43.

24. Quoted in various places (e.g., p. 1) in Jacques Derrida, *Specters of Marx* (New York: Routledge Classics, 2006).

25. Ibid., 31–32.

26. Ibid., 32; emphasis in original.

27. Simon Critchley, "Five Problems in Levinas's View of Politics and the Sketch of a Solution to Them," *Political Theory* 32, no. 2 (2004), 180.

28. Jacques Derrida, *Negotiations (Interventions and Interviews, 1971–2001),* trans. and ed. E. Rottenberg (Stanford, CA: Stanford University Press, 2002), 31.

29. Jacques Derrida, *Politics of Friendship,* trans. G. Collins (London: Verso, 2005), 219.

30. Jacques Derrida, *Limited Inc.* (Evanston, IL: Northwestern University Press, 1988), 152–153.

31. Ibid., 136.

32. Derrida in David Gray Carlson, Drucilla Cornell, and Michel Rosenfeld, *Deconstruction and the Possibility of Justice* (New York: Routledge, 1992), 16.

33. Derrida in ibid., 14–15.

34. Jacques Derrida, *Psyche: Inventions of the Other,* ed. Peggy Kamuf and Elizabeth Rottenberg (Stanford, CA: Stanford University Press, 2007), 39.

35. See, for example, Derrida's "The Principle of Reason: The University in the Eyes of Its Pupils," in Jacques Derrida, *Eyes of the University: Right to Philosophy 2,* trans. Jan Plug (Stanford, CA: Stanford University Press, 2004), where he argues for a similar lack of reason in the *foundation* of the university as a place of reason; or Jacques Derrida and Geoffrey Bennington, *Jacques Derrida,* trans. G. Bennington (Chicago: University of Chicago Press, 1993), 231.

36. See Derrida and Bennington, *Jacques Derrida*, 228–241.

37. Roger T. Ames and David L. Hall, *Daodejing, Making This Life Significant* (New York: Ballantine Books, 2003), 26.

38. Superficially it might be said that in the *Laozi* there is more focus on the attack on "doing," and in the *Zhuangzi* there is more focus on the attack on "discriminating."

39. *Daodejing*, 80. All translations from the *Daodejing* are from Ames and Hall, *Daodejing, Making This Life Significant.*

40. *Daodejing*, 84.

41. *Daodejing*, 103.

42. Ames and Hall, *Daodejing*, 41. The so-called rules mentioned by Ames and Hall include "rules of thumb, habits of mind and action, established customs, fixed standards, received methods, stipulated concepts and categories, commandments, principles, laws of nature, conventions."

43. Ibid., 137.

44. *Daodejing*, 121. Other chapters conveying similar ideas through the "uncarved block" include 15, 19, 32, and 37.

45. *Zhuangzi*, 55, 82. Unless cited otherwise, all translations from the *Zhuangzi* are from Angus C. Graham, *Chuang-Tzu: The Inner Chapters* (London: George Allen and Unwin, 2001).

46. *Zhuangzi*, 57.

47. Burton Watson, *Zhuangzi: Basic Writings* (New York: Columbia University Press, 2003), 36–37.

48. *Zhuangzi*, 75.

49. *Zhuangzi*, 121.

50. *Zhuangzi*, 89–90.

51. *Daodejing*, 127.

52. Graham, *Chuang-Tzu*, 13.

53. *Zhuangzi*, 48.

54. *Zhuangzi*, 149.

55. *Zhuangzi*, 98.

56. Graham, *Chuang-Tzu*, 14.

57. Karyn Lai, "*Ziran* and *Wuwei* in the *Daodejing:* An Ethical Assessment," *Dao: A Journal of Comparative Philosophy* 6, no. 4 (2007), 332. Lai mentions a number of chapters from the *Daodejing* in this context: 12, 18, 19, 20, 37, and 53.

What Is It Like to Be a Moral Being? 24

Amita Chatterjee

> If epistemic curiosity about the world is one tendency that many people have, concern about goodness, rightness and justness also has a powerful presence—manifest or latent—in our minds.
>
> —*Amartya Sen, The Idea of Justice*

> If you experience the pain and pleasure of others while maintaining the distinction between yourself and the other, you have empathetic awareness. You are on your way to becoming a moral animal.
>
> —*Paul Bloom, Descartes' Baby*

I

I am sleeping soundly. I wake up, open my eyes, and find myself in a big building with innumerable rooms set up with gaming tables. I cannot leave this building without playing and winning some of the games, but all the games are unknown to me. I approach one of the tables where people are already playing. I watch the players and try to guess the rules. After a time, I join the play, making very tentative moves. Other players at the table are also watchful. They are wary because they do not know me or the level of my expertise. We are as if enveloped in "a veil of ignorance" and make our moves as best as we can. To finish the game, each of us has to establish some working relationship with the others. How do we go about it? We all hope to win, so we are all competitors. Maybe some of us are naturally smart players. Should we smart ones cooperate with each other, finish the game, and win all the booty? How are we supposed to behave with the dumb players? Should we try to help them become better players or should we keep them in the dark, hoodwink them, and amass the winnings? While I go on winning and some other hapless persons continue to lose, do I feel happy? At some point, do I start wondering whether the rules are fair? What sort of reactions do I anticipate from the regular losers? Do they smell a rat? Do they feel deprived, resigned, outraged? Do all of us have a notion of fair play and do we share the same notion? If our notions of fair play are incommensurate, can we continue to play, not to speak of finishing a game? Are we then eternally trapped in this house of games? Shall we ever be real people in a real world with moral responsibilities?

II

My departure point in this essay is Amartya Sen's idea of justice, developed in his 2009 book of the same title. Here Sen claims to offer an alternative to the extant theories of justice by combining insights derived from Western and Indian moral and economic theories, where ethics and economics are first cousins insofar as they contribute to the general well-being of the human family. What I want to broadly explore in these pages are four aspects of Sen's thinking about justice. First, I will examine the most important points of difference between Sen's and Rawls' ideas of justice. Second, I will look at Sen's ideas as they relate to the *Arthaśāstra,*[1] an important pillar of his theory of justice. Though Sen claims to have derived an important distinction between *nīti* (institutions, a fixed set of rules) and *nyāya* (rules as applied, justice realized), a careful reading of the *Arthaśāstra* shows that the general tenor of this ancient Indian treatise accords better with Rawls' idea of justice than with Sen's. I then look into whether Sen's view can be supported on the basis of some recent experiments in cognitive developmental psychology. And finally, I ask why we need to go beyond Sen's view to have a fully developed theory of justice as a moral value.

Philosophers have a long-standing engagement with justice, both the overarching moral value and the supreme political ideal. It goes back at least to the fourth century BCE in both Greece and India. However ancient it may be, this quest has not yielded a theory of perfect justice; nor has it made much difference in neutralizing the inequalities and imbalances of power prevalent in all societies even in our present era of globalization. Sen's diagnosis of this twofold malady—the unavailability of a theory of perfect justice and inefficacy of existing theories in removing inequities from societies—is that there is a general misconception about the idea of justice. Justice, holds Sen, is so multifaceted and complex an idea that it is unlikely that philosophers would ever agree on what a just society would look like. Hence, rather than running after this will-o'-the-wisp, we should work backward from our innate sense of injustice. Inspired by Charles Dickens' *Great Expectations,* Sen writes in the preface of his own book, "What moves us, reasonably enough, is not the realization that the world falls short of being completely just—which few of us expect—but that there are clearly remediable injustices around us which we want to eliminate."[2] Slavery, the subjugation of women, widespread hunger and deprivation, the lack of schooling for children, and the absence of available and affordable health care are just a few of the palpable injustices one could cite. Unlike philosophers of the Western theoretical tradition led by Hobbes, Rousseau, Kant, Rawls, and the like, Sen equates the idea of justice with the idea of reducing injustice, his beacons being the Buddha, Marx, J. S. Mill, Bentham, Condorcet, Adam Smith, Thomas Paine, and Mary Wollstonecraft.

Because reducing the quantum of injustice in the world involves real people in real-life situations, justice has to be relative to the situation. The answer to the question of what constitutes a just act in a particular situation is necessarily theory driven, and as the theories diverge, so too would the solutions. To use Sen's own example,[3] Anna, Bob, and Carla fight over a flute. Anna claims that she should get the flute because she is the only one who knows how to play. Bob claims that he should get it because he is poor and has no toys of his own. Carla expects to get the flute by virtue of the fact that she made it with her own labor. So who should get the flute? Sen shows that there is no single correct answer to this question because people of different persuasions will give different solutions depending on their theoretical allegience. The economic egalitarian who is committed to removing social inequities will give the flute to Bob because he is the poorest of the three; the libertarian will support Carla's claim because a person has a right to what she has produced. On this point two strange bedfellows—a right-wing libertarian and the early Marx—might agree despite their strong theoretical differences. The utilitarian is likely to vacillate because it is debatable who, Anna or Bob, will derive the greatest pleasure from getting the flute. However, by combining another general principle of "waste not, want not" with the principle of maximum happiness, a utilitarian is likely to give the flute to Anna, who is the only one of the three who knows how to play. What to do now? How to render justice? Should we follow the existing social institution or decide the issue by a coin toss or lottery? What Sen wants to highlight by this example is that there may not be one identifiable just social arrangement on which impartial agreement would emerge. Sen therefore discards the possibility that "transcendental institutionalists" will arrive at a single model of allocation of resources and freedoms.

This sort of theoretical impasse should nevertheless not stand in the way of our ameliorating suffering and reducing injustice because, according to Sen, an institutional blueprint of a just society is neither necessary nor sufficient to make a reasoned choice of policies. To cite Sen's own example, choosing between a Picasso and a Dalí is not helped in the least by knowing that the *Mona Lisa* is the most perfect picture in the world, even if it is possible for us to have a transcendental diagnosis. Similarly, knowing the height of Mount Everest is neither necessary nor sufficient for deciding whether K2 or Kanchenjunga is the higher peak.

This comparative stance brings two points into focus. The first is that one's perceptions and understanding of injustice are always colored by one's values, interests, and customs. How, then, can we ever have any agreement about injustice? Sen says that by the exercise of our critical reasoning, it is possible for us to go beyond and rise above mere self-interest. He is not saying that taking a critical stance will amount to having a view from nowhere. Rather, the critical stance is comparable to that of Adam Smith's "impartial spectator," who can distance himself from local customs and his own viewpoint and perceive the situation from the other's perspective. "We can never survey our own sentiments and motives, we can never form any judgment concerning them; unless we remove ourselves, as it were, from our own natural station, and endeavour to view them as at a certain distance from us. But we can do this in no other way than by endeavouring to view them with the eyes of other people, or as other people are likely to view them."[4] So the stance that an impartial spectator takes not only gives us an intersubjective perspective about the object at hand but also is the first step toward an empathic understanding of others. Empathizing with others means positioning oneself in others' shoes. Once empathy comes, we can move away from the consideration of our own well-being to that of another person. Second, well-being does not comprise only what we can actually attain but also what sort of choices we have in living our lives. In fact, freedom to make choices in our lives can significantly contribute to our well-being. But freedom to choose brings with it responsibility for what we do, and this introduces agency-centered concerns and moral issues. Our freedoms, capabilities, and empowerments lead to a host of justice-centric problems.

That Sen's idea of justice is a development of Rawls' idea of justice as fairness is evident from his reliance on the concept of the impartial spectator. He, however, is deviating from Rawls' model of a social contract made in what Rawls termed "the original position." Rawls' view on the subject is quite well-known,[5] so I will not attempt to summarize it here. Rather, I will be content to point out that any idea of fairness demands avoidance of bias in our evaluations, and the required impartiality, according to Rawls, can be ensured by introducing the narrative of the original position.

> The original position is an imagined position of primordial equality, when the parties involved have no knowledge of their personal identities, or their respective vested interests, within the group as a whole. Their representatives have to choose under this "veil of ignorance," that is, an imagined state of selective ignorance (in particular, ignorance about the distinct particular interests and actual views of a good life—what Rawls calls "comprehensive preferences"), and it is in that state of devised ignorance that the principles of justice are chosen unanimously. The principles of justice in Rawlsian formulation determine the basic social institutions that should govern the society they are, we imagine, about to "create."[6]

It is here that Sen disagrees with Rawls. Without going into Sen's elaborate arguments, I will mention a few salient points of disagreement between these two

Harvard thinkers. Sen, we have seen, argues that even in the original position there may not be any unique choice for one particular set of principles of just institutions. Rather, we are often presented with genuinely conflicting principles, each of which can be universalized. Under such circumstances, we need to fall back on our critical reason as well as our feeling of sympathy to choose one from among those conflicting principles. Hence, we should not look for a fixed set of rules and behavioral norms (*nīti*) to attain justice as fairness; rather, we should look for actual social realizations of justice in the lives of the people (*nyāya*). Sen borrows this distinction from the ancient Indian book of political wisdom, Kautilya's *Arthaśāstra*. A contractarian, thinks Sen, is overly dependent on Enlightenment reason and the principle of give-and-take. Sen rightly points out that our reasonable social behavior is not always guided by the motive of advantage seeking, but rather depends very often on unilateral obligations because of the asymmetry of power. A compassionate being who is interested in reducing the total suffering and injustice in the world would act to strike a social balance the moment she or he realizes that it lies in her or his power to make some difference in the world. Sen borrows this idea from the teachings of Gautama Buddha, recorded in the *Sutta-Nipāta*, which he thinks is also the underlying guiding principle of the human rights activists. More about this later.

III

Let us now look back to the ancient Indian political theory that led Sen to draw a meaningful distinction between *nīti* and *nyāya*, a distintion that bears the major weight of Sen's idea of justice. As mentioned at the beginning of this essay, I find the *Arthaśāstra* to be more in line with the Rawlsian social contract model than with Sen's position.

From the very opening statement it becomes obvious that this political treatise places economics and ethics within the same frame. In the third section of the treatise, it says that righteous and unrighteous acts (*dharmādharmau*) are learned from the three Vedas; wealth and nonwealth from the *Vārtā* (a treatise on agro-economy); the expedient and the inexpedient (*nayānayau*), as well as potency and impotency (*balābale*), from the science of government (*Daṇḍanīti*). In the next section of the *Arthaśāstra*, the subject matter of the science of the *Vārtā* is enumerated as follows. Agriculture, cattle breeding, and trade constitute *Vārtā*, which is most useful because it brings in grains, cattle, gold, forest produce (*kupya*), and free labor (*vishti*). It is by means of the treasury and the army, obtained solely through the *Vārtā*, that the king can control both his own subjects and his enemies.

More interesting and significant for our purpose is the narrative of the origin of kingship found in the *Arthaśāstra*. As the story goes, the land now known as

Bhāratavarsha (India) was once a land of plenty inhabited by simple people, happy and contented, who shared all the gifts of nature and had no notion of private property. Like little children, they were unaware of grief or envy. With malice toward none and protective of one another, they lived peacefully. This age was known as *krta-yuga* or *satya-yuga*. As can be surmised from the current condition of society, there was a fall from this naturalistic Eden, not because of any external demonic force but because the people fell prey to their own desire (*kāma*) and anger (*krodha*). Losing their contentment, some tried to grab land and women and keep them under their own control. Such selfish acts vitiated the atmosphere, and those possessing brute force started oppressing the weaker among them. Thus the Rule of the Stronger Fish (*mātsyanyāya*) came into existence and justice became synonymous with "the interest of the stronger."

Over time, the text says, the oppression gradually eroded the people's resilience to the point where a group of them approached Brahmā, the Purānic Lord of the gods, with their story of woe. Brahmā was sufficiently moved by their appeal to request that Manu, the first man, rule over the earth and protect the people. Manu, however, realized that once greed had raised its head, it would not be easily controlled and evil would take hold of human nature. He therefore declined to be king. But the suffering people were so desperate that they next proposed to pay taxes in the form of surplus food grain to the king's treasury if Manu condescended to become their ruler and protector. Finally, after a long spell of negotiation, Manu agreed to the proposal and became the first king.

It is absolutely clear that according to this treatise a king derives his authority from God and that some sort of a social contract based on mutual advantage was at the root of dynastic rule. Note that there is in this story no myth of the original position, nor were parties to the contract operating under the veil of ignorance. It was God, the all knowing, who chose as king one who was wise among men. Still, without an element of impartiality, justice cannot be upheld. In this story from the *Arthaśāstra* we find posited right from the beginning a universal principle of justice capable of wielding punishment to all, irrespective of their station in life. This principle is known as *daṇḍa*, which literally means the instrument of punishment. This principle did not arise as a result of a social contract but preceded the contract and applied equally to the ruler and the ruled. To prevent the king from turning into a tyrant, God created *daṇḍa* long before instituting kingship. *Daṇḍa* etymologically refers to the ritual staff of an ascetic, which inherited the power of law and became the symbol of discipline. It is supposed to protect the good and punish the evil and thus keep the oppressor in check so that the customary practices of the four castes (the priest and the teacher caste [*brāhmana*], the ruling and the warrior caste [*kṣatriya*], the merchant caste [*vaiśya*], and the serving caste [*śūdra*]), in which traditional Indian society was divided, can sustain the society. In the story, it was not the king but *daṇḍa* that wielded real power; *daṇḍa* was the true leader and the true punisher, ever alert to injustice. A king can check anarchy and rebellion, keep peace and protect personal property, provided he knows how to use *daṇḍa*. Thus we find that the *Arthaśāstra* prescribes a fixed set of comprehensive preferences and social and political institutions in consonance with them. Such fixed social and political practices and the correlative virtues, which are to be described as *nīti*s and not *nyāya*s, are described later.

Daṇḍanīti—norms relating to all-pervading control of the state, according to the *Arthaśāstra*—must be learned by a king. However, *daṇḍa* (punishment) must be tempered with self-discipline (*vinaya*) by a righteuous king. For, says the *Arthaśāstra,* whoever imposes severe punishment becomes repulsive to the people, while he who awards mild punishment becomes contemptible; whoever imposes punishment as deserved becomes respectable. For punishment, when awarded with due consideration, makes the people devoted to righteousness and they work effectively to produce wealth and enjoyment; whereas punishment when ill-awarded, under the influence of greed and anger or owing to ignorance, excites fury even among hermits and ascetics dwelling in forests, not to speak of householders. On the other hand, when the law of punishment is kept in abeyance, it gives rise to disorder, as is implied in the Rule of the Stronger Fish; that is, in the absence of a magistrate, the strong will swallow the weak, but under his protection, the weak resists the strong.

Another important function of *daṇḍa* is to empower the king to acquire what has not been acquired (*yoga*), to safeguard what has been acquired (*kṣema*), and to distribute the excess wealth among the deserving. Though amassing wealth is a duty of the king, it should be duly acquired and not by virtue of any corrupt practice. As indicated by Rawls, the *Arthaśāstra,* too, enjoins practice of a fixed set of virtues commensurate with this form of justice, namely, harmlessness, truthfulness, purity, freedom from spite, abstinence from theft or coercion, and forgiveness. All of these virtues in their other-regarding aspect are supportive of reciprocity and mutual benefit but are not "positional" in nature, nor supportive of the one-way flow of compassion from the powerful to the powerless for the empowerment of the latter and hence inadequate for Sen's theory of justice, where equity and justice demand that social practices and virtues vary depending on the degree of social empowerment. To explain why a socially powerful and economically well-off person should at all feel motivated to help less fortunate persons, Sen moved from the orthodox school of thought to Buddhist philosophy, where compassion (*karunā*) is a virtue that is to be practiced by all if the total quantum of suffering in the world is to be reduced. In the *Sutta-Nipāta,* the Buddha uses an analogy of the responsibility of the mother to her child. A mother nurtures and supports her child, not expecting any future benefit, but out of compassion and understanding that she is in a position to make a big difference in her child's life. It is this compassion leading to empathy that influences people to take altruistic actions and help remove inequalities. Hence, acquisition of virtues like compassion, empathy, and reasonableness makes a being human as well as moral.

IV

Sen begins his book with a quote from Dickens' *Great Expectations:* "In the little world in which children have their existence, there is nothing so finely perceived and finely felt, as injustice."[7] I would like to examine this hypothesis in the light of current experiments conducted by developmental cognitive scientists to determine its validity as well as to ascertain whether human beings are born with an innate sense of injustice or whether this sense of injustice is socially generated. What follows is a paraphrase of a paper published in *Nature.*

Hamlin, Wynn, and Bloom show that "6- and 10-month-old infants take into account an individual's actions towards others in evaluating that individual as appealing or aversive: infants prefer an individual who helps another to one who hinders another, prefer a helping individual to a neutral individual, and prefer a neutral individual to a hindering individual."[8] Previous experiments by developmental cognitive psychologists have established that infants in the first half year of life exhibit preferences for social individuals based on static perceptual features (for example, facial attractiveness and race), and toddlers by eighteen months of age spontaneously engage in cooperative helping behavior. The findings reported by Hamlin, Wynn, and Bloom constitute the first evidence that young infants' social preferences are influenced by others' behavior toward unrelated third parties.

In one experiment, six- and ten-month-old infants saw a character (a "climber" made of wood and with large eyes glued onto it) initially at rest at the bottom of a hill. During a habituation phase, infants saw events in which the climber repeatedly attempted to get up the hill, and on the third attempt the climber either was aided up by a helper who pushed it from behind or was pushed down by a hinderer. The infants saw alternating helping and hindering trials with looking time measured on each trial until their looking time reached a preset criterion indicating they had sufficiently processed these events. It was found in previous studies of which Hamlin and colleagues were aware that infants interpreted similar computer-animated events as instances of helping and hindering and expected the climber subsequently to approach the helper and avoid the hinderer. The experimenters in the Hamlin, Wynn, and Bloom paper asked how infants themselves, as uninvolved and unaffected bystanders, evaluate helpers and hinderers. In the test phase, using the choice measure, the experimenters examined infants' attitudes toward the helper and the hinderer. Infants were encouraged to choose between the two (that is, to reach for one). Infants robustly chose the helper, indicating that they held distinct impressions of the two characters on the basis of their actions toward the climber. Next, in the looking-time measure, infants saw a new display containing climber, helper, and hinderer. The climber alternately approached the helper and the hinderer. It was found that ten-month-olds looked longer at the latter event, indicating surprise when the climber approached one who had previously hindered it. Six-month-olds, however, looked equally to both events, suggesting that they did not attribute to the climber distinct attitudes toward the two characters, despite themselves preferring helper to hinderer in the choice measure. This suggests that the capacity for social evaluation may develop before the ability to infer others' evaluations.

The presence of social evaluation so early in infancy suggests that assessing individuals by the nature of their interactions with others is central to processing the information about the social world, both evolutionarily and developmentally. "The capacity for such evaluations can be seen as a biological adaptation: cooperative behavior such as group hunting, food sharing, and warfare can be beneficial to individual members of a group, but can only successfully evolve if individuals can distinguish free riders from cooperators or reciprocators, those willing to do their fair share."[9] Findings of the 2007 experiments also suggest that preverbal infants may be sensitive to this distinction. "The capacity to evaluate individuals by their social actions may also serve as a foundation for a developing system of moral cognition. Plainly, many aspects of a full-fledged moral system are beyond the grasp of the preverbal infant. Yet the ability to judge differentially those who perform positive and negative social acts may form an essential basis for any system that will eventually contain more abstract concepts of right and wrong, just and unjust."[10] The social evaluations observed in the experiments described do not stem from the infants' own experiences with the actors involved. These subjects had no previous history of interacting with the characters, nor did they themselves experience any consequences of these characters' actions. Their evaluations were made on the basis of witnessed interactions between unknown individuals.

Hamlin and colleagues' findings thus indicate that humans engage in social evaluation far earlier in development than previously thought and support the view that the capacity to evaluate individuals on the basis of their social interactions is universal and unlearned. These initial propensities, however, may get clouded with later contrary social exposures, but the fact that even preverbal infants have likes and dislikes for good guys and bad guys respectively makes Sen's idea of justice more plausible than Rawls'. For these experiments indicate that in real-life situations, we hardly make choices under a veil of ignorance. Six- and ten-month-old infants were performing within a comparative frame. Even if they did not have any idea of absolute goodness or badness, they could easily identify who is a better person and who worse when more than one alternative was present in a social interactive situation. Since we humans are endowed by nature with this innate rudimentary sense of bad, unpleasant, and unjust, and evolution teaches us to sympathize and cooperate with one another, we learn to care for and respect others as having similar sorts of pleasure and pain, expectations and fear. This is a prerequisite of our sincere desire for actualization of the precept "not to do unto others what we do not want to be done to us." Thus, both reason and compassion contribute to our feeling of being moral. This also explains why we feel somewhat relieved, if not happy, when we are convinced that we have been able to make a fair and just move in a given situation.

V

In our world full of inequities and inequalities, the original position is a useless myth. Some of us are strong, some are weak, some are smart, some are dumb, some have access to more knowledge, and some have less. It is never possible to place everybody at par. Moreover, we cannot have a view of events from God's point of view. We are bound to have a particular location and therefore a particular perspective. We can at most imaginatively position ourselves at another's location and attempt to feel how the world appears to others and how they are feeling. Our power to empathize, communicate, reason, and altercate enables us to give due respect to others. In this house of games, we cannot but play with others, but who would play which game should be chosen by each player. Choice implies freedom and freedom depends on knowledge of the rules of the game. Fairness and justice demand that the rules be equally known to all. However, people the world over continue to use knowledge as power, and even a highly empathic person may not empower others with all the rules of the games. That is why a right to information act needs to be enacted separately. It is imperative that we learn to share knowledge and information with others. That alone will prepare the stage for the emergence of fully moral beings. Mere equitable distribution of "primary goods," even if we understand them pretty widely à la Sen, will not give everyone equal rights to governance or simply to live.

NOTES

My thanks to my colleague at Jadavpur University, Dr. Smita Sirker, for her careful reading and editing.

Epigraphs. Amartya Sen, *The Idea of Justice* (London: Allen Lane, 2009), 414. Paul Bloom, *Descartes' Baby* (New York: Basic Books, 2004), 113.

1. R. P. Kangle, ed., *Kautilya's* Arthaśāstra, 3 vols. (Delhi: Motilal Banarasidass, 1988).
2. Sen, *Idea of Justice,* vii.
3. Ibid., 12–14.
4. Ibid., 125.
5. See John Rawls, *A Theory of Justice* (Cambridge, MA: Harvard University Press, 1971); and *Justice as Fairness: A Restatement,* ed. Erin Kelly (Delhi: Universal Law, 2004).
6. Ibid., 54.
7. Ibid., vii.
8. J. K. Hamlin, K. Wynn, and P. Bloom, "Social Evaluation by Preverbal Infants," *Nature* 450 (2007), 557.
9. Ibid., 558.
10. Ibid., 559.

What Is the Value of Poverty? 25

A Comparative Analysis of Aristotle's *Politics* and Dōgen's *Shōbōgenzō Zuimonki*

Steve Bein

Dōgen and Aristotle appear to stand in diametrical opposition to each other on the value of poverty. Dōgen repeatedly admonishes monks and nuns to be poor and advises laypeople that even they would be better off if they gave up all their worldly possessions. Aristotle, on the other hand, famously describes poverty as "the parent of revolution and crime."[1] This marked divergence is noteworthy not because we should expect Dōgen and Aristotle to march in lockstep together but because Aristotelian philosophy and Buddhist philosophy both advocate finding a middle path between extremes. Thus, it is surprising to find two thinkers applying a similar principle and yet reaching such radically disparate conclusions. Aristotle writes as if he wants to see an end to poverty, Dōgen as if he wants to see an end to property ownership.

One might make two observations from the outset. First, Aristotle's position is hardly radical, for it does not take an Aristotle to observe that poverty breeds desperation nor that desperation breeds criminality and political revolution. If that is the order of things, then we might nab Aristotle on a genealogical technicality—on this view poverty is in fact the grandparent of revolution and crime—but in the end Aristotle's famous quotation from *Politics* 2.6 amounts to a reiteration of what is already a commonly held belief. But in that case, Dōgen's position seems all the more radical. Kyoto in the Kamakura era was rife with revolution, criminality, disease, and famine. Dōgen cannot possibly have overlooked the role of poverty in these epidemics, and yet, as Watsuji Tetsurō points out, Dōgen is unusually tight-lipped on the subject, saying only, "You should contemplate impermanence."[2]

Second, Dōgen writes on poverty in regard to monks and nuns, that is, as a personal vow taken by Zen monastics, while Aristotle writes on poverty among laypeople, that is, as a social phenomenon in the *polis*. In this sense Aristotle and Dōgen are not addressing some reified idea called poverty, but rather two different conceptions that, in the interest of linguistic precision, might better have been given two different names. However, Douglas K. Mikkelson has observed that Thomistic Aristotelianism reaches a conclusion quite similar to

Dōgen's, on similarly religious grounds.[3] Even if Aristotle's concern differs from Dōgen's, conceptually speaking the notions of poverty they are working with *do* overlap, even if they are not wholly co-extensive.

Therefore, we may note four propositions: (1) Dōgen is often characterized as a radical in many respects; (2) Aristotle's observation on the relationship of poverty and social upheaval is anything but radical; (3) Dōgen's monastic, individualized conception of poverty is not identical to Aristotle's sociological, politicized conception of poverty; and (4) the foregoing three propositions notwithstanding, we may still find it surprising that Dōgen's view and Aristotle's view seem to be diametrically opposed to each other.

I will argue in this essay that poverty is a multifaceted phenomenon and that, while in some aspects Aristotle and Dōgen are indeed of different minds, in other aspects the gap between them is not nearly so broad as it might appear. I begin by examining Dōgen's view on poverty as Ejō articulated it in the *Shōbōgenzō Zuimonki*. I will then move on to the *Politics* and examine Aristotle's analysis of poverty there. By juxtaposing these two texts I will also develop an image of their authors' views of wealth and property, since these are inextricably intertwined with their views on poverty. I will conclude by comparing the two views and identifying where they agree, where they disagree, and why.

Dōgen on Poverty, Property, and Awakening

"By all means, be poor," Dōgen says, "for if you have a great deal of wealth you will lose your craving for the truth."[4] Throughout the *Zuimonki* Dōgen harps on the necessity of poverty in the pursuit of self-cultivation (*shugyō*, 修行), each time stressing the importance of giving up one's worldly possessions in order to attain awakening.[5] Perhaps the best passage for summing up his assessment of the value of poverty—as well as that of wealth and property—is *Shōbōgenzō Zuimonki*, 3.11. There he recounts the story of Pang, an affluent Chinese layman who threw all his riches into the sea. When others criticized him for not donating his wealth to the poor, Pang said, "I threw it all away because I knew it was harmful. Why would I give something to another person if I knew it to be harmful?" Because of his deep understanding, Dōgen says, the layman Pang "was not inferior to monks."[6]

With characteristic candor, Dōgen says, "Stupid people hoard wealth and are diseased by it."[7] In his view property is more than a burden; it is a kind of affliction. He first left Japan in search of uncorrupted Buddhist praxis, and when he returned, he found his former temple had degenerated so badly that monks now squirreled away valuables in secret vaults. In response to the corruption he said, "If you have wealth, people try to steal it, and if you try to prevent being stolen from, you will immediately grow angry. . . . If you have to hide something, it's better not to own it."[8]

In the same passage he places wealth and material possessions on par with body-mind (*shinjin*, 身心).

> One fears thieves only because one has something to hide from them; throw away all such valuables and the fear disappears as well. It is not only possessions that should be treated this way; it is the same with one's body and life. Even those who kill people think "I should not be killed," and it is because of this that they need to be fearful and cautious. Even if someone is going to kill me, I resolve myself not to think of retribution, and burglars and murderers cease to be a problem.[9]

This, too, is a message that echoes throughout the *Zuimonki:* to attain Buddhist awakening—or even to achieve equanimity, for that matter—one must cast off body and mind (*shinjin datsuraku*, 身心脱落). In *Shōbōgenzō Zuimonki*, 1.16 he says he has never heard of a monk freezing or starving to death while pursuing the way, and in 1.14 he suggests that even if there were such cases, to die practicing self-cultivation is better than any of his alternatives.

This, of course, is exactly the sort of attitude one expects from a great Zen master. But Dōgen goes further than merely likening material wealth to a disease; he also holds that poverty itself is beneficial for self-cultivation. In *Shōbōgenzō Zuimonki* 3.4 he says, "If you desire poverty instead, not only do you avoid anger and shame but you also please the buddhas and sages."[10] This talk of *desiring* poverty reveals an interesting turn: Douglas Mikkelson suggests that in Dōgen's view poverty is to be *obtained* and that one does so by abandoning covetousness.[11] Thus, Dōgen holds not merely that wealth is injurious, nor even that poverty is good for a self-cultivator; as Watsuji put it, for Dōgen "separation from this greed became a *necessary condition* for entering his kingdom of truth."[12]

Incidentally, closer examination of historical events reveals that Dōgen's hagiographers have put a fine polish on Dōgen's position on poverty, which was not as seamlessly constant as they have made it out to be. Dōgen is said to have retreated into the mountains of Echizen due to his disdain for the wealth, debauchery, and corruption of city life. This ignores the fact that he tried unsuccessfully to found several monasteries in Kyoto proper, and that surely a significant factor in his decision to retire to the countryside is that his patron and student Hatano Yoshishige owned land in Echizen and offered it to Dōgen for a monastery. Even if Dōgen believed worldly goods were harmful, he was not so far above wealth and property that he would turn down such a handsome donation. This points to a long-standing tension in this tradition of Buddhist monasticism—monks and nuns are to give up all worldly possessions, yet they may accept donations of food and even valuables from those who have not renounced their wealth—a tension I cannot resolve here but one that is worth noting nonetheless.

In sum, Dōgen's teachings in the *Zuimonki* hold that attachment to wealth is harmful on at least two counts, and perhaps three: it courts anger, fear, and shame; it distracts from self-cultivation; and—if Watsuji is right[13]—it controverts the necessary condition of poverty for Buddhist awakening.

Aristotle on Poverty, Property, and Human Flourishing

"Men fancy that external goods are the cause of happiness," says Aristotle, only then to conclude that this is obviously a mistaken view.[14] As Amartya Sen notes, "Aristotle pointed out, at the very beginning of his *Nicomachean Ethics,* that income and wealth are only instrumentally valued, and we have to go deeper to understand what makes human life rich and human freedoms effective."[15] Dōgen and Aristotle can agree on this much, but not on much else. Indeed, Sen's next sentence includes a point of contention for Dōgen: "As [Aristotle] puts it, 'wealth is evidently not the good we are seeking; for it is merely useful and for the sake of something else.' "

As we have seen, Dōgen disagrees on the usefulness of wealth, but Aristotle contends that "a man *must* have so much property as will enable him to live not only temperately but liberally."[16] Here he disputes Socrates' claim in the *Laws* that in order to live well one must not be impoverished; rather, one must have enough to live temperately. Aristotle's counterargument is that living temperately is not enough, for "temperance will be associated with toil"; better to have people live comfortably, presumably on the supposition that comfortable people are better situated to live in accordance with moral and intellectual excellences.[17]

We have seen the converse of this idea already: namely, the idea that "poverty is the parent of revolution and crime," the full context of which is as follows:

> One would have thought that it was even more necessary to limit population than property; and that the limit should be fixed by calculating the chances of mortality in the children, and of sterility in married persons. The neglect of this subject, which in existing states is so common, is a never-failing cause of poverty among the citizens; and poverty is the parent of revolution and crime.[18]

In point of fact, the bulk of *Politics,* 2.6 concerns neither poverty nor even wealth per se, but rather the proper distribution of wealth across the population—a concern to which population control is every bit as relevant as is distributive justice.

Here we return to a principle point of divergence concerning Dōgen's view on poverty and the Aristotelian view: Dōgen is concerned with how best to realize enlightenment, while Aristotle is concerned with how best to arrange the polis. Given the significant difference between the two philosophers' goals, one might suggest that there is no grounds for fruitful comparison. Aristotle repeatedly returned his attention to politics, while Dōgen claimed to have no interest whatsoever in that arena. Whether we ought to take Dōgen at his word is a different question—his disdainful remarks are arguably a case of sour grapes, written only after his many failures at trying to establish a flourishing monastery in the capital—but it seems certain that, whatever his reasons, Dōgen did not share Aristotle's abiding interest in political affairs. Thus the argument might be made that the two may not be usefully compared on the value of poverty.

But before we reach that conclusion too hastily, we should take note of the fact that both Dōgen and Aristotle argue that the contemplative life is the best sort of life, and both share the goal of human flourishing. It is certainly true that a life of seated meditation is not identical to a life spent exercising theoretical wisdom, and that one ought not to equate satori to eudaimonia, but it is also true that for Dōgen and Aristotle alike, the concern with wealth and poverty is subservient to a concern for how to lead human beings to the best kind of life (however each of them might construe that).

Aristotle describes his own project in precisely these terms. At several points in the *Politics* he indicates that the goal is to establish which kind of political arrangement best facilitates human flourishing:

> Now it is evident that the form of government is best in which every man, whoever he is, can act best and live happily.[19]

> It is the job of the excellent lawgiver to consider, concerning a city and a class of human beings and every other association, how they will partake in the flourishing living that is possible for them.[20]

> A person who is going to make a fitting inquiry into the best political arrangement must first get clear about what the most choiceworthy life is—for if this is unclear, the best political arrangement must remain unclear also.[21]

As Martha C. Nussbaum points out, Aristotle is of two minds about this task. The quoted passages describe what she calls the "distributive conception," which she defines as follows: "DC [distributive conception] tells us to consider the entire group (however specified) and *design* a scheme that will *permit* each and every one of that group to live well."[22] As this passage suggests, Aristotle is less than crystal clear as to which people are members of "the entire group" and which are not. (Women, children, natural slaves, and even farmers are all subject to question.)[23] Nussbaum also observes that the distributive conception itself is in conflict with two alternative principles that appear in the *Politics*.[24] For my purposes here I will assume that Nussbaum is correct in holding that Aristotle does indeed subscribe to the distributive conception and that the question of who counts as worthy of political consideration and who does not is better answered by modern conceptions of universal human rights than by the political schema familiar to Aristotle or to Dōgen. What is most important for present purposes is not which *Homo sapiens* are proper human beings but rather *what the task of politics is,* and according to the distributive conception that task is "securing to its people . . . the necessary conditions for a full good human life. It is to create a context in which anyone at all may choose to function in the ways that are constitutive of a good human life."[25]

As such, "the task of the city cannot be understood apart form [*sic*] a rather substantial account of human good and what it is to function humanly."[26] Of course the task of the legislator must be understood in similar terms. Aristotle's conclusion, according to Nussbaum, is that the legislator's task is to facilitate the training of excellences in young people, to maintain those excellences in adults, and to create and maintain circumstances in which the capabilities for those excellences can be exhibited in practice.[27] Here we may return to the subject of wealth and poverty. If to function humanly is to practice and exhibit moral and intellectual excellence, if the function of the polis and the legislator is to facilitate this human function in every citizen, and if poverty is deleterious to this human function, then it is the obligation of the polis and the legislator to erase poverty as widely and as thoroughly as possible.

Dōgen, Aristotle, and the Different Species of Poverty

There are areas of overlap between Dōgen's view and that of Aristotle. As Martha Nussbaum writes, "[Aristotle] stressed throughout his ethical and political writings that many people are badly educated and therefore want the wrong things, or in the wrong amount."[28] This is in keeping with Dōgen's assertion that "stupid people hoard wealth and are diseased by it."[29] Aristotle and Dōgen independently reach the conclusion that excessive love of self is akin to excessive love of wealth and that both are deleterious to human fulfillment. Though these points of perfect or near-perfect overlap do exist, they are few and far between.

There are also points where they start from common assumptions but reach radically different conclusions. For instance, Aristotle and Dōgen would both agree that property and wealth are valuable not intrinsically but solely based on what they do for their owners. But as to what these do for their owners, the two philosophers could hardly disagree more. An Aristotelian way to approach this question is to first define the ergon of wealth.[30] If, as Dōgen suspects, wealth's characteristic function is to poison the owners' dispositions, then everyone ought to imitate layman Pang and throw it away. On the other hand, if wealth has some other characteristic function—and Aristotle does not clearly define its ergon in the *Politics,* though for present purposes we need not specify what that function might be—then wealth is only *apt* to poison the owners' dispositions. Both Aristotle and Dōgen make this observation, and from this propensity it follows that not *all* of us must throw our wealth away, but rather only those who are most apt to be poisoned by it.

To approach the question by analogy, is wealth more like hemlock or more like rum? That is, is it poisonous to all of us or only to a few, and tolerable or even pleasant for the rest? Aristotle likens wealth more closely to rum, holding that love of it is not a vice; only excessive love of it is vicious.[31] Dōgen likens wealth more closely to hemlock, holding not only that it is best to rid oneself of it but even that it is better to commit it to the sea than to give it to the poor.[32] To put it another way, perhaps both Aristotle and Dōgen can agree that wealth is like rum, but Dōgen believes that all human beings are predisposed to alcoholism, while Aristotle believes only some of us suffer from that predisposition.

At bottom, this is the fundamental disjuncture when it comes to poverty: if Aristotle and Dōgen simply cannot settle on the value of wealth, it is hard to imagine how they might come to an agreement on the value of poverty. Dōgen's assessment of "the necessary conditions for a full good human life"[33] is so much lower than Aristotle's that their assessments of "what the most choiceworthy life is"[34] must necessarily differ. For example, apart from their disagreement on the value of poverty and property, Aristotle and Dōgen are also at odds on the importance and value of leisure. For Aristotle, the "full, good human life" necessarily requires leisure time, whereas for Dōgen, the best life is an ascetic life devoted to strenuous zazen.[35] Dōgen finds menial labor to be quite significant, hence his reverence for the *tenzo*.[36] Aristotle deems menial labor to be a distraction from the development of moral and intellectual excellence.[37]

There is an easy explanation for the difference in views: namely, that Aristotle and Dōgen simply do not see eye to eye on what constitutes the good life. The poverty Dōgen speaks of applies primarily to monastics, whose ideal of the good life stands quite distinct from that of the average citizens with whom Aristotle is concerned. But this explanation is too easy, for Dōgen too draws a distinction between the clergy and the laity, and, contra Aristotle, he says it is no bad thing for laypeople to rid themselves of worldly possessions.

Another relatively simple explanation might be that Dōgen and Aristotle are not of the same mind on the nature of the excellences. There is no obvious reason to deny the theoretical possibility that Aristotelian excellences are of such a nature that property is required to actualize them, while excellences as Dōgen conceives of them are such that poverty is required to actualize them. Indeed, as Nussbaum describes Aristotelian excellences, the possibility is not merely theoretical but actual: "The Aristotelian virtues are, for the most part, dispositions concerned with the reasonable use of external goods: so they are not 'moral' in the sense of being occupied with a noumenal realm that is totally cut off from or independent of the material circumstances of life."[38]

But this explanation also seems too simplistic. If we concede the accuracy of Nussbaum's first claim—that is, if morality for Aristotle is primarily concerned with material goods—then it is true that Dōgen and Aristotle cannot reach an accord. But the first claim is contentious at best, and even if true, it neither entails nor is entailed by the second claim, which is that a "moral" excellence is one occupied with the noumenal and wholly removed from "the material circumstances of life." It seems not only possible but plausible that the moral excellences need not be exclusively either noumenal or mercantile. A third category immediately recommends itself: namely, those excellences that pertain to the *social* circumstances of life. One can arguably go so far as to say that to the extent that Dōgen and Aristotle dwell on moral philosophy, they dwell mostly on this third category of excellences and devote relatively little attention to either of Nussbaum's implicit categories. At least with regard to the moral excellences, Dōgen and Aristotle arguably have more in common with each other than with a noumenalist like Kant or an economist like Adam Smith.

To explain why Dōgen and Aristotle assess the value of poverty so differently, rather than focusing on their views of the good life or of the excellences, it is better to focus on the notions of poverty they employ. As has already been remarked, Aristotle writes of poverty as a sociological phenomenon among the *poloi,* whereas Dōgen writes of poverty as a religious vow undertaken by monastics. Another important difference follows from this, perhaps the most important difference of them all: Dōgen's poverty is *voluntary,* while Aristotle's is not.[39]

Once again one might argue that this difference is so great that Dōgen and Aristotle cannot be usefully compared on the value of poverty. The great taxonomer Aristotle never seems to have imagined the possibility of voluntary poverty, to say nothing of having dealt with it in any depth. The Pythagoreans advocated living a simple life, and Socrates professed an indifference to wealth, but living in poverty is different from living simply. Vows of poverty would not gain any real popularity (to the extent they have ever been popular) until the Cynics, so Aristotle lived in a world without a kind of poverty that Dōgen would have taken for granted. Adopting an impoverished life by consent was beyond Aristotle's ken.

The central importance of consent is obvious in many areas of moral philosophy, certainly including divesting agents of property. (If I have been considering donating my car to charity and you steal it from me and give it to that charity, you have certainly wronged me, even if all other consequences are equal.) Perhaps less obvious is the idea that one can do wrong by *bestowing* property without the recipient's consent. (Suppose I have been contemplating getting a tattoo; if I wake up in the morning to find you have had me tattooed without my consent, my grounds for rectification are surely no less than in the case where you donated my car.)

How, then, is voluntary poverty importantly different from involuntary poverty? A ready answer is that voluntary poverty is undertaken in order to gain some understanding from it, both of oneself and of the notion of ownership. This was certainly one of Dōgen's motivations in advocating the vow of poverty. But in the *Politics* Aristotle himself holds that good people can also learn from involuntary poverty,[40] so the potential for edification is not sufficient to distinguish the two.

Another approach might be to note that poverty can be understood as a psychological condition as well as an economic one, and that we should expect the psychological ramifications of voluntary poverty to be radically different from those associated with involuntary poverty. Aristotle speaks of involuntary poverty, a "poverty of"—that is, a lack of something. The poverty Dōgen has in mind is voluntary, a "poverty for"—that is, a surrendering of something in order to achieve something else. But drawing this distinction may be nothing more than another way of approaching the question of consent. "Poverty for" is a consensually adopted psychological state; "poverty of" is a psychological state one falls into involuntarily. The question of consent is surely important in understanding why Dōgen and Aristotle assess the value of poverty so differently, but it is a question, not an answer.

I suspect easy answers will not suffice and sufficient answers will not be easy to come by. Dōgen is notably silent on the phenomenon of involuntary poverty, just as Aristotle is silent on voluntary poverty. Further, while it is common for people in modern societies to hold the impoverished responsible for their condition, this idea is relatively new, postdating Aristotle by nearly two millennia.[41] Thus, not only does Dōgen withhold comment on Aristotle's subject matter, but the subject itself does not occupy the same philosophical space it did in Aristotle's day.

Plumbing the depths of the nature of consent is too daunting a project for a short essay, but at a minimum I think it is safe to conclude that *if* Aristotle and Dōgen are both concerned with volition and consent in moral decision making—as I think they are—then the strong views Aristotle expresses on involuntary poverty might not extend to voluntary poverty. In other words, it is at least possible, and arguably plausible, that Aristotle's position on voluntary poverty is not so far from Dōgen's as it appears prima facie.

But there remains one concern: namely, that Dōgen's position still appears to be an extremist one and therefore not one that Aristotle is apt to endorse.[42] In *Politics,* 2.7 Aristotle rebukes the legislative approach of Phaleas, "who aims at an equal distribution of property, without asking himself how property is related to good functioning and what the right distribution is for *that* end."[43] Is Dōgen guilty of Phaleas' fallacy? He, too, seems to advocate an equal distribution of goods (though Dōgen would have them distributed across the seafloor, not among the homes of the polis; in either case the result is the same: everyone ends up with the same amount).

As Douglas Mikkelson observes, Aristotle holds that moral excellence is itself an extreme "with regard to what is best and right" and "[the idea] that the proper exercise of virtue is itself a kind of extreme [is one that] resonates within Dōgen and the Buddhist tradition."[44] Thus, one might justify Dōgen's extreme asceticism on Aristotelian terms by appealing to excellence itself as extremist. But another approach is to ask whether it is possible to see Dōgen as something other than an extremist with regard to property. It is easy to see how surrendering all of one's personal property can be construed as excessive generosity, with miserliness as the opposite extreme and Aristotelian liberality as the golden mean. However, it is also possible to see surrendering all of one's personal property as a golden mean itself, bracketed by the deficiency of parting with none of one's property and the excess of giving away not only one's own property but everyone else's as well.

We might characterize that deficiency as "Ayn Rand Syndrome," by which one does no wrong by behaving in a purely egoistic fashion, and its opposite as "Robin Hood Syndrome," by which one reasons that if it is good to give away one's own possessions, it is even better to steal from others and "donate" their possessions as well. This latter disposition is by no means prominent in moral philosophy, but it does appear outside of the Robin Hood stories. The Nick Hornby novel *How to Be Good* envisions what happens to a marriage when one parent decides to be as selfless with his family's possessions as he is with his own. Dōgen himself recounts an episode in which the abbot Eisai gives away Kenninji's valuables—the *sangha*'s nest egg, not his own—and is rebuked by his fellow monks for doing so.[45]

Both Aristotle and Dōgen reject covetousness, and it is hard to imagine either of them endorsing the theft of others' possessions, whether to throw them into the sea or to distribute them among the *poloi*. As such, I suggest both of them would recognize the middle ground between the two (which we might call ascetic generosity) to be morally preferable. If this is accurate, then Dōgen and Aristotle are not so far apart as they may seem. That is, they may be in accord on the value of voluntary poverty, even if they cannot concur on the value of involuntary poverty or on the influence of property ownership.

Deficiency	**Mean**	**Excess**
Donating no personal property (Miserliness)	Donating the proper amount of personal property (Liberality)	Donating all personal property (Overgenerosity)
◄	———	►
Donating no property (Ayn Rand Syndrome) (Pure Individualism)	Donating all personal property (Ascetic Generosity)	Donating all property (Robin Hood Syndrome) (Pure Anticonsumerism)

NOTES

I am indebted to Carl Becker, Thomas P. Kasulis, and Jim McRae for their helpful comments on an earlier version of this essay.

1. *Politics,* 1265b13.

2. Steve Bein, trans., *Purifying Zen: Watsuji Tetsurō's* Shamon Dōgen (Honolulu: University of Hawai'i Press, 2011), 49.

3. Douglas K. Mikkelson, "Aquinas and Dōgen on Poverty and the Religious Life," *Journal of Buddhist Ethics* 13 (2006).

4. Dōgen, *Shōbōgenzō Zuimonki,* 3.11. All Dōgen translations, unless otherwise noted, are my own, based on Watsuji's edition of the *Shōbōgenzō Zuimonki* and taken from Bein, *Purifying Zen.*

5. See Dōgen, *Shōbōgenzō Zuimonki,* 1.14, 1.16, 2.2, 3.4, 3.7, 3.12, 5.5, 5.20, 5.22, 6.3, 6.4.

6. Bein, *Purifying Zen,* 80–81.

7. Ibid., 46.

8. Ibid.

9. Dōgen, *Shōbōgenzō Zuimonki,* 3.4.

10. Bein, *Purifying Zen,* 46.

11. Mikkelson, "Aquinas and Dōgen," 6.

12. *Shamon Dōgen,* my translation, emphasis mine, from Bein, *Purifying Zen,* 46. Watsuji reiterates this message at Bein, *Purifying Zen,* 81: "For Dōgen, separation from the desire for the basic necessities of life was a necessary condition for following the way to the truth."

13. Though Dōgen does not speak in terms of necessary and sufficient conditions, Watsuji is arguably correct, at least with regard to the position Ejō ascribes to Dōgen in the *Zuimonki:* in Dōgen, *Shōbōgenzō Zuimonki,* 1.14, Dōgen "informs his monks that in order to lead the religious life, the essential requisite is to abandon covetousness"; see also Dōgen, *Shōbōgenzō Zuimonki,* 5.20, where Dōgen says, "The first requisite for one who leaves his home to become a monk is to separate Self and from all desires for fame and profit" (translations from Mikkelson, "Aquinas and Dōgen," 6 and 16, respectively).

14. *Politics,* 7.13 (1332a25ff.). Unless indicated otherwise, this and all following translations of the *Politics* are from Benjamin Jowett, trans., *Politics,* in *Great Books of the Western World,* vol. 9, *Aristotle II,* ed. Robert Maynard Hutchins (Chicago: Encyclopaedia Britannica, 1952).

15. Amartya Sen, *Poverty and Inequality* (Stanford, CA: Stanford University Press, 2006), 35.

16. *Politics,* 2.6 (1265a33); emphasis mine.

17. *Politics,* 2.6 (1265a33–34).

18. *Politics,* 1265b5–13.

19. *Politics,* 1324a24–25.

20. *Politics,* 1325a7ff. The translation is Martha C. Nussbaum's, found in "Nature, Function, and Capability: Aristotle on Political Distribution" (Wider Working Papers 31, World Institute for Development Economics Research of the United Nations University, Helsinki, 1987), 3.

21. 1323a14–17; Nussbaum's translation, in "Nature, Function, and Capability," 6–7.

22. Nussbaum's translation, in "Nature, Function, and Capability," 16; emphasis in original.

23. See ibid., 16–17, 20, 25–27.

24. The "holistic conception" (HC), as Nussbaum calls it, holds that a political arrangement is excellent if and only if it mirrors the structure of an excellence in an individual human psyche. Her "whole-part conception" (WP) says that a political arrangement is excellent if and only if its citizens are good as individuals. Ibid., 14–15.

25. Ibid., 6; see also ibid., 25, where Nussbaum describes the task of the legislator, and ibid., 7, where she explains why the task of the polis is both broad and deep.

26. Ibid., 1–2. Cf. *Politics,* 1280b39–1281a4.

27. Nussbaum, "Nature, Function, and Capability," 24–25.

28. Ibid., 13.

29. Dōgen, *Shōbōgenzō Zuimonki,* 3.4.

30. Amartya Sen has taken up this task, seeking to identify the functions of distributable goods in a number of writings; see especially his *Commodities and Capabilities* (Oxford: Oxford University Press, 1999) and "Equality of What?" in Amartya Sen, *Choice, Welfare, and Measurement* (Cambridge, MA: Harvard University Press, 1997).

31. *Politics,* 1263a40–1263b4.

32. Dōgen, *Shōbōgenzō Zuimonki,* 3.11.

33. Nussbaum, "Nature, Function, and Capability," 6.

34. *Politics,* 1323a17.

35. Cf. *Politics,* 7.9–10; and Dōgen, *Shōbōgenzō Zuimonki,* 1.14, 2.6, 2.9, 2.25, 6.4. See also Nussbaum, "Nature, Function, and Capability," 15, 22, 34–35; and Bein, *Purifying Zen,* 26–27, 40, 47, 53–54, 82, 102, 109–110, 112.

36. A *tenzo* was a senior monk in charge of the kitchens. See Dōgen, *Tenzo-kyōkun,* in *Dōgen zenji zenshū,* ed. Ōkubo Dōshū (Tokyo: Chikuma Shobō, 1970), 2:295–303.

37. *Politics,* 1328b39–1329a2.

38. Nussbaum, "Nature, Function, and Capability," 32.

39. Douglas Mikkelson notes this difference as well in his analysis of Aquinas and Dōgen. See his "Aquinas and Dōgen," 4.

40. *Politics,* 1332a19–20.

41. According to Robert Bernasconi, the idea that the poor are to blame for being impoverished does not arise in Europe until the early 1500s. See Robert Bernasconi, "The Philosophy of Poverty and the Poverty of Philosophy," in *The Proceedings of the Twenty-First World Congress of Philosophy,* ed. Ioanna Kuçuradi et al. (Ankara: Philosophical Society of Turkey, 2007), 13:169–170.

42. Mikkelson poses a similar objection both to Sōtō Zen and Thomistic Aristotelianism, in "Aquinas and Dōgen," 17–18.

43. *Politics,* 1266bff.; Nussbaum's translation; emphasis in original.

44. Mikkelson, "Aquinas and Dōgen," 19.

45. Dōgen, *Shōbōgenzō Zuimonki,* 6.15.

Economic Goods, Common Goods, and the Good Life

26

May Sim

How do economic goods, for example, the necessities for life (food, shelter, etc.), relate to the common goods, such as the virtues (justice, moderation, courage, wisdom, etc.), which are good not only for us but also for our relationships with one another; and how do these goods contribute to the good life? Such questions, though not necessarily formulated in these terms, are asked and answered by philosophers from ancient Greece to classical China. Drawing on the wisdoms of Aristotle and Confucius as representatives of these disparate philosophical traditions, I explore their answers to these questions and examine the lessons they offer for evaluating these goods and the implications for practical political policy with respect to such goods today.

Economic goods are parts of what Aristotle calls "external goods," which must be added to the life of intellectual and moral virtues in order for one to be happy.[1] External goods, for Aristotle, are divisible into two types: instrumental external goods such as wealth, friends, and political associates that enable us to perform virtuous actions, and goods that contribute to our blessedness, such as being wellborn (i.e., not born as a slave), having a good family, and not looking totally repulsive. According to Aristotle, if one were born into slavery or the laboring class, one would not have the leisure to engage in the moral-political life or the intellectual life of contemplation. Being utterly repulsive in appearance for him prevents one from being approachable, from making friends, and hence prevents one from achieving moral actions as easily as those who have been blessed with an appearance that doesn't frighten others. Since these activities of political deliberation and intellectual contemplation engage the rational parts of the human soul for him, they are not only proper to human beings but also higher than activities in which our nonrational appetites, desires, and emotions predominate. Being wellborn, for Aristotle, means that one is economically equipped so that one is not preoccupied with procuring the day-to-day necessities of life. Having sufficient wealth enables one to exercise the virtue of generosity (among other virtues such as courage and justice) and have the leisure to deliberate about what is good for the polis as a whole, or the good life, as well as make possible contemplation. In short, economic goods of wealth and property are prerequisites to the flourishing life wherein one can exercise one's rational soul for the contemplation of truths and the deliberation of moral actions.

Even though external goods are required for the life of intellectual and moral virtues, there is a difference between external goods and the virtues. The contrast between "external" goods and the virtues for Aristotle is that, while the latter are up to an individual's own "internal" activities (contemplating and deliberating excellently),[2] the former are dependent on luck or external situations such as being wellborn and wealthy and having a good family and friends. Wealth ensures that the necessities of life are met so that there is the leisure to pursue the moral-political life, the aim of which is to deliberate about the good of the whole human life for everyone living in the polis[3] and/or to engage in the contemplative life[4]—both of which are goods as ends in themselves. In contrast, the moneymaking life is never chosen as an end in itself, for money is good only as a means to other ends: for example, money allows one to secure the basic necessities and be generous.[5] Accordingly, someone who engages solely in a life of moneymaking necessarily leads a slavish existence.[6] More elaborately, a legitimate engagement in moneymaking is natural and limited for Aristotle, as it is directed at taking care of basic necessities that stem from our bodily nature; an illegitimate life of moneymaking is unlimited and unnatural, as its sole purpose is to make more and more money. There is a distinction between two senses of "economic," Ricardo Crespo rightly notes, for Aristotle: first is *oikonomikê,* which means the use of wealth, and second is *chrematistikê,* which means the acquisition of wealth.[7] Crespo emphasizes that even though the end of economics is wealth, the fact that economics is the *use* of wealth suggests that wealth is not unlimited for Aristotle, but is limited to the necessity of life and living well.[8] Accordingly, there is also a distinction between two types of chrematistics for Aristotle. One is subordinated to economics so that it is "limited and natural," while the other is not subordinated and hence is unnatural and "looks unlimitedly for money." Crespo rightly notes that Aristotle disapproves of the latter.

Even though Aristotle regards external goods (property and wealth) as required for human flourishing, because they cater to the bodily needs, they are inferior to the internal goods that arise from the well functioning of the rational soul. Aristotle relegates economics to the household or private realm, which must be satisfied before one can engage in the activities that constitute happiness, namely, the life of politics and philosophy. According to him, a political life engages in the common goods of human beings that can be achieved in action, while a philosophical life engages in the highest human good of wisdom that can be achieved in thought. Both the common and the highest goods result from the exercise of our rational soul and constitute the good life. On the contrary, external goods originate from our nonrational, bodily needs and are merely means to the end of the good life.[9] Accordingly, Aristotle maintains that not only are the common and the highest goods more intimately related to each other than they are related to external goods, but they are also higher than external goods (which are prerequisites rather than pursued in the good life).

Unlike Aristotle's unequivocal account of external goods, Confucius offers a more ambiguous view. On the one hand, he maintains that external economic goods are not a part of the flourishing life. For instance, Confucius thinks that a virtuous person, like his disciple Yan Hui, can be happy with minimal shelter and food, a condition that most people would find unbearable.[10] On the other hand, acknowledging that most people are unlike the virtuous person in the ability to put up with poverty and asceticism, Confucius' approach for the population at large is to make them prosperous first, and then educate them.[11] Upon closer inspection, it is not clear that Confucius completely rejects economic goods for the good life, as he says, "It is a disgrace to remain poor and without rank when the way prevails in the state; it is a disgrace to be wealthy and of noble rank when it does not."[12] This remark seems to insist on the possession of external goods like wealth and honor by serving in government when a state is not corrupt.

In spite of the numerous differences between Aristotle and Confucius with respect to external goods, they share some similar views about them, and their views about the common goods and the good life overlap significantly. My purpose here is to show how the similarities in Aristotle's and Confucius' accounts of external goods (which are due in part to their shared vision of the significance of virtues for human flourishing) can provide resources for remedying our contemporary approach to economic goods in two ways: (1) by showing that the pursuit of economic/external goods as ends in themselves not only skews our perception of the real goods that make us happy, but also prevents us from reaching happiness; and (2) by revealing the natural limits that govern our possession of external goods. Getting clear about the limits of economic goods implies that there are limits to an individual's and a state's possession of external goods. My final argument is that the differences between these authors' views of economic goods can provide resources for understanding the limits of economic growth for nation-states in the global context and support alternative ways of assessing economic growth for a more appropriate use of the world's limited economic resources.

The larger significance of my project is captured in the criticisms of the global impact on the human and nonhuman world by the unlimited pursuit of economic goods as ends in themselves, expressed by environmental critics including Peter S. Wenz and Robert Traer.[13] According to Wenz, consumerism contributes to global warming, which threatens biodiversity by endangering many species and threatening them with extinction. Apart from harming the nonhuman world, Wenz explains that consumerism also harms the poor by increasing the GDP gap between the twenty richest and poorest countries. Consumerism not only robs the poor of their livelihoods through high-yield varieties of wheat and rice crops, but also deprives them of food supplies. Ultimately, consumerism breaks up families and leads to social problems.[14] Similarly, criticizing the economic philosophy of Adam Smith, which maintains that individuals, while pursuing their self-interest, would promote economic growth and thus the common good, Robert Traer argues that "there is no 'invisible hand' that prevents economic growth from damaging the environment and causing global warming."[15]

Let me begin with the first resource in Aristotle's and Confucius' accounts of external goods: that the pursuit of economic/external goods as ends in themselves not only skews our perception of the real goods that make us happy, but also prevents us from reaching happiness. In contrast to Aristotle's account, in which one must already possess external goods in order to serve in government, Confucius' view is that engaging in politics brings external goods to one. External goods,[16] for Aristotle, seem to stem from fortune, as one is either born into a family with external goods or not, while they seem to be objects of choice for Confucius, depending on whether one engages in government service or some other activity. Whereas Aristotle holds that it is not the government's job to secure external goods for its people, since economics concerns the realm of the private household while politics is about the good life for the whole city,[17] Confucius believes that the government is responsible for securing the people's external goods because the political realm is simply the family writ large.[18] That is, external goods belong to the public realm of politics for Confucius. In fact, prosperity of the people is a sign of the legitimacy of their government, or the ruler's accordance with the Way in Confucianism, for it indicates that the ruler is benefiting the people instead of himself. Both the Confucian texts the *Great Learning* and the *Mencius* provide evidence for the ruler's responsibility for the people's material well-being. The *Great Learning* relates the ruler's virtue to his ability to secure his people's wealth: "The ruler will first take pains about *his own* virtue. Possessing virtue will give him the people. Possessing the people will give him the territory. Possessing the territory will give him wealth. Possessing the wealth, he will have resources for expenditure" and "Virtue is the root; wealth is the result."[19] Mencius, too, emphasizes the kind of economic goods due from a good ruler to his people when he asserts, "It has never happened that someone fails to become King when, among his subjects, seventy-year-olds are wearing silk and eating meat, and the black-haired people are neither hungry nor cold."[20] Given the priority of virtue over wealth for Confucius, he would agree with Aristotle that external goods are never to be pursued as ends in themselves. More elaborately, the pursuit of external goods as ends in themselves would make one's existence slavish for Aristotle: "The money maker's life is in a way forced on him [not chosen for itself]; and clearly wealth is not the good we are seeking, since it is [merely] useful, [choice-worthy only] for some other end."[21] Similarly, the Confucians would maintain that a ruler's pursuit of wealth as an end in itself is vicious and will lead to the scattering rather than the uniting of his people, as the *Great Learning* states: "The accumulation of wealth is the way to scatter the people; and the letting it be scattered among them is the way to collect the people" and "The virtuous ruler, by means of his wealth, makes himself more distinguished. The vicious ruler accumulates wealth, at the expense of his life."[22] While this remark about the ruler's making himself more distinguished by wealth might look like a self-serving act rather than one that benefits the people, it is not self-serving because of the role rituals play in Confucian societies. Distinguishing himself by observing the proper rituals over whatever ceremonies the ruler may preside is a way to reinforce the proper performance of rituals by others. Since the proper performance of rituals is key to one's self-cultivation of the virtues, culminating in the highest virtue of humaneness (*ren*, 仁) in which one's love for family members is extended in a graduated manner to others in the community), the ruler's use of wealth to carry out the proper rituals is a service to the entire community, for these rituals offer both opportunities and examples for the proper exercise of ritual proprieties.

In short, both Confucius and Aristotle would agree that the way to the good life or happiness is the pursuit of virtue, and, if anything, external goods are the means to one's virtuous activities. For example, Aristotle deems wealth as enabling one to give to the needy and exercise the virtue of generosity; wealth provides the leisure to engage in the other moral virtues like justice and courage as well as the highest virtue of contemplation.[23] For the Confucians, wealth is for distributing to the people[24] as well as for the proper offering of sacrifices so that the rituals (all important for cultivating the virtues) are preserved in the tradition.[25]

Having discussed Aristotle's and Confucius' views that the pursuit of economic or external goods as ends in themselves can never make us happy, let me move on to the second way these authors' accounts of external goods can help remedy our contemporary approach to economics by showing that there are natural limits with respect to an individual's possession of external goods. Both Aristotle and Confucius agree about the significance of temperance, or the self-control over bodily desires for sex, food, and drink. Without moderation, no other moral virtue can be realized, let alone the highest practical virtue: *phronêsis*, or practical wisdom, for Aristotle and *ren*, or humaneness, for Confucius. While *phronêsis* enables someone to always do the right thing, in the right way, at the right time, to the right people, and with the right motives, *ren* is the highest Confucian virtue, in which, as mentioned earlier, love for one's own family is extended in a graduated manner toward the rest of the community. Aristotle theorizes about temperance; Confucius does not. But there is a theoretical and metaphysical account of moderation in the Confucian text, the

Zhongyong, attributed to Confucius' grandson, Zisi, to which I will appeal for comparison with Aristotle. In general, both Aristotelians and Confucians would agree that excessive indulgence in bodily pleasures prevents one's self-development and moral acts toward others.

For Aristotle, temperance (*sôphrosunê*) consists in a mean state of bodily desires, especially those relating to touch and taste. He says, "The pleasures that concern temperance and intemperance are those that are shared with the animals and so appear slavish and bestial. These pleasures are touch and taste."[26] For Aristotle, corruption by excessive indulgence in such pleasures prevents one's grasp of the proper goals or principles of human good, that is, the moral virtues of courage, generosity, justice, and the like. This is because when one's pursuit is only one's own bodily pleasure, one would not be considering the needs of others in situations requiring virtues like courage or generosity. Consequently, the intemperate will think that his own pleasures of touch and taste are goals of actions[27] and will fail to develop himself and act morally toward others. On the contrary, temperance is a subordination of one's bodily desires to rational deliberation so that one will enjoy the right amount of bodily pleasures at the right time, in the right way, circumstance, and so on. Such self-control over one's bodily desires will in turn enable one to grasp the moral virtues and carry out these virtues with respect to others.

Unlike Aristotle, Confucius doesn't distinguish between pleasures of the soul and pleasures of the body. He doesn't even have the word for "soul" (*psychê*). Confucius also doesn't specify that temperance is concerned only with bodily pleasures. Nevertheless, he maintains that prioritizing one's own bodily pleasures over benefiting others or over self-cultivation is a vice. Praising his disciple's asceticism, he says, "A person of character is this Yan Hui! He has a bamboo bowl of rice to eat, a gourd of water to drink, and a dirty little hovel in which to live. Other people would not be able to endure his hardships, yet . . . this . . . has no effect on his enjoyment."[28] Again, "*Junzi* 君子 make their plans around the way (*dao,* 道) and not around their sustenance. . . . [They] are anxious about the way, and not about poverty."[29]

More elaborately, for Aristotle, all human beings have appetites for nourishment: it is natural to want food and drink when there's a lack. Despite the fact that different people vary in what they find pleasant, Aristotle thinks that there is a natural element in appetites for their proper objects (sex, food, or drink, respectively) that makes some things more pleasant for everyone.[30] Not only does he think that the naturalness of our appetites means that there will be some consensus about the types of object we find pleasant, but it also means that there is a natural limit to our appetites. This natural limit to our appetites, for Aristotle, is the filling of a lack. It is natural for us to eat and drink until we are full. But to exceed the natural limit by eating or drinking beyond that is both gluttonous and slavish. He says, "Eating indiscriminately or drinking until we are too full is exceeding the quantity that accords with nature; for [the object of] natural appetite is the filling of a lack."[31] This argument about what is by nature for our appetites is continuous with Aristotle's claim that there is a limit to the art of acquisition of wealth in economics or household management. The basis of his argument is the limited nature of our bodies, thus the limited basic necessities we need to acquire by wealth to satisfy our bodily needs. Put otherwise, not only is there a limit to the individual's satisfaction of his natural appetites, but there is, as well, a limit to the art of acquisition that is a part of household management. For Aristotle, the art of acquisition that is a part of household management that accords with nature is that which procures "a supply of those goods, capable of accumulation, which are necessary for life and useful for the community of city or household. And it is of these goods that riches in the true sense at all events seem to consist. For the amount of such property sufficient in itself for a good life is not unlimited."[32] With respect to natural appetites, Aristotle maintains that few people are mistaken about their proper objects. Rather, people err by exceeding the limit that is set by nature, namely, filling the lack. On the contrary, Aristotle thinks that people's appetites for distinctive pleasures, for example, for particular types of food and drink, are prone to both qualitative and quantitative errors. That is, they err in not only enjoying the wrong types of objects, but also in enjoying them excessively, in other words, more than what is right for most people.

As I've mentioned, even though Confucius does not theorize about temperance, there is a functional equivalent to it in the Confucian text *Zhongyong*. Consider this passage:

> Prior to the issuing (*fa,* 發) of pleasure, anger, sorrow, or joy, is called the state of equilibrium (*zhong,* 中). After those feelings have been issued, and all are joined according to *zhong,* is called the state of harmony (*he,* 和). *Zhong* is the great root (*da ben,* 大本) of all under heaven (*tian,* 天), and harmony is the path of all under heaven.[33]

To say that *zhong* (equilibrium) is the great root (*da ben*) of all under heaven (*tian*) means that it is the natural source of everything in the world, including our actions and feelings. We are also told that what this source, also called heaven (*tian*), "has mandated (*ming,* 命) is called nature (*xing,* 性)."[34] That this source extends to the whole universe is further supported when the text reads, "When the states of equilibrium and harmony are present, everything under heaven is in place, and all things (*wanwu,* 萬物) will produce."[35] To say that *he* (harmony) is the balance sought in our actions and feelings is comparable to the natural limit Aristotle attributes to our bodily appetites, which limit is achieved when one is temperate. Similarly, that harmony is the path or way (*dao*) to behave (in accordance with *zhong*) is comparable to the Aristotelian mean (*meson*) that constitutes the virtuous way. Notice that Aristotelians and Confucians would agree that appetites are not to be eliminated entirely in the moral life. Rather, they are to be limited. Such a limit is not arbitrary; both prescribe objective standards that are based on nature.

Whereas Aristotle's standard is prescribed by the nature of the human being and what it takes to fill a lack (in food, drink, etc.), the *Zhongyong*'s standard is prescribed by a metaphysical equilibrium (*zhong*), sometimes translated as "mean," that is the origin of all things. Insofar as the metaphysical *zhong* also prescribes our human nature and what is right for it, there is a sense in which the *Zhongyong* would agree with Aristotle's view that our appetites are limited by human nature. The *Zhongyong* and Aristotle also seem akin for the fact that Aristotle, too, speaks of a mean in regulating our appetites and desires. For Aristotle, this mean is between two extremes of excess and defect. But it isn't a numerical mean that is one and the same for everyone. Rather, it is relative to each individual in that it depends on one's being a member of the human species, having capacities for certain actions, and finding oneself in particular circumstances.[36] For example, the mean that is courage for someone rescuing another who is drowning depends on: (1) the fact that he is a human being who is perfected by courage; (2) how good a swimmer he is; and (3) the severity of the storm affecting the sea from which the drowning person is to be rescued. Multiple conditions that are relative to someone, such as self-knowledge and knowledge of one's particular situation, make the Aristotelian mean difficult to achieve. Similarly, the *Zhongyong* expresses the difficulty of attaining what the *zhong* prescribes.

> The Master said, "I know how it is that the path of the Mean is not walked in:—The knowing go beyond it, and the stupid do not come up to it. I know how it is that the path of the Mean is not understood:—The men of talents and virtue go beyond it, and the worthless do not come up to it."[37]

The fact that even those who are said to be talented and to have knowledge can exceed the mean shows how difficult a target it is for the Confucians. The fact that the Confucian *zhong* is cosmic in scope, extending to both human and nonhuman things, contributes to its challenge, as the kind of knowledge that is required to grasp it is not merely restricted to the human as it is for Aristotle. Yet, like Aristotle, the situations that call for adhering to the mean are the everyday occurrences of eating and drinking: "There is no person who does not eat and drink. But few can know flavors."[38]

As Ames and Hall put it,

> The connection between the family and the familiar affairs of the day in the *Zhongyong* is primarily a function of the ritualization of both familial and familiar affairs. That is to say, *li* 禮 as ritual conduct is the primary means whereby one realizes the meaning and efficacy of these fundamental contexts.[39]

In spite of the ubiquity of rituals for the Confucians, the *zhong* still seems more elusive than the Aristotelian mean. Unlike Aristotle, who claims that there is a consensus about the proper objects of our appetites, for example, what is flavorful when it comes to food, the *Zhongyong* maintains that flavors are known only to a few.

Even though the *Zhongyong*'s *zhong*, or mean, like Aristotle's mean, prescribes the limit of one's actions and desires, what one achieves in adhering to this standard is unlike that in Aristotle. This is because, while one actually realizes the Aristotelian mean between the extremes when one has a virtue, say, temperance, the Confucian *zhong* or equilibrium, as the source of all our actions and feelings, is never realizable because it is a source or state *prior* to any stirrings of feelings or desires.[40] Since human beings are never without any stirrings of feelings or desires, what is achieved in adhering to the Confucian *zhong* is a harmony of our feelings, desires, and actions. Put otherwise, one major difference between the two accounts is in the conception of the mean. Whereas the Confucian mean is a standard that preexists all feelings and actions, the Aristotelian mean is a standard that coexists always with feelings and desires. While the Confucian mean is a standard that governs all things in the universe,[41] the Aristotelian mean only governs human actions and doesn't have the cosmic effect of the Confucian mean. Whereas the Confucian mean exists outside of human beings,[42] the Aristotelian mean is an intermediate state *in* the human being that is prescribed by the individual's correct reason.[43] It is the Confucian state of harmony (*he*) that is like the achievement of the mean state in Aristotle, for both are governed by human nature and both are the ways of achieving virtue.

Despite the differences between the Aristotelian mean and the Confucian mean (*zhong*), and the fact that it is the Confucian harmony (*he*) that is comparable to the Aristotelian mean, what is clear is that they agree that an individual's desires and appetites are limited by his human nature. Whether this nature is to be discovered by human reason following Aristotle, or by an adherence to what the *Zhongyong* calls "sincerity" (*cheng*, 誠, or Heaven's Way), such that one can apprehend and do what is right (in accordance with *zhong*) without effort and without exercising thought,[44] both sources agree that cultivation of the virtues is essential to accessing our nature. For instance, Aristotle compares the moderation of our appetites to getting a child to obey his guide. Just as a disobedient child will go astray, appetites that do not follow reason can become insatiable through increasing indulgence in indiscriminate pleasures, eventually expelling rational deliberation.[45] Thus, Aristotle says, "That is why appetites must be moderate and few, and never contrary to reason."[46] By the same token, the *Zhongyong* asserts,

> Hence the sovereign may not neglect the cultivation of his own character. Wishing to cultivate his character, he may not neglect to serve his parents. In order to serve his parents, he may not neglect to acquire knowledge of men. In order to know men, he may not dispense with a knowledge of Heaven.[47]

The cultivation of character in the *Zhongyong*, like other Confucian texts, begins by behaving in accordance with the ritual propriety (*li*) of filial piety (*xiao*, 孝) toward one's parents in the home.[48] Instead of ritual propriety toward family members, the virtues to be cultivated for Aristotle are dictated by the laws legislated by the rulers in a polis, which exercise doesn't originate in the family.[49] In short, not only do the Aristotelians and Confucians agree that our appetites for external goods are to be limited; they agree as well that there is an objective standard that governs the limit. Both hold that one needs to be cultivated in a communal setting in order to understand the limit.

If we compared the two at the level of human nature, so that the standard for the proper limit is dictated by human nature, exemplified by rationality in the *Nicomachean Ethics* and harmony in the *Zhongyong*, the two are quite similar. However, moving beyond the level of human nature, the cosmic *zhong* of the Confucians seems quite different from the rational soul of the Aristotelians as the objective standard for right actions. Nevertheless, to the extent that Aristotle's rational soul is modeled upon the cosmic and metaphysical entity of the primary substance, or God, his ultimate standard of appeal for rationality does not seem as remote from the Confucian cosmic *zhong*. Such subtle comparisons between these two traditions are beyond the scope and relevance of this essay, which focus is more practical than theoretical.

Upon closer inspection, even though the limitation of desires and appetites in order to achieve virtue is difficult for the many according to both Aristotelians and Confucians, the task of virtue is more difficult for the Confucians. In spite of the difficulty, the *Zhongyong*'s account provides us with more resources for thinking about limiting our pursuit of economic goods because it applies not only to the individual context but also to the global context.

More specifically, attaining the limit is more difficult in the *Zhongyong* than in the *Nicomachean Ethics* because the mean that is aimed at is not just relative to an individual, as it is for Aristotle. The knowledge that is required to hit the mean for Aristotle is restricted to self-knowledge, knowledge of the human species, and knowledge of one's circumstances. Such knowledge, though difficult to attain, is not impossible, for practically wise persons do exist for Aristotle. In contrast, the mean in the *Zhongyong* is a metaphysical limit that can never be realized because it requires the absence of any feelings, which is impossible insofar as human beings exist. Moreover, the harmony that can be attained in the *Zhongyong* requires not only knowledge of human beings, one's circumstances, and how to behave appropriately in those circumstances,[50] but also knowledge of heaven.[51] Knowledge of heaven requires the attainment of sincerity (or Heaven's Way).[52] To accomplish this, the *Zhongyong* insists on "the extensive study of what is good, accurate inquiry about it, careful reflection on it, the clear discrimination of it, and the earnest practice of it."[53] Put otherwise, the practice of sincerity calls for both theoretical inquiry of a cosmic good as well as the practice of it. Transcending one's individuality and expanding one's efforts to the whole world is made possible by understanding the source of human nature endowed by Heaven. Tu says, "The quest for self-knowledge may thus be construed as corresponding to a search for an understanding of Heaven."[54] This self-understanding leads to an understanding of the human community and eventually to the whole of nature.[55] This contrasts sharply with Aristotle's requirements for the mean, which are strictly restricted to the human sphere and relative to the individual actor's particular capabilities and circumstances. Such knowledge that is limited to the human realm and to an actor's particularities, for the Aristotelians, seems more accessible than the Confucians' knowledge that extends beyond the human realm to the whole of nature and heaven as the source of everything.

More elaborately, Aristotle separates the theoretical knowledge of truths from the practical knowledge of moral actions and production. The faculty for, as well as the objects of, each of these activities is different. Whereas *nous*, or the speculative part of the soul, deals with unchangeable objects like the first principles and other eternal truths of objects that are either moveable (physics) or immoveable (metaphysics/theology and some mathematics), the deliberative part of the soul deals with changeable objects, like the things upon which we act or produce.[56] Given Aristotle's distinctions in theoretical knowledge, his highest knowledge, which consists in the theoretical contemplation (*theôria*) of truths, excludes the knowledge of things in nature, as things in nature are capable of motion, which motion makes them inferior to the eternal objects of *nous*. Mathematical objects, too, are excluded, even though some of them are immoveable, as they, unlike the eternal highest objects of metaphysical speculation, are incapable of existence separate from matter.[57] Not only are there such sharp separations between different types of theoretical knowledge for Aristotle, but similar separations hold for practical knowledge too. Action differs from production for Aristotle, as the former is an end in itself, whereas the latter has as its end a separate product.[58] For example, a generous action is an end and a good for its own sake, whereas a builder's end is not the act of building but rather the completed house. Such Aristotelian distinctions between the theoretical, practical, and productive realms, not to mention his distinctions within some of these realms, offer an account that contrasts sharply with the unity of theory and practice for the Confucians and their call for careful reflection and discrimination in theoretical knowledge along with the earnest exercise of practical knowledge.

Moreover, there is not a similar extension of one's actions or obligations to others beyond one's polis or to the natural world for Aristotle. On the contrary, the person with sincerity not only completes his own nature so that he has perfect virtue, according to the *Zhongyong;* he also completes the nature of other men, animals, and things. The text states:

> Able to give their full development to the natures of creatures and things, he can assist the transforming and nourishing powers of Heaven and Earth. Able to assist the transforming and nourishing powers of Heaven and Earth, he may with Heaven and Earth form a ternion.[59]

The extensiveness of the sincere person's virtuous actions toward everything in the world offers resources for limiting our appetites for external goods in the global context. Being responsible for helping heaven and earth develop the nature of all things not only puts a limit on the way that nation-states appropriate limited economic resources, but also offers a reminder that there are limits to the pursuit of economic growth. Instead of unlimited economic growth, the *Zhongyong* offers the perspective that other human beings, creatures, and things in the world are to be developed and completed by the virtuous person. It is only in the pursuit of such common goods that one can complete oneself and lead a good life. In contrast, instead of an obligation to develop and nourish the natures of creatures and things around us, Aristotle's view of plants and animals in the world is that they exist for the sake of human beings. Plants and animals are sources of food, clothing, and tools for him. He says,

> After the birth of animals, plants exist for their sake, and that the other animals exist for the sake of man, the tame for use and food, the wild, if not all at least the greater part of them, for food, and for the provision of clothing and various instruments. Now if nature makes nothing incomplete, and nothing in vain, the inference must be that she has made all animals for the sake of man. And so, in one point of view, the art of war is a natural art of acquisition, for the art of acquisition includes hunting, an art which we ought to practice against wild beasts.[60]

Apart from viewing the things in the world around us as means for our good, Aristotle also offers us a more limited perspective regarding economic goods because he relegates them to fortune and restricts them to an individual's, or at most an individual's and the whole polis's, well-being. Consequently, Aristotle's view of external goods is applicable to the good life for individuals and beyond that to individual states.[61] The Confucian account seems applicable beyond individual states, offering resources for a global approach to economic development.

In spite of the difference in breadth between Aristotle's and the *Zhongyong*'s accounts of economic goods, they agree that (1) the pursuit of economic/external goods as ends in themselves will not make us happy, and (2) there are limits to our possession of such goods. Given the *Zhongyong*'s cosmic account of human flourishing, Confucians can offer resources not only for limiting an individual's and a particular nation's consumption of economic goods, which resources can come from the Aristotelians too, but also for limiting our consumption in the global context, which seems too much a stretch for Aristotelians. Both traditions can remind us that human flourishing does not come from external goods and alert us to vices if we pursue economic goods as ends in themselves. Aristotelians and Confucians acknowledge our reliance on external goods for living and point to their proper use for living well. More importantly, each directs us to the natural limit of human consumption, which limit is clear if we understand human nature. Whereas human nature for the Aristotelians is accessible through right reason, knowledge of a cosmic equilibrium that governs both the human and nonhuman spheres is needed for the Confucians. As a standard that is shared by both human and nonhuman beings, the Confucian *zhong* offers a nonanthropocentric way for discoursing about external goods. When humankind is no longer the sole measure of needs, we cannot but ask about the measure and the measured and wonder if our measures to date are adequate or just. If the *zhong* applies to other creatures and things in the world, and harmony (*he*) is our way of realizing the *zhong* (remembering that we can never reach the *zhong* itself since it preexists feelings, desires, and actions), more weight needs to be accorded the nonhuman and the whole cosmos when considering our appropriation of natural resources.

Taking into consideration other creatures and things besides human beings in exercising the virtues is essential to human flourishing in the *Zhongyong*. As such, the unlimited acquisition of external/economic goods like wealth and consumer objects, or acquiring them for their own sakes, won't lead to happiness. On the contrary, limiting our consumption to what we need to live, acquiring enough wealth for our sustenance and whatever is needed to assist others, seems more consistent with the *Zhongyong*'s recommendation that we are to assist heaven and earth in completing the nature of creatures and things in the world. As Peter Wenz has shown us, consumerism not only leads to global warming and threatens biodiversity and species extinction, but also perpetuates the economic gap between the rich and the poor and deprives the poor of their livelihood. In short, the unlimited pursuit of economic goods not only harms the environment, but also results in the breakdown of families, causing social ills.[62] Such excess prevents us from completing our nature and the natures of nonhuman creatures and things, actions recommended by the *Zhongyong* for flourishing. Accordingly, instead of measuring our well-being by looking to the GDP, which measures the quantity of economic activity without considering the quality of life, alternative measures like the "genuine progress indicator (GPI) and the index of sustainable economic welfare (ISEW)," which John B. Cobb Jr. proposes (quoted by Robert Traer) are more compatible with the *Zhongyong*'s philosophy.

> Computation of the ISEW begins with personal consumption, but then adjusts this in relation to income distribution. (Our assumption is that the well-being of the society as a whole is affected by the condition of the poorest.) The index then adds for household services, chiefly the contribution of housewives. It subtracts for "defensive costs," that is, costs that result from economic growth and the social

> changes, such as urbanization, that accompany it. (For example, the cost of commuting to work should not be viewed as an addition to welfare just because it adds to the GNP.) This applies also to the cost of pollution. Since it is an index of *sustainable* welfare, it subtracts for the reduction of natural capital, and adds or subtracts for change in the net international position.[63]

More simply put, instead of assuming that "economic growth and liberalization, with wealth creation,"[64] is the way to manage the environment, Traer suggests that we need to ensure that "economic development is ecologically sustainable."[65] As such, he follows Herman E. Daly and Joshua Farley in their suggestion of a "steady-state economy" measure. This measure would "maintain constant stocks of wealth and people at levels that are sufficient for a long and good life."[66] Echoing this criticism of our contemporary nations' obsession with economic growth and wealth maximization, Peter Wenz says,

> Human beings, like all living things, need to consume to live. However, economic growth, as currently conceived and measured, is unnecessary in the U.S. to meet material needs or foster happiness. And when policies that promote growth increase inequality of income, the results are unhappiness and serious material deprivation.[67]

In short, it is in the starkest difference between the *Zhongyong* and the *Ethics,* a cosmic, as opposed to an individualistic, account of human flourishing, respectively, from which we can derive resources for questioning, on a global scale, our current presuppositions about economic goods and economic growth. Fastening our flourishing to other human beings, nonhuman creatures, and things, the *Zhongyong* would not endorse our current way of measuring human flourishing by focusing on each nation's GDP independently of what is happening to the human and nonhuman things in our own nation and beyond. Instead of a quantitative measure that focuses on economic activity, goods, and wealth, it is the quality of virtue in oneself and others (including the nonhuman realm) that informs the new measure. This new measure of economic goods will focus on common goods like the virtues (e.g., justice, generosity, and temperance), which will in turn contribute to the good life. Not surprisingly, this is a conclusion with which both the Confucians and Aristotelians would agree.

NOTES

1. Terence Irwin, trans., *Aristotle: Nicomachean Ethics* (Indianapolis: Hackett, 1999), 1.8.
2. Ibid., 1.10, 6, 10.
3. See ibid., 8.9, 1160a21–29.
4. Ibid., 10.6–8.

5. Aristotle says, "Riches are a number of *instruments* in domestic and civil economy; it is therefore evident that the acquisition of certain things according to nature is a part both of domestic and civil economy." H. Rackham, trans., *Aristotle: Politics,* Loeb Classical Library no. 264 (Cambridge, MA: Harvard University Press, 1932), 1.8, 1256b; my italics.

6. For an account of Aristotle's thinking on how a capitalistic (chrematistic) society that uses money to acquire more money will lead to our passions ruling our reason, see Spencer J. Pack, "Aristotle's Difficult Relationship with Modern Economic Theory," *Foundations of Science* 13, nos. 3–4 (2008), 270. Pack points to the relevance of Aristotle's understanding of economics for contemporary economists. He says, "The work of Sen and Nussbaum in welfare economics and the proper role of government in society is Aristotelian" (277).

7. Ricardo Crespo, " 'The Economic' According to Aristotle: Ethical, Political and Epistemological Implications," *Foundations of Science* 13, nos. 3–4 (2008), 281–294. Crespo here gives an account of an Aristotelian analysis of economics as a type of human action that can be a virtue that requires other virtues and a science.

8. Ibid., 283.

9. Rackham, *Politics,* 1.2, 1253b23–25: "Since therefore property is a part of a household (*oikias*) and the art of acquiring property a part of household management (*oikonomias*) (for without the necessaries [*tôn anankaiôn*] even life as well as the good life [*eu zên*], is impossible [*adunaton*])."

My assertion that external goods originate from our nonrational, bodily needs is a simplification because both the virtues of honor and friendship are also classified as external goods by Aristotle, and yet they are virtues in themselves and thus are bound up with our rational, deliberative function too. I compare Aristotle and Confucius on the topic of honor in an essay, "Pride or Humility? Aristotle or Confucius?" (invited paper presented at the Inaugural Memorial Lecture of Professor Anthony Cua, Catholic University of America, Washington, DC, April 17, 2009, published under the title, "Rethinking Honor with Aristotle and Confucius," *Review of Metaphysics* 66 [Dec. 2012]: 263–280). A more metaphysical account of these authors' views on friendship is available in my *Remastering Morals with Aristotle and Confucius* (New York: Cambridge University Press, 2007), chap. 7. For another account of Aristotle that emphasizes friendship for the possibility of a life of rationality and hence happiness, see Pedro Tabensky, "Precis of *Happiness: Personhood, Community, Purpose* (Aldershot: Ashgate Publishing Company, 2003)," *South African Journal of Philosophy* 23, no. 4 (2004), 340. For a critique of Tabensky's overemphasis on rationality and friendships for happiness, neglecting the importance of virtues and relationships of dependency, see Peta Bowden, "Happiness and Dependency: Reflections on Happiness: Personhood, Community, Purpose by Pedro Alexis Tabensky," *South African Journal of Philosophy* 23, no. 4 (2004), 395–401.

For another critique of Tabensky's approach to Aristotle, which focuses on his departure from Aristotle's approach by emphasizing unrestricted pluralism for rationality but approves of his use of friendship, see Daniel D. Hutto, "Questing for Happiness: Augmenting Aristotle with Davidson?" *South African Journal of Philosophy* 23, no. 4 (2004), 383–393. The interest in Tabensky's work on rationality is apt for considering the virtuous mean for Aristotle. Add to that his emphasis on friendship, and it is again clear that friendship does not fall so readily into the realm of external goods as I have explained it here. Nevertheless, due to the scope of this essay, which focuses on economic goods, which economic goods originate from our bodily needs, a discussion of how friendship and honor are external goods and also virtues for Aristotle would constitute a digression that is so lengthy as to distract us from my current concern.

10. *Analects,* 6.11; see also 14.10, 15.2. All translations from the *Analects* are from Roger Ames and H. Rosemont Jr., trans., *The Analects of Confucius: A Philosophical Translation* (New York: Ballantine, 1998.)

11. *Analects,* 13.9.

12. *Analects,* 8.13; Ames and Rosemont, *Analects.*

13. The pursuit of economic goods as ends in themselves is the maximization of consumption without limit, which Wenz calls "consumerism." Peter S. Wenz, "Synergistic Environmental Virtues: Consumerism and Human Flourishing," in *Environmental Virtue Ethics,* ed. Ronald Sandler and Philip Cafaro (Lanham, MD: Rowman and Littlefield, 2005), 197–213.

14. Wenz expresses these conclusions regarding the harmful effects of consumerism in ibid., 198, 202, 200, 201, 202–203, respectively.

15. Robert Traer, *Doing Environmental Ethics* (Boulder, CO: Westview Press, 2009), 36. See also Traer's criticisms of economic globalization (40–45) and the flaws of international institutions like the International Monetary Fund, World Bank, and World Trade Organization (43–45).

16. I mean the external goods that contribute to our blessedness instead of those that are instrumental. The former results from fortune for Aristotle, e.g., being wellborn, having a good family, and not looking utterly repulsive. In contrast, instrumental goods for Aristotle, e.g., friends, political connections, and wealth, help us perform virtuous deeds. Irwin, *Nicomachean Ethics,* 1.8, 1099a30–1099b6.

17. Rackham, *Politics,* 1.1, 1253a19–20: "The city-state is prior in nature to the household and to each of us individually," and "Those then who think that the natures of the statesman, the royal ruler, the head of an estate and the master of a family are the same, are mistaken" (1252a7–9).

18. Roger Ames and David Hall observe this distinction between the private and public for Aristotle, which is absent in Confucius. They say that for Aristotle, "The private and the public spheres are not seen as intrinsically connected. That is, the *polis* is not seen as a natural radial extension of the *oikos* any more than the freeman is seen as a natural development of the slave. They have different ends. This view contrasts starkly with classical China in which family (*jia,* 家) serves as a pervasive metaphor for social, political, and even religious relations." Roger T. Ames and David T. Hall, trans., *Focusing the Familiar: A Translation and Philosophical Interpretation of the* Zhongyong (Honolulu: University of Hawai'i Press, 2001), 38.

19. *Great Learning,* 10.6, 10.7; see James Legge, trans., *Confucian Analects, the Great Learning and the Doctrine of the Mean* (New York: Dover, 1971). (Hereafter, when the citation is to the title of one of these three texts, the details of publication are to this volume.)

20. *Mencius,* 1A, 3.4. Bryan W. Van Norden, trans., *The Essential Mengzi* (Indianapolis: Hackett, 2009).

21. Irwin, *Nicomachean Ethics,* 1.5, 1096a7–8.

22. *Great Learning,* 10.9, 10.20; see Legge, *Confucian Analects.* See n. 21 for how the use of wealth in sacrificial ceremonies can make one more distinguished and continue the tradition of one's ritual practices.

23. See Irwin, *Nicomachean Ethics,* 4.1, 1120a25–27: "The generous person will also aim at the fine in his giving, and will give correctly; for he will give to the right people, the right amounts, at the right time, and all the other things that are implied by correct giving." Irwin, *Nicomachean Ethics,* 10.8, 1178b34–1179a2: "But happiness will need external prosperity also, since we are human beings; for our nature is not self-sufficient for [contemplation], but we need a healthy body, and need to have food and the other services provided. . . . Self-sufficiency and action do not depend on excess."

24. "The accumulation of wealth is the way to scatter the people; and the letting it be scattered among them is the way to collect the people" (Legge, *Great Learning,* 10.9).

25. "[Shun] offered his sacrifices in his ancestral temple, and his descendants preserved the sacrifices" (Legge, *Great Learning*, 17.1). Unless otherwise stated, chapter and section numbers, as well as translations of the *Great Learning*, are from Legge.

26. Irwin, *Nicomachean Ethics*, 1118a25–27.

27. Ibid., 6.5.

28. Ames and Rosement, *Analects*, 6.11.

29. Ibid. See *Analects*, 9.27 for how Confucius praises one of his disciples, Zilu, for not being jealous or greedy.

30. Irwin, *Nicomachean Ethics*, 1118a9–14.

31. Ibid., 1119a16–19.

32. Rackham, *Politics*, 1256b28–34. Even though Aristotle emphasizes harm to oneself when one is intemperate, I think that he would agree with Philip Cafaro's analysis that gluttony is harmful to both the glutton and others, as Aristotle thinks that intemperance prevents one from acting virtuously toward others too. Cafaro says, "Gluttony reminds us that the vices, although often selfish, harm both ourselves and others. Food overconsumption harms our health and lowers life expectancy, but it also harms nature. These harms to nature rebound, in turn, and cause new kinds of harm to human and nonhuman beings. . . . Our flourishing is tied up with the flourishing of others." Philip Cafaro, "Gluttony, Arrogance, Greed, and Apathy: An Exploration of Environmental Vice," in *Environmental Virtue Ethics*, ed. Ronald Sandler and Philip Cafaro (Lanham, MD: Rowman and Littlefield, 2005), 142.

33. *Zhongyong*, 1.4; my translation.

34. *Zhongyong*, 1.1; my translation. Following Angus Graham's rejection of translating *xing* as "nature" because it "predisposes us to mistake it for a transcendent origin, which in Mencian doctrine would also be a transcendent end," Ames and Hall endorse Graham's alternative interpretation wherein " '*xing* [性] is conceived in terms of spontaneous development in a certain direction rather than of its origin or goal' " (Ames and Hall, *Focusing the Familiar*, 28). Continuing Graham's words, " '*xing* will be spontaneous process with a direction continually modified by the effects on it of deliberate action' " (ibid., 28; see also ibid., 34, where Ames and Hall explain their use of "creativity" to translate "*cheng*" [frequently rendered "sincerity" or "integrity"] to underscore the central role that individuals play as "co-creative beings" in determining themselves and things in the world). Contrary to Graham and Ames and Hall, I think that an essentialist reading of *xing* that stresses its origin and goal need not preclude the spontaneous effects of human action they wish to emphasize. Rather, an essentialist reading that stresses the origin and goal of human beings has the advantage of articulating our virtue or good (e.g., in the *Zhongyong*'s case, to abide by the standard of the *zhong*, assist heaven and earth in transforming the things and creatures and thus assist in their development), while still allowing for individual variations that arise from one's circumstances and roles; e.g., *Zhongyong*, 14.2 ([Legge, *Doctrine of the Mean*]), states, "The superior man [*junzi*] can find himself in no situation in which he is not himself," mentioning the situations of wealth, honor, and their opposites, as well as sorrow or difficulty. See also *Zhongyong*, 14.3. In other words, just because there is a beginning and an end of human activity (measured by human nature) does not mean that there is no room for individuals to determine themselves. One can transform oneself and other things and creatures in the world in many ways that fit the goal of harmony in accord with equilibrium. Consider Cafaro's arguments against greed and gluttony, Wenz's critique of consumerism, and Traer's cautions against globalization. If practiced, these ways of attending to the world beyond the individual are all consistent with the *Zhongyong*'s view that there is a limit or equilibrium to our pursuits of desires, pleasures, and feelings.

35. *Zhongyong*, 1.5; my translation. For the universality of the *zhong*, see Tu Weiming's commentary on the *Zhongyong*, *Centrality and Commonality* (Albany: State University of

New York Press, 1989). He says that the exemplary person or the "profound person" "believes that the 'middle' path is the most universal and practical way" (30).

36. Irwin, *Nicomachean Ethics,* 2.6, 1106a32–33.

37. Legge, *Great Learning,* 4.1.

38. *Zhongyong,* 4.2; my translation.

39. Ames and Hall, *Focusing the Familiar,* 43.

40. I say more about the difference between the Confucian *zhong* that is never achieved by human beings and the harmony (*he*) that is achievable in chapter 4 of my *Remastering Morals with Aristotle and Confucius.* As such, my reading is sympathetic with that of Tu Weiming when he describes the *zhong* (what he calls "centrality") as "not so much an achieved ideal as a given reality" (*Centrality and Commonality,* 20). However, I disagree with his interpretation that the *zhong* is a "state of mind wherein one is absolutely unperturbed by outside forces" (*Centrality and Commonality,* 20). This seems to be in tension with his assertion that the *zhong* is not an achieved ideal but a given reality.

41. Legge, *Doctrine of the Mean,* 1.5.

42. My interpretation that the *zhong* preexists outside human beings disagrees with Yu Jiyuan's account that the *zhong* is an inner mean that is the state of character of a human being. See Yu Jiyuan, *The Ethics of Confucius and Aristotle: Mirrors of Virtue* (New York: Routledge, 2007). For a detailed account of our differences, see my review of Yu's book, "Yu Jiyuan, *The Ethics of Confucius and Aristotle: Mirrors of Virtue,*" *Dao: A Journal of Comparative Philosophy* 8 (2009), esp. 228–229.

43. Irwin, *Nicomachean Ethics,* 1119b12–21.

44. Legge, *Doctrine of the Mean,* 20.18.

45. Irwin, *Nicomachean Ethics,* 3.12, 1119b3–15.

46. Ibid.

47. Legge, *Great Learning,* 20.7.

48. As Ames and Hall say, "The connection between the family and the familiar affairs of the day in the *Zhongyong* is primarily a function of the ritualization of both familial and familiar affairs. That is to say, *li* 禮 as ritual conduct is the primary means whereby one realizes the meaning and efficacy of these fundamental contexts" (*Focusing the Familiar,* 43; see also ibid., 45, where Ames and Hall relate filial piety [*xiao,* 孝] to *li* by stressing the significance of expressing the appropriate feelings in both).

49. See Irwin, *Nicomachean Ethics,* 5.1, 1129b20–25: "Now the law instructs us to do the actions of a brave person—for instance, not to leave the battle-line, or to flee, or to throw away our weapons; of a temperate person—not to commit adultery or wanton aggression; of a mild person—not to strike or revile another; and similarly requires actions in accord with the other virtues, and prohibits actions in accord with the vices." These actions contrast with those of filial piety for the Confucians in that they concern our relations with those outside the family and don't seem to be particularly relevant to young children.

50. Legge, *Great Learning,* 14.2.

51. Ibid., 20.7.

52. As Tu Weiming puts it, "the human way is, in an ultimate sense, identified with the Way of Heaven because they share the same ontological reality" (*Centrality and Commonality,* 77). Continuing, Tu explains that human beings "can learn to be sincere not because of Heaven's 'grace' but because their nature is originally so endowed" (77). See also ibid., 82, where Tu says, "The reason the sage can form a trinity with heaven and earth, then, is because he follows the Way by realizing that which is inherently in him."

53. Legge, *Great Learning,* 20.19.

54. Tu, *Centrality and Commonality,* 76.

55. Ibid., 78.

56. For Aristotle's distinction between the objects of theory, production, and practice, see W. D. Ross, trans., *"Metaphysics,"* in *The Basic Works of Aristotle,* ed. Richard McKeon

(New York: Modern Library, 2001), 6.I, 1025b19–29: "And since natural science, like other sciences, is in fact about one class of being, i.e. to that sort of substance which has the principle of its movement and rest present in itself, evidently it is neither practical nor productive. For in the case of things made the principle is in the maker—it is either reason or art or some faculty, while in the case of things done it is in the doer—viz. will, for that which is done and that which is willed are the same. Therefore, if all thought is either practical or productive or theoretical, physics must be a theoretical science, but it will theorize about such being as admits of being moved, and about substance-as-defined for the most part only as not separable from matter."

57. For Aristotle's distinction of the three types of theoretical knowledge, see Ross, *Metaphysics,* 6.1, 1026a13–23: "For physics deals with things which exist separately but are not immovable, and some parts of mathematics deal with things which are immovable but presumably do not exist separately, but as embodied in matter; while the first science deals with things which both exist separately and are immovable. Now all causes must be eternal, but especially these; for they are the causes that operate on so much of the divine as appears to us. There must, then, be three theoretical philosophies, mathematics, physics, and what we may call theology, since it is obvious that if the divine is present anywhere, it is present in things of this sort. And the highest science must deal with the highest genus. Thus, while the theoretical sciences are more to be desired than the other sciences, this is more to be desired than the other theoretical sciences."

58. See n. 55 and Irwin, *Nicomachean Ethics,* 6.

59. Legge, *Great Learning,* 22. Commenting on this passage, Tu Weiming holds that on the *Zhongyong*'s account, "self-realization transcends even the restrictions of anthropocentrism" (*Centrality and Commonality,* 54).

60. Rackham, *Politics,* 1.8.

61. That even within a polis the good life is restricted to the fortunate individuals who are citizens for Aristotle is evident when he says, "But a state exists for the sake of a good life, and not for the sake of life only: if life only were the object, slaves and brute animals might form a state, but they cannot, for they have no share in happiness or in a life of free choice" (Rackham, *Politics,* 3.9).

62. See n. 15; emphasis in original.

63. Traer, *Doing Environmental Ethics,* 49.

64. Ibid., 48. Traer is quoting Anthony J. McMichael, Colin D. Butler, and Carl Folke, "New Visions for Addressing Sustainability," *Science* 12 (December 2003), 1919–1920, http://www.sciencemag.org.

65. Traer, *Doing Environmental Ethics,* 48.

66. Herman E. Daly and Joshua Farley quoted in ibid., 48–49.

67. Peter S. Wenz, *Environmental Ethics Today* (New York: Oxford University Press, 2001), 44. See ibid., chap. 11, "Personal Choices, Consumerism, and Human Nature," for Wenz's account of happiness. Even though it differs from the Aristotelians and Confucians in being psychological rather than teleological, we can imagine Aristotelians and Confucians agreeing with his analysis of how excessive consumption does not contribute to our flourishing and how the deprivation of economic necessities adversely affects our lives.

On the Justice of Caring Labor 27

An Alternative Theory of Liberal Egalitarianism to Dworkin's Luck Egalitarianism

Wu Shiu-Ching

Luck egalitarianism (LE), a term coined by Elizabeth Anderson,[1] has been one of the most dominant distributive theories in contemporary egalitarian justice theory.[2] Theorists of LE, including R. Dworkin, R. Arneson, T. Nagel, E. Rakowski, and J. Roemer, have been trying to establish a theory of justice that can reconcile the seemingly incommensurable political values of equality and liberty. To that end, they have proposed that, as far as the distribution of public goods is concerned, social justice would tolerate the inequality of individuals as a fair outcome resulting from personal choices; however, social justice should not tolerate inequality among individuals if the uneven outcome is beyond one's control.

Although LE theorists share this view of accommodating equality and liberty, they disagree about whether the fruits of personal effort should be personally rewarded or socially redistributed. Acknowledging that the use of LE has been too limited to address the vast differences in the redistribution of personal and social resources, Anderson makes a further classification within LE, dividing it into two categories.[3] These categories are the desert-catering luck egalitarianism (DCLE), represented by R. Dworkin and E. Rakowski, and the responsibility-catering luck egalitarianism (RCLE), represented by J. Roemer. Anderson defines both terms as follows.

Desert-catering inequality (DCI). If A and B are equally attributively responsible for some type of conduct x, but A exercises more prudential responsibility than B, then A deserves higher rewards than B for her x-regarding conduct (or greater compensation/assistance from others, if the consequences of x are bad for her).[4]

Responsibility-catering inequality (RCI). If A is attributively responsible for some type of conduct x, then she is substantively responsible for the distributive consequences of x for herself, even if they leave her worse off than others.[5]

According to DCI, individuals who perform the same voluntary act may be rewarded differently because if one puts greater effort into the act than someone else, the greater effort should merit a better outcome. If social distribution cannot reflect the difference between personal efforts regarding the same act, it fails to do justice to the more diligent. Nevertheless, if personal efforts are the same, then one deserves as much as the other despite the market-based option that luck might favor individuals differently. In other words, the difference or inequality among individuals based on their different personal efforts would meet the requirement of being just according to DCI's concept of equality. By contrast, according to RCI, one is responsible for the outcome of the voluntary act irrespective of both the difference of personal efforts and the market-based option luck that might favor individuals differently. All in all, DCI holds that justice should reflect what one deserves, namely, that greater efforts deserve better outcomes and what one deserves should not be offset by market-based option luck. By contrast, RCI holds that justice is akin to participating in a fair game that consists of both just procedures and explicit rules such that anyone who chooses to play the game, such as with gambling, should be responsible for the outcome without complaining about option luck, which is considered a crucial part of playing the game.

Be it DCLE or RCLE, the plausibility of deserts and responsibility in matters of just distribution is at complete odds with the disadvantages confronting the caretakers of the dependent. Under both accounts, caretakers would deserve no social compensation if held responsible for the decision to take care of those in need. Moreover, under both accounts, caretakers would deserve social compensation if it were proven that they had been forced to provide care for those in need. However, as Anderson notes,[6] caregivers who receive social benefits either have been stigmatized as being the least prudent in managing their life's activity (such as using birth control) or the most unfortunate (for having ill and dependent family members who require care) and thus deserving of our pity. As a result, while LE does not fail to provide the social remedy for the inequality of caretakers, the remedy that is based on the incorrect rationale makes them either less prudent than others with regard to self-control or more pitiable than others for having bad luck. Why should someone who voluntarily devotes him- or herself to caring for others be undeserving of social redistribution? How can an egalitarian theory that justifies inequalities for caretakers be considered the ideal for equality? How can both forms of LE, which appear to be the best of both capitalism and socialism, go so wrong?

Due to limited space, I will leave out of the present discussion a detailed analysis of the two modes of LE and will instead focus only on examining R. Dworkin's version of RCLE through feminist critiques. I begin by briefly discussing the main features of Dworkin's theory of justice, particularly his concept of envy-free equal resources, of the luck/choice distinction, and of liberal egalitarianism. I will then proceed to closely examine what is so wrong with Dworkin's egalitarian theory from the critical perspective of the feminist. This will include an examination of the dependence critique, the unequal division of sexual labor, and the capability approach to the just redistribution of public resources. In the second section of this essay, I argue that despite the apparent differences among feminists, an alternative theory of liberal egalitarianism emerges from their critiques.

I end the discussion by arguing that a different voice on liberal egalitarianism has emerged from the feminists' critiques of Dworkin and conclude the essay by presenting three characteristics of the alternative theory: (1) the alternative liberal egalitarian theory would replace envy-free equality with altruistic care and social cooperation as the foundation for the theory of justice; (2) it would reinterpret what Dworkin means by sovereign virtue not in terms of government's obligation to avoid envy among social members but rather in terms of government's responsibility to provide basic care for the protection of human dignity; and (3) with respect to human dignity in general, the dignity of those who provide care is better served by the capability approach than by resource equality as a means for the just distribution of social resources.

A Brief Review of Dworkin's Responsibility-Catering Egalitarianism

> No government is legitimate that does not show equal concern for the fate of all those citizens over whom it claims dominion and from whom it claims allegiance. Equal concern is the sovereign virtue of political community—without it government is only tyranny—and when a nation's wealth is very unequally distributed, as the wealth of even very prosperous nations now is, then its equal concern is suspect.
>
> —*R. Dworkin, Sovereign Virtue*[7]

Envy-Free Equal Resources

According to Dworkin, the sovereign virtue of government is its equal respect and concern for each individual, a virtue that should be realized by distributing resources equally. By resources, Dworkin means both internal resources, such as intelligence, physical ability, and talent, and external resources, such as material goods (food, clothing, and shelter). Dworkin has designed a hypothetical desert-island case to better explain and make sense of his concept of equality of resources.[8] In his imagined desert, each individual is given the same number of clamshells. Each individual can bid for resources that meet his or her needs and preferences on the island through an imagined auction market. Furthermore, to make sure that each individual is satisfied with what she or he bids and trades for, Dworkin uses an envy test as a necessary measure against which the equal division of resources can be tested. The envy test is as follows. If A, after the first round of bidding in the auction, turns out to envy what B has, then the auction must be canceled and started again with a new round of bidding. The auction cannot end until no individual envies what others have in their hands. For Dworkin, the passing of the envy test warrants the sovereign virtue of government within which each individual is both equal in resources and free from envy of what others have in their hands.[9] However, nothing in real life matches what occurs on Dworkin's hypothetical desert island. We are born with different resources; that is, some are smarter, healthier, and richer than others. In real life, each individual not only does not have the same number of clamshells but also is inclined to envy what others have in hand, whether what they have is the result of natural luck or personal merit. Dworkin acknowledges the complaints, but he insists that much can be learned from the thought experiment, which not only provides policy makers the ideal model for the equal distribution of resources but also suggests what society should do to achieve the standards of the ideal case. Given that there is no difference between the situation of those individuals born richer, healthier, or smarter than others and that of individuals who have more clamshells than others at the starting gate, what should society do to realize the equality of resources? In addition to the desert island scenario, Dworkin has created a hypothetical insurance market that, as Dworkin believes, not only can level the differences due to bad natural luck among individuals but also can justify the inequality of outcomes resulting from individuals' different lifetime plans.

Dworkin's insurance market seems to be inspired by the availability of life insurance. However, unlike the market in life insurance, Dworkin's situation serves two different functions, as mentioned earlier. To level the individual differences that arise from bad natural luck, the imagined insurance package can protect individuals born with said bad natural luck. All they have to do is purchase this package, which should be reasonably affordable to them, so that they can have the same quality of life as those who are born with good natural luck. The accessibility of an insurance package that could cover people born with bad luck would erase the differences for those who have fewer clamshells at the start of life.

Dworkin's scenario is not fanciful in that it only reflects what have been the policies of the welfare states, providing allowances to those who are born either disabled (physically or mentally) or poor. Dworkin proposes that, just as in the welfare states, individuals who are born with bad natural luck should be covered immediately and gratis by the insurance package. However, Dworkin also argues that governments should collect money from those who are born with good natural luck so that governments can make up for the tremendous costs of the insurance packages for those who were born disabled and those who are poor. As a result, Dworkin believes that, though individuals might have drawn bad (social and natural) lottery numbers, given the differential taxing system, individuals with bad luck could match up to the lucky ones in terms of the equality of (internal and external) resources.

Dworkin's hypothetical insurance scenario has clarified the equal distribution of resources among those who are born lucky and those who are born unlucky; however, he takes an additional step to demonstrate how the imagined insurance package, if reasonably affordable to everyone, should prevent individuals from envying what others have both on hand and in their lifetime investments and plans. Thus, the accessibility of the package that serves as equal opportunity to insure against both natural and optional luck, based on Dworkin's belief, could compromise what has been incompatible between the starting-gate equality and the end-state inequality due to individual variances of resources arising from different lifetime plans. At this point, Dworkin's insurance package has become fanciful for the obvious reason that the scenario could pass Dworkin's envy test. This scenario demonstrates that as the individual is equal in resources at the starting gate, anyone should be free from being envious of what others might have in their hands as life goes on, given that everyone has an equal opportunity to be insured against risks of all kinds. I will turn next to a more detailed exploration of this second function of the hypothetical insurance case.

Luck/Choice Distinction

To explain how the hypothetical insurance strategy could justify the inequality of outcomes and therefore how that justification could pass the envy test, I will employ another thought experiment. Suppose that A and B are equally talented and devoted to work. Imagine that A and B choose the same (risky) career, such as construction work. Also suppose that there is an insurance policy against life-threatening disasters at risky places of work and that the premium to maintain the basic decent living standard once impacted by a work-related accident is affordable for everyone. If A chooses not to pay the premium and B pays the premium for the basic coverage, then there are four possible outcomes.

1. A has no insurance coverage, and nothing disastrous happens;
2. A has no insurance coverage, and A becomes blind;
3. B has insurance coverage, and nothing disastrous happens;
4. B has insurance coverage, and B becomes blind.

Consider outcomes 1 and 3: the outcome for A is better than the outcome for B because A can turn the premium into personal savings. However, considering both cases 2 and 3 as well as 2 and 4, the outcomes for B are far better than those for A for obvious reasons. Recalling the definition of RCI by Anderson cited earlier in this essay, none of the differences between A and B should demand social redistribution because when everyone has equal opportunity to insure against job accidents, the availability of the insurance market turns those risks that are beyond one's control into something manageable based on one's choices.

As the story goes, if A had an accident at work and became blind and B continues to work and is later promoted to foreman, then there are only two obvious outcomes left, namely, 2 and 3. It is obvious that A would be far worse off than B. Nevertheless, according to RCI, the inequalities between A and B are legitimate, and A should not complain about the unequal outcomes that have resulted due to the way A deliberately chose to manage risk at work. What if, however, A cannot maintain a basic decent living after becoming blind and losing the job? Is it the government's responsibility to provide the needed resources to rescue A? Can the government ignore A's miserable condition without violating its sovereign virtue? The analogy to gambling has been Dworkin's favorite when defending RCI. As we can agree, when C and D choose to gamble, even though C wins a great deal of money and D goes bankrupt, what C gains should not be redistributed to D to cover D's great losses. On the contrary, the redistribution, if performed, would be unfair to C, and as far as justice is concerned, D should be held responsible for choosing the lifestyle of a risk taker.

With respect to Dworkin, if different outcomes among gamblers are justified, then different outcomes between A and B should not be treated any differently because individuals can manage their life risks by choosing to purchase or not to purchase the insurance packages that have been made accessible and affordable to all. According to Dworkin's RCI, what the government should do is not provide rescue programs for individuals like A but instead promote equal opportunity for all to insure themselves against risk.[10] Given that the premium against risk is easily affordable for all, individuals should be responsible for the outcomes of choosing to purchase or not to purchase the insurance. Thus, the hypothetical insurance market scenario can be equated to gambling such that if what the gambler gains should not be redistributed to the losers, those who choose to be risk averse and purchase insurance should not be demanded to compensate those who choose not to purchase insurance coverage.

Dworkin's insurance package strategy is understood as the satisfactory conditions for meeting both the equality of resources at the start and the inequality of outcomes at the end-state. Both forms of distribution or nondistribution, which might seem incompatible on the surface, are justified by Dworkin's luck/choice distinction. As we can agree, no one should be held responsible for matters beyond one's control. Therefore, inequality that results from bad (good) brute luck should be redistributed, whereas inequality that results from personal choices, good or bad, should not be redistributed to those who are worse off, such as gamblers. RCI, as defined by Anderson, only specifies the latter part of Dworkin's luck/choice distinction. I would add the other side of RCI under the title of luck-catering equality (LCE) to complete the description of Dworkin's luck/choice distinction.

Luck-catering equality (LCE). If A is not attributively responsible for some type of conduct x, then she is not substantively responsible for the distributive consequences of x for herself. Therefore, either A should give away part of what she has, if the consequences of x leave her better off than others, or A should have compensation/assistance from others, if the consequences of x leave her worse off than others.

According to LCE, governments are well justified both to collect money from those who are healthy and/or rich and to pay for those who cannot afford insurance against risks. In other words, based on LCE and according to the rights of the people, it is appropriate that those who are more privileged due either to natural talents or to rich families be taxed fairly by their governments. Likewise, based on LCE and according to the rights of the people, it is appropriate that those who are the least privileged be afforded human dignity through the provisions of food, shelter, and education. As is clear with RCI and LCE as two sides of the luck/choice distinction, Dworkin's distributive theory of justice can maintain a balance between both the equality of resources at the start and the inequality of outcomes at the end-state.

Liberal Egalitarianism

According to Dworkin, the luck/choice distinction does not arise from human inclinations. By human nature, we are inclined to envy anyone better off than ourselves. Therefore, based on Dworkin's argument, what should bring us satisfaction regarding lifetime plans and investments, even when we are far worse off than others, must be derived from reasons common to democratic societies, including that human beings are both free and independent. Dworkin invokes two principles as two sides of freedom.[11] They are the principle of equal importance and the principle of special responsibility. The principle of equal importance is defined as the individual's freedom to pursue his or her concept of good without intervention from the government. For example, one may favor gambling over hard work even though gambling is likely to cause one to lose money. The principle of special responsibility is understood as the other side of freedom, in other words, the side that holds individuals fully responsible for their freedom to choose their own lifestyles. Therefore, given that gamblers are likely to be worse off than hard workers in terms of personal incomes, gamblers, by their reasoning, would prefer that there be no legal regulations against gambling; however, gamblers also do not deserve social support to bail them out of personal disasters that arise from their gambling.

Before any liberal state adopts both the policies of nonintervention and no bail-out plan to accommodate the principles of equal importance and special responsibility, Dworkin acknowledges that the sovereign virtue of any political community either should have proper legal regulations against discrimination based on race or sex or should develop public education against both cultural expectations and social coercion of individuals. In this way, each person would be free to choose his or her concept of good under no threat of social discrimination. As a result, personal freedom along with its principles is founded upon two basic tenets directly related to the sovereign virtue of any political community: the principle of authenticity and the principle of independence. The principle of authenticity is defined as a person who in the political sense is free from any form of discrimination and free to choose his or her own concept of good. The principle of independence is quite similar to that of authenticity because it focuses on the importance of personal autonomy in making decisions that should be independent of cultural stereotypes and social coercions.

In summary, the political community that is based on the principles of authenticity and independence should be free from any form of discrimination due to its regulations and educational opportunities and should therefore adopt both policies of nonintervention and no bail-out plans to best accommodate the individual's freedom to choose and accept special responsibility for his or her conduct. The government should equally respect the individual's concept of good, and individuals should be content with outcomes that arise from their lifestyles, even though they may be worse off than others.

These are the main features of Dworkin's theory of justice. To my understanding, the principle of authenticity and the principle of independence, as presented, are the basic assumptions underlying the principle of freedom and the principle of special responsibility. Therefore, both principles should be reflected in Anderson's definition of RCI. Moreover, the absence of the two basic assumptions should remove individuals' responsibility toward their coerced conduct. Thus, the absence of the two basic assumptions should also be reflected within my definition of LCE so that a full and complete description of Dworkin's view of equal libertarianism can be exhausted. Therefore, I would revise both the version of RCI and LCE as follows:

Revised responsibility-catering inequality (RRCI). If A, based on the principle of authenticity and the principle of independence, is attributively responsible for some type of conduct x, then she is substantively responsible for the distributive consequences of x for herself, even if they leave her worse off than others.

Revised luck-catering equality (RLCE). If A is not attributively responsible for some type of conduct x, either because of natural brute luck or because of the absence of the principle of authenticity and the principle of independence, then she is not substantively responsible for the distributive consequences of x for herself. Therefore, either A should give away part of what she has, if the consequences of x leave her better off than others, or A should have compensation/assistance from others, if the consequences of x leave her worse off than others.

In the next section, I will examine how Dworkin's theory of justice within the framework of RRCI and RLCE either has mistreated caretakers or has been ignorant of their disadvantaged positions. To be discussed is the work of Anderson, Eva Kittay, Iris Young, Anne Phillips, Ingrid Robeyns, and Martha Nussbaum.[12] Their critiques can be generally classified into three separate perspectives: the dependency critique, the social division of sexual labor, and the capability approach.

Feminists' Critiques of Dworkin

The Dependency Critique

As Kittay correctly argues in *Love's Labor*,[13] we all need to be cared for when we are small, sick, or old, and we should respond appropriately to others who are in need of care. Therefore, any form of social contract or any theory of just distribution must take into account the provision for caring for those dependent individuals who need care. Given that dependency relations are inevitable human conditions and that care is a precondition in the pursuit of one's concept of good, according to Kittay's dependency critique, the theory of justice reflects the superiority of independence and that individual autonomy is one-sided. As Kittay rightly notes, any theory of just distribution should not only reflect the priority of interdependence in theory but also relieve the caretaker's economic and emotional burden by providing substantial social support. Thus, Kittay provides the third principle as a supplement to Rawls' two principles of justice. To quote:

> To each according to his or her need for care, from each according to his or capacity for care, and such support from social institutions as to make available resources and opportunities to those providing care, so that all will be adequately attended in relations that are sustaining.[14]

As is now evident, Dworkin's theory of justice in both RRCI and RLCE formats fails to satisfy Kittay's principle of justice as it relates to care because, by the definition of RRCI, as far as society is free from any form of discrimination, if equality of sex has been exercised through equal opportunity to education and work, there would be no difference between a surfer who devotes energy and time to recreation and a caretaker who devotes energy and time to caring for dependent family members. Therefore, based on RRCI, the inequality between surfers and hardworking individuals in terms of income is no different from the inequality between caretakers and care-free individuals in terms of economic gains such that if surfers should be responsible for their disadvantages due to their chosen lifestyles, so too should caretakers be held responsible for their economic disadvantages, and as such, they should not be entitled to any social support.

I will discuss in more detail the reasons why, according to Anderson,[15] the (R)RCI has failed the test of care. I will then present the reasons why the RLCE has also failed the test of care.

Based on Anderson's analysis,[16] A, in (R)RCI, refers to both surfers and caretakers. Anderson offers three reasons for Dworkin's justifications for (R)RCI. The first is to preserve plural concepts of the good. The second reason is to protect and be prudent with regard to personal choices. The third reason is to be fair and not burden others with one's lifestyle. According to Anderson's critique, none of these rationales is convincing or plausible, especially when viewed through the perspective of caretaking.

First, Anderson challenges the rationale of the argument that holding A in (R)RCI to equally refer both to self-interested individuals leading luxury lifestyles and to other-oriented individuals leading self-sacrificing lifestyles is to preserve the plural concepts of the good. Even if the rationale holds, however, it does not necessarily follow that government should suspend any form of public support to alleviate the burdens of caretakers. Furthermore, (R)RCI would not provide A any safety net in the form of decent social insurance. As a result, A in general and caretakers in particular are unable to both pursue their concept of good and avoid staking everything on risky choices.

Second, Anderson challenges the rationale that to act prudently means that A in (R)RCI is held responsible for his or her chosen conduct, for better or worse, to make sure that A deliberates alternative options before taking action. Consider the choice to act as a caretaker as an example. The caretaker deliberates alternative options but ultimately decides to devote his or her resources and time to the dependent. Although the caretaker deliberates before opting to care for the vulnerable family member, according to Anderson's analysis, the caretaker will most likely be disadvantaged economically, emotionally, and socially. In other words, the reason the caretaker ends up worse off than others is not because she or he acts without prudence. On the contrary, the caretaker's personal loss is the direct consequence of both her prudent choice and her devotion to vulnerable family members.

Third, given that A in (R)RCI is responsible for his or her worse outcome and that the rationale of fairness is not to burden others for one's lifestyle, Anderson rejects the rationale of fairness of (lifestyles), claiming that it is greatly misleading. According to Anderson, Dworkin's analogy between gambling and caretaking confounds the important distinction between acts of self-interest and acts of social interest. As Anderson correctly points out, buying a luxury car for personal enjoyment is "wholly gratuitous from a social point of view," whereas raising children contributes to the public good shared by all.[17] As far as fairness is concerned, there should be no need to compensate those who are leading luxury lifestyles. Caretakers' lifestyles, however, are not like luxury lifestyles and therefore should be treated differently. Society should provide the social support to caretakers so that society as a whole can be greatly benefited by their devotion to acts of social interest.

With respect to caretaking, just distribution based on the dependency theory is utterly different from Dworkin's just distribution based on RRCI. To clarify the distinctions between RRCI and the dependency theory, I will use a hypothetical scenario. Imagine that A has altruistic parents (Cs) who not only devote themselves to A's education but also save earnings for A to inherit. By contrast, imagine that B has selfish parents (Ds) who spend all their earnings on a luxury lifestyle and, as a result, run out of resources to enhance B's future prospects. According to RRCI, Cs and Ds are like cases because they are all free to pursue different concepts of good, and as a result, both Cs and Ds should be treated alike. That is, Cs and Ds should be held fully accountable for their chosen conduct, good or bad. Because of the other side of RRCI (RLCE), however, B is jealous of what A has in hand, including a good education, good work opportunities, and a financial inheritance. The difference between A and B is the result of brute luck, and therefore the inequality between A and B should be readjusted by taxing policies, as discussed earlier.

To use Dworkin's expression, both RRCI and RLCE are meant to be sensitive to the differences between A and B and should not be sensitive to the differences between Cs and Ds. In fact, the difference between A and B should not be tolerated because neither can be held fully responsibility for something beyond their control. However, RRCI would tolerate the difference between Cs (altruistic parents) and Ds (selfish parents) as a justified inequality because both Cs and Ds, whether due to self-interest or social interest, are like gamblers who are free to choose their personal concept of good. As is obvious by now, RRCI, either implicitly or explicitly, would tolerate the disadvantages of Cs as a result of their devotion to taking care of dependent family members.

For just distribution based on the dependency theory, the case of A, B, Cs, and Ds would invite different kinds of social redistributions of resources for rationales utterly different from those provided by RRCI and RLCE. As is obvious based on Kittay and Anderson, society should provide social support to Cs because of their engagement in acts of social interest that greatly benefit society as a whole and their acknowledgment of the inevitability of the human condition, which is one of vulnerability and dependence without proper care.

As to B's disadvantages due to his family background, although the dependency theory would provide social support for B equal to that of A, the rationale for that support is not based on RLCE because of the failure to pass the envy-free test. Instead, the rationale for the social support of B, as provided by Anderson, Kittay, or Nussbaum,[18] is that society should be responsive to those who are vulnerable and dependent; otherwise, B could not survive the inevitability of the human condition. Therefore, as RLCE aims to eliminate the envy of the least privileged toward those with winning social lottery numbers, the dependency theory aims to maintain the human dignity of the vulnerable.

Furthermore, as RRCI would hold Ds fully responsible for their chosen conduct, even if that would make them far worse off than others, the dependency theory would still provide Ds the basic safety net for reasons that will be disclosed as we continue the discussion in the following section. For now, the reason for the social support of Ds, as we recall Anderson's claim, is that society should protect those individuals who might stake everything on their risky choices.

The Social Division of Sexual Labor: Against Luck/Choice Distinction

Besides the dependent critique based on care, feminists from socialist backgrounds focus on the effects of unequal social institutions, especially the sustaining social division of sexual labor that makes women as a group more vulnerable and less advantaged than men in terms of education, job opportunities, economic achievements, and social status. To highlight the point of the socialist feminists, let us return to the case of Cs (altruistic parents) and Ds (selfish parents), with a minor revision. Take Cs to be those who are devoted to household work and Ds to be those who are devoted to personal careers. According to the socialist feminists, the majority of Cs are predominantly female while the majority Ds, or men, are by contrast career oriented. The phenomenon of such a systematic gender-based distinction in their critique cannot be explained away by the choice of each individual in terms of either his or her career moves or his or her love of caretaking. Instead, the phenomenon of gender-based job segregation, rightly noted by social feminists, must be explained by the enduring social expectations embedded within the division of sexual labor. Okin, Young, Saul, and Phillips[19] have each explained with great insight the social origin of gender injustice and in so doing have found Dworkin's luck/choice distinction to be mistaken. To quote:

> But in closing the gap between social and natural circumstances, it has also turned attention away from the structures that generate and sustain inequality. It has redefined what is predominantly a problem of inter-group relations—the inequalities between rich and poor, male and female, black and white—as a conundrum about luck and choice.[20]

As Phillips correctly points out, regarding the luck/choice distinction at hand, Dworkin not only fails to see the social origin of gender inequality but also comes to the wrong conclusion about personal choices that could have been nothing more than the effects of social expectations and gender-based division of sexual labor.

In Dworkin's defense and in opposition to the social feminists, the RRCI/RLCE is founded on the notion that the luck/choice distinction is meant to provide the protection of personal freedoms in general and women's freedom in particular. RRCI, first and foremost, is meant to be an ideal theory of just distribution based on the condition that the society has been free from any form of discrimination and that the ideal state is founded on the principle of authenticity and the principle of independence whereby any individual is free to choose his or her favored concept of good. Second, Dworkin acknowledges that if sexual discrimination still prevails in the current society, unequal outcomes should be accommodated by RLCE. Third, RRCI is grounded on the priority of freedom encouraging a woman's pursuit of independence. As a corollary, social policies based on RRCI would eliminate, rather than consolidate, gender-based job segregation.

To my understanding, social feminists would oppose all of Dworkin's defenses on the following three accounts. First, as far as the model for equal distribution of resources is concerned, feminists argue that any distributive theory that assumes ideal human conditions—such as life free from vulnerability or a society free from any form of discrimination—is either, at its best, a model of reality that fails completely to grasp what reality is or, at its worst, a model of reality that reflects what social reality is like only according to a number of highly simplified assumptions. For example, the model assumes independence to be a norm of life and is ignorant of the ever-prevalent existence of dependence. While theorists of social justice are satisfied with their ideal model for just distributions, social feminists have questioned how these models could be of any practical use for social change. Social change, for social feminists, does not consist of meeting either the ideal or the pure demands of any distributive model; rather, social change should occur as a result of challenging the ideal of a model whose reality is remote from social reality. Therefore, in contrast to the model of reality depicted through RRCI/RLCE of independence and autonomy, social feminists attempt to work their way out of ever-existing gender-based job segregation using a model of reality that could reflect vulnerability and dependence as norms of social reality.

Second, even though Dworkin provides via RLCE social support for gender injustice resulting from a social division of sexual labor, social feminists, to my understanding, could raise issues regarding the mistreatment and abuse to which caretakers are subjected with respect to the aid they receive. A social policy based on RLCE would mistreat caretakers in particular because, as Anderson rightly points out,[21] those who are dependent on social benefits either have been stigmatized as being least prudent in managing their birth control or classified as the most unfortunate and are thus deserving of our pity. The former form of social dependency is the rationale for both singles and couples without children who complain about bearing the burden for those who decide to have children they cannot afford to raise.[22] As to the latter form of dependency, caretakers with sick and aged family members are considered to be the victims of their forced circumstances and therefore deserving of society's pity because pity has always been accompanied by the feeling that we are lucky to have escaped such degrading and dependent situations. Additionally, social policy based on RLCE tends to abuse caretakers because most of the social support goes to those in need of care, leaving limited resources for the caretakers, who are seen as independent.

Third, social policies based on RRCI/RLCE would, in contrast to Dworkin's thinking, consolidate gender-based job segregation. Again, we return to the case of Cs and Ds to explain this point. Imagine a society with a social welfare policy based on the spirit of RRCI/RLCE, which happens to be common practice among advanced industrial societies. In these societies, women with better education and job opportunities are more likely to choose to be members of Ds (until recently a social class that has been predominately male), leaving their burdens of caretaking and house care to women with poor educations and low job skills. To follow the trend, women with professional skills have become more visible in the population of Ds. Now women from underdeveloped countries have migrated to the households of these professional women to become members of Cs (traditionally predominantly female). Taken together, societies based on the spirit of RRCI/RLCE seem to conform to either intrasociety or intersociety gendered-based sex segregation.

As to this case, RRCI has helped to consolidate the unequal division of sexual labor because RRCI tells any individual in general and any woman in particular, if they are equipped with an education and job skills, that the best choice for men and women is to be members of Ds. As for those who fall into the domain of Cs, the best explanation is none other than the lack of proper education and job training for works other than caretaking. Likewise, with the RRCI/RLCE as a social policy, societies are heading toward either lower birth rates or the prevalence of an international care chain (First World professional women vs. Third World nannies). Worse yet, the prevalence of the international care chain works to consolidate both the persistent gender-based division of sexual labor and the hierarchy of skilled over unskilled workers.

In summary, the distributive model of RRCI/RLCE not only fails to bring an end to the enduring gender-based division of sexual labor, but also fails to alleviate the abuses of caring labor. For social change, social feminists propose an alternative model of reality that could reflect vulnerability and dependency as norms of social reality. With the public support of care and the upgrading of dependency, men and women could engage in dependent relations. Moreover, for a model of reality that projects interdependence as a social reality, social policy that is based on that model could make great strides in terms of both the promotion of the social significance of care work and the public education of caring citizens. Consider military service in Germany as an example. Young militants, both men and women, can choose care work as an alternative to the standard service program. In this way, they "learn what this (care)work is like, how important it is, and how difficult it is."[23] And last, social support for caretakers not only should be free of entrenched stigma attached to either personal imprudence or personal misery but also should be free from abuses by the provision of resources in accordance with their capabilities.

Capability Equality versus Resource Equality

To continue the previous discussion concerning what would be a just distribution of resources so that all in general and caretakers in particular are perceived as equal, feminists, despite their different theoretical positions, are in accord in their acceptance of capability equality, which was founded by Sen and developed with numerous revisions by Nussbaum,[24] to be the rival of both resource equality and welfare equality. There are many cases that can exemplify what it means to be equal in terms of capability. For example, pregnant women require more resources, such as milk, to meet daily standard nutritional needs compared with a non-pregnant person. Imagine a healthy person and a person with a physical impairment. Although both are equally rich, they are different in terms of mobility because there is not adequate access to public space for the impaired person.[25] For the third case, taken from Williams,[26] imagine a crippled individual who has a less easily satisfied but similarly disabled sister. Both are entitled to the access of public space.

As these cases indicate, capability equality that has been attentive to the variations of transforming resources into capability is distinctive from both resource equality and welfare equality. Individuals who are equal in resources have personal variances in translating resources into the ability to do things, as shown in the first case. Furthermore, individuals who are equal in resources end up being different in levels of mobility due to social conditions, as evidenced in the second case. Finally, an individual's capability set should be equal regardless of his or her preference for happiness, as shown in the third case. In all, the capability approach proposes that any just distribution theory should be attentive to both personal conditions, and social conditions that produce "variable resource-capability transformation rates."[27] Nevertheless, the capability approach suggests that any just distribution theory should ignore any personal preferences of happiness with respect to the equality of capability.

Moreover, feminists agree that equality of capability does not suggest that we be equal in our abilities to perform complex functions; however, they all agree that we should be equal with respect to those basic and minimum capabilities, which are open to further deliberations. According to Nussbaum, basic human capabilities should include life, health, food, clothing, shelter, education, mobility, and emotional ties, without which, according to Nussbaum, human beings cannot maintain their dignity.[28] Robeyns contends that basic capabilities consist of both material and nonmaterial dimensions and that the latter refers to family time, emotional well-being, and democratic agency.[29] Taken together, feminists have specified what basic capabilities are, and they have shown that some of these basic capabilities, such as emotional ties with others and participation in communal life, are absent in Dworkin's account of both personal and impersonal resources. For a point of comparison, Robeyns provides the case of the international care chain, indicating that nannies from developing countries do not have equality in emotional capability even though they have equality in resources.[30] Although the nannies could have access to more resources from the international labor market, as Robeyns points out, "they are detached from their family, and their children would more likely abandon them in their old age."[31]

For feminists, the list of basic human capabilities must incorporate both economic resources and emotional bonding to others, without which human beings fail to maintain their human dignity. According to this line of reasoning, Williams contends that feminists argue against any gender-biased social conditions that would set limits on the possibility of incorporating career and family life, especially for women. To make this case, Williams provides as an example a set of twins, Ann and Bob.[32] The twins, as the story goes, are the same in personal and impersonal resources though they are different in terms of the capability of combining career and family in the current society. According to Williams' argument, Bob would be more likely than Ann to find a partner who either will be a homemaker or will try to balance work and family responsibility and who is less likely to be an ideal worker devoted to a full-time career. By contrast, Ann would be more likely than Bob to find a partner who either will be an ideal worker devoted to his career or will balance his work and family responsibility and who is less likely to be a homemaker. As the social division of sex labor goes, Ann's capability to combine career and family is far more difficult than is the case with Bob, who can be both an ideal worker and find a partner who is devoted to raising a child at the same time.

Despite the feminists' efforts to make capability equality a distinct concept of equality, Dworkin opposes their capability approach for two reasons. First, Dworkin posits that the basic capabilities that include emotional bonding and public participation are nothing more than either personal ambitions or personal attitudes related to individual preferences for happiness. Therefore, in response to Williams' imaginary twins scenario, Dworkin argues that while Ann is less likely than Bob to find a partner who wants to be a homemaker, Bob is less likely than Ann to marry a partner who wishes to be a breadwinner.[33] "Ann's chances might be overall greater than Bob's for that reason."[34]

Dworkin further argues that, given a society free from sexual stereotype and gender job segregation, the capability sets of Ann with respect to child rearing are no worse than Bob's, whose capability for domestic work is worse than Ann's. According to Dworkin's critique, if the capability equality approach is, as Williams argues, distinctive to either welfare equality or resource equality, there is no ground to claim that Ann's capacity to raise children is less capable (or valuable) than Bob's ability to work at a career. Ann's capability set is just different from Bob's. Instead, as Dworkin points out,[35] Williams' assessment of Ann's capability set as being less capable than Bob's reinforces the point that capability equality is reducible to equality of welfare. In Williams' judgment, one's capabilities contribute to one's happiness, which is what allows the comparison between the capability sets of Ann and Bob. Therefore, Ann's complaint, if legitimate, only reveals that Williams' defense of capability equality as a distinctive theory is self-defeating.

In all, Dworkin concludes that his view about the capability approach remains intact, namely, that the concept of capability is ambiguous and that, if clearly specified as simple functions reducible to personal or impersonal resources, or if specified as complex functions such as emotional ties to others, then they are indistinguishable from an individual's concept of welfare.

Feminists, as I contend, respond to Dworkin's defenses from two sides. First, the list of basic human capabilities that incorporate both economic resources and emotional bonding to others corresponds to the feminists' model of reality that depicts vulnerability and (inter)dependence as norms of social reality. Thus understood, family time together, emotional bonding to others, and participation in public life are basic capabilities of vulnerable human conditions, not, in contrast to Dworkin's view, complex functions arising from personal ambitions or personal attitudes to the pursuit of happiness. Second, a possible end to capability inequality could not result from the ideal model of just distribution whose reality is remotely detached from social reality. As long as gender-based sex segregation is prevalent in a society, any just distribution theory must be attentive to the social conditions that would set limits on the possibility of incorporating career and family life, especially for women. Along this line of reasoning, when Dworkin dismisses Ann's complaint by contending the legitimacy of Bob's complaint, even though Dworkin is correct with regard to the complaints addressed by both Ann and Bob, the rationale for his argument is wrong. In my view, while Ann's complaint about balancing career and family is legitimate, Bob is equally justified to complain that being an ideal worker comes at the expense of family time and his ability to share in childrearing. Therefore, the solution to Ann's and Bob's problems is not to see them as equal in their capacities, as suggested by Dworkin, because if they are seen as such, their complaints remain unnoticed and go unaddressed. Instead, social policies should work toward incorporating career and family life so that both men and women have the same basic capabilities. To incorporate work and life calls for fundamental social change, such as the revision and transformation of the workplace ethos so that it is "more hospitable to employees who bear an equal or greater share of the costs of child care."[36] More important, feminists argue that workplaces should be accommodating to home care and should reflect the value and significance of care, without which we can barely survive.

> The capabilities approach suggests that a major aim of public policy ought to be the transformation of the workplace, through new flexibility and new ethical norms. These changes and the changes I propose in public education are strongly complementary: as young workers learn to think of care as part of their lives, they become less willing to accept rigid workplaces, and employers who offer flex-time and part-time options will attract the most skilled workers.[37]

Before moving on to the next section, I want to address three more important distinctions between capability equality and resource equality. First, as previously mentioned, social policy based on resource equality tends to abuse caretakers because they are seen as independent persons with more resources (personal or impersonal) than those they care for. By contrast, a social policy based on capability equality would detect the caretaker's rate of transforming resources to capabilities, which is, of course, far lower than it is for those who are not caretakers or who are, at best, tied to those in need of care. Thus, social support for caretakers should justify the protection of the caretaker's personal benefits, and social policies should recognize those who have been dedicated to the service of caring. Caretakers need public facilities such as nannies, day-care centers, and allowances, to maintain their own basic capabilities.

Second, aside from being attentive to the basic capabilities of caretakers, the capability approach also addresses the needs of the least prudent in society. To make this point clear, I will return to an earlier scenario. Imagine Ds (selfish parents) to be like gamblers or to have extravagant lifestyles that cause them to become homeless. According to the capability approach, society should provide Ds with food, shelter, basic medical coverage, and other necessities of life because by failing to sustain these basic human capabilities, Ds cannot maintain their human dignity. Therefore, in contrast to RRCI's suspension of the rescue program for Ds, the capability approach comes to Ds rescue to protect Ds' basic human dignity. The capability approach, which requires social cooperation based on the equal respect of all, does not tolerate insensitivity toward vulnerable members of society and would take any necessary steps to remove obstacles that inhibit their ability to function or to receive the basic capabilities of equal respect for each human being. However, would it be unfair to others to give the social support to Ds, who are supposed to be held responsible for being homeless through their own bad choices? Would social support for Ds encourage other people to likewise act irresponsibly? The reply to these doubts leads us back to the dependency theory discussed in an earlier section of this essay.

Third, capability equality further aims to integrate the political value of liberty as an alternative theory to liberal egalitarianism. Let me address this alternative by returning to the case of the person in a wheelchair. Being human requires certain basic necessities, such as life, health, food, mobility, shelter, and emotional ties. To that end, as Nussbaum points out, public space should be redesigned to accommodate people with impairments so that they can, if they want, move from place to place without barriers. According to the capability approach, society should provide easy access for people with impairments, regardless of whether the public facilities would be widely used by those who have impairments. As a result, the public task is to sustain human dignity and bring out equality of all with respect to basic capabilities, whereas every individual is to some extent free to choose his or her concept of good, just as people in wheelchairs who are given free access to public space might choose to remain secluded. However, some public tasks, such as basic care and compulsory education, are forced on the individual for the sake of human dignity. In other words, if an individual can choose to end the status of being human by one's will, then government should not permit social members to sacrifice human dignity in the name of freedom.

An Alternative Theory of Liberal Egalitarianism

There is an alternative theory of liberal egalitarianism that has emerged from the feminists' critiques, as previously discussed. For comparison, three characteristics, all of which are in great contrast to Dworkin's theory of liberal egalitarianism, are described as follows.

First, as to the basic assumptions underlying the sovereign virtue of any political community, RRCI/RCLE shares both the principle of autonomy and the principle of independence. As thus understood, the ethical individualism of RRCI best accommodates, as a corollary, the view either that the individual's self-interested conduct and envy-free mentality should be both necessary and sufficient for social cooperation or that the individual's lifestyle could differentiate his or her own good from the good of others. The practical implications of RRCI/RCLE, along with its emphasis on the priority of independence and autonomy, are societies inclined to encourage their citizens, women in particular, to be free of the burdens of family. Worse yet, societies rich with nannies from economically underdeveloped nations are inclined to stigmatize a caring labor force as unskilled and therefore unimportant and underpaid.

In contrast, feminists have been critical about the current tide of perception that caretaking is a great personal burden. Instead, the theory alternative to RRCI/RCLE is based on the principle of interdependence and the principle of vulnerability. Therefore, the feminists' alternative theory has replaced envy-free social cooperation with care-based social cooperation.

> The person leaves the state of nature (if, indeed, there remains any use for this fiction) not because it is more mutually advantageous to make a deal with others, but because she can not imagine living well without shared ends and a shared life. Living with and toward others, with both benevolence and justice, is part of the shared public conception of the person that all affirm for political purposes.[38]

The practical implications for public policies under the principle of care should effect both the rectification of caretakers who have been disadvantaged by unfair treatment and the reevaluation of care. For the former, in contrast to RRCI, which rejects Kittay's principle of care by the rationale that government should be neutral to different concepts of good, the alternative liberal egalitarian theorists hold that caretakers deserve social support for their caring conduct, chosen or not, not only because a caring society should not be insensitive to the vulnerability of any member but also because society, as a whole, benefits from the conduct of caretakers, who, in addition to contributing to the public good, set an example of what it means to be a caring citizen. We all benefit from the risks and sacrifices of those engaged in taking care of vulnerable members of society; therefore, a compassionate and just society should take any necessary steps to preserve the human dignity and well-being of its caretakers.

As to the reevaluation of care, the provision of social supports for caretakers promoted by Kittay's principle of care could be the first positive step in eliminating the social stigma attached to caring work. In addition, the importance of care should be widely disseminated through social regulations and public education, such as social policy that requires the structure of a career to accommodate care at home and public education that promotes the cultivation of caring citizens.

Second, in contrast to RRCI/RCLE, which holds Ds responsible for their risky choices, the alternative theory promotes social support of Ds, regardless of the cause of their need, the rationale being to maintain human dignity through the provision of basic human capabilities irrespective of personal choices and responsibilities. To maintain the human dignity of anyone in need is not considered to be unfair to all in general or to caretakers in particular because a caring society should be responsive out of empathy. Such caring in a society is cultivated through social policies and education that have taken interdependence and human vulnerability to be the first priority of human concern. As a corollary, a society that has cultivated altruistic behaviors by meeting Kittay's principle of care would be least resistant to an individual's pursuit of a different concept of good and more responsive to an individual's dire need as a result of his or her risky choices without regard to his or her special responsibility.

Third, as far as equality is concerned, while RRCI/RLCE is a distributive theory that compromises both the equality of resources at the start and inequality of outcomes at the end-state, the alternative theory maintains the equality of basic capabilities throughout the individual's lifetime, a concept closely linked to the underlying principles of human independence and human vulnerability. The equality of the basic capabilities for all, according to the alternative theory, is a form of just distribution that provides social supports for the protection of human dignity in terms of what we, at minimum, are able to do for another human being. Human capabilities, therefore, should not be taken simply as means to an end with respect to human dignity; rather, human capabilities, particularly those basic to life, such as health, food, clothing, shelter, education, mobility, and emotional ties, are essential to human beings.

Conclusion

I have argued that the feminist theory of liberal egalitarianism is an alternative to Dworkin's RRCI/RCLE. In contrast to the principle of freedom and the principle of special responsibility that have served as the basis for the latter form of just distribution, feminists agree that the principles of interdependence and human vulnerability should be the foundation of just social distribution. As understood, these two basic assumptions therefore should be reflected within Kittay's principle of care such that a full and complete description of the alternative theory of equal libertarianism can be exhausted. My revision of Kittay's principle of care is to give to each according to his or her need for the basic capabilities, irrespective of his or her special responsibility, from each according to his or her capacity for care, based on the principle of interdependence and the principle of human vulnerability. According to my principle of care, it is the purpose of social institutions to make available resources and opportunities to both those maintaining basic capabilities and those providing care, so that all will be adequately attended in relations that are sustaining.

NOTES

1. E. S. Anderson, "What Is the Point of Equality?" *Ethics* 109, no. 2 (1999), 287–337.

2. S. Scheffler, "What Is Egalitarianism?" *Philosophy and Public Affairs* 31, no. 1 (2003), 5–39.

3. E. S. Anderson, "How Should Egalitarians Cope with Market Risks?" *Theoretical Inquiries in Law* 9, no. 1 (2008), 239–270.

4. Ibid., 245.

5. Ibid., 244.

6. Anderson, "What Is the Point of Equality?"

7. R. Dworkin, *Sovereign Virtue: The Theory and Practice of Equality* (Cambridge, MA: Harvard University Press, 2000), 1.

8. Ibid., 66–70.

9. J. Heath, "Dworkin's Auction," *Politics, Philosophy and Economics* 3, no. 3 (2004), 332.

10. M. Ousuka, "Luck, Insurance, and Equality," *Ethics* 113, no. 1 (2002), 49.

11. Dworkin, *Sovereign Virtue*, 5.

12. Anderson, "What Is the Point of Equality?"; Anderson, "How Should Egalitarians Cope?"; Eva Kittay, *Love's Labor: Essays on Women, Equality and Dependency* (New York: Routledge, 1999); Iris Young, "Equality of Whom? Social Groups and Judgments of Injustice," *Journal of Political Philosophy* 9, no. 1 (2001), 1–18; Anne Phillips, "Defending Equality of Outcome," *Journal of Political Philosophy* 12, no. 1 (2004), 1–19; Ingrid Robeyns, "Sen's Capability Approach and Gender Inequality: Selecting Relevant Capabilities," *Feminist Economics* 9, nos. 2–3 (2003), 61–92; Ingrid Robeyns, "Is Nancy Fraser's Critique of Theories of Distributive Justice Justified?" *Constellations* 10, no. 4 (2003), 538–553; and Martha Nussbaum, *Women and Human Development: The Capability Approach* (New York: Cambridge University Press, 2000).

13. Kittay, *Love's Labor.*

14. Ibid., 113.

15. Anderson, "What Is the Point of Equality?"; Anderson, "How Should Egalitarians Cope?"

16. Anderson, "How Should Egalitarians Cope?" 254–258.

17. Ibid., 257.

18. Anderson, "What Is the Point of Equality?"; Anderson, "How Should Egalitarians Cope?"; Kittay, *Love's Labor;* or M. Nussbaum, *Frontiers of Justice: Disability, Nationality, Species Membership* (Cambridge, MA: Harvard University Press, 2006).

19. Susan Okin, "Gender Inequality and Cultural Differences," *Political Theory* 22, no. 1 (1994), 5–24; Young, "Equality of Whom?"; Jennifer Saul, *Feminism: Issues and Arguments* (Oxford: Oxford University Press, 2003); and Phillips, "Defending Equality of Outcome."

20. Phillips, "Defending Equality of Outcome," 17.

21. Anderson, "What Is the Point of Equality?" 289.

22. Eric Rakowski, *Equal Justice* (Oxford: Oxford University Press, 1992), 109; K. M. Franke, "Theorizing Yes: An Essay on Feminism, Law, and Desire," *Columbia Law Review* 101, no. 1 (2001), 181–208.

23. Nussbaum, *Frontiers of Justice,* 213.

24. A. Sen, *Inequality Reexamined* (Oxford: Oxford University Press, 1992); and Nussbaum, *Women and Human Development.*

25. Nussbaum, *Frontiers of Justice,* 167.

26. A. Williams, "Dworkin on Capability," *Ethics* 113, no. 1 (2002), 23–39.
27. Ibid., 29.
28. Nussbaum, *Women and Human Development,* 78–80.
29. I. Robeyns, "Assessing Global Poverty and Inequality: Income, Resources, and Capabilities," *Metaphilosophy* 36, no. 1–2 (2005), 46.
30. Ibid., 30–49.
31. Ibid., 41.
32. Williams, "Dworkin on Capability."
33. R. Dworkin, "Sovereign Virtue Revisited," *Ethics* 113, no. 1 (2002), 136–140.
34. Ibid., 136.
35. Ibid., 137.
36. Williams, "Dworkin on Capability," 32.
37. Nussbaum, *Frontiers of Justice,* 215–216.
38. Ibid., 158.

Aging, Equality, and Confucian Selves

28

Steven F. Geisz

A number of authors have recently brought the Confucian tradition into meaningful contact with the theory and practice of democracy. The literature includes accounts of what Confucian democracy is or would be,[1] explorations of the relationship between Confucianism and fundamental features of political liberalism such as rights,[2] and a variety of attempts to link Confucianism and, more broadly, Chinese political theory and practice in general to theories of deliberative democracy in particular.[3] In this essay, I would like to add to this growing discussion by thinking about ways in which a Confucian valuation of and deference to the elderly might challenge and inform liberal democracy.

Liberal democracy aims to treat all adult citizens as politically equal. Once a citizen is over the age of majority, then—at least in standard cases in which a person's right to participate is not curtailed by a felony conviction, for example—she is deemed a full-fledged member of the community and in theory has equal standing with all other adult citizens when it comes to making policy and participating in the political realm in general. While the liberalism of liberal democracy will typically tolerate a significant degree of social and economic inequality among adult citizens as the necessary by-product of valuing individual property rights and other kinds of individual freedoms, it is committed to the fundamental idea that all adult citizens are and must be treated as *political* equals.

In what follows, I want to consider three main questions. First: Is there any plausible alternative to a standard "all adult citizens have equal political standing" model of democracy that could be drawn from a specifically Confucian valuing of elder members of the community? Second: Insofar as there is a plausible alternative, what might it reveal about differences between how liberalism and Confucianism think of human selves as located in time? Third: What sort of difference would it make if the Confucian valuing of age were implemented via informal social norms, on the one hand, or via explicit institutional mechanisms and procedures, on the other?

I will begin by outlining a hypothetical Confucian version of deliberative democracy that allocates opportunity within a democratic community's deliberative forums so as to allocate political power in a way that tracks the age of adult citizens. I will consider the ways in which such a Confucian version of deliberative democracy is related to other proposals for Confucian democracy and various ways it might provide a plausible alternative to standard liberal versions of deliberative democracy. Specifically, I will focus on the ways that such a hypothetical Confucian deliberative democracy treats all citizens as politically equal over the course of an average lifetime, even though it does not treat all adult citizens as political equals at any given time. By comparing and contrasting the synchronic equality of standard liberal versions of deliberative democracy with the diachronic equality of this hypothetical, Confucian-inspired deliberative democracy and by considering the ways in which such a Confucian-inspired deliberative democracy is a formalized version of what Confucian ritual propriety aims to achieve, we can identify an independently interesting Confucian notion of human selves as essentially extended in time. Finally, I will consider the differences between infusing a Confucian valuing of the elderly into democracy via informal mechanisms and doing so via more formal institutional structures and procedures.

Age, Speaking Time, and Democratic Deliberation

There are many facets to the Confucian tradition, and there are multiple ways in which one might try to apply the Confucian valuing of the elderly to contemporary community life. Confucianism emphasizes the virtue of *xiao* (孝), or filial piety, and at least part of that virtue involves a specific sort of deference toward older family members. Beyond that, the Confucian virtue of *li* (禮), or ritual propriety, demands among other things that one behave deferentially toward elder members of one's community, and that one do so in ways that track subtle differences in status that are partially a function of an individual's age.

A Confucian deference toward the elderly is enmeshed in various other Confucian virtues, and the quick gloss I have given only hints at the ways in which such deference is grounded in the overall tradition. And, admittedly, Confucianism is not unique among the traditions of China—much less the traditions of other cultures—in its insistence that people deserve some sort of deference simply on account of their age. Nevertheless, both the degree to which Confucianism values the aged and the centrality of that value to the tradition makes deference toward the elderly a defining characteristic of the Confucian tradition.

In order to consider whether Confucianism can provide a plausible alternative to the "all adult citizens have equal political standing" model of liberal democracy, in what follows I will consider first a specific Confucian-inspired variation on the liberal deliberative democracy proposed by a number of theorists. Some stage setting will be helpful. Deliberative democratic theory comes in many forms, but they all insist that something important is missing in the preference-combining mechanisms that are at the heart of aggregative democracy. Deliberative democrats typically identify what is missing as one or more of the following: the rationality or rational justifiability of the results of the policy-making process; significant opportunity for the policy preferences of community members to be transformed by the decision-making process;[4] or the overall legitimacy of the process.[5] Often, what is seen as lacking involves all three.

In order to improve upon aggregative democracy, the deliberative democratic solution is to add deliberation to the democratic process. Details vary depending on the specific proposal, but the general idea is to set up a deliberative forum and then coax, encourage, or possibly even require community members to work together to try to reach meaningful agreement on policy by engaging in deliberation with one another. Ideally, such deliberation will lead to agreement about important community decisions, but, if the deliberation fails to reach meaningful agreement, the processes of aggregative voting and other hardball political activities such as bargaining can come into play in addition to—and, importantly, *after*—deliberation in order to set policy.

I want to focus on the kind of political-liberalism-inspired deliberation that is associated with the touchstone work of Gutmann and Thompson,[6] but which is widely supported by deliberative democrats, especially those who are broadly liberal in their commitments and outlook.[7] Gutmann and Thompson allow that both the electoral mechanisms of aggregative democracy and the associated processes of political bargaining might be fine ways of establishing policy in some cases, but in other cases—especially where there is deeply entrenched, morally charged disagreement within a community—the legitimacy of the community decision-making process requires that members of the community come together and discuss their policy preferences in a rather constrained way. Specifically, Gutmann and Thompson require that community members offer explicit *reasons* in support of their preferred policies, rather than merely expressing their support for such policies. According to the ideal of such deliberative democracy, one should not just announce the policy preferences one has, at least in situations in which there is morally charged disagreement. One must also offer reasons in support of one's preferences. Moreover, reason giving must take place in a particular way. The reasons must be framed in terms of the *common good* (not in terms of mere self-interest), and they must be *publicly accessible* (meaning, roughly, that the truth and relevance of what is offered as a reason in support of a policy position must be assessable equally by all members of a community). Beyond constraints on the reasons themselves, the explicit reason-giving process must be marked by the exemplification of particular virtues by the deliberators—broadly liberal virtues such as *tolerance* for difference of opinion and more specific virtues such as *reciprocity*.[8]

On this kind of liberal deliberation, the entire deliberative process aims to support the political equality that is at the heart of political liberalism, and to protect and insulate it from both economic and social inequalities.[9] In concrete terms, liberal deliberation protects political equality by providing a forum that heads off the aggregative mechanism of voting. The motivation for wanting to do so is that mere voting processes are seen as ineliminably susceptible to the influences of economic and social inequalities and are therefore potentially damaging to the enjoyment of political equality. In addition, the strictures on the appropriate exchange of reasons that are essential to the deliberative forum serve to limit self-interested bargaining of the sort that happens in association not only with aggregative voting, but with many other kinds of political situations. Though the motivation for limiting such bargaining might seem obvious, it will still help to highlight it here: self-interested bargaining will (it seems[10]) be driven by and will reinforce (and possibly even exacerbate) the economic and social inequalities that exist in a community.[11]

The feature of liberal deliberation involving the defense of political equality is typically manifest in part by giving everyone in a community an equal say within the deliberative forum. At a most basic level, this usually means giving everyone an equal amount of time in which to speak, and it often also involves the introduction of structural features such as the presence of a moderator whose job involves adjusting for emerging patterns of dominance in the conversation (or at least those patterns of conversational dominance that are not driven solely by prowess in logical argumentation).[12]

What might a specifically Confucian-inspired alternative to liberal deliberation be? There are a number of different avenues we might take here, and indeed there are suggestions already available in the literature.[13] Suppose we think of Confucian deliberation as aiming to fill the same role in an eventual Confucian version of deliberative democracy as liberal deliberation is to fill in an eventual liberal deliberative democracy. That is, Confucian deliberation will be added to full-blown aggregative democracy as a kind of decision-making forum of first resort, at least in the case of deep, morally charged disagreement about policy within an otherwise established democratic community.[14] Ideally, for the decisions for which this forum is appropriate, agreement will be reached by deliberation, and the mechanisms of aggregation and political bargaining will be used only as a last resort.

Confucian deliberation could be similar to the proposed liberal deliberation in some ways, but there would be crucial differences. For example, rather than explicit reason giving as the definitive feature of deliberation, Confucian deliberation could be guided by speech acts constrained by the social pragmatics embodied in Confucian ritual (*lǐ*, 禮) and tradition. Depending on what features of Confucian ritual are emphasized, we could come up with a Confucian version of democratic deliberative democracy that, for example, downplays

Gutmann and Thompson's explicit-reason-giving requirement in favor of a requirement that one's policy preferences be expressed in accord with Confucian ritual and get supported via speech acts that are broadly constrained by Confucian social pragmatics. I will not explore that possibility in much detail in what follows but will focus instead on a hypothetical Confucian deliberative forum within which the Confucian valuation of the elderly is made explicit by allocating speaking time to participants in a way that tracks the participants' ages. Such a Confucian deliberative forum will highlight and defend a version of a specifically Confucian social hierarchy based on age.[15]

There are two broad ways in which a Confucian deference to age could be incorporated into democratic deliberation. First, the deference could be produced as a result of ritual-inspired deferent behavior on the part of participants in the forum who have internalized Confucian social pragmatics, even without explicitly allocating extra speaking time to people the older they get. If the majority of the participants in the deliberative forum were to have a tendency to defer to elder members of the community by refraining from certain kinds of criticism and by taking the utterances of their elders more seriously than the utterances of younger members of the community, then the deliberative forum would be marked by a Confucian deference to the aged, even in the absence of any explicit changes to the procedures that constitute a non-Confucian, Gutmann-and-Thompson-style deliberative forum.

Alternatively, the Confucian deference to the elderly could be incorporated into a democratic deliberative forum in a more obvious and explicit way. In concrete terms, imagine an up-and-running Confucian deliberative forum in which community members come together to communicate about policy choices, prior to allowing political bargaining and aggregative voting mechanisms to run their course and determine policy. In this forum, the amount of *say* that any given person has is determined by that person's age in the following way: the older a person is, the more speaking time she has.

As one way to pump intuitions, imagine that every person over a given age—say, age eighteen—is admitted to the deliberative forum, but that mere admittance does not confer any privilege to speak. For every five years a person is aged over twenty, one minute is given to that person's allotted speaking time in the deliberative forum. Thus, twenty-year-olds are allowed only to attend silently and learn from the deliberative forum, forty-year-old participants each are allotted four minutes to speak, and eighty-year-olds would each be allotted twelve minutes to speak. Variations in the algorithm used to determine speaking time would track different conceptions of the appropriate privileges of age. My concern here is not with the exact details of the amount of time a person has and how that amount is calculated. Rather, I introduce this example as one way to think about how a Confucian respect for age might be incorporated into a working deliberative forum. However such Confucian deliberation gets spelled out in detail, it will reject the basic requirement of standard liberal versions of democratic deliberation that everyone in the forum have an equal chance to speak.

Such a proposal could provide a plausible way to introduce some sort of deliberation into various cultural contexts, depending on how deeply infused a Confucian valuing of age is in a given context. My hope is that the proposal might help in thinking about how to improve actual governance in various real-world contexts, but evaluating the likelihood that such Confucian deliberation could be implemented is not my concern here. Rather, I am interested primarily in how we might evaluate this ideal of Confucian deliberation vis-à-vis the ideal of standard "all citizens are political equals" deliberation put forward by liberal deliberative democrats such as Gutmann and Thompson.

It might seem as if the proposal of introducing a deliberative forum that allocates additional speaking time to people depending on how old they are would be politically naive, at least if the proposal is meant literally. As I discuss later, there is value to considering such a proposal, even if it never would be implemented, because a fine-grained look at potential objections to the proposal and how they compare and contrast to objections that could be raised against more straightforwardly liberal proposals for deliberative democracy reveals important information about standard liberal assumptions about the nature of political equality and about ways of thinking about political selves through time. However, even when taken as a literal proposal for how to structure a deliberative democratic forum in a Confucian cultural setting, the hypothetical Confucian deliberative forum I am considering is no more naive or improbable than other proposals that have been made in the literature on Confucianism or even implemented as real-world experiments by deliberative democrats. Daniel A. Bell, for instance, has considered concrete ways in which a community might work Confucian commitments into democracy, and he even explicitly suggests that seating arrangements could manifest respect for the elderly in deliberative forums by allowing the elderly to have better seating positions.[16] James Fishkin and his collaborators have theorized about and experimented in real-world situations—both in and outside of China—with various sorts of deliberative forums that, from the perspective of many people who are entrenched in a nondeliberative vision of democracy that emphasizes hardball political bargaining and the messy amorality of so many contemporary political campaigns, would look equally far-fetched. For instance, in what Fishkin, Baogang He, and Alice Shu describe as the first Chinese deliberative poll, the town of Zeguo in Zhejiang Province conducted a policy poll after a kind of deliberative forum that included "Chinese indigenous deliberative methods" such as having "democratic heart-to-heart talk[s]."[17] So even if at first the Confucianism-inspired deliberative forum I am considering here seems unlikely ever to be implemented, it is not obviously more implausible than other proposals in the literature, and, in any case, we should be cautious about relying too heavily on our initial conceptions of what is possible and probable when trying to think about the possibilities of democracy.

So before moving on to a detailed consideration of objections that might be raised to this hypothetical Confucian-inspired deliberative forum and what those objections reveal to us, I want to make clear the following:

1. I am here considering a hypothetical system in which older participants are given more speaking time in a democratic deliberative forum than younger participants, *and this is meant literally.*
2. Even if the forum in question were not literally to allocate additional speaking time to older participants, the consideration of the situation in which literal speaking time is allocated unequally is helpful to us in understanding the ways in which a Confucian deliberative democracy might look different than a more straightforwardly liberal deliberative democracy.
3. Regardless of whether or not such a Confucian deliberative forum is ever implemented, the consideration of it and the comparison of it to the kinds of deliberative democratic experiments conducted by people like James Fishkin and advocated by Amy Gutmann and Dennis Thompson helps us understand important assumptions about the nature of liberal democracy and its conceptions of fairness.

Evaluating a Confucian Age-Privileging Deliberative Forum

At the very start, it might seem as if the inequality of allotted speaking time in this Confucian-inspired deliberative forum would be unfair and ad hoc—that there is something prima facie unjust about the unequal allotted speaking times in Confucian deliberation, at least in contrast to the liberal alternative.

How might a defender of Confucian deliberation respond? On the one hand, such an objection might seem simply to amount to an insistence that a person's age is not a legitimate factor in determining the amount of say she should have in community decision making (at least for anyone at or above the age of majority). If that is what the objection amounts to, a defender of Confucian deliberation could simply say that the objection begs the central question against Confucian deliberation.

Leaving aside the line of response to the initial objection that such inequality in speaking time would be unjust, I want to explore a way in which the social inequality expressed in the unequal allotment of speaking time might—in spite of first appearances—really be perfectly compatible with a kind of meaningful political equality, even a political equality that liberals should recognize. If so, then even though the proposed Confucian deliberation is driven by an acceptance of a particular social hierarchy involving age that is prima facie incompatible with a liberal insistence on keeping such social inequalities out of the political process (at least insofar as we are talking only about people over the age of majority), on closer analysis the Confucian alternative is not as antithetical to meaningful political equality as it at first seems.

Assuming variation in age within a community, there is, of course, going to be unequal say in an individual Confucian deliberative session, considered in itself. However, if we begin by looking at individual community members rather than individual deliberative sessions, then, over the course of an average human life-span, we see that every person's opportunity to speak in the totality of Confucian deliberation sessions that she can be expected to attend is equal to the opportunity of everyone else. Over the course of an average lifetime, everyone will have an equal amount of time to participate in a Confucian deliberative forum. It is only if we look at participation in deliberation at the temporal scale of an individual deliberative session (or at a scale of time that encompasses a small or relatively low number of deliberative sessions) that the inequality of allotted speaking times seems to lead to age-driven inequality of opportunity to participate in political discussion and decision making.

Of course, some people will in fact not live as long as others, and consequently their actual amount of participation in the political decision making of a community that adopts this sort of Confucian deliberative democracy will be less than that of others in the community who live longer. However, this is not a telling objection. On the one hand, such inequalities in life-span are arguably beyond the scope of concerns about the sort of fairness of political processes. Furthermore, if we look at the amount of participation a person has in *liberal* deliberation over the course of her lifetime in a liberal deliberative democracy, those with shorter life-spans will have less overall chance to participate than those with longer life-spans. (Admittedly, the problem may still be bigger in this regard for Confucian deliberation, since in the case of a Confucian deliberation, a person's overall amount of participation per year lived beyond the age of majority is only equalized at the time a person reaches the high end of the expected life-span in a community.)

Perhaps the best response on the part of a defender of Confucian deliberation to a worry about differing life-spans is as follows: if we think of inequalities in actual life-span as a special case of inequalities in health more generally, then it is not obvious that Confucian deliberation is any worse off than liberal deliberation in this regard. Liberal deliberation, even in the quasi-ideal version we have been discussing, requires relatively robust health on the part of its practitioners. If the differences in actual health of community members is not thought to be a problem for the fairness of liberal deliberation, then it is not clear why differences in actual age span should undermine the sense in which Confucian deliberation allows for equality of say over the course of an average life-span.

On the other hand, insofar as either health in general or expected life-span in particular correlates with factors that we do not want to have influence a person's ability to participate in a deliberative forum (be it liberal or Confucian), then we may want to think of ways to correct for that. Specifically, if health/life-span in a community correlates with socioeconomic class, racial/ethnic identity, gender/sex, or sexual orientation (or even with factors such as religious or political affiliation), then we may want to think about correcting for that in the allotment of time given to speakers in the deliberative forum. The issues here are tricky, and my hunch is that many of them are best left untouched, but the important point is that *if* we are worried about unfairness in the case of Confucian deliberation, we should be *equally* worried about it in the case of liberal deliberation, and there are ways in which we might correct for at least some of the unfairnesses in both kinds of deliberation.

Of course, if allotting more speaking time in any given deliberative session to people who are older does not compromise political equality over the span of a typical human lifetime, then there are other, *non*-Confucian forms of deliberation that award age-dependent speaking times that are *also* not a threat to political equality on the scale of a typical lifetime. I have in mind possible proposals that would award more time to *younger* participants rather than to older participants (or even crazy, complicated proposals that would award more time to a person as her age approaches forty, then decreasing time as her age approaches fifty-one, and then increasing time until her age approaches sixty-four, and then gradually decreasing time as she ages from there on out). Such non- (or even anti-) Confucian proposals for structuring speaking-time allotments in deliberation would also, it seems, not create political inequalities based on age over the course of a lifetime. I presume other factors could be used to rule them out (although "the young have more say" proposal might have its own merits, especially if we think about giving them more time to learn how to participate and then later to use their increased skills more efficiently in the shorter allotted times that come with increasing age). My point here is that a great many age-dependent ways of allotting deliberation opportunity (or even of allotting political "say" more broadly) might have their particular merits or demerits relative to liberal, "everyone has equal say" deliberation, but the only way in which the age-dependent unequal-speaking-time proposal clearly seems to create a condition of unequal political opportunity is if we insist on looking at a person's opportunity to participate in political decision making on a scale of time that is less than that of a full human lifetime. (In this regard, the Confucian proposal and the suggested non-Confucian, "young say more" proposals differ significantly from proposals that would allot speaking time in deliberation based upon gender/sex, racial or ethnic identity, economic class membership, etc.)

I have considered a specific alternative to the "all adult citizens have equal political standing" model of liberal democracy by considering a hypothetical

Confucian-inspired modification of a liberal deliberative democratic forum. However, we could also explore similar elder-favoring modifications of other, *non*-deliberation-focused democratic practices, such as voting schemes that allocate more votes to citizens as they age. On such a model, we might allow every citizen of voting age to get an additional vote for every so many years they are aged beyond the legal voting age. We might consider variations that would allow voters who have multiple age-determined votes in any given election the opportunity to spread their allocated votes among the available candidates or ballot-option possibilities, or we might stick to models that require all of a voter's allocated votes to be given to a single candidate or single answer to a ballot question. And, of course, different ways of valuing age might be encoded in the voting procedure by how many additional votes we give to an individual on account of her age. While there will be important differences between a model of deliberative democracy that allocates speaking opportunities within a deliberative forum in a way that tracks age and a voting scheme that allocates votes in accord with a voter's age, what remains the same is the general idea that such an elder-valuing modification of liberal democracy provides a way of ensuring political equality over the course of an average lifetime while institutionalizing age-based political inequality at any given moment.

Selves through Time, and Democratic Institutions

The exploration of what time scale to use when asking about equality or inequality of political opportunity highlights a feature of Confucianism that is obvious when thinking about that tradition in some contexts but that is sometimes neglected when thinking about Confucian approaches to politics and political theory: Confucianism emphasizes our situatedness as individuals in time and as members of communities that extend through time. Conversely, political liberalism can be seen (at least in many of its manifestations) as treating people as relatively dehistoricized beings. By thinking of people as rational, autonomous agents and at the same time thinking of rationality and autonomy as being universal and (in some sense) culturally and historically transcendent, political liberalism arguably conceives of people as being outside the histories of their individual lives and the histories of their communities. Confucianism, in contrast, emphasizes the way in which historical tradition and the progression of time infuse a community and an individual human life (at least when a human life is appropriately lived). It insists that we look at people as beings that live through extended periods of time, changing in significant ways as they do so, and filling different roles within a community as they age and master ritual, virtue, and so on.

At one level of description, we can say that a Confucian-inspired democratic political system that allocates political opportunity within a democracy at least partially in accord with age sees life as a journey of the self through time, whereas standard political liberalism sees all adults as having "made it," as it were, once they have reached the age of majority. The Confucian-inspired deliberative forum and the corresponding voting schema considered earlier institutionalize an acknowledgment that people tend to change with age, and they make this fact central to a person's political standing within a democracy in a way that standard liberal democracy does not, since standard liberal democracy does not mark the fact that there is such expected change in adults as they age within the political procedures of democracy themselves.

Of course, to be fair, liberals *can* acknowledge that, among the adults who are deemed to be political equals within a community, there are likely going to be differences in political perspective and preference, not to mention wisdom and general state of mind, that correlate at least roughly with a person's age. After all, almost everyone acknowledges that as most people age, they tend to develop a kind of perspective that is informed by past experiences and often contains a kind of wisdom that is lacking in youth (although, in contrast, some people instead simply become more jaded or narrow-minded as they age). And, of course, there are the expectable losses in a person's cognitive and emotional capacities that do or will likely accompany old age in many of us.

Although political liberalism does not attempt to work those expectable changes over the course of a lifetime into the institutional framework of democracy in any way (except insofar as it does not allow children to participate fully in political decision making), there seems to be no reason to think that liberalism itself is ultimately incompatible with a conception of selfhood as essentially amounting to a progressive journey through time than is the sort of Confucianism expressed in *Analects* 2.4:

> The Master said: "From fifteen, my heart-and-mind was set upon learning; from thirty I took my stance; from forty I was no longer doubtful; from fifty I realized the propensities of *tian* (*tianming* 天命); from sixty my ear was attuned; from seventy I could give my heart-and-mind free reign without overstepping the boundaries."[18]

In short, the liberal vision of all adult citizens as having political equality at all moments does not make explicit what might reasonably be expected to happen to a person as she journeys through adulthood, but its vision of responsible adult participation in a political community is at least minimally *compatible* with acknowledging that citizenship plays out against a complex backdrop of aging and changing individual selves.

Nevertheless, standard political liberalism sees expected age-dependent differences between and changes over time in adult citizens as being *irrelevant* to their status as political equals, in the same way that differences in economic status and non-age-related social status are seen as being irrelevant to the kind of political equality on which liberalism focuses. Just as economic and non-age-dependent social status are deemed irrelevant to political standing by liberalism (except insofar as what liberalism takes to be extreme cases of economic or social privilege might bubble over and undermine meaningful political equality), likewise differences in social status and perspective that at least roughly correlate with age are deemed irrelevant (but again, except insofar as those differences might bubble over and make a difference in political equality—but here liberalism tends to see only being younger than the age of majority as an age-relevant difference that legitimately impacts the relative political standing of citizens). Political liberalism in effect abstracts away from age-dependent differences among adult citizens, at least when theorizing about public policy and political decision making.

Seen in this way, the Confucian-inspired approach is arguably preferable, since the liberal version might be taken to amount to a willful ignorance of the expectable effects of aging: since people *do* tend to develop as they age—and do so in roughly predictable ways—why shouldn't our political institutions and practices take that into account by awarding more political responsibility to citizens as they age, especially since doing so is compatible with a meaningful political equality, albeit one that is visible only diachronically rather than synchronically? Even if the particular details of the Confucian deliberative forum or the age-tracking voting schema discussed earlier as examples are not acceptable, it still might seem as if *some* Confucian-inspired schema of institutionalizing age-dependent political status would track a relevant feature of human life—the obvious fact that we tend to change with age. If a Confucian-inspired democracy tracks that change while a standard liberal democracy does not, isn't that in itself a point in favor of the Confucian-inspired form of democracy?

Age or Youth?

Of course, even if we are open to the notion of developing democratic institutions and practices that track age while maintaining political equality over the course of an average adult lifetime, it is not obvious that correlating increased political influence with increasing age is in all cases better than, say, correlating increased political influence with youth. Consider the common wisdom one often hears scientists or mathematicians express, at least in certain kinds of conversations, according to which great and innovative discoveries are rarely made by anyone over the age of thirty, or consider the ways in which some businesses in certain situations—say, the dot-com heyday of the late 1990s and early 2000s—tend to turn to youthful leadership precisely because young CEOs are seen as being more likely than older business leaders to better guide certain kinds of organizations in times of rapid change. Such situations in which common wisdom (whatever that is) trumpets the comparative value of a youthful perspective are at least arguably the exception rather than the rule when thinking about what sort of age-correlated judgment and perspective are most likely to contain the most insight and wisdom. At the same time, however, there are scientific mentors and various management consultants—not to mention many, many other people—who think there are cases where the predictable perspectives of the aged are *less* likely to be on the mark than those of the young might. The mere fact of this tendency to privilege youth should give us pause in thinking that a Confucian-inspired age-dependent democratic political scheme provides a viable alternative to an "all adult citizens are always politically equal" scheme, even if we are willing to say that there is no relevant difference in the kind of political equality among citizens in the two schemes that would lead us to favor one over the other on that basis alone.

We might also worry that a Confucian-inspired age-dependent democratic system would tend to favor certain policy choices over others. In other words, by giving the elderly more say, the system would tend to be conservative or simply to favor policies that benefit the elderly, or whatever. Here we would need empirical data to nail down whether any particular policy choices would be likely to be favored by a Confucian-inspired system in general, but it seems reasonable to suppose that an age-favoring democratic procedure would be likely to shift the policy outcomes in somewhat predictable ways. Regardless of whether such policy outcomes are acceptable, the mere fact that age-favoring procedures could be expected to benefit some policy choices over others might seem to show that there is something wrong with building such age-tracking mechanisms into democratic institutions, since doing so is not merely a procedural change but instead amounts to taking a de facto political stand on substantive issues.

To the extent that we feel the pull of such an objection, we must already be committed to some broadly liberal democratic conception of state neutrality, at least among policy options that are equally likely to protect basic liberal democratic rights. But even if we accept that the institutional mechanisms of a democracy should be as neutral as possible vis-à-vis the likely policy debates they are intended to resolve, the mere fact that a Confucian-inspired age-dependent set of democratic institutions is likely to favor some policy choices over others in contrast to a more straightforwardly liberal set of institutions does not give us reason to favor the liberal set of institutions, since they themselves can be seen as favoring *their own set of policy choices.* At this level of description, there seems to be no set of policy choices that is obviously *the* set that is more neutral overall. Even if we can predict which kinds of policy choices would emerge from a Confucian age-dependent democratic system and which would emerge from a liberal "all adult citizens are always politically equal" system *and* we are committed to the idea that the democratic institutions themselves be as neutral as possible with regard to associated substantive policy choices, there still is no good reason to favor the non-Confucian system over the Confucian one on the basis of which is more neutral.

Informal and Formal Mechanisms of Implementation

I have considered the pros and cons of formalized versions of a Confucian-inspired age-valuing democratic procedure—either in the form of a deliberative forum that allocates speaking time on the basis of age or, more briefly, in the form of a voting mechanism that allocates more votes per election to citizens as they age. I turn now to a deliberative forum where Confucian norms of valuing the elderly do their work only informally. Imagine a deliberative-democratic forum in which the explicit procedures that guide deliberation are of a non-Confucian sort and where official speaking time is allocated equally to all participants. Even if a moderator were present at this imaginary forum to enforce time limits, if the people participating are acculturated in Confucian norms of deference to the elderly, then younger participants might be expected to limit their own speaking time to something shorter than the maximum. Maybe the younger members would allocate their unused speaking time to older participants, if that is allowed. There are numerous other ways in which Confucian-inspired norms could play out informally in a deliberative forum, even in the absence of any explicit measures to enforce them. Younger speakers could make reference to what elder members have previously said as they give their own remarks in the forum; younger members could signal their deference to elder members in subtle ways by what they say and how they say it; elder members could have their say toward the end of the deliberation session such that their temporal position in the order of speakers would be analogous to the privileged seats at the table at a Chinese dinner banquet;[19] or, all else being equal, it could simply be that everyone participating in the forum would take the comments of the most elderly more seriously than those of younger participants. Depending on how deep Confucian values run, we can easily picture a situation in which the de facto age deference manifested within a deliberative forum, however explicitly structured to allocate equal speaking opportunities to all, might approximate or even equal the age deference of the Confucian-inspired deliberative forum discussed earlier.

It is more difficult to imagine a case in which Confucian age deference so strongly influences a non-age-tracking voting procedure. But even in that case there are ways in which informal Confucian valuation of the elderly might influence voting outcomes. Even if every citizen has only one vote in an election, the background valuing of the elderly in a Confucian community might significantly influence election outcomes, despite there being no explicit mechanism encoding that Confucian value in the voting procedures themselves.

In short, in communities in which Confucian values are strong and widely held, we might find a Confucian-influenced age-deference system in effect grafted onto straightforwardly liberal democratic institutions and procedures in such a way that the overall functioning and outcome of the institutions will significantly approximate what we would get with an explicitly Confucian age-valuing model of the sort discussed previously. In assessing democratic institutions that are infused by Confucian age deference but without any formal structuring to reinforce that deference, it seems there could be no real objection from advocates of straightforward liberalism. Yes, these institutions would be influenced by Confucianism, perhaps even heavily, but the policy-forming mechanisms themselves would not encode the values of a specifically Confucian conception of the good society. In that way, it would seem possible to have a Confucian-inspired democracy, at least in the dimension of deference to valuing of the aged, without in most cases raising any liberal hackles. Of course, if the Confucian valuation of the aged becomes so strong or gets manifested in such a way that it muffles the voices of younger members or somehow interferes with the policy-making decisions of the community, defenders of liberalism would object.[20] In moderation, though, a set of deliberative or voting procedures that do not mark age deference explicitly and formally but that are influenced informally by the Confucian age deference might approximate the features of the explicit age-valuing mechanisms discussed previously, but in a way that is more tolerable, and indeed more likely to be manifest, in real-world communities.

To the extent that the informal mechanisms would approximate the more formal versions of Confucian-inspired age-valuing democracy, they would still encode a vision of the self as extended through time. And, as in the case of the formal models considered in this chapter, participation in the democratic practices would influence the way people act and think about themselves. True, the way in which the vision of the self is extended through time would make a practical difference in the minds and self-conceptions of participants in those more formalized versions of age-valuing democratic procedures, but even then the influence on participants would presumably be subtle. Whether or not the Confucian age deference were formalized in the deliberative forum or the voting procedures, participants would probably not be influenced in such a way that they would think explicitly of themselves as being extended in time. Rather they might be expected to learn those lessons more slowly, and largely without being conscious of it, by participating over time in the democratic institutions that are age valuing. So these explorations into the ways to work age valuing into deliberative or nondeliberative democracy in explicit ways would be relevant to any kind of liberal democracy in a significantly Confucian context. The extent to which the Confucian-inspired valuation of the elderly impacts people through the conception of the self through time that it encodes is an open question—one perhaps best answered by social scientists doing empirical work.

Conclusion

I have considered in this essay two different kinds of democratic decision-making procedures. First, there is a straightforward liberal kind of procedure that tries to ensure political equality among citizens at all moments. In deliberative democracy, such a procedure allocates equal speaking time within the deliberative forum. Not only does such an "all adult citizens are always political equals" model of democracy attempt to abstract away from differences between citizens in terms of their economic and non-age-based social statuses, but it also—as we have seen in the Confucian-inspired procedures discussed in this chapter—attempts to abstract away from the expectable changes and developments in a person's faculties of judgment and perspective as she ages.

Second, there is a Confucian-inspired procedure that privileges age and favors the elderly either (1) by allocating increased speaking time in deliberative forums to older participants or (2) by allocating increased votes to citizens as they age. This Confucian-inspired alternative can, like the standard liberal approach, abstract away from differences in economic and non-age-based social status in order to emphasize some sort of real or imagined political equality among citizens, but the kind of political equality here is one that is manifest only at the scale of complete human lifetimes. Importantly, the Confucian-inspired procedures do not abstract away from expectable changes in a person's faculties of judgment as she ages.

Although I have introduced this Confucian alternative in contrast to a standard liberal model of deliberative democracy, it might be more proper to see it as potentially only a variation of liberal deliberative democracy, since, as I have argued, it is compatible with protecting a kind of political equality in the face of property-rights-derived differences in economic and other social status. I have considered various ways in which one might try to defend the standard liberal model over the Confucian one, but the upshot of the investigation is that neither the liberal model nor the Confucian model is clearly preferable in all cases. That, in itself, is of interest.

The Confucian-inspired model does seem likely to reinforce among its participants a conception of the self as something that is essentially spread out in time and subject to a predictable sort of development and growth over time. This might be something to count in favor of the Confucian approach—but even here, it is not clear whether it is a good thing. Getting people to think, however explicitly, about themselves—or at least their political selves—as being on a journey through time might encourage them to take longer-term perspectives on political questions, and it might encourage people to be patient and more thoughtful as they gradually move up in influence as they participate in democratic institutions over the years. But it could alternatively encourage complacency among the young, or even a kind of self-centered arrogance among the elderly.

So, it seems as if there is a hypothetical, Confucian-inspired, age-valuing alternative to a standard version of liberal democracy, and it seems as if it is at least potentially as legitimate as the standard, "all adult citizens always have equal political status" model. Whether it really would be a preferable alternative would depend on a host of microlevel considerations that will vary with particular context and the needs of various communities. At the very least, such an alternative is worth considering when thinking about ways to encourage democratization on the small and even large scale in Confucian-friendly cultural contexts, and it points to an often unnoticed way in which democratic institutions can shape our sense of ourselves as beings located in and developing through time.

NOTES

Earlier versions of this paper were presented at the 2008 Central Division Meeting of the American Philosophy Association (under the title "Deliberation, Ritual, and Equality") during a special session sponsored by the APA Committee on the Status of Asian & Asian-American Philosophers and Philosophies and at the 2007 Southeastern Conference of the Association of Asian Studies meeting (under the title "Deliberative Interactions and Confucian Perspectives [Liberal and Confucian Deliberation]"). I benefited from feedback received from the audiences and the other participants in both of those sessions, and I am grateful to Brooke Ackerly for serving as the formal commentator for the session at the 2007 presentation. I received particularly helpful feedback from Daniel A. Bell on one of those earlier versions of the paper. I also wish to thank the audience at the Tenth East West Philosophers' Conference for their feedback after my presentation of the more mature version of this paper in May 2011 and at least one anonymous reviewer for additional feedback.

1. Daniel A. Bell, "Deliberative Democracy with Chinese Characteristics: A Comment on Baogang He's Research," in *The Search for Deliberative Democracy in China,* ed. Ethan J. Leib and Baogang He (New York: Palgrave, 2006), 149–157; Daniel A. Bell, *Beyond Liberal Democracy: Political Thinking for an East Asian Context* (Princeton, NJ: Princeton University Press, 2006); Brook A. Ackerly, "Is Liberalism the Only Way toward Democracy? Confucianism and Democracy," *Political Theory* 3, no. 4 (August 2005), 547–576; Sor-hoon Tan, *Confucian Democracy: A Deweyan Reconstruction* (Albany: State University of New York Press, 2004); various contributions in Daniel A. Bell and Hahm Chaibong, eds., *Confucianism for the Modern World* (New York: Cambridge University Press, 2003).

2. See various contributions in Kwong-loi Shun and David B. Wong, eds., *Confucian Ethics: A Comparative Study of Self, Autonomy, and Community* (New York: Cambridge

University Press, 2004); and Will Kymlicka and Baogang He, eds., *Multiculturalism in Asia* (New York: Oxford University Press, 2005).

3. Ethan J. Leib and Baogang He, eds., *The Search for Deliberative Democracy in China* (New York: Palgrave, 2006).

4. John S. Dryzek, *Deliberative Democracy and Beyond: Liberals, Critics, Contestations* (New York: Oxford University Press, 2001).

5. Amy Gutmann and Dennis Thompson, *Democracy and Disagreement* (Cambridge, MA: Harvard University Press, 1996); and Amy Gutmann and Dennis Thompson, *Why Deliberative Democracy?* (Princeton, NJ: Princeton University Press, 2004).

6. Ibid.

7. While many deliberative democrats are liberal in the overall outlook, many others (especially those heavily influenced by the work of Habermas) advocate nonliberal versions of deliberation. Dryzek (*Deliberative Democracy*), for instance, advocates a kind of nonliberal deliberation that allows more room for rhetoric and other nonargument-based forms of political communication in the deliberative forum.

8. Reciprocity in this context is, roughly, the virtue not only of being disposed to offer reasons the offering of which shows appropriate respect to one's interlocutors, but also of being disposed to listen to and seriously consider the reasons offered by others and to do so with an attitude of openness to being convinced of the merits of a position that one heretofore thought of as wrongheaded or immoral.

9. By "social inequalities" I mean the kinds of differences in status and influence often associated with gender/sex, race, ethnicity, sexual orientation, education level, religious or other group affiliation, etc. All such sources of social status are, of course, tied in complex ways to economic status.

10. I say "it seems" because there are important complexities to political bargaining that potentially make it not really as antithetical to the goals of deliberative democrats as they often seem to think. I explore some of these complexities in "Deliberative Democracy, Bargaining, and What Doesn't Get Said" (conference paper delivered at the 2006 meeting of the Southern Society for Philosophy and Psychology and at the American Philosophical Association's 2007 Central Division Meeting).

11. Beyond heading off both aggregative voting mechanisms and bargaining processes, liberal deliberation also seeks to minimize the influence of rhetoric and emotional appeal. After all, the vision of political equality inherent in political liberalism goes hand in hand with a conception of a person as an autonomous agent, which in most cases is defined in terms of the notion of a *rational* agent freely making decisions for herself on the basis of reason. The nonargumentative means of persuasion typified by rhetoric and emotional appeal are thus threats to the exercise of rational control by people of their decision-making processes. Consequently, rhetoric and emotional appeal are seen as threats to the exercise of political equality. See Dryzek, *Deliberative Democracy,* for a nonliberal version of deliberative democracy that explicitly allows for some kinds of rhetoric and emotional appeal to be proper parts of the deliberative process.

12. See James S. Fishkin, "Realizing Deliberative Democracy: Strategies for Democratic Consultation," in *Search for Deliberative Democracy in China*, 37–52, as well as his earlier work.

13. Daniel A. Bell has developed a proposal for a Confucian kind of deliberative democracy in the form of a "House of Scholars" in the following publications: "Democratic Deliberation: The Problem of Implementation," in *Deliberative Politics: Essays on Democracy and Disagreement,* ed. Stephen Macedo (New York: Oxford University Press, 1999), 70–87; *East Meets West: Human Rights and Democracy in East Asia* (Princeton, NJ: Princeton University Press, 2000); "Deliberative Democracy with Chinese Characteristics: A Comment on Baogang He's Research," in *Search for Deliberative Democracy in China*,

149–157; and *Beyond Liberal Democracy*, esp. chap. 6. Other proposals for forms of deliberation that are compatible with a Chinese cultural context, if not with a specifically Confucian worldview, include various essays in Leib and He, *Search for Deliberative Democracy in China*, esp. Chen Shenyong's contribution, "Native Resources of Deliberative Politics in China." Also relevant here is the outline of a specifically Confucian version of democracy in Ackerly, "Is Liberalism the Only Way toward Democracy?"

14. This differs from many of the proposals and accounts of deliberation and deliberative democracy in Leib and He, *Search for Deliberative Democracy in China*, where the concern is more often with infusing deliberation and aspects of deliberative democracy in the current or near-current real-world political environment.

15. I will set aside two aspects of the traditional Confucian hierarchy: the assumed unequal standing of rulers and ruled and the prescribed inequality of men and women. With regard to the ruler/ruled inequality, while it is central to classical and premodern Confucianism, I take it to be antithetical to Confucian *democracy*, and the Confucian deliberation I am exploring is supposed to function in a Confucian deliberative democracy in the way liberal deliberation is supposed to function in a liberal deliberative democracy. Ackerly presents a vision of Confucian democracy that retains elements of Confucian hierarchy that can arguably be thought of as being in part a ruler/ruled hierarchy. Ackerly opposes what she calls "exploitable hierarchy," not hierarchy per se (see Ackerly, "Is Liberalism the Only Way toward Democracy?" esp. 557 and 567–578). Though it is not perfectly clear, it seems to me that Ackerly would allow a kind of social hierarchy that includes what I am thinking of as the ruler/ruled inequality to be a part of something meaningfully called "Confucian *democracy*"—albeit with the proviso that the hierarchy not be what she calls "exploitable." It depends on whether or not nonexploitable hierarchy could allow for an inequality of ruler(s) and ruled. In any case, I am not considering any such hierarchy—exploitable or not—in the hypothetical Confucian deliberative democracy I discuss.

As for the man/woman inequality, in line with what a number of commentators have suggested (see Ackerly, "Is Liberalism the Only Way toward Democracy?" 557 and 574n54), if we allow contemporary political liberalism to treat men and women as political equals in spite of the history of the cultures from which such liberalisms emerged, there is no reason (or at least no *obvious* reason) why we could not analogously detach Confucianism from the gender inequalities of its history, even while retaining some of the other social hierarchies from its history.

By thinking about age and bracketing the other sources of social inequality that are part of classical Confucianism, I do not mean to indicate that age inequality could function by itself in such a way as to give us a distinctively Confucian way of life, nor do I claim that Confucianism lends itself easily to the breaking off of particular features and separating them from the rest. I only mean to say that we have to begin somewhere, and I think we can begin by thinking about ways in which the age dimension of an unequal Confucian social hierarchy might challenge and inform a liberal ideal of democratic deliberation.

16. See Bell, "Deliberative Democracy with Chinese Characteristics," 151.

17. See James S. Fishkin, Baogang He, and Alice Shu, "The First Chinese Deliberative Poll," in *Search for Deliberative Democracy in China*, 229–244 (esp. 237–238); as well James S. Fishkin, "Realizing Deliberative Democracy: Strategies for Democratic Consultation," in *Search for Deliberative Democracy in China*, 37–52; and Fishkin's earlier work.

18. *Analects*, 2.4; translation from Roger T. Ames and Henry Rosemont Jr., trans., *The Analects of Confucius: A Philosophical Translation* (New York: Ballantine Books, 1998).

19. See again Bell, "Deliberative Democracy with Chinese Characteristics," 151, where he discusses seating arrangements in Chinese deliberative forums.

20. And, indeed, we can imagine John Stuart Mill objecting, especially if the Confucian influence becomes the sort of strong social pressure he worries about in *On Liberty* (1859; Mineola, NY: Dover Publications, 2002) as being an infringement on individual liberty even in the absence of explicit legal sanctions. Mill himself is, to say the least, not a fan of the "despotism of custom" that he thinks is characteristic of China in the nineteenth century; see Mill, *On Liberty,* chap. 3.

Institutional Power Matters 29

THE ROLE OF INSTITUTIONAL POWER IN INTERNATIONAL DEVELOPMENT

Lori Keleher

> There is a deep complementarity between individual agency and social arrangements. It is important to give simultaneous recognition to the centrality of individual freedom and to the force of social influences on the extent and reach of individual freedom.
>
> —*Amartya Sen, Development as Freedom*

> Gender relations do not operate in a social vacuum, but are products of the ways in which institutions are organized and reconstituted over time.
>
> —*Naila Kabeer, "From Feminist Insights to an Analytic Framework"*

Academics and practitioners working in international economic development often cite the critical role of empowerment within development; however, relatively little attention has been paid to institutional power.[1] Institutionalized power plays an important role in generating, reinforcing, and reproducing the inequalities that prevent or limit various groups of individuals—most notably women—from acting as agents, engaging in empowerment processes, or being empowered. In other words, we cannot adequately address the role of empowerment with development without properly understanding the role of institutionalized power in empowerment. This essay seeks to briefly explain what institutionalized power is and the significant role it plays in the sort of empowerment that is critical to international development. In what follows, I first introduce several key concepts, including *institutionalized power* and *empowerment,* before explaining the important role that institutionalized power plays in generating, reinforcing, and reproducing dangerous inequalities. I conclude by listing some of the aspects of institutionalized power that I argue call for more attention within international development.

Key Concepts

The concept of *institutionalized power* has roots in Marxist and socialist thought as well as in various strands of feminist philosophy and economics.[2]

Institutionalized power can be understood as power that exists as a result of *social differences*—including inequalities—present in the *social relations,* which are *systematically* generated, reinforced, and reproduced by both formal and informal institutions. Institutions at work within a given society may include the international community, the state, the legal system, the military, the political system, the political party, the market, the firm, the banking system, the church, the village, the community, the tribal council, the household, the family, marriage, and many others.

These institutions embody frameworks of "rules," or patterns of behavior, that define social groups and social relations. Both formal and informal institutions may explicitly profess (and sometimes strive for) one official set of rules—which may include, for example, "all are equal before the law"—while actually operating within another, unofficial and often implicit framework of rules—for example, a system in which black people who murder white people are much more likely to be sentenced to death than white people who murder black people.[3] An adequate analysis of institutionalized power requires us to look beyond the official, explicit rules of institutions and to understand the unofficial, but powerful, social rules of intuitional frameworks. Social rules are not absolute. There may be exceptions to the rules, and the rules may change over time.

Social groups are social categories that are created, perpetuated, and recreated by institutions. Examples of social categories include women, men, the elderly, wives, homosexuals, widows, the able-bodied, Christians, Hindus, Muslims, and Brahmans. Institutionalized norms determine how individual group members (are expected to) relate to one another in the context of society.

Social relations are the structural relationships of social groups. *Gender relations* are one type of social relation. Gender relations describe the relationships between men and women within a given society or institutional framework.[4] As products of institutions, such relationships define the roles, responsibilities, and freedoms and, in turn, the power shares of individual group members, including who does what, who gets what, who decides what, who has access to what, who controls what (and whom), who serves whom, and so forth. The differences in the roles, responsibilities, freedoms, membership conditions, and relative power shares of social groups are *social differences.* Social differences between men and women are *gender differences.*

Unfortunately, the power available to the individual members of the different social groups in the institutionalized relations of society is often unequal. Moreover, the inequalities of institutionalized power found in social relations often result in a relative deprivation of some groups (including women) and a relative privileging of others (including men). Social groups, social relations, and social differences are all products of changeable social patterns. Institutions—which are controlled by privileged groups—on the other hand, tend to work to reinforce current social patterns and, in turn, social inequalities, thereby confirming the greater share of social power (control) and advantages of the privileged groups and the *oppression* of other social groups.[5]

Empowerment, within the context of international development, can be helpfully understood as the enhancement of individual agency or the expansion of the set of the substantive freedoms (or capabilities[6]) that allow an individual to do or be something valuable.[7] For example, an individual could be said to be empowered, or to be experiencing empowerment, when she gains the real freedom to vote in an election that influences her life or to be literate or well nourished. I use the phrase "real freedom" in an attempt to exclude hollow "freedoms." A case of a hollow freedom is when voting rights are formally granted on paper but nullified in practice due, for example, to violence at the polls, fraudulent elections, or other circumstances, such as an institutionalized social rule that says that "(good) women do not themselves participate in politics, but leave such matters to men."

Empowerment is not an all-or-nothing concept. Rather, it is a more-or-less concept. Each of us can be understood as being more or less empowered at various points in our lives. An individual's empowerment can be the result of her own engagement and labor either alone or in cooperation with others. For example, when someone works to grow a garden or works with others to open a village clinic, she is engaging in an empowering process. An individual's empowerment can also be the result of the actions of others. For example, when barriers are removed so that a child is able to attend school or access medical care, the child experiences empowerment, even if she did not herself work for the freedom.

Oppression occurs when the members of a social group are systematically denied various valuable freedoms by virtue of the fact that they are members of that group. For example, women are oppressed *as women* when women are systematically denied certain freedoms—to become literate, to work outside the home, to choose whom they marry, and by no coincidence whom they have sex with—*because* they are women, that is, because it is not deemed to be the role or the place of women to do such things within the relevant institutional framework. Thus, individuals are oppressed by virtue of membership in a social group. But this is not to say that all individuals who experience a serious deprivation of valuable freedoms are oppressed.

It is not necessary for an individual to be a member of an oppressed group to experience a significant deprivation of freedom. When poverty is understood as a lack of capabilities, or valuable freedoms (as within the human development capability approach), all poor individuals are by definition deprived of valuable freedoms. Thus, even members of privileged social groups can be poor in terms of income, or even capabilities.

Moreover, individuals and groups can experience *disempowerment* without experiencing oppression. For example, an individual, a family, or even an entire community might experience disempowerment—a reduction in the real freedoms they enjoy—after a tragic event like a flood or a fire. But this sort of disempowerment is distinct from oppression, which is a social-political phenomenon. Of course, individuals, families, and entire communities may be forced to live in undesirable disaster-prone areas like floodplains because they are members of an oppressed social group. In such cases, oppression and disempowerment occur as related *phenomena,* but they remain distinct *concepts.*

Empowerment, as I have defined it, within the context of international development is focused on the individual as the object of moral concern. Perhaps it is because empowerment efforts often focus on the *individual* and because institutionalized power results in the oppression of members of social *groups* that institutionalized power issues are underrepresented in the empowerment literature. However, because individuals are members of social groups, any approach to development with a normative concern for individuals must also be concerned with the institutionalized power of social groups. In the following section I seek to explain just two of the ways in which privileged groups use institutionalized power to reinforce current social patterns, and, in turn, social inequalities, and oppression.

Before moving on, I want to make clear that any consideration of inequality or oppression within the context of development reveals the painful reality that women are by far the largest and most consistently oppressed group. I believe that it is for this reason that "empowerment issues" are frequently equated with or reduced to "women's issues." I submit that such a reduction is a mistake. When we reduce all social empowerment to female empowerment, we fail to recognize not only the limitations of the social category of men, but also the complex reality that individuals participate in more than one social group and that such participation can result in cross-cutting inequalities in the structural hierarchy of society. Any adequate theory of empowerment must recognize that institutionalized social power creates and sustains not only inequalities rooted in the social relationships of gender, but also inequalities that exist in relationships among other social groups or categories including caste, race, social-economic class, age, marital status, educational status, sexual orientation, religion, tribe, and so forth.

The varieties of social inequalities notwithstanding, there is no country in which women are treated as well as men.[8] Furthermore, as economist Nalia Kabeer rightly points out, gender is by far the most significant social relation because "for any given category of disadvantaged groups in society, women, by and large, suffer from all of the disadvantages of men in their class but in an intensified form as a result of direct gender discrimination in the allocation of resources and responsibilities."[9] Thus, while we must be careful not to commit the common mistake of simply reducing empowerment issues to women's issues, we are justified in focusing on gender relations and the inequalities that affect the lives of women when discussing and analyzing institutional social power.

How Institutions Generate, Reinforce, and Reproduce Inequalities

Institutions work to generate, reinforce, and reproduce the current system and perpetuate the inequalities of social relations in at least two ways.[10] First, institutions conflate social categories with natural categories and thereby allow social differences to appear to be fixed natural and objective facts about *the way things are*. Second, institutions defend current social systems—oppression, inequalities, and all—as essential to a valuable and valued culture, thereby allowing social differences to appear to be cultural treasures that reflect *the way things ought to be*. Before explaining why social inequalities can be oppressive and even deadly, I will consider each of the two ways in which institutions work to generate, reinforce, and reproduce inequalities of societies.

Within the institutions that make up society, the *social-political* categories of various groups, including race, ethnicity, caste, tribe, and even social class (through phrases like "blue blood"), are often conflated with related biological categories and cited as a basis for various social roles and inequalities. For example, the social categories of gender ("woman" and "man") are often conflated with the significantly different biological categories of sex ("female" and "male"). Male and female human beings exhibit basic biological differences: for example, different reproductive organs and different chromosomal makeups.[11] For the most part, however, male and female human beings are biologically similar.

Both males and females are helpless at birth, susceptible to disease, injury, and death. Both require nutritious food, clean water, protection from harsh environments, and at times medical attention to survive. Both are capable of learning language, new concepts, and skills. Both are capable of reasoning, performing difficult tasks, introspection, making sense of the world, having hopes, fears, goals, and plans of their own, and cooperating with others. They are both capable of feeling pain and pleasure and sorrow and joy, and of being cruel and kind. These few biological differences and many biological similarities are (all but) universal for males and females.[12] They occur throughout history, across cultural and geographical boundaries, in every subgroup of every society.

In contrast to sex differences, gender differences are neither universal nor fixed. The roles attributed to women and men are products of social practice that can, and often do, vary from one society to another and change over time. As the Oxfam *Guide to Gender-Analysis Frameworks* explains:

> Sex is a fact of human biology; gender is not. The experience of being male or female differs dramatically from culture to culture. The concept of gender is used by sociologists to describe all the socially given attributes, roles, activities, and responsibilities connected to being a male or a female in a given society. Our gender identity determines how we are perceived, and how we are expected to think and act as women and men, because of the way society is organized.[13]

However, when biological sex differences are conflated with constructed gender differences, the socially determined attributes of "women" and "men" created within a particular society are perceived to be fixed natural traits that are rooted in biology and hence are taken to be brute, immutable facts about the world. When traits of social differences such as gender are taken to be natural biological traits, the different roles, responsibilities, freedoms, membership requirements, and relative power shares of social groups are *mis*understood to be natural and therefore unchangeable facts about groups of human beings. Moreover, in many cultures, there is a further institutionalized suggestion that, even if we could change such "natural traits," to do so would be to defy the wishes of the divine or do violence to nature. Either way, attempts to change the socially constructed and oppressive gender roles *mis*taken as natural are often considered a moral wrong.

Consider, for example, that in many societies formal and informal institutions encourage the belief that because (some) females bear children and males do not, women are *categorically* and *naturally* more qualified parents than men. It is often inferred from this culturally constructed belief that all and only women should rear children. In some cases, it is further inferred that women who do not or cannot have children are not "real" or "good" women. In extreme—but certainly not uncommon—cases, the role of women is restricted entirely to the domestic sphere. Indeed, in some cultures (for example, in parts of rural India[14]), women are entirely secluded from public view as a matter of proper behavior. This practice is known as purdah (which is derived from the Hindi word *parda,* or "curtain"). According to the prescriptions of purdah, women are forbidden from appearing in public and must "follow complex rules of veiling the body especially in the presence of relatives linked by marriage and before strange men."[15]

When women are associated with or restricted to the domestic sphere, their participation in institutionalized public-sphere activities—for example, the market, the state, or the academy—is formally or informally restricted. The dubious, unofficial, and often implicit grounds for their restriction are that, because women are designed by nature or by God for the domestic sphere, it would be unnatural (hence, wrong) for them to participate in the public sphere. In addition to the social stigma of being a "bad" woman, women who participate in the public sphere often do not receive the same privileges as men in the public sphere. "The importance of purdah is not limited to family life; rather, these practices all involve restrictions on female activity and access to power and the control of vital resources in a male-dominated society. Restriction and restraint for women in virtually every aspect of life are the basic essentials of purdah."[16]

It is worth noting that even women who enjoy significantly more freedom are often restricted within the public sphere. Working women in the United States earn less in the public sphere and do more housework in the private sphere than their male counterparts.[17] The so-called stay-at-home moms in the United States often feel excluded from public-sphere-based social communities. This social phenomenon in the United States is called "the Mommy Wars" and is an example of what some feminists call the double bind of oppression, where there is no empowering choice for women. Writing in the *Washington Post,* Tracy Thompson states: "Feminists say they value sisterhood, but behind the scenes, stay-at-home mothers often criticize office-going moms for neglecting their kids, and working mothers often disparage their at-home counterparts for getting some sort of retro free ride."[18] I am not suggesting that the obstacles middle-class women face in the United States are as dire as those faced in rural India. Rather, I wish to make clear that inequalities rooted in the conflation of sex and gender can be found everywhere and at every economic level. The bottom line is that conflating biological traits like sex and culturally constructed traits like gender is one way that oppressive gender roles are systematically generated, reinforced, and reproduced.

However, despite the institutionalized beliefs of members of a given society, gender roles and relations are not natural or fixed facts. Indeed, gender roles and relations can and do change. For example, more women play key roles in the public sphere of many societies today than they did in past generations. Moreover, gender roles and relations can and do vary. Even a cursory examination of social roles in various societies reveals enough differences to make it clear that gender roles are not unchangeable facts about the world. As economist Naila Kabeer explains:

> Some societies allow large areas of overlap in the lives of men and women while others are organized in ways which maintain a very rigid segregation between the world of men and the world of women, what men do and what women do. What they tend to share is the idea that their own way of organizing roles and relations between women and men is the "natural" and hence, only way of doing it. In many South-east Asian societies, it is believed that women are naturally more commercial and concerned with money and they play a prominent role in trade and commerce. In much of South Asia, of course, women are considered to be hopeless with money, and financial matters are entrusted to men.[19]

As the world becomes increasingly connected through technological advances, including easier travel, the internet, and satellite television, it becomes clear that there is more than one way to understand social relations and roles, and, in turn, it becomes increasingly difficult to defend social roles as universal objective biological facts. Of course, as discussed in the example given previously, even in technologically advanced—or well-developed—and relatively heterogeneous societies like the United States, institutions continue to produce, reinforce, and re-create social roles and relations—including inequalities—that are often defended as "natural" on biological grounds.

Another common line of defense for the inequalities generated and sustained by institutionalized power is that social relations are a matter of culture and therefore a valuable and treasured aspect of identity for all involved. As Kabeer observes, "A defense based on the sanctity of culture . . . moves us away from disputes over *facts* to disputes over *values*."[20] Thus, the fact that human beings, regardless of race, ethnicity, religious tradition, caste, or gender, all share overwhelming biologically similarities while maintaining very different social roles within different societies poses little or no threat to institutionalized power inequities justified by appeals to cultural values. Moreover, the rules of official institutions that explicitly call for equal treatment of all can be quickly denounced on the grounds that social differences, and even inequalities, are a valued part of the informal, or "extra-institutional," culture.

Unlike biological facts, cultural norms and values are not expected to be independent facts about the world; instead, they exist in the values and belief systems of society members. Of course, in many cases, appeals to the sanctity of culture are intended to justify a particular society's brand of gender relations that conflate biological sex with gender. Moreover, in some cases, culture is conflated with biology in a different sense. Arguments are made that by being born into Culture X from parents of Culture X, one is inextricably tied to the values of Culture X as a matter of *fact* or nature: "It is in her blood." Yet such beliefs about membership in the cultural community are themselves products of culture that vary greatly from society to society. For our present purposes, culture can be understood as the collective value system of a social community.

The formal and informal institutions of a culture often work to generate, reinforce, and re-create the values and beliefs of the culture, sometimes simply for the sake of reinforcing and re-creating them—that is, for the sake of tradition. Many of the values and beliefs of cultures are about social roles and relations. Unfortunately, in many societies the role of some social groups, often women, is one of subordination reinforced by institutionalized violence justified as a part of the relevant culture. As economist Kanchan Mathur explains:

> In some societies, the threat and practice of violence is used to ensure women remain within socially-defined boundaries of behavior and space; in others their status as "property" of male family members deprives them of rights over their own bodies and sexuality within the familial sphere; in yet others, violence against women may constitute a legitimized and routinised aspect of prevailing cultural definitions of gender.[21]

Institutions, limited social roles, inequalities, and even practices of violence are all defended with appeals to the sanctity of culture. In some cases, many of the individuals who are trapped in subordinate roles in which they are denied rights and subjected to violence are among those who defend the oppressive practices of their cultures.

Consider the practice of female genital mutilation (FGM), or female circumcision, which takes place in twenty-eight African countries as well as several other parts of the world including the United States. FGM is a procedure in which all or part of the external female genitalia is removed, usually with crude, unsterilized instruments (including dirty pieces of broken glass and old razor blades) and without anesthetic.[22] FGM is an institutionalized practice reinforced by the market, the family, religion, marriage, the community, and various overlapping institutional forces.

Performing FGMs is an established trade for some women, who depend on the practice for their livelihood. FGM is believed to ensure marital fidelity, enhance fertility, and promote child survival. Because FGM makes intercourse extremely painful, it may limit infidelity, but it can also lead to sexual dysfunction, which undermines fertility. Moreover, FGM increases the risks of child and maternal mortality during labor. Nevertheless, men will refuse to marry (and to pay dowries for) girls[23] who have not been circumcised. In societies that practice FGM, female genitalia are believed to be unsightly and dirty; removing them is therefore deemed necessary to promote health. In fact, the procedure often results in infections and in some cases death. Some mistakenly believe that Islam requires FGM. However, while some Muslim women are circumcised, the practice is neither universal among Muslim women nor exclusive to Muslim women. Moreover, FGM predates the Islamic faith. The procedure is often considered a right of passage into womanhood.[24]

Citing the above social norms as their reasons for practicing FGM, some families who want to promote or preserve their good name in the community look past the pain, health issues, and risk of death as they subject their young daughters to the procedure. Likewise, girls who want to be viewed as "good women" and eligible for marriage within the community agree to endure the procedure despite the pain and the risks. In doing so, both the families and their daughters reinforce and re-create the social roles of the "good family" and "good woman" within their society.

The United Nations, World Health Organization, and several other national and international organizations recognize female genital mutilation as an act of institutionalized violence against women. Girls who are subjected to FGM lack several valuable freedoms, including the freedom to be healthy and the freedom of bodily integrity. Yet countless men *and* women have defended the excruciatingly painful, ultimately unhealthy, and sometimes deadly practice as a traditional act sacred to their culture and often reject the criticism and concerns of the United Nations and World Health Organization as mere outsider interference. For example, Eunice Sitatian Kaelo, a Masai woman from Kenya, describes her mother as saying, "Female circumcision is our culture. Why should we be forced to abandon it when we were born into it? Abandoning our culture would be annoying our ancestors. It would bring a curse to the entire community."[25]

Defending oppression and violence against women as a valued and valuable part of culture is often successful because, at first blush, it seems that many women *choose* FGM as a way of honoring their culture and that discontinuing the practice would undermine their agency. However, it is unlikely that most women are acting as authentic agents when they defend female circumcision on the grounds of cultural sanctity. The violence perpetuated by oppressive institutions often renders autonomous agency impossible. Girls who submit to FGM may "choose" FGM as the lesser of two evils: a girl can either risk her life by submitting to an excruciatingly painful procedure and gain community acceptance, or she can refuse FGM, shame her family, and be ostracized by her community and its resources, which might also lead to her death. This "choice" seems even less like an act of agency when one considers that many girls are subjected to FGM as children between the ages of four and ten.[26]

It is often difficult from within the confines of any society to recognize the institutional patterns that we take to be part of our lives, even when they result in terrible inequalities, oppression, violence, and death. As Simone Weil tells us, "Someone who does not see a pane of glass is not aware of not seeing it."[27] Unlike most victims of FGM, agents have some understanding of their choices.[28] As a Masai, Kaelo was proud to be circumcised as a young teenager during a coming-of-age ceremony that apparently pleased her family and increased her status in the community. However, having become more aware of the risks involved, Kaelo has more recently declared it her life's ambition to abolish the procedure among the Masai.[29]

Whether defended as matters of fact or in the name of cultural sanctity, institutionalized power too often results in the relative deprivation of the members of some social groups and privileging of others by confining individuals to certain narrow—often oppressive—social roles. These social roles are continuously reinforced and re-created by formal and informal institutions through both official and implicit social rules. Rigid institutionalized social roles prevent development of agency and limit the expansion of the set of real freedoms of individual members of social groups. For members of underprivileged or subordinate social groups, these limitations frequently result in social, sometimes violent, oppression as well as grave material deprivation and even death.

In many cases, honoring the responsibilities and privileges associated with social relations is taken to be so important that doing so is on par with—or even trumps—meeting the universal biological needs of some socially disadvantaged human beings. In the case of gender relations, such inequalities result in the oppression and death of millions of women throughout the world. Economist Amartya Sen uses the phrase "missing women" to refer to the many women who would be alive today if their access to medical treatment, food, and other essential needs had been equal to the access enjoyed by the men in their communities.

Sen uses female-to-male survival ratios to determine the number of missing women at more than 100 million. In North America and Europe, where most women have reliable access to the resources they need to meet their essential needs, there are 1.05 females for every male. This female-to-male ratio is much lower in parts of the world—particularly in Asia and North Africa—where millions of women are "missing" in the sense that they have died prematurely due to avoidable gender biases in terms of access to essential resources. In parts of North India, for example, the female-to-male ratio is .86.[30] Sen demonstrates, moreover, that the differences in female-to-male ratios are not strictly determined by the availability of resources or economic growth within a region but are primarily correlated with differences in institutionalized gender relations.

Consider the range of female-to-male ratios in India. In the northwestern states of Haryana and Punjab, which have experienced rapid economic growth since independence and have higher per capita incomes than other Indian states, the female-to-male ratios are very low: 0.86 and 0.87, respectively. However, in the southern part of the country, ratios are relatively high: 0.99 in Tamil Nadu, 0.98 in Andhra, and most notably 1.06 in Kerala. As Sen explains:

> These regional patterns of female-male ratios are consistent with what is known of the character of gender relations in different parts of the country. The northwestern states, for instance, are notorious for highly unequal gender relations, some symptoms of which include the continued practice of female seclusion, low female labour-hour force participation rates, a large gender gap in literacy rates, extremely restricted female property rights, strong boy preferences in fertility decisions, widespread neglect of female children, and drastic separation of a married woman from her family. In all these respects, the social standing of women is relatively better in south India.[31]

Furthermore, Kerala, where the female-to-male ratio is 1.06 (higher than for any of the major regions in the world except Eastern Europe),[32] represents "a major success in the expansion of female literacy, considerable prominence of women in influential social and professional activities, and a tradition of matriliny."[33]

The institutionalized values of societies reflected in these statistical social differences are also responsible for the fact that many "women tend to fare quite badly in relative terms compared with men, even in the same families."[34] Girls and women are often not valued as much within the household and therefore do not enjoy the same basic freedoms as boys and men, including the freedom to be well nourished. This institutionalized practice holds true, even when there are sufficient resources to ensure proper nourishment for the whole family, and in spite of periods of economic growth. In fact, Sen has found that in many parts of India "higher levels of poverty tend to go with higher female-male ratios," which, he suggests, may be because "the partnership aspect of gender relations is stronger in poorer households, where survival depends on effective cooperation, than among privileged households where women tend to have more dependent and symbolic position."[35] Sen further suggests that this "more dependent" feature of the role of women within the household may affect the status of women in different classes and castes differently. This leads to the conclusion that, at least in some important cases, the systematic deprivation of women is likely to be defended as a matter of culture.

It is a well-supported social anthropological hypothesis that as a region experiences economic growth, the lower castes engage in a process of emulation of higher—more patriarchal—castes,[36] in which the role of women is limited and subservient. Tragically, the lifestyle of women plays the role of some sort of a social status symbol in this process: a stay-at-home wife is thought to be a sign of success. In other words, as lower castes experience some economic gains, the role of women is often more restricted in the household, and this restricted role is correlated with the deprivation and low survival rates of women and girls. Thus, Sen's work can be understood as showing that, insofar as economic expansion or upward economic mobility has an influence on female-to-male ratios in regions of India where society reinforces and re-creates patriarchal gender relations, it seems that economic growth actually leads to some *intensification* of gender bias. Sen concludes that "achieving greater gender equality involves a process of active social change which is not automatically linked with economic growth."[37] Sen shows that development, understood as an increase in GDP, does not promise a remedy for—*and may actually intensify*—the sort of institutionalized gender bias that generates the social power inequalities that in turn result in the premature deaths of girls and women. Sen also provides evidence that human development efforts that target the empowerment of women and girls, that is, the expansion of the set of real freedoms women enjoy and agency enhancement, are very effective in mitigating gender bias in survival rates. Statistics show that freedoms that are likely to give women more voice in the home, including education and paid work, are among the most significant variables in raising female-to-male ratios.[38] As Sen writes,

> Working outside the home and earning an independent income tend to have a clear impact on enhancing the social standing of women in the household and society. Her contribution to the prosperity of the family is then more visible, and she also has more voice, because of being less dependent on others. Further, outside employment often has useful "educational" effects, in terms of exposure to the world outside the household, making her agency more effective. Similarly, women's education strengthens women's agency and also tends to make it more informed and skilled.[39]

Sen's work on missing women and the correlation between institutional power and female survival rates makes clear the importance of institutionalized power differences in both formal and informal institutions. It is clear that it is the *social* standing of women in the household and society and not simply GNP, or even household income, that must be changed if women are to be empowered as effective agents and to enjoy the basic freedoms that enhance their well-being and make possible their survival.

Conclusion

In light of the gravity of inequalities resulting from institutionalized social rules, it is clear that anyone interested in promoting the empowerment of women or any marginalized group should give attention to the important role that institutionalized social power plays in generating, reinforcing, and reproducing such oppressive and deadly inequalities. The modest goal of this essay has been to explain institutional power and the critical role it plays in generating, reinforcing, and reproducing inequalities. I have not attempted here to provide an explanation for how international development can account for institutional power.[40] However, I conclude with a partial list of guidelines for those working toward such an account. I believe the items in the following list are necessary, though not sufficient, for a complete account of institutional power and empowerment in development. I provide the list in the hope of stirring debate on this issue and in an effort to provide the reader with a clearer idea of the sort of engagement of the issue I believe is needed.

1. *Directly engage institutional power issues.* When we focus on GNP or economic income, we miss some of the social causes of human misery and lack of freedom. This is not to say that GNP is a useless indicator, only that institutional power issues must also be directly engaged.
2. *Recognize the power of both formal public-sphere institutions, such as the government, and informal private-sphere institutions, such as the family.* Securing formal voting rights in public elections on paper may do very little to empower people if the social power generated within the informal private sphere restricts their freedom to vote in public elections.
3. *Recognize both the official and the unofficial rules of institutions.* Recall that an institution can claim to support equality (e.g., all are equal before the law) while systematically undermining it (e.g., in the United States blacks who kill whites are more likely to get the death penalty than whites who kill blacks).
4. *Recognize that changes in patterns generated in one sphere of institutions can have a great impact on other institutional spheres.* For example, formal public-sphere institutions (e.g., providing public education for women) can have a great influence on the patterns of informal private-sphere institutions (e.g., more equitable food distribution in the home).

5. *Recognize the importance of social relations.* It is a matter of logic that as the social role of women changes, the role of men will change too. We must be aware of such changes and work toward institutional patterns that promote human flourishing. For example, children of employed women do better (in terms of nutrition and survival) in homes where there is a more balanced division of household labor than in homes where women work a double day of domestic labor and public-sphere employment.[41] Members of households in which unemployed husbands of employed wives not only shun domestic work as "women's work" but also beat and rape their wives as a way of coping with what the World Bank calls "gender anxiety" are far from flourishing.[42]

NOTES

Epigraphs. Amartya Sen, *Development as Freedom* (New York: Alfred A. Knopf, 1999). Naila Kabeer, "From Feminist Insights to an Analytic Framework: An Institutional Perspective on Gender Equality," in *Institutions, Relations, and Outcomes: Framework and Case Studies for Gender Aware Planning*, ed. Naila Kabeer and Ramya Subrahmanian (London: Zed Books, 1999), 4.

1. I am not arguing that *no one* working on empowerment is paying attention to institutionalized power. There are of course some good philosophers and social economists working on these issues, including Naila Kabeer, Christine Koggel, Deepa Narayan, and others. My claim is the more modest one that *more* attention should be paid to institutionalized power by those concerned with the role of empowerment in development.

2. The relevant concept of power is central to several—but not all—feminist schools of thought, including what Rosemarie Tong has called Marxist, socialist, postmodern, and radical feminism. Power also plays a role in feminist economic approaches that draw on these philosophical feminist theories. See, for example, Naila Kabeer's Social Relations Approach discussed in her *Reverse Realities: Gender Hierarchies in Development Thought* (London: Verso, Institute for Development Studies, 1994).

3. According to Amnesty International's report "Death by Discrimination: The Continuing Role of Race in Capital Cases" (http://web.amnesty.org/library/index/engamr510462003, accessed January 26, 2012), "Even though blacks and whites are murder victims in nearly equal numbers of crimes, 80% of people executed since the death penalty was reinstated [in the United States in 1977] have been executed for murders involving white victims."

4. For the sake of simplicity, I restrict gender to the categories "women" and "men." As I do so, I am only too aware that, in making this move, I am privileging these traditionally received gender categories and excluding those who do not identify with either.

5. I am not offering an argument against institutions in general. Rather, I am attempting to explain how oppressive institutional power can be generated and sustained.

6. I have in mind here the capabilities of the human development capability approach as pioneered by economist Amartya Sen and philosopher Martha Nussbaum.

7. I argue for the usefulness of this definition of empowerment in my paper, Lori Keleher, "Sen and Nussbaum: Agency and Capability-Expansion," *Ethics and Economics* 1, no. 2 (June 2014), 54–70, and in my dissertation: Lori Keleher, "Empowerment and

International Development" (PhD diss., University of Maryland, 2007), http://drum.lib.umd.edu/handle/1903/7584.

8. According to the findings of the United Nations Development Program's 2010 Human Development Index (HDI) and Gender Inequality Index (GII).

9. Naila Kabeer and Ramya Subrahmanian, eds., *Institutions, Relations, and Outcomes* (New Delhi, India: Zubaan Books, 1999), 21.

10. Several people, including Naila Kabeer (Kabeer and Subrahmanian, *Institutions, Relations, and Outcomes*), have observed these two ways in which power relationships are persevered.

11. Even what I am calling the "biological categories" of sex are not as neat and absolute as they are often portrayed. "Male" and "female" may be considered clear and tidy natural categories when compared to the relatively messy social categories of "men" and "women." But even the seemingly tidy dichotomies of "male" and "female" have trouble with, for example, hermaphrodites, abnormal chromosomal makeups, and elective sex changes in which reproductive organs are transformed while chromosomal makeups remain the same. Moreover, the degree to which biological categories are constructed is debated in both biology and feminist theory. For example, Judith Butler has argued that the category "sex" is "as culturally constructed as gender" (*Gender Trouble: Feminism and the Subversion of Identity* [New York: Routledge, 1990], 7).

12. See n. 14.

13. Candida March, Ines Smyth, and Maitrayee Mukhopadhyay, *A Guide to Gender-Analysis Frameworks* (London: Oxfam GB, 1999), 19.

14. Barbara D. Miller, "Female Labor Participation and Female Seclusion in Rural India: A Regional View," *Economic Development and Cultural Change* 30, no. 4 (July 1982), 777–794.

15. James Heitzman and Robert L. Worden, eds., *India: A Country Study* (Washington, DC: GPO for the Library of Congress, 1995), http://countrystudies.us/india/84.htm, accessed January 26, 2012.

16. Ibid.

17. U.S. Department of Labor, Bureau of Labor Statistics, 2011, http://www.bls.gov/home.htm.

18. See Tracy Thompson, "A War Inside Your Head," *Washington Post*, February 15, 1998, http://www.washingtonpost.com/wp-srv/national/longterm/mommywars/mommy.htm, accessed January 26, 2012. Men who care for children—especially men who care for children full-time—or do not have a robust public-sphere involvement deviate from the socially determined role for men. Consequently they are often excluded from many of the privileges granted to men (or "real men") in society. The often-implicit grounds for their exclusion are that men are not designed for domestic participation. So individuals—both females and males—are socially penalized, often by exclusion, for deviating from the assigned gender roles of their society.

19. Kabeer and Subrahmanian, *Institutions, Relations, and Outcomes*, 21.

20. Ibid., 7; emphasis in original.

21. Kanchan Mathur, "The Emergence of Violence against Women as an Issue in the Women's Development Programme, Rajastan," in Kabeer and Subrahmanian, *Institutions, Relations, and Outcomes*, 288.

22. World Health Organization, "Female Genital Mutilation Fact Sheet," no. 241 (June 2010), http://www.who.int/mediacentre/factsheets/fs241/en/.

23. A distinct but related oppressive cultural practice takes place in *some* communities that practice FGM, where girls as young as nine years old are often given by their families for marriages to men with multiple wives in exchange for dowries.

24. World Health Organization, "Female Genital Mutilation Fact Sheet."

25. Ledama Olekina, "FGM: Maasai Women Speak Out," *Cultural Survival Quarterly* 4, no. 28 (December 2004).

26. According to the UK-based organization Forward. See "Female Genital Mutilation," Forward, n.d., http://www.forwarduk.org.uk/key-issues/fgm.

27. Peter Winch, *Simone Weil: "The Just Balance"* (New York: Cambridge University Press, 1989), 106.

28. What exactly it means to understand a choice and how well one must understand a choice in order to act as an agent are interesting and important epistemological questions. They are also beyond the scope of this essay. I believe there is a correlation between understanding one's choices and agency. However, for my present purposes it is sufficient to say that a young girl between four and ten years old acting on the encouragement of her parents (the institution of the family) or a potential husband is very unlikely to be acting as an autonomous agent. I am offering an inductive argument. It is, of course, still logically possible that some girls do choose FGM. The possibility is greater still that some women actually choose FGM. My purpose here is not to fully explore agency with regard to FGM. (For such an explanation see Diana Tietjens Meyers, "Feminism and Women's Autonomy: The Challenge of Female Genital Cutting," *Metaphilosophy* 5 [2000].) Rather, it is to provide an example in which women and girls are systematically pressured into acting against their own interests in the name of culture; the fact that some, the likelihood that a great many, are so pressured is enough for my purposes.

29. Tara Tidwell Cullen, "A Woman's Approach to Dealing with a Perilous Right of Passage," *Christian Science Monitor*, June 8, 2005, http://www.csmonitor.com/2005/0608/p15s02-woaf.html, accessed January 26, 2012.

30. Amartya Sen, *Rationality and Freedom* (Cambridge, MA: Harvard University Press, 2002), 231.

31. Ibid.

32. Ibid.

33. Ibid.

34. Ibid., 229.

35. Ibid.

36. See ibid., 243n35, for more on this process of emulation, called the *Sanskritization* process.

37. Ibid., 243.

38. See ibid., 245–257; Sen, *Development as Freedom*, 190–192; and M. Murthi, A. C. Guio, and J. P. Dereze, "Mortality, Fertility, and Gender Bias in India," *Population and Development Review* 21 (1995).

39. Sen, *Development as Freedom*, 191–192.

40. I hope to provide an account, or at least make progress toward an account, in future work.

41. Sen, *Development as Freedom*, 195–200.

42. Deepa Narayan, *Voices of the Poor* (New York: Oxford University Press, 2000), 174–215.

The Value of Diversity 30

BUDDHIST REFLECTIONS ON MORE EQUITABLY ORIENTING GLOBAL INTERDEPENDENCE

Peter D. Hershock

One of Buddhism's central insights is that our conflicts, troubles, and suffering can be positively and sustainably addressed only on the basis of things "as they have come to be" (Skt. *yathabhutam*) and not simply as they are at present. Histories matter, in other words. A second insight, and one with powerful contemporary resonances, is that all things arise interdependently. Strongly interpreted, this means that relationality is more basic than "things-related." Interdependence is not a contingent, external relation among essentially separate entities; it is internal or constitutive. In short, interdependence entails interpenetration. Seeing this is to see that conflicts, troubles, and suffering are expressions of interdependence gone awry—a function of our karma or how the relational outcomes and opportunities we experience are inflected by our own values, intentions, and actions.

These insights suggest that there may be significant liabilities associated with the common liberal assumption that the individual—moral agent, rational decision maker, citizen, consumer, corporation, or nation-state—is the basic and proper unit of economic, political, and ethical analysis. Insisting that the individual is ontologically and critically foundational, especially in an era of increasingly complex global interdependence, is like insisting on eating soup with a fork. We have crossed a historical threshold beyond which continued allegiance to the idea that things and beings exist independently of one another becomes problematic. Insisting on such an atomistic or entity-positing ontology severely compromises our capacities for responding both to the creative possibilities of widening and deepening global interdependence and to the novel risks, threats, and hazards generated by its predominant motive forces of modernization, industrialization, and marketization.

In what follows, I make use of Buddhist concepts of interdependence, karma, and nonduality to rethink the meanings of and means to greater global equity, challenging the identification of equity with individual equality of opportunity and instead arguing in favor of understanding equity as a relational function of enhanced diversity. In doing so, I hope to open prospects for moving beyond tensions between modern universalisms with their ethics of sameness and postmodern particularisms with their ethics of difference. Such movement has considerable theoretical merit, but it also opens an oblique middle way beyond the practical stalemate between the politics of recognition (participatory equality) and the politics of redistribution (economic justice). This stalemate is in many ways emblematic of the modern divorce of ethics and economics. Getting beyond the impasse is not only critical to eventual reconciliation; it is crucial to overcoming our manifest impotence with respect to the globally widening disparities of wealth, income, and resource use that together constitute the single greatest obstacle to realizing truly shared human-with-planetary flourishing.

Geographies of Difference: When Interdependence Means Increasing Inequality

In keeping with the Buddhist insight that we can effectively respond to troubles or conflicts only on the basis of how they have come to be, I want to begin with a synoptic overview of how income, wealth, and resource use are presently distributed. Consider the following representative statistics.[1]

As of 2005, the richest 5 percent of the world's population earned approximately one-third of all global income; the richest 10 percent, just over half; and the richest 20 percent, fully three-quarters. The poorest 5 percent and 10 percent of the world's people earned 0.2 percent and 0.7 percent, respectively, of global income, and the bottom 40 percent took home a mere 5 percent.[2] To put this in more graphic terms, the richest 1 percent of the world's people earned as much as the poorest 60 percent (or 4.3 billion people).[3]

Disparities of wealth and consumption are even more pronounced. The top 1 percent of the world's households currently hold 40 percent of global assets; the top 2 percent hold 51 percent; the top 5 percent hold 71 percent; and the top 10 percent, just over 86 percent. Meanwhile, the bottom 50 percent—nearly 3.5 billion people—possess just 1 percent of global wealth.[4] Indeed in 2000, the 492 billionaires in the world were worth \$2.16 trillion, or 1.7 percent of the global total, more than twice that of the world's poorest 3.5 billion people. By 2010, the number of billionaires had risen to 1,210, with combined holdings in excess of \$4.5 trillion, or nearly 2.4 percent of total global wealth.[5] Not surprisingly, the richest 20 percent of the world's people account for 86 percent of global consumption; the poorest 20 percent, just 1.3 percent.[6] Broken down into decile rankings,[7] this consumption gap is even more striking:

% of total	.05	1.0	1.4	1.9	2.4	3.3	4.8	8.1	17.6	59
Decile	1	2	3	4	5	6	7	8	9	10

That is, the top 10 percent of the world's people consume more than the rest of the world combined, with the 4.7 billion least advantaged people (70 percent of the world population) accounting for just 10.5 percent of global consumption.

It might be said that data is history stripped of narrative. And it is possible that these inequalities of income, wealth, and consumption do not tell the whole story. Over roughly the last two-and-a-half centuries, global investment in modernization, industrialization, and marketization have resulted in dramatically extended average life expectancies; increasing educational opportunities and achievements; and vastly expanded freedoms of choice. Viewed in absolute aggregate terms, the era of industrial modernization and the ascent of free-market economies has been one of rising incomes, phenomenal wealth production, and expanding life options for all. And given these much-celebrated gains, there are many—especially in the global North—who would regard their underlying, manifestly uneven geographies of social, economic, and political power and advantage as a developmental necessity, a basic condition for realizing the kinds of economic growth needed to lift the world's poor out of absolute poverty.[8]

Yet there is also considerable evidence that the means to such absolute gains, for example, in wealth and income, are afflicting the majority of the world's people with a decreasing share of the benefits of free-market globalization. In 1820, the wealth and income gap between the richest 20 percent of countries in the world and the poorest 20 percent stood at a ratio of 3 to 1. By 1913, that ratio had increased to 11 to 1; in 1950 it was 35 to 1; in 1973, 44 to 1; in 1992, 72 to 1; and in 1998, 86 to 1.[9] Today, four out of every five people on the planet live in countries where income inequalities are increasing while a mere 5 percent live in countries where they are decreasing.[10] And among those countries with rising inequality, the United States—the global champion of neoliberal globalization over the past quarter century—is a powerful frontrunner. For example, whereas the top 1 percent of the population earned 8 percent of total U.S. income in 1976, by 2007 this had risen to 23.5 percent. Indeed, of the total increase of U.S. income from 1980 to 2007, the top 1 percent received 80 percent. In terms of wealth, the holdings of the top 1 percent went from 19 percent in 1976 to 35 percent in 2007. In that year, just prior to the home mortgage crisis and recession that dealt a near-mortal blow to the American middle class and poor, the top 20 percent of the population possessed 85 percent of U.S. wealth, whereas the bottom 40 percent had a staggeringly small one-third of 1 percent.[11]

It is tempting to see trends like these as an index of corporate greed or an indictment of the generations of national and global leaders who have failed to square ideals of government *by* the people with the realities of governing *for* the people. Although tempting, such ad hominem denunciations of corporate and personal bad faith fall short of what is needed to more equitably orient global dynamics. Indicative of the nature of the problem is the fact that the single best predictor of where one stands on the increasingly steep slopes of global advantage is not the class into which one is born, but the country.[12] Seen in that light, the hierarchies of wealth and power associated with contemporary global economic dynamics cannot be attributed solely to the morally suspect doings of an oligarchic elite but are, rather, evidence of long-standing systemic biases.

Recognizing this is a positive step in the direction of righting historical wrongs. But it is not enough. For many of those living on the commanding heights of developmental advantage, the structural origins of inequality can be seen as warrant for the ethically sterile belief that the global geography of advantage is simply a combined result of historical accident and developmental necessity. And, granted the ontological and critical primacy of the individual, it is a short side step from there to seeing the plight of those that the World Bank describes as lacking even "the hope of a dignified life"—one-fifth of all humanity—as a plight for which no one is ultimately responsible.

Against this view, I propose that, while increasingly skewed distributions of income, wealth, and resources cannot be attributed solely to the moral deficiencies of the rich, they also cannot be dismissed as an essentially anonymous function of geographical luck, historical accident, or developmental necessity. They are recursively amplifying, relationally manifest effects of a structurally embodied and internally conflicted constellation of values—a pattern of eventuation not only in which each of us has a share but also in which we are each in a position to meaningfully intervene.

Buddhism as Values-Transforming Practice

The pivotal Buddhist insight that all things arise interdependently brings with it the realization that liberation from trouble and suffering is a process of reconfiguring relational dynamics, a process that the Buddha averred was possible only because of karma. This claim confounded many of the Buddha's interlocutors. In pre-Buddhist India, karma was understood as an unrelenting and inescapable system of just deserts, a deterministic moral law mandating that for every action there would be determinate results. Good actions will invariably bring good results, and bad actions will just as invariably bring bad results, each in accordance with an unchanging and overarching cosmic moral order (Skt. *ṛta*).

In contrast, the Buddhist teaching of karma is that, if one pays close and sustained enough attention, a recursively dynamic consonance becomes evident between the complexion of our values, intentions, and actions and the patterns of outcome and opportunity we experience. The operation of karma ensures that all purposely undertaken actions result in experienced consequences, and that all experienced realities imply responsibility. Yet precisely because all things arise in dynamic interdependence, the topography of our own experience is always open to revision. There are no inevitable outcomes and no ultimately intractable situations. Improvisation is always possible.

From a Buddhist perspective, then, liberation from trouble and suffering first and foremost entails an ongoing critique of self, a critique carried out through realizing that we are relationally constituted and that troubling or conflicted patterns of interdependence reflect inconsistencies and conflicts among our own values and interests. This is the function of the practical emphasis in Buddhism on dissolving the conditions that sustain our own ignorance, habit formations, and cravings. But many of our most dearly held values are products of our familial, cultural, and historical circumstances. And because of this, Buddhist practice also involves a resolute critique of the values-embodying cultural, political, economic, and technological institutions and practices that inform and shape our lives as relationally constituted persons-in-community.

From a karmic perspective, because interdependence is always in some significant degree also interpenetration, the acute unevenness with which the benefits and costs of economic growth are now distributed cannot be dismissed as an historical legacy for which we have no (or only theoretical) responsibility. Neither can it be excused as a result of processes or forces in the face of which we are effectively helpless. It is a recursively dynamic function of how the processes of global interdependence are being inflected by dominant complexions of values, intentions, and practices, a dynamic in which we are each intimately and responsibly implicated.

The Karma of Free-Market Globalization

Because of its axiological character, Stephen Toulmin's historical analysis of modernity offers an apt jumping-off point for understanding the karma of mounting global inequality.[13] According to Toulmin, the origins of modernity can be traced to a convergence of political, economic, social, cultural, and technoscientific dynamics on a "hidden agenda" of cosmopolitanism, an agenda structured by a historically distinctive set of values including universality, equality, autonomy, sovereignty, objectivity, choice, competition, and control.

Deepening alignment of social, political, economic, and technological dynamics with this cosmopolitan agenda—especially over the first two centuries of modernization, from roughly 1750 to 1950—resulted, among other things, in the progressive, emancipatory dissolution of traditional communities and their replacement by abstract, equality- and rights-claiming collectives of freely associating individuals. Over the same period, accelerating processes of scientific and technological advancement brought about revolutionary expansions of human capacities for choice and control.[14] In combination, these manifestations of modernity's cosmopolitan agenda played crucial roles in the rise of civil society, the emergence of Western democracies, the ascent of classical liberalism, and the normative assertion of the autonomous, rational individual as the basic unit of ethical, economic, and political analysis.

Yet the dual valorization of freedom and control that has characterized modernity[15] has also ensured that its progressively emancipatory dynamics have always been shadowed ironically by no less progressively disciplinary ones. The dissolution of traditional social, economic, political, cultural, and epistemic structures opened historically unprecedented spaces for the consolidation of new kinds and constellations of power.[16] One outcome of this reconfiguring of power dynamics is that, although inequality among societies continued to increase during this period, inequality within societies generally decreased. The dislodging of traditional elites—and the dismantling of political, economic, and social institutions that had guaranteed their privileges—had the effect of opening spaces for the emergence and growth of mercantile and middle classes. The premodern pattern of widespread equality for a poor majority and extraordinary wealth and income for an extremely small minority gave way to a more gradual distribution curve, an increasingly differentiated pattern of income and opportunity distribution.[17]

Nevertheless, as powerful as the modern idea/ideal of the individual proved to be as a tool for reconfiguring global power dynamics, it was not immune to the disciplinary dimensions of nationalization, industrialization, and marketization. These processes at once made possible and required the production of new kinds of populations, including loyal citizens, increasingly differentiated kinds of workers, and ever more imaginatively stimulated and choice-exercising consumers. The birth of the individual in its various incarnations as moral agent, social contractor, citizen, entrepreneurial competitor, and consumer was crucial to the progressive freeing of men, women, and children from involuntary conscription into culturally specified roles—first and foremost as fathers, mothers, sons, and daughters. But it was also an instrumental part of the so-called creative destruction needed by new elites to realize novel but by no means symmetrically beneficial kinds of global order.

There is now general recognition that a shift in modernization processes occurred sometime in the mid-twentieth century. This shift has been variously described as the advent of a postindustrial world,[18] as the birth of the knowledge society,[19] as the rise of global informational capitalism,[20] and as the emergence of a global attention economy in which consumption and wealth/income distributions are shaped primarily by globally shifting attractors for and flows of attention.[21] Understanding this transition is crucial to understanding the evolving dynamics of inequality among and within societies and in discerning imperatives and potentials for new means to and meanings of enhancing equity.

Let me now focus on two dimensions of this transition: networks and reflexive modernization.

The Network Society

The global communications advances made possible by Cold War computing and communications research have dramatically altered the global organizational dynamics of power, resulting in the advent of what Manuel Castells refers to as global network society. There are two key factors in what Anthony Giddens has called these new "structurations" of power dynamics. First, although the value of membership in a hierarchy is a function of distance from the center/top of the hierarchy, in networks, membership value is a dual function of the quantity of nodes in the net and the informational quality of their connections to it. Second, network growth is shaped by both negative/stabilizing feedback and positive feedback that accelerates interactions and amplifies differentiation. That is, network growth is not centrally determined but is instead an emergent and uncertainty-heightening function of the informational contributions made by/through all of its nodes. Thus, while network growth is invariably values coordinated, at least beyond certain thresholds of interactive scale and scope, networks begin serving as multipliers and magnifiers of difference. Network-enabled global informational capitalism not only accelerates the constitutive flows of globalization; it does so in ways that unpredictably intensify and amplify both integrating and fragmenting potentials.

Reflexive Modernization and World Risk Society

Although the ironic pairing of systemic vitality and volatility is a feature of all networks, it takes on particularly troubling significance when the processes of global informational capitalism and industrial modernization cross thresholds of scale, scope, and complexity to become structurally reflexive. Beyond this point, it is no longer possible to externalize the environmental, health, social, economic, and cultural costs of sustained growth, and economic growth comes increasingly to depend on the ironic production of risks, threats, and volatilities as a function of the successes—not failures—of emerging systems of complex interdependence. This marks the advent of what has been called "reflexive modernization" and "world risk society,"[22] the advent of global relational dynamics in which continued economic growth entails the production of unpredictable risks and hazards in the face of which responsible decisions must be made.

One of the key features of reflexive modernization is the percolation of the threats, risks, and hazards associated with continued growth into virtually every aspect of life, along with expanding individual decision-making responsibilities.

This manifests on one hand as an expansion of emancipatory (especially market-designed and market-delivered) freedoms of choice. On the other hand, it brings an intensification of disciplinary compulsions to choose, which increase pressures for each individual to define the terms of his or her life, to challenge existing social forms (especially those related to work, family, and gender), and to construct his or her own identity and life narrative under conditions of continuously heightening ambiguity, uncertainty, and risk.[23] Moreover, just as decision-making resources are far from evenly distributed, so too are the costs and benefits produced by continued industrial modernization. Hence, increasing compulsions to choose easily translate into ever-more exacerbated divisions between globalization and development winners and losers.

Problems, Predicaments, and the Aporia of Difference

Viewed through the critical lenses of global networks and reflexive modernization, a disturbing picture comes into focus: economic vitality and hence political legitimacy are implicated in the emergence of increasingly uneven geographies of development, opportunity, and risk that are caused not by primarily external factors but by recursively amplifying internal ones. As I would describe it, we are not only in an era of change but in the midst of a change of eras defined by a shift from the era-defining dominance of problem-solution to that of predicament-resolution.

Problems occur when existing strategies and techniques fail to bring about ends that we intend to continue to pursue. Solutions consist in the realization of new means of furthering already existing patterns of aims and interests. The invention of the gas-hybrid engine is a solution to the problem of high automotive carbon emissions, a solution that enables the continuation of customary transportation practices, extending rather than calling into question the culture, economics, and politics of the automobile. Predicaments arise when we are made aware of competition or conflict among our own values, aims, and interests. Predicaments cannot be solved; they can only be resolved. Resolution of a predicament implies both enhanced clarity about how things have come to be as they are and more thoroughly and deeply coordinated commitments, and results in a significant revision or reconfiguration of relevant values, aims, and practices. Global hunger and anthropogenic climate change are not problems; they are predicaments. We know full well how to ensure that all of the world's people have adequate nutrition and how to reduce (if not reverse) human impacts on climate. What stands in the way are not technical barriers but conflicts among social, economic, political, and cultural values.

The problem-to-predicament transition marks a global shift from the predominance of the technical to that of the ethical. At the same time, however, the processes involved in bringing about this transition ensure the growing obsolescence of universalistic ethics of "the same." The globalization-driven multiplication and magnification of differences and the problem-to-predicament transition together compel recognition of a troubling *aporia* of difference. On the one hand, we find ourselves faced locally, nationally, regionally, and globally with intensifying imperatives to more fully recognize and respect differences, going beyond mere tolerance of difference and otherness to enabling them to matter more than ever before. The politics of recognition and respect that have developed over especially the past quarter century are a key manifestation of growing awareness of these imperatives. On the other hand, we find ourselves faced with equally intensifying needs to join in ever more robust and sustainable forms of global collective action, subsuming our differences within shared and deepening commitments.[24]

Relinquishing Commitment to the Free-Market Agenda of Modern Globalization

In combination, the advent of network-structured reflexive modernization and world risk society, the problem-to-predicament transition, and the manifest intensification of the *aporia* of difference have three important practical implications.

First, they make quite clear that continuing to take the individual as the basic unit of economic, political, and ethical analysis is no longer tenable. Not only would doing so serve to continue absolving the drivers of rising inequality from apt and significant critical engagement; it would also prohibit effective engagement with manifestly intensifying imperatives for coordinated responses to the very real risks, threats, and hazards being produced in pursuit of continued economic vitality and political legitimacy.

Second, especially in the context of a fully relational ontology, they force recognition that relatively widening gaps in the distribution of income, wealth, consumption, costs, risks, and hazards are in fact also an index of progressive relational disadvantage. Maintaining otherwise is simply to commit the fallacy of composition, the fallacy that whatever is good for each and every one of us (as individuals) must be good for all of us (as a relationally constituted whole).[25] The structural maintenance and intensification of relational disadvantage for an overwhelming global majority is equivalent to an impoverishing diminution of their contributory relevance to others—their exclusion from the process of predicament resolution and their sentencing to what Zygmunt Bauman has aptly termed "wasted lives."[26]

Finally, they impel recognition that in a world of increasing social, economic, and political differentiation, and ever more acutely uneven geographies of development, continuing to define equity as a function of comparative equality of opportunity is to relegate equity to the status of an increasingly distant and abstract ideal for which no one is responsible.[27] Rights to participate are not identical to participatory rights of way. Consider that the United Nations estimated in 1998 that $40 billion would have sufficed to meet the Millennium Development Goals of providing basic education, water, sanitation, prenatal health care, and basic health and nutrition coverage for everyone in the developing world, a commitment made by all UN member nations.[28] In the same year, Americans spent $8 billion on cosmetics, Europeans spent $11 billion on ice cream and $50 billion on cigarettes, and Americans and Europeans together spent $17 billion on pet foods and $210 billion on alcoholic drinks. More than $400 billion were spent globally on narcotics and nearly $800 billion on the military. Today, 2.75 billion people still lack basic sanitation and 1.2 billion lack adequate clean water, resulting in one-half of all men, women, and children in the developing world being out of school or work each day from water-originated illness. More than 900 million people continue to live in hunger, and one-third of all children in the developing world are so malnourished that they are likely to suffer irreversible retardations of motor and cognitive development.

We are not all the same. As powerful an ideal as the modern value of equality has been, in reality it remains a fiction. And while fictions can be powerful, their power is never absolute or eternal. The global failure to meet the Millennium Development Goals is not a matter of technical problems; it is evidence of a profound and unresolved predicament. To address it, we need a conception of equity that is practically effective in working with existing processes of differentiation, orienting them in ways that are conducive to the pursuit of truly shared flourishing rather than some universal but potentially coercive common goal.

Differentiation and the Reconciliation of Economics with Justice

If modern ethics of "the same" and their ideal of global unification afford at best partial responses to the issues of justice posed by globalization-driven inequalities, it might be supposed that postmodern ethics of "difference" and their ideal of free variation could offer useful resources for reconceiving equity. But however much postmodern constructions of the ethical salience of difference evidence a systematic inversion of key modern values, they remain aligned with a core constellation of modern commitments to promoting independence, autonomy, equality, tolerance, and choice. And to this extent, they remain wedded to de facto strategies of disarming differences and are just as impotent as modern universalisms in responding to the contemporary *aporia* of difference and in generating the depths of cross-cultural resolve needed to address truly global predicaments. For guidance in reconciling the politics of recognition with that of redistribution, and for reconciling growth with justice, we need a more nuanced conception of difference and a qualitatively robust ethics of interdependence.

A first step in this direction is to refuse to see sameness and difference in dualistic terms, according to which sameness implies conceptually rich mutual identification and difference refers to a conceptually vacuous and purely external relation. Such a nondualistic understanding of sameness and difference was offered by the Chinese Buddhist philosopher Fazang (643–712) in his explanation of how the teaching that all beings have Buddha-nature (*fo-xing*) could be reconciled with manifest ill will, conflict, and unalleviated suffering. For Fazang, this is because all things are the same precisely insofar as they differ meaningfully from and for one another. That is, all things ultimately *are* what they *mean* for one another. Buddhist nonduality is not an erasure of difference but rather a restoration of the logically excluded middle way between sameness and difference. To borrow a distinction framed by Jean-Luc Nancy,[29] Buddha-nature is not a structural essence that we have in common; it is a relational dynamic in which we each have a distinctive contributory share. The nonduality of sameness and difference does not depend on *whether* things differ or not, but on *how* they do so.

For contemporary purposes, we can begin fleshing out this nondualistic understanding of sameness and difference by distinguishing between variation and diversification as distinct directions and qualities of differentiation processes. Variety is a quantitative index of apparent multiplicity, a function of simple coexistence. Consisting of nothing more than things *being different*, variety can be seen at a glance and imposed at will. Diversity is a qualitative index of a specific kind and direction of relational dynamics, a function of complex and coordination-enriching interdependence. Diversification is a process of *becoming different*, which occurs and becomes evident, if at all, when differentiation is activated as the basis of mutual contribution to sustainably shared welfare. Diversity cannot be seen at a glance, and it cannot be imposed. It is an emergent relational achievement. Whereas variety is conceptually exhausted by the fact that things *differ from* one another, diversity entails that things in some significant degree also *differ for* one another. Zoos are high in species variety; ecosystems are high in diversity.

Going beyond Comparative Equity

Distinguishing in this way between two kinds of differentiation processes helps clarify the imperatives we have for delinking equity from its now standard identification with achieving equality of opportunity: the pursuit of functional guarantees of our essential sameness. So defined, equity is critically neutral with respect to whether the differentiation processes now required for economic growth are inflected toward increasing variety or diversity. As long as absolute gains in opportunity, income, and real-life options are enjoyed by all, the means to these gains—whether socialist or capitalist, for example—are of no particular relevance. Yet from a Buddhist perspective in which poverty is understood not as a material lack of possessions (income, wealth, and property) but rather as an index of the erosion of possibilities for valued contribution,[30] this neutrality has the troubling implication that equity can be promoted by means that exacerbate relational impoverishment, contributing to the erosion of conditions conducive to the emergence and enhancement of social, economic, political, and ecological diversity.

At a theoretical level, this means that identifying equity with generic equality of opportunity rather than specific relational outcomes runs the risk of normalizing indifference about the means to and meanings of our differences, an indifference that bars equity from playing any substantive conceptual role in alloying the politics of recognition (respect for differences) with that of redistribution (economic justice). But the shortcomings of agnosticism regarding the means to improved life options are not only those of omission.

It has been recognized since the early twentieth century and the work of economists like Thorstein Veblen that sustaining industrially powered economic growth requires not only a geographic expansion of markets but also a maximization of the density of consumption by increasing opportunities for consumption and amplifying compulsions to choose—the commodification of every possible aspect of daily life paired with the production of ever new and intensifying forms of desire. Through the technological advances of the last century, it has become possible to commoditize the full spectrum of basic human needs, including food, clothing, shelter, basic education, and medical care, but extending now as well to the needs for felt belonging and meaning making. These advances have undoubtedly brought unprecedented expansions of individual capacities for exercising experiential choice and control. But as part of the dynamics of global informational capitalism and world risk society, the industrial proliferation of options for what amount to ever more individuated and fleetingly satisfying acts of consumption and affiliation are not innocent of systematic impacts on relational quality.

Nicholas Georgescu-Roegen[31] has argued that, when viewed thermodynamically or in terms of energy conversions, industrial production is a dissipative not a generative process. In other words, industrial production consists in the social transfer of entropy from developmental centers to peripheries, the creation of a necessarily asymmetric pattern of both material and semiotic flows.[32] This process involves dismembering ecological and social relations to release the material and social or attentional energies bound therein, exchanging the resultant resources for industrially produced goods and services, which, to ensure sufficient throughput to support growth, must be ever more rapidly consumed. Economic growth thus entails an ongoing compression of the extraction-production-consumption cycle. In traditional economic terms, this means a recursively accelerating relationship between supply and demand. But in thermodynamic terms, it means the accelerating export of high-entropy waste to industrial peripheries. Beyond certain thresholds, this process entails the systematic degradation of natural and social environments: the progressive compromise therein of relational complexity, resilience, and adaptive capacity.

The potential for compression in the production-consumption-waste cycle for most material goods and services is, of course, limited. A fast-food meal, for example, offers some satisfaction for at least a number of hours. This is not the case for electronically transmitted informational and experiential goods and services that are effectively converted to waste upon consumption.[33] And it is telling to note in this regard that, whereas the global oil industry had all-time high revenues of $1.7 trillion in 2007, global media and entertainment revenues reached $1.6 trillion, evidencing a near balance of material and attentional energies in fueling the global economy. But the revenue transfer from consuming peripheries to producing centers tells only a small part of the story. Media and information consumption also involves the irreversible export of attention from the immediate relational dynamics of the family, neighborhood, and local community—an ongoing depletion of the most basic resource needed for relational enhancement.

To put this in perspective, the amount of time spent watching television now globally averages three hours per day, with people in so-called advanced countries like the United States averaging closer to four and a half hours. That is, something on the order of 15 to 20 billion hours per day are spent consuming televised entertainment and news, with many billions more devoted to internet surfing, listening to radio, watching films, playing video games, and so on. The attention energy thus spent on market- and media-delivered experiential goods and services is not lost, of course, though the satisfactions derived may be ephemeral. It is, however, attention energy that is no longer available for use in appreciating—that is, both sympathetically understanding and adding value to—immediate relational dynamics.[34] And, just as homes and gardens deprived of attention will sooner or later fall into ruin, so too will communities, neighborhoods, families, schools, children, and the elderly.

The creative destruction brought about by the industrial export of attention will result in new markets for individually targeted material, mental, and emotional commodities and in new opportunities for elective affiliation. But the benefits of the resulting increase in economic activity will not be symmetrically distributed. And, because of the constellation of values presently informing the accelerating interactions and amplifying differentiation needed to sustain growth, they will come at considerable relational costs.

The industrially powered extraction and export of attention is inversely related to appreciation of the immediate relational dynamics constituting us as persons-in-community. Advocates of social media as a force for opening global civil spaces hope that this is simply a prelude to realizing geographically disparate, but nevertheless relationally robust, communities of common interest. The global dominance of values central to free-market liberalism—equality, autonomy, independence, toleration, competition, choice, and control—makes this very unlikely, however. In karmic terms, this combination of values tends to bias interactivity and differentiation toward the fusion of expanded freedoms of individual choice with contracting scopes of commitment, coordination, and mutual contribution. This fusion is conducive to the progressive identification of the optimal with the optional, which is at considerable odds with generating the relational resources needed for predicament resolution.

The recursively accelerating production of goods and services and populations in need of them is, at present, conducive to an entropy-increasing bias of differentiation processes away from diversification toward variation. And given this, the neutrality of equality of opportunity with respect to the means to and meanings of growth has become counterproductive. The deferral and contraction of commitments that are instrumental to the growth of the global economy, as it has come to be, fosters the erosion of precisely the kinds of relational resources needed to engage effectively in predicament resolution and in shared revisions of the meaning of our global interdependence. For equity to perform the critical function needed in an era of complex global interdependence, it cannot be neutral with respect to either the meanings of or the means to justice.

Relational Equity: Realizing Diversity-Enriching Modes of Interdependence

One possible route to a more pragmatically sound conception of equity is to follow Nancy Fraser in resisting any decoupling of the cultural politics of difference from the social politics of equality,[35] rejecting the false either/or choice between redistribution and recognition since it is now apparent that justice requires both. Fraser herself argues for beginning from a deontological conception of justice grounded in equal rights to pursue social esteem under fair conditions of equal opportunity, at least tacitly affirming the need for a relational conception of equity that expresses critical sensitivity to issues of difference. For Fraser, the intersubjectivity of esteem offers pragmatically grounded hope for bridging the gap between subjective claims for recognition and objective claims for redistribution. But under present conditions, the intersubjectivity of esteem will not carry us quite far enough in closing this gap.

The advent of a global attention economy signals a profound—and profoundly asymmetric—alteration of the conditions for realizing social esteem. The extraction and local-to-global export of attention that is now crucial to sustaining global economic growth amounts to a systematic and yet effectively invisible colonization of consciousness. This represents a phase shift in the power relations of global colonialism that is driven and supported by the derivation of economic value from technological appropriations of the social, political, and cultural dynamics of belonging and meaning making.[36] Effectively bridging the needs for both recognition and redistribution requires challenging the karma—the constellation of values, intentions, institutions, and practices—that informs the conception of equity as a comparative index of essentially external relations among individual persons, communities, or classes. This means abandoning allegiance both to the ontological primacy of the individual and to the priority granted to the values of independence, equality, and autonomy in liberal rights discourses grounded in universalistic constructions of human nature. It also means abandoning particularistic efforts informed by the same values that would seek to open routes to justice through identity politics and their fundamental insistence on rights to substantially vary or differ from one another. As Jock Young has pointed out, it is "just as community collapses [that] identity is invented."[37] In Zygmunt Bauman's evocative phrasing, identity is the "ghost of deceased community"—a political construct put to instrumental use as "a potent tool in the hard labour of the 'invention of community' masquerading as community-resurrection."[38]

Yet simply eschewing both deontological alchemies for the transformation of humanity and identitarian efforts to "raise the dead" does not, in and of itself, articulate a clear way forward. We can begin doing so by recognizing that, if all things are relationally constituted, equity must be seen as a relational value or modality of appreciation, a distinctive quality of interdependence. Given the irreducibly dynamic nature of interdependence, this means that equity should not be taken to be a static goal or destination (for instance, participatory access for all) at which we might reasonably hope to arrive someday. Rather, equity should be understood as a direction or pattern of eventuation. Formulated in more positive and specifically Buddhist terms, equity consists in the ongoing realization of *kusala,* or superlative arcs of change.

Unlike the distinctions between good and evil or what is fair and unfair, the Buddhist distinction between the *kusala* and *akusala* is not a dichotomy. From the perspective of Buddhist practice, the entire spectrum of conventionally defined possibilities from good to bad—including all the intervening shades of not quite good or bad—is *akusala*. The *kusala* implicates us in movement oblique to that entire spectrum in the direction of realized virtuosity. Equity, in other words, is a qualitative function of the ongoing realization of relational virtuosity: the realization of conditions for relating freely in the expression of shared means to and meanings of relational flourishing. Understood in this way, equity is enhanced insofar as differentiation processes evidence *kusala* patterns of values coordination. As is made clear in the *Sakkapañha Sutta* (*Digha Nikāya*, 21), engaging in values coordination of this sort is a process of joint karma revision, the result of which is a liberating dissolution of the conditions for conflict, trouble, and suffering. That is, equity occurs as a recursive, predicament-resolving function of the prevalence of both capacities for and commitments to furthering our own self-interests in ways that are deemed valuable by others. In short, there ultimately can be no equity without diversity.

Seen in this way, equity neither derives from nor merely thrives in diversity; rather, equity and diversity are co-constituting. Put somewhat differently, equity is not something achieved *through* diversity; equity is an achievement *of* diversity. This is analogous to the relationship between Buddhist practice and awakening, especially as understood in the East Asian traditions of Chan, Sôn, and Zen: rather than being achieved through practice (which implies practice is undertaken instrumentally with a goal in mind), awakening is realized as an achievement of practice. To use a much more mundane example, learning to successfully hit a tennis ball with a deeply satisfying "thwack" is not a goal we arrive at through practicing how to swing—something like the cake we get as a result of faithfully following a recipe—but rather by hitting tennis balls. That is, the successful tennis shot is not a *product of our efforts;* it is the situation-conditioned *perfection of effort.* Similarly, establishing an equitable arc of relational transformation is not a product of diversification processes—of realizing differences that mediate mutual contribution to sustainably shared flourishing—it is their ongoing consummation.

Like the modern ideal of achieving equality of opportunity, achieving relational equity in the terms just outlined has among its aims the ending of all forms of social, economic, political, and cultural exclusion. But because of their origins in the insight that all things arise interdependently, commitments to achieving relational equity would carry us well beyond the anthropocentric pursuit of equal rights to access and participation in at least three important ways. First, they would entail going beyond the liberal opposition of exclusion to actively appreciating mutual inclusion. Second, they would compel extending the ambit of inclusion or equity considerations to encompass both other species and ecological and environmental systems, an expansion practically compelled by our apparent ability to affect planetary processes adversely and irreversibly. Finally, because diversity is an emergent quality of complex relational dynamics, and because commitments to achieving relational equity would thus require us to address ongoing and intrinsically unpredictable challenges, we would be compelled to refrain from identifying the pursuit of equity with the pursuit of individual empowerment.

If we accept that power is an index of individual agents' abilities to break bonds and unilaterally escape dependency,[39] exercising power expresses a denial of mutual inclusion, a denial of our interdependence and interpenetration. In other words, power implies both an ability to control situational dynamics or determine how things turn out and a willingness to ignore the meanings of our actions for others in order to retain and augment that ability. As such, power implies a karmic bias toward variation that renders it counterproductive as either means to or meaning of achieved equity. Extending and enhancing inclusion in the ways needed to pursue relational equity require not power but strength, a demonstration of capacities for and commitments to responding to situational dynamics in ways that would lead to truly shared and superlative arcs of relational transformation. As a function of achieved diversity, equity cannot be forced; it can only be elicited by deepening and expanding engagement in accordance with the values of mutual contribution and appreciation.

The work of realizing a more equitable world thus resembles the work of bodhisattvas, those enlightening beings in Buddhism who vow to bring about liberating relational dynamics for all sentient beings, knowing full well that sentient beings are numberless and that the manifestations of their karma are inherently unpredictable. This is profoundly sobering. To use a distinction usefully framed by James Carse,[40] realizing a more equitable world is not a finite game, an activity that can be undertaken in order to finish and win. Instead, it is akin to infinite games like marriage, where the point is not to finish and win but to improve the quality of play in such a way as to intensify the interest and commitments of everyone involved. Yet as sobering as this realization may be, it is also deeply comforting. Affirming that there is no equity without diversity is ultimately to affirm that realizing a more equitable world can never be just *your* task or *mine;* it is and will always and irreducibly be *ours.*

NOTES

1. Calculations of income and wealth disparities are fraught with technical difficulties in terms of both data availability and the underlying mathematical operations involved. Especially when the aim is global per capita comparisons of income/wealth, assumptions made in addressing these difficulties can lead to vastly underestimating global disparities. For a brief discussion and response, see Branco Milanovic, "Global Income Inequality: A Review," *World Economics* 7, no. 1 (January–March 2006), 131–157, http://www2.unine.ch/repository/default/content/sites/inequality08/files/shared/ documents/Milanovic1.pdf, accessed April 5, 2011.

2. Milanovic, "Global Income Inequality," 142; United Nations Development Program, *Human Development Report, 2007/2008* (New York: Palgrave Macmillan, 2007).

3. Branco Milanovic, *Worlds Apart: Measuring International and Global Inequality* (Princeton, NJ: Princeton University Press, 2007).

4. James B. Davies, with Susanna Sandström, Anthony Sharrocks, and Edward N. Wolff, "World Distribution of Household Wealth" (United Nations Discussion Paper 2008/3).

5. See Luisa Kroll and Kerry A. Dolan, "World's Billionaires 2011: A Record Year in Numbers, Money and Impact," *Forbes,* March 9, 2011, http://www.forbes.com/2011/03/08/world-billionaires-2011-intro.html.

6. UNDP, *Human Development Report, 2007/2008.*

7. World Bank, *World Development Indicators, 2008* (Washington, DC: World Bank, 2008).

8. In support of such a view, one could cite World Bank comparisons of global per capita incomes in 1981 and 2005. These show that the portion of the world's population living on less than $2/day PPP dropped from 69.4 percent (2.542 billion people) to 47 percent (2.564 billion people) (World Bank, *World Development Indicators 2010* [Washington, DC: World Bank, 2010]).

9. United Nations Development Program, *Human Development Report, 1999* (New York: Oxford University Press, 1999). Here it might also be noted that, along such key measures as real GDP growth, increased life expectancy, reduced infant, child, and adult mortality, literacy, and education, a contrast of the two-decade period from 1960 to 1980 with that from 1980 to 2000 shows a clear decline in progress over the more recent decades, when free-market economics and neoliberal ideology came into global ascendance. Mark Weisbrot, with Dean Baker, Egor Kraev, and Judy Chen, "The Scorecard on Globalization 1980–2000: Twenty Years of Diminished Progress" (briefing paper of the Center for Economic and Policy Research, July 11, 2001), http://www.cepr.net/documents/publications/globalization_2001_07_11.pdf.

10. UNDP, *Human Development Report, 2007/2008.*

11. Robert Reich, *After-Shock: The Next Economy and America's Future* (New York: Alfred A. Knopf, 2010).

12. Milanovic, *Worlds Apart.*

13. Stephen Toulmin, *Cosmopolis: The Hidden Agenda of Modernity* (Chicago: University of Chicago Press, 1990).

14. See, for example, James Beniger, *The Control Revolution: Technological and Economic Origins of the Information Age* (Cambridge, MA: Harvard University Press, 1986); and Peter D. Hershock, *Reinventing the Wheel: A Buddhist Response to the Information Age* (Albany: State University of New York Press, 1999).

15. Peter Wagner, *A Sociology of Modernity, Liberty and Discipline* (London: Routledge, 1994).

16. Michel Foucault, *Discipline and Punish: The Birth of the Prison,* trans. Alan Sheridan (New York: Vintage Books, 1995).

17. Branko Milanovic, Peter H. Lindert, and Jeffrey G. Williamson, "Pre-Industrial Inequality," *Economic Journal* 121 (March 2011), 255–272.

18. Daniel Bell, *The Coming Post-Industrial Society* (New York: Harper Colophon, 1972).

19. Nico Stehr, *Knowledge Societies* (London: Sage Publications, 1994).

20. Manual Castells has written on global informational capitalism in his three-volume work *The Information Age: Economy, Society and Culture* (Cambridge, MA: Blackwell): vol. 1, *The Rise of the Network Society* (1996); vol. 2, *The Power of Identity* (1997); and vol. 3, *End of Millennium* (1998).

21. Georg Franck, "The Economy of Attention," first published in *Merkur*, nos. 534–535 (July 1999), and available in English translation at http://www.heise.de/tp/r4/artikel/5/5567/1.html, accessed November 23, 2009; Richard A. Lanham, *The Economics of Attention: Style and Substance in the Age of Information* (Chicago: University of Chicago Press, 2006); Hershock, *Reinventing the Wheel;* Peter D. Hershock, *Buddhism in the Public Sphere: Reorienting Global Interdependence* (London: Routledge, 2006); and Thomas H. Davenport and John C. Beck, *The Attention Economy: Understanding the New Currency of Business* (Cambridge, MA: Harvard Business School Press, 2002).

22. Ulrich Beck, Anthony Giddens, and Scott Lash, *Reflexive Modernization: Politics, Tradition and Aesthetics in the Modern Social Order* (Stanford, CA: Stanford University Press, 1994); Ulrich Beck, *Risk Society: Towards a New Modernity* (London: Sage Publications, 1992); Ulrich Beck, *World Risk Society* (London: Polity Press, 1992).

23. Anthony Giddens, *The Transformation of Intimacy* (London: Polity, 1992).

24. This is most evident and imperative, perhaps, in regard to the predicament posed by anthropogenic climate change, a predicament that clearly requires a reconfiguration of global economic, political, social, cultural, and technological values and priorities.

25. For example, while enabling any single Chinese citizen to drive a personal car may be good for him or her individually, enabling every Chinese citizen to do so will eventually result in widespread traffic gridlock, a phenomenal rise in urban air pollution, increased contribution of the Chinese economy to the conditions for intensifying climate change, and a host of other impacts familiar to all who have seen, for example, the automotive transformation of Bangkok, Jakarta, and other major Asian cities.

26. Zygmunt Bauman, *Wasted Lives: Modernity and Its Outcasts* (Oxford: Polity Press, 2004).

27. This modern conception of equity contrasts in important ways with premodern Aristotelian and medieval European framings of equity in terms of institutionally expressed sensitivity to the fact that there are times when the universal application of a given law will unfairly disadvantage a particular person or group precisely because of how they differ from others.

28. United Nations Development Program, *Human Development Report 1998* (New York: Oxford University Press, 1998).

29. Jean-Luc Nancy, *Being Singular Plural,* trans. Robert D. Richardson and Anne E. O'Byrne (Stanford, CA: Stanford University Press, 2000).

30. For a discussion of a Buddhist concept of poverty, see Peter D. Hershock, "Poverty Alleviation: A Buddhist Perspective," *Journal of Bhutan Studies* 11 (Winter 2004).

31. Nicholas Georgescu-Roegen, *The Entropy Law and the Economic Process* (Cambridge, MA: Harvard University Press, 1971).

32. Alf Hornborg, *The Power of the Machine: Global Inequalities of Economy, Technology and Environment* (Walnut Creek, CA: AltaMira Press, 2001). It should be noted that center and periphery here are relational terms and do not refer to stable geographical locations. The centers of the global economy are, in other words, zones of intense energy conversion and consequent wealth accumulation that can change physical location as circumstances demand, hence the much-noted mobility of global capital.

33. This compression is nowhere more dramatically illustrated than in the world's major stock exchanges, where the effective lifetime of a piece of information is seventeen seconds.

34. Attention alone is not, of course, all that is needed to address urban blight, community breakdown, and familial malaise, but without it no sustained response is possible and the momentum of the system and its informing values will prevail. Attention is necessary, but not sufficient.

35. Nancy Fraser, "Recognition without Ethics," in *Recognition and Difference: Politics, Identity, Multiculture,* ed. Scott Lash and Mike Featherstone (Thousand Oaks, CA: Sage Publications, 2002).

36. See Hershock's *Reinventing the Wheel* and *Buddhism in the Public Sphere.*
37. Jock Young, *The Exclusive Society: Social Exclusion, Crime and Difference in Late Modernity* (Thousand Oaks, CA: Sage Publications, 1999), 164.
38. Zygmunt Bauman, "The Great War of Recognition," in *Recognition and Difference*, 142.
39. Bauman, "Great War of Recognition," 140.
40. James P. Carse, *Finite and Infinite Games: A Vision of Life as Play and Possibility* (New York: Ballantine Books, 1987).

Contributors

Roger T. Ames is professor of philosophy and editor of *Philosophy East and West*. His recent publications include translations of Chinese classics: *Sun-tzu: The Art of Warfare* (1993); *Sun Pin: The Art of Warfare* (1996) and *Tracing Dao to Its Source* (1997) (both with D. C. Lau); the *Confucian Analects* (1998) and the *Classic of Family Reverence: A Philosophical Translation of the* Xiaojing (2008) (both with H. Rosemont); and *Focusing the Familiar: A Translation and Philosophical Interpretation of the* Zhongyong (2001) and *A Philosophical Translation of the* Daodejing*: Making This Life Significant* (2001) (both with D. L. Hall). He has also authored many interpretative studies of Chinese philosophy and culture: *Thinking through Confucius* (1987), *Anticipating China: Thinking through the Narratives of Chinese and Western Culture* (1995), and *Thinking from the Han: Self, Truth, and Transcendence in Chinese and Western Culture* (1997) (all with D. L. Hall). Recently he has undertaken several projects that entail the intersection of contemporary issues and cultural understanding. His *Democracy of the Dead: Dewey, Confucius, and the Hope for Democracy in China* (with D. L. Hall) (1999) is a product of this effort. Almost all of his publications are now available in Chinese translation, including his philosophical translations of Chinese canonical texts. *Confucian Role Ethics: A Vocabulary* (2011), his most recent monograph that evolved from the endowed Ch'ien Mu lectures at the Chinese University of Hong Kong, is an argument that this tradition has a sui generis vision of the moral life.

James Behuniak Jr. received his PhD from the University of Hawai'i in 2002 and is currently associate professor of philosophy at Colby College. He works in the areas of Chinese philosophy and American philosophy and is the author of *Mencius on Becoming Human* (State University of New York Press, 2005) and coeditor with Roger T. Ames of 孟子心性之學 *Studies of Mencius on Feeling and Nature* (Beijing: Social Sciences Academic Press, 2004). He has authored several articles in Chinese and comparative philosophy for edited volumes and for journals, such as *Philosophy East and West; Dao: A Journal of Comparative Philosophy; Journal of Chinese Philosophy;* and *Asian Philosophy.*

Steve Bein is visiting assistant professor of philosophy and history at the State University of New York, Geneseo. He teaches courses in ethics, Asian and comparative philosophy, Asian intellectual history, and Buddhism. His *Purifying Zen* is the first English translation of Watsuji Tetsurō's groundbreaking treatise on Dōgen. Most recently he is the author of *Compassion and Moral Guidance,* an East-West comparative study of the role of compassion in ethical decision making. He received his MA and PhD in philosophy from the University of Hawai'i at Mānoa and studied at Nanzan University and Ōbirin University under the auspices of the Crown Prince Akihito Scholarship Foundation.

Nalini Bhushan is professor of philosophy and director of the South Asia Concentration at Smith College. She was educated in Chennai, South India, and received her PhD in philosophy at the University of Michigan, Ann Arbor. Most recently she edited *Indian Philosophy in English: From Renaissance to Independence* (Oxford University Press, 2011, with Jay L. Garfield) and *Contrary Thinking: Selected Essays of Daya Krishna (*Oxford University Press, 2011, with Daniel Raveh and Jay L. Garfield). Presently she is conducting an in-depth study of the work of little-known professional philosophers in the Indian academy, against the complicated backdrop of traditional Indian encounters with cosmopolitan modernity, in the context of British colonial rule.

Purushottama Bilimoria (PhD, La Trobe University) was educated in New Zealand, Australia, and India and has held fellowships at Oxford and Harvard Universities and visiting professorships at the State University of New York, Boston University, and the University of California, Santa Barbara. He is currently a Chancellor's Public Scholar and visiting professor/scholar with the Institute of International Studies, Religious Studies Program and Department of Philosophy at the University of California, Berkeley. He divides his time as a visiting professor of philosophy and comparative studies at Deakin University, senior fellow at Melbourne University Australia, and "mentor" at the newly established Sanchi University in Bopal, India. He was formerly a visiting professor at Emory University (1999–2000), where he was at the Center for the Study of Public Scholarship as a Rockefeller Fellow. He was also a Ford Foundation–funded nominee working (with Renuka Sharma) on personal law in India for the Islamic Family Law International Project in the Emory Law School. He has been a visiting professor at the State University of New York, Stony Brook, attached to the Center for India Studies, Asian and Asian American Studies, Philosophy, and the Humanities Research Institute. He was also associated as an adjunct with the Department of Religion, Columbia University, where he was a recipient of a John Templeton Foundation Grant for developing research and pedagogical projects on science and spirituality in India. Purushottama has published in areas of his expertise: philosophy, Indian ethics, personal law, postsecular critiques, and diaspora studies. He is an editor in chief of *Sophia* (an international journal of philosophy and religion, with Milton Springer) and coeditor of the newly founded *Journal of Dharma Studies* (also with Springer).

Steven Burik is currently assistant professor in philosophy at Singapore Management University. He holds a PhD in comparative philosophy from the National University of Singapore. His research interests are mainly in continental philosophy (Heidegger, Derrida) and Chinese philosophy (Daoism). His works include *The End of Comparative Philosophy and the Task of Comparative Thinking* (State University of New York Press), a co-authored, forthcoming textbook in Critical Thinking, and papers in various journals, including *Philosophy East and West* and *Comparative and Continental Philosophy.*

Amita Chatterjee is retired professor of philosophy and emeritus professor, School of Cognitive Science, Jadavpur University, Kolkata. She was also the first vice-chancellor of Presidency University, Kolkata. She is the author with Smia Sirker of *Understanding Vagueness* (1994) and *Mental Reasoning: Experiments and Theories* (2009) and editor of *Bharatiya Dharmaniti* (1998) and *Perspectives on Consciousness* (2003). She jointly edited *Manodarshan* (2003), *Some Philosophical Issues on Indian Logic* (2003), and two volumes on *Philosophical Concepts Relevant to Sciences in Indian Tradition* (2006) for the Project of History of Indian Science, Philosophy and Culture. Her areas of specialization are logic and Navya-Nyāya, analytic philosophy, philosophy of mind, and cognitive science. She has published articles in national and international journals of repute and her articles have been included in important anthologies. She has coedited *J. N. Mohanty's Lectures on Kant's Critique of Pure Reason* (2013). Currently she is editor of *Journal of Indian Council of Philosophical Research.*

Baoyan Cheng is associate professor in the Department of Educational Foundations at the University of Hawai'i at Mānoa. She specializes in comparative and international education, and her research focuses on equity and cultural issues. Her recent publications include *Student Loans in China: Efficiency, Equity and Social Justice* (Lexington Books, 2011) and a book chapter in the edited volume *Student Financing of Higher Education: A Comparative Perspective* (Routledge, 2013).

Gordon Davis teaches in the Department of Philosophy at Carleton University in Ottawa, Canada. Since finishing his doctorate at the University of Oxford in

2005, he has published articles in ethical theory, political philosophy, and the history of philosophy, with an emphasis in recent years on the comparative history of philosophy, in particular on theoretical comparisons between Western and Buddhist moral philosophy and their implications for methodologies in meta-ethics.

Jay L. Garfield is Kwan Im Thong Hood Cho Temple Professor of Humanities and Head of Studies in Philosophy at Yale-NUS College, Professor of Philosophy at the National University of Singapore, Professor of Philosophy at Melbourne University, Adjunct Professor of Philosophy at the Central University of Tibetan Studies and Doris Silbert Professor in the Humanities and Professor of Philosophy at Smith College. He is the author of more than ninety articles addressing questions in the philosophy of mind, the foundations of cognitive science, developmental psycholinguistics, philosophical logic, ethics, hermeneutics and translation theory, Buddhist philosophy and cross-cultural interpretation, and the history of Indian philosophy in the nineteenth and twentieth centuries. Garfield's most recent books are his translation, with the venerable professor Geshe Ngawang Samten, of the fourteenth–fifteenth-century Tibetan philosopher Tsong Khapa's commentary on Nāgārjuna's *Mūlamadhyamakakārikā* (*Ocean of Reasoning*, 2002), *Empty Words: Buddhist Philosophy and Cross-Cultural Interpretation* (2006), *Buddhist Philosophy: Essential Readings* (coeditor with William Edelglass, 2009), *Pointing at the Moon: Buddhism, Logic, Analysis* (coedited with Mario D'Amato and Tom Tillemans, 2009), all from Oxford University Press, and *Trans-Buddhism: Transmission, Translation and Transformation* (coedited with Nalini Bhushan and Abraham Zablocki, University of Massachusetts Press, 2009), *Moonshadows: Conventional Truth in Buddhist Philosophy* (with the Cowherds, Oxford University Press, 2010), *The Oxford Handbook of World Philosophy* (edited with William Edelglass, Oxford University Press, 2010), *Western Idealism and Its Critics* (CUTS Press, 2011), *Indian Philosophy in English from Renaissance to Independence* (with Nalini Bhushan, Oxford University Press, 2011), *Sweet Reason: A Field Guide to Modern Logic* (with Jim Henle and Tom Tymoczko, Wiley-Blackwell, 2011), and *Contrary Thinking: Selected Papers of Daya Krishna* (edited with Nalini Bhushan and Daniel Raveh, Oxford University Press, 2011). Garfield's *Engaging Buddhism: Why It Matters to Philosophy* will be published by Oxford University Press in 2015, as will his edited collections *Madhyamaka and Yogācāra: Allies or Rivals* (with Jan Westerhoff) and *The Moon Points Back: Buddhism, Logic and Analytic Philosophy* (with Yasuo Deguchi, Graham Priest, and Koji Tanaka). He is currently working on a new book on Buddhist ethics with the Cowherds and a collection of translations of commentaries on Dignāga's *Alaṃbanāparīkṣā* with an international team of collaborators, as well as a history of philosophy in the Indian renaissance with Nalini Bhushan.

Steven F. Geisz is associate professor of philosophy and chair of the Department of Philosophy and Religion at the University of Tampa. He received his PhD in philosophy from Duke University. He has published articles in, among others, *Philosophy East and West,* the *Philosophical Forum,* and *Journal of Applied Philosophy.* His research is on classical Chinese philosophy, philosophy of mind and language, and political philosophy.

Peter D. Hershock is codirector of the Asian Studies Development Program at the East-West Center in Honolulu, Hawai'i. His research has focused on the philosophical dimensions of Buddhism and on using Buddhist conceptual resources to address contemporary issues. His books include *Liberating Intimacy: Enlightenment and Social Virtuosity in Ch'an Buddhism* (1996), *Reinventing the Wheel: A Buddhist Response to the Information Age* (1999), *Technology and Cultural Values on the Edge of the Third Millennium* (edited, 2004), *Chan Buddhism* (2005), *Buddhism in the Public Sphere: Reorienting Global Interdependence* (2006), *Changing Education: Leadership, Innovation and Development in a Globalizing Asia Pacific* (edited, 2007), *Educations and Their Purposes: A Conversation among Cultures* (edited, 2008), and *Valuing Diversity: Buddhist Reflection on Realizing a More Equitable Global Future* (2012).

Larry A. Hickman is director of the Center for Dewey Studies and professor of philosophy at Southern Illinois University Carbondale. He is the author of *Modern Theories of Higher Level Predicates* (1980), *John Dewey's Pragmatic Technology* (1990), *Philosophical Tools for Technological Culture* (2001), and *Pragmatism as Post-Postmodernism* (2007). He is the editor or coeditor of more than a dozen volumes, including *Technology as a Human Affair* (1990), *Reading Dewey* (1998), *The Essential Dewey* (with Thomas Alexander, 1998), *The Correspondence of John Dewey* (1999, 2001, 2005, and 2008), *John Dewey: Between Pragmatism and Constructivism* (with Stefan Neubert and Kersten Reich, 2008), *John Dewey's Educational Philosophy in International Perspective* (with Giuseppe Spadafora, 2009), and *The Class Lectures of John Dewey,* vol. 1, *Political Philosophy, Logic, Ethics* (with Donald F. Koch, 2010).

Kathleen M. Higgins is a professor of philosophy at the University of Texas at Austin. She is author of *Nietzsche's "Zarathustra"* (1987; rev. 2010), *The Music of Our Lives* (1991; rev. 2011), *A Short History of Philosophy* (with Robert C. Solomon, 1996), *A Passion for Wisdom* (with Robert C. Solomon, 1997), *Comic Relief: Nietzsche's "Gay Science"* (2000), *What Nietzsche Really Said* (with Robert C. Solomon, 2000), and *The Music between Us: Is Music the Universal Language?* (2012). She is coeditor with Robert C. Solomon of *From Africa to Zen: An Invitation to World Philosophy* (Rowman and Littlefield, 2003) and *World Philosophy: A Text with Readings* (McGraw-Hill, 1995). She is editor or coeditor of numerous other books on such topics as Nietzsche, German idealism, ethics, aesthetics, and love.

Heidi M. Hurd is David C. Baum Professor of Law and Professor of Philosophy Co-Director, Program in Law and Philosophy at the University of Illinois. She is the author of *Moral Combat* (Cambridge University Press, 1999), which has been widely reviewed and translated into multiple languages. She has two books forthcoming from Oxford University Press: one coauthored with Ralph Brubaker on the moral underpinnings of debt forgiveness through bankruptcy discharge, entitled *Debts and the Demands of Conscience,* and the other coauthored with Michael Moore on topics in criminal law, entitled *Essays in Criminal Law Theory.* Her numerous articles in the areas of criminal law, torts, legal philosophy, and political theory have appeared in the nation's top law and philosophy journals, including the *Yale Law Journal, Stanford Law Review, Michigan Law Review, Legal Theory, Law and Philosophy, Chicago Law Forum, Notre Dame Law Review, Journal of Contemporary Legal Issues, Boston University Law Review, Australian Journal of Legal Philosophy,* and *Southern California Law Review.* She has given well over one hundred lectures and paper presentations at conferences and gatherings across the United States and Europe, as well as in Israel, Japan, South Korea, Taiwan, Uganda, Argentina, Canada, and Australia. She regularly teaches criminal law, torts, evidence, and environmental policy, as well as philosophy courses in moral theory and political philosophy.

Thomas P. Kasulis is professor of comparative studies at Ohio State University, where he teaches philosophy, religious studies, and East Asian studies. He is a former president of the Society for Asian and Comparative Philosophy and of the American Society for the Study of Religion. His books from the University of Hawai'i Press include *Zen Action/Zen Person, Intimacy or Integrity: Philosophy and Cultural Difference, Shinto: The Way Home,* and the coedited *Japanese Philosophy: A Sourcebook.* He is currently writing a history of Japanese philosophy.

Workineh Kelbessa is an associate professor of philosophy at Addis Ababa University, Ethiopia. He obtained his BA in philosophy from Addis Ababa University, his master's in the politics of alternative development strategies from the Institute of Social Studies, the Netherlands, and his PhD in environmental ethics from Cardiff University, UK. He is the author of *Traditional Oromo Attitudes towards the Environment: An Argument for Environmentally Sound Development* (2001) and *Indigenous and Modern Environmental Ethics: A Study of the Indigenous Oromo Environmental Ethic and Modern Issues of Environment and Development* (2011). He has also published many articles in refereed journals and chapters in books in the fields of environmental ethics, African philosophy, globalization, philosophy of sex, and indigenous knowledge. He is a former Fellow of the Alexander von Humboldt Foundation and a member of the executive committee of the International Development Ethics Association and the editorial advisory board of the journal *Environmental Ethics*. He is currently completing a book on African philosophy of sex and the HIV/AIDS epidemic.

Lori Keleher is an assistant professor in the Department of Philosophy at New Mexico State University in Las Cruces, New Mexico, where she teaches courses on international development ethics as well as in several other areas of philosophy. She has been on the executive board of the International Development Ethics Association (IDEA) since 2006, and cochair of the Human Development Capability Approach (HDCA) Ethics and Development Thematic Group since 2007. She has published articles on development ethics and in ancient philosophy.

Oliver Leaman is professor of philosophy and Zantker Professor of Judaic Studies at the University of Kentucky. He previously taught in England and the Middle East. He writes mainly in the areas of Islamic and Jewish thought, and his most recent publications are *Islam: The Key Facts,* cowritten with Kecia Al, and *Jewish Thought: An Introduction* (both published by Routledge) and *Islamic Philosophy* (Wiley). His edition of *Ninian Smart's World Philosophies* appeared in 2009. His latest books are *Judaism: An Introduction* (I. B. Tauris, 2011) and *Controversies in Contemporary Islam* (Routledge, 2013).

James McRae earned his PhD in comparative philosophy from the University of Hawai'i at Mānoa in 2006, specializing in ethics and Japanese thought. He is currently an associate professor of philosophy and religion and the coordinator for Asian studies at Westminster College in Fulton, Missouri. His publications include the books *The Philosophy of Ang Lee* (with Robert Arp and Adam Barkman, University Press of Kentucky, 2013) and *Environmental Philosophy in Asian Traditions of Thought* (with J. Baird Callicott, State University of New York Press, 2014).

Jin Y. Park is associate professor of philosophy and religion, and director of the Asian Studies Program, at American University. Her research focuses on Zen and Huayan Buddhism, Buddhist-postmodern comparative philosophy, Buddhist ethics, social and political dimensions of Buddhist philosophy, and the Buddhist encounter with modernity in Korea. Her book-length publications include: *Reflections of a Zen Buddhist Nun: Essays by Zen Master Kim Iryŏp* (translator, 2014), *Makers of Modern Korean Buddhism* (editor, 2010), *Merleau-Ponty and*

Buddhism (coeditor, 2009), *Buddhism and Postmodernity: Zen, Huayan and the Possibility of Buddhist Postmodern Ethics* (2008), and *Buddhisms and Deconstructions* (editor, 2006).

James Peterman teaches philosophy at Sewanee: The University of the South, where his teaching and research focus on the intersection of topics in epistemology, medical ethics, traditions of honor, and early Chinese philosophy. Having published articles in the United States and abroad on early Chinese philosophy, he has recently completed a manuscript on Wittgenstein and Confucius, *Whose Tradition? Which Dao? Confucius and Wittgenstein on Moral Learning and Reflection* (Albany: State University of New York Press, forthcoming). Moreover, he has recently been named director of Community Engaged Learning, Sewanee's academic community engagement program, as well as director of Sewanee's Bonner Leader Program, a scholarship and service internship program affiliated with the Bonner Foundation (http://www.bonner.org).

Naoko Saito is associate professor at the Graduate School of Education, University of Kyoto. Her area of research is American philosophy and Pragmatism and its implications for education. She has been working as a mediator in cross-cultural settings, especially between Japan and Anglo-American cultures, and more recently European cultures. She is the author of *The Gleam of Light: Moral Perfectionism and Education in Dewey and Emerson* (2005) and *Uchinaru Hikari to Kyoiku: Pragmatism no SaiKochiku* (The Gleam of Light: Reconstruction in Pragmatism, 2009), a Japanese adaptation of *The Gleam of Light,* as well as numerous articles. In collaboration with Paul Standish, she has coauthored *Democracy and Education from Dewey to Cavell* (forthcoming, 2014) and has coedited the collections *Education and the Kyoto School of Philosophy* (2012), *Stanley Cavell and the Education of Grownups* (2012), *Walden in Tokyo: Stanley Cavell and the Thought of Other Cultures* (forthcoming, 2015), and *Honyaku no Sanaka ni aru Shakai-Seigi* (Social Justice in Translation; University of Tokyo Press, 2014) She is the translator of *The Senses of Walden* (2005), the first book of Cavell's to be published in Japanese, and of *Beyond the Self: Wittgenstein, Heidegger, Levinas and the Limits of Language* by Paul Standish (2012).

May Sim is associate professor of philosophy, director of the Boston Area Colloquium in Ancient Philosophy, president of the Metaphysical Society of America (2013), and former director of Asian studies at the College of the Holy Cross. She is the author of *Remastering Morals with Aristotle and Confucius* (Cambridge University Press, 2007) and more than forty essays comparing Eastern and Western philosophies in the areas of metaphysics, ethics, education, the environment, natural law, and human rights. She is contributing editor of *The Crossroads of Norm and Nature: Essays on Aristotle's Ethics and Metaphysics* (Rowman and Littlefield, 1995) and *From Puzzles to Principles? Essays on Aristotle's Dialectic* (Lexington Press, 1999). She is completing a book on a Confucian account of human rights, and working on a manuscript on Metaphysics and Ethics, East and West.

Robert Smid is a senior lecturer in philosophy and religion at Curry College in Milton, Massachusetts. He earned his PhD in religious studies with a concentration in philosophy of religion from Boston University in 2007, under the direction of Robert Neville and John Berthrong. He is the author of *Methodologies of Comparative Philosophy: The Pragmatist and Process Traditions* (State University of New York Press, 2009), as well as a number of articles published in the *American Journal of Theology and Philosophy, East-West Connections,* and elsewhere.

Paul Standish is head of the Centre for Philosophy at the Institute of Education, London. His research addresses a range of philosophical questions in relation to education, and he is particularly interested in creative tensions between philosophical traditions. Recent books include *Stanley Cavell and the Education of Grownups* (Fordham University Press, 2012) and *Education and the Kyoto School of Philosophy: Pedagogy for Human Transformation* (Springer, 2012), both coedited with Saito Naoko, *Jiko-o Koete: Wittgenstein, Heidegger, Levinas, Gengo no Genkai* (Beyond the Self: Wittgenstein, Heidegger, Levinas and the Limits of Language) (Hosei University Press, 2012, trans. Saito Naoko), and *Tetsugaku no Subject Tenkan: Standish cho* Jiko o Koete *o Meguru Taiwa* (Replacing the Subject of Philosophy: Dialogue on Standish's *Beyond the Self*) (University of Tokyo Press, 2015, ed. Saito Naoko). With Kwak Duck-Joo he has coedited a special issue of the *Asia Pacific Educational Research Journal* entitled *Cultivating Humanity and Transforming the Knowledge Society* (2014). He is associate editor and was editor (2001–2011) of the *Journal of Philosophy of Education.*

Kenneth W. Stikkers is professor of philosophy and Africana studies at Southern Illinois University Carbondale and professor of economics and sociology at the Autonomous University of Sinaloa, in Mexico. He earned his PhD in philosophy at DePaul University, and he specializes in and has authored numerous articles on the philosophy of the social sciences, especially economics, and historical and thematic links between classical American and contemporary continental philosophies. He edited the English translation of Max Scheler's *Problem of a Sociology of Knowledge* and is the author of *Utopian Visions Past, Present, and Future: Rethinking the Ethical Foundations of Economy* and coeditor of *Wealth and Well-Being.* Forthcoming are *Economics as Moral Philosophy* and a collection of the writings of the late Native American philosopher Rober Bunge, cited in the essay in this volume. Stikkers is the recipient of the Helen Potter Award for contributions to social economic theory, and he is former president of the Society for the Advancement of American Philosophy.

Karsten J. Struhl teaches political and cross-cultural philosophy at John Jay College of Criminal Justice (CUNY) and the New School University. He has coedited *Philosophy Now* (Random House, 1972, 1975, 1980), *Ethics in Perspective* (Random House, 1975), and *The Philosophical Quest: A Cross-Cultural Reader* (McGraw-Hill, 1995, 2000). He writes about such topics as ideology, human nature, just war theory, global ethics, radical democracy, visions of communism, ecology, Marxism, and Buddhist philosophy. His articles have appeared in a variety of journals, books, and encyclopedias.

Meera Sushila Viswanathan is an associate professor in the Departments of Comparative Literature and East Asian Studies at Brown University. Her research has centered on classical Japanese poetry and prose; Western medieval court literature; and comparative poetics and aesthetics. Her publications include "An Investigation into Essence: Kuki Shūzō's '*Iki' no Kōzō*" (1989); "Poetry, Play and the Court in the *Tosa Nikki*" (1991); "In Pursuit of the *Yamamba:* The Question of Female Resistance" (1996). In addition, she teaches courses on feminist literature and literary theory, theories of ekphrasis, and travel literature.

Wu Shiu-Ching is professor of philosophy at National Chung Cheng University, Republic of China. She received her bachelor's degree in philosophy from National Taiwan University and her PhD in philosophy at Temple University. Her recent research interests focus on all kinds of feminist theories, as well as their practical implications. She teaches courses on feminist epistemologies, feminist philosophy of science, moral particularism, ethics of care, and applied ethics. She has published articles in Taiwan's leading journals on the normativity of care ethics, the comparative study of care ethics and moral particularism, and care ethicists' assessment of Stephen Darwall's rational care theory of welfare.

Xu Di is a professor in the Department of Education Foundations, College of Education, University of Hawai'i at Mānoa. She is a member of the Board of Examiners for the National Council of Accreditation of Teacher Education (NCATE, now Council for the Accreditation of Educator Preparation, CAEP), which has been providing national accreditations for teacher education programs in the United States since 2007. Her recent publication focuses on bridging the Eastern and Western philosophy for educational practices and includes "The Wisdom from the East: A Holistic Theory and Practice of Health and Wellness" (2013), "Spiritual Heritage and Education Today" (2013), "Taoism:

Origin, Essence, and Practice" (2013), and "A Reading of Lao Zi for Educational Philosophers Today" (2012). In addition, she published *A Comparison of the Educational Ideas and Practices of John Dewey and Mao Zedong in China* (1992), and various chapters and articles on teacher education, educational foundations, multicultural education, international education, and ESL education. She was a visiting scholar and research associate at Philosophy of Educational Research Center at Harvard University (1999–2000), a visiting professor in Peking University (2011, 2009, and 1997), and an exchange professor at National Kaohsiung University in Taiwan (1998).

T. Yamauchi is emeritus professor at Osaka University of Education. He has taught at Kyoto University, Osaka University, and others. His main publications are on the moral philosophy of R. M. Hare. He has translated many books by Callicott, Hare, Singer, and others into Japanese. His articles include "The Confucian Environmental Ethics of Ogyu Sorai," in J. B. Callicott and J. Macrae, eds., *Environmental Philosophy in the Asian Traditions of Thought* (State University of New York Press, 2014), "Wang Yang-ming," in A. J. Palmer and P. B. Corcaran, eds., *Fifty Key Thinkers on the Environment* (Routledge, 2002), "Is Hare's Fanatic Possible?" *Bulletin of the Japan Society of British Society* 9 (1986), and many others.

Yang Liuxin is an associate professor in the Institute of Moral Education at the Peking University of China. He teaches in the area of moral and civic education, and his primary research interest is in Chinese classical ethics and moral education. He is the author of *Human Capital and Modernization of China* (2003, Shandong University Press), and is the translator of *Understanding John Dewey* (by James Campbell, 1995, Open Court, in Chinese 2010, Peking University Press). Among his recent articles are "Educating beyond Language: Thoughts on Moral Cultivation in *Yizhuan*" (*The Journal of Humanitics,* 2011) and "On the Philosophy of Education of Classical Confucianism in *Xueji*" (*Lanzhou Academic Journal,* 2010). He was a visiting scholar in the Department of Education Foundations at the University of Hawai'i during the academic year 2007–2008. He received the grant of the Canada-China Scholars Exchange Program from Canada (DFAIT), and has been a visiting scholar in the University of Toronto for research on "global citizenship education of the western world" during the academic year 2013–2014.

Index

Abe Hiroshi, 75–76
abstraction, perils of, 161, 164–165
Adorno, Theodore, 110
aging, 22, 142–156, 483–502
Alesina, Alberto F., 238
Alexander the Great, 201, 359
Ambedkar, B. R., 307
Ames, Roger T., 11, 19, 237, 242, 256, 312–313, 409–410, 448, 456–458
Analects of Confucius (*Lunyu*), 143, 146–147, 153, 168–169, 175–178, 180–181, 190, 244, 493
Anand, Mulk Raj, 270–271
anattā (no-self), 163
Anaximander, 404, 406
ancestor reverence, 149–150
Anderson, Elizabeth, 460–461, 466, 468–472
Anscombe, Elizabeth, 179
anthropology, and economic theory, 214–228
Aquinas, Thomas, 359, 429
Arab Spring, 2, 389–390
Arendt, Hannah, 216
Aries, Philippe, 222
Aristotle, 6–7, 20–21, 53, 61, 107, 166, 171, 201, 315, 359, 364, 429–440, 441–459
Arneson, R., 460
Arsić, Branka, 334
Arthaśāstra, 20, 198, 205, 208, 422–424
Asia Pacific Economic Cooperation (APEC), ix
Aśoka, 198, 200–201, 208
Attfield, Robin, 367
Augustine, 171
Ayres, Clarence, 232

Baily, Greg, 201
Balala, Mah-Hanaan, 277
Bardhan, Pranab, 198, 203
Barnard, Chester I., 76–77
Bataille, Georges, 219
Bauman, Zygmunt, 527, 533
Behuniak, James, Jr., 16
Bein, Steve, 20
Bell, Daniel A., 234–235, 488, 500
Bentham, Jeremy, 172–174, 301, 420
Bergson, Henri, 36–37, 46
Berlin, Isaiah, 4
Bhagavad Gītā, 263, 269
Bhagwati, Jagdish, 208
Bhattacharyya, K. C., 15, 259–261, 264–265, 269–270
Bhushan, Nalini, 14
Bilimoria, Purushottama, 12
Birtchnell, Thomas, 203
Bishop, Pauahi, 157–158, 178–179
Bloom, Irene, 253
Bloom, Paul, 418, 425–426
Boaz, David, 283
Braithwaite, John, 128, 130–132, 136–137
Brohman, John, 353
Buddhist ethics, 8, 9, 16, 23, 109–124, 221, 296–311, 392–396, 429–440, 519–538. *See also* Huayan Buddhism
Buffett, Warren, 193–194
Bunge, Robert, 221–222
Burik, Steven, 19

Callicott, J. Baird, 75, 337, 346, 349
capabilities approach, 11, 205, 209, 364, 474–477, 516
capitalism, the moral equivalent of, 194–196

Carse, James, 535
Cavell, Stanley, 16–17, 312–314, 316–321, 333–334
Chakraborty, S. K., 204
Chappell, David, 297–298
Chatterjee, Amita, 19
Cheng Baoyan, 11, 22
Chen Wen-Yan, 328
Churchill, Winston, 188
Cobb, John B., Jr., 453–454
communitarian ethics, 14, 241, 248–256, 258
Confucian ethics, 11–12, 146–151, 163–164, 167–170, 174–178, 241–258, 337–350, 483–502
Confucianism, 10, 11, 13–14, 20, 125–141, 142–156, 166–170, 174–178, 229–240; Japanese, 17–18, 337–350
Confucius, 441–459
conspicuous consumption, the moral equivalent of, 186, 191–194
Crespo, Ricardo, 442
Critchley, Simon, 406–407
Crocker, David, 362, 364–365

Dahrendorf, Ralf, 59
Daly, Herman E., 368, 454
Daodejing, 16, 283–285, 287–292, 410–411
Daoist ethics, 16, 19, 151, 400–401, 409–415
Dasgupta, Partha, 198–200, 207
Davis, Gordon, 16
death, 221–225
Deloria, Ella, 221
democracy, Confucian, 483–502
Derrida, Jacques, 19, 111, 116–119, 122, 406–409, 413–415
development: economic, 351–374; international, 503–518
Dewey, John, 13–14, 165, 229–240
Dharmaśāstra, 205
Dickens, Charles, 419, 425
Dilthey, William, 4
diversity, 23; value of, 519–538
Dōgen, 30, 429–440
Dorn, James, 284, 288–289
Dorrien, Gary, 248
Dower, Nigel, 351, 363
Dushun, 35, 121
Dworkin, Ronald, 21, 460–482

Eastman, Charles Alexander, 223–224
economics: and anthropology, 214–228; Confucian, 241–258, 286–288; Daoist, 283–295; evolutionary, 230–233; Islamic, 15, 272–282; neoclassical, 229–233; and rights, 296–311
egalitarianism, 460–482
Einstein, Albert, 394
Ekins, Paul, 359
Ellison, Ralph, 120–121
Emerson, Ralph Waldo, 316–318, 334–335
Engles, Friedrich, 3–4, 377–378, 382, 397
English, hegemony of, 326–335
environmental ethics, 9, 18, 68–81, 82–108, 186–191, 337–350, 351–374, 383–385
epistemology, 37–38
equity, 6; and interdependence, 519–538
ethics, of Watsuji, 68–81; and universalism, 171–173. *See also* Buddhist ethics; communitarian ethics; Confucian ethics; Daoist ethics; environmental ethics; global ethics; socialist ethics

family, 142–156, 168–171
Farley, Joshua, 454
Fazang, 118, 529
fear, 43–45
filial piety (*xiao*), 11, 22, 136, 142–156, 168–170, 175, 177, 340, 450, 484; and governance, 151–154
Fingarette, Herbert, 135
Fishkin, James, 488
Florida, Robert, 297–298
Foucault, Michel, 225, 329, 331
Francione, Gary, 95
Franklin, Benjamin, 226
Fraser, Nancy, 532
Friedman, Milton, 229, 283
Fromm, Erich, 222

Gaddhafi, Muammar, 390
Galbraith, John Kenneth, 233
Gandhi, Indira, 202
Gandhi, Mahatma, 14–15, 200–202, 206, 259–271
Garfield, Jay L., 14, 297–298
Gates, Bill, 193–194, 224
Gecko, Gordon, 195
Geisz, Steven F., 22
General Agreement on Tariffs and Trade (GATT), 257

Georgescu-Roegen, Nicholas, 530
Geras, Norman, 19, 378–381, 396
GEW (gross economic wisdom), 199
gift giving, 214, 218–226
global ethics, 385–392
Gombrich, Richard, 304–305
Goodman, Charles, 299
Goodpaster, Kenneth, 96
Gore, Al, 188
Goulet, Denis, 357, 360–367
GNH (gross national happiness), 199
Graham, A. C., 412, 457
Gramm, Phil, 234
Great Depression, 216, 234
Great Learning (*daxue*), 149–150, 175, 286, 346, 444–445
greed, 39–43, 48
Griffin, James, 301–311
Guo Qiyong, 169, 180
Gutmann, Amy, 485–487

Hall, David L., 237, 242, 256, 409–410, 448, 456–458
Hamlet, 406
Hamlin, J. K., 425–426
Hardin, Garrett, 234
Hare, R. M., 341–346
harmony (*he*), Chinese conception of, 243–248, 252–256, 449–450
Hartwick, E., 358
Hassan, Muhammad, 276
Hawai'i, Kingdom of, 157–158
Hawken, Paul, 352
Hayek, Friedrich, 229, 233, 283
He Baogang, 488
Hegel, G. W. F., 51, 171, 301, 378
Heidegger, Martin, 19, 400–406, 416
Heilbroner, Robert, 215–216
Held, Virginia, 61
Hershock, Peter D., 23, 119, 161, 312–313
Hickman, Larry A., 13
Higgins, Kathleen M., 12
Himmelfarb, Gertrude, 51–52, 55–56
Hobbes, Thomas, 215–216, 420
Holland, Alan, 366–367
Holocaust, 379–381
holograph, 32–36
Homer-Dixon, Thomas F., 73–74
Huayan Buddhism, 10, 35–36, 39, 48, 112–113
Huggins, Nathan, 219, 221
human nature, 214–216, 225
Hume, David, 301
Hurd, Heidi M., 9

Ienaga Saburō, 49
Ihara, Craig, 297
Ii Naosuke, 193
Ik people, 379
Inada, Kenneth, 297–298
Indra's net, 34–36, 39
institutionalized power, 503–518
International Development Ethics Association (IDEA), 364
International Monetary Fund (IMF), 357, 370, 388

James, William, 12, 185–186, 194–196, 230, 237
Jefferson, Thomas, 301
Jigme Singye Wangchuck, King, 195
Junger, Peter, 297
justice: defined, 158–159; of caring labor, 460–482; Derrida on, 408–409; Heidegger on, 403–406; and reconciliation with economics, 528–529; as relational virtuosity, 167–168; social justice, 324–336. See also *niti* (institutionalized justice); *nyāya* (realized justice)

Kabeer, Naila, 503, 506, 509
Kahan, Dan, 125–127, 132–134,140
Kaibara Ekken, 340–341
Kamehameha I, 157
Kant, Immanuel, 54, 171–174, 198, 263, 299, 304, 314–315, 381, 420, 436
Kantor, Jay, 96
karma, 23, 519, 522–525
karuṇā (compassion), 163
Kasulis, Thomas P., 8, 18, 23
Kelbessa, Workineh, 18
Keleher, Lori, 22
Kennedy, John F., 44
Keown, Damien, 297–298
Kershaw, Ian, 380
Keynes, John Maynard, 216–218, 229, 352
Khayed, Rasem, 276
Kim Iryŏp, 112–114
King, Martin Luther, Jr., 211, 255
Kittay, Eva, 468, 470, 479–480
knowing, detached and engaged, 33–34, 43, 46–47
Krishna, Daya, 198, 205

Kristeva, Julia, 112
Kuki Shūzō, 49
Küng, Hans, 386
kusula (superlative practices), 533–534
Kymlikca, Will, 300
kyōsei (symbiosis), 9, 76–79

Lai, Karyn, 7, 414
Lakota, 221–224
Lansmann, Claude, 380
Lau, D. C., 290–292
Leaman, Oliver, 15
Lebret, L. J., 359
Leopold, Aldo, 74–75, 341, 346, 348
Liu Qingping, 169, 180
Liu Wei-Zhi, 328
Locke, John, 171, 218, 269, 301
Lopez, Barry, 360
love, 45–46
Lyotard, Jean-François, 110–111

Mabbett, Ian, 201
Macaulay, Thomas, 260
Marcel, Gabriel, 222
Marglin, Stephen, 217
Marom, Yotam, 391
Marx, Karl, 3–4, 50, 55, 199, 222, 263, 306, 311, 326, 330–331, 356, 377–378, 382, 397, 420, 503
Mathur, Kanchan, 510
Matilal, Bimal K., 201
Mauss, Marcel, 54, 219–220, 223
McCormick, Ken, 283–284, 288–290, 292
McRae, James, 8
Mead, George Herbert, 4
Mencius, 144–145, 150–154, 245–248, 286–287, 444
Menger, Carl, 217
Merleau-Ponty, Maurice, 120
mettā (desire to remove suffering), 163
Miki Kiyoshi, 49
Mikkelson, Douglas K., 429–431, 437–438
Mill, John Stuart, 128, 172–174, 263, 301, 304, 306, 315, 420, 502
Mish'alani, James, 96
misplaced concreteness, fallacy of, 164
Miyadai, Shinji, 314
Modi, Narendra, 207–209
Moeller, Hans-Georg, 291–292
Morgan, Edmund S., 221
Mubarak, Hosni, 390
Muelder, Walter G., 14, 241, 243, 248–258
Muhammad, 273–274, 276, 279
Myrdal, Gunnar, 359

Naess, Arne, 346
Nagel, Thomas, 460
Nancy, Jean-Luc, 5, 529
Navajo, 219–220
Nietzsche, Friedrich, 12, 52–53, 60–61, 63, 189, 194–196, 317, 401, 403
Ninomiya Sontoku, 344–347
Nishi Amane, 331
Nishida Kitarō, 49, 51–52, 57–58, 331
niti (institutional justice), 159, 161, 422
nonhuman entities, and welfare, 91–93; and rights, 93–103; and virtue, 103–107
Nordhaus, William B., 368
Nussbaum, Martha, 10–11, 125–141, 205, 209, 364–365, 433–436, 468, 471, 474–475, 516
nyāya (realized justice), 159, 161, 422

Occidentalism, 332–333
Occupy Wall Street (OWS), 2, 39, 390–392
Ogyū Sorai, 18, 341–344
O'Neill, John, 96

Palma, G., 355
Panagariya, Arvind, 208
Park, Jin Y., 9
Peet, R., 358
Peterman, James, 10
Phillips, Anne, 468, 471–472
Phillips, D. Z., 126, 135–136
Platonic cosmology, 338–340, 345
Pogge, Thomas, 209
Polanyi, Karl, 1, 214–215, 235, 285
Politics, 429–430, 432–434, 437
Pollock, David, 360–361
Popper, Karl, 46
Pŏpsŏng, 121
postcoloniality, 198–213
poverty, the value of, 429–440
Pragmatism, 165–166
pratītyasamutpāda (dependent co-arising), 163
propriety (*li*), 143–145, 166, 484, 486–487
Putnam, Hilary, 165–166
Pythagoras, 171

Qin Xiao, 237–238
Qur'an, 272–281

Rakowski, E., 460
rational choice theory, 161
Rawls, John, 16–17, 19–20, 62, 159–160, 174, 198, 210–211, 312–315, 317, 325–326, 333, 419–422, 424, 468
Regan, Tom, 95, 97
Reiman, Jeffrey, 114–116, 121
relations, internal and external, 27–33, 42–43
Ricardo, David, 3, 50
Robbins, Lionel, 216–217, 230–231
Robeyns, Ingrid, 468, 475
Rockwell, W. Ted, 231
Roemer, J., 460
Rolston, Holmes, 96
Rosser, J. Barkley, Jr., 235
Rothbard, Murray, 287
Rousseau, Jean-Jacques, 171, 269, 420
Ryan, Paul, 235

sacrifice for the common good, the moral equivalent of, 186–191
Sagoff, Mark, 368–369
Sahlins, Marshall, 215–217, 226
Sai Baba, Sri Sathya, 199–200, 204
Saito, Naoko, 16
Saito, Yuriko, 187, 192–193
Sakai Naoki, 329–332
Sakkapañhā Sutta, 534
Salt and Iron Debates, 246, 254, 257
Sandel, Michael, 16–17, 312–323
scarcity, 214–218, 229–233
Schumacher, E. F., 109–111
Sen, Amartya, 9, 11–13, 19–20, 109, 159–164, 198, 203, 205, 207–211, 213, 363–364, 432, 440, 474, 503, 513–516; and individualism, 161–163; on justice, 418–428
shame penalties, 125–141
shari'ah law, 273, 277–280
Sharma, Arvind, 198, 203–204
Shaw, George Bernard, 387
Shen Nong, 285
Shōbōgenzō, 429–431
Shu, Alice, 488
shukan (epistemological subject), 330–333
Shuowen jiezi, 153, 243
shutai (subject of praxis), 330–333, 335
Sim, May, 20, 179
Simmel, Georg, 4, 8, 54–60
simple location, fallacy of, 161, 166
Singer, Milton, 199–200
Singer, Peter, 188–189, 194, 301, 341–342, 346
Slingerland, Edward, 290–291
Smid, Robert, 14
Smith, Adam, 1, 3, 50, 160, 192, 218, 283, 288, 420–421, 436, 444
Sober, Elliott, 96
socialist ethics, 18, 377–399; as a global ethic, 385–392
Solow, Robert, 368
Somarantne, G. A., 203
Sōseki Natsume, 51, 62–65
Spencer, Herbert, 224–225
Spengler, Oswald, 53–56
Standish, Paul, 17
Stannard, David, 220–221
Stepaniants, Marietta, x
Stikkers, Kenneth W., 13
Stone, Oliver, 195
Streeten, Paul, 363
Struhl, Karsten J., 18
Susman, Margaret, 56–57
Sutta-Nipāta, 163, 422, 424
Suzuki Akira, 329–330
swadeshi, 259, 261, 263–265
swaraj, 259, 261, 263–265
Swearer, Donald, 297–298

Tagore, Rabindranath, 14–15, 204, 259–271
Taylor, Romeyn, 286
Tempels, Placide, 359–360
Thompson, Dennis, 485–487
Thoreau, Henry David, 312, 315, 319–320
Tobin, James, 368
Toulmin, Stephen, 523
Traer, Robert, 443–444
transcendentalism, 160, 164–165
Trotsky, Leon, 385
Truman, Harry, 353
Tucker, M. E., 337
Turnbull, Collin, 379
Tu Wei-ming, 337, 451, 458

United Nations Declaration of Human Rights, 386

value, 49–57; Daoism on, 409–415; Derrida on, 406–408; and diversity, 519–538; Heidegger on, 401–403
Veblen, Thorstein, 14, 191–192, 229–232, 235, 530

Vesterlund, Lise, 197
Vimalakīrti Sūtra, 45–46
Viswanathan, Meera Sushila, 8
Vivekananda, Swami, 260
von Mises, Ludwig, 217

Walker, Scott, 390
Wang, Jessica Ching-Sze, 236
Wang Yangming, 340
war, moral equivalent of, 185–186
Watsuji Tetsurō, 8–9, 49, 51, 57–65, 68–81, 330–331, 429
Weber, Max, 199–201, 224
well-field system, 246–247, 253–256
Wenz, Peter S., 443–444, 453–454
Whitehead, A. N., 161, 164–165, 179
Wilkinson, Tara Loader, 193
Williams, Bernard, 10, 130–132, 136–137, 140, 163, 474–476
Wissenschaft paradigm, 8, 27–48
Wittgenstein, Ludwig, 10, 126, 318–319
Wogaman, J. Philip, 249
Wolff, Richard, 391–392
Wollstonecraft, Mary, 420
World Bank, 357, 370, 388
Wu Shiu-Ching, 21
wuwei, 283, 287–292
Wynn, K., 425–26

Xiaojing, 152
Xu Di, 11, 22
Xunzi, 287

Yang Liuxin, 11, 22
Yang Shen-Keng, 327–328
Yao Xinzhong, 245–246
Young, Iris, 468
Young, Jock, 533

Zhang Dainian, 243, 257
Zhongyong (*Focusing the Familiar*), 147–148, 151, 177, 244, 346, 446–454
Zhuangzi, 400, 411–414
Zhu Xi, 340–342
Zuo zhuan, 244